ZARTMAN, I. William ed.   Man, state, and society in the contempo-
rary Maghrib.   Praeger, 1973.   531p   map   tab   bibl   68-16096.
15.00, 6.95 pa.
Half of a two-volume study of the Maghrib.   While this volume deals
with the contemporary era, its companion will be historical.   Zartman,
a noted writer on North African politics, has compiled an impressive
list of 40 articles, some of which have been translated from French
publications.   The greatest gap is in the area of society.   For example,
social groups are interpreted as the ruling political and military elites.
While these sections are valuable, the book needs more material that
would explain other societal topics such as the contemporary family,
tribe, poverty, social mores, and religion.   Although the guidelines for
this work exclude selections published in book length, some of the
material used in books like Reuben Levy's *The social structure of Islam*
(1957) would supply this missing material.   The addition of Libya to the
Maghrib, which is not done by some North African writers, is welcome.   This makes sense in light of Mu' Ammar al-Qadhdhafi's aggressive Libyan policy toward contemporary North Africa and the Middle
East.   Undergraduate and graduate libraries should add this book to
their North African collection.

Man, State,
and Society
in the
Contemporary
Maghrib

Man, State, and Society in the Contemporary Maghrib

EDITED BY
I. William Zartman

PRAEGER PUBLISHERS
New York · Washington · London

PRAEGER PUBLISHERS
111 Fourth Avenue, New York, N.Y. 10003, U.S.A.
5, Cromwell Place, London SW7 2JL, England

Published in the United States of America in 1973
by Praeger Publishers, Inc.

Library of Congress Catalog Card Number: 68–16096

Printed in the United States of America

To the memory of Roger Letourneau, teacher of North Africa

And to the collaborators of this collection who have passed away — Frantz Fanon
        Mohammed ben Yussef
        Henri de Monfety
        Damien Helie

CONTENTS

ACKNOWLEDGMENTS

This book was compiled in order to help English-speakers better understand a world in which they are a minority. It touches only a part of that world, but a part that has been twice separated from our grasp: once because it has its own indigenous Muslim and Arab culture, and then again because it has long been the realm of French scholarship as well as political interest. Thus, the process of finding the best work on the area has often involved translating studies that are in a different scholarly tradition and a different style of expression (as distinct from a mere difference in language). In this search, we have gone through more than three hundred articles, a task that would not have been possible without the diligent and tireless assistance of Mrs. Susan Denvir, to whom I am most grateful. I am also appreciative of the advice of Clement Henry Moore, Roger le Tourneau, Stuart Schaar, and Philippe Cabanius.

Several guidelines were established for choosing the articles, in addition to those concerning subject matter. Selections were excluded if they had already appeared in book form, and out-of-print or otherwise unavailable works were preferred to more readily available ones. Articles employing a particular disciplinary approach have been preferred to purely substantive studies. In some cases, the selection required simply has not been written; I have had to make do, or do without. I have also tried to include a reasonable selection of the major authors on the Maghrib, and whenever possible, of the Maghribis themselves. Those who have been omitted have, I hope, been paid the proper respect in the notes. Most of the articles have not been abridged; those that were are so indicated in the text. Footnotes were abridged when necessary, and cross-references and a few additional footnotes were added. In some way or another, all of these selections are out of date. They were not chosen for timeliness, however, but for the way they present a particular subject matter. In each case, later articles — if they exist — have not done as well.

The translation — a mammoth task in itself — was taken over with characteristic energy and flair by my wife, assisted on individual articles by Monique Fouques du Parc, Janie Julianelli, Hassan Abdin Mohammed, and Francoise de Messey; Professor David Wolitzky checked the psychological terms and expressions. The statistical tables were compiled by Ahmed Rhazaoui, with the additional help of the Center of Research and Study of Mediterranean Society at the University of Aix.

I am deeply grateful to all those named above, and to the authors, publishers, and reviews that gave permission to reprint. I am, of course, responsible for the results. My only hope is that this book will serve to increase our understanding of the Maghrib, both by presenting the sound analytical work that is available and by suggesting areas where further research is needed.

Although an appropriate acknowledgement has been given in each essay, I should like to emphasize my indebtedness and appreciation to the following publishers for granting me permission to reprint copyrighted material:

American Universities Field Staff; African-American Institute (*Africa Report*); American Geographical Society of New York (*Geographical Review*); Basil Blackwell & Mott Ltd *(Bulletin of the Oxford University Institute of Economics and Statistics); Confluent,* Paris; Frank Cass & Co *(Middle Eastern Studies)*; Centre des Hautes Etudes Administratives sur l'Afrique et l'Asie Moderne *(L'Afrique et L'Asie)*; Documentation Française *(Maghreb)*; Department of State, Office of External Research; *Esprit; Government and Opposition*; Institute of Current World Affairs; International Institute of Differing Civilizations, Brussels *(Civilisations); Journal of Developing Areas*; Middle East Institute, Washington *(Middle East Journal)*; Princeton University Conferences, Annual Conference on the Middle East; Société Française de Psychologie *(Psychologie Française)*; Society for Applied Anthropology *(Human Organization); Temps Modernes*; United Nations; UNESCO; and the official information services of Algeria, Libya, Morocco, and Tunisia.

In addition to the essays previously published or previously delivered as conference papers, two chapters of this volume appear here for the first time and are based by their authors — Damien Helie and Jacques Roumani — on their doctoral dissertations for the University of Algiers and Princeton University, respectively.

I. William Zartman

New York City
June, 1972

INTRODUCTION

Comparisons, similarities, and differences are relative. Men, states, and societies in the contemporary Maghrib differ, but on the whole they resemble each other more than they do outsiders. Thus it is possible to make meaningful comparisons among them; the constants enable us to focus attention on the variables. This means that a study of Libyan oil workers, Tunisian villages, Algerian shanty-towns, or Moroccan students also tells us something about Moroccan migrant workers, Algerian local structures, Tunisian urbanization, or Libyan youth. It is true that students of developing societies make such claims for sectoral comparisons the world over. The internal similarities of Maghribi societies, however, also tie together the young and the old, the urban and the rural dwellers in the region, with their similar — if not common — culture, problems, goals, and power, and these elements set them off to a greater or lesser degree from the rest of the world.

The whole region was launched by Capsian culture, touched by Carthage, and ruled by Rome. Its Berber base was converted and acculturated by the Muslim Arabs. Three of the four societies (Algeria, Libya, Tunisia) were parts of the Ottoman Empire; a different three (Algeria, Morocco, Tunisia) fell under the French. Each had a different type of nationalist movement, but all passed through similar stages. Although the independent political systems vary greatly, they must deal with nearly identical problems. As the camera zooms into detailed focus, differences among the societies rise in relief. Yet both the cultural base and the rates of change by which development is measured remain similar. The developmental process means that the national factor is stronger today than ever before, raising the possibility of a growing differentiation of species, but it also means that the components, challenges, means, and responses of each nation are necessarily still quite alike.

It thus seems paradoxical that North Africa is better known as a region of case studies and archetypes than as an area of controlled comparisons. Whatever the reason, it is significant — and regrettable — that there are so few comparative studies of nationalized colonial land, of urban migration, of educational systems, or of reactions to the politics of colonization.[1] Instead, the focus has been not only on the Tunisian education system, the Algerian Army, or the Moroccan tribe but, more broadly, on Tunisia as the single-party model, Algeria as the paradigm of revolution, or Morocco as *the* segmentary society.[2] Yet to regret the absence of the comparative approach is no reason to deplore or belittle the case studies. They are often excellent, and their value is increased if they are considered as laying the groundwork for future comparisons, both at the national and the subnational level.[3]

The value in studying the Maghrib, then, is that it can teach us about more than merely the North African societies themselves. As comparative instances of alternatives (one of the closest things the social sciences have to the controlled experiment), the societies show the impact of differentiating variables. As single cases, they stand as models for the analysis of other societies.

The component studies in this collection are arranged by subject matter rather than by country. The introductory selection presents the general characteristics of the region. Part II ranges over the spectrum of values and attitudes, from traditional to modern and, more frequently, their mix. Part III reviews the same spectrum through the personalities of leading Maghribi politicians, and Part IV presents the aggregate personalities of important elite groups. Part V deals with the political mechanisms through which leaders, groups, and populations interact, and the final part with the problems the Maghribis must solve if they are to dominate their environment.

Notes

1. An important exception is Douglas E. Ashford, *National Development and Local Reform* (Princeton, N.J.: Princeton University Press, 1967), although Pakistan replaces Algeria in the tripartite comparison.

2. Quality examples are Clement Henry Moore, *Tunisia Since Independence* (Berkeley: University of California Press, 1965); Lars Rudebeck, *Party and People* (New York: Praeger, Publishers, 1969); William B. Quandt, *Revolution and Political Leadership: Algeria 1954–1968* (Cambridge, Mass.: The M.I.T. Press, 1969); David and Marina Ottoway, *Algeria: The Making of a Socialist Revolution* (Berkeley: University of California Press, 1969); John Waterbury, *The Commander of the Faithful: The Moroccan Political Elite, a Study in Segmented Politics* (New York: Columbia University Press, 1970); and David M. Hart, *Turbans, Triggerfingers and Tribalism* (Princeton, N.J.: Princeton University Press, pending).

3. On the national level, Clement Henry Moore, *Politics in North Africa* (Boston: Little, Brown, 1970); on the subnational level, Werner Plum, *Gewerkschaften in Maghreb* (Hannover: Verlag für Literature and Zeitgeschehen, 1962).

ONE

The Background

1

A NOTE ON THE MAGHRIB

CHARLES F. GALLAGHER

The western wing of the Arab World, long known in Arabic as the Maghrib —
that is, the place of the setting sun, or the West — forms the northwestern
quadrant of the African continent, an area of more than 2 million square miles.
In size it is two-thirds the area of the continental United States, and it comprises
the four nations of Morocco, Algeria, Tunisia, and Libya, together with Saharan
areas and many parts of Mauritania that are considered *terra irredenta* by
Moroccan nationalists. The region possesses a long-standing ethnic homogeneity
and also a strong cultural unity, which in the years since its various members
became independent has been expressing itself through a profound historical
transition accompanying the end of more than a century of intensive European
settler colonialism.[1]

Within the past fifteen years, the Maghrib has changed as much as or more
than most other regions in a rapidly changing world.   Its member states achieved
independence beginning with Libya (1951), Morocco and Tunisia (1956), and,
finally, after a bitter and bloody struggle, Algeria (1962). In the process, at least
four-fifths of the resident European elite — once numbering 2 million persons,
and forming about 7 per cent of the total population of the region just after
World War II — departed permanently. During this same period, however, a
heavy influx of North Africans, mainly Algerians, into Europe, in search of
work, created new human ties of another kind that are reflected both in the
continuingly close economic relationship of the Maghrib countries with their
European neighbors and in their efforts in recent years to arrange some kind of
accommodation with the European Economic Community. . . .

A limited amount of technical cooperation on a regional level has been
instituted with the active encouragement of the United Nations and other
international bodies. The North African countries likewise form part of the
Arab World and are all members of the Arab League, although Tunisia has
boycotted that institution as an instrument of the hegemonistic policies of
Egypt. Here, too, there is an abatement of the often extreme tensions of
yesteryear, which leaves the impression that the Maghrib as a whole, and each

American Universities Field Staff Report, North Africa Series, XIII, No. 6 Copyright
©1967, American Universities Field Staff, Inc. Reprinted by permission.

The article was written in May, 1967; bracketed material has been added by the editor
to bring it up to date.

country within it, is more soberly concerned with its own internal preoccupations and is more properly engaged in tending its own interests than was the case a while back. Not the least factor contributing to this trend is the increasing importance of oil and gas to the economies of Libya and Algeria and, very recently, to Tunisia potentially, together with the increasingly complex relations this entails with Europe.

The states of the Maghrib share three distinctive geographical features that separate the region from the rest of the continent and make it into what the first Arab conquerors called an "island on the land." These are the desert, the high mountains of the Atlas, and the inland sea that gives life to a Mediterranean countryside along a thin strip of the northern coast.

The southern and eastern approaches of the area are made up by the world's greatest desert, the Sahara, which has in historical times been much more a barrier than an avenue of communication — despite the emergence of a new Africanist school stressing the importance of trans-Saharan contacts. The Sahara is encyclopedic in its diversity; high, arid mountains range up to 10,000 feet in the lunar-looking southern reaches of Algeria and Libya and are bounded on the north by ancient, submerged seas, which have stored the petroleum products that now enrich their possessors. High steppe, rock desert, floating dunes, and incidental fertile oases coexist in a region that, with little or no rain on the whole, is still occasionally subject to disastrous flash floods. To the north, the Sahara is mostly cut off from the sea by a long, continuous mountain chain — the Atlas, with many variant regional names — which stretches out like a backbone from west to east, beginning in southwestern Morocco and finally running into the Mediterranean in the Tripolitanian province of western Libya. East of that, the Jebel Akhdar of Cyrenaica forms a geographical, but not geological, extension of the chain and serves in an attentuated way the same function as the main Atlas group: to turn the coastal strip north of the mountains into a productive, Mediterranean-type enclave to the degree that it is adequately protected from Saharan wind and sand by the mountain barrier. This relatively fertile region is widest where the Atlas is highest and thickest, as in Morocco, where the 13,600-foot peaks of the High Atlas shelter the wide plains of northwestern Morocco, made more fruitful by abundant Atlantic rainfall. The Atlas diminishes in altitude from west to east; it is little more than 7,500 feet in Algeria, the highest point in Tunisia is just over 5,000 feet, and the mountains peter out in Tripolitania as little more than hills of 2,500 feet. Accordingly, the fertile Tell of northern Algeria is a narrower, Chilean-shaped, serpentine area; more than two-thirds of Tunisia lies in the arid center-south below the main Atlas dorsal; and the coastal strip that is cultivable in Libya gives out before the Gulf of Sirte, where the desert finally comes down to the sea.

Everywhere the fertile land is Mediterranean in its physical make-up: both olives and cork trees flourish; oak-types and chaparral scrub brush make up a *maquis* cover not unlike that of Spain, southern France, or parts of California; and the principal crops include figs, almonds, olives, and grapes and (owing to European influence) their wine. Fruit trees are found at higher altitudes, and in the desert regions the date is the staple crop.

Lest this description seem too enthusiastic, the debit side of the geography of the Maghrib should be stressed. The land is in good part high, uneven, and thirsty. Rainfall is irregular and often disastrous in its unpredictability. The Sahara hovering nearby keeps alive the specter of periodic climatic excesses when searing *sharqi* winds blow off the desert and parch the earth. Much of the region is a high plateau, going up 3,000 feet, which offers disadvantages in both winter and summer; Morocco, especially, has aptly been described as "a cold country with a hot sun." Internal communications have been difficult at most times in both Morocco and Algeria because the shape of these countries is excentric, and intermontane valleys are often sharply cut off from one another. Rainfall may be abundant, as in the Rif in Morocco or Kabylia in Algeria (more than sixty inches in some places), and still run wasted off the sharp slopes; on the contrary, it may be deficient, as in Marrakesh (eight inches) but permit a limited oasis-type culture depending on skilled irrigation procedure, or virtually nonexistent, as in southern Tunisia, where less than one inch falls. Nevertheless, the southern and southeastern slopes of the Rif away from the rainfall side are semiarid and denuded, while southern Tunisia and parts of the Algerian pre-Sahara have suffered floods that made thousands homeless. If he wishes, the American reader may establish a tenuous parallel with conditions in California. There are great similarities but at least two important differences, both derogatory to the Maghrib: (1) human beings and their animals have not systematically deforested and eroded California for a thousand years, as has been the case in the Maghrib; and (2) there is as yet no technique for technological control in the Maghrib corresponding in degree to that available in California for the maximization of capricious or deficient natural endowments.

The southern shore of the Mediterranean and its hinterlands in some depth have long been the realm of a complex human stock, white in skin color and sharing a Hamitic tongue and a culture — based on stock-raising, some agriculture, the use of domestic animals, and the firing of hard-core pottery — seemingly imported from the East in the late Neolithic period. These people were the "Libyans" found by the Greeks in earliest classical days, the "Afariq" (who gave their name to the entire continent), cousins of, but resistant to, the invading Phoenicians, who established the first empire in Northern Africa at Carthage around 800 B.C. Greco-Roman writers generally referred to them, as to many others, as barbarians (*barbaroi*), and the name "Berber," carried over into Arabic when Islam appeared in Northern Africa in the seventh century, took root and is used today by both Oriental and Western intruders to designate the original inhabitants. At the bottom, this culture and stock are still there; North Africa today, from the Siwa oasis of western Egypt to Agadir in Morocco and from Tamanrasset and the Tibesti to Kabylia, is still overwhelmingly Berber in blood and rural lifeways, although in thirteen centuries it has become thoroughly Arabized in language, in civilization, and, up to a point, in self-view.

In the course of history, many other peoples have introduced their genes into the physical make-up of the inhabitants. Beginning in the first millennium before Christ, the area has seen the arrival of Phoenicians, Greeks, Latins, Jews, Indo-Germanic groups like the Vandals (and latter-day Europeans), and, most important of all, the Arabs. The last came in two great waves, mainly in the seventh and eighth and the eleventh and twelfth centuries. Among some groups and in some places — especially in the large, traditional cities but also in some tribal areas — they have remained an intact entity; elsewhere, they have much modified the ethnic pool by blending in. In any discussion of racial origins in this area, however, two facts should be stressed. One is that much of all of this is becoming increasingly academic as the new concept of a modern nationalism based on the nation-state arises. The other is that although a division between Arab and Berber does indeed exist and has always existed (to be exploited by the colonizing powers in the hope of extracting political advantage therefrom), the line does not cut exactly as Westerners usually think it does. The difference is primarily linguistic, and exactness would compel the use of the terms "Berberophone" and "Arabophone." Berber as a language has given enormous ground to Arabic, morphologically and syntactically as well as geographically, its use today being restricted to refuge mountain areas, where it is preserved to a greater extent by monolingual women than by bilingual men, who are usually forced to communicate in the national language, which is, everywhere, Arabic. Corollary to this is the fact that, while it might be technically correct to speak of the population of the Maghrib today as being mainly Arabized Berbers, the cross-linkage of Arabism and Islam is so effective that, for most of the dwellers in the area, integration into the religion and participation in the traditional-universalistic socio-religious system of Islam has led to a large-scale surrender of identity, with a concomitant identification with the importers and leading sponsors of that religion, the Arabs from the Middle East.

The population of the Maghrib [in 1970] was estimated at more than 30 million inhabitants, most of whom are concentrated in the more fertile coastal regions described above. Because large desert areas are empty or sparsely populated, real density is much higher than over-all figures indicate, and in some extremely overcrowded regions, such as Kabylia and the Rif, overpopulation has long been a problem that has had to be resolved by temporary or permanent emigration.

In recent years the region has become much more homogeneous than before, the rural-urban balance has shifted sharply, and demographic pressure has been accentuated to an alarming degree. [Fewer than] 300,000 Europeans remain in the four Maghrib states, of the 2 million present two decades ago, and perhaps [one-tenth] of a Jewish population estimated to have been 500,000 at the end of World War II. Muslims thus constitute almost 99 per cent of the total resident population, as compared to only 88 per cent in 1950. Intensive, rapid, and haphazard urbanization, brought about by pressure on the land and underemployment rather than by an industrial boom — and in Algeria by the dislocation of the war as well — has vigorously continued since World War II and much changed the physiognomy of the large coastal cities. The populations of Casablanca and Algiers have more than trebled in the past generation, and the enormous shanty-towns surrounding them continue to absorb tens of thousands of new arrivals each year as best they can. Both of these agglomerations contain well over 1 million persons at present, and the same process is taking place in Tunis. Tripoli, the latest and most rapidly growing mushroom town, has somewhat different origins, owing its growth to the oil boom and the inflationary upheavals that Libya is experiencing, with the result that good agricultural land in the coastal provinces is being abandoned by farmers who come to the city seeking, usually in vain, to share in the bonanza that has increased national income tenfold within eight years.

The rapid rate of increase of the population — running at or near 3 per cent a year in all the countries save Libya, for which accurate figures are not available — is clearly a major obstacle to development of any kind and has recently become a source of concern to the Maghrib governments. Education and social services have suffered everywhere because of this excessive growth and the fact that over 40 per cent of the population is under fifteen years of age in Morocco (46 per cent), Algeria (42 per cent), and Tunisia (42 per cent). Each of these countries has recently taken some steps with respect to family planning, but it is far too early to predict the results . . . .

The Maghrib entered history just before the end of the second millennium B.C., with the founding of Phoenician settlements on the shores of modern Tunisia, followed by factories stretching out beyond the Strait of Gibraltar. Carthage, the successor to the Phoenician traders, exploited the region and did business with it, but there was no real colonization nor much civilizing influence except in the immediate hinterland of the city in northern Tunisia. Roman legions garrisoned all North Africa, but Roman civilization was found only at selected points in Tunisia, eastern Algeria, and coastal Libya, while most of the country was protected by a Chinese-like wall of fortifications, the *limes*. As Roman power waned in the early centuries of the Christian era, the Berbers reasserted their control in much of the area and assisted in the destruction of the Empire.

When the Arabs moved into the Maghrib after A.D. 650, they found both the Rum, the name given to a sedentary population of Latin culture under Byzantine rule along the coast of Tunisia, and the warlike Berbers, who inhabited the interior. The former capitulated quickly, but the conquest of the Berbers was protracted and difficult. No sooner was it accomplished than a revolt made North Africa virtually independent again, and for several centuries thereafter free Berber states floated on the fringe of the Arab caliphate, adopting and discarding with enthusiasm a variety of Muslim heresies.

In the middle of the eleventh century, a group of veiled nomads from the Sahara, the Murabitin or Almoravids, swept into Morocco and subdued it, as well as much of Spain that had been the fief of the caliphate of Córdoba. Their successors, the Muwahhidin or Almohads, were the only true North African dynasty in history, ruling the region as far east as Tripoli and holding half of Spain for a century. With the succeeding dynasty, the Merinids in Fes and their offshoots among the Hafsids in Tunis, North Africa reached the apogee of its traditional civilization and compared favorably with the merchant states of Italy and Spain of the same period. In Fes, Granada, Tlemcen, and Tunis, architecture, music, and literature flourished, and such remarkable writers as ibn Khaldun and ibn Batuta came to prominence.

The Maghrib was largely untouched by the Crusades, but the area was increasingly involved in the futile defense of Muslim Spain from the Reconquest of Spain and Portugal. From 1400 on, Iberian activity spilled over onto the North African coast, and an intermittent series of religious wars continued for centuries, with periodic European occupation of many of the coastal cities, from Agadir to Tripoli. In the interior, much of the region withdrew into an isolation within which was fermented a religious reform and revival based on the appeal of local and often fundamentalist saints, as well as on the charisma of sharifian families (that is, descended from the Prophet). Also exhibiting a well-founded xenophobia, the North Africans found partial release for these sentiments by striking back at the Europeans through a satisfying and profitable piracy that continued from the sixteenth to the early nineteenth century.

Ever since the Middle Ages, European impact on the Maghrib has been heavy and unrelenting, whether negatively or positively; and particularly the "century of colonization," which began with the French arrival in Algiers in 1830, has had a seemingly permanent effect in the fields of politics, economics, and cultural and social change. The historical problem of European colonization is distilled in the Maghrib, for here, as nowhere else in their empire-building, Europeans (French, Italian, and Spanish) went to settle, in their eyes permanently, in the midst of a pre-existing alien society with a complex folk culture, a high traditional civilization, and a world religion close in spirit to Christianity, although doctrinally and psychosocially deeply opposed to it.

In retrospect, the closeness of the relationship between Europe and the Maghrib dictated that there be either total assimilation or violent resistance. In fact, both were attempted, and both actually coexisted for some time. The French made a determined effort at assimilation, especially in Algeria, and in the period between the two world wars, it would have been either a foresighted or a brave pundit who would have predicted a breakaway of their North African provinces in the near future. Italy under Fascism made Libya the "fourth shore" of its Mediterranean dream; and Spain looked on its possession of the two shores surrounding the Pillars of Hercules as a natural and eternal right.

On the other hand, the history of the region after 1830 can also be read as that of an area never fully conquered. In Algeria, resistance continued for a generation, flaring up bitterly in Kabylia in 1857 and in 1870–71 before subsiding for two generations. Tunisia pursued a more moderate path of political opposition, but took it early and persistently; political activity began in earnest soon after the turn of the century, and from the 1911 Tunis riots on, an unbroken continuity of resistance confronted the protector, culminating in the 1934–38 period, which saw the formation and outlawing of the Neo-Destour (the New Constitution Party). The Senusi brotherhood of Cyrenaica put up a violent struggle against Italian domination in the 1920's and was crushed or harried into exile only during the decade preceding World War II. Morocco provides the best example of all: it took more than twenty years to "pacify" the country (1912–34), immediately after which the armed struggle in the countryside gave way to a new, ideologically based urban opposition that eventually completed the task of restoring national independence.

The year 1930 may fairly be considered the turning point almost everywhere. A nascent nationalism in the modern sense was stirred in its Islamic roots by a French decree attempting to alienate Moroccan Berbers from orthodox Muslim jurisprudence. That decade saw the growth of the Neo-Destour in Tunisia, the precursors of the Istiqlal and other minor parties in Morocco, and a marked stepping up of political activity, which had begun after World War I among the Algerians in France, by Ferhat 'Abbas and the religious leaders in Algeria itself. The Popular Front (1936–38) in France first encouraged, but ultimately disappointed, nationalist hopes; these, however, were revived by World War II, and rightly so. Paradoxically, Libya benefited first through having had the good fortune to belong to a loser, for the United Nations trusteeship in that country relinquished power to a sovereign Libya at the end of 1951. Tunisia won internal autonomy in 1955 following a pledge made the preceding year, largely under the pressure of events in the then French states of Indochina, and formal independence for the country came early in 1956. At almost exactly the same time, Morocco became sovereign once again, after forty-four years of protectorate status, during the last three of which an armed resistance movement in the cities, protesting the exiling of Sultan (later King) Mohammed V, threatened to make the country untenable for France. Already, two years before, in November, 1954, the Algerian revolution had broken out. It lasted eight years, reduced much of rural Algeria to desolation, permanently changed the nature of Algerian society, brought down the Fourth Republic and its parliamentary government system in France in 1958, and pushed the homeland to the brink of civil war on two occasions. In terms of a general overturn of the whole of a society, as well as in the number of lives lost, it was without question the most violent anticolonial revolution of this generation. After Algeria's accession to independence in July, 1962, it made an abortive attempt to place itself in the vanguard of the anticolonial movement in southern Africa and elsewhere, as well as to maintain a strategically independent position somewhere between the Afro-Asian bloc, the positive neutralists as they then existed, and the Communist bloc countries, showing at the same time a special sympathy for the position of such "loners" as Cuba and Yugoslavia. The 1965 coup put an end to the more spectacular Algerian foreign-policy initiatives for a while, however, and looked at later, in the perspective of the [ten] years since independence, the country appears still to be in a state of shock from the disturbances of the revolution. It is hard to avoid the conclusion that it will be a good while before Algeria emerges from this state and is able to make coherent efforts to develop a positive sense of identity and personality.

The four independent countries of the Maghrib show much variety in the degree and quality of their political development, as well as in the kinds of national political organizations. Morocco and [until recently] Libya were among the world's few remaining monarchies, while Algeria and Tunisia are republics dominated by single parties which label themselves socialist. Yet, in many respects both kingdoms have had more in common with one or another of the republics than with each other, and vice versa. Morocco is a long-established country, secure in its traditions and historically cemented by a national dynasty which has ruled for three centuries, while Libya is a geographical expression made into a country by the vagaries of international politics – a country whose sense of national being is rudimentary, with a nebulous personality and traditions that are still unformed. Tunisia, like Morocco, has long been a center of Muslim civilization in the area, and indeed for most of recorded history the Tunis region has been the cultural heartland of the North African littoral. The existence of a solid middle class and a bulwarking village hinterland of unique quality, together with the rapid growth of a younger group whose education is modern, combine to give a special flavor to a country which has been and is still quite homogeneous, tranquil, and comparatively open to fruitful external influences. On the other hand, its socialist neighbor, Algeria – which functioned through most of history as a corridor between Tunisia and Morocco, and which suffered from some 130 years of direct French rule that utterly suppressed what consciousness of the self existed – is still lacking the pillars of cultural tradition which support its neighbors on both sides. As a result, Algeria is today faced with the problem of having to create both a personality and institutions out of the void left behind by an especially ruthless colonialism and the chaos engendered by the revolution.

The historical anatomy of each country-area is reflected in the political organization of the corresponding nation today. Effective political power in Morocco is wielded by the king alone, in conjunction with a small group of ministers and technicians whom he appoints and shuffles periodically. The country became a constitutional monarchy in 1962, but the period of limited multiparty parliamentary government that ensued (1963-65) was one of political feuding and demagoguery, stagnation, and economic decline. Parliament was dissolved in 1965 and full powers were assumed by the king, who is a modern, active, European-trained politician but also in good part still a traditional autocrat, one who governs by a combination of intrigue, intelligence, drive, and the still great prestige he holds among large segments of the common people, especially those in rural areas. [Little of this style has been changed by the introduction of new constitutions in 1970 and 1972.]

In Libya, although the lines of power moved in seemingly similar fashion between an authoritarian royal family and weak political groupings, the underlying causes were different. Libya's chief political task has been to fashion a nation out of dissimilar and noncomplementary regions scattered across vast and largely empty spaces. The two main regions, Tripolitania and Cyrenaica, are distant from and previously unconnected with each other; and they developed sharp antagonisms as a result of their different responses to Italian rule in this century. The king, chosen from the Senusi brotherhood, has symbolized the unyielding Cyrenaican resistance to foreign control, a resistance that the more numerous and urban Tripolitanians did not participate in. Tripolitanian guilt has been assuaged by feelings of superiority toward the Cyrenaicans, who in turn affect to despise the former for their cowardice. Until 1963, Libya was a clumsy, three-headed federal state (the lightly populated Fezzan oases forming the third member of the then "United Kingdom of Libya"), with internal provincial customs barriers and an unwieldy system of three rotating capitals. The transformation of the country into a unified state has at least laid the groundwork for a potential reduction of mutual suspicions, although it may take some time before a true nation-state emerges in Libya. [The Arabist coup of the military in 1969, with no discernable regional attachments, may foster this development.]

The political system in independent Tunisia has been the result of the high degree of national integration and sophistication that the country achieved during its thirty-year-long period of working and preparing for independence. Alone in the Maghrib — and also uniquely among Arab states — Tunisia has had a functioning, mass-oriented, and mass-supported political party that has operated in both urban and rural areas for some three decades. The Destourian Socialist Party (PSD) (founded in 1934 as the Neo-Destour, and renamed in 1964), has done much to bring a majority of Tunisians into active participation in the task of nation-building; and its founder, Habib Bourguiba, president of the republic since 1959, chief architect of the political and social transformation of Tunisia, and leader of the struggle for independence, may legitimately be considered the "father of his country."

The PSD operates in Tunisia through a widespread system of local cells, regional federations, and committees responsible to the central party organization. It supervises and controls a number of affiliated organizations that deal with labor, education, women's affairs, student affairs, agriculture, commerce, and industry — that is, in short, it has a hand in every aspect of national activity. As virtually a single party, although it has worked a national-front system, the PSD is so overwhelmingly dominant that for operational purposes there is almost no difference between the state and the party. Most ministers are active party members who either double as local regional officials or spend their free time ranging through the countryside in campaigns of indoctrination and "explanation." The crucial turning point in modern Tunisian political history was the dethronement of a traditional bourgeoisie centered in Tunis by the party as a part of the steady evolution that Tunisia underwent in the years between 1930 and 1955. Out of this came a new Tunisian class — drawn from a wide spectrum of professional persons, lawyers, journalists, younger members of the urban middle and upper classes, some merchants and tradesmen, labor, youth, and, above all, women, whose emancipation in independent Tunisia has outstripped that in any other Arab country.[2]

Certain recent signs, however, suggest that the very success of the Destour in creating this new society, which has expanded so very rapidly in the past few years, may be the source of difficulties at a higher level of development. Government by charisma, personal whim, and an increasingly touchy authoritarianism — which is not, however, by any means a police-state totalitarianism — appears to be disenchanting ever larger numbers of educated young people and the younger members of the broadening elite. Since the early 1960's, there has been restiveness both among students abroad and within the ranks of the General Union of Tunisian Students (UGET), and also, most notably, among many trade unionists of the General Union of Tunisian Workers (UGTT), which is probably the most solidly constructed movement of its kind in any Arab or African country. The student demonstrations of 1966 were a clear sign of a disaffection that masks not only a deep crisis of generations but also a widespread feeling of discontent — a feeling that seems to stem principally from the fact that freedom of expression and the political evolution of the country have not paralleled the dramatic social progress made since independence. Although Bourguiba and the Destour have remarkable achievements to their credit — indeed, the balance since independence is very heavily positive — there is no doubt that they have lost the unquestioning confidence of much of the society that they have brought into being . . . .[3]

Algeria officially terms itself a "popular and democratic republic" and professes to follow a "specifically Algerian socialism." In fact, these phrases mask an incoherent ideology never explicitly defined (although described emotionally and at length in the Charters of Tripoli and Algiers) and also never put into practice. They also conceal a continuing undercover struggle between elments influenced by secular, Marxist principles and others who would have Algeria give primacy to Islamic values. Finally, they hide the fact that, since the coup of June 19, 1965, Algeria is a military dictatorship in which final power is in the hands of a twenty-four-man revolutionary council composed in the main of army officers.[4]

Since independence, word and deed, theory and practice, have more often than not been difficult to disentangle in Algeria. The single-party National

Liberation Front (FLN) theoretically guides a decentralized state modeled along the lines of a "people's democracy" with Yugoslav overtones. In reality, there is no party except for the façade;[5] the decentralization of state-owned sectors of agriculture (nationalized after the departure of European farmers in 1962) has hardly begun; and the nationalization of small businesses has been halted and reversed, with some properties being returned to their owners. Likewise, the new Algeria proclaimed a new deal for the workers and peasants, but labor unrest has grown to the point where massive arrests took place in mid-1966 and urban workers must be counted among the active opponents of the regime. Plans have been made to complete the transformation of the agrarian sector by nationalizing large Algerian-held properties – relatively few in number – and by turning state farms into independent accounting units. These underline the peasant origins of the revolution and the continuing concern of the authorities with the *fellahin,* in contrast to the lack of mutual comprehension found in relations between the government and the urban proletariat.

The 1965 coup that overthrew ben Bella at least had the advantage of replacing the hysteria of a near-paranoid head of state with the self-effacing group headed by Colonel Houari Boumedienne – aptly described as "a man of few deeds as well as few words" – which has produced the semi-stability of mediocrity. Of course, the regime in Algeria today suffers from the disadvantages of following in the footsteps of a demagogue and of having to face problems that will be virtually insuperable in the immediate future . . . . Without a functioning party to galvanize the population, especially in the rural areas; without the cohesion of effective leadership; and with virtually separate ministries, which often work at cross-purposes and of which only a few can be considered competent – Algeria has felt a steady drain of its once-vigorous revolutionary *élan.* Given the complexity of the economic and social problems confronting the country, and the limited abilities of not only most of the leadership but also of many middle- and lower-level cadres, it would seem likely that matters will not improve for some time to come – and they may well get worse before they get better.

Throughout most of their history the countries of the Maghrib have shared similar economies. These are based on Mediterranean-type agriculture, extensive stock-raising in the drier regions and the steppes, and some subsidiary oasis cultivation in the southern extremities. Emphasis on one or another of these may have varied both in time and by region – depending on climatic changes and irregularities of water, vegetation cover, and the like – but generally the resemblances have outweighed the dissimilarities.

From the days of Roman Africa to the modern farms of Morocco, and from the Libyan shores to the sheltered valley of the Sus around Agadir, the principal subsistence crops have been the hard cereals, durum wheat and barley, plus figs and olives. More recently, the main cash crops for export have consisted of citrus fruits, olives and their oil, specialty vegetables, and wine. Beginning in this century, the extractive industries have played an important role; phosphates have for some time been the principal earner in Morocco, and iron ore, lead, cobalt, zinc, and antimony are found in the area. Since World War II, a complex of secondary and processing industries has been developed. Fish and vegetable canning, fruit-juice processing, tanning, cement, glass, and paper industries, shoemaking and leatherware, plus a growing textile industry, form the core of this growth. In many fields here, as with the newer industrial endeavors, similarity in the economic structure leads to outright rivalry; several of the countries, for example, have either under construction or in planning their own steel mills, oil refineries, and chemical complexes.

The long and intricate relationship with colonialist Europe has further shaped the economies of the Maghrib countries along roughly parallel lines. All have been distorted by the so-called "dual economy" pattern, in which modern, European-type agriculture, industrial circuit, processing, and shipping facilities, and export market economies were superimposed on and alongside local cultivation methods and traditional ways in commerce and artisanry. Today the European farmer is physically gone from all the countries except Morocco, and in most cases the state has assumed the responsibility for agricultural progress and reform. The situation is more fluid in industry, but it can be said that much direct European control, and more influence, persists in Morocco and Libya, while in Algeria and Tunisia the legacy, although more abstract, is certainly not absent.

Today, however, there are increasingly divergent trends in the economy of each country, which could shape their future development along increasingly separate lines unless regional economic cooperation, so far of a quite restrained nature, succeeds in guiding them toward mutually complementary patterns. The state-farm system in Algeria has become a permanent feature of the landscape, but the essential problem, which is that there are two few estates to divide up and too many farmers on limited areas of land, has not really been tackled. Tunisia initiated a system of voluntary production cooperatives a few years back; this has had a moderate success, but the same problems of agrarian overpopulation and imbalance can be found in that country. Only recently, Morocco, under the prodding of the International Bank for Reconstruction and Development and the United Nations Food and Agricultural Organization, began seriously concentrating on agricultural reform and the improvement of farming techniques, but it is still too early to tell whether a sustained effort will be made, and, if so, what result can be obtained.

In two countries — Libya and Algeria — oil production has become a very important source of revenue. Libya's production of 72 million metric tons in 1966 raised it in the short span of seven years to sixth place among world producers, coming after Iran and preceding Iraq. Income to the government from oil receipts was increased to nearly $400 million in 1966, and [to more than $1 billion in 1970]. Per capita income in Libya, a theoretical figure at best, amounted to about $300 in 1966, or more than seven times what it had been in 1958 before oil was discovered. The government's five-year development plan — amounting to $475 million and programed through March, 1968 — was an effort to translate money into social progress, but it was hampered by human inefficiency, technical gaps, shortages, and corruption. [It was suspended by the military coup of September, 1969.] The mushrooming nature of Libyan society is reflected in the sharp inflation existing in wages, rents, and all prices save those of staple foods. The impact of oil has not been so dramatic in nearby Algeria, which has a much larger population and a smaller production, that is [46] million metric tons in [1969] (as compared with 26 million in 1965). Algeria signed a preferential agreement with France in 1965 covering oil policies with respect to joint prospecting and sales, and it has since been at odds with non-French foreign companies on several occasions, although some joint operations are carried out with them by Sonatrach, the state-owned oil corporation. Revenues [amounted to $250 million in 1969]; they are channeled through Sonatrach, which is active in all sectors of the petroleum industry and the subsidiary chemical industries that are derived from it.

Morocco and Tunisia, on the other hand, are relatively poor in oil, although Tunisia has made one fairly sizable strike and there are still possibilities of other discoveries. Both countries, however, are profiting from the tourist boom that exists throughout the Mediterranean and that got under way in Morocco and Tunisia in the early 1960's. The International Bank for Reconstruction and Development recommended tourist development along with agriculture and selective education as one of the fields of concentration for Morocco, and the enlarged infrastructure is being rapidly put into place there, as it is in Tunisia also. Morocco expects 1 million tourists by [1972, compared with 760,000 in 1969], and they could bring in from $160 to $200 million; Tunisia's figures for tourists have been running about half those of Morocco, with shorter stays and somewhat less money spent. Nevertheless, tourism should be the principal foreign currency earner for both states by [the 1970's].

In the end, however, the basic problems of the Maghrib cannot be solved without a thoroughgoing revision of existing traditional rural and urban structures that are inadequate to support the socio-economic growth of modern nation-states. This would require long-range, well-integrated plans for investments in human skills through education; for the use of surplus labor for productive purposes in public-works projects, especially in rural areas; and for a greater sense of urgency in agreeing to regional cooperation in the joint use of energy sources and the joint planning of industrial projects (some of which are already redundantly springing into being in several of the countries).[6] Negotiations [completed] by Morocco and Tunisia [in 1969 for partial] association with the European Economic Community are a constructive and probably necessary step in this direction.

The place of the countries of the Maghrib in human activities, their relationship to other nearby areas, and the meaning of their past and present have all been the subject of much speculation and comment. For my own part, I have suggested elsewhere that the terms that come most often to mind in these respects are permanence, cohabitation, responsibility, and identity. The first refers to the remarkable persistence of a peasant society and a traditional culture over more than two millennia in the face of incoming civilizations from the Middle East and Europe. The penetration of Muslim-Arab society in the Maghrib has been steady and pervasive through long centuries, and it has been fortified by the Arab renaissance of thought and socio-political activity during recent decades. Equally important perhaps is the modernist and largely Mediterranean culture imported along with European colonialism during the past century, which has generated a new wave of urban North African culture that mixes both external and internal elements in haphazard profusion.

Yet out of this mixture — now further complicated by a tenuous but nonetheless real sense of belonging to Africa as a whole — has come a modern Maghrib whose individual states, although each different from the other, have used all the borrowed and bestowed items in their cultural toolbox to make something unique and quite different from all other societies. The diversities and the similarities within the region reinforce each other; and the ambiguities with which the Maghrib is still cloaked finally fascinate us more than the reality of past achievements or the specific quality of the monuments and historical records. The subtle receptivity the Maghrib has shown in assimilating or rejecting this or that cultural item, in the midst of a deep inner indifference, makes it a fertile field for the student of comparative development, whether in history, anthropology, or modern politics. In the end, the greatest compliment that may be paid to the Maghrib is that it has preserved a full integrity at the same time that it has undergone attacks and encroachments upon its personality as severe, or indeed more severe, than any other society in generally similar colonial circumstances — even while hearing more clearly and intensely than most the siren call inviting it to abandon itself and embrace the other. Several years ago, the distinguished British social scientist Ernest Gellner put his finger on what is possibly the major focus of our interest, when he noted:

> Nature appears to have designed this island ["Jazirat al Maghrib" in Arabic, or the "Island of the West"] so as to provide the sociologist with a controlled experiment, a contrast with Mediterranean Europe, in which many factors are held constant. . . . Despite its similarity to Southern Europe and proximity to it, it has not shared in its historical development, until it became forcibly incorporated in it by colonial expansion. Why?

It is precisely because this question has not been properly answered that both the past and the present of the Maghrib compel our attention. And it is because the conditions of its incorporation by force into a European framework have been exchanged for the possibility of voluntary cooperation and interaction — with other areas as well as with Europe — that its future has an extraordinary appeal both in terms of inter-area and other comparative studies and as a laboratory for observing the kind of change and interchange that is rapidly intensifying among societies everywhere in our time. The extreme fluidity of the age poses searching psychological problems of security and identity to all the inhabitants of the Maghrib, but it equally suggests the opportunities still open to a culture that, in comparison with many, is still relatively open-ended and has a considerable area of choice in which to operate. The Maghrib might be envied for the fact that the material difficulties of its future are at least matched by the complexity of the cultural challenges facing it.[6]

Notes

1. See also by Charles F. Gallagher, American Universities Field Staff Report, North Africa Series, X, No. 2 (February, 1964), "Rural Reform and Revolution"; American Universities Field Staff Report, North Africa Series, X, No. 3 (March, 1964), "Industrialization and Development"; and *The United States and North Africa* (Cambridge, Mass.: Harvard University Press, 1963).

2. See Henri de Montety, "Old Families...," pp. 171–80 in this reader.

3. See Edouard Meric, "The Destourian Socialist Party...," pp. 285–95 in this reader.

4. See I. William Zartman, "The Algerian Army...," pp. 211–24 in this reader.

5. See William H. Lewis, "The Decline of Algeria's FLN," pp. 330–39 in this reader.

6. See A.F. Ewing et al. "Industrial Coordination...," pp. 475–92 in this reader.

TWO

Values and Attitudes

The basic ingredient of North African
attitudes is the area's Islamic background.
It is only an apparent paradox that this
must be understood in a dialectic context. North Africa — like any other
culture area — can never be wholly
Frenchified or Westernized; it can only
produce its own synthetic reactions to
imported change, combining its past heritage with antithetical notions of secularization, materialism, revolution, and nationalism. Nor can this synthesis be a
single, linear evolution toward one inevitable outcome. The reaction to antithetical ideas can as often be retrenchment

or the rediscovery of history as it can be acceptance of new notions at their face — and often locally inappropriate — value.

It is also paradoxical that the removal of a modernized upper class through revolution does not clear the way for revolutionary modernism but for the emergence of a mass that is at once uprooted and profoundly traditional. When the change is evolutionary, the maintenance of a modernized, intellectual elite — often in strong contrast to the alienated and unevolved mass — produces a gap between followers and leaders that is not present in revolutionary change and that forces the elite to relate to the traditional culture. In both revolution and evolution, therefore, the weight of traditional values and attitudes is at least as great as the weight of modernism (often it is greater). Both local and foreign observers too often mistake direction for position: societies with a strong, coherent tradition — such as the Islamic societies of the Maghrib — may be moving toward modern attitudes, but they are still deeply impregnated with tradition. All of this is not to deny modernization, development, or "progress"; it is only to suggest that where a people came from may be more important than the direction in which they are headed.

Such is the broad focus of the following studies of North African attitudes, although each article has very much its own point of view. The evolution of the Islamic tradition in the face of challenges — or at least of "differentness" — from the outside is examined by Jean Dejeux. Dejeux notes the dual colonial reaction of imitation and revolt — after centuries of defensiveness and withdrawal — and the unsettling effects of this reaction on traditional assurance and identity. These themes reappear often in subsequent selections, although Dejeux's unsecularized Westernism is his very own. L. Carl Brown discusses the socio-political implications of Islam today, with particular attention to the major Islamic institutions of North Africa — the sects and the 'ulema. More than a valueless humanistic synthesis or a consciously reformed structure, Brown foresees an experimental society, changing as it meets change.

Two selections treat the problem of confronting this heritage while at the same time satisfying contemporary needs and values. Ernest Gellner compares two Moroccan efforts at reconciling past and present, each claiming in its fashion that modernity does not represent a change but is merely an extension of the past; by historicizing modernism and rooting change in the past, the unsettling aspects of modernization are removed. Raymond Vallin examines the problems of fitting the "square pegs" of socialism into round Islamic holes. Islamicizing socialism may be a matter merely of pasting labels, but socializing Islam creates more concrete resistance.

Two other selections analyze "the price of upsetting the equilibrium and the internal dynamism of the Muslim societies" (as Dejeux puts it) that is the down payment of modernization. Frantz Fanon, writing as a trained psychiatrist rather than in his more familiar role as ideologue for the Algerian revolution, portrays the bewilderment of the North African expatriate in France. Pierre Bourdieu analyzes the same dehumanizing process in Algerian colonial society; his depiction of an ideological (magical) but prerevolutionary stage of attitudes is important to an understanding of both the background and the current status of Algerian society and politics.

The last two articles in this section deal with the role of education in modernization. Jacques Selosse, in an unusual psychological study of Moroccan school graduates, shows the uprootedness of those former pupils who have lived in areas of cross-cultural contact, as compared with the more solid base values of the more traditional sector. In the final selection, Douglas E. Ashford examines the changes in attitude of future elites in the Maghrib, with particular attention to personal and national components to attitudinal change.

Despite their different methodologies — most of which, after all, may be summarized under the label of interviewing, whether quantified, conceptually categorized, or simply ingested — the studies included here are all pioneer works. A few of them have skillfully interpreted old data to establish a basis for understanding; others have created new data to build on that base. Psychological studies, survey research, content analyses, depth interviews, and similar techniques have been only little used in North Africa.[1] Because the societies of the Maghrib are in general more open than those in other parts of Africa and the Arab world, these techniques can be used effectively. It is not only a question of introducing new techniques, however, for a great deal remains to be done on the historical components of Maghribi attitudes, and particularly on independent Maghribi history.

Note

1. A few published titles include Horace Miner and George de Vos, *Oasis and Casbah* (Ann Arbor: University of Michigan Press, 1960); Douglas E. Ashford, *Perspectives of a Moroccan Nationalist* (Totowa, N.J.: Bedminster Press, 1966), Michigan; Clement H. Moore and Arlie R. Hochschild, "Student Unions in North African Politics," in S. M. Lipset and P. G. Altbach, eds., *Students in Revolt* (Boston: Houghton Mifflin, 1969); John Simmons "Factors Associated with School Achievement," in John Badeau, ed., *North Africa Between Colonialism and Sovereignty* (pending, Columbia); and Mark Tessler, "Cultural Modernity: Evidence from Tunisia," *Social Science Quarterly* (Sept.,1971); John Sigler, "News Flow in the North African International Subsystem," *International Studies Quarterly* (Dec., 1969).

2

MEETING OF TWO WORLDS IN THE MAGHRIB

JEAN DEJEUX

This study seeks to sketch a portrait of the original relations between Islamic and Western cultures in the Maghrib, of later relations between Muslims and non-Muslims, and, finally, of prospects opened today by an Islam viewed by some of its elites as a vehicle to a universal humanism. We could almost venture a summary, descriptive title: from closed to open Islam.

The Islamic realities in the Maghrib are quite complex. As also happens in other religious surroundings, the real world is often far removed from theory and fine ideas. It therefore seems pretentious to attempt, in only a few pages, to discern the shape of yesterday's realities and tomorrow's prospectives. Nevertheless, in considering the relations between two worlds — Islamic and Western (which is theoretically Christian) — we may distinguish two phases: yesterday, withdrawal and commitment (introverted Islam); today, openness and dialogue (extroverted Islam). This, then, is not a study of abstractions: Islam is not seen in the light of ideas but in the life of the Muslim societies of the Maghrib.

An interpenetration of cultures and civilizations is as manifest in the Maghrib as anywhere else. The Islamic world of premechanized North Africa has to invest considerable effort in adapting to the industrial era of which it stands on the threshold. "Change or disappear," wrote Mohammed 'Aziz Lahbabi, concluding a series of meditations on national cultures and human civilization.[1] But how to change and still remain true to oneself, to one's essential values? It is not enough to call oneself "submissive" to God to find in this basic attitude the way to survive the steamroller of the technical world's "materialism" and of civilization's "modernism". In the end, one has to lose both aggressive and defensive attitudes in order to open up to others, to universalize and accept entry into the concert of nations, provided with a score that is in harmony with the rest.

YESTERDAY, WITHDRAWAL AND COMMITMENT

Before discussing the original relations between the two cultures, we have to ask if meaningful relations were possible at all, and to admit, in answer, that "the heart was not in it." A quick look at the sociohistorical aspect of the

Translated, by permission, from *Confluent*, No. 34 (October, 1963), pp. 759–80.

problems shows in fact that the "hedgehog" tactic (to use military terminology) adopted by Muslim societies did not help the meeting of the Muslim and Christian worlds. It is true that some values were exchanged, but Islamic Maghrib was on the defensive.

The image that comes to mind is one Jacques Berque likes to use, a variety of Arab rose, the "starred polygon." It evokes an alternation: on one hand, meditation and withdrawal within oneself and into the ancestral cave (the grotto of *Nedjma,* where the vital strengths of the race are concentrated), and on the other, the display of forces shown by the offensive angles of the geometric figure; or the internal angels *(arkan)* recalling the *zawiya* (corners of the *ribat* [fortress] where the soldiers prepared for the jihad [holy war]), and the aggressiveness of the outgoing angles, with warriors surging from the grotto and its refuges. It also evokes the maze, the labyrinth of the casbahs, and, ultimately, a mystery. In fact, it is a concrete reality, both offensive and biting, impersonal, mysterious, concealed, and unknown. . . .

This starred polygon, which to us recalls a Vauban fortress, can symbolize Maghribi societies, bristling with protruding bastions, nurturing mysterious cavils in their folds, and preserving in their most secret and concealed parts hidden corners where ammunition is stored. Through a reaction of defense and counteracculturation, Maghribi Islam became withdrawn and frozen. Seen from the outside, it was an impassive world, a world occupied with bare survival, with protecting itself in order to prevent absorption by others and to defend its own personality.

A DEFENSIVE WORLD PREPARES ITS REVENGE

Before closing in on itself, Maghribi Islam was influenced by its centrifugal nature. "Extremist" tendencies flourished, as, for example, the Kharijite schism, the Malekite reaction, the devastating invasion of the Hilalis, and the puritan reform of the Almohads. At one time, its advanced columns came as far as Poitiers. The Spanish Reconquest, in turn, certainly did not make any friends among those expelled from the Iberian Peninsula.

Islamic society withdrew into itself, suspicious and strong in its superiority complex as a "chosen people." It became "committed" and xenophobic when the Portuguese and the Spanish began to land on the North African shores in the fifteenth century. During the sixteenth century, the marabouts preaching in the countryside missed no opportunity to galvanize the masses against the invaders. Since then, and especially after the conquest years of 1830, 1881, and 1912, Muslim sensitivity reacted strongly against everything that appeared as an attack or a seizure. Almost without exception, the periodic revolts after 1830, especially in Algeria, whatever their true cause, took place in the name of Islam. Few disturbances arose without the jihad serving as a powerful trigger, without religious fanaticism in the background acting as a flag or a sign of momentary cohesion for dispersed tribes. Down to the present, Islam has served as a link and a politico-religious bond among different Maghribi groups, unified under Muslim symbols such as the Ramadan fast and religious festivals, the fez and the veil, or a sacred practice or custom used ostensibly as a reaction of counteracculturation. . . . It is not without significance that the maraboutic brotherhoods often headed the jihad. In any case, "it is almost a sure assumption that the Islamic faith – or better, devotion – was displayed more vividly after the European arrival then before, and after thirty years of Protectorate than after ten."[2]

A CLOSED WORLD WITH A RELIGIOUS SUPERIORITY COMPLEX

The seemingly closed fortress of the Islamic world tried to keep pure against contamination by the outside world. Everything was disrupted, a whole new social world had replaced the old order, but deep in their hearts its members felt strong. Withdrawn into themselves, the Muslims kept their conscience clear by repeating to one another and by hearing from the religious chiefs that "Yours is the best community that has been made for men: you order what is proper, forbid what is reprehensible, and believe in Allah" (Qoran, III, 106-110).

Two factors had a role in this hedgehog tactic adopted by the invested Maghribi societies: the European occupation, or colonization, and the Muslim superiority complex.

An Algerian writer, Malek Bennabi, in *Vocation of Islam*, described all this intelligently:

In its Mediterranean site, Islam's contact with Christian thought may not have brought spiritual enrichment but it did not impose transformation either. Contact between the two religious views came in a colonialist context, which seriously distorted the real meaning of Christian thought in Muslim eyes. The Muslim could easily feel superior to a rapacious and presumably Christian settler, established in injustice and exploitation. On this level he had no inferiority complex, no need to reassess his views or his faith. The moral apathy of Mediterranean Muslim peoples can probably be attributed to a large extent to this kind of righteous pride, to this religious self-sufficiency, that they implicitly compared with colonialist Christianity.[3]

This world, satisfied with possessing truth and perfection, was therefore under no pressure to emerge from itself and discover other cultural horizons. Withdrawn and dormant, it was in fact morally and intellectually paralyzed. Bennabi criticizes the self-satisfied attitude that made the people say, "Islam is a perfect religion. We are Muslims, therefore we are perfect." . . .

The colonial situation certainly could not bring forth public confessions from popular leaders. No one will demean himself or confess his mistakes when the enemy is looking. But neither did the clear conscience and "chosen people" mentality help raise questions in the preindependence period.

Talbi, in an excellent talk in Paris in 1960, said that one must avoid the "complacent and satisfied optimism born of a more or less voluntary delusion that has been one of the great calamities of Muslim civilization. By depriving this civilization of the incentive of creative dissatisfaction, it prepared it euphorically for the strangulation of death." Bennabi had his own terrible word for it: "colonizability," which, understandably, many regarded as offensive. Yet, an Algerian novelist took it up again in her first book: "Worst of all is the lethargy, the somnolence. We hear only of settlers and colonialism. But the real evil is our mentality of the colonized, of colonizables. That is what must be changed, that is what we have to tell them in our own language."[4] . . .

THE NON-MUSLIM WORLD COPIED BUT NOT "UNDERSTOOD"

Thus, because of colonization and the Islamic mentality, the "other world" of the West and of Christianity has not yet really been understood.

Albert Memmi, in his *The Colonizer and Colonized*[5] has sufficiently demonstrated the colonized's dual reaction. He first tries, in a disorganized fashion, to imitate the model. He tries to be "modern" in dress, furnishings, transportation. He learns to speak the other's language for immediate needs and future claims. . . . The intellectual genius ibn Khaldun, in his *Prolegomena,* accurately describes the imitation of the Galacians by the Andalusian Muslims. . . .

The second reaction of the colonized is the one of revolt, ending in independence. Before that time, Western borrowings were above all utilitarian: they would be useful one day in defeating the source. The colonized knew how to use the lessons of such movies as *The Great Train Robbery* or *Spartacus,* which today excite young Algerians who attend Parisian movie theaters. "Your teachers made me read Rousseau and French Revolution," answered Yacine Kateb when asked at what point his awakening to political realities had begun. "I can assure you that in our young minds the wild ideas came to the forefront. We took them very seriously."

But besides the lessons of the European revolutions and the French Resistance, besides the "conglomerate morain of utensils, clothes, gestures and languages" that Europe was pushing forward (Berque), what was retained? We will let Bennabi explain once more.

> The student goes forth with blinders that prevent him from contemplating civilization except from its abstract or futile side. He is able to see only the outcome, not the evolution, of civilization. Guided from the beginning by the sense of utility, he cannot perceive obscure but creative energies — above all, creative of moral and social values that make a civilized man superior to a primitive one. He will not see the child learning the meaning of and respect for life by petting a cat or growing a flower, nor the plower stopping at the end of a row to judge his work and commune with the earth, which is the embryo of the synthesis in all civilization. Nor will he have learned the lesson of "madmen" like Bernard Palissy, who burned his last piece of furniture and even his floorboards to obtain enamel. In general, the Muslim student did not experience Europe, he read it: he learned instead of understanding.[6]

Moreover, how many Muslims from North Africa set out to discover the West? The clichés and stereotypes about the West were as numerous in Muslim countries as clichés about Muslims were in the West. In the end, I am forced to conclude that Muslim Maghrib lacked — and still lacks — students of the West who can help the Maghrib to discover the values of the Christian world.[7] To be sure, there have been Western caricatures of Islam that the Muslims rightly contest. But the knowledge of Islam is more profound and more objective in the West than is North African Muslims' knowledge of Christianity, which is often reduced to a few clichés and simplistic formulas without meaning. One cannot appreciate what one does not understand.

TODAY: OPENING AND DIALOGUE

In saying "today," I encroach a bit on the future, at least in hope, and also look back on the recent past. We do not start at zero. Some of today's reforms and declarations of good intentions for the future have doubtless been possible because of independence. But they have also been possible because of the European presence, which, although no doubt colonialist, was not entirely negative. The Moroccan novelist Driss Chraibi dared to write in 1956 in the weekly *Demain:* "I am convinced that European colonialism was necessary and salutary to the Muslim world. Its very excesses, joined to the sure values of Europe, have been the ferment, the yeast, of the social revival that we are now witnessing."

Good intentions and, occasionally, good relations were not totally lacking. Without going as far back as the letter of Gregory VII to the emir an-Nasir of the Kalaa of the Beni Hammad, we can recall, for example, the stands and exhortations of Ferhat 'Abbas — who is today in disgrace — for a fruitful confrontation of Christians and Muslims in North Africa. "Christianity and Islam have chosen to settle in this Mediterranean soil," he wrote in the *République Algérienne* of February 13, 1953, "as they did in the Middle Ages in Spain. They can live in symbiosis complementing and enriching one another. This can bridge the chasm that the era of violence has opened between them. They can at last make our country a meeting place." . . .[8]

"The Muslim world has felt a terrible shock from Western civilization," noted Mourad Kiouane. In fact, the electric shocks of 1830, 1881, and 1912 unleashed an awakening of consciousness. Little by little, the eruption of technical, organizational Western civilization forced the Maghribi world to come out of its torpor, but at the price of upsetting the equilibrium and the internal dynamisms of the Muslim societies. If, therefore, the picture of the Islam of yesterday is generally true, black as it might be, if in the aggregate the Muslim world has not been provoked into "rethinking its faith," as Bennabi said, it is also undeniable that on several levels powerful phenomena have acted in favor of acculturation and more or less important men have begun to nourish other attitudes and to borrow new ways.

But deadlock and opposition were not only characteristics; often the imperviousness was only apparent. Even if former stratifications reappear and if inviolable areas open up to give vent to deeply repressed sentiments, bursting forth today in the joyous exuberance of feeling "free," progress nevertheless has been made. Perhaps all these new phenomena noted in the Maghribi societies are not due to acculturation, given the previous colonial relations. But just as animist Berbers acquired a certain universalist dimension through Islamic acculturation, so contemporary Muslims are influenced by the Western presence. It is difficult to draw up a balance sheet, for there have been many imponderables. But new values have appeared on several levels. Bilingualism is one important factor, even if in the Maghrib it is a difficult phenomenon to study. There are others. There were personal contacts in schools and universities, in the army and the administration, and, in a few cases, in mixed marriages. The European, by rubbing elbows with the Muslims, took on some of their habits and customs, some of the Mediterranean ways of life and action. But the European presence had an even stronger impact on Maghribi society. Education was responsible for a good deal of the transfer of new ideas and attitudes, but even more so "the effect of the general climate" (George Hardy) of the French presence. Finally, one must mention the Algerian workers in France: more than 3 million in the last fifty years. They have certainly — and visibly — been influenced by current ideas. . . .

POLYGAMY BECOMES INADMISSIBLE IN THE TWENTIETH CENTURY

The terrible shock of the European rush into North Africa and then of independence permitted the breakup of a closed world and the condition for new reforms.

Three main foci needed development: family, state, and individual. When President Bourguiba declared that "polygamy has become inadmissible in the twentieth century," it sounded to Europeans like a public avowal that things were changing. Of course, this is not the criterion for the over-all evolution of a country, but it shows that, on the level of family realities, some values were transferred. Monogamy was already practiced in the Tunisian cities, but Bourguiba's reform officially sanctioned a large, active women's rights movement. Other marriage reforms followed: Obligatory consent of the two parties, discontinuation of repudiation, and so on. In Morocco, polygamy is not forbidden but simply made more difficult. Women's rights are increasingly being recognized, and as the societies develop the role of women will doubtless grow in importance. North African workers in France have observed authentic Christian households and have appreciated the place of the wife in these homes. A young man wants to choose his wife instead of having one imposed on him, and both man and wife hope to build a home that will no longer be the extended family of the past but rather a stable and united couple. Much remains to be done to reform false ideas about sexuality and the morals of the married man, to inculcate an aspiration to higher values in marriage. Young people must be taught to adapt to the demands of a mixed society. In short we must have an education in love.

There is a general desire for states that are not totalitarian but democratic, in which "the people" are given a voice; there is talk of liberty for everyone but also of a single party. The crucial point is secularity, a concept unknown in Islam. But in North Africa, at least, again depending on the individual and the different levels of society, the tendency is more and more toward a concept of Islam as a "private religion." . . . In Islam, "what is involved is nothing less than a cultural revolution that aims at establishing religion as such, at delimiting it on the level of logic, at defining (in the full sense of the word): its boundaries would then be recognized . . . [it is] the mutation from an integrating to an integrated religion [that is involved]"[9] But because the partisans of secularity have to take the traditional sectors of society into account, the constitutions use formulas such as "Tunisia is a free state. . . . Its religion is Islam." Furthermore, North Africa confuses clericalism and church, secularity and secularism or even atheism. The notion of tolerance must also be taught: ordinarily it is only relative,[10] as in the other countries with Muslim majority.

Lastly, the idea of the human personality is making its way little by little into North African mentalities. There is a declared intention to respect not only the freedom of others, the freedom of conscience, but also other basic liberties, within the natural limits of law and order in the society. . . .

The values concerning women and monogamy are human values born in the West, but with few exceptions, they are generally not recognized as such. Truths are easily "Islamized," as the writer Savvas Pacha said at the end of the last century, Muslim psychology is generally averse to the notion of borrowing. Thus there is always an attempt to locate these values — or at least their roots — in the Qoran. Yet the Muslim values are not purely and simply equivalent to Christian values. They are not comparable through similarity, but only through analogy.

"Let us shake off immobilism," is the title of a pamphlet by Mahjoub ben Milad, Professor at the Tunis Normal School. "I am convinced," he wrote, "that nothing like that [rediscovery of spiritual interest] will ever come if the Oriental countries do not shake the accumulated dust of centuries of decadence from their spiritual structure and if they do not boldly turn for support to a reconsideration of their spiritual heritage, completely, penetratingly and unfailingly." Courageous, lucid self-criticism has tended in that direction in Tunisia, in particular by writers, professors, and trade unionists, as early as the first years of independence. Studies have been conducted by several journals, colloquia have been held and new periodicals came into being that question, criticize, propose reforms, and call for "an immense cleansing of our cultural past in order to clean all traces of decadence from it" (Mahmoud Messadi)[11] . . . .

The most lucid among the Maghribis know very well the direction that the crisis in North Africa is taking. We have only to read again the talk given by Talbi in Paris,[12] which courageously describes the superficiality of Islam in the youth, the situation of the non-"catechized" masses, and the religion "apparently unable to grasp the seriousness of the stakes," outside the circuit of current events, and perceived only as a cohesive factor or "a kind of patriotism." Behind the façade, the structure faces collapse: "This Islam is at the mercy of any demagogue." Everyone, for that matter, knows that minds are already preoccupied with Marx: encumbering "myths" and "superstructures" are swept away by groups and publications of the so-called friends of the people. Everywhere, a formerly sacred world, previously under the law of the Qoran, is being "profaned." Movies, radio, television, press all propagate images, ideas, slogans, ways of thinking and acting that are not Muslim. The ideas and habits of yesteryear are called into question. Often the whirlwind creates a vacuum: "I come to you to rediscover my soul," said an Algerian!

How to change and not lose one's soul? The Maghribis feel that the colonial experience depersonalized them, upsetting the old equilibrium and destroying the original human values of an archaic or premechanized communal society. But this change in traditional behavior is inherent in the changes necessary for joining the industrial era. Some obvious human values have nevertheless had an impact on the individual, thanks to the encounter with humanist and Christian aspects of the West. What the Maghribis should hold on to are the values of solidarity and mutual help that have been their strength, as well as the spiritual values, which are sometimes considered superfluous but which are in fact the only elements capable of supplying "the spiritual supplement" necessary to the new world. A religious sense, a feeling for the family, a tradition of hospitality, all must remain, for without them the forces of collectivism already threaten to dehumanize the authentic personalization that has already begun to take shape.

IN SEARCH OF A NEW HUMANISM

The profound significance of today's crisis is the rupture with a closed, quiet universe and the thirst for a new universal and nonsectarian humanism. . . .

Research into this new humanism is only one aspect of religious thought. Let us not delude ourselves. "There are possibilities, even signs of renewal and impetus," said Talbi, speaking of Islam as a whole, "but if we are to be objective and rigorous we cannot say that there is presently a real rebirth and growth."[13] To believe that there has been a profound re-evaluation just because other words have been used would be harmful. But the very fact that there is concern is already important.

We can see the tendency toward a new humanism in the studies of professors and essayists, in contemporary novels and poetry. For the moment, it consists mainly of aspirations, declarations and affirmations, lacking in depth and insufficiently documented. There is talk of "a new scale of values" (Mahmoud Messadi), a desire to "promote man" (Ahmed ben Salah), a wish to "reconcile man with himself." Man valued as such must "cut himself a path toward the goal of universal man" (Jean Amrouche).[14] Having discovered the power of man, one Maghribi even wrote that "man is the supreme value of everything else." It is difficult to know how far these formulas go: Vague humanitarianism? Hazy socialism?

We can ask on what this humanism is based. Lahbabi writes that "in order to be a true humanism, realistic personalism would have to put God 'between parenthesis,' that is, make him neither an accused, an obstacle, or an absolute motor."[15] He believes that the individual in Jean Lacroix's personalism is limited by transcendence from on high. In his view, Lacroix's and Mounier's positions are not free of the heavy weight with which medieval speculations have charged the word "person," a concept understandable only in reference to a being without end, perfect and transcending the individual.[16] Rejecting this supposed limitation, the author seems to arrive at an anthropocentric humanism, cut off from a foundation in God that should ensure its values. The transcendency we are discussing here seems to have been understood by Lahbabi as totalitarian and oppressive, a divine, arbitrary voluntarism taking away all freedom from the human person. However, a healthy notion of transcendency is not an obstacle to the self-assertion of the individual. Furthermore, if faith in God is reduced to a quarrel of religious faiths or to dogmatic differences, one can only reject that basis of belief. Rightly understood, however, it is the only fundamental attitude: "Faith in God preserves faith in man."[17] Retained on the level of essential values, faith cannot be a source of oppositions. Cut off from the "roots of heaven," despite the generous intention to bring together believers and disbelievers (Marxists), one might end up with an eclectic doctrine that satisfies no one.

This brotherly humanism should make it possible to bring up the mass in a true spirit of tolerance, not because God will have been relegated "between parenthesis" (since faith in God unites believers and should inspire respect toward unbelievers, who also enjoy the same sun, to use an analogy), but because religious barriers and even the spirit of *dhimmi* [protected non-Muslims] will have been transcended. Brotherly humanism need not be limited to man as a member of the Prophet's community.

If we do not want to talk of religious faith, however, let us speak with Jacques Maritain of temporal and secular "faith," the essential criteria for "living together" in a terrestrial pluralistic city. Maritain's goal is thus *purely practical*. His points of convergence should be admitted by every civilized man of good sense: basic political and social rights and liberties. What is important for the inhabitants of this pluralist world is to agree on the same practical conclusions, "as long as they cherish, perhaps for completely different reasons, truth and intelligence, human dignity, liberty, brotherly love, and the absolute value of the moral good." In that case, there is absolutely no need to try to justify these practical positions — or at least at such lengths — since some philosophical and theological convictions will remain divergent.[18]

In order that these principles will not remain simply fine ideas, it is necessary for different levels of society to be educated in the direction of this pluralism and universalism. This is how the wish of Jean Amrouche must be interpreted: "Can [Algeria] effectively fulfill the role that we are hoping for, to become a multiracial nation that will overcome the antagonisms of race and religion? Will it become something that is not found anywhere else in the world, the fatherland of man overcoming its weighty components: religious, linguistic, emotional, and mythological? This is the big question."[19]

Relations and fruitful encounters were established between Islam and Christianity in Spain in the twelfth and thirteenth centuries, and also in the Italian cultural centers, although the Muslim influence must not be exaggerated.[20] Conditions are very different today. When we ask the Maghribis what their religious culture has to offer the West, the answers are often embarrassed.

Several levels must be distinguished. A purely sentimental return to Arabo-Muslim myths would not be beneficial. In the twentieth century, these myths could serve no other purpose than a demagogic orchestration of a revolution for which the masses demand an Islamic symbol. We understand "the attachment to the Arabo-Islamic culture without which the intellectual feels himself uprooted and cut from his people," but this attachment is not without ambiguities.[21] "It cannot be, in any case, a nostalgic withdrawal into the past," said a proposal of the Federation in France of the National Liberation Front (FLN). But there is no agreement on the positive and original content of Islam, not as it was in the Middle Ages but as it can be appreciated today, taking into account acculturation and influence of Western ideas. . . .

Today, more than ever, it is necessary to open to others. Léopold Sédar Senghor, for example, is not afraid to call himself a "cultural half-breed," just as he declared that "all the great civilizations were [and] are civilizations of cultural — and indeed biological — mixtures." How is that meeting of cultures understood in the Maghrib?

Toward what destiny is Islam heading? "Will it end," Talbi asked, "by making a doctrine out of secularization of the law, consecrating . . . the separation of the spiritual from the temporal? If so Islam would make room for a world-wide ecumenical civilization, even if it were to persist as a living but personal faith inspiring feelings and attitudes." In any case, it would be an illusion to believe in a world-wide religion made by men, in a vague and inconsistent universal syncretism qualified as "transcendent unity of religion."

We are for the moment in an interregnum, according to Paul Ricoeur: "We are on the threshold of a true dialogue."[22]

But original relations can be established or intensified in the Maghrib, land of confluence, only if the Muslim societies open themselves to pluralism and if the youth is educated with this in mind. The thirst for learning is great. But the conditions for a true dialogue will not be fulfilled if people remain content to "read" Europe, to learn instead of understand, if they do not emerge from their complacency and discover the meaning of concern and of seeking.

Notes

1. Mohammed Aziz Lahbabi, *Du clos à l'ouvert,* published by the Comité du Maghreb (Casablanca: Dar el-Kitab, 1961).

2. Jacques Berque, "Vers une étude des comportements en Afrique du Nord," *Revue Africaine,* 1956, p. 553.

3. Malek Bennabi, *Vocation de l'Islam* (Paris: Editions du Seuil, 1954), pp. 165—66.

4. Assia Djebar, *La Soif* (Paris: Julliard, 1957), pp. 70—71.

5. Albert Memmi *The Colonizer and the Colonized* (Boston: Beacon Press, 1966).

6. Bennabi, *op. cit.,* pp. 60—61.

7. See Francois Bonjean, "Quelques causes d'incompréhension entre l'Islam et l'Occident," *Cahiers du Sud,* 1947, p. 33. On the same point of Christian doctrine, Lahbabi wrote: "I am ashamed to note that compared with eminent Islamologists, such as the Dominican Father *Anawait,* Louis Gardet, or Father Hayek, there are no or only a few Muslims who, to my knowledge, are able to describe Catholic, Protestant, and Orthodox theologies objectively without polemics or repeated clichés." *Confluent,* No. 20 (March, 1958), p. 82.

8. See also 'Abbas, *La Nuit coloniale* (Paris: Julliard, 1962), pp. 174—75.

9. J. Poirier, "Droit Musulman et développement économique," *Cahiers de l'I.S.E.A. Humanités,* special issue, No. 120 (December, 1961), p. 217.

10. See Moulay Ahmed 'Alaoui's interview in *Témoignage Chrétien* (April 13, 1962), p. 927, on the banning of Catholic broadcasts on the Moroccan radio.

11. Demeerseman calls the "generation of Independence," in Tunisia "the generation of self-criticism." See his excellent study on Tunisian personality in *IBLA,* Nos. 95—96 (1961), pp. 223—49.

12. See *Confluent,* No. 8 (June-July, 1960), pp. 398—405.

13. A Muslim lawyer, Asaf A. A. Fyzee, declared: "To answer this question, we would have to know if Islam can today produce a spiritual intelligence as Ghazzali or ibn Khaldun, or St. Thomas Aquinas, or Luther, or even Barth, Kierkegaard, Maritain, or Berdayef. But the question still remains: If there were such a man and if he were willing to speak out, would his voice be heard?" Conference on Islam (Paris: Centre National de Recherches Scientifiques, 1956), p. 131.

14. *Confluent,* No. 22 (June, 1962), pp. 461—63.

15. Mohammed Aziz Lahbabi, *De l'être à la personne* (Paris: Presses Universitaires de France, 1954), p. 347.

16. *Ibid,* p. 171; see also pp. 344—47.

17. Jacques Maritain, *Le Philosophe dans la cité* (Paris: Alsatia, 1960), p. 173.

18. Jacques Maritain, *L'Homme et l'état* (Paris: Presses Universitaires de France, 1953), pp. 100—106.

19. *Afrique-Action,* February 13, 1961.

20. P. Chenu, *Confluent,* Nos. 11—14 (1961), L. Gardet and M. Anawati, *Introduction à la théorie musulmane* (Paris: Vrin, 1949), chap. ii; G. von Grunebaum, *Medieval Islam* (Chicago: University of Chicago Press, 1946).

21. See Georges Laveau, in Francois Perroux, ed., *L'Algérie de demain* (Paris: Presses Universitaires de France, 1963), p. 230.

22. *Esprit,* No. 10 (October, 1961), pp. 439—53.

3

ISLAM'S ROLE IN NORTH AFRICA

L. CARL BROWN

The role of Islam in modern North Africa[1] (and, for that matter, in the Middle East as well) is as elusive as quicksilver. With a bit of sophistical reasoning it is not too hard to show an "essentially Islamic" base to all kinds of activities and movements in North Africa. Stacking the cards in the other direction, it becomes no less difficult to argue that Islam is more or less irrelevant to the major problems North Africa is confronting today.

Perhaps a better approach to the subject avoids these extremes by recognizing that it is not quite within the Islamic framework that problems are being faced in the area. North Africa today is characterized not so much by a clash of the religious and the secular as by a more general confrontation of old and new — a confrontation that cuts across religious, political, economic, and even familial institutions. For example, to isolate Islamic modernism from this over-all context of a revolutionary struggle between old and new is to distort its significance. In the same way, to view other religious developments as essentially a rearguard action against an encroaching secularism is to assume a dichotomy that is not at all that sharp in day-to-day life.

Islam in modern North Africa is one part in the total pattern of a society, once traditionalist and scorning change, that is becoming more and more oriented toward the dynamic. The burden of proof has shifted. The revulsion against *bid 'a* (blameworthy innovation) has given way to a fascination for *nahda* (renaissance).[2]

In this present flux there are many "Islams." There are several who would claim to speak for Islam. There are infinitely more who are either indifferent or inclined to postpone consideration of religious matters. There are almost none (an important point, perhaps too often ignored) espousing a frontal attack against Islam. Islam in North Africa does not lend itself to anything approaching European anticlericalism.

THE IMPACT OF ISLAM

On now to a few brief statements that may help to clarify the role of Islam in North Africa today (keeping in mind the difficulties and reservations suggested above):

31

1.   By Eastern Arab standards, there is a great uniformity in North African Islam (and has been for centuries, since the fall of the Almohads). Except for the very small Mzabite community in south central Algeria and the few remaining Kharijites on the Tunisian island of Djerba, all North African Moslems are Sunni, and the vast majority follow the same school of law (Maleiki).

2.   Also, unlike the Arab East, there are very few remaining native Christians in North Africa. (The last handful of Christian dioceses disappeared in the 1150's, at the time of Almohad persecution.)

3.   For these above two reasons, Islam is the most important common denominator in the Maghrib. As a symbol of unity and identity, Islam is to North Africa what Arab nationalism is to the Arab East. In the Maghrib, Islam can be appealed to as the means of transcending such basic differences as those between Arab and Berber, just as a common Arabness can be used in the Arab East in an attempt to unite Sunnis, Shi'ites, and the many Christian communities.

4.   From the late medieval period right up to the present century, North Africa was the Islamic area *par excellence,* where Muslim mysticism had flourished in the form of mass religious brotherhoods. In all Muslim countries, the brotherhoods with their veneration of the sheikh deemed to have powers of intervention with the divine *(baraka)* have served as the major vehicle for introducing unorthodox practices and popular superstitions. Many French writers have seen this as no more than a pre-Islamic Berber tendency toward anthropolatry, but this idea seems of dubious value, since the same institutions have flourished (sometimes still survive) in the Arab East, Turkey, Islamic Black Africa, and elsewhere.

Historically, the brotherhoods have been the major institutional means of extending Islam (albeit a somewhat distorted version) out into the countryside. In a time of extreme political decentralization (which characterized the premodern period), the brotherhoods also served political functions – providing asylum, mediating between the tribes and the central government, rallying political protest movements against the central government, and so on.

5.   One of the most imposing changes that has taken place in the last few generations in North Africa has been the rapid decline of these Muslim brotherhoods – mainly the result of modernization. The increased power of the central state apparatus, which modern colonization brought, has rendered their former political role obsolete. At the same time, the concomitant increase in influence of the urban (and also cultural) centers, plus the now rapid increase in literacy, have conspired to make the brotherhoods – representatives of a popular, antirational, and usually provincial form of Islam – less appealing.

The brotherhoods also (quite consistent with their venerable political traditions of mediating with central political authority) cooperated with the French, a stance that earned them the enmity of the rising nationalist movements.

However, such a pervasive network as the brotherhoods does not virtually disappear without leaving traces. A few random examples might suggest the complexity of this development (which needs much more research):

In the 1930's many Moroccan peasants thought of the nationalists as "a new religious brotherhood."

During the colonial period, local meetings of nationalist political parties, in both Morocco and Tunisia, were often held in former *zawiyas*. The tomb of Tunisian trade-union leader Ferhat Hached (assassinated by French terrorists in 1952) is now visited on Fridays by pious Muslim women, which suggests that "Sidi Ferhat" has become to a certain class of people not so much a nationalist martyr as a Muslim saint.

A final example is the paradoxical synthesis of Western left-wing ideology with old-fashioned veneration of the sheikh that was evident in the movement led by Algeria's Messali Hajdj.

To the extent that the aims of modernization are achieved, there is every reason to believe that new, more impersonal groupings, such as political parties, trade unions, sports and professional clubs, can fill the social role formerly monopolized by the brotherhoods. At best, there will be only transitional difficulties. However, in the event of a really serious socio-political breakdown, a much more fundamentalist Muslim organization (adapting many brotherhood principles of organization) could well quickly appear, perhaps something like Muslim Brethren of the Arab East.

6. The brotherhoods would almost certainly have declined in any case, but the rapidity of their fall and the thoroughness of their disgrace was in large measure the result of Islamic reformism in North Africa. Ideologically linked with the *salafiya* movement of Mohammed Abduh (1849–1905) and the *al-Manar* group, reformism in North Africa was of great (and often unrecognized) importance not only in combating the brotherhoods but also in working for a restoration of the Arabo-Muslim identity. In all three countries, Islamic reformism has been closely lined with early nationalism.

The Muslim reformers were of greatest importance and maintained their separate identity longest in Algeria. There a group active since the 1920's under the leadership of Abd al-Hamid ben Badis organized, in 1931, the Algerian Association of 'Ulema, which continued to exist right up until merging with the National Liberation Front (FLN). The Algerian Association of 'Ulema, by creating rudimentary Qoranic schools, combating the divisiveness and heterodoxy inherent in the brotherhoods, and generally fostering a sense of Algerian Muslim identity, did as much as any single organization to prepare the ground for the eventual armed struggle under the aegis of the FLN.

In Tunisia, the early nationalist and leader of the original Destour, Abd al-Aziz al-Tha'albi, was basically a Muslim reformer à la Mohammed Abduh, but Islamic reformism took a back seat much earlier in Tunisia to the Western-trained modernists under Bourguiba. (Note, however, that Bourguiba and those who, in 1934, would form the Neo-Destour did not take an anti-Islamic position. Rather, they effectively posed in those early years as the real defenders of Tunisia's Islamic personality.)

Islamic reformism was the major stimulus behind the early nationalist stirrings beginning in Morocco in the late 1920's, and the present leader of the Istiqlal, 'Allal al-Fassi, whose political career began at this time, is a classic representative of both the strength and weaknesses of Islamic reformism today.

In all three countries, Islamic reformism was in the forefront of the campaigns: (a) against the brotherhoods; (b) in favor of expanding Arabic and Islamic education; (c) in favor of reforming traditional religious education in order to make it more adaptable to modern requirements; (d) in general terms, against anything smacking of "assimilation" (as often noted, it was ben Badis who answered the assimilationist argument of Ferhat 'Abbas in 1936 that the Algerian nation did not exist).

Yet today, when considering the present lowly status of those spokesmen of Islamic reformism (for example, after independence a few members of the Algerian Association of 'Ulema were given posts in the unimportant Habous Ministry),[3] one is tempted to ask if the role of these Muslim reformers was not basically that of unwittingly clearing away roadblocks for a thoroughgoing secularism.

7.   The above question leads to another striking phenomenon in present-day North Africa: the decline of the old religious elite. In a sense, just as with the religious brotherhoods, the decline in power and prestige of the orthodox 'ulema has also been a result of modernism brought or at least accelerated by the colonial situation. Even the active role played by the reformist 'ulema in the nationalist movements (especially in Algeria) was not enough to retrieve their position.[4]

The 'ulema as a class in all three countries have already lost or are fast losing any institutional base from which to exert power or influence: (a) they have lost control of education (a monopoly of the 'ulema class in the premodern period); (b) they are losing their last foothold in the legal profession (the shari'a courts) with the establishment of a single, national system of courts, as in Tunisia; (c) they have lost or are losing the emoluments coming from administration of religious trust properties (habous).

The profession of Muslim "cleric" has lost prestige, and as a result fewer qualified young people train to become 'ulema. A social history of the "old families" in all three countries showing how these families (often of the 'ulema class for generations) have sent their sons to Western or Western-type schools would illustrate the point.

8.   It is also true that Islam (as is the case with any religion in a time of revolutionary social change) is often caught in a cross fire, used as a justification for things sanctioned simply by tradition and, generally, found in uneasy alliance with lost causes. The whole campaign of female emancipation is a classic example, but there are many others.

9.   Still, postindependence constitutions of the three countries designate Islam as the state religion. The Tunisian president must be a Muslim, and in the Moroccan constitution the king is given the caliphal title of commander of the faithful. There is almost no antireligious (or anticlerical) feeling in North Africa (admittedly there would be little need for such an attitude, given the declining state of the 'ulema). It is also worth noting that Bourguiba's famous campaign against the Ramadan fast was based on a rather strained interpretation of permissible exceptions according to shari'a law, that the major resistance came from the masses and not the 'ulema, and, in any case, Bourguiba is atypical even for Tunisia in his frontal assault on Islamic practices.

ISLAM AND POLITICS

A few tentative conclusions somewhat more directly linked to politics and international relations might now be suggested:

1.   The Muslim religious institution — the Muslim "church" — in North

Africa is in such disarray that it is quite meaningless to talk of "whither Islam" in terms of what the orthodox 'ulema class are thinking or doing. There will be no serious confrontation of the 'ulema with any North African government unless there is something approaching a complete breakdown of government control and effectiveness. The rise of the Qiyam (Values) Society, which caused quite a stir early in 1964, says quite a bit about the continued instability and lack of consensus in Algeria, but this group appears to have had little chance of playing an important role.

2.   The educated elite in all three countries are absorbed with a certain idea of progress, a new humanism or this-worldliness that is, of course, basically Western in inspiration. They are in a mood more concerned with getting things done than pondering eternal verities. There is no prejudice against Islam in their viewpoint. Even those many who think of themselves as Marxists would tend to find the antireligious aspects of Marxism somewhat irrelevant. To them, at the moment, Islam is more nearly a matter of self-identification vis-à-vis the "other." They have, in effect, not rejected Islam but rather nationalized it (a position not unlike that of the agnostic Zionist).

3.   There is no reason why the intensity of the common Muslim identity vis-à-vis the outsider (so strong during the colonial period and the struggle for independence) should not subside, at least in the next few years. The removal of the *colon* population as an ever-present threat and attraction and even the radical decline in the native North African Jewish population has left North Africa today an even more religiously uniform country.[5]

4.   On the other hand, there is a certain uneasiness and feeling of estrangement that — other things being equal (a major exception at the moment) — would incline even the Western-trained elite toward increased rapprochement with the Arab (and Muslim) East.

5.   An argument advanced by several Western Arabists and scholars suggests that the "crisis" that finds an Islam still reluctant to leave the cocoon of its medieval synthesis pitted against the requirements of the modern world must be resolved before any of these Islamic societies can turn effectively to other problems. In effect, until a new Ghazzali . . . nothing but trouble for the Muslim countries.

Perhaps this viewpoint should be rejected. Does history bear out the implicit assumption that societies must solve their problems first, or that they must have (or believe that they have) coherent value systems in order to act effectively, or that the blueprint comes before the experimentation?

There are, in fact, some amazing new ideas about Islam being advanced by modern Western-trained North African Muslims. Most of these views would curl the hair of traditionally trained orientalists. They involve such ideas as the separation of church and state, or that the interpretation of ritual requirements is a matter between the individual believer and God, or that the chief of state in a democratic Muslim state can express the consensus *(ijma')* of the religious community.

It is also stimulating to see that the best of these new ideas are well beyond the pitifully simple apologetics that have characterized, and all too often still characterize, the writings of the traditionally trained Muslims. Examples of the apologetic tendency may be seen in earlier attempts to identify Islamic values with those of the French Revolution; or, during the heyday of democratic liberalism, to insist that Islam created the first democratic society;[6] or — a later and still popular tendency — to say that Islam was the first socialist society.[7] On the other hand, these new ideas about Islam advanced by certain modern North African Muslims are infinitely more sophisticated and represent a genuine "internalization" of certain Western values. The ideas of those in North Africa who seek a synthesis between their own culture and Western education will probably not soon jell into a consistent new philosophy. North Africa (for that matter, the Arab East as well) will continue its experimentation in creating a dynamic society institutionally adjusted to the requirements of continuous change. Unless there is a complete breakdown that could leave the way open for a reactionary group assuming a religious coloration, there is no reason why the new "Ghazzali" cannot be kept waiting in the wings indefinitely.

Notes

1. Especially helpful from among the writings of the North African Muslims themselves on this subject are: Malek Bennabi, *Vocation de l'Islam* (Paris: Editions du Seuil, 1954); Mohammed Aziz Lahbabi, *Le Personnalisme musulman* (Paris: Presses Universitaires de France, 1964); and the special issue of *Confluent,* Nos. 41-42 (June-July, 1964) entitled "Comment les Musulmans du Maghrib comprennent, vivent et pratiquent l'Islam?" An excellent general appreciation of North African Islam within its historical setting is Roger Le Tourneau, "North Africa: Rigorism and Bewilderment," in G. von Grunebaum, *Unity and Variety in Muslim Civilization* (Chicago: University of Chicago Press, 1955). Those interested in following this subject in greater detail will find a longer bibiography at the conclusion of chap. v in Leon Carl Brown (ed.), *State and Society in Independent North Africa* (Washington, D.C.: The Middle East Institute, 1966).

2. See Jean Dejeux, "Meeting of Two Worlds in the Maghrib," pp. 21-30 in this reader.

3. For other views on the Habous Ministry, see Raymond Vallin, "Muslim Socialism in Algeria," pp. 50-65 in this reader.

4. See 'Allal al-Fassi, "The Mission of the Ulema," pp. 151-58 in this reader.

5. See "Les Juifs dans l'Afrique du Nord — leur situation et leurs problemes en 1968," *Maghrib,* No. 27 (May-June, 1968).

6. See Ernest Gellner, "The Struggle for Morocco's Past," pp. 37-49 in this reader.

7. See Raymond Vallin, "Muslim Socialism in Algeria," pp. 50—64 in this reader.

4

THE STRUGGLE FOR MOROCCO'S PAST

ERNEST GELLNER

There are at present two dominant political parties and trends in Morocco. The key figure of one is 'Allal al-Fassi, and of the other, Mehdi ben Barka. Both parties spring from the split in the Istiqlal in 1959. [Ben Barka was assassinated in 1965 but the party lives on.]

Roughly speaking, ben Barka's is the left party of the urban working class and of the radical and occidentalized intellectuals; al-Fassi's is the party of the old traditional bourgeoisie and of the countryside.

It so happens that, in 1958, two years after independence and before the split, two books by Moroccans about Moroccan history appeared, one with an introduction by al-Fassi, the other with an introduction by ben Barka. The two books were not aimed at each other; nor, apparently, was either written in the knowledge that the other was appearing. Superficially, they are not comparable: ben 'Abdallah's *Les grands courants de la civilisation du Maghrib,*[1] with an introduction by al-Fassi, clearly has a wider scope than Lahbabi's *Le Gouvernement marocain à l'aube du XXème siècle,* with an introduction by ben Barka.

The two volumes appeared at a time when the split was not yet openly acknowledged, whether or not it was foreseen or contemplated. But few things could illustrate the spirit and state of mind of groups of people better than the manner in which they view their own national past. By juxtaposing these two volumes, we are conveniently presented with two contrasted spiritual self-portraits, more revealing perhaps than formal statements of position (which, in Morocco as elsewhere, tend to be abstract, emotive, noncommittal, and often indistinguishable from party to party). History is the most powerful of political projectionists. The past may or may not explain the present, but the present reveals itself in its manipulation of the past. . . .

The reasoning in 'Allal al-Fassi's introduction is interesting enough to be reported in full. He explains frankly and simply the reasons, as they appear to him, for the need for the kind of historical study of which the book is an example. Colonialists invoke the backwardness of Arab and Muslim lands and justify occupation as the only way to bring them the benefits of "modern methods," held by them to be the exclusive property of the West. Al-Fassi

Reprinted, by permission, from *The Middle East Journal,* XV (Winter, 1961), 79-90.

reports the following impressions from his own *tournées de propagande* in Europe, Africa, Asia, and America: the *élite internationale* shows little interest in the "monstrosities of colonialism," because they suppose these might equally be committed by native authoritarians. International public opinion, he remarks, is intrigued by whether the strivings for independence really spring from the people as a whole or merely from a minority that is itself inspired by Western civilization. From these premises, al-Fassi concludes (by a slight but reasonable jump in the argument) that many people believe colonial countries to lack a glorious past of their own civilization. Hence, al-Fassi goes on, he became convinced of the need to assist the national struggle by bringing to light the truth concerning the national heritage. These reasons lead him to give a warm welcome to the present work; and he proceeds to make some extremely flattering references to the personality of the author, including the fact that, while bicultural, he has not allowed foreign training to alienate him from his "essence, the national culture, and its high spirituality."

The essay, of some 130 pages, that receives this praise is in effect an inventory of the virtues that can be discerned in Moroccan history and civilization, and sometimes – and here it becomes most amusing – a *tu quoque* demonstration that a variety of vices are also found in European civilization. For instance, the chapter on "Islam and Women" unravels the piquant fact that, apparently, the medieval Council of Mâcon discussed the question whether women were endowed with souls at all. (The point is: People in whose civilization woman finds her very status as a human being in dispute presume to criticize underdeveloped lands for the position they accord women!) Other chapters similarly discuss the position of religious minorities, of social security, and so on, in Morocco and the Muslim world and contrast it with conditions elsewhere. There is even a passage, directed perhaps at the English part of international public opinion, that draws attention to the fact that animals receive much better treatment from Arabs than they do from Europeans.

There are also chapters dealing with specifically Moroccan or North African issues. The association of Barbary with piracy is challenged; so is the dissociation of Berbers from Islam. Claims are made for cultural and scientific achievements, such as the dominant influence of Morocco on Latin American culture (through the Andalusian heritage) or the discovery of the circulation of the blood prior to Harvey, and so on.

In brief, the whole work is a typical example of a kind of reaction one frequently finds among students and intellectuals from "underdeveloped" countries; a sense of injury at the contempt they think they encounter for their own civilization, producing a determined attempt to attribute to it the virtues that they think the critics find lacking; an inclination to (again) *tu quoque* countercharges, combined with a not quite comfortably consistent admission of the need to change and of the fact that just recently things have been not too good (but this attributed to a temporary decline or, indeed, to the machinations and aggression of the detractors). The whole betrays a certain naïveté, in two ways: (a) the methods employed – selective, uncritical – themselves provide an example of the lack of sophistication that is being denied (ben 'Abdallah's scissors-and-paste method would shock ibn Khaldun as much as Ranke); and (b) there is an acceptance at their face value of "Western standards" that are being emulated, standards that in fact may have only a Sunday-school status with the

Westerners themselves and be honored by them in reality with but a very qualified or partial respect.

The "underdeveloped" intellectual who argues in this manner is in effect engaged in an inner dialogue, in which the imagined protagonist is modeled on the cruder of the European denigrators of non-European "backwardness," one of those "old Africa hands" who, as Sir Charles Snow remarked, generally looks as if it would not take Neanderthal man five years to catch up on him. But since, taking it all in all, such old hands are as typical of industrialized societies as more sophisticated liberals, it should not surprise us that the underdeveloped intellectual should strive to argue with them. His naïveté lies perhaps in the belief that such people really would be affected in their opinions by discoveries of past historical greatness. The tough Europeans of Casablanca and Algiers are, no doubt, in their own way, very worthy people, but they did not flee poverty in Marseilles, Alsace, Valencia, or Naples in order to bring the light of Descartes, Goethe, or Dante to Africa. If it is discovered that these lights have African equivalents, it would not move them very much.

The inner dialogue with an imagined opponent of this type is what gives the work its general tone. Officially, however, the protagonist is not the crude European denigrator of "backward" people, but the anything but crude historians and sociologists who, so to speak, provided the French protectorate in Morocco with its intellectual rationale. The French domination of Morocco was carried out, culturally, on the highest possible plane. It is common enough for emergent nations to have to revive or invent a national history: it is less common for them to be faced with an oppressor who has put as much skilled, indeed loving, care into his own historiographical view of the situation. The French administration in Morocco had a sociological section, a kind of highbrow intelligence unit initially concerned with aiding the pacification of the tribes and, later, when tribal dissidence ceased, with understanding the new and even more dangerous dissidence of the rising proletarian *bidonvilles*.

The official protagonists of ben 'Abdallah's work — treated with utmost courtesy and respect — are such men as the historian Henri Terasse and the sociologist Robert Montagne. Their work, and that of other sociologists of the school, did not, of course, contain any crude denigration of Moroccans as backward. Theirs was never the tone of conversations in Casablanca bars. On the contrary, they contained an element of romanticism, even of a Moroccan *mystique*. Nevertheless, or all the more, they offended the susceptibilities of the Moroccan intellectuals, who came to understand what was being done. A liberal Catholic Frenchman, Ignace Lepp, who published a general volume on Morocco at the time of the Franco-Moroccan political crisis, comments on the situation:

In all the schools of Morocco . . . the French nation was exalted. . . . The principal figure in the battle of Poitiers was obviously Charles Martel. . . . [The] first reaction [of the Moroccan pupils] was inevitably humiliation. . . . So the Westernized youth began to speak of the "Moroccan nation" in roughly the same terms as we use in our textbooks. . . . In the nationalist weekly *al-Istiqlal*, . . . a Moroccan refashioned in his own style *L'Histoire du Maroc* by Professor Henri Terasse, whose objectivity appeared to the Moroccan elites as an insult. . . Not only the work of Terasse but also certain chapters of *Révolution au Maroc* by Robert Montagne . . . contributed to exasperate the xenophobic complex.[2]

The Moroccan referred to by Lepp is ben 'Abdallah. In his own introduction to the volume under discussion, he remarks (p. 13) that an earlier form of the work had appeared in *al-Istiqlal* (a form that had been enriched with the present plethora of quotations at the suggestion of Si Balafrej, then secretary of the Istiqlal party, later foreign minister and the second prime minister of independent Morocco — a suggestion whose fulfillment is, perhaps, responsible for the magpie texture, so to speak, of the book).

What is this view that, officially, ben 'Abdallah combats (while in an emotional sense rebutting all European denigrators)? Henri Terasse's *Histoire du Maroc*[3] is an extremely useful and worthy book, though indeed in some ways it is a bit of a Franco-Moroccan *1066 and All That*. The author is a little given to neat balance sheets at the end of chapters, listing Good Things and Bad Things, which does, however, enable one to discern easily the values that underlie such grading. These values and assumptions are in part such as one would expect and, perhaps, share: it is assumed that the ultimate and proper destiny of any territory is to grow to be a centralized nation and state, and that *frondes* (which in Morocco had the habit of being permanent under the name of *siba*) were a bad thing. The political moral drawn from this is — to put it rather bluntly — that given the marked and carefully recorded failure of Morocco to become a European — type nation-state, the French Protectorate was necessary to help it attain this universally valid and inherently good end.

There are also some assumptions or attitudes more specifically tied to the Moroccan situation: looking back at the great Berber dynasties of Morocco's Middle Ages, the author cannot but regret their decision, at the moment of their greatest glory, to bring in defeated Arab tribes (which turned out to be the thin end of the Arab wedge) and thus seal the Arab destiny of Morocco — a bit of a retrojected "Berber policy"? (If so, it is a little inconsistent — for if Morocco had stayed a purely Berber country, the protecting power need not and could not have protected Berber idiosyncrasy.) Or again, the later emergence of sharifian dynasties is applauded, as only the charisma of descent from the Prophet could by then, it appears, save Morocco from chaos. (A reflection, perhaps, of the French stress of the religious position of the sultan during the Protectorate — while ben 'Abdallah, as shown, is concerned with the king as a member of a national dynasty.)

Robert Montagne's sociological theories complemented this historical interpretation. He perceptively stressed the manner in which, in general, the nominal political units in Africa and Asia are *not* like European centralized nation-states,[4] even when modern maps and international terminology make them appear so. (One might reflect here, however, that as this is a general characteristic, not so much should be made of the specific failure of Moroccan dynasties to achieve what would have been an oddity anyway.) In his crucial *Révolution au Maroc*,[5] a brilliant analysis wholly mistaken in all its immediate and specific predictions, he further stresses the precariousness of Moroccan politics and loyalties, the archaic nature of the monarchy, the centrifugal and traditional nature of rural Morocco — all of these showing that the time is not yet ripe for the modernist aspirations of the young Moroccan intellectuals or for an attempt by the king to support them and to provide effective leadership. The book was, in fact, a justification of the French coup of 1953 — the exile of the king — and events have shown the analysis, as actually presented, to be wholly wrong. The king, the young intellectuals, the explosive new proletariat, and, in the end, the countryside, combined to attain independence. (It is hard to build precise and immediate predictions on sociological analyses, for they cannot exclude short-term political alliances between even the most disparate of partners. In the longer run, however, the analysis may still be applicable: today, the new intellectuals are more or less in opposition again, and the king, supported by the more traditional sections of the population, *is* the government.)

These, then, are the opponents with whom ben 'Abdallah polemicizes – plus, perhaps, the man in the Casablanca bar for whom the *indigènes* were not at all *évolués*. What does he produce in reply? Simple denials and counteraccusation, supported by a hodgepodge of disparate quotations, an adulation of the monarchy. It is intended to show that, by the Europeans' own nominal or overt standard (whose effective application or social roots are left unscrutinized), the Moroccan has no need to be ashamed – though it is conceded that, nevertheless, some changes are now called for: reference is made, by 'Allal al-Fassi in his preface, to the need to throw light on the "road which Morocco took spontaneously in search of the very methods of detailed organization which today it borrows directly from the West" (p. 11).

The section of his book for which ben 'Abdallah earns this commendation – to have shown how Morocco was already spontaneously moving in the direction of modernity – is a summary of a projected constitution in 1908 (four years before the establishment of the Protectorate). Little information is given concerning the context of this project, nor is there any discussion of the social conditions of its effective implementation.

In brief, the book can be read as the self-defense of a justly angry, offended man, but one who has not taken the measure of his opponents nor exploited their real weaknesses, and one who betrays his own: moreover, this instinctive, passionate, immediate reaction contains few indications of what he will do when the injury is righted, and indeed it does not suggest a deep preoccupation with the question. He will show his detractors there was no justice in their charges; he will also improve himself to leave no excuse for them.

The contrasted volume is Lahbabi's *Le Gouvernement marocain à l'aube du XXième siecle,*[6] with a preface by Mehdi ben Barka. In reading this book, and the preface, we enter a different world. There is, indeed, in the preface, a slight touch of whitewashing the Moroccan past: "The Moroccan government before the Protectorate, although archaic, . . . was neither illogical nor completely impotent as our adversaries enjoy depicting us" (p. 3).

But this whitewashing, qualified and careful, such as it is, is not allowed to be an end in itself: These are not the remarks of a man preoccupied with redressing a past insult. On the contrary, the matter is only invoked to draw from it a contemporary implication. The above passage is followed immediately by the following: "The intelligent sovereigns of the nineteenth century till the eve of the Protectorate were strong believers in reform. . . . To construct a modern and democratic state today, with firmness, is to follow faithfully in their footsteps."

Like 'Allal al-Fassi, he is sensitive to the suspicion that political aspirations may be but foreign borrowings of intellectuals, but again, the rejection of this is used to point a present moral (p. 4): "Lahbabi's thesis shows that our appeals to democracy are not – as some claim – . . . mere borrowings from the outside presented by intellectuals without a grasp of reality. To the contrary . . . . "

It should incidentally be noted that at the time ben Barka's group was not in opposition (any more than was 'Allal al-Fassi — and, indeed, the two had not split): so these invocations of democracy cannot be treated as simple rhetoric or opposition. On the contrary, they have a definite content, as will emerge.

What is Lahbabi's thesis? First of all be it noted that he does have one: his work coherently argues a case, it is not a scissors-and-paste rebuttal of a generalized insult. In fact, there are two central positions that he tries to establish. Both are issues of constitutional law. The first concerns the status of the Moroccan monarchy; the second the status of delegation (of powers) in Muslim law, with special reference to Moroccan practices.

Concerning the monarchy, he denies the thesis of absolute power, which has hitherto been widely accepted as theoretically valid. On the issue of delegation, he denies a specific right of absolute monarchy, namely to delegate such powers as it pleases to whom it pleases. This second thesis is far more than a mere technical point of law: Lahbabi maintains that the French Protectorate in Morocco was (in terms of legal theory) based on the reasoning that the sultan is an absolute monarch and is fully entitled to delegate his powers as he wishes — even to foreigners — and hence may, for instance, choose to request the French Republic to take over a few of his tasks that he happens to find irksome or beyond his powers, such as, for instance, the running of his country. If, on the other hand, he is neither absolute nor entitled to delegate powers as he wishes — as Lahbabi maintains — the whole argument collapses.

Lahbabi's thesis, if accepted, completely revolutionizes the customary view[7] of the situation held not merely by the French but also, I think, by most nationally oriented Moroccans. The usual view is that the Moroccan monarchy *was* absolute (limited only by the actual sociological limits of its power); that the French exploited its weakness first to impose the Protectorate and then to usurp successively more and more of the Monarchy rights. (This was known as *administration directe* — as opposed to mere advice and technical assistance, held to be at least less objectionable and compatible with the original purpose of "protection" — and it was the central complaint of the nationalists against the Protectorate administration.) Lahbabi's counterclaim is that the absolutism was invented *ex post* — contrary to the true constitutional position — by the French, so that it could in conjunction with the theory of "delegation" provide a rationalization of their rule.

The really striking thing about Lahbabi's thesis is its double-edged nature. It is indeed a polemic against the French — like ben 'Abdallah's book, though concerned with a specific issue rather than the general and diffuse matter of the merits of a whole civilization — but while arguing with a position attributed to them, it draws conclusions pregnant with implications for the present and the future. In fact, for anyone acquainted with the atmosphere of postindependence Morocco, Lahbabi's book, with its rather cool and dispassionate treatment of the monarchy, must come as a bit of a surprise. One can only assume that two facts helped to camouflage the tendency of his argument: one, the somewhat dry and legal-historical form in which it appears, and two, that on the surface, it was, as indicated, an argument against an alleged French position.

In Lahbabi's case, the polemic with the French looks more like a means than an end — the end being a view of Morocco's past relevant to the present. After all, the French Protectorate is dead and gone, and not much is gained by refuting a rationalization of it. Moreover, it is questionable whether this (or any other) rationalization was ever of much importance. Lahbabi's refutation of the doctrine of delegation refers a good deal to alleged misunderstandings of the medieval Muslim jurist Mawardi, whose doctrines were relevant to delegation. But one may well wonder whether Marshal Lyautey carried a copy of Mawardi on his campaigns — or if he did, whether the fate of Morocco was allowed to hinge on the interpretation of medieval Muslim legal thought. If, on the other hand, both the French conquest and present royalist tendencies can be shown to spring from the same and mistaken doctrine, this is a far more important matter.

It is worth looking at Lahbabi's arguments in a little more detail. His book falls into two parts: the first is concerned with the delimitation of royal sovereignty, the second with the notion of delegation.

In the first part, Lahbabi begins by denying absolute, legislative or constitutive authority to the monarchy either as sultan or as khalif, basing himself on facts both of recent or of distant Moroccan history. For instance, he supports the contention that the Moroccan theory of the khalifate differs in its reality from the "pure," oriental theory by invoking the fact that medieval Moroccan dynasties were not even of Qoranish origin — let alone descendants of the Prophet. The denial of the legislative power of the sultan is supported by reference to the content and role of the sultan's decrees *(dahirs)* as late as the beginnings of this century. In fact, Lahbabi maintains that Moroccan legislation is based in reality neither exclusively on a static Qoranic law, and less still on royal decree, but on "legislation by judges." (It is not quite clear whether he means case law or legal treatises, or both.)

The central and most interesting part, however, of Lahbabi's treatment of the sovereignty of the Moroccan sultan comes in his discussion of the institution of *bayca* (a kind of act of submission or recognition). His argument here constitutes a fascinating polemic and contrast with the French interpretation of Moroccan history. The French interpretation concentrated on the failure of old Morocco to be a unified, centralized, effective national state (the implication being that the modern Moroccan state, for the control of which the nationalists were striving, was a creation of the French). Their main piece of supporting evidence for this claim — a point on which they displayed "insistence, clumsy in its persistence" (Lahbabi, p. 200) — was the permanent division of Morocco into *bled al-makhzen* and *bled as-siba*, or the pale where the government's writ ran, and the area of permanent tribal dissidence. This distinction and its corollaries are indeed the central theme both of Terasse's history and of Montagne's sociology.

Lahbabi does not, in effect, deny the facts on which this distinction is based. He merely reinterprets them radically. He redefines the two terms: *"Bled al-makhzen . . .* territory where the population has *consented* to the delegation of higher administrative powers to the sultan. *Bled as-siba . . .* territories which *do not want* to delegate the right to administer themselves to the sultan" (p. 41, italics added).

In brief: the *same* facts, the existence of dissident areas, which were used by the French to illustrate the failure and impotence of Moroccan government, are used by Lahbabi to provide the basis for a consent (and hence anti-absolutist) theory of the Moroccan historical constitution.

Which of the two interpretations is correct? Was dissidence, *siba,* due to recognition of the need for consent for valid government, or was it merely a sign of the lack of power on the part of the would-be absolutist central government?

This question could only be given a clear and simple answer if "force" and "consent" were, sociologically, neatly separable notions. In the mythologies of political or legal theory, perhaps they are: in the real life of societies, they are not. People give their consent to what they are socially constrained to do anyway, or what is sanctioned by the possibility of force that need not be overtly displayed. On the other hand, people may be visibly forced to comply with the orders of an authority whose power is, however, in the end based on their own beliefs or assumptions and thus, in a latent kind of way, on their own consent.

In the concrete case under consideration, it is quite possible to argue either way. There can be no doubt but that the area of dissidence correlated very highly with mountainous and inaccessible terrain — in other words, with the physical possibility of evading the arm of central authority, with the inability of central power to assert itself. This can be invoked to show that relative power, and not an act of choice, determined submission and dissidence, and hence that it is illegitimate to invoke these brute facts of power in an attempt to retroject a "consent theory" onto the constitutional past of Morocco.

On the other side, however, it may be argued that submission was not always dictated by violence but followed on deliberation; and it is obvious that these deliberations were guided not merely by consideration of the strength of central power but also by the anticipation of how it would use its authority if that authority were granted — a social contract situation indeed! (To appreciate the full reality of the situation, one should add that generally, and particularly in marginal areas on the borders of dissidence, officials and representatives of central government were not so much appointees as people whose *de facto* local authority was recognized, underwritten, and utilized by central government. Thus a subtle interplay of force and consent applies not merely to the recognition of, but equally to recognition by central government. That this was the situation would hardly be disputed by either side to the historical argument.)

A further argument that might be used in support of the government-by-consent interpretation is this: the tribes who chose to remain dissident nevertheless "recognized the spiritual authority" of the central sharifian power. This point, again, is admitted by both sides, and, indeed, it is stressed by the French historian. The most striking illustration occurs when a royal expedition into dissident lands is defeated, and the captured sharifian sultan is nevertheless treated with great respect by his dissident tribal captors and allowed to return to his capital. It is not quite clear what this proves: certainly, the dissidence was not simply self-defense of small tribal groups but dissidence from something specific and permanent whose position was recognized and conceptualized. It was a kind of permanent relationship, like legal separation — which obviously is different from the state of never having been married. (One might add that here again we find a kind of symmetry: the royal army might well treat with respect, and exile rather than liquidate, the religious leaders and personnel among dissident rebels. This point might cancel out any conclusions drawn from the previously-cited episode.)

Given the scarcity of first-hand data on this matter (of recognition and dissidence by tribal Morocco of its national dynasty), it is worth putting on record my experiences in this connection in a part of the country — the central High Atlas — which for various obvious geographical reasons (the extensiveness and ruggedness of the mountains) was at the very heart of the old *siba* dissidence. I first began working in this area in 1954, twenty-one years after the *siba* had been terminated by French conquest, nominally on behalf of the sultan. There were of course plenty of older — or even middle-aged — men who remembered the previous political condition.

In brief summary, I should say this about it: *siba* had certainly been a fact — there is no question of it being an *ex post* invention of historians or sociologists. It had been a stable condition. The term and the concept were frequently employed and automatically understood. *"Lokt n'siba"* ("in the time of dissidence") was a frequent opening of a sentence. It was a concept with a contrast and, indeed, the very contrast that the historians and sociologists attributed it with: *makhzen,* government.

The question of whether to submit to central government or not, whether by bowing to *force majeure* or by voluntary recognition, simply did not arise for the tribes at the very heart of the mountains and the dissident area. They were separated from the "land of government" by the extensive territory of other dissident tribes, so neither the choice nor the fatality of a social contract was available to them.

The tribes closer to the governmental pale, however, did unmistakably remember resisting it by violence (successfully). In the shadowy area along the ill-defined boundary between *makhzen* and *siba,* a curious phenomenon could also be found: local families might receive governmental appointment which could be totally ineffective, or even kept dark by them.

Was this resistance to "spiritually recognized" authority also held to be shameful — a feeling that should be a sign of a moral acceptance of central authority? When I was told of this past resistance, it was done in a manner suggesting that it was indeed shameful — or at any rate, that a certain ambivalence was felt about it. It is possible that this shame or ambivalence was, as it were, added in retrospect: by the time my informants were telling me about these things, modern nationalist ideas and values had had some time to make their local impact. I have no way of deciding whether the story would have been told in the same way, with the same emotional accompaniments, and so on, thirty years earlier. However, there is one reasonably significant piece of local evidence on this matter that is not open to this kind of suspicion: one of the most turbulent, feud-addicted, thieving of the local tribes, which is cut off on a very stony and arid plateau (on which in the past it could often have been left with no alternative other than raiding more fortunately placed neighbors), a tribe somewhat feared and despised by its neighbors, is reputed according to local legend to be in the sorry position in which it is as a punishment for defying the sultan. This legend obviously antedates the diffusion of modern nationalism in the recesses of the Atlas, and thus provides some evidence for an earlier sense of "national" unity — or at any rate, moral recognition of a religiously based dynasty over what is now a national territory.

Other traditional legends that are to be found in this region do take cognizance of the existence, albeit distant, of a central dynasty. But they take cognizance of it in a curious way: the story is told of the sultan Mawlay Isma'il (contemporary of Louis XIV, and a folk figure) as wandering locally prior to his accession, during a painful interregnum, and achieving his crown thanks to a prophecy, plus endowment by magical power accorded him by the local thaumaturges, the holy lineages who provided locally the hereditary arbitrators for the dissident tribes. I have come across a number of variants of this legend, which plainly has and is meant to have a moral — namely, the ultimate moral authority of the local dynasty of "saints" (who, in fact, were of purely local importance and of no significance at the national level). The legend, which has no basis in historical fact, in effect makes local saints into ultimate arbitrators, indeed, into king-makers. But in so doing, in the course of rather naïvely buttressing their genuine local influence by inventing for them a spurious national one, the legend implicitly recognizes the existence of the national dynasty, which is merely "made," but for some reason, not replaced, by the local marabout.

What this kind of traditional belief would entail if incorporated into the premises of the reconstruction of the law and custom of Morocco's historic constitution, I do not propose to speculate. It would be an academic exercise, as those whose voices count in such reconstructions are not likely to make use of this particular fact. (Though other "facts," of about similar status, are sometimes invoked: for instance, local legends of Arabian origins of Berber tribes are taken seriously by the modern Moroccan administrators and used as evidence for denying an Arab-Berber dualism.)

There is, however, a serious point that hinges on this and that will have to be faced by anyone trying to extract a modern-type political or constitutional theory from the realities of Morocco's past, and that is the proliferation of persons claiming sharifian descent (that is, descent from the Prophet). Even if we discount all those whose claim would be disallowed by others and restrict ourselves to, as it were, officially recognized ones, their number is, as in some other Muslim countries, very considerable. In towns they form something between a guild and an estate; in the countryside, they form important lineages. For instance, the holy men of "my" region who claim to have been instrumental in the enthroning of Mawlay Isma'il, themselves claim sharifian descent *via* the first (Idrisid) Moroccan dynasty. This matter must raise difficulties for any rigorous theocratic, divine-right theory in that the basis for the divine right is diffused too widely, leaving excessive *spielraum* for dispute and chaos or for choice of ruler by consent, according to the way you care to look at it. (The French authorities were the last to utilize the ambiguity of the rulers, not merely in imposing the unfortunate ben 'Arafa in 1953 but equally in choosing the present king for succession from among his brothers earlier.) Lahbabi bypasses this issue, as indicated, by appealing to the medieval Berber dynasties, which did not claim sharifian descent at all; but in doing so, he would seem to be contradicting the spirit of more recent centuries of Moroccan history and, indeed, the way in which dissidents expressed their moral recognition of central government. He is, of course, in harmony with the present official attitude, which in its very political terminology stresses the "national monarchy" rather than "religious empire" aspect of the king's position.

It is worth noting that the normal recognition of the central dynasty is a fact liable to cut both for and against Lahbabi's thesis. It does support the claim that there existed a moral community, parts of which did and parts of which did not also submit to its political authority. On the other hand, the moral recognition was based on a religious premise that, if valid at all, should be valid generally and leave no room for legitimate withdrawal of consent, so that Lahbabi's doctrine of monarchy-by-consent lapses. (And conversely, consent makes the satisfaction of the religious condition redundant.) Lahbabi's treatment of the religious premise is somewhat cavalier: in another connection, he reports how, in 1907, the population of Marrakesh deposed one sultan and named another, "on the condition that he defend the Moroccan territory or, *to use the terminology of the period,* that he be the sultan of the jihad" (p. 61, italics added).

One may feel that his easy assumption that the religious concepts are simply the "terminology of the period" for permanent realities of national sentiment and self-defense, somewhat begs the crucial issue in this matter.

One should add that Lahbabi's use of the fact of dissidence to buttress a consent theory of government (which normally can be supported in Islamic contexts only in a rather weaker form by appealing to the ruler's consultation of jurists and so forth) is most original. It is also far more interesting than the usual handling of the historical fact of tribal dissidence by other Moroccans, who tend to square the stress on national unity with the historical fact that half the tribes were engaged in resisting it, by appealing to the distinction between "good and beloved king" and "bad oppressive local representatives." "Sultan good — qaid bad" might be a slogan of this attitude — one for which many parallels could no doubt be found in peasant rebellions, in theology, and even in the discontent of populations under Stalinism. This attitude seems to have some very deep root in the unwillingness of the human heart to believe that the top management (of country or universe) is bad, a preference for attributing evils to its lower executive agents or advisors, of whose wickedness the top management is held to be ignorant or in any case not responsible. This type of interpretation of the past is very common in Morocco now, but it is not employed by Lahbabi.

One might of course object to the whole approach to these problems via political or legal theory. With regard to political theory, one never seems to know whether the "theory" is meant to be opposed to practice or to fact — whether we are getting a summary of the norms or of the reality. With regard to legal and constitutional theory, the situation is even worse. Does such a theory draw merely on that which is written *and* morally recognized by the participants in the situation? But these two categories may diverge; and different things may be written in different places, and different things recognized by different people. Above all, legal theory must (a) *interpret* that which is written, and (b) *invoke the actual reality of behavior,* the social context in which the rules operate, the unwritten assumptions within which the explicit norms are embedded. But how much of it? As we have seen, Lahbabi does both: he interprets the old religious terminology as being simply an old mode of expression, and he invokes, in a striking original manner, the salient features of traditional Moroccan society to arrive at a new theory of the moral basis of its politics.

The difficulties — the ultimate indeterminateness, as it seems to the layman, the nonlawyer — of legal constitutional theory arises from the fact that it must invoke *some* social reality to make any sense of the rules, but never quite *all* of it, for then it would fail to be normative, fail in its purpose of providing a basis for condemning deviations from the valid norm. (Some social reality must remain excluded as deviant.) The theory we get depends on where we choose to draw the line, between what is evidence of constitutional practice and what is deviance.

But this type of difficulty arises with particular and perhaps decisive and concrete relevance for anyone who, like Lahbabi, attempts to employ this approach in an "underdeveloped" country. *Ex hypothesi* — and the hypothesis would not be denied, presumably, by Lahbabi, and certainly not by ben Barka — an underdeveloped country such as Morocco stands before a necessary social transformation, and the break with the past has been both fundamental and speedy. But this being so, what can follow, legitimately, for the future of Moroccan politics from interpretations of the past, interpretations that have to invoke social contexts that are either gone or destined to go? (It should be remembered that Lahbabi is no kind of revivalist romantic: his discussion of the past merely has a kind of aura of legal timelessness, and its aims are forward-looking. He is not invoking the past in order to idealize or to strive to return. Morocco in general does not seem to produce this phenomenon: there are traditionalists but not revivalists. This is superficially surprising in a country whose immense aesthetic appeal springs from the survival of so much — architecturally, sartorially, socially — from the past.)

Rural Morocco today does not appear to have the option of dissidence; the one or two attempts in this direction since independence were crushed with surprising ease. (Real dissidence is more conceivable among the industrial proletariat than among the tribes.) Officials today, since independence, *are* officials, appointed from the center and transferable from place to place; they are not simply local notables whose power is ratified from the capital. The qaid really is an official, and not a notable. Above all, though it may be true that the French misused a mistaken theory of delegation to build up an administrative machinery of their own, that present Moroccan state is not a continuation of the pre-French one, it is a continuation of the French-built structure with Moroccan personnel. Still, it would be wrong to conclude from all this that nothing follows from Lahbabi's analysis. The crucial thing that does follow is that if, in the future, there is open resistance to the monarchy, or to some specific act of it such as, for instance, the nomination by the ruling monarch of his successor, then such a resistance will be able to invoke, rightly or wrongly, Morocco's past as well as its future. . . .

Emergent countries have a particular need of guiding historical ideologies. Recent historical interpretations by Moroccans have been particularly illuminating, in being neatly contrasted and being endowed with political patrons who happen to be the two crucial politicians in the country. The two works provide insight into the different outlooks of two generations. One is a work of reassurance, eclectic, given to taking Western values at their face value, and displaying a contradiction between its own protestations and the way in which they are substantiated. It also displays no consistent or sharp preoccupation with the future.

The other is a coherent and elegant refutation of a Western position, a technically excellent utilization of a sophisticated technique, and a work in which the study of the past is clearly oriented toward implications in the present and future — implications whose radicalism is obscured or camouflaged only by their abstract and scholarly form.

The struggle for Morocco's past is, of course, a struggle for its future.

Notes

1. Casablanca: Imprimerie du Midi, 1958. See also 'Allal al-Fassi, "The Mission of the Islamic 'Ulema," pp. 151-58 in this reader.

2. Ignace Lepp. *Midi Sonne au Maroc* (Paris: Aubier, 1954), p. 155.

3. Henri Terasse, *Histoire du Maroc des origines à l'établissement du Protectorat français* (2 vols.; Casablanca: Editions Atlantides, 1949).

4. He did this particularly in his Paris inaugural lecture (published in English in *The Cambridge Journal*).

5. Robert Montagne, *Revolution au Maroc* (Paris: Editions France Empire, 1953).

6. Rabat: Editions Techniques Nord-Africaines, 1958.

7. It has been widely assumed that Morocco is, in theory, an absolute monarchy or theocracy. For instance, Neville Barbour (ed.), *A Survey of North West Africa (The Maghrib)* (London: Royal Institute of International Affairs, 1959), says (p. 109): "Morocco cannot be called a democracy, since all power is legally concentrated in the hands of the King." It is true, however, that the book goes on to qualify this by appealing to contemporary fact where Lahbabi appeals to a past one: "But neither is it an absolute monarchy since political parties play a significant role." The contributor on the Moroccan aspect of Mr. Barbour's survey is M. André Adam, the French official retained by the independent Moroccan government, who runs its Administrative Staff College and who is also a very distinguished sociologist and Moroccan expert of great standing.

5

MUSLIM SOCIALISM IN ALGERIA

RAYMOND VALLIN

... The war of liberation gave an unusual impetus to socialist ideas. Socialism had already been discussed at the Soummam Congress of August 20, 1956,[1] and at about the same time by Abbane Ramdane, who foresaw a peasant revolution and an agrarian reform. In the autumn of 1960, the labor leaders of the General Union of Algerian Workers (UGTA) and such Provisional Government (GPRA) leaders as President Benyussef ben Khedda announced "the unyielding determination of the National Liberation Front (FLN) to bring a social or socialist revolution to Algeria."[2] Soon after, Lakhdar ben Tobbal, GPRA minister of state, said that "the Algeria of tomorrow has to be socialist. . . . This idea, however, was not accepted by the former leaders." Another GPRA leader declared in the United States: "Algeria is 100 per cent socialist."[3] Thereafter, the Algerian political orientation seemed established, and ben Bella confirmed it in Cairo a few months later, in April, 1962: "Algeria will have a socialist government. . . . It will have an agrarian reform."[4]

The Tripoli program, made public in July, 1962, contained the aspirations of the top leadership, although in moderate terms: liberal socialism (limitation of rural property to 1,500 acres, facilities for foreign investment and capital transfers, consumption and transformation industries left to private enterprises) and mild social revolution, tempered by respect for Islam and tradition. Such a program should have evoked great popular interest, if not enthusiasm. But at that time public attention was focused on more pressing political problems, and it was not until November, 1962 — January, 1963, that the program was fully reported and explained on the radio and in the newspapers. The program was drawn up in Hammamet, Tunisia, in May, 1962, and subsequently adopted by the National Council of the Algerian Revolution (CNRA) in Tripoli in June. It acknowledged that the Algerian insurrection had been only the beginning of a democratic and social revolution, but the word "socialism" was not expressly used.

That did not take long to come. In early August, ben Bella, then GPRA vice president, declared in Oran: "To us, socialism means liquidation of privileges. . . . We want an Algerian socialism, born of our national experience

Translated, by permission, from *L'Afrique et l'Asie,* No. 66 (Spring, 1964), pp. 21–42, and No. 69 (Winter, 1965), pp. 14–32.

and benefiting from the experiences of the socialist countries."[5] At the same time, the FLN Arabic press explained Nasser's doctrine of Arab socialism under the title: "A New Step Toward the Arab Revolution."[6]

In the beginning of November it became clear from frequent official use of the new key word [socialism] *(ishtirakiya)* that a turning point had been reached and, on January 12, the minister of habous [religious property], Tewfiq Madani, embroidered on Nasser's ideas of socialism in Islam by saying, "Islam is a socialist religion, it is a religion of equity."[7]

At the time, these words seemed quite innocuous. Only higher education and land abandoned by the settlers had been put under socialist rule, and no one saw any problem in these takeovers. Furthermore, the word socialism expressed to Algerian ears the idea of collective enterprise and participation. This etymological peculiarity was then used to present socialism as an extension of the traditional *towiza,* or village mutual aid, practiced throughout the Maghrib.[8]

The reformists, overjoyed that their idea had finally found official favor, put the emphasis on the obligation to work, an initiative that jeopardized the sacred *mektub* ("it is written") so often used to avoid work or study. There was still no question of attacking private property, which was guaranteed by the Qoran itself.

Moreover, a purge of religious leaders was threatening to provoke a reaction in conservative circles. Thus, the government had to appear more fundamentalist than the traditionalists it was eliminating. The Ramadan fast and the charity offering that ended it were made national duties on January 25, 1963, and discreet references were made to the principles of Tripoli, which implicitly recognized Islam as the state religion.

With the religious leaders purged and replaced for the most part by modernists, the March, 1963, decrees on land nationalization and management committee brought new changes. There was a danger that measures that "accelerated the class struggle" and were clearly prejudicial to the idea of private property would be denounced as a violation of Islamic law. The minister of habous was probably given the difficult task of justifying the decrees. To realize just how difficult this was, it is worth recalling how seventh-century Islam, which appeared and spread as a revolutionary egalitarian movement capable of rallying the Oriental masses oppressed by Byzantium or Ctesiphon, has retrogressed through the centuries. Ottoman Islam and its brother, the Islam of the marabouts and zawyas in North Africa — so aptly termed "old turban" Islam — had a highly bourgeois, even reactionary, nature until recent years. Without mentioning slavery, which existed in Algeria until the second half of the nineteenth century and which still exists in some Middle Eastern states, it is clear that, until very recently, the ideal social type was not the worker or the man of action. The respected man was the solid citizen, the trader, the civil servant, the *qadi,* the doctor — in brief, the "notables" of Islam. But the rich notables and the bourgeoisie were precisely those who must first be brought into line and eliminated if necessary. Thus, the antibourgeois Islam again appeared, the Islam of Medina when Mohammed and his successors were fighting the Meccan oligarchy.

In April, 1963, ben Bella openly preached socialism, supported by a huge propaganda campaign.[9] In May, religious justifications in hand, the minister of habous broadcast appropriate sermon themes for the Friday services and published a journal in Arabic, *al-Ma'rifa* (Knowledge), where Islamic socialism was officially exalted.

The press soon pushed the theme further, perhaps too far. Islam no longer simply "tolerated" socialism, it identified with it. In its first issue, *al-Ma'rifa* presented Abu Dharr, companion of the Prophet, as the father of socialism and the promoter of class struggle. The daily *al-Sha'b* (The People), in an editorial described the Prophet himself as the advocate of a "revolution of the poor against the rich," sending the Mecca feudalists "through a Turkish bath."[10]

The ideal Muslim state was a "City of God" striving to assure the moral and material happiness of men on earth within the framework of God-revealed norms. In such a system, the sacred directed the secular and the main responsibility of authority was to apply the religious law, the *shari'a*. Such a state was theocratic, except that there were no priests but rather a "priesthood of believers." It did not postulate the equality of the citizens but established a hierarchy deduced from the sacred texts: God and his law, the Prophet, the leaders, the believers — men and women, tributaries, slaves. The Qoran made clear, furthermore, that "we have raised some of them above others, in a hierarchy, so that some take others for their service."[11] Official interpreters[12] explain that "some" are the rich and "the others" the poor. Islam was thus far from being a classless society and far, too, from abolishing the exploitation of man by man, as preached by socialism.

Unequal on the social and economic levels, the believers were nevertheless equal before the law, through a fraternal solidarity[13] that was to transcend and replace the idea of the tribe, the family, or the *bani amm*. The chief of state, a virtual substitute for Mohammed, was also a brother but was endowed with almost absolute political power, since he was to apply a code of life derived from Revelation. He was elected by representative believers and could be restrained by any citizen qualified in jurisprudence. He made the decisions. He submitted them to the *shura* (legal advisors), and then to the people (or their representatives), who accepted or rejected them.

This organization was incorporated in the Algerian constitution adopted by referendum on September 8, 1963. A presidential regime was created, with the Islamic *shura* replaced by a Political Bureau headed by ben Bella and a National Assembly that is not elected but appointed. . . .

Yet democracy was for a long time, and still is, a magic word. . . . [Several years before the revolutionary war broke out], the Algerian essayist Mourad Kiouane wrote that "democracy is the formula which is closest to the Islamic idea. . . . This affinity does not go beyond principles. When it comes to their realization, democracy and Islam take different paths. If democracy admits that one man is worth one vote, and that a cheat or a rascal can govern, Islam does not. . . . In an Islamic state, the mechanism of voting has to be so divided so as to make voting impossible for categories of men or women unable to bear all its risks. . . . Government of the people, by the people, for the people is only partially true in Islam."[17] Is it only a coincidence that in 1955, in choosing the motto for the FLN, its leaders marked the difference by changing the initial word: *"Revolution* by the people and for the people"?

Later, Mohammed Bouaroudj, an authorized spokesman for independent and socialist Algeria, commented on the notion of sovereignty and explained the position of Islam with regard to the exercise of power by the people:[15] In Islam, "man transcends all political values and social guaranties." The human being has an ideal value, a quasi-sanctity, explicit in the Qoranic verse, "We honor Adam's son," which bestows on him a kind of divine trust and vicariat, along with responsibility for his actions. Nevertheless, Islam does not go so far as to trust the management of the state to the common man: "In Islam, democracy is by no means a simple political matter of giving power to the masses. It is made of sentiment, emotion, and personal and social criteria which instill democracy in the popular mind even before a constitution has legislated on its behalf. The result is that democracy is not necessarily linked to a legal religious text, following the Qoran or the hadith, but rather is part of the very foundations of Islam."

After this balanced preamble, Bouaroudj insisted at length on the Muslims' right to censure authority, citing the example of 'Omar, who declared, at the time of his accession to the khalifat, "If any one among us should find any deviation, let him correct me," To which a Bedouin in the crowd answered: "By God, if we see deviation in you, we will correct it with our swords!"

To Bouaroudj, this signified "the right to revolt against corrupt rulers" and is confirmed by the hadiths: "If there are people in my community who are afraid to say, 'You oppressor' to a tyrant, we will not pay any attention to them," and "the best testimony is a word of truth before an unjust imam." Finally, several verses of the Qoran,[16] including the famous commandment to do good, establish "the right to revolution, which is in itself a way of acting that we would call today the principle of popular censure."

By nationalizing first abandoned property and then all colonial property, the new regime obviously won great popular support, both in rural and in urban areas, since the measures legalized a *de facto* situation that had developed gradually after July, 1962, and also reassured the thousands of squatters who occupied the houses, villas, and industries of the "fleeing" Europeans. It is evident that the popular appeal of these measures would have been even greater if the government had allowed the Algerian occupants to become the legal owners of the vacated holdings. Many such hopes were disappointed, but the state substitute for individual ownership, with or without socialism, was finally accepted. For the Algerian state was only following an age-old tradition common to the Middle East, according to which conquered or vacant lands belong to the imam or the prince. . . .[17]

In Algeria, the first religious commentary justifying the widespread nationalizations appeared in June, 1963, in the National Student Union (UNEA) press. Taking up the ideas of Sibai,[18] the newspaper first cited the hadith — "Men are associated in three elements: water, fodder, and fire" — as evidence that Islam provided for the nationalization of certain natural goods. In particular, "everything that is necessary to man is amenable to nationalization." Turning to private property, the article recalled that Islamic law forbids greed (seizure or forced sale), that the habous is a kind of nationalization for religious purposes, that Khalif 'Omar created a communal grazing area in Ribdah for the cattle of poor Muslims, and finally that Mohammed himself ordered a palm tree pulled out of a private wall because the tree was an abusive imposition on the owner of the place. It then concluded that Islam "institutes nationalization."

Another article recalled with satisfaction Khalif 'Omar's refusal to hand over to the Muslims the lands seized from the defeated Emperor Chosroes, giving this as an example of nationalization, when in fact the decision was based on accepted tribal practices of the time.

In August, 1963, two articles in *al-Ma'rifa* undertook a canonical examination of the limitation of private wealth. In the first,[19] Ahmed Charabaci made it clear that Islam did not oppose wealth. and a comfortable life so long as they were not illicitly earned and did not give rise to forbidden actions. Furthermore, he added, the hadith asserts that private wealth is inviolable: "All Muslims must respect each other, their family, their goods, and their honor," and "not only does Islam not forbid gain and possession; it urges work, production and ownership." But, of course, as in everything else, there is a limit, and it is up to the authorities to make sure that the limit is respected. . . . Furthermore, Islam suggests that while wealth should be spent without excess, on the owner and his family, a part should be set aside for God (tithe and charity) *and for country.*[20]

The author thus concluded that Islam was neutral, favoring neither the millionaire nor the proletariat; a Muslim "must not have such a large fortune as to endanger or inconvenience others." Islam, therefore, certainly does not encourage the "tyranny of wealth" and even less "the creation of a social class that owns everything, alongside a class of have-nots." In fact, Islam "does not want its followers to be poor or deprived, living like monks or isolated from the world, sunk in poverty and humiliation on this earth." Nor does it "combat honest wealth that is pure and proper in its means and origin, but it condemns ill-gotten and corrupt riches, hoarding, stinginess, and avarice. It combats the acquisition of wealth rooted in sin."

This statement, which developed Kawakibi's ideas,[21] obviously could not justify the systematic takeover of middle class property by the Algerian state, even if the bourgeoisie had "bled the people to death" (to use Algerian socialist press terminology). A new exegesis was needed and it appeared in the October issue of *al-Ma'rifa.*[22] This time, Dr. Bahi al-Khawli envisaged the right of the Islamic state to take over, purely and simply, whatever was required for "the public use," the only limitation being the minimal living wage of the citizen. The author built his thesis on the "holy communication" cited by Tabarani and Imam Ahmad ibn Hanbal: "We provided you with wealth with which to worship and pay the legal tithe," and on a controversial verse: "Those who accumulate wealth and do not spend it in the way of God are to be warned of a painful torture."[23] The Qoran also condemned squanderers, whom it called "the Devil's brothers."[24]

At first analysis, the author asserted that merely meant that "all property belongs to God," with men only the temporary users, enjoying the usufruct of divine goods. Then, having recalled that in Islam man does not have the liberty to spend his money as he pleases, and that, on the contrary, he must budget his expenses in accordance with divine norms, al-Khawli went on to say: "The imam — that is to say, the chief of state — continually considers the possessions of the individual in order to be able to take away what is necessary for the spiritual sanitary, subsistence, educational, war and other needs of 'society.' "

However, he agreed that the verse has been given very different interpretations. Abu Dharr said that no one may spend his income only for his family; the remainder belongs to God. 'Ali said that the spending of one's income, even for his family, is limited; the remainder belongs to God. 'Abdallah ben 'Omar said to each his income and his possessions; once the tithe is paid, the remainder belongs to the one who earned it. Subsequently, lawyers have agreed that the theories of Abu Dharr and 'Ali represent the ideal way, and 'Abdallah states "what was allowed."

In sum, according to al-Khawli, Islam placed the means of acquiring wealth into general categories but did not limit individual income; the individual could dispose of his revenue only according to the rules of his society and the demands of the times; the individual was God's treasurer (*amin*), responsible for what remained after expenses made according to God's commandment and offering the rest to the political leader (*wali l-amr*) when the community needed it.

These quotations indicate how long Islam has been concerned with the social problem of wealth and how its choice has been made. We may say that after the seventh century, the urban spirit of "free enterprise" won out over bedouin collectivism and that the present mode of Muslim socialism is not, after all, so different from certain tendencies of early Islam. The difference is that the earlier theoreticians of collectivism have been disavowed by the orthodox consensus, and are more or less accused of *shi'ism*.

Contestable or not, an attempt to reinterpret dogma merits attention, in order to appreciate its sources and its success. Educated Muslim Algerians have generally looked to Islam as a model for lawmaking. Islamic society (*umma*), with its constraints and its collectivism but also with its fraternal warmth, can easily recall the socialist ideal of brotherhood, and this affinity is often expressed. "For the people," said an Algerian civil servant, "Islam is a kind of socialism."[25]

But it is only "a kind of" socialism, since, for many reasons, not all related to religion, socialism has long meant atheistic materialism, moral disorder, and even anarchy. World events have also associated it with the struggle against colonialism and underdevelopment. Because of this, it has attracted the young especially, who also have seen in it a political way to greater liberties, and in more concrete terms to the "libertinism" that traditional Islam prohibits or blames: the right to appear in public with one's fiancée or wife, the abolition of the veil and the claustration of women, the right to drink alcohol, the right to go to parties to dance, and so on.

Ben Bella's first years at the head of the government were instructive in this regard. In the region of Algiers under the tight control of wilaya IV, all alcoholic beverages were prohibited to Muslims and the *junud* enforced the rule. A more liberal ben Bella relaxed the prohibition, since he believed that drinking was an individual matter. He rallied the liberal youth (60% of the Algerian population is under twenty) and became the undisputed leader after overcoming wilayism. Then came the decrees of December 28, 1963, forbidding Muslims to drink alcohol, closing down cafes, and raising taxes on alcoholic beverages; these were accompanied by speeches by Mohammed Khider on the duty of observing Ramadan, and other obligations.

Islamic commandments had been questioned and had to be restored, but there was strong disappointment, doubled by a fear of secularism. In fact, along with the declarations and the new laws, a wave of Marxist propaganda was released in Algeria in 1963. The national press printed daily eulogies of the Soviet countries and China, of Marx, Lenin, and Mao. People were thus led to believe that the government was thinking of Marxizing the country and liquidating Islam, despite such affectations as the arguments on "Islamic socialism," which little by little came to be regarded as only an alibi for the Communists. . . .

Islamic socialism also caused concern among religious people and prominent personalities known for their religious zeal, who considered it imprudent, if not sacrilegious, to erase thirteen centuries of consensus on individual property and fall into an arbitrary collectivism whose origins were foreign to Algeria and to Islam.

Their irritation became apparent in a meeting organized on January 5, 1964, by the al-Qiyam (Values) Association in the House of the People, where 3,000–4,000 people heard the regime's religious and political orientation questioned obliquely (as was necessary). The solutions advanced by the speakers did not rouse much enthusiasm since, torn between prejudice and regression, they had advocated a "return to tradition" that was both depressing and frightening: the enforcement of prayer through police force and of orthodoxy through village watchdog committees. The socialist press found it easy to make fun of these advocates of the Middle Ages and the Inquisition. . . .

After the al-Qiyam debate, other reactions came to light that were more balanced and more capable of arousing the interest of the sophisticated public. A case in point was the informal talk of Professor Jamaleddine Baghdadi in Algiers on February 5, 1964, under the auspices of the UGTA, which has been actively interested in this religious-political question. Baghdadi, an excellent speaker in Arabic with a profound knowledge of Western culture, outlined socialist doctrine and history from Plato to Lenin by way of Mohammed and Abu Dharr, before coming to the materialistic socialism of Marx, which he denounced. He showed on one hand that, even though it has an important place in Islam, economic concerns are not the focal point of Muslim doctrine, and, on the other, that Islam advocates brotherhood and love and would not tolerate either materialism or the principle of a "bloody repression," since it is based on a philosophy of the golden mean.

At the time, the regime was being challenged by a scattered regional and Berber opposition hardened by the unfortunate and brutal repression of October, 1963, and purporting to be socialist, according to its name: Front of the Socialist Forces (FFS); ideas such as those of Baghdadi seemed to contradict the drastic tendencies of the government.[26] In any case, the UGTA delegates who heard Baghdadi reacted unfavorably, despite the applause of the audience and even of Labor Minister Nekkache. The Union spokesmen disavowed Baghdadi, who soon afterwards was accused of being "objectively and basically conservative" because he had questioned the necessity of class struggle and disavowed bloody revolutions and the *zakat*.[27]

Although "objective," the condemnation did not satisfy all the militants. Soon after, one of them openly and soundly questioned it: "The controversy with Professor Baghdadi is ridiculous. At the time of the khalifas of Medina, there were no 'means of production' but only a rich minority who refused to pay the *zakat*. Socialism has nothing to do with it."[28]

The Ramadan fast — rigorously observed, with the help of volunteers from the FLN — had just ended, and foreign political observers spoke of "rifts" in Algerian socialism between the "revolutionaries" under the FLN banner and among the President's advisors, and the "religious" under Khider and the 'ulema of all schools, with the supposed help of Mzab, Colonel Chaabani, and the

UGTA. The "religious" reaction was quite vocal, since Mohammed Harbi, director of *Révolution Africaine* and principal revolutionary theoretician of the FLN, spoke out for the "respect of Islamic values." Furthermore, discussions in the capital tended to focus on these values, and Malek Bennabi, former *'alim* and author of *The Vocation of Islam,* who surprisingly became the oracle of socialism, denounced "the excessive assimilation of Islam and Marxism" and warned his readers against "foreign ideologies that seek to substitute themselves for the true aspirations of the people," and, instead of a dogmatic Islam that "petrified thoughts," recommended another, modern Islam, which "tends to be universalist and works for the renovation of Arab civilization."[29] A short time later, however, Noureddine Hassani dampened the "religious" group's hopes through a ponderous doctrinal speech on the theme "Socialism and the Criteria of Development in Algeria." A courageous member of his audience replied: "Islam cannot identify with Marxism as a mean of economic development and must therefore create a doctrine defining the bases of an Algerian Islamic socialism. . . ."[30]

The next element in the debate came from Sheikh Bachir Ibrahimi, former president of the Association of 'Ulema, who was welcomed with honor at the end of 1962 by the chief of state but then became suspect to the point of being put several months under house arrest. "Our country is moving slowly but surely toward civil war, a moral crisis such as we have never before encountered, and insurmountable economic difficulties. The leaders do not seem to realize that our people are crying above all for unity, peace, and prosperity, and that the theoretical bases of their action should be taken not from foreign doctrines but from our Arabo-Islamic ones. The time has come when the leaders should give the example, when only probity and competence should decide. The time has come to restore the value of the much-used term, 'fraternity,' and to return to the principle of consultation, so dear to the Prophet."[31]

The FLN press did not react, but the Arabic newspaper of the UGTA two weeks later "executed" the sheikh in a brutal pamphlet cleverly entitled, "The 'Ulema of Evil."[32] The sheikh and his followers were denounced as enemies of socialism and as a "corrupt clique" that abused the tolerance of the militants. "If such people protest against the importation of socialist ideas, the pamphlet concluded, why do they not criticize the capitalist economy, lipstick, and automobiles? Are they not also imported?"[33]

The labor unions, outraged, were still not satisfied. On July 8, they vehemently accused other "corrupt cliques" like the Muslim Brotherhood, with whom the 'ulema had ties before 1954, the Mzab reformists, the Habous "Ministry", and finally such individuals as Professor Hamza Boubekeur, director of the Paris Mosque, and, surprisingly, sheikhs Kheireddine and Bajoud, accused of "criminal activities," and other less-well-known reformists as Hadj Nacer, labelled a "blind peacock" and smuggler.

In fact, despite the imams' considerable following, and even with the construction of some forty new mosques since 1962, there is a feeling of a decline in popular religion. The time is past when Islam was a refuge against assimilation or a weapon of psychological war. Beneath the respect paid to it lies a good deal of indifference. People no longer pray in public, the pious are ridiculed, and the faithful who practice their religion are becoming rare, less than 1%, from personal observations in Algiers. Maghribi Islam of the fraternities and marabouts seems to be the greatest loser. Its chiefs, already strongly criticized, have become suspect and live a retired life. They are considered as sorcerers and storytellers in the public markets. Their visitors and financial supporters are viewed as naïve or reactionary, for the regime has little sympathy with the "techniques of salvation" and even less with private competition to socialist organizations.

Ben Bella gave his own views on the subject in May, 1964, while visiting Moscow: "We are carrying out a successful fight against backwardness, superstition, and the reactionary and conservative habits of thought." Reassured by this presidential declaration, the Algerian press during the summer castigated the vestiges of superstition and saint worship. The Constantine newspaper *al-Nasr (Victory)* denounced the revival of maraboutism in Ain M'Lila, explaining that "the drought causes our poor brothers to organize maraboutic orgies (*zerdas*) to bring rain." This folklore[34] could be excused, according to the newspaper, if it were not mixed up with "Rabelaisian meals and dances," "exploited for goals contrary to Islam and revolutionary principles," and so on. Furthermore, if nothing were done, "justice and happiness would be overcome by the onslaught of retrograde and degrading methods. . . . Already in the villages and *duars,* marches are organized, pilgrimages to the *zawiyas* . . . . are becoming more frequent . . . . Evil forces which take up their worthless task again."[35]

About the same time, the UGTA took the offensive to the talebs, so-called dentists and doctors, who dare to practice in the center of the capital and "commit murder in the name of Islam with impunity," as well as other swindlers, vendors of amulets and phylacteries, organizers of rigged lotteries, and so on, down to the "shopkeeper bourgeoisie". who are "associated in this crime."[36] The Algiers Communist newspaper, *Alger Républicain,*[37] pointed out with indignation the case of a taleb doctor from Oued Smar whose patient had died from suspect intravenous injections. The official party press[38] denounced the progress of maraboutism in Tiaret and a few months later, its Arabic newspaper *al-Sha'b (The People)*[39] published a diatribe against the wizard from Batna, a man with a yellow turban who was accused of cupidity, imposture, impiety, and charged with being a "stranger" known to none, and finally — curiously, for a socialist press — "the devil's vicar."(This kind of problem is generally discussed only in the Arabic-language newspapers, a face-saving measure, since few foreigners are able to read them . . . .

June, 1964, brought a new argument to Islamic socialism through the speech given by Madani to inaugurate a new mosque in Bou Saada. "Our socialist Revolution is compatible with Islam since it is the will of the people."[40] The sentence was revealing for its use of the notion of *ijma',* unanimous consent of the believers, which allows the community to legitimize its wishes within the framework of Muslim law. The principle of *ijma'* contains the potentiality for reform, allowing Islam to adapt itself and eventually to get rid of tyrants or unjust and ineffective imams. This potentiality perhaps explains why its exercise was made so difficult over the centuries, being first subject to the agreement of eminent lawyers who were supposed to represent the people, then finally taken from the jurists through the artifice of "closing the door of *ijtihad*" (prohibiting interpretation the texts). In sum, the believers were pushed away from authority to make way for the specialists, who in turn have been silenced. There has never been an ecumenical council in Islam. Madani, in fact, posed the question of the infallibility of the community, forgetting the restrictive measures imposed during the Middle Ages of Islam and assuming a popular unanimity in favor of socialism.

Along with this appeal to the people, a Marxist interpretation has been given to the birth of Islam. A first attempt of this kind took place in 1963, in an editorial in *al-Sha'b,* which declared that Islam began as "a revolution of the poor against the rich."[41] This theory, novel although not illogical or historically inaccurate, was taken up and developed by the UGTA in a Marxist version of the Sura Nabawiya, whose tone was so peremptory that no one dared question it: "Each time that the Good People brandished the torch of Right and Liberty on the behalf of tortured humanity, the reactionary clique called down the vengeance of the Apostle and his companions in order to oppose the Prophet . . . . "[42] Compared with this neglected but truly modern Sura, the articles of Egyptian scholars in al-Ma'rifa seemed mild indeed, especially after the attacks of the UGTA press against the bourgeois and the oppressive classes.

"Can a bourgeois be Muslim?" asked the newspaper. Obviously not, since he "tends" to possess the means of production, lives in luxury, and opposes the Revolution. "The trashcan of history" is a good place for the bourgeoisie, proclaimed another article, which called Algeria "the model of Arabism and Islam" and even "the ideal model for all of Africa."[43] These appeals for the elimination of the bourgeoisie were a prelude to the confiscation measures soon to affect them under the guise of recovering "ill-acquired property," while week after week a formidable Communistic campaign unfolded on the radio, accompanied by readings from the Qoran and traditional Muslim greetings . . . .

If most of the people were apathetic or resigned, those who were a bit more aware of what was going on became alarmed; echoes of the regime's unpopularity were so strong by the eve of the general elections of September, 1964, that the government had to move away from the Communists. On September 3, 1964, the complete Arabization of the first year of primary school was announced, along with mandatory religious training. Several Marxist personalities were excluded from the government, including Mohammed Harbi, who on October 31 gave up his position as director of *Révolution Africaine* to 'Amer Ouzegane, first recognized advocate of specifically Algerian socialism. A "detente" appeared to have been reached, and ben Bella returned once more to the familiar theme of Islamo-socialist coexistence: "In developing all these human qualities, we also achieve an original synthesis between the values of Islam and these of a humanistic and scientific socialism."[44]

The occasion was propitious for the "religious" to make their voices heard. The Habous press took their position rather brutally, through excerpts from a speech of one of its inspectors in the Kabylia: "The agents of atheism and Communism are paid propagandists who would like to soil the reputation of religion and its members. Beware! Impose your existence on the enemies, be witnesses in the Algerian society! Through your firmness and decisiveness, religion will win out."[45]

Révolution Africaine published an article defending scientific socialism but the "religious" paid no attention to it, and the UGTA soon printed an editorial promoting religious teaching in the public schools. "Faced with this irresistible wave [in favor of Islam], some intellectuals whose sympathy for Marxism is well

known will acknowledge the Arab and Muslim reality of Algeria. Indeed, the
UGTA made sure that on several occasions some organizations and personalities
gave their public support to the cultural and spiritual direction that the country
is taking . . . . "[46] The editorial contained chosen citations from Madani and ben
Bella: "We will present this socialism to the entire world and we will say to the
people: If you are taken with the socialism of Karl Marx, well, we take pride in
the socialism of Mohammed!" "In [the Soviet Union], you can laugh at religion
as you please. In Algeria, we have triumphed because of our religion, and we will
conquer only through Islam."

After such pronouncements, it would have seemed that Algerian Islamic
socialism would have been accepted. But political events do not always follow a
straight line, especially in Arab countries, where at least Western legend assures
us that directness is never the shortest way. The November 1 celebrations hardly
confirmed the rejection of revolutionary ideas "imposed from abroad." A poem
by Malek Haddad published on that day reads:

> [In] this Arab Algeria that I know by heart
> [In] this Islamic Algeria where Lenin is at home
> On this November 1 when the firefly appears
>   I say it
>   I proclaim it
> Down on your knees before the day which nears![47]

A few days later, French-speaking Muslims listening to Radio Algiers[48] lost their
last illusions (if they had any left). An evening variety program began with a
French poem about evolution, persistently explaining the world "from the
amoeba to men by way of the monkey." Then followed a long, bitterly ironic
denunciation of these "poor people" with rusty brains who think that the
"world has been created for man," with the sun and moon to light him, animals
to serve him, and vegetables to feed him. Such a parody of the Qoranic
revelation was in direct conflict with the president's assurances and even more
with the teaching of Islam in the schools.

Although it had suddenly become the champion of an Islamo-Marxist
symbiosis, the UGTA Arabic press was suspended without warning or comment
after its pro-religion editorial. On December 2, Madani left the Habous Ministry,
Sheikh Bayoud was rumored to be in jail with other reformists, Hadj Nacer was
in voluntary exile, and Sheikh Ibrahimi retired from public life. The purge of old
spiritual leaders neutralized the 'ulema, long considered to be leading authorities
of Algerian nationalism, pioneers of militant Arabism, and examples of the
Muslim social ideal. Their departure marked the end of an era that, in retrospect,
might well appear as the golden age of Algerian Islam. For, through one of those
ironies of which politics sometimes has the secret, the 'ulema, professional
protestors who fought so long for freedom of religious practice, handed down to
their successors, the Habous, a centralized state apparatus without equal in
Islam, to our knowledge.

This innocuous — and admittedly secondary — ministry has powers that in
fact are dictatorial: it hires and fires religious leaders, directs the Qoranic schools
and Islamic centers, administers the habous and the mosques, has an almost
uncontested monopoly over religious books and texts, and each week determines

the subject of the Friday sermon (*khotba*) for the entire country. Such centralization amounts to making an imamate out of the government, an alarming power for the neighboring states but one that might also for the moment enable it to exert pressure in favor of reforms where religion will be at stake . . . .

But there are other critical areas where real or supposed religious interference has posed problems that challenge the regime. Two of the main ones are Arabization and women's emancipation, which the Tripoli Program as well as the FLN charter considered to be options as irreversible as socialism itself.

In 1962, the change from the colonial language, French, to the sacred language of Islam, Arabic, appeared to some intellectual Arabic-speaking militants as merely a matter of issuing decrees. Legislation and public enthusiasm would take care of everything: the purest Arabic would be spoken everywhere, from primary school to the university, proving [the Egyptian intellectual] Taha Hussain and other pessimists wrong. Two years have gone by, and the former assurance has been replaced by discouragement. Not only did Arabization require the training of Arabic-speaking teachers and the importation of Arabic printers and typesetters, but it also presupposed much work to modernize the language, since books in chemistry, electronics, or nuclear physics, for example, could not be translated into present-day Arabic. Even worse, leaders in schools and literacy programs were not sure which Arabic [— spoken, written, Algerian, Middle Eastern —] should be taught. Pending a decision, French is still being used in schools and administration, to the disappointment of the Arabists. . . . For the time being, the Algerian towns are slowly being covered with official signs in good Arabic with some commercial signs in dialect. Arabization continues, especially through radio and television, which teach modern Arabic by using it every day, but also through the press, which has made striking progress since 1962. It is therefore not impossible to imagine Algeria Arabized in fifteen years and ready to produce in Arabic books that will meet its ambitions.

The situation is less satisfactory with regard to the emancipation of women. The veil, forced marriage, exorbitant dowries, elaborate wedding festivities, nonparticipation of women in social life — although not a part of the formal religion — are considered essential by the majority of the people. To eliminate them would pose delicate social and political problems, in view of the widespread traditionalism and integrism of the majority of the religious or parareligious leaders. The government could scarcely count on them in any case, and it has preferred to address itself directly to the national organizations and their clientele. Nevertheless, a campaign was launched, and in October, 1964, the press published the results: 600,000 girls were enrolled in school; women from the National Union of Algerian Women (UNFA) had built a school in Tlemcen; women were now seen in the weekly markets in the countryside.

On November 15, 1964, a vigorous editorial in the new Arabic weekly *al-Shabab* (The Youth) opened fire:

Our revolution has not accepted and will not accept the subordination of women whatever the justification, whether in the name of a deviant notion of Islam, in the name of tradition, or in order to preserve special privileges . . . . To those who exploit Islam and take cover under moral values, we say that whatever is done for the working class is moral and that whatever is hostile to it is immoral. As the holy apostle said: "The hand of God is with the collectivity."

This remarkable pamphlet is based once more on *ijma'*, the general consent of the community. The argument is strong if the community does agree. But is this the case? The following week, the same newspaper lined up the demands of the "youth" and called for reductions in the dowry (*mahr*) paid by the groom ($1,800 and three sheep is the current rate in Batna); co-education, since "the meeting of boys and girls is imposed by the twentieth century way of life"; and abolition of forced marriage (*jabr*) . . . .[49]

But this account would be incomplete without the thesis of the "religious" who rallied to socialism, for it brings a new element into the preceding discussion. Two citations from *Révolution Africaine* will suffice in closing this study:

"Purely from the mental point of view [sic], it is not given to women to give lessons to men. From the point of view of physical and biological structures of the brain, man is superior."[50]

"The woman in the home is therefore an alienation of the feminine personality in a capitalistic regime . . . . In principle, no religious, legal, or political obstacles to a true promotion of women exist here. There are only prejudices surviving from a feudal mentality."[51]

In the present state of mind, and contrary to a hundred solemn affirmations, the practical perspectives of socialism arouse only moderate enthusiasm. People do not mind working but they prefer a direct and exclusive profit and a rhythm that is suited to the country and to themselves. Few people are eager to work overtime for a brighter tomorrow, which might take a quarter of a century to come about . . . . Finally, collective work, where one's own personality is drowned in a group instead of being seen for its own worth, is not appreciated. This trait, already apparent in the Berbers, who have a long individualistic tradition, is even truer of the Arabs, whose ideals do not include manual labor, much less work for someone else.

Algerian independence has profoundly modified not only the economy but also the implantation of the people and the social structures. One family head out of three is unemployed, 90% of the skilled workers live abroad, mostly in France; thousands of persons unprepared for such roles have become blue-collar workers or laborers, and thousands more have entered the army.

In this already somber social picture, a confused popular revolution has been taking place that has taken its roots from the occupation of vacant lands, legalized thereafter by a strong government that came out of a small civil war. All this was done in the name of socialism, despite the fact that neither the social structures nor the religious traditions had prepared the country for it. For two years, this government, advised by a group of Communist figures, tried to impose a Marxist-Leninist ideology. It stumbled over several roadblocks (only hinted at because outside the scope of this study), but above all over serious Islamic religious reactions. To contain or eventually eliminate them, the regime has taken over all religious organizations, purged their former leaders, and discretely advanced the cause of an Islamic socialism, received with many a reservation. After many heated politico-religious controversies, the regime during its third year in power seemed to put the Marxist theories on ice and to pursue its experiments in its own form of socialism, with Islam as the state religion and Arabic as the official language.

Notes

1. See Maurice Maschino, "Entretien avec un Syndicaliste Algérien," *Les Temps Modernes*, Nos. 175—76 (October-November,1960), pp. 517—30.
2. *Le Monde*, December 26, 1961 reporting *al-Ahram* (Cairo).
3. Radio Luxembourg, January, 31, 1963.
4. Agence France-Presse despatch, April 1, 1962.
5. See ben Bella's interview with *L'Unità*, pp. 124—26 in this reader.
6. *Al-Moudjahid*, July 30 — August 3, 1962.
7. See *Combat*, July 24, 1961: "The state established by Islam and founded by Mohammed was the first socialist state. Mohammed was the first to adopt a policy of nationalization." This statement was refuted by the Syrian mufti al-Tantaoui the following October.
8. See R. and C. Descloitres and J. C. Reverdy, "Urban Organization and Social Structure in Algeria," pp. 424—38 in this reader.
9. Ben Bella's speech to the Congress of the Former Prisoners, April 26, 1963.
10. *Al-Sha'b*, May 24, 1963.
11. Qoran, XLIII, 32.
12. For example, the commentary of al-Jalalain, currently used in al-Azhar University in Cairo.
13. Qoran, IX, 11.
14. See Mourad Kiouane, "La Démocratie selon l'Islam," in *Jeune Islam*, No. 1 (May, 1949), p. 8.
15. See Mohammed Bouaroudj, "The Notion of Sovereignty in Islam" (in Arabic), *al-Ma'rifa*, 1963), pp. 22—27.
16.Qoran, IV, 77; XXXI, 16; III, 1000; III, 106. The modernists see in this principle the right of the community to control the affairs of state and not, as in the past, the right to intervene in one's neighbor's affairs to bring him back to orthodoxy.
17. In Algeria, until 1865, personal ownership of land was the exception nd collective property the rule. The repression of the 1871 revolt made it possible fir the settlers to buy up large collective landholdings. See A. Noushi, Enquete sur le niveau de vie des populations constantinoises (Paris: Presses Universitaires de France, 1962).
18. *Le Socialisme en Islam* (Damascus, 1959), cited in *Orient*, No. 20 (4th quarter, 1959), p. 117.
19. Ahmed Charabaci, "Ishtirakiya al-Islam" ("Socialism in Islam"), *al-Ma'rifa*, No. 4 (August, 1965), pp. 3—8.
20. It is the purpose of the legal tithe, the *zakat*, to be used for the needs of the community, which is here called Fatherland for the cause.
21. 1849—1902. Kawakibi expressed in 1900 the idea that fortune should not become excessive since too great riches lead to a decrease in morality.
22. Dr. Bahi al-Khawli, "al-Maslaha al-'amma fil-Islam" ("The Public Good in Islam"), *al-Ma'rifa*, No. 5 (October, 1963), pp. 71—73.
23. Qoran, IX, 34; in the story of the Revelation the doctors (Jews) and the Monks (Christian) ate the wealth of the people.
24. Qoran, XV, 29.
25. Mohammed Ahcen, *Révolution Africaine*, 1964), p. 12.
26. Ben Bella at a meeting in the Place des Martyrs, January 11, 1964: "We will shoot them!"
27. *Révolution et Travail* (UGTA French-language newspaper), No. 27 (February 27, 1964), p. 2.
28. *Al-Thawra wal-'Amal (Revolution and Labor)*, March 4, 1963.
29. Talk on "Problems of Ideology," in Algiers, February 24, 1964.
30. Talk in al-Biar, March 9, 1964.
31. Declaration to Reuters, April 16, 1964.

32. Title of a controversial article by Sheikh Bachir, in 1950, in which the Catholic Church and missionaries were accused of being "colonialist agents."

33. *Al-Thawra wal-'Amal,* April 29, 1964.

34. Folklore is fashionable again after having been looked down upon for thirty years. The festivals of Sidi Hosni, Sidi Abdelkader, and Sidi al-Hourani were celebrated in Oran in 1964 with official support to revive folklore.

35. May 15 1964.

36. *Al-Thawra wal-'Amal,* May 28, 1964.

37. *Alger Republicain,* June 13, 1964.

38. *Al-Moudjahid,* No. 219 (June 18, 1964), p. 2.

39. *Al-Sha'b,* October 14, 1964.

40. Speech given on June 29 and reported in *Alger République,* June 30, 1964.

41. *Al-Sha'b,* May 24, 1964.

42. *Al-Thawra wal-'Amal,* June 23, 1964.

43. *Ibid.* May 28, 1964.

44. Ben Bella on Radio Algiers, September 23, 1964.

45. *Al-Ma'rifa,* No. 14 (August, 1964), pp. 108—16.

46. *Al-Thawra wal-'Amal,* August 6, 1964.

47. *L'Algérien,* November 1, 1964. This newspaper is published in French for Algerians in France.

48. Radio Algiers, November 8, 1964.

49. It is to be noted that the Malikite Mufti of Algiers, Baba Ameur, took the stand in another article in *al-Shabab* of supporting total freedom of marriage

50. Tidjani Hachemi, cited in *Révolution Africaine,* December 12, 1964.

51. M. A. Ouzegane, in *ibid.*

6

CONTRIBUTION TO THE STUDY OF MOROCCAN ATTITUDES

JACQUES SELOSSE

Psychological research on socio-cultural variations has been carried out on the effects of three essential variables on the attitudes of young urban Muslim Moroccans:

1. *Sex.* Although age and sex are basic distinctions in social-structure analysis, age distinctions have been eliminated as much as possible by limiting the present study to young adults between twenty and thirty years old.

2. *Education.* [Under the French Protectorate], the Direction of Public Instruction established a system of Franco-Muslim schools to prepare students for examinations equivalent to those for French [primary and secondary] diplomas. Their teaching staff was almost entirely French. Some "Muslim" schools also provided a modernized curriculum similar to that of the Franco-Muslim schools, but with emphasis on Arabic and religious education, taught mostly by Moroccans who were active nationalists. These schools were modern in comparison with the traditional *msid* and the primary and secondary cycles of the Qarawiyin and ben Yussef schools.

3. *Urbanization.* All the respondents were from one of three urban structures: European towns, medinas, or villages. Although this classification may appear oversimplified to one who knows the diversity of Moroccan towns, it nevertheless covers urban structures whose scope and social patterns are quite varied. The respondents have been divided according to the place where they lived for more than ten years:

A. The "new city," a creation of the Protectorate with a geometrical layout to facilitate commercial, industrial, and administrative contract, was mainly inhabited by Europeans. Moroccan families, through either emancipation or professional and social obligations, also lived there, although mostly on the outskirts in "shanty-towns."

B. The "medina" is the traditional Muslim city whose commercial and

Translated, by permission, from *Psychologie Française*, VI, No. 3 (July, 1961), 218-29, and VII, No. 4 (October, 1962), 312-15.

religious activities determine the system of communications. Enclosed by high walls, each of the medina's quarters (*derbs*) has its own separate character. The layout is concentric around the mosque or the kasbah, suggesting a self-centered movement of withdrawal and self-defense.[1]

C. The villages grew up at a water point or a crossroads. Trading or tribal centers, their activities vary according to season and are focused on the *suq* (market)[2] . . . .

The survey was initially conducted with a sample of 483 respondents (293 men, 190 women), from which 237 sets of answers were retained (162 men and 75 women) from respondents who fulfilled the following criteria: (1) at least a sixth-grade education, (2) residence in a European town, medina, or village for at least ten years, and (3) active membership in a socio-cultural, labor, or political association. The survey was conducted after November 28, 1955, when the first independent government of Si Bekkai was formed[3] . . .

The following analysis of Rorschach test results, limited to "intimate resonance types," brings out certain dominant socio-cultural characteristics that help us understand the attitudes of the population.

TABLE 1

(*in per cent*)

	Men	Women	Franco-Muslim	Muslim	New Cities	Medinas	Villages
Introverted	48	39	41	46	35	43	51
Extroverted	34	39	42	32	39	36	30
Inhibited (coarcted)	10	10	9	10	15	10	11
Mixed	8	12	8	12	11	11	8

The introverted type is dominant (44 per cent). The mixed type is only 10 per cent, compared with European samples of the same age group, where it is about 21 per cent. The inhibited type is relatively large, numbering 10 per cent of the Moroccan sample, against only 3 per cent for a similar European sample. Men were more introverted than women, and former students from Franco-Muslim schools were more extroverted than those from Muslim schools. This variable is very significant among women; in fact, nearly half the women who attended Franco-Muslim schools were extroverted, compared to one-third of the alumnae of Muslim schools. Muslim education showed the highest percentage not only of introverts but also of mixed types. The inhabitants of European towns were most extroverted and least introverted; villagers were most introverted and least extroverted.

The analysis of sentence-completion tests was undertaken on two levels: frequency ("typicality") scores were established by weighting the phrases used to complete the sentences, and attitudes were discovered through content analysis of the answers. The measure of frequency was arrived at by dividing the sample population according to scores based on values assigned to attitudinal associations in the answers to the sentences to be completed. Four points were given for positive answers, that is to associations with a dynamic, realistic, proversive content, and three points to associations having an inhibiting, retrospective, and conflictual content.

The content analysis brought out the extreme ambivalence of feelings and seemed to justify giving the highest weighting to positive and inhibiting associations. Furthermore, the large number of "neutral" answers required that a higher coefficient be applied to significant answers. Thus, two points were given for a "neutral" — banal, descriptive, or passive — answer. Ambiguous, omitted, or incomplete answers were given one point.

On the basis of these frequency scores, a curve was drawn that was sufficiently regular to establish three categories for the sample population:

Nonconformist attitudes: scores above 266 (15 per cent of the sample);

Accepted attitudes: scores from 265 to 226 (43 per cent of the sample);

Conformist attitudes: scores of 225 to 186 (33 per cent of the sample);

Marginal (subnormal) attitudes: scores below 186 (9 per cent of the sample).

Divided according to constituent types obtained with the Rorschach test, the sample fell into the following percentage categories:

TABLE 2
(in per cent)

	Introverted	Extroverted	Inhibited	Mixed
Non conformist	14	16	4	20
Accepted	45	37	33	60
Conformist	36	37	33	20
Marginal	5	10	30	—

The covariation of the two types is thus evident.

TABLE 3
(in per cent)
ASSOCIATIONS

	Positive	Inhibited	Neutral	Ambiguous	Long Answers	Median Frequency Score
Men	18	16	46	20	2	234
Women	18	20	39	23	2.5	236
Muslim	19	18	42	21	3	238
Franco-Muslim	17	17	45	21	1	231
New cities	18	20	44	18	2.5	237
Medinas	18	17	42	23	1.5	227
Villages	16	17	48	19	2.5	227
Introverted	18	18	45	19	2	239
Extroverted	17	18	44	21	2	235
Inhibited	13	15	38	34	1.5	210
Mixed	22	20	40	18	3	243

No difference is statistically significant; the results therefore have only a descriptive value. Nevertheless, the study was significant for the "urbanization" variable and the frequency scores. Respondents living in the European towns had a higher frequency score than did inhabitants of medinas and villages. Table 3 shows the tendency to "neutralize" the content of the answers among the respondents from villages, who provided the highest percentage of introverts (51 per cent). People in the medinas had a tendency toward ambiguity, while city-dwellers tried hard to express themselves either positively or negatively (the highest number of extroverts are found among them).

After having thus characterized and "typified" the sample according to its constitutent and tendential characteristics, the results of the associations derived from the completion questionnaires were divided into sixteen personality factors. Since logical induction did not always determine content in the completion test, the analysis utilized only the associations obtained from the words and not the extension of the sentence itself. The first nine factors concern family and interpersonal relations.

1. *Attitudes toward the mother.* We did not find significant variation on account of sex. Respondents from Muslim schools emphasized the affective behavior of a mother toward her children, while respondents from Franco-Muslim schools emphasized the person in her maternal status, preferring her to all other members of the family. The personal qualities of the mother were most appreciated by those who lived in European towns, while for the others her signs of affection toward her children were most important.

2. *Attitudes toward the father.* No significant variation was seen between the sexes. The Muslim-school respondents underlined the educative qualities of the father and the wishes that they addressed to him were of a religious nature, while respondents from Franco-Muslim schools gave more weight to their father's personal qualities. This group expressed criticism and praise with equal force. The wishes they expressed toward their fathers were for good health. There were no significant differences due to urbanization.

3. *Attitudes toward the family.* Men emphasized the educative qualities of the family, notably its importance for the future of the children. Women appreciated a positive attitude toward progress in general, as well as domestic virtues. While respondents from Muslim schools distinguished their own family from others, insisting upon its originality, its socio-economic status, and its egualitarian treatment of its children, respondents from Franco-Muslim schools ascribed particular qualities to their family and felt they had a right to privileged treatment within the family. Urbanization did not seem to influence these attitudes significantly. Perception of family status and role differed therefore according to education. Respondents from Franco-Muslim schools gave more weight to their parents' personal virtues than to their family position. If they remained attached to the particular characteristics of their parents, they acknowledged having been the recipient of particular attention from them. Women seemed interested in the role of parental attitudes toward progress rather than toward education, although in fact the two values are complementary. The influence of urbanization was evident only in the educative attitudes of the mothers, which were encouraged by people living in the European towns.

4. *Attitudes toward the sexes.* This is an intrusion into the private domain, a taboo. Respondents from Muslim schools are the only ones to express characteristics that differentiated them from the bulk of the sample: They noted with equal intensity the civic role of women and their inadequate education.

5. *Attitudes toward heterosexual relationships.* The couple is conceived of

by respondents from Muslim schools as the place where affection and familial feelings are expressed. The contractual aspect prevails over any other. Respondents from Franco-Muslim schools expressed envy and jealousy at the sight of a happy couple. Married life was considered a natural social necessity by respondents from Muslim schools and was presented as an agreement between partners, while for respondents from Franco-Muslim schools, it was an ideal to be pursued and attained. Men especially expressed that point of view; women appeared much more reserved.

6. *Attitudes toward friends and social relations.* Men evaluated their relations according to two criteria: the aid, assistance, and understanding they could count on in their social relations, and the climate of moral conformism in which their social exchanges took place. Respondents from Muslim schools chose their friends for their socio-cultural, political, and intellectual qualities. Their personal attitudes toward others were guided by a desire to be seen, appreciated, and esteemed (the honor complex). For respondents from Franco-Muslim schools, social relations were limited to a select cell, sometimes reduced to members of their family. Freedom of expression, of appreciation, and of self-criticism were the qualities most appreciated. Spontaneity and frankness were the virtues asked of friends. People in European towns had stricter selective criteria for their friends than people from traditional towns and villages.

7. *Attitudes toward superiors.* Men evaluated their superiors essentially on the basis of the attitude those superiors adopted toward them. The interest a superior showed toward the respondent was considered most important. Those from Muslim schools mainly criticized the negative attitudes of the superior vis-à-vis the respondents and also his presumed political shortcomings. But they easily adopted a respectful attitude in their relations with him. People from Franco-Muslim schools also gave much weight to the superior's personal attitude toward them, although they seemed to have a natural esteem that sprang from the recognition that he possessed technical superiority. But they were willing to modify their behavior in a very opportunistic way, depending on the circumstances. Respondents from the villages felt that the attitude of the superior was more frequently one of carping than of encouragement.

8. *Attitudes toward subordinates.* Men showed a positive attitude toward subordinates. People from Muslim schools were ready to participate in a common task with their subordinates; they showed a certain concern for their collaborators and expressed feelings of gratitude toward them. But those from Franco-Muslim schools wanted to be obeyed and felt guilt feelings toward their subordinates. The ambivalence of the attitudes is clear; the superiority feelings that Franco-Muslim education seemed to confer appeared poorly assimilated and gave rise to conflict.

9. *Attitudes toward colleagues.* In this case, the women expressed themselves with more intensity: individual qualities were the most appreciated. Respondents from Muslim schools appreciated the qualities of social and political (civic) participation, as well as reciprocal esteem and friendship that should govern interpersonal relationship. Respondents from Franco-Muslim schools extolled human qualities in others and emphasized personal virtues. Inhabitants of European towns gave more emphasis to political participation and social qualities in their colleagues than did the inhabitants of medinas and villages. Thus, on the level of the respondents' participation in the activities of

social groups, two attitudes appeared clearly, one reflecting a national and civic community and the other narrowly and critically personalistic.

These differences were even more apparent in situation analysis. The next seven factors concern subjective attitudes.

1. *Respondents' fears and worries.* For men, personal problems of inhibition were dominant. Every new relationship was feared as an occasion for frustration and injustice. Socio-cultural traditions were considered as hindering the respondents' happiness and development. For women, it was not so much interpersonal relationships as the "world" that was perceived as a source of conflict fraught with danger. Respondents from Muslim schools dreaded any new situation and at the same time, feared cultural traditions and their own inhibitions, while respondents from Franco-Muslim schools were careful to give their fears a more precise, limited, and objective content. An attempt to adjust to reality seemed to prevail. Inhabitants of the medinas were less preoccupied with their personal problems than were those from European towns or villages.

2. *Guilt.* Personal defeats attributed to personality weaknesses were considered to be a source of guilt feelings among Muslim-school respondents, whereas circumstances (failure in studies, material privations, lack of leisure) were considered a source of regret by Franco-Muslim school respondents. Respondents from European towns cited their family as the source of their guilt feelings more frequently than did the other groups. The dichotomy between personal and circumstantial responsibility is a reflection of the two characteristics of behavior already mentioned: submission and revindication.

3. *Respondents' abilities and productivity.* Men found their abilities adequate to confront any situation. Women, more unassuming but more realistic, limited their ambition to getting a job, which for a Moroccan woman represents an escape from the gynaeceum and the acquisition of her autonomy. Muslim school respondents found a point of honor in the personal justification of their abilities, whatever their effectiveness, while respondents from Franco-Muslim schools tried to adjust their abilities to a social position while displaying an acceptance of their destiny.

4. *Attitudes toward the past.* Women felt nostalgia for their childhood, men missed the pleasures of their youth. The present confronted both of them with the reality of a competitive world for which they did not feel prepared. Respondents from Muslim schools looked on the past as a period of construction and preparation for the future, whereas the respondents from Franco-Muslim schools saw the past cut up into periods, which were differently appreciated. Respondents living in European towns felt their childhood experiences more painfully than those from medinas and villages.

5. *Attitudes toward the future.* While women looked to the future with serenity and even confidence, men saw it as something difficult to build. Muslim school respondents were less worried about their future than people from Franco-Muslim schools. Medina-dwellers thought that tomorrow would be better than today, while those from the villages and European towns showed feelings of anxiety concerning their future.

6. *Goals pursued.* Goals pursued by Muslim-school respondents were essentially linked to the idea of social, political, and individual development. People from Franco-Muslim schools were sensitive to the pleasures of life and tried to reserve time for leisure and recreative activities; at the same time, they were eager to

consolidate their professional status through work. It became apparent that increasing their knowledge and enjoying their private life were the foremost goals of the European town-dwellers, whereas for medina and village inhabitants, political and social interests were dominant. Thus, it seems that at the recreative level a new dimension could be added to the different social characteristics already cited, illustrating a social "theoretical and political" type and an "economic and domineering" type. Aesthetic and religious values seemed secondary to these dominants but were used to support them.

7. *Views on life.* In their conception of life, only one difference between sexes was of any significance: Women were more positive and more optimistic than men. Education, on the other hand, provided several variables. Respondents from Muslim schools recognized and advocated the political, social, and national values of life, while respondents from Franco-Muslim schools cited individual values. The sample appeared to be neatly divided. Those who discovered the individual personality did so through withdrawal, which appeared basically selfish. The particular won out over the social. This self-consciousness seemed to occur at the individual level; it had not yet reached a level of personalism. Liberalism meant liberation of the individual but brought with it anxiety at the level of social group participation. Franco-Muslim school respondents looked on life as a struggle whose outcome was uncertain, and more often than their friends from Muslim schools they turned to their sacred and theoretical values. Optimism was more discernible in people from Muslim than from Franco-Muslim schools.

Thus, the discovery of the individual and his inherent value was obtained at the cost of fear of alienation and dependence. Respondents from Franco-Muslim schools also felt themselves outsiders in a society where Arab culture dominates; they saw their cultural models disappearing, or at least decreasing.

Among the young city-dwellers, pessimism was strongest and social and economic constraints were felt sharply. The resultant behavior was divided between submission, on the one hand, and hope of being recognized and thus able to express oneself, on the other. Yet for medina inhabitants, daily life was conducted in a serene surrounding, where the only event was participation in the community's social activities. Economic restraints were well accepted. There were as many optimists as pessimists among this group. The village-dwellers were the most "self-determined" and were eager to make their way in life. But their feeling was somber; in fact, passivity traits seemed to outweigh reactivity traits. . . .

The third test was projective, designed to study reactions and attitudes through the use of ten photographic montages illustrating the urban and industrial evolution of Morocco. The test complemented the investigation of Moroccan personality undertaken with Rorschach and completion tests.

The stories' heroes were frequently of the opposite sex from the respondent. (However, respondents often avoided personalizing their heroes and instead used such general concepts as progress, science, independence, sanitation, justice, religion, and politics.) Analysis of the heroes' behavior brought out certain common characteristics. Attitudes of resistance appeared, directed against an outside world that was considered dangerous and frustrating. Social relations were quite often a source of dependence and were felt to be alienating. Tradition

TABLE 4

Themes in Stories, Ranked by Frequency of Mention

Theme	Sample	Men	Women	Franco-Muslim	Muslim	New City	Medina	Village
Women's social status	1	1	3	1	3	1	1	6
Women as a factor of social evolution	12	28	5	16	17	11	20	13
Individual sentimental life	15	14	9	10	20	25	21	16
Marriage as sexual emancipation	28	30	20	32	31	23	32	27
Resolution of shanty-town problems	2	2	6	3	4	3	8	2
Fidelity to Islam	3	5	1	2	6	4	3	1
Urbanization as an improvement on the *bled*	4	9	4	7	1	6	2	12
Generalized education	5	4	7	4	9	5	5	5
Social hygiene	6	6	2	5	13	13	4	14
Civilization and hedonism	7	7	8	6	10	2	6	4
Work as a socio-economic necessity	13	8	28	25	14	2	9	9
Criticism of parasitism, search for skills	8	3	14	24	7	7	7	8
Concern for Islamic tradition	10	12	10	13	8	9	14	3
Hospitality as an Arabo-Muslim virtue	19	11	25	11	15	14	22	18
Return to family and tribal values	23	22	24	30	11	16	26	24
Charity as a Muslim virtue	26	23	31	19	23	19	33	22
The sultan, royalty	27	24	18	18	24	30	23	25
Class-consciousness	16	16	26	8	2	21	10	21
Need for social policy	18	19	13	23	18	18	13	7
Search for social justice	22	25	12	26	16	17	17	28
Generational conflicts	21	21	17	20	22	12	25	21
Xenophobia	30	29	27	27	30	29	30	29
Critical judgment on human responsibilities	25	26	19	17	26	20	27	23
Fidelity to the *bled*, criticism of cities	9	13	11	12	12	22	16	15
Urbanization	17	15	15	9	21	31	24	11
Socio-economic value of crafts and tourism	24	20	22	22	19	15	15	26
Unemployment as a socio-economic problem	29	27	33	29	28	27	18	30
Critical situation of socio-economic status	31	32	29	28	33	33	28	31
Love for children	11	10	16	15	5	8	11	17
Social change as a cause of inadaptation	20	17	21	14	29	28	19	19
Isolation of youth	32	31	32	33	27	26	31	32
Dress as a symbol of evolution	14	18	23	21	25	24	12	10
Children as a factor of revolution	33	33	30	31	32	32	29	33

(side margin: Marriage as sexual emancipation)

and custom weighed on the free decision of individuals. This dependence in new situations reflected at the same time avidity, insatiability, and recourse to protection. It came out, too, in certain forms of social parasitism, against which the respondents rebelled. In an opposite but quite complementary way, we discerned manifestations that suggested a search for power. This search was above all motivated by the call for social justice and economic equality; the desire to possess seemed, in fact, to be a desire to participate.

Attachment to material goods was expressed through the desire for their better distribution. Equipment and recreation were sought on a community basis. Notions of a social ethic appeared. Nevertheless, feelings of exclusive possessiveness showed up, especially in close personal relations. The span of relations narrowed as selection became more rigorous. Probably this possession of "the other," expressed in either a homosexual or heterosexual way, constituted a defense against anxiety caused by changes in the social structure. From this point of view, individual love can be conceived of as a product of cultural development.

As in every transculturation situation, a dialectic movement reflected the alternance of personal options. The following scheme is usual: negative factors linked to life in the *bled* or artisanry were expressed by dependence, submission, indirect domination, frustration, and avidity. Positive factors linked with urban life ánd industrialization led to possession, participation, solidarity, enjoyment. Despite the weight of the past, rich in its accomplished historicity, the future introduced the theme of a new era. Certainly it is just a timid beginning. Before taking advantage of progress, the essential prerequisite to enjoying technical liberty, the respondents valued the present, thus putting off their emancipation and postponing their commitment. The attitudes of the urban sample testified to a true awareness of their new social position, on the one hand, and to an objective appreciation of the new situation created by the impact of a technical civilization, on the other. This awareness is at the base of all social transformation. It modifies the perception of the social norms, it sanctions new values and in this way helps in the evolution of Moroccan society in its quest for a new equilibrium.

Notes

1. See Jean Dejeux, "The Meeting of Two Worlds in the Maghrib," pp. 21—30 in this reader.

2. See Marvin Mikesell, "The Role of Tribal Markets . . . , pp. 415—23 in this reader.

3. To simplify the presentation of a battery of tests, they will be divided artificially into tests of level and personality tests.

a. Tests of level include: (1) the P.M. 38; (2) the Ballar test, modified and reduced to twenty-five questions; (3) the Terman Verbal or "best answer" test; (4) the commissions test.

b. Personality tests make a "constitutive" analysis by means of the Rorschach test, to which were added two sentence-completion tests — the questionnaires of the Stein-Sacks completion test — for purposes of verification (test-retest). A test of interpretation, based on ten pictures of scenes from everyday life, was analyzed by projective content. Finally, there was a graphic production test (the drawing of a tree, the Koch-Stora test). For the results of the tree test, see Jacques Selosse, "Le test de l'arbre: enquête expérimentale appliquée à une population citadine," *Revue de Psychologie des Peuples,* XVIII, No. 3 (1963), 283—304. For general results, see also Jacques Selosse, "Perception du changement social par une population citadine marocaine," *Revue Française de Psychologie,* April-May, 1963. For a comparable study, see Jean Cuisenier and Abdelqader Zghal, "Changements culturels en milieu rural tunisien," *Cahiers de Tunisie,* IX, Nos. 29—30 (1960), 51—74.

7

THE NORTH AFRICAN SYNDROME

FRANTZ FANON

It is often said that man is continuously searching for himself and that he denies himself when he stops the search. But it seems that there is one basic dimension of all human problems that can be described. More precisely, all the questions asked of man by man may be summarized as follows: "Did my acts of omission or commission contribute to the devaluation of human reality?" The question could also be posed this way: "'In every situation, did I call upon the man that is within me?'" I want to use these questions to show that a theory of inhumanity might find its laws and corollaries in the particular case of North Africans who emigrated to France.

All these men who are hungry, who are cold, who are afraid, who frighten us, who step on the jealous emerald of our dreams, who distort the fragile curve of our smiles, all these men confronting us, who ask no questions of their own and to whom our questions are strange — who are they?

I ask you, I ask myself. Who are they, these creatures longing for humanity who lean against the invisible but terribly sharp (I know from experience) borders of an integral recognition? Who are they really, these creatures, who hide and are concealed by social truth under the [French racist] names [for North Africans]: *bicot, bounioule, arabe, raton, sidi, mon z'ami?*

Thesis I: That the behavior of the North African often provokes a suspicion about the reality of his illness on the part of medical personnel. Except in emergency cases (intestinal obstruction, wounds, accidents), the North African makes his appearance enveloped in vagueness. He has a headache, a stomach-ache, a back injury, he hurts all over. He is in terrible pain, his face betrays it, it is the sort of suffering that you cannot ignore.

"What is it, my friend?"

"I am going to die, doctor." His voice is broken, so low you cannot even hear it.

"Where does it hurt?"

"All over, doctor."

Above all, do not ask for the precise details; you would not get anywhere. For example, in diagnosing an ulcer, it is important to know the timing of the pains. But the North African seems hostile to any standard notion of timing. It is

Translated, by permission, from *Esprit* (February, 1952), 237-48.

not that he does not understand, since he often comes with an interpreter. It is as if it were painful for him to go back to where he no longer is. The past for him is a burning path; his hope is not to suffer again, not to be face to face once more with his past. This present pain which tortures his face muscles is enough for him. He does not understand that someone wants to impose again on him — even if only through its memory — the pain that has just passed. He does not understand why the doctor is asking so many questions.

"Where does it hurt?"

"In my belly." (He points to the chest and abdomen.)

"When?"

"All the time."

"Even at night?"

"Especially then."

"It hurts more at night than during the day?"

"No, all the time."

"But more at night?"

"No, all the time."

"And where does it hurt most?" There again he shows his chest and abdomen.

And so it goes. Outside, patients are waiting, and what is more serious is that you have a feeling that time will not change anything. So the patient leaves with a probable diagnosis and an approximate therapy based on it.

"Follow this prescription for a month. If you don't feel better, come see me again."

Then one of two things happen.

1. The patient does not feel better immediately and comes back to see the doctor three or four days later. This turns us against him, since we know that medicine should be allowed some time to take charge (if we may use that expression) of the sore. We try to make him understand that fact, or rather he is told that fact. But our patient does not hear us. He *is* his pain, he refuses to understand what we tell him. The next step takes him to the proposition: It is because I am an Arab that they do not treat me like the others.

2. The patient does not feel better immediately, but he does not go back to the same doctor. He goes somewhere else. He starts with the idea that to obtain satisfaction one must try all the doors, and he continues to knock. He knocks insistently, shyly, naïvely, with rage. He knocks, the door opens. The door always opens. And he tells of his pain, which becomes more and more his own. He describes it now with volubility. He catches it in the air, pushes it right under his doctor's nose. He takes it, touches it with his ten fingers, develops it, displays it. It grows before his very eyes. He seizes it on every part of his body, and after fifteen minutes of explanations, with gestures, the interpreter (matter of fact as he must be) translates for us: "He says that he has a bellyache."

All these incursions into space, all these spasms on his face, all these staring glances only meant vague pain. We feel left out of what was said during the explanation. The comedy or the drama starts all over again: approximate diagnosis and therapy.

There is no reason for the wheel to stop. One day someone will take an X-ray that will show an ulcer or a gastritis, or even more likely will show nothing at all. We will say simply that his pain is "functional."

This notion is important and deserves commentary. A thing is said to be vague when it lacks consistency or objective reality. The pain felt by a North African for which we cannot find a cause is declared inconsistent, unreal. And the North African *is* the-one-who-does-not-like-to-work. All his actions will be judged by that *a priori* criterion.

A North African comes to the medical center for listlessness, feebleness, debility. He is given an active treatment of invigorants. After twenty days he is discharged. But then he is back with a new illness.

"My heart is jumping all over inside." "My head is bursting."

Faced with the fear of being discharged, it may be asked whether the lassitude for which he was treated did not come from a kind of vertigo. Then you begin to wonder whether you were not being used by this patient, whom you never understood very well, anyway. Suspicion arises. From then on, you will look at the alleged symptoms with distrust. This is especially true in winter. Some clinics are literally inundated with North Africans when cold weather comes around. It feels so good to be in a hospital ward at that time.

In one ward, a doctor is lecturing a European suffering from sciatica, who walks all day long from one ward to another. The doctor is trying to explain that in his particular case, rest is part of the treatment. With North Africans, he tells us, it is quite different; there is no need to recommend rest, they always stay in bed.

Faced with this pain without cause, this illness spread throughout and all over the body, this continual suffering, the easiest attitude at which one more or less rapidly arrives is the denial of all compassion. In the end, the North African is a pretender, a liar, a good-for-nothing, a lazy loafer, and, finally, a thief.

Thesis II: That the medical personnel's behavior is often already set. The North African does not appear with a racial characteristic but rather with characteristics established by the European. To put it differently, the North African, because he has come, automatically enters into a preexisting order.

A few years ago, a trend appeared in the medical profession that soon came to be called neo-hypocratism. This tendency requires that, when confronted with the patient, the doctor does not pay as much attention to the organic diagnosis as to the motive behind it. But this new trend has not yet reached the medical school where pathology is taught. There is a built-in vice in the doctor's thoughts, a vice that is extremely dangerous. Let us observe it in action.

I have an emergency call from a patient. It is 2:00 A.M. The room is dirty, the patient is dirty, his parents are dirty. Everyone is crying. Everyone is yelling at one another. There is a strange feeling that death is not far away. The young doctor braces himself. He bends "objectively" over this abdomen, which looks like any other.

He touches, he feels, he taps, he asks, but gets only wailing in return. He touches again, taps vigorously, the abdomen contracts, defends itself. He "does not see anything." What if it were a case for surgery? If he were to let something go unnoticed? His diagnosis is negative but he does not dare to go. After some hesitation, he directs his patient to a medical center with a diagnosis for intestinal surgery. Three days later, who comes to meet him in his office? The "intestinal surgery," smiling, completely cured. What the patient does not know is that he has trampled on a very demanding medical theory.

Medical analysis goes from symptoms to lesion. In professional meetings, at international congresses, everyone agrees on the importance of the neuro-vegetative systems, the brain, endocrine glands, psychosomatic links, and sympathalgies, but medical students are still taught that every symptom has a lesion. A sick man is someone who, while claiming to suffer from a headache, buzzing in the ears, or dizziness, is in fact suffering from arterial hypertension. But if the doctor does not find hypertension or a brain tumor, or anything else positive, then he will find medical analysis at fault; and since all analysis is analysis of something, he will find the patient at fault — an intractable, undisciplined patient, who does not know the rules of the game. The rule in all its rigor reads: Every symptom presupposes a lesion.

What am I going to do with this patient? From the ward where I sent him for probably surgery, he comes back to me with a diagnosis of the "North African syndrome." And it is true that the young doctor who just starts practicing feels he is meeting Molière face to face through the North African *malade imaginaire*. If Molière (I am going to say something silly, but all these lines are written to make explicit, and even exaggerate, a bigger idiocy) had had the privilege of living in our twentieth century, he certainly would not have written his *Imaginary Patient*. For today, no one can doubt that Argan is sick, really sick!

"What, rascal? Am I sick? Am I sick, you impudent man?"

North African syndrome. Today, the North African who comes for a checkup carries the dead weight of all his people: all these people who show only symptoms, all these people of whom we said, "nothing concrete" (read: "no visible lesion"). But the patient who is there, in front of me, this body that I am forced to suppose inhabited by consciousness, this body that is not quite a body anymore or rather that feels itself twice as much a body because it is transfixed with fright, this body that forces me to listen to it without being willing to let me know what is wrong, pushes me instead to revolt.

"Where does it hurt?"

"In the stomach," and he shows his liver. I begin to lose my temper. I tell him that his stomach is on the left and that what he showed me was his liver. He is not disturbed, and continues to feel his mysterious belly with his hand: "All this hurts." I know that in "all this" there are three organs, or five or six, to be more exact. Each one has its own pathology; this new pathology invented by the Arabs does not interest me. It is a pseudo-pathology. The Arab is a pseudo-patient.

In every Arab there is an "imaginary patient." The new doctor, like the young student who has never seen a sick Arab, *knows* (see the old medical tradition) that "these people are all charlatans." That is really something to think about. Faced with an Arab, the student or the doctor is inclined to use the *tu* form [the familiar form of address in French]. It is nicer, we are told; it makes them feel at ease; they are used to it. (I am sorry, I feel incapable of analyzing this phenomenon without dropping the objective attitude that I had set for myself).

"I can't help it," an intern told me. "I can't approach them the same way as my other patients." Yes! I can't help it. If you could know what I "can't help" in my life. If you could know what it is in my life that torments me, even in the hours when other people fall asleep. If you could only know. But you will not know.

The medical personnel discover the existence of the North African syndrome not so much by experiment but by oral tradition. The North African takes his place in the asymptomatic syndrome and is automatically viewed in terms of indiscipline (see medical discipline), of inconsistency (in regard to the law: every symptom is related to a lesion), of insincerity (he says that "it hurts," but we know that there is nothing to bear out that fact). There is a mobile idea there, on the limits of my bad faith, and when an Arab reveals himself through the words, "Doctor, I am going to die," this idea that has been roaming in my head will impose itself and dictate my behavior. Really, these people are not responsible.

Thesis III: That even the best minds and the purest intentions occur in a context and hence must be approached through a situational diagnosis. Dr. Stern, in an article on psychosomatic medicine, inspired by the work of Heinrich Meng, writes:

> One not only has to find out which organ is sick, what is the nature of the organic lesions, whether they exist, and what virus has attacked the organism. It is not enough to know the patient's somatic constitution, one must also try to know what Meng calls his situation, that is to say his relations with those around him, his occupations, his preoccupations, his sexual activity, his feelings of security or insecurity, the dangers that threaten him; and also his evolution, the history of his life. You have to make a diagnosis of the situation.

Dr. Stern has laid out a superb plan. Let us follow it.

1. Relations with his environment. Shall we really talk about it? Is there not something comical in talking about the relations of a North African with his French environment. Has he any relations? Has he an environment? Is he not alone? Are they not alone? Do they not look absurd to us, are they not out of place, in the subway or on the bus? Where do they come from? Where are they going? From time to time you might see them working on a building, but you do not *see* them, you just notice them, you glimpse them. Environment? Relations? There is no contact, there are only clashes. Do you know how much love and kindness the word "contact" contains? *Are* there any contacts? *Are* there any relations?

2. Occupation and preoccupations. He works, he is employed, he keeps himself busy, he is given something to do. His concerns? I do not think that this word even exists in their language. Concerned about what? In France you might say: He is concerned about finding a job. In North Africa: he is busy trying to find a job.

Pardon me, ma'am, but could you tell me what you think preoccupies North Africans?

3. Sexuality. I already know what you are going to say: Sexuality is a question of rape. To show the extent to which an inherent misperception study can be prejudicial to the authentic explanation of a phenomenon, I would like to cite a doctoral thesis in medicine presented in Lyon, in 1951, by Dr. Leon Mugniery.

In the industrial center of St. Etienne, eight out of ten married prostitutes.

Most of the others live in an accidental cohabitation of short duration, sometimes maritally. Often they take a prostitute or two into their home and bring their friends to her.

For prostitution seems to play an important role in North African society.... It comes from the strong sexual drive that is characteristic of these hot-blooded Mediterranean people.

There is no doubt that we can raise many objections and give many examples to prove that attempts to house the North African decently have always ended in failure.

Most of the men are young (25 to 35 years old), with strong sexual needs that the ties of mixed marriages are only able to satisfy for a short time, for whom homosexualism is always a disastrous temptation.

There are few solutions to this problem: either one must help regroup these families in France and bring over Arab girls and women, despite the risks inherent in an invasion of this kind by Arab families, or has to accept the idea of brothels for them.

If we were not to pay attention to these factors, we would run the risk of exposing ourselves to more and more attempted rape cases, examples of which are reported again and again in the newspapers. Public morality has more to fear from these facts than from licensed brothels.

And, in concluding, Doctor Mugniery denounces the errors of French Government in capital letters: "THE GRANTING OF FRENCH NATIONALITY BESTOWING EQUAL RIGHTS SEEMS TO HAVE BEEN TOO HASTY AND IS BASED MORE ON SENTIMENTAL AND POLITICAL REASONS THEN ON THE SOCIAL AND INTELLECTUAL EVOLUTION OF A RACE WITH SOME TRAITS OF A REFINED CIVILIZATION BUT WITH A SOCIAL, FAMILY, AND SANITARY BEHAVIOR THAT IS STILL AT THE PRIMITIVE STAGE."

Is there anything more to say? Do we have to take these absurb sentences one by one? Must we remind Professor Mugniery that if the North Africans in France have to be content with prostitutes, it is first because there are some, and second because there are no Arab women.

4. His internal feelings. No reality? One might just as well refer to the feelings of a stone! Internal tensions! What a joke!

5. His feeling of security or insecurity. The first is to be ruled out. The North African is in a state of continual insecurity. I wonder if it would not be a good idea to reveal to the middle-class Frenchman that it is a curse to be a North African. The North African is never secure. He has some rights, you will answer, but he does not know them. Ah! Ah! He only has to become aware of them.

Awareness, ah yes! We are back on firm ground. Rights, Duty, Nationality, Equality, many wonderful things! The North African on the doorstep of the French Nation — his own, too, we are told — lives in the political realm, on the civic level, an imbroglio that no one wants to see. What is the connection with the North African who is in a hospital? Precisely, there is one.

6. The dangers that threaten him. Threatened in his effectivity, threatened in his social activity, threatened in his belonging to the city, the North African combines all the conditions that make him a sick man. Without family, without love, without human relations, without communication with the collectivity, the first awareness of himself will be in a neurotic setting, at pathological level. He will feel empty, lifeless, battling with death, a death beyond death, dead while still alive. What is more pathetic than to see this robust, muscular man tell us in a truly broken voice, "Doctor, I am going to die."

7. His evolution and the story of his life. We should say, rather, the story of his death, daily repeated: a death in the streetcar, a death during medical consultation, a death with the prostitutes, a death in the shop, a death in the movie theater, a multiple death in the newspapers, a death in the fear of all "the proper people" to go out after midnight. A death, yes a DEATH.

All this is all right, they will tell us, but what is the solution? You know them well, they are vague, flabby.

"We have to be on their backs."

"We have to push them out of the hospital."

"If you listened to them, they would forever be convalescent."

"They do not know how to explain their illness."

And they are liars,

And then they are thieves ("to steal like an Arab").

And then, and yet, and furthermore . . . .

The Arab is a thief.

All Arabs are thieves.

They are a slothful race,

Dirty,

Disgusting.

There is nothing you can do with them.

Absolutely nothing.

Sure, it is hard for them, too,

To be as they are.

But you have to admit that it is not our fault.

On the contrary, it is our fault.

On the contrary, the fault is *yours*.

How so? Men come and go through the hall that you have built for them, where you did not place benches for them to rest, where you have constructed scarecrows that wildly slap their faces, that hurt their heads, their chests, their hearts,

Where they do not find any room,

Where you do not make any room for them,

And you dare tell me that you are not interested!

That it is not your fault!

How so! This man that you transform into a thing when you systematically call him "Mohammed," that you reconstruct, or rather dissolve, because of an idea, an idea that you know is disgusting. (You know it perfectly well, you take something away from him, something for which you yourself were once ready to give up something, even life.) Well, *here is a man:* don't you have the impression of draining him of his substance?

Well, let them stay home!

Oh yes! here is the tragedy. Let them stay home! Only they have been told that they are French. They learned it in school, in the street, in the army (where they had shoes to fit their feet), on the battlefield. They have been fed with France, where in their body and "soul" there was a place for something supposedly great.

Now they are told over and over again that they are on "our soil." That if they are unhappy, they can go back to their own kasbah. For there again is a problem. Whatever the troubles encountered in France, some say, the North African will be happier at home . . . .

Studies made in England show that children who were well fed and had a private nursemaid but who lived outside their family surroundings showed signs of morbidity that were twice as strong as those encountered in children not as well cared for but living with their families. Without going that far, let us think about all the people who live a life without future in their country and refuse good jobs in foreign lands. What is the use of having a good job when it does not lead to family life, when it does not permit enjoyment of the good life in society? The science of psychoanalysis considers expatriation a factor of morbidity. That is quite right.

These considerations help us to conclude:

1. The North African will never be happier in Europe than at home, since we require him to live without his familiar environment. Cut off from his origins and cut off from his future, he is a thing thrown into a roaring way of life, bent under the law of inertia.

2. There is manifest and abject bad faith in this proposal. If the standard of living(?) at the disposal of the North African in France is higher than the one he was used to at home, it means that there is much to do in his own country, in that "other part of France."

There are buildings to be built, schools to be opened, roads to be laid out, ghettos to be demolished, towns to be erected, men, women, children, and more children to smile at. There is work to be done at home, human work, work that is part of the meaning of a family, not work for a poor room or a flophouse. Throughout all French territory (metropole and French Union) there are tears to dry, inhuman behavior to correct, words like *mon z'ami* to wipe out, men to make more human, places like Moncey Street to open to traffic.

Your solution, sir?

Do not push me any further. Do not force me to tell you what you should know, sir. If you do not see the man in front of you, how am I to suppose that you can see the real man in yourself?

If you don't want the man who is front of you, how can I believe in the man that might be you?

If you don't insist on bringing out the man, if you don't sacrifice the man who is in you so the man who is living on this earth can be more than a body, more than a Mohammed, by what magic am I to be certain that you, too, are worthy of my love?

8

THE ALGERIAN SUBPROLETARIAT

PIERRE BOURDIEU

Awareness of unemployment comes together with a certain way of experiencing its duration, itself inseparable from the new meaning given to work.

Entrance into the money economy is coupled with the discovery of time as something that can be wasted, that is, the distinction between empty, or lost, time and full, or well-filled, time.[1] These are unknown notions in the logic of a precapitalist economy. Time flows away, punctuated by the divisions of the technical and ritual calendar that impose a specific moment, duration, and rhythm on every activity. If, as often shown, punctuated time is not measured time, it is because there is no equality or uniformity in intervals lived in an autistic experience. The passage of time is comprehended by means that are like many lived experiences: either the impressionistic grasp of qualitatives touches of the world, such as "when the sun touches the earth," or a corporal experience, like *thaoulasth,* which means "when the coldness of the early morning makes you shiver as in fever" *(thaoula).* These signposts are not milestones, which would suppose the notion of regular and measured intervals; they determine islets of duration that are not understood as parts of a continuous line but make up many units closed on themselves and juxtaposed. For example, the week is often called *es-suq,* which means the lapse of time between two markets.

The experience of duration, which comes with the experience of activity, has no reference other than itself. As proof, if the unit of duration is the time necessary to achieve a well-defined task — for example, plowing a piece of land with a pair of oxen, or walking to the nearby market — space is inversely appraised as duration or, better, in reference to the activity accomplished within a definite lapse of time, the day of plowing or of walking. But the basis of all the equivalences, the unique experience of the activity, can only be brought back to oneself; so, unconscious of time as coercion and limit, it is its own measure of itself.

The result is that if we deem this time "empty" or "ill filled," it is only because we refer it to a completely extraneous measure. If it appears to us as time in which nothing or very little happens — and is this not what we mean

Translated, by permission from *Les Temps Modernes,* No. 199 (1962), pp. 1031–51.

when we speak of potential underemployment? — it means simply that what happens is not what we expected. The nature and the number of events that we keep to constitute time sequences, hence their tempo, depend on the principle of selection that we use implicitly and that underlies the ideas we have about work and, therefore, about life itself. We are like the man from the city who thinks that nothing happens in a small village because he rejects what fills up the life of the villagers as uninteresting.

But is this not true of the time of the unemployed or, more generally, of the subproletariat? If it looks empty to us, are we not comparing it to an extraneous standard? The time devoted to the search for work, the time spent in waiting at the placement office, can only be defined in negative terms, in opposition to time for leisure and time for work. It is not time past but time lost or spent. But in this case, it is lived as it is: the experience of duration felt by the unemployed includes a reference — explicit or implicit — to the capitalist vision of work and time, a condition of awareness of unemployment. The attitude of peasants who call themselves unemployed without undergoing any decisive change in their objective situation is significant: the duality of the systems of reference inclines them toward reflection and they discover in traditional activity an unknowing unemployment. Unworked time is empty time, in opposition to the time of the traditionalist economy that, with the only aim of allowing the duration of the group, could not deem an experience of duration empty when it was itself its own measure.

Thus, unemployment as the consciousness of being unemployed is the aberrant by-product of an economic and social order that does not offer everyone the possibility of achieving the goal it imposes as an absolute necessity — a money income — and which makes the people who achieve it see as badly filled time any activity that misses it. But because unemployment, irregular employment, and work as mere occupation do not furnish the minimum security and assurance about the present and immediate future that is provided by permanent employment and a steady salary, they prevent any effort to rationalize economic behavior in reference to a future aim, and they enclose all existence within an obsession with the morrow, a fascination with the immediate.

The unemployed, vendors on the sly, resellers of a bunch of bananas or a pack of cigarettes, small traders, traditional craftsmen, and all those people whose profit is as much as handout as a tip — watchmen, porters, errandboys — are they sure enough of the present to try to make sure of the future? Are not they condemned to improvidence and fatalist renunciation, expressing a total distrust of the future, inspired by awareness of their inability to control the present? "When you are not sure of today," an unemployed man in Constantine said, "how can you be sure of tomorrow?" A fisherman in Oran said, "The more I make, the more I eat; the less I make, the less I eat." Those two striking statements express the heart of subproletarian existence. The sole aim of activity is to fulfill immediate needs. "I earn my piece of bread and that's all." "What I make, I eat." "I barely earn my children's bread."[2] Here is the end of the old tradition of providence. The man in the city begins to resemble the traditional peasant's image of him: "What the day worked, the night ate." Sometimes, traditional behavior returns, absolutely aberrant in its new context and inspired by an obsession with subsistence. "I have supplies ready," said a small grocer from Oran who makes a dollar a day, "If ever I don't make any money, I still eat." Such traditionalism of despair is as inconsistent as hand-to-mouth existence. But is it possible to hope beyond the present, beyond daily bread, when this essential objective is hardly fulfilled? "Wages are just enough to break even, but not enough to get ahead," according to an unskilled worker in a Constantine fishmarket. Because sacrifices are made mainly on consumption, the income may increase but no savings (or even the idea of savings) appear, so much greater are the needs than the means. When asked if they have any savings, most of the subproletarians laugh or become angry.[3] "Savings?" a driver answers with a smile in Orleansville. "The day I am paid, I get sick, I do not know what to do. I live from hand to mouth." Of course, they try to reduce expenses as much as possible, but they never keep any real accounts. "I do the shopping myself," says a tailor in Oran, "I don't keep track and I don't know how much I spend. I don't have savings; if I had any, I would have opened a bazaar" – he laughs – "where everything would be expensive or cheap, according to whether you were well off or not. When you have money, everything looks cheap and you spend. You don't give a damn." Caught in the vicious circle of poverty, these men are too much imprisoned in hand-to-mouth existence even to think of saving, although saving would be the only escape from such a life.[4]

The kind of payment, especially in the case of day-laborers, intermittent or steady, tends to be an obstacle, the rationalization of the economic behavior. "It is better to be paid by the month than by the day," says an occasional docker in Algiers, "If we are paid daily, we never save anything. After work, we buy food and the money is all gone. It is as if we had made nothing. When you are paid by the month, you can put something aside to buy things, you don't have to worry." If this is a psychological illusion, it deserves analysis, all the more since the insecurity created by daily payment can only increase when the work is intermittent. By cutting up income into small sums immediately exchangeable for goods used the same day, daily payment leads to the exclusion of equipment expenditures that can only be thought of (and paid off) within a long period, and to the imprisonment of the worker in the hand-to-mouth existence that is synonymous with an absence of planning.[5]

For the subproletarians, the only way to survive is through the use of credit. Despite their deep dislike of debts, a hangover from their peasant past, they all have debts, at least at the grocer's and the baker's.[6] The phenomenon is so common that it may be considered an aspect of urbanization and a necessary condition of adaptation to urban life.[7] The credit of confidence has assumed the role occupied in the village society on one hand by reserves and on the other by exchanges of gifts and services in the name of solidarity.[8] Thanks to credit, the poorest can eat every day, despite the irregularity of their income. But does the merchant get what he expected? We must quote the bus driver who, after several years as a milkman, knows the small shopkeeper's situation well: "The shopkeeper goes on supplying and supplying even more, and if, for example, he 'sells' $40 worth, he only gets $30; the next month he hardly gets $20. This already makes $30 in debts. The shopkeepers have thousands of dollars that never come in, but they can't do anything about it. If they refuse credit, they lose customers, they will not get their money back anyway, and they will not even get the little they are used to. Also, they cannot refuse because they are not selling luxuries, but the family food. Besides, the shopkeeper does the same with the wholesaler. All this leads to confusion in bookkeeping, although in reality, there are not many shopkeepers who keep books. Many don't even know how to write."[9]

The small shopkeeper and the subproletarian are linked together, the first because he must sell on credit if he wants to sell, the second because he can only buy on credit. But the small shopkeeper does not grant credit only in his own interest: The shopkeeper who would refuse credit to a father in distress would be dishonored in the eyes of the people since, beyond a certain level, credit tends to mingle with mutual aid or assistance and also because the kasbah or the shanty-town constitutes a group of interacquaintances, the members of which are linked by a sort of fraternity and thus by the obligations of solidarity. Whatever their personal reasons, the shopkeepers provide a valuable social function: by advancing food when people are badly off, waiting for payment until the money comes in, they assure their poorest customers a minimum of security in an existence haunted by insecurity. Credit allows the customers to avoid budgeting, since it tends almost automatically to make it possible to stagger an essentially irregular income. The mechanism is all the more paradoxical since the small shopkeepers seldom keep accounts, draw directly on cash for the family needs, are often unaware of the notion of profit, and expect nothing but subsistence from their activity. "Where is the profit now?" a small shopkeeper of Sidi-bel-Abbes said. "Today I work for credit. I take goods on credit and when I have sold all of them, then I pay the wholesaler. Sometimes I have some money left over and sometimes not; then I have to borrow elsewhere." Through these incongruities in the credit chain— from wholesaler to retailer (who does not keep accounts) to customer (who does not keep accounts, either)— a kind of balance is achieved that enables the most disfavored classes, the shopkeepers and the customers, to subsist.

This kind of quasi-automatic regulation is one of the complicated mechanisms that allow the poorest to attain a precarious balance, at the subsistence level, without any calculation and rationalization of the family economy. Thus, for example, though it is true that the imperatives of broad solidarity sometimes can be obstacles to the formation of a capitalist class, forcing those who succeed to help the rest, fraternal mutual aid does allow uprooted country folk to get over poverty and distress by helping them achieve a certain indispensable security, the help in kind or in money that allows them to live while they look for a job or are unemployed, including sometimes even work itself and often lodging. Similarly, if the joint ownership that is part of chosen or imposed cohabitation often prevents modernization and long-term investments, it nevertheless assures subsistence to the poorest, through a plurality of wages that tends to offset the irregularity and lowness of the income. In short, it would appear that incoherence and uncertainty were their own limit; among other things, the general lack of regularity and rationalization in expenses as well as in income leaves some room for adjustment. But from this it also follows that the introduction of a single regular expense, such as rent in low-cost housing projects, is often enough to endanger or destroy the hazardous balance.

This existence abandoned to incoherence has no real meaning in the logic of traditionalism or of a capitalist economy. It would be useless to try to understand each concrete existence as a discontinuous series of actions, some of them related to traditional patterns, others to capitalist patterns. As a matter of fact, like an ambiguous form, each behavior can be analyzed twice, since each is naturally related to a dual logic; just as capitalistic ways of behavior imposed by necessity differ from those integrated into a capitalistic way of living, so traditionalist behavior as forced regression is separated from original traditional behavior by the abyss caused by awareness of the transformations of the context. So it is, for example, that the hand-to-mouth existence of the subproletarian or the proletarianized *fellah* is totally different from the secure life the *fellah* used to enjoy. In one case, the search for subsistence is a unique and generally accepted aim, guaranteed by customary rules; in the other, the acquisition of just enough to survive is the aim imposed on an exploited class by economic necessity. Because the context is changing and the change is recognized, and because the economic assurances and the psychological security of an integrated society and a living tradition are disappearing, perilous improvisation replaces traditional providence and comfortable stereotyped behavior. Thus, unemployment or irregular work leads to behavioral disorganization that may misleadingly appear as an innovation growing out of a conversion of attitudes. Traditionalism of despair and lack of planning are two sides of the same reality.

As a matter of fact, unemployment and irregular work have only a destructive effect. They sweep away traditions and traditionalism but prevent the achievement of a rational plan of living, the condition for the adaptation to a capitalist economy. "I live by *baraka* (luck)," an unemployed worker says, and life for most of the subproletariat, enclosed in the present, is indeed a perpetual miracle. It is as if the lack of steady employment and of a minimum regular income prevented rational planning in economic behavior or, more generally, in all behavior; as if the will to survive or to endure prevented the existence of an ambition to undertake or to foresee.

In fact, what is it "to live from hand to mouth"? Far from being the announcement of the future in present behavior or the organization of the present in regard to an abstract future, set out by calculation and rationally related to its antecedents, the present day is lived without any reference — intuitive or rational — to the following day. The day-laborer, after his daily payment, buys the bread or the *couscous* he will eat that night, without thinking of what will happen the day after, because the situation prevents it. The parceling out of time into discontinuous units tends to condemn the individual to immediate fulfillment of immediate needs. The consciousness, obsessed by the uncertainty of a morrow always in doubt, is mesmerized, fascinated by an aim that imposes itself with absolute urgency. Therefore, the repression of the immediate answer to objective suggestions and solicitations and, by the same token, the sacrifice of immediate and urgent aims in favor of ends perceived and rationally selected, are unthinkable, because the primary needs are not of the kind that can be postponed or ignored. This is why we cannot expect the rational ranking of aims that is the condition of the capitalist calculation, the basis of rational behavior according to the capitalist reason. In fact, saving — like investment, or the mere distribution of expenses over time — assumes that all the aims of the activity have already been put into perspective or, better, that a life plan — a coherent system with a hierarchy of foreseen or contemplated aims integrated into the present — is already established, so that present activity makes sense only in regard to a conceived and desired future and that, reciprocally, the contemplated future takes root in present behavior. . . .

If it is always necessary for opinions that commit the future to be ranked according to their immediacy, from the dream to the project rooted in present behavior, we must not forget that the degree of commitment in the expressed opinion depends upon the degree of accessibility of the contemplated future; and that future is more or less accessible according to the material living conditions and the social status of the individual, as well as the area of the existence involved. For example, opinions about the future of the children, which assume two-generations' level of life, are even more haphazard than the appraisal of needs.

Of course, the most incoherent opinions about the future are to be found among the unemployed, the small shopkeepers, and the unskilled workmen. Thus, an unemployed man in Constantine, who owns nothing, figures that the income necessary for his family's needs is $400 per month. When asked about the future he wants for his children, he says: "They would go to school; when they would be educated enough, they would make their own choice. But I cannot send them to school. If I could, I would like them to be taught for a long time so that they could be doctors or lawyers. But I have no help. I have the right to dream." We see the same gap between imaginary aspirations and the actual situation in an unemployed man in Saida who, after having said he was afraid that he would have to take his children out of school for lack of money, wanted his daughter "to go to the end, until she succeeds, until the end of high school, if she can, or the end of junior high; this way, she can work as a teacher."

Another unemployed man in Constantine says, "You need education but to have education you need money." And, speaking of his daughters' education, "I will send them to Algiers, Paris, and even farther; they will go to the end." And, finally, "We can't have the children educated. When you make 80 cents a day, what can you do? I sent my daughter to a summer camp. I had to buy her clothes to send her. And I can tell you, it cost me a lot." These are the same people who, when asked if they wish to keep their children in school after the primary degree, often answer, "Yes, to the end," or, like an unskilled worker in Oran, "Nothing but the best."

The same lack of discrimination, the same lack of realism, characterizes opinions about the work of women. In fact, it is among the poorest people that we find the highest rate of peremptory and absolute answers, positive or negative. Similarly, when asked about the reasons for unemployment, the subproletarians often avoid answering, or give curt or contradictory opinions: "I am not educated." "Those are strange questions you are asking." "There are too many people around. Everybody is looking for a job. If I was educated, I could tell you, but unfortunately I don't even understand the numbers on a yardstick. How can you ask me things like that?" (unemployed man in Constantine). Most of these men soon learn that the experience of working in a modern business is no less distressing and disconcerting than the experience of unemployment. Country folk who are "deruralized" without being urbanized must discover and learn everything about the technical world and the urban world at the same time (the French language, work disciplines, technical skills, measuring tools). Always being told what to do, they are not expected to understand what they have to do. Never sure of anything, either of working today or of working again tomorrow, these objects of determinism cannot find in themselves, or in their work, or in the business reasons to stick to a job that they may lose the next day. Can we then be surprised that they cannot put together a system of coherent opinions about a condition so deeply marked with instability and incoherence? . . .

Because he is never up with the world, because his continuous efforts to overcome insecurity strike insurmountable obstacles, because there is so little chance that he will reach his most essential and most coveted aims by an active and rational approach, he is brought to a magical perception of the universe. Life lived as a gamble, as *qmar,* gives way to personalized powers such as "pull," the *baraka* of the subproletariat. Far from being caused by free will, it either assures symbolic and dreamlike satisfactions or it fills the world with friendly and hostile powers. The magical perception of the world is the only recourse for an individual faced with a world that forbids any plan with a reasonable chance for success. With no choice but to obey the arbitrary decrees of the world, even concerning his essential values, he understands the world as filled with powers fighting over a prize that is his own destiny. "Pull" is not a fact of his experience but of mythical reason, that is to say, both an omnipresent power and a universal explication. To prove it, it is enough to notice that the idea is usually as indeterminate as possible. It is those who have never experienced its effectiveness who talk most about it, while the luckiest often deny its existence and explain success — starting with their own — through merit only.

If it had specific powers, such as procuring work, we might consider "pull" as one of those "functional gods" characteristic of the Roman religion for, like them, it acts within daily life and familiar surroundings. Instead, it is a kind of manna or *baraka,* a force at once impersonal and personalized, omnipresent and localized, that moves and drives the social world. "Pull comes first, you bet! You can't get ahead just by hard work. The way I see it, what works is pull, like that, direct" (porter, Oran). "We live in a special case where pull makes the machine work" (commercial clerk, Alger). "These days everything works with influence, even the machines!"(unskilled tobacco factory worker, Constantine). Thus, more deeply, pull appears to be the appropriate language of a life that cannot be explained rationally because it is nothing but fatality, chance, and arbitrariness. Faced with a world that offers itself as the expectation of meaningful explanation but that undoes and denounces any attempt to impose meaning, the man who does not stop trying to decipher and explain, to judge and reason, has no other resort but words: verbalism is the last resort of reason that refuses to give up. . . .

"Malevolent pull," that is: discrimination, settlers, Spaniards or Italians, mechanization, all those personalized and hostile powers known through concrete experience, are transfigured by mythical reason. Thus, the machine is described as a work-eating monster: "There are too many machines. The machines take the work" (waiter, Affreville). "The machines steal the bread of the people" (laborer, Constantine). "We must get rid of machines. Machines kill labor" (watchman, Tizi-Ouzou). Interjection or exclamation, the magic-mythical language does not serve to enunciate or even indicate the world but to express feelings. The coherence of the ideological universe is not based on logical rules but on the unity of feeling: Is there anything that the destitute and deprived can oppose to a hostile world haunted by magic powers, if not the belief in magic? . . .

Prisoners of the colonial order, which is understood as the diabolical work of

an evil spirit bent on surprising and defeating human will, what can they invoke
if not a power of the same nature and size? What can they await if not a miracle,
when all rational behavior is — and knows that it is — condemned to failure?
Waiting for the future miracle, in the individual as well as the collective order,
often coincides with resignation in the present: "In a Muslim state, there will be
no more *bakshish,* no more influence," says a porter in Oran. "We will walk
straight. First, begging will be eliminated, the government will take it over." The
myth of a paradise lost, the reverse of a future paradise, is also heard: "There is a
lot of unemployment because a lot of refugees, persecuted by both sides, have
come to town. Before 'the events' [the revolutionary war], we had everything for
nothing" *(fellah,* a refugee in Saida). . . . Since it cannot be explained by necessary and objective reasons, failure, in the shape of unemployment, for example,
seems caused by hostile intention, objectively incarnate in the social order. This
magic-mythical vision of the world feeds on the relation with the European fore-
man, boss, or settler: through them, objective malignancy has a face, a look, and
also a perfectly appropriate language.

The suffering imposed by this most inhuman situation is not reason enough
to conceive another economic and social order. To the contrary, it seems that
only when material living conditions permit another conception of the economic
and social order can suffering be imputed to a system explicitly understood as
unjust and inadmissible. Unable to understand this, the subproletarians tend to
accept their suffering as habitual or, better, as *natural,* as an unavoidable
component of their life. Indeed, poverty clings to them with a necessity so total
that there is no possible escape, all the more since they consider it the common
fate of all Algerians, or at least of everyone they know. In addition, their lack of
a minimum of security and education prevents a clear understanding of the total
change in the social order that would be necessary to abolish the causes. A driver
in Oran, after a visit of his poor shack and his shabby children, added: "There,
that's my life. Only the salary is not all right. The rest, we are made for it." "To
each his fate." "Everyone has his luck." "It is what God wants for me."
"Mektub." There are many common formulas that no longer express confident
surrender, as in the old tradition, but rather the resignation associated with
despair or revolt. The subproletarians *are* poverty and destitution, pain and
misfortune; they are not detached enough from their condition to regard it
objectively. . . .

They never reach an awareness of the system's responsibility for their lack of
education and of professional skills. . . . Consequently, unable to understand the
system and their role in it, they cannot link the improvement of their situation
to a radical transformation of the system; their aspirations, their demands, and
even their revolt take place within the framework and logic of the system. Thus,
"influence," that product of the system, is seen as the only means to bend the
systematic inflexibility of the system. In short, if poverty is lived as an
unavoidable component of the very condition of people whose nature is to be
without, rather than as a result of exploitation, it is because absolute alienation
deprives the person of the very awareness of alienation.

So we must avoid seeing the subproletarians' revolt as the expression of a real
revolutionary conscience. Indignent protest against objective wickedness may
coincide with acceptance of the objective order. Revolting against established
wickedness does not necessarily mean questioning the order that underlies the

wickedness. Revolt and protest may be ways of accepting inferiority by confessing it. Is that not the deeper meaning of the protesters' behavior as they stubbornly aim at the impossible as if — through substitution — to hide or offset a fundamentally recognized inferiority? As a matter of fact, "povertism" lives on the same logic as effective quasi-systematization; by substituting intention for necessity, one puts oneself at the mercy of the arbitrary orders of that very power of which he is a victim but from which, in spite of everything, he expects charity in the form of the fulfillment of his vital hopes. The same people who say, "They don't want to give us work" also say, "They don't give us enough." More often, rebelliousness, feeding on resentment, mingles with submissive resignation. In fact, the feeling of subordination, which generates ambiguous attitudes, replaces the awareness of alienation, which gives rise to revolutionary attitudes. Because any individual or collective project is forbidden them, the subproletarians tend to see themselves in the same way that they are seen by the ruling caste. "We are made for that," they say more or less explicitly (and the others: "They are used to it"). Like racism, povertism is an essentialism.

Thus those who are *in* the condition of the subproletariat cannot comprehend it, since to do so would presuppose their ability to plan an escape. Because it is impossible not to take it as it is, the dream of escaping only means experiencing the weight of necessity more cruelly. In exile from the present, these men can get away from it only through dreams, which bring immediate, that is, magical, fulfillment by making a sharp distinction between present injustice and pain, and a future Utopia. "I don't think women and girls should work right now. Afterwards yes, when it will all be over, when the evil spirit will be gone, and when there will be gold louis on the ground, when there will be a Muslim state: on that day, she may go out; I will not say anything to her about it" (dealer in old clothes, Oran).

Notes

1. See Pierre Bourdieu, "The Attitude of the Algerian Peasant Toward Time," in Julian Pitt-Rivers (ed.), *Peasant in the Mediterranean* (The Hague: Mouton, 1964), pp. 55—72. See also Pierre Bourdieu, A. Darbel, J. P. Rivet, and C. Seibel, *Travail et Travailleurs en Algérie* (The Hague: Mouton, 1963); and Pierre Bourdieu and A. Sayad, *Le Déracinement* (Paris: Minuit, 1964).

2. See Frantz Fanon, "The North African Syndrome," pp. 74—82 in this reader; and R. and C. Descloitres and J. C. Reverdy, "Urban Organization and Social Structures in Algeria," pp. 427—38 in this reader.

3. An analysis of family budgets indicates that the amount spent for food increases with the revenue to a certain level.

4. Schumpeter has well indicated the function of savings: "The role of the entrepreneurs' savings is to make them forget the necessity of day-to-day routine imposed by the concern for earning their daily bread and give them the leisure to look ahead and hammer out their plans." *(Capitalism, Socialism and Democracy).* But we should not forget that saving itself requires the ability to be a little above the daily routines; with three exceptions — a worker whose monthly income was only $43 and two coffee-shop keepers who declared $60 and $80 — everyone who said that he had some savings had a permanent job and an income over $100.

5. We met also protests against the weekly payment system. Since job stability in Algeria depends upon the length of the period of payment, the preference for monthly payment is thus reinforced.

6. The peasant aversion to credit tied in with the whole system of value, and particularly of morality and honor, is expressed by a peasant from Ouled Hamida: "I can't make ends meet. . . . The problem of credit is this: I don't like to borrow, because I feel uneasy and I blush when I see my creditor; furthermore, the people here don't give credit to newcomers because they don't offer any guarantees: no source of income, no salary. The grocer refuses to give credit; he is afraid that everyone will leave once peace has come and then he won't be reimbursed. He only gives credit to people who own cattle or to his cousins from the same *ferka* — those he knows."

7. Debts sometimes are very high. Thus, a cleaning woman who in Oran earns $36 a month owed $120 to her grocer. A clerk in a cloth shop from Tlemcen owed the grocer $100. "I owe at least $130," said a painter from Saidia, "two months' work. I got in debt when my daughter got married. In a Muslim wedding you have to provide a trousseau and jewelry. All this is expensive. I save on everything to pay back my debts. I don't eat well and even cigarettes I buy on credit from the grocer."

8. See R. and C. Descloitres and J.C. Reverdy, pp. 424—38 in this reader.

9. Seventy-eight and one-half per cent of shopkeepers do not have any diploma; 20.3 per cent have a primary-school diploma and 1.1 per cent have a high-school diploma. A more detailed study showed 70 per cent illiteracy; this percentage is probably even higher among the very small shopkeepers.

9

SECOND- AND THIRD-GENERATION ELITES IN THE MAGHRIB

DOUGLAS E. ASHFORD

Because of the disproportionate influence of the second-generation group and political concern for the contentment of the third-generation group, it is easy to receive an impression that the privileged young people of Morocco, Tunisia, and Algeria are much more numerous than they are in fact. Although both generations are sometimes treated rather coolly by the elder nationalists, youthful skills and vigor have been eagerly sought by all branches of government and also, more recently, by the growing private sector of the economy. This also tends to make the talented young people a focus of popular concern and to underscore their problems. It is advisable, however, to start with as accurate estimates of their actual numbers as the records permit. There are also limited data on the professional trends among educated youth.

Without prejudice to their contribution to North Africa in other respects, it must be noted that the French did not seriously embark on the problem of secondary and advanced education for Muslims until the end of World War II. A few extremely fortunate men were able to pursue their educations in France, but probably not more than a hundred or so from each country annually. In the late 1940's, the political revival of the North African countries coincided with the swing toward the right in French politics. When the elder nationalists began to realize that their policy of boycotting French education was self-defeating, the French policy shifted to look more cautiously on the rapid advancement of the North Africans.

Algeria was probably the most successful in getting a respectable number of young persons into the "liberal professions," but this was done at the price of nearly isolating the emergent Muslim middle class from the problems of Algeria. Thus, a man like Ferhat 'Abbas, now an elder nationalist, found himself in the well-known dilemma of being estranged from his countrymen and unaccepted by the French in the 1930's. Morocco and Tunisia have largely

From "Second and Third Generation Elites in the Maghrib" (U.S. Department of State, Bureau of Intelligence and Research, Policy Research Study, November, 1963), pp. 9—11, 36—41, 46—48, 52—55. Reprinted by permission. This paper was originally prepared under contract with the Department of State. The author is solely responsible for its contents, including the accuracy of both statements of fact and interpretative comments. Sponsorship by the Department of State does not imply official endorsement of the conclusions expressed.

escaped this type of problem because of their later development. There are a few artistic types, such as Driss Chraibi, who reside in France and rather profitably display their alienation for the public, but this attitude is losing popularity as the real problems of North Africa become better known.

For each of the North African countries, the present second-generation group is roughly 10,000 young men. There are almost no women in the group. The second generation were attending secondary schools in the early 1950's. In Morocco, in 1953, there were 1,174 Muslims in European secondary schools, 481 in technical schools, and 5,120 in Muslim secondary schools. Seldom were more than a fourth of those with the baccalaureate accepted for the "superior" or university level. Until independence, secondary-school education was limited to the cities throughout North Africa. In 1952, there were only 54 Moroccan Muslim secondary-school teachers out of the very modest total supply of 225.

The situation was better for the Tunisian second-generation group. In 1955 there were 250 Tunisians in normal schools, 7,346 in secondary schools, and 7,688 in technical schools. Although technical school secondary education is usually terminal, and the rate of attrition between the *"bac"* and the *licence* is fierce, the Tunisians, with a third of the Moroccan population, were very clearly doing proportionately much better than the Moroccans. The Tunisians were noticeably better off in other respects according to the 1956 census. There were 174 Muslim secondary-school teachers at that time, out of a total of 405. Thus, there is some hard evidence that Tunisians had more opportunities to become second-generation leaders. The larger accumulation of young leaders may partially account for the decidedly middle-class outlook of Tunisian youth.

French statistics for Algeria are controversial but do not indicate major gains over neighbors, despite 130 years of French rule. In 1954, there were 7,421 Muslims attending secondary schools and 618 in the superior cycle. Of course, educational facilities were much greater in Algeria, where the University of Algiers has a long history and where there was a large European minority. Although selected Algerians did gain prominent positions and enjoy modern professional status, opportunities in Algeria appear to have been proportionately more restricted than in either Morocco or Tunisia.

The second generation in all three countries often includes persons with only a secondary education, but it is doubtful if a secondary education will qualify a member of the third generation to occupy an important post. Naturally, French educational principles will continue to be very influential, and the bac is highly regarded, especially when one is fully qualified. The second generation of necessity included those with secondary education if it was to participate in a political revolution and persuasively claim that the nation was prepared for self-rule. For example, there were only 202 Tunisians in French universities in 1938. A university education was definitely the exception until very recently, although many third-generation youth now talk as though everyone should be entitled to advanced training.

The present second generation in Tunisia has few university graduates. There were 578 university students in 1949, and 946 in 1953. In the 1940's and even in the 1950's a college education was a guarantee of success, something that may tend to be less true for the third generation as time passes. There are now slightly more than 3,000 university students in Tunisia, according to the students' organization. Nearly half are in science, about a third in letters, and the rest in law. Small numbers are also accounted for by the traditional university of Zitouna, which Bourguiba is rapidly merging with the University of Tunis, and by agricultural institutions. Judging from Tunisian figures on those completing the *bac* early in the 1960's, these figures appear to be accurate.

Following the pattern in much of the less-developed portion of the world, Tunisians have been attracted to the professions providing the most prestige and income. The Tunisian government, however, has taken vigorous measures to guide university students into careers appropriate to the country's needs. There are no reliable figures for judging the success of the government's effort, but a breakdown by faculty is available for Tunisians attending only French universities in 1957. Of the 1,138 students in France, of whom 800 were in Paris, about 350 were in letters, about 150 in law, a little over 200 in science, and about 400 in medicine and pharmacy. Allowance must be made for the varying length of the courses, but still the Tunisians seem to show considerable interest in the less glorified university pursuits.

The Moroccans appear to have been less successful in guiding the young into careers beneficial to an underdeveloped nation, and this may create particular problems for the third generation. According to the Moroccan Five-Year Plan, there were just under 2,500 university students in 1959. Of these, about 1,500 were in law, 800 in letters, and under 200 in science. This probably does not include medicine and pharmacy, but it is doubtful if the medical careers were attracting more than science as a whole. The historical trends within Moroccan education substantiate these figures: the 1953 census indicated that there were 140 Muslims at the Rabat Institute for Advanced Study, the nucleus from which the present faculty of letters in Rabat has grown; 127 Muslims attending the legal center; and 220 attending the scientific center. As in many other problems, the Moroccans have yet to take a hard look at the professional pattern of their third-generation youth.

Trends within Moroccan education indicate how important careful planning will be, and also that the third-generation group of leaders will take on increasing importance. There were more than 5,000 university-level students enrolled in the fall of 1962, nearly double the number enrolled three years before. The government hopes that there will be 14,000 in university and advanced technical schools by 1967 — Moroccan goals often are optimistic. The University of Rabat added a Faculty of Medicine in 1962, and a variety of specialized faculties were added at Fes. An advanced normal school is being constructed with UNESCO funds, and an engineering college will open shortly in Rabat. The student community is rapidly becoming large enough in Morocco to represent a political and social element placing severe demands on government, and encompassing persons whose vitality and skills are needed in Morocco's reconstruction.

If a university education is the criterion for joining the third-generation group, about 500 students a year qualify by completing their advanced education. Some take more than four years, and quite a few fall by the wayside. There are also some losses to firms and other agencies outside the country. The figures for secondary-school completions are probably at least twice those for university education. In Tunisia there are plans to increase the number of secondary students rapidly. By 1968, the country [hoped] to be producing over 3,000 fully prepared secondary students a year, although steps will also be taken to encourage these youths to enter technical and higher clerical positions.

Because the third-generation youth are participating in a much better integrated society than did their elders of the second generation, the secondary-school graduates will no doubt approach the level of political awareness of the university-trained third generation; hence it may be appropriate to consider them members of the third-generation elite — or potential elite — even if they do not attain advanced education.

The new Algerian government has not yet had time to consider long-run educational policy, although the ben Bella regime had made known its dependence on French assistance and methods. French rule did not bring the Algerians special advantages, except for the small number of middle-class Muslims admitted to professional schools. In 1944, for example, only 130,000 Muslims were in school, or about 8 per cent of the eligible students (at this time 90 per cent of the French youth in Algeria were in school). French plans called for enrollment of a million and a half Algerians by 1964, or about three-fifths of the eligible students. These proposals were not energetically backed until 1958, and have no doubt been seriously upset by the departure of the Algerian French community. The rapid expansion of secondary and technical schools in the last few years of French rule could have unsettling effects. Most of the new students have enjoyed their advanced educational status long enough to have a stake in continuing, and to have expectations of receiving the kind of security and prestige associated with higher education. In 1960, there were almost 37,000 Muslims in secondary schools (compared with 11,000 in 1954) and 20,000 in technical schools (compared with 9,000 in 1954). The skills and talent represented by this educational investment will be badly needed in the reconstruction of Algeria.

In a consideration of the education of future leaders in North Africa, perhaps the most important quantitative indicator is the trend. The numbers of secondary-school and university-trained people will increase rapidly over the coming decades. Hopefully, the rate of increase will be greater than that of the population as a whole, something that has not been true over the past years. For the second generation the trend is toward a diminishing importance in public life. They are entering into middle age and, as their personal interests become defined, losing the political preoccupations of their youth. The third generation is less known but undoubtedly more important.

UNSTABLE VALUES AND POLITICAL CHANGE

To go more deeply into the unstable values of the second and third generations it is necessary to understand a little about the intellectual blinders that many Western scholars have worn as they conducted inquiries in Africa and Asia. For several generations, studies of the non-West were strongly influenced by missionaries, businessmen, and others with specialized concern in the less familiar societies. The tendency was to magnify the unusual problems and irremovable peculiarities of such societies. Naturally, the dramatic actions and strange habits of the new society were perceived more strongly. Often the visitor lacked disciplinary training and had little intellectual base for a more clinical evaluation.

Over the past decade the intellectual blinders of the West have gradually fallen away. The movement has been from a narrow cultural absolutism, though uncritical relativism, to more objective evaluation. Even highly literary observers, who might be most tempted to romanticize strange settings, are beginning to look more critically on the cruelty and poverty that underlies exotic social systems. Koestler has recently questioned whether our own culturally ingrained feelings of respect for others' religion and our unfamiliarity with the harmful consequences of certain religious practices might have led us to be excessively tolerant of some Oriental cultural idiosyncrasies. The same trend can be identified among social scientists. Lines of comparability were first suggested by anthropologists and economists, who had the habits of working with more precise variables and knowing more exactly what data were relevant to their inquiry. More recently there have been similar suggestions from sociologists and political scientists.

Recent scholarship does not pretend to explain all the curiosities of the non-West. Indeed, one of the important assumptions of much contemporary social science is that all variables cannot be studied simultaneously. In preliminary inquiry, problems must be broken down into their components, and agreed, explicit means of measurement must be used. This does not mean that the less familiar society is without unique characteristics or even that such singularities may not be an integral part of the social system. The point is rather that knowledge can derive cumulative benefits by working from a known base. The discovery of similarities increases the possibility of profiting from past experiences and applying the experience of past decisions.

From this it follows that there may be some advantages in focusing on the most important and most familiar new variable in the lives of young elites. The new factor is the nation. It has become the focus of instability and uncertainty for millions of people in Africa and Asia, but it is also a structure fairly well known to the more developed societies. In recent work on Africa, scholars have frequently underscored the novelty of the *national* economy, a *national* legal system, and *national* political institutions. These are problems with which the West is familiar, and it should not be too modest about its accomplishment despite the aberrant political systems developed with fascist and Communist values. Even the failures provide some instruction on how the individual can be related to the nation in a modern setting. The traditional religions, family structures, tribal patterns, and even existing cultural values may not be as important as once thought in constructing an empirically based interpretation of the young leaders' problems that is scaled to the needs of the new nation and yet rooted in the accumulated knowledge of the advanced nations.

The situation of the talented young man of the second or third generation may be made more intelligible by considering where such a person might turn for national values. There are, first, his elders. They are likely to have the nationalists' simplified, self-confirming view of the nation. To them, creating the country symbolized the victory over "colonialism" and the chance to revive Arab culture. The elders do not tend to see the nation as a vehicle for social change. Its mere existence vindicates the sacrifices of the nationalist struggle and thereby provides personal satisfaction. It must also be added that many elder statesmen of Morocco and Tunisia, and perhaps also in Algeria, are most interested in their personal affairs. To some extent they are withdrawn and conservative, as are their counterparts all over the world, and many are still deeply rooted in traditional life. The void between youth and elder is, therefore, twofold in the changing society: they are separated by age and oriented to different societies. Enough of the old society remains to protect the elders' ways, but not enough to reassure the youth that the old society represents a viable alternative for the future.

Another possible course of action for the third generation is to identify with the more vigorous, more successful members of the second generation. In Morocco, men like Bouabid and ben Barka, though gradually passing into middle age, are widely envied by ambitious youth. These men portray the nation as an instrument of forced social change. As was demonstrated by the Unity Road scheme, the attractive second-generation leaders are more concerned with ways to associate the mass with the nation than with ways to constructively orient the talented youth to the nation. Progressive politicians are certainly aware of the country's need for cadres, but their thinking often assumes that young people will simply not be able to resist the attraction of social revolution. The bright young politicians are undoubtedly persuasive, but it is not so clear that a more privileged young person sees himself, in ben Barka's phrase, as a "true militant citizen." The young citizen may be determined, but he is not at all sure how his militancy can be expressed.

A third possibility for youth is to orient his political thinking toward the world. International affairs may displace domestic affairs as a field of reference. There are important indications that this does take place, just as it tends to occur in the pre-independence phase. Finding the national frame of reference proscribed by the colonial power, the past generation therefore tended to look toward international agencies for solutions that could only come from the powers involved. In a somewhat different way, the young man of the third generation also seeks a frame of reference through international affairs. International activities provide him with a feeling of solidarity and mutual support that he often fails to find in his own society.

There are very few youth manifestoes that are not equally divided between national and international affairs, and often there is more discussion of the international sector. This is not so much an indication of lack of interest in domestic problems as of the inability of domestic politics to attract interest. In a developing nation there are not many highly controversial problems, and those that are controversial are generally carefully regulated by the government. The weak orientation to the nation as a vehicle of change means that young people tend to look elsewhere for action. In general, this is lamentable since it means in turn that the national image is not adapted to changing conditions and young people continue to neglect their country as an effective instrument of change through individual participation. The distinction is important since they do understand that the government can affect their destiny. Indeed, they may feel the overpowering aspect of government too strongly. It is precisely this remote, helpless attitude toward political life that needs to be changed.

International affairs lack many of the hazards of national political action. Someone else can always be blamed, and nearly always some colonial or suspected imperialist power is involved. The international realm of action is, therefore, less risky to one's individual position. The obligations are vague, and there are usually many loopholes. The character of international exchange also means that the language is so abstract and diplomatic that few specific, immediate questions need to be dealt with. Everyone can agree with minimum sacrifice of his own interest, although the price is that less can in fact be accomplished. The United Nations simply cannot replace a national government, whatever may be suggested by many youth publications.

The internationalist response has the interesting characteristic of nearly always being politically uncontroversial. Since it is often superficial and vague, both left and right can use it in national politics. It is just as easy for al-Fassi to rhapsodize about Mauritania as it is for Bourguiba to mobilize his people over Bizerte. International values solve domestic problems by making them uncontroversial or by submerging them so that they need not be resolved for the moment. During the Congo crisis, one party could rally over the injustice to Lumumba, while the less progressive party could pontificate over the United Nations police action. Neither is wrong, and neither risks being called to account for his position in a way that might endanger his influence. In addition to the practical political advantages of the internationalist solution, it bears a certain similarity to past nationalist experience. Thus, there are many attractive aspects to the internationalist appeal, all of which share the same evasive character.

There is another important form of evasion of practical politics. As the number of highly skilled technical persons increases in the developing country, there is sometimes a growing tendency to look for relief from meaningful exchange on the national level by stressing the technical aspect of government. In a sense, the technique is allowed to replace the substance of government. The temptation is natural in a country like Tunisia, where a growing number of bright, skilled young officials find no political outlet and cannot afford the diversion of their effort that the Neo-Destour demands of successful militants. Like the stress on international affairs, the technical alternative is a ready-made substitute for more direct contact with national politics. It is less controversial and sometimes endows itself with pseudo-scientific glamour. One does not have to make difficult choices as he is forced to do in the real business of governing. There is a small possibility, which the enthusiast can easily magnify, that political solutions can be found by wholly rational means. If this can be done, the difficult questions of political responsibility and political participation are automatically resolved. This school of thought is particularly highly developed among a group of French bureaucrats and may have spread to North Africa from them.

The stress on the technician is, therefore, a prepared rationalization for avoiding national politics. One does not need to decide on political values since there is a mathematically calculable optimum solution. Furthermore, the informed young citizen can see how few alternatives often do exist in a country having limited resources and overwhelming problems. This is possibly an important stimulus for the constant emphasis on the shortage of cadres and the pressing need for more professional training for every skilled person. In practice it may be that less advanced training and more direct experience with the real problems of the country would benefit the country more. But this would run counter to the evasive character of the entire response. There are other attractions of the technician's orientation. It brings security with irresponsibility. One just calculates, gives the best possible solution, and hopes for the best without individually associating himself with the consequences. By following this highly unrealistic version of human interaction, he supposedly enhances his value to his nation. His national obligations are paid, he incurs little risk, and when he is right, he becomes indispensable. No matter what happens, he has the security of the entrenched civil servant.

There is nearly always a large measure of this kind of thinking among both the progressives and conservatives of a changing country. Like the internationalist response, it is used to avoid decision no matter where the citizen rests in the political spectrum. For the conservative it provides a defense against mounting social pressures that might endanger his position, and at the same time it dissipates those pressures so that they do minimum damage. In practice this has often meant that change takes place so slowly that little or no relief is felt, and the society explodes. However, this line of thought can also be detected in the progressives' discussion of highly organized, centrally directed work forces that are hopefully to construct highly skilled productive facilities with unskilled labor. Bourguiba's *"lutte contre sous-développement"* is certainly an example of this kind of thinking just as much as Hassan II's *"promotion nationale."* This is not to say that such movements are not potentially useful and cannot make important contributions, but their value is diminished if they become substitutes for more profound social and political adjustments that bring the individual into more meaningful contact with government. As such projects advance, however, there is every reason to think they will also increase pressure for effective participation and swell the numbers of citizens trying to find an effective contact between their personal lives and their country.

The most difficult part of national development is creating an effective set of intermediate values for the second- and third-generation groups. The elders' strength is not that they are psychologically better grounded for present-day national affairs, but that they are still more deeply rooted in the past. They do not feel the uncertainty of young people because they are not concerned with the new nation as a vehicle for change. This also means that they tend to be less productive, less imaginative citizens. Older people are more complacent, more satisfied in nearly every society because age always gives a certain recognition and privilege. But older nationalists often are not fully aware of the pressures of the future. Their complacency is something more than the usual complacency of old age. They do not fully understand the explosive force of the nation they often have helped create.

The talented young people know they live in an environment that is rapidly changing. But the pattern that changes the least is the group closest to them: their family. If they wished to retreat from national affairs, they could find solace in the traditional family structure. Likewise, the young person has friends and immediate group associates. Though he exists in a less complex pattern of group relationships than that of the young person in the advanced society, the university student or the young civil servant in Morocco or Tunisia is not as personally isolated as is often assumed. Neither are the bonds of family and parents as worn as youthful unrest sometimes suggests. The immediate needs of his personality can be filled, and, in the face of defeat, he can even get a certain consolation from the old structure. Thus, the roots of the society in a rapidly developing country may not be so weak as it is sometimes argued. The lines of family affection may be undergoing strain as the country grows, but the nature of these relationships makes them pliable. The problem is that family ties are simply not applicable to the major problem area confronting the young citizen. There is no reason to expect the family structure of the new country to perform functions not performed by families in the West.

There is also unmistakable evidence that the second- and third-generation citizen does not lack ultimate values. He is as religious as his counterpart in most advanced societies. His tendency to give religion less emphasis is dramatized by his elders' tendency to make religion into a criterion for all the problems of contemporary society. Undergoing the process of modernization means learning that religious dogma does not explicate every life situation. This does not mean, however, that religion is less important for individual motivation, but only that it is not the sole frame of reference. Furthermore, the second and third generation are unquestionably reliable patriots. Their ultimate allegiance to the nation is not in doubt. An individual's vague, barely intellectualized construct of the ultimate values of human life does not often conflict with daily problems as long as he lives within a traditional society; habitual values and habitual actions coexist and reinforce each other. Uncertainty arises once life becomes complex and as decisions must be made concerning less well-defined, less familiar situations. It is, therefore, the intermediate values that are difficult to acquire. Much of the behavior of the second and third generation can be usefully interpreted in this way. The multiplicity of new situations that is an inescapable part of living in a modern society necessitates the formation of values to govern actions between the ultimate imponderables of life and an intimate, more emotional questioning of daily affairs. If suitable and rewarding, this new orientation will be harmonious with ultimate values and will make the relations with the closest groups more satisfying.

To say only that the young Tunisian or young Moroccan lacks values is misleading. His relations to his family appear to be as harmonious and satisfying as those of most youth throughout the world. Furthermore, the second- or third-generation North African does not lack religious sensitivity, though he may not practice his religion more scrupulously than his counterpart in more advanced societies. Both avenues of inquiry follow conventional lines. If a person is not contented, the facile assumption is often made that it is an intimate relationship like family or a powerful relationship like religion that is disrupted. Important as these concerns are to the young North African, and probably to all the young people of Africa and Asia, it is quite possibly another problem area that creates youthful uncertainty. His personal values must be reconciled with a new framework for action, one whose importance has been stressed throughout the childhood of the young person. The nation has taken on great importance, but the youth may not know quite what to do about it.

It is natural, therefore, that he should take great interest in social action, philosophers, and intellectuals. In a very real sense, the journalist is the action-oriented social observer. He is providing raw data for the person seeking familiarity, and he is generally careful about forcing his views on the reader concerning the best course of action. The fellow-traveling intellectual, and the Communist as well, also responds to the needs of the bewildered student or confused young official. The Marxist framework is an action framework. Indeed, the socialist is guaranteed social action and given historic reassurance that social change will take place. Nothing could be more appropriate to the mentality of the second and third generation, but this does not necessarily mean that only the most radical political and economic analysis can appeal to such a mentality. Nor does it mean that the mass-action approach of Ardant and others will necessarily solve all the problems of the developing nations. However, those wishing to appeal to the young person of Africa or Asia can profit from clearly understanding the nature of the emotional and intellectual need of the maturing, talented youth. Above all, it should be remembered that he is not *without* values, but that he only lacks values that are appropriate to the new field of action that independence and subsequent national development open up.

OPINION FORMATION AND POLITICAL CHANGE

The early phase of a nation's development has almost always been characterized by a remarkable degree of extreme nationalist feeling. Attitudes toward the nation are naturally influenced and shaped in this period by the exhilaration and excitement of independence. The image of the nation tends to be highly abstract, idealized, and emotionally charged. The nationalist is unusually sensitive to criticism, suspicious of nonnationalists of even his own citizenship, and often inhibited in adopting foreign ideas. His attitudinal views on the nation are very likely similar to those of members of more advanced societies in periods of extreme nationalist sentiment. There is some cross-cultural research to provide empirical proof of such similarities.

As the country encounters the obstacles to its own development, a period of assessment begins. The appeals that have sustained the highly affective image begin to lose their persuasiveness. Individuals return to their jobs and homes, and more immediate perceptual fields of family, friends, and local community take on more importance. The shift in perceptual emphasis means that there will be relatively less affective attachment to the remote framework of national activity, and relatively more interest in local affairs and the tangible benefits to be drawn from independence. Increasingly, the nation tends to be viewed as an instrument of action more than as an inspiration for sacrifice. Once this assessment begins, a source of potentially severe conflict is created. The nation is obviously not all that it was claimed to be, nor is it omnipotent in the face of the complexities of modernization. Very little is known of the complexities of this attitudinal transformation, but the upheavals and chaos that are social manifestations of perceptual tension and uncertainty are all too well known.

The transitional period is characterized by the decreasing importance of the affective aspects of the nation and the increasing importance of the cognitive aspects of the nation. The continuum between compulsive, driving loyalty and critical evaluation is the shift toward thinking of the nation in terms of achievement. There is some prima facie evidence of this shift in Nasser's concern with "Arab socialism" and Bourguiba's innovation of "Destourian socialism." These are not so much new doctrines as new ways of thinking about the country which are partly introduced by the leader's own realization of the inadequacy of the affective image for mobilizing developmental forces, and by the citizens' growing level of articulation and interest in government.

This is not to say that the emotional pitch of the nationalist phase cannot be sustained for long periods, but only that it becomes less and less appropriate to the problems confronting the rapidly changing country. The affective image is reinforced by irredentist campaigns. Morocco exhibits what is surely the classic example of this; a theme that was once almost openly sneered upon by politicians and shunned by the monarchy has now become a central policy and greatly distracts from immediate matters of government, However, the affective image is also hard to sustain and always in danger of summarily disappearing with an international settlement.

Enough is known of how highly affective attitudes operate in the person's perceptual world to suggest how inhibiting they may be in the non-West. The more important question of developing the cognitive elements of one's attitudes is much less understood. There is, however, considerable inferential evidence to be found in Lerner's study of "empathy." The person who can imagine himself in other roles is clearly less inhibited and more versatile attitudinally. Of course, a person having considerable "psychic mobility," to use Lerner's phrase, may also have some highly affective attitudes on more general topics — rather like the citizen of an advanced society who betrays a racial prejudice. Nevertheless, such a person is always vulnerable to severe conflict, and there is much historical evidence that the integrative tendencies of the modernization process tend to create such conflict — just as the prejudiced person finds it increasingly difficult to disparage the intellectual qualities and social contribution of Negroes. Similar implications can be found in the study of political effectiveness in the American voting studies.

Once the trend toward augmentation of cognitive elements in attitudes toward national affairs is established, it becomes a matter of applying what is known of the dynamics of attitudinal change to the non-Western situation. There have been two central propositions in the explication of cognitive conflict: the magnitude of the conflict and the person's level of tolerance of conflict. It is quite apparent that the magnitude of such conflict must be extremely high in the nationalist phase. There have been some studies in Ghana and Egypt that reveal this kind of conflict very clearly. There is, of course, much first-hand evidence in the use of the irredentist goal, the colonialist "plot," and the "enemy within" to sustain the discipline and sense of sacrifice of the early developmental phases. Where the magnitude of dissonance is great, such appeals serve to reduce the conflict by making adjustment to conflicting cognitive elements unnecessary. It is interesting to note that a study shows Egyptian professionals, who very likely find it more difficult to accept the emotional image and to ignore the cognitive stress, tend to become ambivalent. This may well be a form of adjustment to attitudinal conflict that cannot be resolved within the social system and therefore is resolved by withdrawal. Such a reaction has real costs for the new nation, however, and there is reason to think that it may eventually become positively injurious to national development.

The theory of cognitive conflict states that where magnitude of conflict is very great, as appears to be the case in the new nation, there will be greater forces in favor of attitudinal change. The developing country has such problems of attitudinal adaptation, however, because in addition to the wide diversity of individual advancement and different individual problems created thereby, the tolerance level is low. The perceptual world of the early phase created the conditions of low level of tolerance of conflict. Although the potential magnitude of conflict may be very great once a cognitive element that contradicts the affective image is perceived, it appears that the new participant's low level of tolerance of conflict makes such perceptual instructions very difficult. Evidence that their ideas of national affairs may be incomplete, inadequate, or distorted is very likely to be rejected.

Where the evidence cannot be rejected, the member of the new nation may make attitudinal concessions by "fragmenting" his views. The affective and cognitive aspects may be related to disconnected parts of the person's perceptual world. Such tendencies are readily apparent in the new nation's views on nuclear testing, neutralism, and foreign aid. Perhaps the international world is more easily fragmented to suit perceptual needs than the national and more immediate frames of reference, where the evidence is more difficult to ignore. However, the same tendencies can be observed in the internal politics of most new nations as well, especially in adjusting to the needs of "democracy" and individual expression. Rationalizations of one-party rule and police methods often rest on such fragmented attitudes.

Where the tolerance level becomes such that the person cannot make an adjustment in the existing conceptual framework, he might begin to examine his system of beliefs. This is clearly what is underway in the two generational groups of North Africa. Psychologists tend to assume such attitudinal reconciliations are most difficult where serious personality maladjustments are involved — but the psychologists may be excessively influenced by the modern societies in which their work has generally been done. Consensual standards in the developing countries are still rudimentary and not widely accepted. Interpersonal relations are still governed by standards of the traditional life, which was not oriented to change and did not encourage much individual selectivity.

Being able to give specific, concrete meaning to ideas is an important source of personal stability and effectiveness; and this is substantially valid in opinion formation in the new countries as a whole. If the new citizens, in this case the young elites, cannot envisage how the problems of the country relate to their values and aspirations, the result will be political uncertainty and evasiveness. The second and third generations in Morocco and Tunisia evidence this uncertainty. It is reflected in their organizations, in their reaction to the newly formed governments, and in their discussion of the future. It is not the stuff that can be manipulated in the usual sense of the word. The young people of North Africa, and probably most of Africa and Asia, have a serious psychological void in their political and social thinking. The void cannot be filled with foreign ideas, although socialist values represent much that they desire. The final solution is part and parcel of the growth of the country, and only in the integration of values and ideas will they discover a precise, effective meaning for the newly formed nation.

The psychological suspension of the second and third generations cannot be altered from outside, but the environment can be affected and youth can be encouraged to acquire the skills and knowledge that will help them to understand the complexity of a modern society. Excessive concern about youth may actually do some harm. They are already in a situation where much of the harshness and impersonal selectivity of the day-to-day world has been removed. Extreme indifference to their needs and aspirations might alienate youth, but too much concern becomes over-protective and can only heighten the over-simplified image of the world that many young people already have. There are signs that some third-generation youth are beginning to realize that they cannot aspire to the rapid promotion that members of the second generation group have enjoyed. Learning to live within the limits of environment is a critical step in the process of maturation, and should certainly be encouraged in every possible way. . . .

CONCLUSION

Some generally clear-cut lines of development for second- and third-generation groups can be foreseen within the existing North African political systems. Morocco is ruled by an intelligent, imaginative young monarch. Hassan II has displayed considerable leadership, but has also been extremely reluctant to delegate power or to implement effectively many of the programs he has ostensibly supported. It is doubtful if he intends to allow influence to be shared in any manner he cannot himself personally oversee. . . .

The king's cautious view toward social change creates considerable skepticism among third-generation youth. Many willingly submit in order to be assured of sinecures in the lower ranks of the civil service or in government-financed enterprises. Many maintain a careful neutrality while inwardly being resentful and discontented. A sizable proportion, perhaps half of the university group, are openly critical of the regime and work for the National Union of Popular Forces (UNFP). The existence of a king underscores the personalization of power, which contributes to the evasiveness and uncertainty of political attitudes. Moreover, Hassan II is in a position of opposing the party associated with progress and based on the industrial segment of the society. His technique of surrounding himself with generally less imaginative men who are pliable to his demands is widely known among young people. . . . The royal family and much of the palace entourage, not unmixed with indulgence of favoritism and corruption, is discussed freely. It is difficult to see how such impressions of authority could be expected to generate constructive, determined attitudes toward the future of Morocco. Many young people are simply cowed, but others are alienated, and many are repelled. Very clearly, little is done to give youth an image of government as an instrument for change within which each person can individually seek his role and make his contribution.

The situation is not much more favorable for second-generation leaders in Morocco. Many, of course, are committed to one camp or the other in the developing struggle for power. By far the largest proportion are secure in government and commercial jobs, although some of the recent strikes suggest that many civil servants may be gravitating toward the UNFP as the malaise of the government becomes more costly to the nation's future. The most unfortunate aspect of the present system so far as the second-generation leaders are concerned is how the amorphous situation drives both Istiqlal and UNFP sympathizers into less productive activities. Only the trade-union leaders, who preserve direct popular contact by virtue of their organizational positions, seem to have increased their concrete, precise knowledge of the country — and this knowledge is generally confined to the cities where they run the urban municipal councils. (One of the unforeseen benefits of the elections was to involve the trade-union leaders in some of the practical problems of government.) With the withdrawal of many other second-generation leaders, Moroco losing considerable energy and talent.

Although little is known of the internal divisions the Algerians face in the development of their country, some less precise observations can be made of the young Algerian leaders. The leaders of the government are industrious and competent. This may be part of the revolutionary zeal that the Algerians are still able to sustain. The young Algerian has had seven years to think about what he will do in a free country. The entire third generation has come of age during the war. The injustices of the French regime are more deeply engraved in the minds of Algerians than in Moroccans and Tunisians.

The National Liberation Front (FLN) comprised a mixture of peoples from all parts of Algeria. It has made a lasting contribution to the integration of ethnic types and instructed young Algerians in ways of overcoming the diversity of their country. The Moroccan resistance never spread far from the cities except for a few tribally based armies in the isolated mountain areas. The Tunisians' resistance effort was the source of renewed ill-feeling between the south and north of the country, and the disarmament of the guerrillas was part of the bitter misunderstanding between Bourguiba and Salah ben Youssef. The fight for Algerian liberation has also created divisions, but it has probably created more unity of an enduring kind. . . .

The Tunisian regime provides grounds for optimism in the immediate future, but it is doubtful if the present system of single-party rule will be able to bring about an effective integration of the growing numbers of articulate young people over a long period without major concessions. The problem may very likely be brought to a climax with the death of Bourguiba. Though pushing through secular reform, the Tunisian government's mode of operation is rather like the more traditionally inclined Moroccan government. The difference is that the Neo-Destour, and ultimately the president, provide one-man rule for Tunisia in much the same way as the monarch does for Morocco. In the distribution of prestige and security the two systems are similar, although there are crucial differences in their ability to introduce basic social reforms and to enlist mass support. The talented second-generation leader has been faced with a dilemma similar to his Moroccan colleague. Success is determined largely by reconciling oneself to the existing institutions, and there is no meaningful alternative.

However, the Tunisian system has been able to appeal to more capable second-generation leaders by its efficiency and productivity. Unsettled young officials would make formidable opposition leaders but for the government's success in keeping them fully occupied with serious tasks. To a large extent, Bourguiba's positive response to economic planning is evidence of his awareness of the importance of keeping the energetic, imaginative young Tunisians busy. He has also had the foresight to protect discreetly the positions of the upper-middle-class young Tunisians, whose families provided much of the party's early support. Except for the Bizerte affair (which might be evidence of Bourguiba's failing powers), he has been extraordinarily successful in keeping the second-generation group engrossed in the concrete problems of the country and convinced that he is the man best suited to reconstruct Tunisia.

Until recently, there has been no serious doubt that the president is indispensable. Developing a more advanced society, however, also generates self-regulating mechanisms to provide social harmony and to introduce changes. Authoritarian leadership is not well suited to a smooth-running, prosperous society. The full development of Tunisia is still far off, but there are many candid young officials and professional men who feel that they are ready to have a larger voice in their own affairs — or, more exactly, that the Neo-Destour has too large a voice in their affairs. Some have fallen into easy compliance with the system, and a few are apathetic. But a measure of Bourguiba's success is the growing capacity of Tunisians to think independently and concretely about their problems. He has sustained the interest of most capable second-generation leaders..

The reasons for the relative moderation of Tunisian youth can be sought within the general theory suggested here. Growing up in a society where some major advances toward modernization have been made and where the goals of the modernized youth have been widely accepted, they do not feel driven to more extremist solutions. Although there are very likely proportionately more doctrinaire Communists operating in Tunisia than in Morocco, the Tunisian Communists must operate in a less hospitable social environment. They could be undercut and, indeed, often do find themselves undercut, on domestic issues. They would unquestionably have more difficulty in generating acts of violence among Tunisians than among Moroccans. The intent to construct a new society is not in doubt in Tunisia. The third-generation group of Tunisia is sometimes described disparagingly by other North African youth, because it is not understood that young Tunisians, though living in an amorphous political setting, do not view the future with despair. Bourguiba's calculated risk is how long one can withhold means of political expression from a group that is making rapid gains in other areas of human activity. . . .

THREE

Leaders and Personalities

A speech can sometimes serve to make a portrait of the speaker. In each of the following selections, a North African political figure presents not only a discourse on a particular subject but also, through that subject and his treatment of it, a revelation of his own personality, style, and political approach. Six of the leaders included here were at one time heads of state: two kings of Morocco (the father and his successor son), a president and the chairman of the Revolutionary Council of Algeria (the leader and the supplanting colonel), the president of Tunisia (who has thrice been his own successor), and the chairman of the Revolutionary Command Council of republican Libya.[1] Two others represent the poles of influential political leadership: the Morocan *salafi 'alim* who is leader of the Istiqlal party, and the Trotskyite intellectual who was advisor to the Algerian president. This latter group could be extended indefinitely: immediate candidates would include a Tunisian socialist labor leader and planner (Ahmed ben Salah),[2] a Moroccan bourgeois liberal and palace advisor (Ahmed Reda Guedira), an Algerian liberal nationalist (Ferhat 'Abbas),[3] and the three North African martyrs: a Tunisian Islamic radical (Salah ben Youssef), a Moroccan activist intellectual (Mehdi ben Barka),[4] and an Algerian alternate leader (Mohammed Khider).

Some of the speeches in this section were made at the time of taking office. Thus, Mohammed V's first Speech from the Throne after independence tells of his accomplishments over the past year, his immediate plans for his country, and his dreams for its future. His presentation is factual, compassionate, sincere — and royal. Ahmed ben Bella and Houari Boumedienne, each speaking at the time of his takeover, are both clearly different from the king. Ben Bella is very much concerned with the revolutionary masses, Boumedienne with the revolutionary state. Ben Bella appears less frustrated by his six years in a French prison than does Boumedienne by his three years in a Benbellist government. Ben Bella, the "idealist," is more careful of the meaning of his words than is the "realist," Boumedienne. Mu'ammer Qadhdhafi, recently a captain but now successor to a king, tells of the secret preludes to his takeover and of the vast panoramas of the future. (His predecessor is not included in this collection because he never said much and little of it was significant).

The speeches of Hassan II and Habib Bourguiba were made later in their careers. Hassan speaks twice — in a moment of joy after his constitution has been accepted in a referendum, and, three years later, in a moment of disappointment, after the constitution and its institutions had been sent back to the shop for an indefinite period of reworking. Hassan's explanations reveal him as being urbane, clever, adroit — and also royal. Bourguiba's speech is a summation made from the vantage point of ten years in power. All of the elements of "Bourguibism" are there: socialism, realism, personalism, and anticolonialism, combined with a desire for unity, justice, and development. The result is one of those lectures in civic education that have made the president the schoolmaster of his people.

The speeches of 'Allal al-Fassi[5] and Mohammed Harbi[6] were both delivered at a moment of downswing in their careers. (Al-Fassi had failed to form a government as premier-designate some months earlier, and his party's activist wing had broken away from his control; Harbi was about to be removed as editor of *Révolution Africaine* and was losing influence with ben Bella.) But their message is independent of their personal fortunes. Both speak of social change and the role of an institution in it; all Fassi's institution is the 'ulema, the religious notables, and Harbi's the party, the revolutionary vanguard. The importance of the message is not lessened by the fact that each institution was politically weak in the country concerned.

These selections are valuable for what they reveal about the speakers and for their authoritative comments on local political and social change. But they do not constitute in-depth studies of the leaders. Little work on leadership and personality has been done in North Africa from any disciplinary approach.

Bourguiba,[7] Mohammed V,[8] Hassan II,[9] and ben Bella[10] have all had their foreign biographers, who have produced works that are interesting but more anecdotal than rigorous. There is also the composite profile — the "insightful caricature" — from the inside[11] or the outside,[12] which may actually tell more than the unusual life stories of unique national leaders. But perhaps we can learn most from the unabashedly anecdotal: the novel.[13] Until sophisticated and nonethnocentric social or political psychological studies of North African leadership personalities can be made — and even afterwards, for that matter — fiction will remain the most truthful mirror of personality in the context of change.

Notes

1. Speeches of each head of state are available, individually or collected in volumes, from this country's diplomatic missions.

2. Between 1956 and 1969, when he was removed from office, some of ben Salah's speeches were published by the Tunisian Information Ministry.

3. See Ferhat 'Abbas, *La Nuit coloniale* (Paris: Julliard, 1962), and Amar Naroun, *Ferhat Abbas: les chemins de la souveraineté* (Paris: Denoel, 1961).

4. See Mehdi ben Barka, *Les Problèmes d'édification du Maroc et du Maghreb* (Paris: Plon, 1959) and *Option révolutionnaire au Maroc* (Paris: Maspero, 1966). He also wrote editorials as editor of *al-Istiqlal* in 1956—58. See also articles in *New Outlook* II, Nos. 3—4 (November, 1958); *Review of International Affairs* (Yugoslavia), IX, (November 1, 1958), 8—10; and *Africa South in Exile,* V, No. 2 (January-March, 1961), 96—101. See also Ernest Gellner, "The Struggle for Morocco's Past," pp. 37—49 in this reader; 'Abdelkader ben Barka, *El Mehdi ben Barka mon frère* (Paris: Laffont, 1966); S. Sarne, *L'affaire ben Barka* (Paris: Table Ronde, 1966); Roger Muratet, *On a tué ben Barka* (Paris: Plon, 1967); and François Cavighioli, *Ben Barka chez les judges* (Paris: Table Ronde, 1967).

5. See *L'Autocritique,* which appeared serialized in *al-Istiqlal,* and *The Independence Movement in Arab North Africa* (Washington, D.C.: American Council of Learned Societies, 1954); his articles also appeared in five issues of *La Pensée,* which were published by the Ministry of Islamic Affairs, 1962—63, when he was minister. See also articles in *New Outlook,* II, Nos. 3—4 (November, 1958), 43—45, and *Etudes Méditerranéennes,* No. 1 (Summer, 1957), pp. 21—25. See also Amnon Cohen, "Allal al-Fassi: His Ideas," I *Asian and African Studies* 3:121—164 (1967); E I J Rosenthal, *Islam in the Modern National State* (New York: Cambridge University Press, 1965), 154—178; and the dissertation of Fouad Masriah for Princeton University, 1972.

6. Mohammed Harbi, "L'Algérie et ses réalités," *Economie et Politique,* No. 130 (May, 1965), pp. 52-60. His editorials appeared frequently in *Révolution Africaine* in 1963 and 1964.

7. Jean Lacouture, *Cinq hommes et la France* (Paris: Editions du Seuil, 1961); Felix Garras, *Bourguiba et la naissance d'une nation* (Paris: Julliard, 1956); Jean Rous, *Bourguiba, L'homme de l'action de l'Afrique* (Paris: Didier, 1969). See also Bourguiba, *La Tunisie et la France* (Paris: Juilard, 1954, and 2nd ed., Tunis: Ministry of Information, 1970); Henry Christman, *Bourghiba* (New York: Africana, 1972).

8. Lacouture, *op. cit;* Rom Landau, *Mohammed V, King of Morocco* (Rabat, 1957).

9. Marvin Howe, *The Prince and I* (New York: John Day, 1955); Rom Landau, *Hassan II, King of Morocco* (London: George Allen & Unwin, 1962).

10. Robert Merle, *Ben Bella* (New York: Walker, 1966); Georges Vaucher, *Sous les cedres d'Ifrane* (Paris: Julliard, 1962).

11. Two superb examples are the composite of Albert Memmi's "inside-outside" experience as a North African Jew, *The Colonizer and Colonized* (Boston: Beacon Press, 1967), and the autobiographical fantasies transcribed by Paul Bowles from the Maghribia

of Mohammed Charhadi, *Life Full of Holes* (New York: Grove Press, 1964); and of Mohammed Mrabet, *Love with a Few Hairs* (New York: George Braziller, 1968).

12. Douglas E. Ashford, *Perspectives of a Moroccan Nationalist* (Totowa, N.J.: Bedminster, 1964); Henri de Montety, *Femmes de Tunisie* (Paris: Mouton, 1958).

13. This topic is beyond our scope here. The best single treatment is found in David Gordon, *North Africa's French Legacy* (Cambridge, Mass.: Harvard Center for Middle Eastern Studies, 1964): also Abdelkrim Khatibi, *Le Roman Maghrébin* (Paris: Maspero, 1968). Good anthologies are CPM, *Anthologie Maghrébine* (Paris: Hachette, 1965), and Albert Memmi, *et al., Une anthologie des écrivains maghrébins d'expression française* (Paris: Presence Africaine, 1965).

10

THE FIRST ANNIVERSARY OF THE KING'S RETURN TO MOROCCO

MOHAMMED V

Faithful subjects:

The Feast of the Throne, a noble tradition through which the people manifest their attachment and their fidelity to the king, culminates these "Three Glorious Days" that We are celebrating for the first time in an independent and unified Morocco. November 16 marked the anniversary of Our return from exile, the starting point of our national revival, the beginning of the end of the Protectorate, and the start of an era of emancipation and liberty. Yesterday, Independence Day, We proclaimed the independence and territorial unity of Our country, in the name of the whole Moroccan nation. Today, We celebrate the Feast of the Throne that links us to Our glorious past and the most brilliant epochs of Our civilization. Thus, these three national festivals recall to Us memories of glory, victory, rebirth, and liberty.

God would not have allowed Us to enjoy these benefits if there had not been a perfect understanding between the Sovereign and His people, creating this communion of feeling and ideas and unifying us in sacrifice and in the sacred struggle for Our ideals. The Sovereign who today is addressing you, proud to have accomplished His duty toward the nation, notes with pleasure the heroic behavior of His people, who were able to sustain constant efforts, lead a continuing fight, and accept sacrifices for the sacred cause of the Fatherland, that is, of Our liberty, Our independence, and our unity. Let us give thanks to God who has watched over us and prevented disaster from falling on Our path.

A year has passed since Our return, a year of effort and continued action. We owed it to Ourselves to act fully so as to allow the Moroccan nation to acceed to the rank that it deserves among other nations, and for which its illustrious past, marked by great accomplishments, qualifies it. Let Us remember that on this day a year ago We addressed you in these words: "On the occasion of this happy day, it is Our pleasure to announce to you the end of the Protectorate and the

Speech of November 18, 1956; translated from Mohammed V, *Le Maroc à l'heure de l'indépendance* (Rabat: Ministry of Information, [n.d.]), pp. 27–35, 38–40.

advent of our liberty and independence." What yesterday was only a happy announcement has now become reality. Our country enjoys its full liberty and all the attributes of sovereignty.

On the threshold of the second year of this new era, it is Our duty to reflect over the past year and to establish the balance sheet of Our accomplishments. This work has imposed unceasing and inhuman efforts on us and has demanded of us all possible means to achieve the most in the time allotted to us. The task is even more remarkable when we consider that it has been accomplished in such a short time. Had We not armed Ourselves with patience, perseverance, and devotion, We would not have been able to accomplish it in this amount of time. Thereafter, We will trace the program for the months to come, for the foundations We are building must be harmonious and solidly grounded. Similarly, the nation must be aware of the results obtained and of the distance still to be covered, and it must remain united in action, guided by the same thoughts so that We can advance toward greater accomplishments without loss of time.

Upon Our return to Our country, Our first concern was to form a real government, to which We gave the task of taking over the powers exercised by the Protectorate authorities, of building the political, administrative, social, and economic foundations of a new Morocco, of beginning negotiations with France so as to put an end to the old regime and establish new relations with her based on mutual understanding, liberty, and equality. We Ourselves went to Paris to direct these negotiations, which ended with the solemn declaration of March 2, 1956, by which France recognized Our independence and Our right to exercise all the attributes of sovereignty.

After preparatory talks with Spain, We went to Madrid, where we were warmly greeted by the Spanish people. This welcome touched Us very much and is a testimony of Spanish-Moroccan friendship. The negotiations that we conducted in a cordial and confident climate with the Spanish chief of state, Generalissimo Franco, brought us to the joint declaration of April 7, by which Spain recognized Our independence and unity. On the way back, We stopped in Tetuan, the northern capital, to emphasize this unity. We were overjoyed to see Our subjects in the north show the same attachment to the Throne and the same fidelity to the Fatherland as their brothers in the south.

In taking over the direction of national security, We have sought to ensure individual, public, and collective security in an atmosphere of confidence and collaboration between the responsible authorities and the entire people. We have undertaken the creation of a National Army and it is Our desire that it be the strength of the nation, the spearhead of all activity, and the symbol of state prestige. After setting up a Ministry of National Defense, We have appointed Our Crown Prince, Moulay Hassan, as chief of staff of the Royal Armed Forces, and We ordered him, alongside the minister of national defense, to exert all his efforts to create this army and give it a national character susceptible of arousing pride and heroism among all our citizens. The Crown Prince has proven his capabilities and his diplomatic qualities during technical conversations with the responsible authorities of France, and in a short time has organized the Royal Army; he continued that task by negotiating with Spain and proceeded to integrate the soldiers of the north into the National Army; the task was finally completed with the integration of the Liberation Army, whose members had accomplished prestigious acts for the liberation of their fatherland; it is Our duty to allow them to take part in the organization that has the task of defending the idea for which they fought. Thus the Royal Armed Forces today number 30,000 men.

In order to give this army Moroccan leadership, We have sent a number of missions to advanced military schools in France and Spain, with the result that, in a short while, competent officers will be coming back to Morocco to ensure the country's defense, along with their comrades.

In order to tighten relations among different parts of the Kingdom, on one hand, and with the central power, on the other, We have created provinces whose governors, qaids, and pashas will form a special corps, in accordance with their services. We have achieved the separation of powers: We have abolished the customary tribunals and abrogated the Berber Dahir. We have established fifty-two delegate judge courts, which have received the judicial powers previously held by two hundred qaids. We have Moroccanized the foreign tribunals and put an end to capitulatory privileges.

Our economic policy is based upon just distribution, intensified production adapted to the country's needs, development of a cooperative spirit among all individuals, establishment of commercial exchanges with foreign states in accordance with the economic interests of the country, and, finally, encouragement of foreign capital investment.

The public works have had the objective of fighting underemployment, developing cities, and accelerating the training of Moroccan cadres. To this end, We have drained and irrigated several regions in the Kingdom so as to render 32,000 additional acres useful. We have inaugurated the Meshra Homadi dam on the Moulouya River. We have distributed land in the Gharb, which has just been drained. A further drainage program will allow Us to recover thousands of acres on the left bank of the Sebou River. In Oujda, We have inaugurated an electric transformer that can generate up to 50,000 volts. We sent forty students to technical schools to specialize in public works. Since January, We have increased the salary of agricultural workers by one-third. Thanks to the intensive training of agricultural cadres, Our country can count on forty more agricultural agents. We have encouraged the creation of agricultural unions. We have been concerned with the realization of an agrarian reform and, not satisfied with merely distributing land to the farmers, We have also worked to reform the agricultural methods and to encourage the use of modern machinery. We have provided important credits for building many dwellings in the countryside, especially in the deprived Northern Zone.

We have been also concerned with workers' problems and demands. We gave the Moroccan Labor Union [UMT] the former labor exchanges of Casablanca and Kenitra, where union men could meet to study their problems and defend their interests in security and liberty.

We have given our cultural policy a national impetus so as to assure all our youth an education inspired by the spiritual principles of Islam and Arab culture, leaving place for a thorough knowledge of the country's history. Our objective remains free, compulsory education for all our children, girls as well as boys. During the past year, 1,000 new classrooms were opened to welcome over 70,000 pupils; this increase in the school body is a testimony to the Moroccan youth's enthusiasm for study. We have begun the Moroccanization of the

Education Ministry and made an effort to give scholarships to students now studying in Arab countries and in Europe.

We have begun to Arabize education which We will have completed it in the primary schools within three years. We have opened religious institutes in Oujda and Taroudant, allowing us to increase the number of students. We have decided to send study missions to several capitals so as to be able to fulfill the scientific and technical needs of the country. We have been concerned with everything that could raise the intellectual and physical level of the youth, while at the same time encouraging every means of elementary and physical education.

To allow religious foundations to regain their proper place in spiritual guidance, We have organized courses, issued directives for a new spirit in the Friday sermons, and formed new 'ulema's associations with the task of organizing lectures on theology and law throughout the country. In the social field, the Habous Ministry has substantially raised the salary of religious figures, has, on Our instructions, adopted the families of the martyrs who died for the sacred cause of the country, and has participated in giving assistance to students in religious education.

We have tried our best to Moroccanize the hospitals, and have set up schools to provide intensive courses for Moroccan nurses. We have also decided to give to these establishments a uniform status so as to eliminate all discrimination. We have fought contagious diseases with all Our means. We presided over the creation of a National Association for Assistance to the Children of the Martyrs for Independence, with the aim of taking care of these orphans and improving their living conditions, in reward for their fathers' sacrifice for the Fatherland and national dignity.

As part of our desire to consolidate the state and reinforce its organs, We set up a Crown Council for consultation whenever circumstances require it and We judge necessary; to this council We have appointed figures capable of carrying out their high responsibilities. By setting up a Consultative National Council, We have wished to guide Our people toward that democracy which remains Our fundamental objective. In the speech with which We opened this council, We proclaimed Our desire to see Our people participate in the management of state affairs. We also wanted to establish a direct contact between Ourselves and Our people and thus revive the tradition of our glorious ancestors: it is for that purpose that We have instituted the Bureau of Surveys and Guidance under Our authority. Such is the balance sheet of Our and Our Government's accomplishments over the past year . . . .

Morocco's accession to parliamentary life based on general elections demands all Our attention. To attain this goal, We will follow the natural process by first calling for the organization of municipal and rural elections, then the creation of regional assemblies, and, finally, the convocation of a Constituent Assembly to draw up a constitution within the concept of a constitutional Arab, Muslim, democratic monarchy.

In the field of education, We will devote Our efforts to intensifying children's education and increasing the number of students, setting up a university, continuing the work of Arabization, generalizing teaching, and sending cultural missions abroad. On the judicial level, We will organize regional appeal courts, create a national court of appeal, and promulgate legal codes solidly based on Muslim law.

We will also proceed in the distribution of land We will recover in accordance with the program We have set for Ourselves.

The Ministry of National Economy, which now includes finances, trade, and industrial production, will draw up a general plan. This plan will have as its goal the improvement of the standard of living, the increase of production, and the revival of industry and crafts. We will open negotiations with interested nations so as to put an end to the limitations imposed on Our sovereignty regarding customs duties, so that We will be free to trade with other countries and protect our national production.

We will work out labor statutes adapted to the workers' aspirations and in accordance with the needs of our production. We will continue Our efforts against unemployment: To this end We will set up construction plans and public works. We have created a ministry whose special mission is to reorganize the civil service, regulate its nature, and define the role of each ministry and each civil servant. This ministry will contribute to forming badly needed cadres and will enable Morocco to benefit from the help of French, Spanish, or other technicians until Moroccans are ready to take over.

The Urban Services will for its part work to eliminate the shanty towns and replace them with low-cost housing. . . .

We will not go on explaining to you the program that We have set for Ourselves: We only promise what We are sure to be able to accomplish. We make a formal commitment before God and Our people to spare no efforts for the good of the country and its greatness, for the well-being and prosperity of Our brothers and sisters. As in the past, We were able to achieve independence only through an intimate union between Ourselves and Our people, so we are convinced that we will be successful in the future only if We have the help of God and the support of Our subjects.

We stand in need of a real mobilization that will turn all of us into soldiers in the service of Our country, for its reconstruction, and for the liberty of its inhabitants.

We invite Frenchmen, Spaniards, and foreigners living in Our country to continue their constructive activities, which Morocco greatly needs. We give them the assurance that they will be respected and protected. We live in a time when solidarity among men is a necessity for the good of all.

11

THE PASSAGE AND SUSPENSION OF THE
MOROCCAN CONSTITUTION

HASSAN II

THE 1962 REFERENDUM

At this time last night the president of the Supreme Court brought Me the official final results of the referendum. I need not tell you that this confirmation of what we all knew gave Me intense pleasure and, I must say, one of these new joys that are not only unmixed but, even more, are absolute.

Indeed, it was the realization of the wish of My beloved father, H.M. Mohammed V — God rest his soul — and of all the generations of Moroccans who have militated, fought, suffered, and given of their freedom or their lives. At last, this constitution consecrated Morocco as a modern state in the full meaning of the word, for without any kind of coercion, Morocco decided the organization of its everyday life; the relationships between its members, between state and individuals, between state and collectivities, within a framework accepted by all, examined and evaluated by all. . . .

The Moroccan constitution is not what is called a "granted" constitution. I think it unnecessary to give a lecture in philology, because one has only to look into a dictionary or a basic text on constitutional law. A "granted" constitution becomes obligatory for everyone as soon as it is sealed; it is promulgated without any direct or indirect consultation with the people. The Moroccan constitution is a "nongranted" constitution, it allowed the King to ask the entire electorate, women and men: Do you or do you not agree with what I propose? The people were offered an alternative: Yes, the constitution is good; No, we do it over. But neither the referendum nor the people who answered to it ever questioned the principle of the monarchy or of the person who represents the monarchy.

Why a referendum? Because it is the simplest and most sincere — not to say most innocent — expression of democracy. It allows every man and woman to

Speeches of December 13, 1962, and June 7, 1965; translated from Hassan II, *Le Maroc en Marche* (Rabat: Ministry of Information, 1965), pp. 203—9, 517—21.

say what he or she has to say without any intermediary between him and his king. And, to the extent that we may consider Jean-Jacques Rousseau the father of an old-fashioned but basically pure democracy, we can say that the referendum, as a pure and orthodox formulation, is the formula that has been and should be used. Why should I accept intermediaries, whatever their number or qualities, between My people and Myself? Why should I imagine that three hundred, or four hundred, or two hundred and fifty people could be the representatives of three and one-half or four and one-half million electors? Can I not trust My subjects' political judgment? Should I consider them as minors, unable to distinguish between good and evil, between right and wrong, lacking any political sense, political instincts, or political education, and needing a go-between, a channel, to be able to make a judgment? No. This nation has been reacting for centuries; and every time, its reactions have been civilized, orderly, pugnacious, audacious, and thus realistic, prudent, conservative of the best in its history and its past.

It has been said that the Moroccans have never advanced to the level of a nation or a people. I answer very simply: ibn Toffeil, Avicenne, the Giralda, Moulay Idriss the Conqueror, Moulay Ismail al-Alawi, Mansur the Golden, and others I won't mention! I answer very simply that Andalusian music, the *pastilla* that you and others like to eat, the sculptured plaster, the carved wood, all this is civilization, and it cannot advance, flourish, or survive except within a framework where the leaders have the advancement of their country and their civilization at heart. Finally, I tell them: Gentlemen, if Europe knows algebra and the Ptolemaic system, if the philosophies of Socrates and Plato are known, it is through the Arabs, and especially through Morocco. For these and many other reasons I decided that the Moroccan people were of age, that they deserved — not only deserved but had a right to ask for — direct consultation, with no intermediaries, no dispensary that hands out constitutional pills, more or less degenerating, like tranquilizers, which are forbidden nowadays. And, thank God, that is why we do not have to fear constitutional malformations or monstrosities.

There is one thing I want everyone to know, and it is what I will say to the representatives when I open the parliament — with the help of God: "Gentlemen, My ministers are My collaborators. You, you are My ministers." And by giving them this responsibility in conceiving and planning, I will lead them to be trained by difficulties.

Why do people insist on seeing enemies in parliament? They will not be the King's enemies and the King will not be their enemy, because Our constitution is not the outcome of demands or riots but of more or less quiet and peaceful requests. It came through a train of thought, a daily operation, imperceptible but real, between the people, the King, and He who was the Crown Prince. For the Crown Prince has the fortune to have been brought up by His father within and among the people: the Crown Prince had the fortune to take a part, here in the Mechouar, on January 11, 1944, in the nationalist demonstration before the palace. For five years, on his summer vacation, the Crown Prince had the fortune to play soccer on the beach of Ain-Diab with people who are today excellent soccer-players, or perhaps haberdashers or Coca-Cola salesmen. The Crown Prince kicked these fellows in the shins, and got kicked back. So why try to separate the representatives and the King? No, gentlemen. The representatives represent a people who said "Yes" to Hassan II, who said "Yes" to the monarchy for today and for tomorrow, as long as the monarchy continues to do its duty.

It is certain that the keys to success, the keys to permanence, are not in the hands of the people, for the people will always be sound and good; they are in the hands of those who have to rule over Morocco, who have to preside over the destinies of this country. The constitution does not give them powers; it gives them tasks, it gives them obligations. *The constitution makes Us a referee.* I am sure that many said: Oh, the King has enormous powers! But gentlemen, know that the King took just enough to be able to intervene when things are bad, or to help them get better. I will give you a very simple example: imagine two soccer teams on a field, take away the referee's right to blow a whistle and dismiss a player, and play, gentlemen. It is simple as that.

Finally, there is a very important part of the constitution: the consecration of judicial independence, up to the Superior Council of the Magistrates. All the magistrates are elected by their peers. All of them. And the only appointed member of this council is the King, who appoints his justice minister, who is vice president, and two or three other magistrates. The fact remains that We, the appointed members — some by Me, some by destiny — are a minority. But minority against what? Why always speak of a minority against a majority? Why must a constitution always be against something? The fact is that Morocco wanted to prove that it was getting out of one sphere into another, it wanted to prove that a country on the road to development can reconcile freedom and efficiency. And that is why it "canonized" public liberties.

There will always be people who will say: the single party is forbidden, in order that the King may divide and rule. I say no! It is not because of that; it is simply because, if you accept a single party in Morocco, as a logical consequence you have to accept Me as the president, the secretary general of the union, of the party, of the cells. . . . . It is obvious. Where there is hierarchy, there is power. And that is inadmissible. Or else I am president of the party. And nobody ever saw a king at the same time president of a party, member of a party, or supporting a party. A king is above parties. Gentlemen, this is the only explanation I will give for the prohibition of the single party. I will leave it to the partisans, to members of the political parties, to give other explanations. . . .

At last, at last — and this is important — with this constitution, I guarantee to everyone the right to take part, directly or indirectly, not only in management but above all in control: in the twentieth century, control is more important than management.

Was all this created ex nihilo? No. Really, My task has been greatly simplified. For everything about personal status, judicial guarantees, public liberties, labor rights, political liberties, freedom of press, the right to set up business, the right to go to court, all this, like many other things, Mohammed V achieved before he died. In less than six years. And Mohammed V kept his promises, more than any man could have kept them when confronted daily with thousands of problems, including that of having faithless collaborators.

Then popular representation had to be organized. So We created a House of Representatives, elected, as you know, by universal suffrage. But experience has shown that assemblies elected by universal suffrage are not always appropriate for the difficulties of the situation. Sometimes, they discuss "politics" and "public matters" rather than matters that in the twentieth century represent real, everyday democracy, the democracy of the daily problems.

That is why I decided to add a second assembly. It will not be, as some may think, a "brake," a place where matters are thought over and sent to the "ice-box," but, on the contrary, a motor. Those who are doubly represented — whether by the Chamber of Agriculture, the Chamber of Commerce, the Chamber of Industry, the Chamber of Handicrafts, or the labor unions, or, lastly, the local or regional assemblies — see everyday what democracy is: "Give us a canal." "Build us schools." "Make us an Operation Plow under such-and-such conditions." "Give us seeds of a certain quality." "Organize the territory in such way. . . . "

For democracy in the twentieth century — as Professor Duverger said in his book that I had to defend in front of him for My law degree — democracy is the power of everyone for the benefit of everyone, through an elite elected by everyone. The elite does not create itself. It is not a *deus ex machina,* as in the theater. It comes to life in the cells. And we need diversity not only in training but also in the way the Moroccan people get their political education. . . .

Finally, I say to those who, at the last minute, wanted to involve God in the constitution: I will involve Him in it. I involve God in it because I think that each man, whether he is a painter, a pianist, a cook, a cabinetmaker, or let's say, a constitution-maker, when inspired, needs God's help and a pure mind which will not alter the intentions he has to write down on the paper. There are those who say, What? Islam is only in the sixth paragraph? No, gentlemen, Islam is in the Preamble: "Morocco is a Muslim state." And then again in Article 6 (I do not give any numerical value to articles). When we say that Morocco is a Muslim state, that the state religion is the Muslim religion, we mean that it is as a Muslim state, following true Islam, the real concept of Islam, that Morocco pledges the free practice of religions. Naturally, [within] the juridical notion of public order and morality.

Complete freedom will be granted to the practice of the Hebrew and Christian religions. They are "religions of the Book." They are religions accepted by Islam. Not only accepted, but we are advised to believe in their prophets. This does not mean that tomorrow, Morocco will accept sun worship, or fetishism in public places, or that it will accept the Bahai sect or other sects that are pure heresies. Morocco is a Muslim state, tolerating the religions of the Book that admit the unity and indivisibility of God, namely, the eternal and universal religions that are the Hebrew and the Christian religions. . . .

THE 1965 SUSPENSION

Praise to God.

My dear people. . . .

The parties, organizations, and individuals We consulted gave Us written answers that We studied with the greatest care, We discovered that it was impossible to reconcile their contradictory demands and conditions. So We increased Our efforts by calling Our interlocutors to direct and frank talks, but still We could not reach national unity. Faced with the impossibility of forming a coalition government, it would have been natural to have a program of public safety imposed by a government backed by a coherent parliamentary majority, conscious of its responsibilities, able to give a serious and positive character to the work of the parliament and able to support the executive's efforts in the rapid accomplishment of the tasks from which you, dear people, expect so much. But, it was impossible to find a majority that could provide the necessary parliamentary backing for the formation of a stable government.

Unable to find either a government of national union or a parliamentary majority, We faced two options: to remain faithful to the virtues of democracy, which We have always considered the best and most efficient way, or to resign Ourselves to maintaining a parliamentary system that has only given rise to fruitless discussions and that, if it continued, would injure that very democracy, Our moral values, Our dignity, and Our creative genius. We are convinced that the paralysis caused by futile parliamentary debates would result in nothing but disappointment and condemnation of democracy. But democracy is one of the fundamental acquisitions of Our people, and We are determined to protect it by securing the conditions necessary for it to flourish and be freely practiced. And so we find before Us several solutions, from which We must choose the most suitable to get out of the crisis.

We could choose to abandon the parliament to its negative ways; but We could not think of such an eventuality, because of Our responsibilities and Our duty to protect the rights of citizens and groups, and also because of Our duties under the constitution as king, "symbol of national unity, guarantor of the permanence and continuity of the state." Nor could We once more compose a government and let it take its chances in seeking parliamentary support. We knew that no government could find support from a divided parliament, unable to provide a majority aware of its responsibilities. Could We, then, permit instability to be established in the country, and see governments without support follow one another, in order to prove that no parliamentary majority existed? We had a duty to spare Our country and Our people a series of sterile experiments that would only have ended in administrative, social, and economic degradation, and would have impaired the morale of Our people and the good name of Our country.

A third solution was also possible: to use Our constitutional prerogatives to dissolve the House of Representatives and hold new elections within forty days, as provided by the constitution. But We did not want to expose the country to the harsh shock of an unexpected electoral campaign, taking place in the heat of passions and the clash of individual ambitions and interests. Besides, even without those considerations, if new elections were to take place in the present situation, they would not produce a less divided or more coherent parliament.

As a matter of fact, the constitution, in its present form, contains provisions that do not guarantee conditions for the normal operation of parliamentary institutions. Moreover, the constitution is incomplete and imprecise, and there are hindrances to its proper application. So we must revise some articles in order to perfect Our constitution in the light of past experience, to avoid a crisis of authority and a dangerous instability in the country.

To cope with this critical situation, We have decided, by the responsibilities that are Ours and that oblige Us to safeguard the future of Our people and the continuity of the state, and in order to protect the country from the dangers that threaten it, to use Our constitutional prerogatives, which empower Us to take all necessary measures for the institutions' return to their normal operations, when minds will have regained their serenity and passions cooled. Such conditions are indispensable for an era of union that We continually seek for the mobilization of Our people and the undertaking of constructive efforts.

My dear people: Today, we sealed the royal decree that sets up a state of emergency. Until the institutions return to their normal operations, We will take all legislative and administrative measures necessary for the conduct of state affairs. The state of emergency will not impair the democratic liberties guaranteed by the constitution. Political parties and labor unions will continue their legal activities in order and respect for the law. . . .

Every constitution, like every human work, is imperfect and can be revised. The experience of the last two years of parliamentary life shows the need to revise some articles of Our constitution. This revision, dear people, will be submitted to you in a referendum. . . . The constitutional monarchy is a definitive national acquisition. From now on, Our common ambition is that our constitution correspond genuinely to our realities, and that it guarantee the exercise of democracy in stability and harmony among constitutional institutions. . . . The country demands a strong power, a fair power, a steady power. This is why we have to take a series of measures and carry them out with rapidity, firmness, and effectiveness.

The era of decay and negligence in state management is over. A new era for the country begins, an era of responsibility in all fields and at all levels, an era of good citizenship and respect for law and state authority, an era in which every honest citizen will find the place he deserves. From now on, We take direct responsibility for the executive power, adding heavy responsibilities to those We already bear. In doing so, I am convinced of your maturity, your civic spirit, your attachment to Our Self, to the Throne, your impatient desire to see projects accomplished that We will undertake together for your prosperity. All of this will give you a new enthusiasm to reach the goals We have set for Ourselves. We are counting on all Our subjects, without exception, to surmount this decisive stage together and, after the revision of the constitution and the calm organization of new elections, to arrive at the restoration of effective functioning of the parliamentary institutions.

12

AN INTERVIEW WITH BEN BELLA

MARIA ANTONIETTA MACCIOCCHI

"What is the political outlook of Algeria?" "Socialism, socialism," ben Bella answered, and he returned to the expression frequently in the conversation, as if he wanted to take every opportunity to pull it out of the shadows and transfer it into concrete terms.

"But what do you mean by socialism? Can you give any examples?"

"Analogies in this field are almost always superficial or misleading. We want an Algerian socialism, born of our national experience, benefiting from the experience of socialist countries."

I asked him what immediate steps he thought should be taken to bring about this type of transformation in a country emerging from semi-feudalism and colonialism.

"For us it is of prime importance to initiate immediately an agrarian reform; ours is a country that has inherited a peasant-based economy. There are 7 million peasants, 1 million peasant families, who constitute the fundamental structure of the country. The peasant population is the decisive force in the country, the backbone of the Liberation Army in every region, in every village, in the country, and in the *bled*."

I asked him what kind of agrarian reform he envisaged, since the problem is complex; many of the French settler lands have been mechanized and are large modern agricultural enterprises.

"An agrarian reform," ben Bella said, "that collectivizes land and gives it to agricultural cooperatives that would be entrusted with its management and exploitation. . . . The course we want to follow will also be carried out through peasant assemblies and congresses. We want to encourage agrarian reform from below because the mass of peasants favor it and are participating personally in all phases of its creation through the development of a widespread movement in the countryside."

It seemed clear that ben Bella considers the poor peasants the fundamental revolutionary force of Algeria.

Translated from an interview published in *L'Unità*, August 12, 1962, p. 3.

"The poor peasants, the principal victims of land speculation and of colonial exploitation, are without any doubt the force that stands at the base of the revolutionary transformation of society. Where is our proletariat? It is not very numerous, dispersed, concentrated in rudimentary nuclei or abroad. The revolutionary mass is basically rural. . . . the Cuban revolution took a similar point of departure: a peasant mass in arms for agrarian independence and reform. Even tsarist Russia was a peasant country."

I asked ben Bella why he had emphasized the Arab component of the Algerian revolution.

"When I say that we are Arabs," ben Bella said, "I don't even remotely think of stressing racial questions of skin or blood. I don't know how much of the Arab or the Roman there is in my blood; that's not what interests me. But I have a way of being and of thinking in life; I have certain ethics, a fixed inheritance of culture and of civilization, my humanism and my personal moral values. Arabism, for me, is above all the way to underline our neutralism, for example, in foreign policy. It is a neutralism that is active and dynamic, that is capable of acting in order to impose peace; it should not be confused with the neutralism of those who remain uninvolved in the problems of our times."

"It also seems to me," I interjected, "that what I have called your Arabism is an attempt to oppose every form of compromise with neocolonialist forces."

Ben Bella, who had spoken in a composed, almost timid way, at times staring at his desk, at this point became aroused, and exclaimed:

"That is the big question: Neocolonialism! When one asks us why we are divided after the CNRA at Tripoli,[1] when one asks us what is the rift which opened in a group of men all united in the same faith to expel the oppressor, well then, I tell you that at the bottom of the dissension among us lay the question: What is our attitude toward neocolonialism? In other words, what is the ideological content of the Algerian revolution? I have asserted that neocolonialism is like the plague for us. I have always taken the position that it represents the perpetuation of old privileges in new forms. Colonialism has been modernized, it has become more up to date, less crude; it has realized that the people cannot be dominated by the whip, by machine-guns, by bloody repression. So it looks for other means, more progressive systems of domination: an enlightened colonialism, so to speak, based on a fictitious equality, with colonial peace hanging over our land and at the same time with economic and military domination of key points of our society. But this means a new form of slavery and oppression.

"We have not been divided by personal ambition, as the Western press claims. The problem is not the position that each of us occupies but the ideas on which our unity of action must be based. The Political Bureau, today, is a team that has the same political thought and that is unanimous in its actions, ideals, and policy, in wanting to block the way to neocolonial compromise.

"We maintain that either there is a revolution going on in this country — and we will be able to carry out agrarian reform and all the other reforms of which I will speak extensively in our congress — and consequently we will be able to proceed with our forces on this path, or else that Algeria will become a revised and corrected version of all the other African governments that accept neocolonialism. Money always — or almost always — implies a political counterpart, 'If we give in to this perspective, we would end up turning our backs on the revolution.' "

I asked him what kind of relations he intends to have with the socialist countries and the Soviet Union. He answered that the Algerian leaders have the same attitude toward the socialist camp as other underdeveloped countries that have enjoyed its support and economic cooperation. They are for peaceful coexistence and neutralism, but there is more: they acknowledge the ideological help of the socialist camp through its doctrine and through its accomplishments, all of which indicates conclusively that the Algerian revolution has a socialist orientation.

I then brought up the controversial question of the role of the army.

"The role of the army is set out in the Tripoli Program," ben Bella said. "It is necessary to work out its reconversion, not because it constitutes the base for a military dictatorship but because without the support of this mass of men we would be unable to construct the new Algeria. We have magnificent cadres, politically educated. The best of them should take their place in the party, for the future of the country is in the party. We need a new army of pioneers to create the infrastructure of the country, to construct roads, houses, and schools, besides defending the frontiers."

Since he had raised the subject, I asked if he was still considering the creation of a single party in Algeria.

"Certainly," ben Bella stated, "The single party is, in practice, the National Liberation Front [FLN]. As was the case in the struggle for liberation, everything must take place within it. United, we have obtained our independence, and united, we must proceed toward an even greater goal: the creation of a socialist country."

"And the Algerian Communist Party [PCA]?" I asked

"We must maintain the union of the workers and the peasants with us, as achieved during the struggle. The militants of the PCA are invited to enter the Front, to help us in the Front, to consolidate our bonds with the masses within the Front; their cadres could be the cadres of the Front, the leaders of the Front, according to their merits and their labors."

What does the politics of Nasser mean to ben Bella?

"One cannot avoid the fact that Nasser, unlike others, has really thrown the colonialists out of his country. As far as the internal regime, I cannot judge, I cannot go into its merits; it is a particular type of experiment. In any case, it is profoundly different from the concrete reality of a country like ours, which has fought for seven years and where the people push toward a socialist perspective.

"Speaking of concrete reality," I said, "do you not fear that your long stay in prison may have removed you from it, as some of your antagonists say?"

Ben Bella was not disturbed but smiled, replying that "prisons are revolutionary academies" and asking if those who were imprisoned under fascism became detached from the concrete reality of their country.

Note

1. See P.J. Vatikiotis, "Tradition and Political Leadership: The Example of Algeria," pp. 309—29 in this reader.

13

THE THIRD ANNIVERSARY OF ALGERIAN INDEPENDENCE

HOUARI BOUMEDIENNE

People of Algeria: Three years after independence, our country again confronts its destiny. At this decisive moment, the thoughts of each of us go out to our glorious martyrs and to all patriots who risked their lives for a free and independent Algeria. The memories of seven and a half years of war always nourish the feelings of a people who have been put to the test, and they exalt the revolutionary action of the militants who show themselves worthy of pursuing the task of the glorious artisans of national independence.

On June 19, in a proclamation read to the Nation, the Revolutionary Council underlined the seriousness of the situation that led it to take on historic responsibilities. The reign of mystification and uncertainty is over. The page has been irrevocably turned. The morbid deviations of personal power have profoundly changed our institutions. The confusion and concentration of power and the liquidation of the revolutionary cadres have turned a policy of docility into a system of government. In trying to muzzle and tame the vital forces of the Nation, in hardening and freezing the governing bodies of the country, in hoping to create the myth of the "providential man," the dictator deliberately violated revolutionary legitimacy.

The results are a sad legacy: the breakdown of authority into political and administrative fiefs, a demagogic conception of socialism, delinquency of the state, and paralysis of the party. The situation is as deplorable in the economic and social fields. Spectacular but isolated actions, improvised decisions, made at conferences or at chance meetings, that were in fact aimed only at psychological-ly conditioning the masses or individuals and at covering up the incoherence and contradictions of a harmful policy of dissipating national resources and state funds.

But one cannot try with impunity to subjugate an entire nation that has fought and suffered for the triumph of revolutionary principles and the attainment of a better future. Despite misleading appearances, personal power bore within itself the seeds of its own destruction. That is why the revolutionary outbreak of June 19 was written in the historical logic of our Revolution.

Speech of July 5, 1965; translated from Houari Boumédienne, *Les discours du Président Boumedienne* (Algiers: Information Ministry, 1966), pp. 12—20.

People of Algeria: In bringing an end to personal power, the Revolutionary Council has re-established revolutionary legitimacy. The continuity of the Algerian Revolution is henceforth ensured. The revolutionary principles that inspired our struggle for liberation are returning, strengthened and vigorous. The fundamental options contained in the Tripoli Program and the Charter of Algiers have again found the spirit of November 1 and the revolutionary conditions necessary for their realization.

In this sense, socialism is part of our historical heritage. It did not have to await some demagogic make-believe to become a reality in our national policy. It is the expression of the will and aspirations of our people, the fruit of their revolutionary combat.

People of Algeria: On June 19, the Revolutionary Council took on historic commitments. Since June 19, the performance of the country's activities, the proper functioning of public affairs, have been handled normally, in security and order. The stability and confidence that prevails in the country, despite the subversive and reactionary attempts of a few professional troublemakers, show how fragile was the order built on mystification and lies. The swift downfall of the tyrant has ripped away the deceptive veil that concealed a sad reality.

The attempt at depersonalizing our people has failed badly. On the contrary, it has served to reaffirm their revolutionary conscience. The adherence of the masses and all the national leaders to the proclamation of June 19 shows strikingly how exactly events responded to the impatient expectation of all our people. The National People's Army, born of the people and serving the people, vigilant guardian of the sacred principles of the Revolution, has accomplished its mission in contributing decisively to the reinstatement of revolutionary legitimacy.

People of Algeria: On June 19, the Revolutionary Council, the highest body of the nation, committed itself to ensuring the permanence of the Revolution by rehabilitating our historical values, by restoring to the people their trampled dignity, their confiscated sovereignty, by giving back to our party — the FLN [National Liberation Front] — its true revolutionary avant-garde role, and by setting up a serious and organized state.

The FLN will be a dynamic avant-garde revolutionary party functioning according to the rules of democratic centralism and composed of experienced militants. In accordance with the Tripoli Program and the Charter of Algiers, it will have the job of elaborating, guiding, inspiring, and controlling, and not of managing or replacing the state. Toward this end, an authentic congress will be called to freely designate the party organs.

On the other hand, it is important to build a state based on morality and a real social commitment, respecting our Arab and Islamic values. We have to moralize our institutions, to build an effective state machinery capable of ensuring revolutionary order and discipline and of preventing the agents of the state and administration from any form of pressure or solicitation. State action will be assured of continuity through the stability, skills, and effectiveness of its dynamic administration.

In a word, to make the state the true executor of a coherent policy is one of the essential tasks of the Revolution. The state institutions, drafted within legitimate state bodies, will enable the popular will to express itself and to endow itself with a constitution that conforms to the principles of the Revolution and from which all seeds of personal power are eradicated.

Justice will be equal for all. It will be devoid of arbitrariness and of all pressure. It will not be the instrument of one man but will serve the Revolution. All these rationally conceived institutions will enable the life of the Nation to be organized internally as well as externally.

People of Algeria: In the framework of institutions and operations adopted to the needs of the people, the economic and social development of our country will forcefully determine the guidelines of our national policy; an administration rationally organized and planned in relation to our fundamental options will be the main goal of the Revolutionary Council.

Three years after our independence, what is the real state of our economy? The results obtained have not been equal to the sacrifices agreed to by our people, to their legitimate ambitions, or to our real possibilities. If the worst has been avoided and if some advantages have been safeguarded, it is above all thanks to the political maturity of the peasants and workers. For it is they and they alone who have brought self-management to farms and industries. And if the cult of personality tried to turn this to personal profit, in reality it only legalized an accomplished fact. But by refusing to organize the socialist sector seriously, it made it possible to scatter the revolutionary forces, turn the workers' interest away from self-management, and waste and dissipate productive capital.

The evolution of the economy for the last three years has been characterized by a drop in production, a loss of productive capital, stagnation in other sectors, widening territorial and sectoral disparities, economic disorganization creating a climate of insecurity that renders the association of the masses and the emulation of the workers impossible, and hoarding and a total absence of investment. This serious situation is the result of activism, sterile agitation, improvisation, and approximation being turned into methods of government, scorning Algerian realities. Hasty and anarchic measures, a blind tendency to idealize reality based only on its spectacular and gratuitous aspects, have ruined the efforts of the working masses and the good cadres of the nation.

At the financial level, a policy of prestige and noisy publicity has led to a deplorable mismanagement of public funds. It is demagogic and irresponsible to put the problems of building socialism outside the true realities of our country. It is not a matter of dividing up the booty and consuming it; it is a question of transforming the economy of our country and of mobilizing all the energy of the nation to that end.

We should first call upon our internal resources. International aid on a basis of equality and noninterference in our internal affairs can only be supplementary. We must also create conditions of security so as to ensure a sizeable increase in national investment within the framework of our socialist options, an effective mobilization of hoarded savings, and real participation of the entire nation in economic reconstruction. Most of the economic problems at the present stage are those of economic direction and working methods. The spirit of haste, the absence of planning, blind authoritarianism coupled with anarchy and disorder, euphoric optimism, refusal to face the truth because it is not always agreeable to hear it, all of which prevailed until June 19, must be banned forever.

From now on, verbal socialism is dead; the building of a socialist economy has begun. Future generations will not remember the words, they will judge the acts. We must work for them conscientiously and with determination. There will be no more place for the noisy improvisation and waste that jeopardized the principle of self-management, one of the basic ingredients of our socialist option. In the agricultural sector, the agrarian reform, which has been justified by the role played by the peasants in the Revolution, will achieve the participation of the masses in the development of the country, thanks to the institutional structures.

People of Algeria: In the field of foreign policy, ever since November 1, 1954, the Algerian Revolution joined the vast movement of people who fight for liberty and human dignity. Today as yesterday, Algeria intends to remain faithful to this basic option and to work continuously to reinforce a solidarity forged in combat with all oppressed people. . . .

People of Algeria: The credibility of our country on the international scene remains determined above all by a clear awareness of the seriousness of the hour. The economic and financial situation is seriously mortgaged by the reign of indifference and the systematic depletion of our public resources for the sole purpose of prestige and personal political benefits. Reconstruction is possible, but the way is one of strict austerity imposed on all sectors, first of all on the party and state. A greater civic sense is demanded of the citizenry and a cult of the public good must be imposed on the leaders. There is especially an urgent and imperative need for organization, seriousness, and constant efforts.

But our policy, taking into account the legitimate ambition of the country, will be based on the reality of our means. In short, the future of our country will depend on the will of each Algerian and his attachment to the principles for which the best among us fought and died. The Revolutionary Council is anxious to honor the commitments proclaimed on June 19, 1965. It will devote itself to the difficult task that has been assigned to it. It will work untiringly toward progress, justice, and the well-being of all.

Glory to our Martyrs!

14

A VISIT TO FEZZAN

MU'AMMAR AL-QADHDHAFI

"In the name of God, Who has upheld right against wrong and eliminated the latter. Thanks be to God, Who has pulled down the idols and broken the shackles which fettered this people for long years."

Brethren: I convey to you the greetings of struggle, of strife, and of revolution and bring you the greetings of the armed forces, which risked total destruction for the sake of the people.

The armed forces, which throughout the period of preparation for the revolution were vulnerable to ruin, did not hesitate or falter in their determination to bring nearer the day of revolution.

The armed forces never hesitate at any moment or on any day to enter the battle, with all its risks, and to assume their grave responsibilities, out of faith in their status as the vanguard and protective shield of the people and also as an effective power that can challenge injustice, pull down the idols, and break the shackles so that the forces of the Arab people in Libya may be unleashed to build and produce.

When they left their barracks on the 1st of September, the armed forces believed that they truly reflected the profound revolutionary feeling that fills the hearts of this people, and that their role was not yet over. They are still fully prepared to strike firmly, violently, and rapidly at the people's enemies.

Brethren: The armed forces are an integral and inseparable part of this people, and when they proclaimed the principles of liberty, socialism, and unity, they produced nothing new. It is the people who believe in liberty, socialism, and unity and inspired the armed forces, their vanguard, which imposed them on the enemies of the people with the force of arms. Thus, it is the people who are the teachers, the inspirers, and the pioneers.

LIBYAN PEOPLE'S STRUGGLE

Brethren: Freedom is the natural right of every individual, but the Arab people in Libya have been deprived of it for many years. The Libyan people have suffered much for the sake of liberty and sacrificed as much as any other people to that end. They confronted the hordes of invaders — the Italians, at a

Speech of September 22, 1969; issued by Libyan National Cultural Center, 1970.

time when they were defenseless — to defend liberty at any cost. But we never lost faith that the enormous sacrifices made by the Arab people in Libya would not pass unrewarded, and that the day would inevitably come when this people would emerge victorious. In the end, this people wrested freedom from darkness and the depth of despair. They proclaimed it to the world at large, and with all vigor rushed forward to achieve full unity with their armed forces. Within the span of twenty days, this people proved to the world that this revolution is the people's own revolution and that what happened on the 1st of September was far removed from a military coup.

The role of the armed forces on the 1st of September was merely the role of a commando vanguard, after which the people, imbued with faith in freedom, socialism, social justice, and all-embracing Arab unity, proclaimed to the world that what happened in Libya was a profound revolution by the people, and that this revolution will continue until the people have reached their noble objectives, and that the armed forces will "keep their finger on the trigger" at all times to defend the people's revolution, protect the people's gains, and consolidate the people's victories.

The armed forces will never rise above the people nor will they monopolize the country's rule, out of faith in the fact that the people are the ruler, the master, and the "king of kings." So, down with the kings, and long live the people! The thrones that existed against the people's will, the chairs and palaces made by imperialism with the people's blood, sweat, and legitimate right fell down in a minute, for they had been based on injustice and despotism.

The rulers brought by imperialism, the thrones made by imperialism, and the palaces built with the people's right were toppled with one stroke, and it was proven to the world that what the people build with their free and unrestricted will shall be everlasting, and what is imposed on the people with force shall vanish into thin air. What imperialism has done has already vanished, giving way to what the people are building with their free will, which was unleashed on September 1.

PRINCIPLES OF THE REVOLUTION

Brethren: Socialism, which this people proclaimed on the 1st of September, was essential for the people's life. It was necessary to dissolve class distinctions and to bring about the emancipation of the mass of this people from the grip of poverty, so that the Arab man in Libya might enjoy an honorable human life.

God has not created this people poor, nor has He imposed poverty on them, nor created them slaves. God has also not imposed slavery on this people, nor has He created them a backward people, nor imposed backwardness on them. It was the vicious and the charlatans who made a slave of this people, who were born free.

It was also the wicked who robbed this people's wealth; it was the greedy, the rapacious, and the agents of imperialism who sucked this people's riches and forcibly imposed poverty on them. Socialism is a noble principle which no one can profane, but the enemies of the people want this people to be backward and wish to see them poor, even inflicting poverty on them. They cast doubt on the socialism of Islam, on Arabism, and on the September 1st revolution.

Those who usurped the wealth of this people and sucked their blood are casting doubts on socialism: the socialism of Islam; but the conscious people, the noble and revolutionary people, will never accept an alternative to social justice. The people, who have rushed forward on the road of progress, who have broken the fetters, will on no account allow themselves to be misled by propaganda or diverted from the path of socialism by prejudiced elements. The conscious and noble people know how to achieve social justice .... This people will never hesitate nor will they halt their great historic march toward liberty, socialism, and unity.

The enemies of Arab unity, agents of Zionism and imperialism, occupants of thrones and chairs, those motivated by selfish interests, and the enemies of Arabism and Islam, are a stumbling block on the road to Arab unity. But the people, who have surged forward, broken the shackles and trodden on idols, will impose freedom, socialism, and Arab unity by force on the enemies of Arabism and Islam ....

Freedom, socialism, and unity are not the outcome of the 1st of September, nor the fruit of one day or night; they have been deeply embedded in the heart of this people for centuries past. Freedom was not born on September 1st. For its sake the Arab people in Libya had offered thousands of victims throughout the ages. History and the world bear witness to the enormity of the sacrifices made by the Arab people in Libya out of faith in freedom. Socialism was also familiar to this people, for the Islamic religion, which has been many centuries in existence, is a socialist creed. Socialism therefore was not born on September 1st; socialism is social justice.

The Arab people are the most persistent of all the world's peoples in their defense of justice. They have borne the banners of that justice high throughout history and across continents and dark seas.

Arab unity was not the fruit of September 1st, for it has existed since time immemorial and will remain forever. It fills the hearts of the Arabs from the Ocean to the Gulf. The demand for Arab unity is, therefore, tantamount to placing things in their true perspective. There is also nothing new in the quest for that unity; it is no novelty. What is to be abhorred is regionalism, the frittering away of the Arab homeland, and the division of the Arab people's ranks. Unity is eternal, it has existed among the Arabs for thousands of years. Regionalism is the innovation that came to be imposed by imperialism and maintained by its agents. The stands of this people through history confirm that unity is deep-seated in their hearts, as well as their faith in unity. The land of Palestine since 1948 bears witness to the truth and existence of this unity. Arab blood from the Ocean to the Gulf has mixed on the land of Palestine in defense of the Arab lands from the Ocean to the Gulf.

The Holy Land, Brethren, imposes unity on us. The inevitability of the struggle between the Arab people, imperialism, and world Zionism renders inevitable the achievement of unity and the quest for unity. The inevitability of historic strife between the Arab people and its enemies also involves inevitable unity which now constitutes the solid road to the Holy Land. Unity also provides a protective shield for the gains of the Arab people; it is the safe road leading up to the Holy Land.

LIBERATION OF THE HOLY LAND

We lost the Holy Land when we were separated; when we were divided into parties and factions, and when the Arab world fell into fragments.

Faith in the Arabism of Palestine is one of the greatest supports of Arab unity. Palestine cannot be restored by negative means, by classes or by donations. It can be reached only by the march of the Arab masses, free of fetters, restrictions, and narrow regionalism. We will arrive at Palestine, Brethren, when we have pulled down the walls which impede the fusion of the Arab people in the battle. We will reach the Holy Land when we have removed the borders and the partitions. We will reach the Holy Land with arms and with men, but only when we have the borders. The battle to free Palestine must extend from Syria to North Africa. We shall liberate Palestine when the Arab land has become one solid front. What is going on in the occupied land of Palestine affirms the necessity of unity. The ferocity of imperialism and Zionism also emphasize the necessity of Arab unity as well as the imperialist challenge to the Arabs. Arab unity therefore, will serve as a strong and decisive answer to the challenge of both imperialism and world Zionism . . . .

REVOLUTIONARY FEZZAN

Brethren: We have come to Fezzan before any other area for many reasons. Firstly, because it is the most undeveloped province of Libya. Attempts were made to impose slavery on Fezzan, but it insisted on its sovereignty and freedom. History bears witness to the battles Fezzan has fought in defense of and out of faith in freedom. But the forgerers have obliterated Fezzan's brilliant history.

Now that the dark has been dispelled, with God's power, Fezzan has rushed onward in resolute defense of freedom, socialism, and unity. The rapacious, the dominating elements, and the vested interests have imposed backwardness on Fezzan. They have robbed Fezzan of both its wealth and its freedom, otherwise it would not have been backward. However, the revolution, which truly expresses the interests of the poor, wronged, and toiling classes of the people, firmly believing that backwardness should not be the lot of Fezzan and that it should enjoy its natural and legitimate right of freedom, wishes to affirm that Fezzan is worthy of liberty, of progress, and of making a positive and constructive contribution to the building of a unified and progressive society.

The time is now ripe, Brethren, for the masses of the Arab people in Fezzan to take a positive part in the battle for freedom, socialism, and unity. Slavery will no longer be imposed on the noble people of Fezzan, who shall henceforth be master on their land, free to shape their own fate. Backwardness will no longer be imposed on Fezzan. Shackles will break and barriers fall down for the Arab people in Fezzan to fuse with the other Arab peoples and build a society of welfare, freedom, and prosperity. But this cannot be achieved with words or slogans, for we must prove to the world that the masses of the people who had been fettered in the past have now come to the open to build their future with their own hands. Fezzan will no longer be a forgotten quantity as it was in the ages of darkness and backwardness. The progressive revolutionary tide will rather extend to cover its neglected villages, and to create a society of freedom and welfare in the deep and remote parts of Fezzan.

Brethren: I wish you to prove to the world that the Arab man in Fezzan, when he is liberated, can turn the barren desert into green land. I wish you to substantiate the fact that the Arab person in Fezzan, when he gains his liberty, can bring life back to our villages on which death had been imposed. I wish you to prove to the world in a practical way that the Arab people in every part of Fezzan are worthy of revolution, and that revolution is a natural right of this people, that life can flourish and progress in every part of Fezzan's distant areas, that forgotten Fezzan can catch up with the world, and that technology can make its way to every remote village of Fezzan.

This, Brethren, cannot be done for you by anyone; it can be done only by your own hands. You must rush forward from your villages, from your cottages, from the heart of the desert and of the oases to build and to shape your fate with your hands in the way you like.

Brethren: We wish that this tumultuous and profound enthusiasm should turn into the power of work and construction. We wish that these forces and these giant energies which have been unleashed from their prison should head toward production, construction, and industrialization to build a progressive Fezzan and make a positive contribution to the country's progress.

Brethren: The age of tutelage, of sovereignty over the people, of domination, and of the monopoly of rule has gone for good. With God's help, the time when your destiny was decided in palaces and dance halls is past. From now on, your fate will no longer be sealed by telephone contacts or foreign correspondence, nor will it be decided inside palaces.

Brethren: We have started our tour with Fezzan for several reasons. The good land of Fezzan invokes memories dear to our hearts. Not long ago I was with you as a student in the school nearby. I was subjected then to the same injustices as you suffer today. I sustained despotism, gross injustice, domination, and slavery. Until the recent past I was one of you, and will remain one of you, forever sharing your feelings. . . .

It is the backwardness suffered by the masses of the Arab people in Fezzan, the injustice and the slavery that were imposed on Fezzan, that inspired many officers of the armed forces to join the revolution. The officers of the armed forces come from areas very similar to Fezzan, which suffer the same backwardness, oblivion, and slavery. The officers of the armed forces who touched off the revolution of September 1st as the vanguard of this people experience your feelings. They have not come down from palaces, thrones, or other countries. Nor have they come through false heritage but rather from the people, the villages of the people, and the ranks of the people. They have come forward from the desert and the old and noble towns and villages.

Brethren: The revolution will not consist of mere visits and speeches. It will rather extend to every house, village, and cottage. The revolution will grow stronger through your daily fusion with it, and will also become more profound, firm, and extensive. It will be more capable of telling the world that what happened in Libya was not a military coup but a tumultuous popular revolution.

We shall always meet, Brethren, and our meetings, as I said, will be in the spheres of production, in every forgotten village, forest, and district of Fezzan. Our future meetings will be meetings of workers, of farmers, of soldiers, and of militants. We will not meet on forums but on production fields to turn the neglected barren desert into green lands. We will raise instruments of modern civilization in our hands instead of slogans. We will have the means to defend the people's victories and gains. We shall always meet in production fields, and until we next meet, may God's peace and blessings be upon you.

15

DESTOURIAN SOCIALISM AND NATIONAL UNITY

HABIB BOURGUIBA

I am happy and agreeably surprised to see you here in such numbers. You know how much I like to have direct contact with you and with the people. Since I realize the importance of the subjects discussed by the Party commissions and notably by the Commission for Socialist Studies, I have decided to participate in your deliberations. I know that your weekly meetings are attended with assiduity, and I appreciate the participation of elements of your elite and especially of university lecturers. The active collaboration of intellectuals and of teachers, whose task is to train tomorrow's cadres, gives me great satisfaction.

I have followed your discussions with interest. They eloquently illustrate the originality of our national movement, which has always avoided shutting itself up within the tight framework of a party in the classical sense of the term. The national movement is striving to lead the popular masses, raise them up and make of them a striking-force at the service of the nation.

Politics give rise not only to problems of ideological choice, but also to problems of strategy. For it is not enough to fix an objective; one has to consider how to attain it. Our aim was to better the condition of the Tunisian people. Its condition was far from brilliant fifty or eighty years ago. Everyone knew this, not only the campaigners but also the other citizens. But knowing so was not enough. How were we to achieve our aim? We had to work out an adequate strategy. We had to know how to navigate our ship of state and bring it safely into harbor: to liberate our country, bring about national unity and build up an efficient state. It was a vitally important and most difficult task; one that provoked heated feelings and controversies.

The calmness of your discussions confirms me in my conviction that Tunisia is in good shape. I am now sure that the work of renewal will be relentlessly pursued. In our present struggle, as in our past one, perseverance must be the rule. Our battle for development and human betterment requires the cooperation of several generations. We have started the process. From now on our efforts will be uninterrupted. The supreme objective, passed on from one generation to another, will go on arousing Tunisians to action and devotion to duty.

After listening to your speeches and observations, I wished for reasons of

Excerpts from a speech delivered on March 1, 1966, at the headquarters of the Coordination Committee for Tunis and Suburbs.

137

efficacy to take part in your discussions. It is helpful for young campaigners
and even for members of the Government to hear me express my opinions on
the numerous problems you have to discuss. I also want future generations to
benefit from what I say. Moreover, hearing you expound your viewpoints on our
choices and options may lead me to make certain adjustments to the policy I
have adopted.

MOTIVES OF MY LINE OF ACTION

In the course of your discussions, you have striven to analyze the motives of
my line of action. What led me to choose the path that was and remains mine?
What was the origin of our Destourian socialism? What is its authenticity based
on? What is my conception of national unity? Why have we rejected class
warfare? These are the questions you are asking yourselves. I am ready to give
you the necessary explanations . . . .

As I said in my speech at Cairo University, the fundamental originality of our
Destourian socialism is that it is based on the objective realities of our country.
It proscribes sectarianism and fights against doctrinaire tendencies. It is thus a
continuous creation. Its creed is the will to attain our objectives by shortcuts
and at the least cost. To do this, we must progressively overcome the resistance
inspired by myths and old customs often originating in an obscurantist past.
How can we do this? Our natural inclination is to choose persuasive means. But
we do not exclude, where necessary, recourse to coercion, but coercion well
gauged and reduced to a minimum. However that may be, Destourian socialism
is primarily concerned with objectives. The ways and means are not fixed
beforehand. They are in accordance with the development of the action and
with circumstances.

Studies have been made on the relations between different utopian and
scientific forms of socialism in the world, not to mention Stalinism and Titoism
and the borrowings made by Destourian socialism from these forms of socialism.
The theories on which they are based being highly controversial, it seems to me
that it would be a waste of time to go into them. Besides such an approach to
the question implies that we are bound to justify our Destourian socialism by
finding historical precedents for it, as if we were obliged to paint our socialism in
some Marxist color to render it acceptable. I do not agree with this
approach. . . .

THE DEVELOPMENT OF MARXISM

Revolutions and political doctrines are the work of men with a passion for
justice, of the unrelenting enemies of tyranny and oppression. Many among
them, such as Jean-Jacques Rousseau, Montesquieu, and Marx himself, were
simply theorists who never took part in any militant action but served as
inspirers and sources of reference for the revolutionary movements.

There is no doubt Marx was moved by the social injustices of his times and
the destitution of the working class. He was deeply affected. Reflecting on the
economic conditions of his century, he made a strict analysis and discovered that
the concentration of the means of production in the hands of a minority was the
root of all the ill. This concentration encouraged the exploitation of a great

number of workers by a minority of the propertied. He concluded that in order to put an end to social injustice. it was necessary to destroy capitalism.

From the dialectical standpoint, his reasoning was perfectly coherent. It is true that he who has the means of production in his hands tends to pay low wages to his workers so as to guarantee the profitability of his enterprise and ensure the maximum of profits, especially when there is an abundance of labor on the market.

Marx affirmed by extrapolation that, unless good order were established, capitalist society would inevitably evolve toward a growing proletarianization of the laboring masses and an ever-greater concentration of the means of production. He forecast among other things that small and medium-size industrial enterprises would sooner or later be absorbed by the trusts, with whom they would not be able to compete for long. Their owners would be brought down in the social scale to swell the ranks of the proletariat.

THE ROLE OF THE STATE THAT MARX DID NOT FORESEE

But Marx could not foresee that a dynamic intervention by the state would be able to break this determinism. Today, the state fixes minimum salaries, and the association of the workers in the management of the enterprise and profit-sharing with them are developing.

As for limited-liability companies, are they not financed by thousands of shareholders who no longer have the least power or right of supervision over the management of the business? They are lucky if at the end of the year they get some meager dividends. The power to take decisions has passed into the hands of directors, who, even without holding any shares, are entrusted with the direction of the company because of their competence. If incompetent men were placed at the head of these companies, they would be doomed to bankruptcy, the workers to unemployment, and the shareholders to financial ruin. This is what is happening today in the industrialized countries, such as Great Britain, the United States, France, and Germany, to which Marx referred.

If he had lived long enough, Marx would have been astonished to see his ideas spread, contrary to his forecasts, in the underdeveloped countries rather than in the industrialized ones. Who would have thought that Marxism would one day take root in Russia, a country that was far from being developed and that had industry in an embryonic state? This historical event was the outcome of military defeat.

Lenin was no doubt a socialist, a Marxist. But ideological conflicts opposed him to other tendencies no less socialist and Marxist. He was given an unhoped-for opportunity by the military collapse of the Russian Empire. The tsar, his government, and his army had lost all their prestige. Their authority had been seriously shaken. The Russian people were weary of the war. Lenin signed the Peace of Brest Litovsk.

But when after acceding to power he wanted to apply the theories of Karl Marx to the letter and set up a dictatorship of the proletariat, he found out that the proportion of workers to the total population (1–1.5 per cent) was so feeble that there could be no question of doing so. He blithely brought in the peasants. Marxism in its original form had already been left behind: "Marxism-Leninism" took its place. Karl Marx had not envisaged the joining of the peasantry to the industrial proletariat, the chief object of his preoccupations. But such details could not be allowed to stop the success of the Communist revolution. To win over the peasants to the new regime, the latifundia, the vast domains belonging to the tsarist aristocracy, were distributed to them. Land and peace then were the two factors for the success of the Soviet Communist Party.

This party was not composed merely of workers, but also of intellectuals, such as Lenin himself (who was, incidentally, of aristocratic origin), and idealistic philosophers who, distressed by the workers' condition, were calling for a rise in the living standards of the proletarians. The agrarian reform gave the peasant a plot of land. At first the results were disastrous. There was famine because of the bad exploitation of agricultural land. These are the inevitable consequences of all hastily conceived land reform. It was then necessary to regroup the peasants into sovkhozes and kolkhozes. Friction then developed between the authorities and the peasants, who, just after winning their freedom, had to submit to the exorbitant instructions of the Party. There were disputes, often violent ones, over the choice of crops. Hatred was cultivated, and blood watered the land. Anyone calling the official doctrine into question was accused of deviationism and treason. Economic problems were dealt with by gunshot and peoples tribunals were called to the rescue. And the bourgeoisie, the scapegoat for every failure, was denounced in connection with everything.

The authorities had to go back on their steps. The period of the New Economic Policy gave the peasants a breather. And today the authorities seem to understand that profits may be an objective criterion for economic efficiency.

Over forty years later, they were in the same position. For the state to keep its authority, it had to give the people an enemy to destroy. In a carefully maintained atmosphere of war, successive foes were handed over to public vengeance. When the Tsarists, Mensheviks, and deviationists had been thus liquidated, imperialism, colonialism, and America were denounced. Now we see the government of Peking holding up the threat of American aggression against China. Who believes in it? By maintaining a state of alarm, a people can be kept under the yoke of a merciless dictatorship. And the workers, for whom the revolution was carried out, are the victims.

THE TUNISIAN APPROACH

Our approach to the problem is quite different. The reason why we did not make the same mistakes after coming to power is perhaps that the dominant trait in my character is acute sensitivity. I have learned that the other day Mr. Chedli Fitouri said in a declaration, "The President must have rare sensitivity." He was right. Since my earliest youth I have always suffered in the face of injustice and tyranny. I am not speaking merely of the acts of injustice committed by the French against Tunisians and by capitalists or employers against the workers, but also of the injustice of which women were the victims when they were kept in an inferior status by men.

I have this sensitivity in regard to all Tunisians without discrimination. There is often talk of the "petty bourgeoisie" of small traders and small proprietors and how to distinguish between the small and the large so as to integrate the former and exclude the latter. Such twaddle is part of Communist propaganda and can have no sense in Tunisia.

At a certain period in this country, injustice and exploitation prevailed. Furthermore, relations between Tunisians were often somewhat tainted with scorn. The citizens of the capital despised the provincials and the Soussians despised the inhabitants of the neighboring villages. This was perhaps a sign of underdevelopment. As for women they were the object of the utmost disdain. What did it matter if one repudiated one's wife after thirty years of marriage? (I have already told you the story of the man who, near the end of his life, after being married for twenty-five years, repudiated his wife, who was for him an encumbrance and the companion of his bad days, so as to be more sure of deserving paradise by ending his days in Mecca near to the Prophet.)

This was the situation in Tunisia, a situation to which no sensitive being could remain indifferent. As for me, experience sharpened my sensitivity. I sat side-by-side with French and Italian pupils at the *lycée*. Then I lived abroad, where a certain justice prevailed. How could we have admitted of its being otherwise in Tunisia? Under the pretext of French domination of our country or that might is right?

Because of my acute sensitivity, because I suffered so much from the spectacle of injustice, I sympathized with the unhappiness of others. In this respect I was just like the trade-unionist Mohammed Ali or any other worker. I was quite different from certain Old Destourians who did not condescend to mix with the down-at-heel. According to them, it was better to keep the working class and ordinary folk out of politics, for which only the genteel were fitted.

Why should I be called bourgeois? I come from the Sahel, from a modest family that toiled and suffered. Maybe it was this life of struggle that stamped me. After Zarrouk's punitive expedition in the Sahel, my family was ruined. My father found nothing better to do than enlist in the army. For twenty-five years he lived away from Monastir, his native town. His mode of living was modest. At the most he kept up appearances.

What distinguished my family from what are called the masses was not the degree of wealth but rather a sense of dignity. For anyone living in need and seeking nevertheless to keep up appearances has to make sure that his comportment and outward appearance inspire respect and esteem. Only the slovenly let themselves neglect their appearance — and being a worker is no excuse. It is necessary to teach everyone — worker, peasant, or bourgeois — the notion of self-respect, cleanliness, and good appearance. Have we not also seen certain heads of state sporting negligent attire, to say the least, so as to pose as revolutionaries? For my part, I am no partisan of such mystification.

Frequently, families belonging to what are called the middle classes have to face up to need. They do so with dignity. Whatever the slenderness of their resources they succeed by dint of economy in ensuring for their members a decent standard of living. I was brought up in such a background. It in no way differed from that in which many of our fellow citizens live in the towns and in the country. I owe my sensitivity to this background. I have always fought for the permanent elimination of injustice and destitution. It is a daily combat, and one that is hard and difficult.

Injustice appears in the most diverse forms, from that of men toward women, to that of the French gendarme toward the "native auxiliary" left to do all the dirty tasks and treated with the utmost disdain.

THE MOST REVOLTING FORM OF INJUSTICE

But the most revolting form of injustice is that of subjecting a whole people to the colonialist yoke. We were determined to attack this injustice. The colonial administration with all its accompanying humiliations had implanted itself everywhere with such subtlety that Tunisians were no longer even aware of the fact. Tunisians accepted their lot as if it had been inherent in the very nature of existence. Even more, they had become so used to colonialism that they came to have apprehensions about the end of the colonial era and wonder what would happen if the Protectorate disappeared. This reminds one of the attitude of emancipated slaves suddenly left to fend for themselves. The very notion of freedom was losing all attraction for them, as if they had been hesitating to run in the great adventure of life and shoulder their own responsibilities. They had become used to being led by one potentate or another — the resident general, the civil controller, the gendarme, the qaid, the sheikh, and so on. With the passing of time, they had come to accept abuse of authority, humiliation, and extortion, which are the by-products of foreign domination.

But another and even graver reason made me resolved to undertake and dedicate my life to this great adventure: the fate that was waiting for the Tunisian people if the efforts of the Protectorate went on unchecked; a fate even gloomier than its lot on the eve of French occupation.

The Protectorate was in fact a machine carefully adjusted to crush Tunisian personality.

When I published a study on the budget in the first number of *Action Tunisienne,* on November 1, 1931, I was endeavoring to make Tunisians aware of this process of annihilating the national personality. I also wanted it to be known in France that we had discerned the purposes of the Protectorate. I remember the figures of speech I used in my tours through Tunisia and especially in the Sahel. I compared the Protectorate to an oil-press, which slowly and inexorably crushes the filters full of olive pulp to extract the oil. The ultimate aim of the operation is to transform the olives full of oil into dehydrated cakes. I told the Sahelians that we were like the olives in the oil-press, controlled from outside. Whatever we did we could not escape from the grip for as long as we were controlled from outside; our position was bound to lead to an even gloomier future, if things continued in this way.

Certain persons came to tell me about abuses committed by the authorities such as the sheikhs, the qaids, and the civil controllers. I asked them to join the party. Some of them showed their fear of being arrested or losing their jobs if they joined, or tried to convince me that their cases were urgent and required immediate intervention so as to put an end to an injustice or right a wrong. I then insisted on the necessity of joining the ranks of the party, which alone could assemble the popular masses and change the course of events.

This is how I analyzed the situation in the country and how I tried to re-educate the Tunisian people. On the one hand, I showed the fate being prepared for it by the Protectorate and, on the other hand, the connection between the Protectorate and the abuses every citizen suffered from in his daily life. I showed the link there was between the need for freedom and the action of the party. I assured my listeners that the day we were strong enough to recover our sovereignty the foreign hands operating the oil-press would let go their grip.

Tunisians were far from seeing the correlation between the end of oppression and adherence to the Neo-Destour. They were not accustomed to such language. The leaders of the Old Destour were careful to avoid such reasoning. They were content to write fine articles in such newspapers as *La Voix du Tunisien,* in which they complained about the discriminating salary paid to Tunisian civil servants, the lack of street lighting in the medina or the bad functioning of a street fountain in some "native" quarter. This was their conception of the struggle.

Meanwhile, I strove to explain in word and writing that we had lost control of the levers of the state and that, instead of bewailing our lot, we should get organized so as to win back control of the levers of the state.

So the sensitivity I spoke of before gave place to reflection. Once the danger had been seen and the situation analyzed, the objective could be defined. I studied in a rational manner the path to follow and drew up a plan of action. Certain persons could not understand what connection there could be between recovering national sovereignty and our visits to the Souassi, Frashish, and Hamama tribes. They esteemed that these bedouins understood nothing about politics and had no role to play. I thought, on the contrary, that it was necessary to awaken the consciousness of the masses so as to mobilize them for the fight for freedom, and that we had to keep in direct and permanent contact with them.

These contacts enabled me to raise from a heterogeneous people shock troops capable of standing up to the authority of the Protectorate. What matter that the timorous gave way at the first ordeal! By our untiring educational effort, a greater number of campaigners came to swell our ranks. I was thus able to launch an assault against the Protectorate. It began with street demonstrations and meetings. I was arrested many times. I was deported to some remote corners and detained in some prisons in Tunisia and France. I did not yield.

My methodical approach enabled me to detect the regime's weaknesses, to work out a long-term strategy that brought my action to its culmination, that is, to the total independence of Tunisia and to full and complete sovereignty.

The situation required a mind capable of translating sentiment into thought and thought into action, and of resolutely continuing this action until final success. But even during the hardest moments of the struggle, even from my jail, where I was awaiting death, I felt, as a fighter, satisfaction at having performed my duty until the end, with neither weakness nor surrender of principles.

Thus, at the outset, there was one sensible man, who "sensed" the danger. He spoke to his fellow-citizens to make them aware of the danger threatening their existence as individuals and as a nation, but also and above all to mobilize them as instruments of their own liberation. To lead his people to freedom, this man did not wait for liberators to come from outside, from the Sublime Porte or Emperor Wilhelm II. He devoted his life to the happiness of his people. Responsibly and loyally, he applied this method of informing Tunisians about their duties, their rights and the part they were called upon to play in the life of their country. As an example, I shall only mention a young campaigner from Porto Farina, who said to his executioners before his execution: "I was expecting to die. My blood is the tribute that Tunisia must pay in order to achieve independence."

Statements like this are significant. They show a high morale. I am sure that this young man had attended more than one meeting, that he had heard me speak, that he had observed my attitude during the trials of strength, that he had grasped the spirit of our movement and the importance of what was at stake. This is why he consented to make the supreme sacrifice and faced death with the calmness given by faith.

During these ordeals, certain campaigners weakened, but those who remained steadfast were entirely won over to us. They showed themselves ready to make every sacrifice for the cause to which they devoted themselves. They clearly saw the objective. They knew what difficulties and what obstacles remained. They were convinced that, though they themselves might not attain the goal, their sacrifice would certainly facilitate the task of those who took over.

In 1952, when I prepared campaigners for the final struggle, I told them it was necessary to pay the blood tax. The fight had to be accepted, even if the blood of our combatants flowed. France had to be forced to make the supreme choice, by proving that, despite the disproportion between the forces involved, despite manhunts, summary condemnations, barbarous repression, and so on, the Tunisian people were resolved to hold out to the end. Forced to choose the lesser evil, France could not but come to terms with Bourguiba. Around me, people were skeptical. But my resolution was unshakable. "It will be hard," I said.

We should have to hold out as long as necessary, and this might be a long time. Nevertheless, victory would be ours in the end. While France had might on her side, we had the strength of resistance and perseverance on ours. On every occasion, I quoted the example of the rope that eventually wears down the lip of the well.

In this way, we spent more than twenty years struggling to make the French leaders change their policy and negotiate with the Neo-Destour. When they had agreed to come to terms, a new plan of action was put into application: it consisted in facilitating concessions from the adversary by seeing to it that his legitimate interests were safeguarded. Everyone was satisfied. The stick and the carrot proved effective.

Our action therefore demanded tenacity and patience; if the adversary had succeeded in eluding us, it would have been inefficacious. This is why we always tried to convince them that, far from solving the problem, repression only made it worse.

Here there is a constant feature of my action. In actual fact, my calculations allowed for repression. Just like a button being pressed, my arrest was to set in motion a carefully constructed machine, which would be ready to function. Our campaigners were vigilant. We understood each other perfectly. The time had come for direct action. The imprisonment of Bourguiba meant war between France and the Neo-Destour. We had to remain lucid, for this war would only finish in the event of agreement between the two antagonists. At the first signs of willingness to negotiate on the part of our adversary, we were ready to exploit the situation.

Thus, by our own means and without the slightest help from any alliance, we succeeded in standing up to a great power and progressively making it come to terms with us. In this way, we opened the path of emancipation to other peoples.

This method, known as the policy of stages, or Bourguibism, is a form of psychological warfare. It was necessary to take into account the state of mind not only of Tunisians but also of our adversary. Firmness and flexibility had to be kept in due proportion.

We readily admit there was a fair element of luck in our successes. This providential good fortune was that the very man who set the movement going survived every ordeal. Need I tell you, I did not imagine it would be possible? However, I was thoroughly convinced that my strategy and tactics were effective and that they were the only valid ones in the national and international context. In a letter to Dr. Thameur written from Fort Saint-Nicolas, I stated my views. I thought I would never leave prison, and I wanted to warn my comrades.

However, fortunately for my country, I survived the vicissitudes of the struggle. Of course, my death would not have diminished the intrinsic value of my method in any way. Theoretically, it appears perfectly logical; in practice, it seems to be easy, with its alternation of firmness and flexibility. But this would be to neglect the intangible factors that sometimes govern a man's behavior without his knowledge: the fear that grips him at the very moment he launches a trial of strength; recourse to Byzantinism to excuse setbacks; refusal of the adversary's invitation to act, falsely termed "provocation." But this was of little importance; I had confidence in the people, knowing their combativity. To me, Tunisians are all Bourguibas and will always be able to make the best of a bad situation.

This was the basis on which our great epic, this stirring national adventure, was conducted from 1931 to 1964, like a game of chess. Remember: 1931 was the year of the triumphant celebration of the Protectorate's fiftieth anniversary. After that, the country's history was marked by a long series of struggles followed by truces, which went on until checkmate in the form of total decolonization.

Once independence had been recognized, we realized that we were not at the end of our troubles. Our independence was in form only. We indeed had a national government, but French troops still occupied the country, our economy was an appendage of the French economy, and we were being stifled by one-way customs legislation. And over and above all, anarchy prevailed in the country, and was only held in check by French force. There was a general scramble: the fellaga were getting out of hand and each claimed to have defeated France. We were on the edge of the precipice and in danger of losing the fruit of all our sacrifices.

PROBLEMS OF VICTORY

It was inevitable that, in these circumstances, the country should have experienced what I have termed the problems of victory. It is historically true that there were injustices and that exploitation was reintroduced. The exploitation of the people by colonization was replaced by another form of exploitation it would be idle to deny. Here the Marxist analysis has proved exact to a certain extent. Old customs, old economic structures, especially agricultural structures, and archaic modes of production encouraged the circulation of wealth under conditions that were inadmissible to one's reason and revolting to one's conscience. There were what I have called "strategic positions" secured by some people in the distribution circuits. Some individual had only to pick up his phone to have large quantities of goods at his disposal. He laid down the law in the market by distributing goods in accordance with his personal interest. He did not hesitate to participate in black market activities. The consumer paid docilely without asking where his money went. The state was quite indifferent to all this. The public authorities did not even consider the question of whether they had anything to say about the production-distribution circuit. Goods circulated freely and reached the consumer only after costly detours. In this way, injustices crept in without anyone realizing that he was still being exploited as he had formerly been by foreign settlers. Moreover, Tunisians had not noticed they were undergoing colonialist exploitation until it was quite late. The settlers had not taken the Tunisians' cloaks or cows from them. Their method was much more subtle. Dispossession was brought about by budgetary means: to pay their taxes, Tunisians had to sell their cloaks or their cows and the fiscal income passed to the other side. In the meantime, Tunisians and Frenchmen made friends, without the former ever suspecting that the latter lived by the sweat of Tunisian brows and without perceiving the causes of their continued regression.

There were also economic reasons for this regression. The economic structures inherited from colonization caused bottlenecks: the structures of production, of distribution and of the circulation of wealth often allowed one class to be exploited by another. This had to be changed. Some wholesalers operated in Tunis; others lived in Marseilles. They all gained a fat living from the small girl or small boy who went to the local grocer to buy an ounce or so of tea: small profits make large fortunes.

Once independence had been reconquered, our movement might have come to accept the situation. This would have been inadmissible. When injustice comes to the notice of anyone in a position of responsibility, he must put an end to it. Of course, we are all Tunisians and we are all of us free from foreign domination. This is no reason for us to accept another form of national domination, this time with all the damage that may result for the nation as a whole. So to put an end to the matter I had imports handled by a state company and I fixed a reasonable profit margin for traders. The huge profits, amounting to hundreds of millions, will now go to building up industrial and agricultural enterprises, instead of swelling the fortunes of wholesalers and brokers.

We shall thus have remedied a catastrophic situation without using violence. It is indeed a revolution whose aim is to banish injustice and exploitation and install equity and true fraternity. There is no need to proclaim an abstract principle *a priori* or to look for the solution in Karl Marx's *Capital*. My method is to refer to the facts of the Tunisian situation.

Likewise for production. Certain forms of production give rise to pauperism and dry up the sources of production. We therefore had to reorganize the system of land tenure. Vast areas of land were abandoned because they were habous lands or indivisible. Because of disagreement between the co-heirs, none of whom consented to make any sacrifices that might profit the others, scores of thousands of acres were condemned to sterility. As I was responsible for the country's interests, I could not allow such a substantial source of wealth to be wasted. I therefore abolished habous property and shared out the lands which had now reverted to the status of straightforward property. Everything that stands in the way of the development of production must be done away with.

It is however not enough to destroy obstacles: production must be stimulated at the same time. This is a creative task. Mere encouragement such as raising wages or prices is not enough. When justice is established, production is stimulated. The people are convinced of the government's sincerity and sense of responsibility. They understand that the government uses its power of compulsion, not for the benefit of one class only but for the benefit of the entire nation. And the stronger the people's conviction, the greater is their enthusiasm.

This brought us to adopt socialism, more especially a humanitarian type of socialism, and we decided to solve our problems progressively, on the basis of existing structures and taking account of Tunisia's special circumstances. We first of all had to encourage production and see to it that incomes were distributed with greater justice. We then had to organize the utilization of production in a suitable manner. This last item is very important, for production may in its turn be transformed into a means of production. This is the problem of reinvestment. It is important that investment lead to as high a rate of production as possible, so that new wealth be created.

Hence the need for a policy of austerity: consumption is reduced so that a larger share of production can be capitalized instead of being hoarded. If an owner is unable to exploit his capital, others more qualified can replace him. The accumulation of capital as practiced at one time by capitalists in liberal regimes may be undertaken either by the state or by private persons in agreement with the state. The use of capital and the utilization of production must be brought under state direction. A producer may be allowed to dispose of his entire production; new services may also be assigned to the enterprise. In such cases, the state contents itself with directing and coordinating economic activities. Why go further when the heads of enterprises willingly follow the advice they are given, because of its utility? Is it really necessary to hang people in order to deserve the title of revolutionary? Frankly, I do not think so, so long as they show their willingness and work within the framework of the general interest.

NATIONAL UNITY

The question of national unity, that is, the collective march of all the "social categories" of a nation toward common objectives, arises in this connection. I must here mention my dislike of the term "class" and other such labels that correspond to nothing. In fact, as I have already said, I do not know quite whether I am bourgeois or worker. The movement I had the good fortune to impress on the country throughout thirty-five years assembled people of towns and country without distinction. Read the names of our martyrs again: they came from all social categories. Only one category is missing: the Communists; not one of them will be found on the list.

You would not wish me, now that we are independent, to seek out the "wicked bourgeoisie" and give them a bad time! Of course not. We are all of us here united fraternally and I shall never consent to destroy our national unanimity and exclude certain elements of the nation in order to deserve the title of Marxist socialist. I do not despair of men without having put them to the test. I do not believe in the class struggle. I do not believe in fratricidal struggles. Everyone is free to try to make a reasonable profit, in accordance with his personal tendencies. It is quite legitimate. But at the same time we are engaged in developing among citizens a love of their neighbor. For each of us — and this is a feature of man's superiority over animals — has an altruistic side to him, as a result of which he tends to devote himself to his fellowman and give what we call "God's share." There is an element of sentiment in man. Was it not that element — the heart's share — that led to the sacrifice made by our martyrs, who fell at Ghar el Melh, Moknine, Ksar Hellal, Monastir, and nearly everywhere else? Man is so made that he is able to feel real pleasure when he places himself at the service of others in the name of justice and charity.

We want to cultivate these virtues among the Tunisian people. We want to make them become aware of these noble values. And we have had comforting reports from the workers and the bourgeoisie, the well-to-do and the more modest classes. Besides, selfishness, opportunism, and the tendency to exploit others are not the monopoly of the bourgeoisie. We have sometimes come across these traits among workers and even among certain trade unionists who do not let slip any opportunity to exploit their unfortunate comrades more ferociously than the worst of employers would do.

The question therefore is one of men, not of class. The bourgeoisie and the proletariat, the ideas of Karl Marx and Lenin are all outmoded notions! What is really in question is the intellectual short-sightedness of certain individuals obsessed by their immediate interests, who in spite of their comfortable position try, for example, to transfer currency clandestinely. They think they are doing well for themselves. In actual fact, they are sapping the foundations of the state that protects them. I should also mention those swindlers who export crates of rotten fruit. These various traffickers are now pondering their misdeeds in jail.

We must everywhere and always raise citizens' moral and intellectual level so that they understand that their own interest coincides with the collective interest.

FRATERNITY AND JUSTICE SHALL TRIUMPH

This is the essential point. When this truth is understood and accepted and the sense of fraternity and justice triumphs, a fine human mutation will have been accomplished. Without this harmony, as we well know, the national struggle would not have culminated in victory. Today, we have far greater means than before, and our greatest victory is indeed this shoulder-to-shoulder contribution to the effort of development. When wealth is distributed, each will want to have his share, but we shall have been sufficiently united by a common destiny to avoid clashes with sordid individual interests.

Substituting the dictatorship of the proletariat for the dictatorship of capital does not mean that dictatorship itself is abolished. Both forms crush human dignity.

Woolly-minded thinkers, reformers looking for guinea pigs, clutter the world up with theories. For our part, we prefer to open up people's minds. For us, the dignity of man is at stake. We think man is perfectible, and we refuse to believe that there are men who are irremediably bad. We first of all give them the benefit of the doubt, and we make the necessary effort of persuasion in order to strengthen our ranks. In the battle we are waging, we need these ranks to be closer and minds to be more open. We thus hope that our collective effort will lead to great human betterment. Our battle against underdevelopment is intended to liberate man from the dominion of hunger, ignorance, and sordid individualism.

I am convinced that this meeting and others in the future will help to unite our ranks and show the aims and outlines of our action with greater clarity and precision. They will also help to convince the people that state and Party leaders are not working to serve their own interests or their class' interests — that is, if they indeed belong to a class.

In this connection, we should mention the complaints of Communists who make a great fuss about demanding trade union liberties in non-Communist countries, although these same liberties do not exist in Communist countries. If we adopted Communism, there would no longer be any question of liberty at all. A trade unionist is a citizen like anyone else. His membership in a union for the defense of his corporate interests does not relieve him of his obligations toward his country. Communist propaganda tries to detach him from his country and bind him to one class in opposition to the other classes in the nation.

In reality, these class distinctions are often arbitrary. If workers constitute an antibourgeois class in their trade unions, what are we to say of teachers and civil servants who are trade unionists? Are they not bourgeois in reality?

These considerations of class are therefore paradoxical. They are harmful. They foster the hatred of workers toward the wealthy and even toward intellectuals. Is it not a fact that in some countries intellectuals are even taken for impostors? For, having kept intellectuals out of office, such regimes have proved incapable of managing the affairs of state.

At all levels, in the government and in the factory, in the civil service and in industry, management requires a good stock of the necessary knowledge. What is primordial is proper qualification and competence. The amount of wealth is immaterial to the question. It would be inconceivable to have an ordinary laborer at the head of a state, on the pretext that he belonged to the working class.

It is quite aberrant to exclude a valuable man from office because he belongs to the bourgeoisie and put in his place an officer or former resistance fighter on the pretext that these latter belong to some revolutionary movement. Through incompetence, they would be paralyzed and thus incapable of solving the problems facing them and deteriorating their country's situation. Owing to their limited imagination, they would be powerless to struggle against unemployment and poverty, although their country had substantial natural wealth.

Those one tends to regard as privileged people are in fact people who have degrees and the qualifications required for key posts in the state, and it is thanks to their competence that national affairs are administered properly.

It is our constant concern to train competent people. Our success is ensured by the renewal of the party's cadres and the strengthening of our militant ardor through recruitment from the rising generations.

The national movement must not remain the monopoly of "veteran campaigners" who were imprisoned in the past. New faces, young people who did not suffer imprisonment but who have aptitudes and a part to play must in their turn break through and accede to posts of responsibility.

Thanks to our unity and to the militant spirit that I guard vigilantly and that has strong roots in our past of struggle, we have been able to undertake this immense task and give it a human imprint. Through our concern for efficacity, man's condition must be improved and his betterment insured. This is the ultimate aim of our combat, which is also intended as a contribution to the progress of human civilization.

16

MISSION OF THE ISLAMIC 'ULEMA

'ALLAL AL-FASSI

"In the Name of Allah, the Merciful, the Compassionate. Call thou to the way of thy Lord with wisdom and good admonition, and dispute with them in the better way. Surely thy Lord knows very well those who have gone astray from His way, and He knows very well those who are guided."

I would like to thank the Department of Higher Education in the Ministry of National Education for organizing public lectures in which the 'ulema discuss the problems and means of renovating Islamic culture in the light of contemporary human evolution and in accordance with the spirit of Islamic education as perceived by the Great Educator [the Prophet], peace be upon him. In this lecture, I will deal with the role of the 'ulema or the objectives and methods essential to their [holy] message.

It seems that the role of the 'ulema has always been the same whether in ancient or modern times; it is closely related to the nature of the Prophet's message. The means which they use to correct and elucidate distortions in human thought are an integral part of this message which they explain and defend. It is appropriate here to quote a hadith [saying of the Prophet] in which the Prophet describes the 'ulema: "The 'ulema are the heirs of the prophets. They [however] inherited nothing — not even a dinar or *dirham* — except knowledge; a great deal would accrue to him who partakes from their knowledge."

Since the prophets had preached the doctrine and delivered the message, it is the duty of the 'ulema not only to preserve this heritage and transmit it honestly but also to defend it by using and innovating different means. The Prophet said the following regarding this [in a hadith]: "This Faith [Islam] shall be delivered by the successors who would defend it against the distortions of exaggeration and the abrogations of ignorance." This hadith has thus defined the duties of the 'ulema in three main ways:

1. To correct any deviation from religion that might be caused by over-zeal for the Faith itself.

Speech delivered to a conference of Moroccan 'ulema, in September, 1959; translated and published here by courtesy of Hassan Abdin Mohammed.

2. To expurgate plagarisms of liars who infuse in the religion things that do not belong in it and that are contradictory to the concept of Unity [of Allah].
3. To correct the assumption of the ignorant who, by seeking to satisfy their instincts, undermine their own beliefs.

This presupposes, naturally, that the 'ulema themselves are knowledgeable in Islam and are acquainted with other religious and human ideas of different times. They would have to learn about human beings, languages, historical and technological developments, all aspects of human civilizations and the way these civilizations shape human achievements. The message of Islam, accordingly, becomes a core around which knowledge, scientific discoveries, innovations, and constructive methods revolve; then religion and culture become one and the same.

If we study the history of Arabic thought in the early Islamic period – the period of the brilliant renaissance in the sciences – we will find that religion was a strong motivation behind almost every achievement . . . . The revolutionary reform that Islam created in Arab society was in itself a pool of new knowledge to which the Prophet was the first school [the first to understand and teach this new knowledge]. From this school came the first 'ulema, who dispersed themselves to deliver the message and spread knowledge. Shortly afterwards, and due to the rising need for understanding means, objectives, and reasons, new Islamic sciences began to crystallize and Arabic thought began to bloom; the use of new arguments and new evidence against adversaries became imperative. Philosophical and abstract sciences began to form and, as a result, the interaction of different human cultures was made possible under the Islamic states.

Many 'ulema and Orientalists later on have paid great attention to the impact of Islam on Arabic knowledge; they have agreed that religion [Islam] was not only the direct stimulus for the creation and perpetuation of a healthy scholarly atmosphere in Islamic society but also for the assimilation of previous knowledge. In his book *The Aspects of Arabic Thought,* Dr. Kamal al-Yazji, a young Arab writer, confirms this conclusion; in fact, he reaffirms what George Bastide, I. Goldzieher, and al-Farabi concluded much earlier.

If you understand this, you would then know that using every possible [legitimate] means to find the truth was in fact a tradition of the Prophet, the caliphs, and the Companions; do not ever think that any of these sciences is taboo, because they are essentially a way of finding truth. Accordingly, it is pointless to contend that science is contrary to Islam, because such contentions are obviously groundless.

There is no doubt that the Qarawiyin 'ulema are conscious of the necessity of using all means for renovation; they have also recognized the impact of Islam on the sciences. The late Mustafa Sadiq al-Rafi'ay made the following comment on the contribution of Islam to the scientific discoveries: "The Holy Qoran was the main reason for the scientific achievements of the Islamic world; most of the sciences have drawn from the Qoran in one way or another. The commoners of the early times of Islam pressed the 'ulema to interpret religion in the light of the new theoretical sciences . . . to establish a link between them and the Qoran."[1]

However, I do not subscribe to al-Rafi'ay's last interpretation about the commoners' pressure on the 'ulema; indeed, the opposite seems to be the case . . . and, in fact, the author recognizes this earlier.

Nevertheless, the dispute between the Salafi 'ulema and the theoreticians relates to a different question: Should we stick to the letter of the Qoran and the Sunnah and thus concede that we can add nothing to our traditional knowledge or would it not be more useful to devise new means of solving our problems and improving the understanding of the Islamic community? This difference in the degree of our certainty is obviously a difference in the degree of our knowledge.

The Qoran, which had great impact on the invention and diversification of the sciences, would not disapprove of or frown upon new approaches and methods for the attainment of knowledge. Actually, it is the Qoran that enlightened the Muslim intellect and induced the individual to decipher the secrets of the universe.

By living up to their responsibilities, the early 'ulema opened new horizons for Islamic thought and devised an empirical method quite different from that upon which Aristotelean logic is based. Mr. Briffault, in his book *The Making of Humanity,* stated that Bacon had learned the Arabic language and sciences and made little original contribution himself in introducing Europe to the empirical method. Bacon was simply one of those scholars who transmitted Islamic knowledge and methodology to Christian Europe. Briffault also added that empirical method of the Arabs spread in the times of Bacon . . . [and] people in Europe were very interested in it.[2]

Therefore the need to explain the legacy of Islam . . . had induced the 'ulema to investigate, above all, the truth of knowledge. On the other hand, the message of Islam itself had liberated Arabic thought from all traditional restrictions and limitations; it made it capable of distinguishing between what conforms with rationality and what is revered simply because it constitutes an inherited tradition.

The scholars of human civilization have agreed that the distinctive feature of Arabic civilization lies in its ability to incorporate and assimilate diverse aspects of knowledge using empirical methods. The Arabs have excelled in innovations but also in intelligent and honest copying. Georges Bastide summarizes this concept as follows: "The effectiveness of any civilization is primarily due to the interaction of environment and culture in every stage of human experience. The absence of this effectiveness is conducive to savagery."[3] This means that the efforts of the Arabs were devoted to the employment of human capabilities to develop a high morality; in other words, to move toward a better realization of the self. Nature should act as a catalyst in the process of building a creative civilization. The sciences are useless unless they help reveal the value of human experience; yet science should not be used to falsify any of the human values. The objective is therefore to promote the success of human experience, which starts from observation and depends, ultimately, on the intellect for the evaluation of different phenomena.

The Prophet's prophecy of a community where the 'ulema would revive the Faith and reform society did not mean that Islamic society will not degenerate; it simply affirmed the permanence of the Islamic doctrine that is embodied in the Qoran. It is the believers who need a continuous effort if they wish to

remain in the high level bestowed on them by Islam. The reformers can only sow
the seeds of reform that will not come to fruition without the involvement and
participation of the whole nation; collective efforts will undoubtedly enforce
individual efforts, and reform can take place only when corruption in society has
reached a point beyond which reform becomes an urgent need.

Some of the 'ulema have lost track of the correct Sunnah, Arabic thought,
and Islamic civilization. They contented themselves with false abstractions put
forward and diffused by nations hostile to Islam in order to disrupt and weaken
society. However, this did not, fortunately, affect the important sources of
Islam, because the Qoran had been compiled earlier, and no one doubts that its
present form is the authentic and original one. Similarly, the hadith is available
in its abrogated and correct versions. Whatever alterations that have been made
were in details and additions that resulted from controversies. These controversies
led sometimes to distortions, which are mentioned by the prophet in the hadith
quoted above.

Some sociologists of religion argue that the evolution of religions affects even
the doctrine and its rituals. But if this is true in actual reality about Christianity,
where controversies have questioned the doctrine, it certainly is not the case in
Islam. In Islam, according to the *ijma'* [consensus] of different sects and viewpoints, the core of the doctrine is the Unity of Allah and the Message of the
Prophet. Goldzieher accepted this when he said: "It is impossible to equate the
Islamic beliefs with the basic religious elements in any Christian church." There
are no synods in Islam in which doctrinal or religious controversies could be
resolved and principles established to be binding on all Muslims; also there is no
priesthood or religious hierarchy in Islam and no one single interpretation of
holy texts has won unanimity. In the introduction to his translation of *The
Principles of the Sociology of Religions,* Dr. Mohammed Gasim challenges
Bastide's contention that the Islamic beliefs have undergone a process of
evolution.[4] According to Gasim, the absence of a religious hierarchy in Islam is
mainly because the relationship between the individual believer and Allah is
direct; it does not require an intermediary. The author has also pointed to the
tolerance among Muslims to prove that controversies did not in fact question the
basic beliefs but stemmed, instead, from difference on details which were open
for *ijtihad* [exercise of individual judgment in interpreting Qoranic texts and
hadith].

In recent times many 'ulema in the Islamic world have tried to investigate the
reasons for the dormancy of Islamic societies. Among them was Sheikh
Mohammed Abduh, who made the following remarks after his tour of the
Ottoman Empire:

1. The Islamic peoples have accepted ideas which were alien to Islam; these
   ideas were introduced by foreigners as well as conjurers. Moreover, the
   people have accepted [uncritically] all that has been transmitted from
   earlier times and consequently they deprived themselves of the right to use
   their own judgment.
2. Another reason for the stagnation was the tyranny of caliphs and Muslim
   leaders who denied the people freedom of thought. They were encouraged
   in this by hypocritical 'ulema, who either commended the rulers' actions
   or misinterpreted the shari'a to justify political expediency.[5]

Unless they return to the true religion, the Islamic peoples will not regain their pride and dignity. The return will be made possible only by the reopening of the "gates" of *ijtihad* and the repudiation of tyranny and absolutism. To believe in Allah would obviously require a repudiation of atheism. Mohammed Abduh once said, "I have often called the attention of the people to two important questions: Firstly, the liberation of thought from the shackles of imitation and classifical interpretations of religion that go back to the period before controversies [schisms]. Religion should be viewed as one of the checks and balances on the inadequacies of the human mind. Secondly, the reform of the Arabic language."[6]

Abduh also added. "I have also directed the attention of the people to an important issue so often neglected despite its paramountcy in social life, namely, to distinguish between the right of the government to obedience and the right of the people to justice."[7]

All these factors — a return to the original sources of Islam, *ijtihad,* and the realization of the distinction between the rights of the state and those of the individual — will make possible a new era of constructive culture described by Goldzieher in the last chapters of his book about the schools of Islamic exegesis, as a product of the *salafiya* movement.[8] Dr. Mohammed al-Sabhi confirms Goldzieher's conclusion by arguing that the school of Mohammed Abduh was different from the revivalist movement in India, because the former was an independent and evolutionary development of Islamic society.[9] Nevertheless, revivalists in Islam, whether Indian or Arabic, have always entertained the same objectives. They have sought to restore the original sources of religion, to liberate the people from superstition, to reopen the "gates" of *ijtihad,* and to look for a new consensus based on religious principles reconcilable with the facts of human development in technology and economics.

Unfortunately, there was hardly enough time for the Islamic peoples to rethink their situation. Western colonialism, with its material resources, industrial capabilities, and subtle rhetoric devastated the Islamic world; the latter was faced with the problem of defending its independence and resisting colonial attacks on its spiritual values. The social institutions of colonialism were by far more destructive than the military and political institutions.

It was the British who started the campaign in India; they organized a movement that sought to replace religion by secular ideologies. They found in Sayid Ahmad Khan an able agitator and collaborator. The missionaries had also prepared a handful of young Indians who endorsed colonialism by glorifying Western culture and degrading that of Islam. The colonialist campaign was extended to the Arab countries; France used the Sufi sheikhs and some of the 'ulema, while Russia successfully directed native movements in the Soviet Union according to a master plan.

Apart from its role of economic exploitation, which has always been resented and resisted by the colonized, colonialism succeeded in idealizing and perpetuating the image of the West. Western experiences have become — or rather have been made — a standard according to which things and ideas of the East [Orient] should be evaluated. This is intellectual slavery, which to many Islamic thinkers is even worse than the Crusades.

The Islamic peoples have awakened today to the fact that their sons are as far away from their religion as the Spaniards were at the beginning of the ninth century. Father Ijaro described the Spanish situation as follows:

My Christian brethren have a deep appreciation of Arabic poetry and fiction. They study the works of Islamic theologians and philosophers, not to criticize them but to copy their style. Today you can hardly find any of our scholars who can read the Latin commentaries on the Holy Books. Alas! Our Christian youth are ignorant of any literature or language apart from Arabic; they read and study Arabic books with earnest and enthusiasm. They build complete libraries at great expense and do not cease praising the heritage of the Arabs. On the other hand, if you mention the Christian books they protest that these are not worthy of their attention. Alas! The Christians have forgotten their language; not even one in a thousand is capable of writing a letter to a friend in correct Latin. But if they have to write in Arabic they would distinguish themselves. Indeed, some of them write even better poetry than the Arabs.[10]

It is paradoxical that Father Ijaro's description of his coreligionists should be appropriate to the state of the Islamic peoples at the present moment. The Christian world has changed. Can we change too?

Some of the reasons for the present stagnation are to be found in the thought of some of the 'ulema. The retrogression of Islamic studies and the isolation of the religious institutes from intellectual life in the East and the Maghrib was partly due to the fact that the traditional 'ulema have failed to listen to reformers like Mohammed Abduh, Jamal al-Din al-Afghani, and other contemporary thinkers. This retrogression has created an almost unbridgeable gap between classical Arabic studies and the new Western thought. The latter is being taught to young Muslims either directly in Western institutes or indirectly in their Islamic counterparts, which simply reproduced Western culture without any criticism. If the present situation persists, and if the Islamic institutes do not take a more positive attitude toward Arabic and Islam, it will not be very long before atheism dominates the towns and the countryside. Everyone will become an imitator of the West, which is undoubtedly moving toward the rejection of religion.

What should we therefore do to fill this vacuum? The answer is simple and clear. The Islamic institutes should regain their influence and responsibility in the protection of religion and language; the 'ulema in these institutes would have to play the classical role that has been assigned to them by Islam. In the same way that the early 'ulema had coped with intellectual developments and innovations — by logically reconciling these with Islam — the contemporary 'ulema should direct their attention to the revitalization and modernization of Islamic institutes, so that they may open new horizons of knowledge as well as, its objectives, and consequently, the role of the 'ulema; similarly, the present situation in the Islamic world calls for a redefinition of knowledge and its objectives.

The primary objective is, however, to end the existing isolation between the intellectuals and the masses on the one hand and authentic Islamic knowledge on the other. This would, of course, require an end to the isolation which separates the 'ulema from contemporary scientific [modern] life.

The Islamic world witnesses today a surging movement for the modernization of educational curricula that have been damaged by colonialism. This reformist movement is active in the Maghrib, Tunisia, and the rest of the Islamic countries. But the original institutes [i.e., al-Azhar] have either drawn inward for fear of criticism or simply ignored the whole problem. The role of these institutes requires that they occupy a prominent position within the system of national education; indeed, they are flexible enough and adapted to entrench their activities deep in the national culture.

Higher education should address itself to two things: a healthy revival of the Arabic language and the establishment of shari'a and theology institutes. This will facilitate the growth, of a unified code of Islamic laws embodying legislation on matters of justice and behavior. Besides, the revival of comparative religious and ethical studies would further the development of a dialectic capable of refuting allegations and distortions. Although the Arabic curricula are continually improving in the Middle East, their counterparts in the Maghrib still suffer from the lack of content and style. It is therefore imperative that the 'ulema and the linguists pay more attention to Arabic and particularly to the problem of Arabization.

Theology, on the other hand, should be studied in the shari'a institutes according to the plan suggested by Dr. Abdelrazaq al-Sanhuri, which runs as follows:[11]

Theological studies should take a comparative approach, with special emphasis on two points: firstly, a detailed study of the history and development of Islamic theology in the period preceding the four major *mathahib* [plural of *mathab,* school of theology]. Secondly, all theological schools — *shi'ah, zahirite,* and *khawarij* — should be studied so that different currents of legal thought could crystallize into general themes. These themes could then be compared to the principles of modern Western theology in such a way that similarities and differences become clear. The above approach will elucidate the basic prepositions of Islamic theology, its details and logic.

Whenever the need for the adaptation of Islamic theology is felt to be pressing, it should not be neglected; those parts of it that are flexible enough to coexist with the facts of modern living should remain unchanged. In both cases, theology would remain authentic and devoid of all foreign elements. According to our analysis, the following aspects of Islamic theology need more research and investigation:

1. The history of Islamic theology with special emphasis on the pre-*mathahib* period.
2. Reassessment of the classical interpretations of theological principles.
3. Comparative analysis of the different schools of theology in Islam.
4. Comparison of Islamic theology with modern Western legal codes.

The objective behind a new approach in these studies is to revitalize theology and draw some general conclusions as a basis for modern shari'a laws and this, of course, requires a detailed and scholarly treatment.

Another specialized institute should also be established to deal with questions of doctrine and ethics, i.e., the basis and logic of the Islamic dogma, the social and practical implications of ethical behavior, the sociology of religion, social psychology, and so on. However, what the Islamic institutes need most, apart from programs and research, is a strong commitment on the part of educationalists to their message of creating a new generation responsible and capable enough to reconstruct what has been corrupted. This new generation could hardly achieve anything unless the 'ulema themselves set a good example to be followed; practice is the best means of education.

It is needless to say that the role of the Qarawiyin 'ulema is great. It is not the betterment of salaries and pensions but rather an undertaking to preach and practice Islam with open minds. The 'ulema's fulfillment of their role is indispensable to a new revival of Islam, because it will determine the direction of Maghribi Islam. May Allah guide our 'ulema and leaders toward this achievement.

Notes

1. Mustafa Sadiq al-Rafi'ay, *Tarikh al-'Arabi* (Ā History of Arabic Literature), II, 18.

2. Ali Sami al-Nashar, *Manahij al-Bahth al-Mufakri al-Islam (Research Methods of Islamic Thinkers)* (Cairo, 1966).

3. Georges Bastide, *Mirages et certitudes de la civilisation* (Paris: Presses Universitaires de France, 1953).

4. Georges Bastide, *The Principles of the Sociology of Religions,* trans. Mohammed Gasim, p. 7.

5. Rashid Rida, *Tarikh al-Ustaz al-Imam (Biography of Mohammed Abdulh),* I, p.11.

6. *Ibid.*

7. *Ibid.*

8. I. Goldzieher, *Le Dogme et la loi de l'Islam: historire du dèveloppement dogmatique et juridique de la religion musulmane,* translated into French by Flex Arin (Paris, 1958).

9. Mohammed al-Sabhi, *al-Fikr al-Islami al-Hadith wa silatuhu bil ist 'amar al-Gharbi (Modern Islamic Thought and Its Relation to Western Colonialism),* pp. 84 ff.

10. *Majallat al-Muslimun (Muslim Journal),* VI, No. 5, p.7.

11. *Al-'Alam al-'Arabi (The Arab World Journal),* II, p. 23.

17

THE PARTY AND THE STATE

MOHAMMED HARBI

There are broad social forces in Algeria that are opposed to the bourgeoisie, neocolonialism, and imperialism, in a word, to the old order. This statement would be incomplete if we did not point out that among these forces there are some that are not ready to accept or help the transformation of social relations and the revolutionary transition to socialism. Furthermore, among these forces there are great differences in the degree of intensity and awareness. We should not forget that the socialist option is quite new, so that the gap between revolutionary possibilities and subjective factors (organization, slogans, and so on) remains great. In many sectors, the dream of internal peace between the forces of revolution and those of reaction, the hope for social and political change without a fierce struggle to the bitter end, is not receding despite the lessons of several crises since July, 1962.

The problems of party and state are at the center of all the discussions among militants in the country. This is quite proper, since the results of the current struggles depend in part on their positive appreciation. Clarification of the most elementary notions of socialism, which bourgeois ideology tries to empty of content, and the constant denunciation of falsifiers and "revolutionaries" weighed down by thousands of little daily intrigues are also an integral part of the triumph of the socialist revolution. Building ramparts against the harmful activities of utopian liberals, who yesterday advocated coexistence between communities and today preach coexistence between classes, and blocking the new-style marabouts, who tend to pervert the consciousness of the masses and then leave them defenseless before the spokesman of the rich, are other tasks to be carried out without respite or weakness. But enough of generalities.

Before discussing the problem of party-state relations in a country that is laying the material bases of socialism, we should point out that state and party are not and cannot be independent because of the nature of the society in which they develop (although this does not mean that they passively reflect the objective conditions of their frame of action). Let us take the case of a bourgeois democracy.

In a bourgeois system, the existence of parties is dominated by their context,

Speech delivered before a cultural conference organized by the New Algeria Committee in Algiers, October 6-21, 1964.

that is by capitalist property relations. On the political level, the bourgeoisie, as a ruling class (even if it does not always act homogeneously), acts as if on the basis of production; it takes over the functions of management and decision and pushes out the workers. At the same time, it creates instruments to control society, which makes it possible to allow the citizenry to participate in public life. Among these instruments are the parties — and the legal existence of labor parties in countries with a bourgeois system of government does not alter our view of them. Through their militants and their organs of training and information, the parties form public opinion. Competition among them safeguards the appearance of democracy, allowing dissatisfaction to be tapped and channeled, while providing a safety-valve, an alternative, in a word, a "state of reserve."

In this system, the leadership and the organization of the party in power blend into those of the state. The state and the party apparatus, socially heterogeneous, with elements from different social stratas, but united in their goal — the defense of the bourgeois order — are inseparable. The conclusion is clear: in a bourgeois parliamentary democracy, the party in power becomes part of the state machinery. It does not take it over; it only manages it for the benefit of the bourgeois caste. The primacy of the state over the party (as in Britain) or parties (as in West Germany), is the rule.

In such a system, the state not only appears as a coercive apparatus whose role is to guarantee the capitalist system of production through the legal monopoly of force (this role comes into the open only in a social crisis, when the workers challenge the pre-eminence of the bourgeoisie). It also appears as the decisive force in the functioning of society. (This impression is supported by the current changes in modern capitalism, where the state plays an ever increasing role in economic as well as social matters, further increasing its domination over the governed.) In such a system, there is both democracy and dictatorship: dictatorship of the bourgeoisie over the social classes, which are condemned to choose the sauce with which they are to be eaten; democracy for the bourgeoisie — a very small minority. As you see, we are far from the crass mystification that presents the state as the embodiment of the general will and takes the reality out of human relations.

This digression on state and party in the bourgeois system was designed to show what the state and party are not, and cannot be, in a society seeking to lay the foundations of socialism. They cannot be the embodiment of an authoritarian centralization of social life. They cannot be the instruments for maintaining the separation of the governing and the governed, the leaders and the followers. Experiments in some of the socialist countries, which remain linked to a particular phase of the workers' movement, cannot turn the results of their practices into the necessary categories of evolution in human society. To see the problem of party and state in a new light, we must therefore return to a correct definition of socialism . . . .

DEFINING SOCIALISM

We soon understand why it is wrong to define socialism as the nationalization of the means of production. The nationalization of all means of production and their management by the state — in other words, by socially heterogeneous institutions — leaves in the background another contradiction between master and executor.

But, some will say with sophistry, with the elimination of private property and the liquidation of the economic and political domination of the bourgeoisie, class contradictions disappear and are replaced by other nonantagonistic contradictions. Then society evolves peacefully, since it bears within itself a solution to the contradictions arising within it. This remark is incomplete because it makes all the contradictions in the societies evolving from capitalism to socialism equivalent to internal contradictions of the people, and systematically excludes contradictions between the people and those who want to put themselves above them socially or politically.

The experiments of Poland and Hungary are sufficiently clear. They show that conflicts are determined by different or opposed interests, and that is where one must start in order to understand them. To proceed otherwise is to turn the theory of scientific socialism into a simple doctrine of social progress, leaving dialectics in the bushes. As the National Liberation Front's [Tripoli] program rightly pointed out, socialism differs from capitalism not only because it eliminates private property but also because of its tendency to abolish all executive apparatus that is separated from society. Socialism can only be man's conscious organization of his own life in all fields; a radical transformation of all the values born within the capitalist system.

For our definition of socialism to be correct, however, it must be completed. A consummated socialism corresponds to a very high level of productive forces; it means economic abundance, abolition of the market and of money, and full expansion of man's capacities. Questions of party and state, and their relations, do not arise in such a framework, where man as producer, consumer, and member of the collectivity is master of his destiny. "As long as the proletariat still needs a state, it is not for purposes of liberty but to repress adversaries; and the day when it will be possible to speak of liberty, the state will cease to exist as such" (Engels).

This period of uninterrupted change, when the people exercise their domination on a minority of exploiters is therefore defined as a period of transition. In the Charter of Algiers, it is described as follows: "The period of transition is one in which the political organization of society prepares for socialism by beginning with the abolition of exploitation of man by man, the establishment of the material foundations for the rapid development of productive forces, and the liberation of the creative activity of the workers. None of these requirements can be given priority over the others because they are an inseparable whole."

During this period of development, the desire to provide for all the needs of society runs up against objective limitations: first economic (weak productive forces) and then human (stigma of the capitalist society from which the transitional society evolves). At the political level, these limitations mean the maintenance of state power. In his report to the party congress, Secretary General ben Bella defined that power: "Our state belongs to the workers and to all who profess socialism. Through it and the mobilization of the masses, the enemies of socialism will be destroyed. In our task of state-building, our main goal must be to reduce the distance between governing and governed as much as possible, to associate all citizens and particularly the producers in the job of leadership and planning. Self-management is a step toward that direction."

If I have insisted on this long exposé of the content of socialism and the nature of the state during the transitional period, it was to prevent the mystification that turns state property and state management into a sacred formula of socialism. It was also to explain that there is no other way of bridging the gap between leaders and agents except through the progressive transfer of economic, social, and political power to the workers. Only in that way can new social relations be substituted for the former capitalistic relations. It is clear that this transfer depends on the political conditions in which a socialist revolution evolves. Before coming to the party and the state, I had to emphasize that in its content as in its form, the socialist state is a special kind of state, whose action seeks to enlarge socialist democracy at the productive and political levels, even when the effects of capitalistic survivals and economic pressures demand constraint. In conclusion, we might say that during that transition period, the state plays an important part in the liquidation of capitalist tendencies and forces hostile to socialism and helps lay the foundations for the construction of socialism. But in accordance with this, it must prepare for an increasingly direct management of the economy by the producers, act in a way that the economic and social content of the socialist system takes root and becomes an everyday fact, and make it possible progressively to push the use of coercion into the background.

THE REVOLUTIONARY PARTY

Until now, I have not spoken about the revolutionary party in a country building socialism, or of its role vis-à-vis the state. In order to do this, it was first necessary to set things straight and to discard the confusions often purposely kept alive about socialism and about the nature of the transitional period. Unlike bourgeois political movements, the socialist revolutionary party is not a refuge for professional politicians prowling around the state institutions in order to infiltrate them. Nor is it a meeting place for specialists who know how to explain everything but refuse to change anything. Its form, its content, its methods are set by its mission: Build socialism, make man his own master by freeing him from oppression. Its *raison d'être* is to organize and regroup the workers, express their aspirations, win them the help and sympathy of the working masses – the unorganized citizens whose interests coincide with those of the workers. Thus it gathers the most aware, most active, most devoted, and most disinterested of the workers, poor peasants, and anonymous laborers who make up the vital forces of the progressive social processes.

Because of the place they hold vis-à-vis the means of production, the workers and the nonspeculating peasants create the future and are at the same time a result of it. It is their position that gives them an avant-garde character, and for this reason the revolutionary party must lean on them, solidify their alliance, extract them from bourgeois influence and ideology, in a word, organize them to move society and direct activities so as to build socialism. It must accomplish this role without replacing the workers, whose militants are only their most conscious fraction, and without turning the other mass organizations into mere conveyor belts.

A revolutionary party degenerates as soon as its leaders and its militants act as if they were commanding troops. From the moment they no longer understand or are no longer convinced, a people can easily be misled by obscure forces. With the people, there is progress; without them, one only marks time, even if he thinks he is advancing. In summary, the party is the incarnation of the unity of leadership. It draws up the general guidelines, controls their application, and through its militants makes the state move in the same direction, along with all the other organizations that shape society. But to exercise its leading role satisfactorily, the party needs the ideological and practical unity of its members and must avoid becoming a managerial apparatus if it is to remain a factor of mobilization, organization, and formation of the masses. That is where it differs from the state, which is above all a factor of power. If, therefore, the party wants to keep its avant-garde character, maintain ties with the masses, and cultivate their confidence, it should not be simply a factor of power. In fact, that is where the problem begins. For it is through the state and its institutions that the party acquires its power, engages its struggle against capitalistic tendencies and antisocialistic manifestations, in a word, creates the conditions for a new order. But to understand the dangers that threaten the party, we must return to the obstacles that it will face, the objective and subjective phenomena that push it to fuse with the state apparatus.

1.   As a result of the low level of productive forces, which renders the workers numerically and culturally weak, the economic and political activities of bourgeois society and the pressure of economic middle classes (speculating peasants, traders, and so on) acquire particular weight.

2.   The undeveloped social consciousness of the masses and the weakness of their material resources enable the privileged classes to bring out the conservative attitudes among the working masses and force the revolutionary power into transactions and compromises. Moreover, the survival of exploiting classes in certain sectors of the economy and the persistence of market forces pose problems that are beyond administrative regulation.

3.   The strata that act inside the state apparatus are characterized by particularly heterogeneous social origins. Among these strata, the weight of proletarian and peasant representatives is nil. It is only in the lower levels of production and in the self-managed sector that one finds a large proportion of leaders from the masses. This situation gives real strength to the bourgeois and pro-bourgeois elements, who enjoy an actual cultural monopoly in the country. I will go even further. The war and the revolution have caused a real metamorphosis of the Algerian middle strata and even of certain privileged people. Because of the rapidity of the revolutionary transformation, a very clear discordance arises between the change in the social position of the former privileged classes (from owners to nonowners) and the much slower change in their mentality, their way of thinking and behaving. With independence, hundreds of people were pushed into responsible posts while still bourgeois subjectively (although not in terms of their situation).

4.   The methods of leadership and action inherited from clandestinity and the war constitute a brake to a free confrontation of opinions.

5.   The privileged strata pushed off the stage by the revolution never willingly accept their condition. This forces the state to forbid all propaganda, to repress all activities that look to the past. But the experience of many socialist

countries proves how easy it is to interpret constructive criticism, conceived in a socialist spirit and questioning methods foreign to the revolutionary spirit, as an antirevolutionary attitude. There is always the danger that limitations on the democratic life of the country — necessary because of the dangers passed by the enemies of socialism — may be transferred to the party.

6.   Foreign technical assistance, important and useful for the country, exerts an influence in certain fields that is not always in harmony with the country's policy of consolidating the independence of the party and the state. Our state apparatus is still not completely ours: On January 1, 1964, out of 134,550 budgetary posts, we find 76,861 Algerians, 16,292 foreigners, and 41,427 vacant posts. In category A, there are 3,950 foreigners and 6,266 Algerians. In category B, there are 10,234 foreigners and 13,568 Algerians.

7.   When it takes over, the party puts its best and most influential officers and leaders into the state machinery. Their role is to guarantee the control of the party over the state. But once in the state, the representatives of the party find themselves in a contradictory situation, crisscrossed by currents expressing different if not divergent interests: the interests of peasants, of the lower middle class, of the debris of the former ruling classes, and of the technicians who exert pressure on them, trying to push them into a middle way, inciting them to reduce the autonomous activity of the masses and to exclude them from the organization of production, in short, to subordinate party policy to the interests of the varied forces acting on the state. In Algeria, this pressure of the adverse environment, which in fact tends to subordinate the party to the state and deviate the course of the revolution, finds its strength in the shortage of cadres and the monopoly of culture and experience that is still in the hands of the enemies of socialism. It also finds echoes among honest leaders who do not understand that the hostility of lower party organisms to certain state institutions is not a challenge of state authority but the unequivocal manifestation of social antagonism, the normal attitude of those who bore the burden of war, accepted sacrifices, and see yesterday's spectators taking over today's positions of responsibility.

We have just reviewed the factors acting in favor of the fusion of party and state machinery. However, we must add that the negative influence of those factors may be worsened if, in the social composition of the party and its organisms, the forces whose future is linked to the building of socialism — I mean the workers — are numerically inferior to the other social classes. Everyone knows the bitterness of the struggles that the middle-class elements, left to themselves, provoke in order to ensure a rapid rise in the state hierarchy — their wrong conception of the party, their use of the party against the state, and of the state against the party. Everyone knows, too, that those struggles were made easier by the conditions of Algeria's accession to independence. The state came before the party. The building of the revolutionary party and the principles of policy and organization on which it is based, did not appear clearly until the adoption of the Charter of Algiers. Therefore, its homogeneity and the ideological unity of its members are not an immediate fact. They can only be the product of struggle.

REPERCUSSIONS OF THE PARTY-STATE FUSION

Let us now examine the possible effects on the party of its fusion with the state or its subordination to it — in short, of its bureaucratization.

1. Because of its use of various means belonging to the production system to strengthen itself, the state, by the internal logic of its development, tends to separate itself from society, to impose itself as a force above society, and to sanctify its role. This *etatisation* of social life restricts the influence of the working masses on the current evolution, as well as their ties with the party. It causes "bureaucratism," which is a serious deformation in the building of socialism. I would like to take a minute here to give a precise definition of this term.

In many circles, "bureaucratism" is used in reference to defects in the administration: the flood of papers, the delays in the achievement of everyday matters. This conception is wrong and even harmful, because it tends to bring discredit on civil servants in general and to make them the scapegoat of the masses. It is all the more harmful since we know that the execution of all functions of leadership by the producers is impossible the day after the revolution — in any country, but especially in those that lag behind culturally. So when we speak of the bureaucracy we do not mean all civil servants but only those who, extending their grasp on the state and the economy, try to take advantage of their situation to crystallize social inequalities and acquire new privileges.

2. The second consequence is the shift of policy-making centers from democratic organisms to those where hierarchy dominates, and also the intervention of the state in the life of the party. Problems are no longer solved through collective discussions but through formal decisions taken by limited groups inside state institutions and transferred in an authoritarian manner to the rank and file. Slogans replace explications. The perennials and the opportunists take precedence over the militants. The experience of the party, which means the experience of all its members, is pushed into the background. Its wealth in comparison with the state vanishes, with negative effects on its internal cohesion. As a result, incomprehension confuses the party's vigor, and what is most serious is that this difficulty does not mean that the decisions taken are wrong but that they are not understood and assimilated.

3. The third consequence is that the creative activity of the masses is again brought into question. Every autonomous initiative is interpreted as a transgression of party prerogatives. The central organisms make all the decisions, and if they do not, we wait. The masses are called on to create and construct, without any possibility for initiative to develop.

This mistrust of the masses, the tendency of specialists to subordinate the party to themselves, to consort with members who are inside the state, and to destroy local initiative, worsens the separation between leaders and masses, a separation that is all the more fraught with possible consequences as those masses compare their standard of living and their needs with those of the state agents.

In this respect, it is time to face the arguments that aim at justifying exorbitant salaries and wide differences in wage scales. A society progressing to socialism must work from the beginning for the greatest possible equalization. There are real inconveniences in equality of remuneration for work. The political and psychological consequences of a situation in which one group can satisfy its secondary needs while a majority still struggles for a minimum cannot be overlooked by any man caring for social justice, and even less by a socialist. The justification of high salaries by reference to training expenses becomes meaningless when these expenses are borne by society. Anyway, the possible exceptions justified by the shortage of leaders — still very real today — cannot concern party members, who are given the socialist maximum along with all the other militants in positions of leadership.

We see that a fair conception of the relationship between the state and the revolutionary party is crucial for the harmonious building of socialism. It is all the more decisive when party and state develop within the framework of defined social relations, without any clear and precise boundary between bourgeoisie and working masses. Moreover, the working classes themselves, because of the influence of middle-class ideology, contain reactionary currents in their midst. The distinction between the state and party is necessary to the socialist revolution. This means that every precaution must be taken to keep under party control the party militants who receive state responsibilities. This is the only way to protect them from the temptation of melting with elements from outside the party and of mixing the state apparatus into internal party matters. It also means that one must avoid systematically emptying the party of substance by depriving it of the majority of its influential officials and leaders, to the benefit of the state and the administration.

But the democratic control of the party leaders and democratic party life are not enough. To eradicate the roots of "bureaucratism," it is also necessary to deny any material advantage to the performance of the leadership functions and to give the management of the means of production to the workers. Management by the workers is one aspect of the reorganization of society in a socialist way, but is not a guarantee. Only the existence of adequate political institutions, of ways of functioning for the society, which radically break with everything that, in any way, has to do with the capitalist machinery, can constitute an efficient brake to the bureaucratic tendencies of the apparatus. But this is conditioned by an understanding and explanation of the institutions and how they work; consequently, it is necessary to give the maximum information on all matters discussed within the party and state organisms, especially the economic organisms. In a socialist country, it would be nonsense for a leader to justify a position by telling the workers and militants, that "there are things you do not know and do not understand." When you base a leadership role on the ignorance of those you want to set free from alienation, of those you want to emancipate, you already place yourself above them.

In conclusion, we can affirm that the leading role of the party and its pre-eminence are a *sine qua non* condition of the road to socialism. Thanks to its leading part, pressure groups will be prevented from taking over organs of the state apparatus for their profit. Thanks to the unity of direction that it produces inside the state, to its power of action, control and education, the division into deeply divergent tendencies that exists at the institutional level will be overcome. In our country, the self-management helps this enterprise by releasing creative energies. Its existence is the best protection against bureaucratic deformation. The battle to implant it and for its eventual success is also a battle for the construction of a new, popular state. That is why this acquisition must be the starting point for laying down the basis for the reorganization of Algerian society and for achieving communal reform, which is the prelude to the remodeling of communal structures and the achievement of the slogan: "Power to the workers."

FOUR

Elites and Social Groups

As a transitional society, North Africa must be understood above all through its elites and their component social groups. The elites enjoyed a privileged position in traditional North African society, where everyone "knew his place." But it was also the elites — both old and new — that began to reshape society in the process of modernization. This process will have to continue for some time before such a degree of social mobility is achieved that "elite" can lose its stratified connotations. The elite may be modernizing, but the elite-mass structure is not. Even at the beginning of the 1970's, and even in revolutionary parts of North Africa, elite is still a stratum that one attains and occupies, rather than a role that is open to all. Whether in an Algeria born of a revolutionary war or a Morocco born of a bourgeois-led independence struggle, there is much that is ascriptive mixed in with achievement criteria in elite definitions (even if "ascriptive" has taken on a new meaning: birth at the right time, place, and social position to have been available for nationalist militancy).

The process of elite transformation is insightfully portrayed in a classic (and hitherto classified) study of 1939 by Henri de Montety, a long-time civil servant with the Protectorate. Montety shows that profound social changes were transforming Tunisian society even before the political changes brought about by the nationalist struggle. Octave Marais, who more than two decades later occupied a similar position in the independent Moroccan administration, gives a global description of a society whose elite transformation indeed brought political change, but whose elite then tended to stand still, expanding in place but not continuing the process of social change. A closer focus on a segment of this elite is presented by James R. Shuster; his picture of a status-quo and technocracy-oriented bureaucracy is accurate not only for Morocco but also for Algeria, Libya, and Tunisia, although in those countries the bureaucracy is not always as integrated into the ruling class as it is in Morocco. It is in Algeria that a truly new class has emerged: the military; its origins, values, and roles make it the crucible of a "new man" in Algerian society, although more in the Soviet than the transitional sense, as I. William Zartman shows.

Much more work needs to be done on North African elites. The values, roles, origins, continuity, and cohesion of most of the important social groups, and the personal, programmatic, and generational fissures within them are simply unknown. Some work is being done on students;[1] a surprising amount of attention has been given the military,[2] considering the difficulty of gaining information, but much more could fruitfully be undertaken. Business elites and religious groups — notably, 'ulema and sects — have been almost totally neglected, as have the extremely important family interrelations. In an area where Fes battles its offspring, Casablanca; where Tunis confronts the towns of the Sahel; where Algiers rules over its three beylics of Oran, Medea, and Constantine; and where Benghazi takes its revenge on Tripoli by abandoning it in summer for the alternate capital of Beida, urban elites in all their forms, factions, and alliances are the face — if not the body — of the society.

Notes

1. Clement Henry Moore and Arlie R. Hochschild, "Student Unions in North African Politics," *Daedalus,* Winter, 1968, pp. 21–50.

2. Chapters on the Moroccan army may be found in I. William Zartman, *Problems of New Power* (New York: Atherton Press, 1964), and Leo Hamon (ed.), *Le Role extra-militaire des armées dans le Tiers Monde* (Paris: Presses Universitaires de France, 1966); and on the Tunisian army in Hamon (ed.), op. cit. On the 1971 military uprising, see John Waterbury, "The Coup Manque," American Universities Field Staff Report, North Africa Series, XV, No. 1 (1971); and "Le putsch du 10 juillet 1971 au Maroc," *Maghreb,* No. 47, pp. 11-19 (1971).

18

OLD FAMILIES AND NEW ELITES IN TUNISIA

HENRI DE MONTETY

In 1880, the Regency of Tunis had a population of about 1,300,000, including 700,000 bedouins and 600,000 town-dwellers. Tunis alone had between 60,000 and 80,000 people. The other principal towns were Sfax, Sousse, Kairouan, Mahdia, Monastir, Bizerte, le Kef, and Beja. There were also large villages spread out along the coast, especially in the Sahel [central Mediterranean littoral]. The oases of the south contained some important settlements, and Berber villages were nestled here and there in the mountains.

The rest of the territory was settled by bedouin tribes, some Berber or Arab but most of mixed blood. These tribes had maintained some sort of cohesion in the south, where they led a seminomadic life. They were sedentarized and segmented in the center and in the Tell mountains.

Northern and southern tribes, small Berber villages and ksour [fortified villages of the oases] did not show much difference from similar populations in the neighboring Maghribi states. But the eastern coastal strip, with a dense, refined, and industrious urban population, formed a province clearly apart from the hinterland.

The political and administrative structure was strongly centered on Tunis, the capital and cultural center. Around the bey and his court gravitated the administration, army, and 'ulema. The central power in the provinces was represented by the qaids [tribal leaders], holders of all powers except the shari'a jurisdiction exercised by the qadis [judges]. Even though the ties between the beylical administration and its subjects had always been loose, the entire territory acknowledged its authority.

Tunis was not only the political capital of a strongly centralized state but also the intellectual pole of the eastern Maghrib. This had been the case ever since it had won from Kairouan the primacy in Islamic science and converted the Zitouna Grand Mosque into a university, in the mid-nineteenth century. Moreover, in La Goulette, the only harbor regularly visited by European ships, it had an open window to Europe and the Orient.

The unitary constitution of the regency, centered on the capital, whose

Translated, by permission, from Henri de Montety, "Enquête sur les vieilles familles et les nouvelles élites en Tunisie" (mimeo; Paris, 1939), pp. 1–3, 37–67.

prestige far overshadowed that of the other towns, soon engendered a feeling of national cohesion, in which are to be found the deep roots of modern Tunisian nationalism. In this respect, Tunisia was in a very different position from Algeria, which was an agglomeration of villages and tribes with few cities and no real capital, and from Morocco, where Fes and Marrakesh fought for first place while two-thirds of the country escaped the authority of the sultan.

This pre-eminent position of Tunis was a powerful magnet for the social elites. Most of the leading provincial families came there to stay (just as French nobles went to Paris and Versailles) and made large fortunes. This elite concentration gave an added luster to the capital.

Other towns in the regency were not without their importance. Kairouan, Mahdia, and Monastir preserved the memory of a glorious past. Others, like Sfax and Sousse, began to make a place for themselves in the economic and intellectual life of the country. All were craft and market centers, well known to a large clientele; some were true provincial centers. All interstitial space between these cities, apart from a more or less extensive garden zone, was inhabited by tribes who had continual relations with the towns, coming to their suqs (markets) and maintaining contacts with notables, although preserving a feeling of proud independence from the city dwellers. . . .

OLD FAMILIES IN NEW STRUCTURES

Under the French Protectorate, . . . the former aristocrats still occupy an important place, especially in positions of authority, of traditional culture, and of officialdom. They have often been able to conquer the largest share of the new structures, especially as lawyers, secular judges, and Old Destour leaders. Thus it cannot be said that the old families were pushed out of the social order by a new elite: they resisted, maintained themselves in their former positions with the support of the government, and went into new jobs concurrently with the new elements.

Nevertheless, despite the important place they still enjoy in the social structure, the role of the old families is already diminished by the simple fact that they have had to share their influence and authority with the new elite, as the waves of new aspirants storm the gates of command posts. On the other hand, the members of old families who complete with newcomers for the new jobs have adapted to modern civilization and have received the same education and training as their competitors. . .

Old families who have completely disappeared from the scene are, in fact, relatively few. When we examine the biographies of two hundred famous Tunisians of the nineteenth century, written by the historian ben Dhiaf, we notice that at least half the families cited still hold good positions. Many in the other half have simply faded away. Those that have fallen on bad times or out of favor and have ceased to play any role do not represent more than one-tenth of the number cited by the historian. The decline of aristocratic families generally occurred because of political disgrace. . . . Other mamluk [former Turkish] families, having also incurred disgrace and depleted their fortunes, have been able to maintain an honorable life due to help from the beylical family to whom they were related. . . The Slims, one of whom became minister, split into two branches: one, under former qaid Mahmoud, sunk into mediocrity, the sons doing menial jobs; the other, headed by Adel, has kept its fortune and rank. It is to this branch that the Neo-Destourian leader Mongi Slim belongs. . . .

Sons of makhzen [government] and mamluk families have looked for other possibilities outside the traditional positions of authority, either in the lower civil service or in the liberal professions: some became farmers to develop the land held by their family, while others became lawyers (20% are of mamluk and makhzen origin), physicians (25%), and pharmacists (14%). The mamluks also find opportunities in the political structures. The Destour Party was founded by a mamluk, Bach Hamba, and there were four mamluks among the twenty Destour leaders in 1938. On the other hand, no makhzen representative could be found in the Destour leadership. The number of mamluk or makhzen families who choose to remain in the hereditary traditional administration is dwindling, despite constant Protectorate efforts to make administrative posts available to them. The ranks of the beylical army offer a refuge to these scions and are almost entirely filled with mamluks. . . .

The search for new directions is observed to a lesser extent in the 'ulema cast and the maraboutic [saintly] families. Despite the fact that the 'ulema enjoy preponderance in the shara'a structure and remain with their eyes turned toward their traditional destiny, a few young men from their rank timidly enter the administration, either in posts of authority (5% of the qaids and khalifas) or secular judiciary (8%). Even fewer are those entering the new liberal professions (only one lawyer and three physicians), and none as yet has gone into secular education. A few members of the maraboutic bourgeoisie are found in official political organs, such as the Grand Council and municipal councils, but no one from the 'ulema or the maraboutic families is active in the Old or Neo-Destour leadership.

But it is the baldi [city] bourgeois who has done most to adapt himself to the conditions of modern life and who, emerging from his traditional role of craftsman, trader or farmer, inundates the administrative, professional, and political structures, moving ahead of the new elite and successfully competing with it on the intellectual level. In positions of authority formerly reserved for the makhzen and mamluk families, the baldi bourgeoisie already holds 20%. Secular law practice offers them a large field (26% of the posts). They have conquered the professional positions in the Grand Mosque (15%). But they do not seem to be tempted by secular teaching, where they have not even one member.

The liberal professions, which are more suited to the bourgeois temperament, open their doors to a large baldi contigent (30% of the lawyers, 25% of the physicians, and 30% of the pharmacists). But it is above all in the official political sector that the Tunis and provincial baldi make up the largest percentage (60% in the Grand Council, 80% of municipal council and economic chambers). This can be explained by the character of the bourgeoisie that makes up the traditional and natural elite of the Tunisian population in the city as well as villages. The baldi make up an important part, 30% of the Old Destour leadership, although some of them have gone to the Neo-Destour. . . .

In the old provincial families, there was a similar evolution, although it is interesting to note that they have been far less influenced than the Tunisois by the pernicious effect of the modern economic system. Most of them have kept all their property. Many of them even seem to have prospered under the

Protectorate and to have improved their social position compared to the aristocracy. . . .

The baldi bourgeoisie is definitely the transitional element between the old and new elite: it belongs to the first by heredity and social condition, and to the second by its intellectualism and its direction. There is a complete intermediary span between the old bourgeois families, wrapped up in their traditions, and the intellectual petty bourgeoisie, from which most of the new elite comes.

Thus, it is often difficult to know where the old elite ends and the new begins. If we put into the first category a family of notaries or small Sahelian landowners whose sons have risen to high positions, and into the second a family of wealthy craftsmen or large landowners whose descendants work in lower administrative jobs, it must be recognized that convention makes up part of the criteria used, and that there is no real difference between a Bourguiba or a Zouitin, petty bourgeois of Sahel, for example, and a Kaak or Essafi, old baldi of Tunis.

If the old families hold a weaker position in the social structure, it is because this structure has undergone prodigious development and distortion, and new elements have made their way into it. The decline of the old families is relative and uneven . . . . A survey of the modern social structures shows that the old families have kept a preponderant place in the representative bodies: 90% of the municipal councilors, 95% of the economic chambers, 85% of the Grand Council. This is easily explained since the municipal councilors were chosen by the government, and the economic chambers and Grand Council were elected by a college of notables who are easily impressed by the prestige of the old families.

Among the principal figures of Tunisian nationalism, 70% of the Old Destour leadership comes from the old families, whereas these families do not count for more than 15% in the Neo-Destour leadership. This characteristic is also noticeable, although to a lesser extent, at the lower levels of the Destour; the Old Destour cell leaders include 20% of representatives from the former local elite, while none are members of the Neo-Destourian cells.

In the administration, the old families stand firm on several levels: authoritative functions (78%) and higher positions in the ministries (about 70%). But in these posts, the progressive introduction of recruitment by examination tends to diminish their number; thus, in the corps of qaids and khalifas, the proportion of old families, which stood at 85% before the institution of the examination, has dropped to 30% in the contingent recruited thereafter. In the lower jobs of sheikhs, *amins,* and secretaries to the qaids, whose appointment is in the hands of the government, the old local elite remains in place in 70–80% of the cases. It is because of this recruiting by competitive examination that the percentage of old families has fallen so low among the secular judges (39%) and even more so among the professors of the Zitouna Grand Mosque (43%). It is strange that the old families have excluded themselves from some of the new positions. For example, they did not try to enter either secular education (5% of the secondary teachers and no primary teachers) or the interpreters for the French administration (5%) which did not require examinations.

Not only have the old families maintained their preponderant role in the business world, but they have also acquired a leading position in the new liberal professions: lawyers (75%), physicians (50%), pharmacists (45%).

Thus, in the lower positions, aside from administrative clerks and schoolteachers, the old local families have maintained their predominance, whether they are in positions of authority chosen by the government (although infiltrated by popular elements from the Zitouna) or small managers and medium landowners (which change only slowly). However, these lesser local elites, who kept their secondary rank, make up the seedbed from which the new intellectual elite of higher cadres are recruited in large numbers.

THE NEW TUNISIAN ELITES

The new conditions in which Tunisian society finds itself as a result of its accession to modern civilization, the profound changes in the structures of authority and influence, the development of individual values, and the fading of the caste spirit have had the effect of bringing about a new ruling elite. This new elite is no longer a group of well-to-do or well-known families with a hereditary moral and administrative authority over the masses. It is a group of individuals selected for their abilities or, even more, for their intellectual training. It is a self-creating elite that can be renewed in less than a generation.

At present, the new elite is still far from a majority in the different compartments of the social structure. The old clans still keep up a strong front, holding on to most positions of authority or officialdom and surviving by the sheer force of their traditions and the support that the Protectorate finds in them. Although parts of the old ruling class have made the transition from the old order to the new, acquired intellectual values, and found a place in the new social order, in doing so they have in a sense laid the first foundations of the new elite.

Thus, for the sake of accuracy and clarity, it would be more appropriate not to contrast the "old first families" with a "new elite" but rather to speak of "new elites" and distinguish those which came from old roots, through renovation and adaption to the new order, from those made up of truly new elements, coming out of "secondary families" or even from the mass. Thus, a rough sketch of the social structure in modern Tunisia [by 1939] would show:

1. The "great families" who have kept their moral authority and social role through tradition. They still enjoy an important place in the administrative positions of authority, especially in tribal leadership, and in the official political bodies; in the judiciary and high positions of Islamic culture, their impact is already diminishing.

2. The "new elite" emerging from some of the "great families," who through their intellectual abilities or their know-how have obtained jobs in the new social structure. The important percentage of jobs taken by scions of "old families" in the liberal professions, secular judiciary, high administrative posts, and in the Old Destour, have already been noted.

3. The "new elite" emerging from the petty bourgeoisie or ordinary families who have made their way to positions of responsibility have obtained an increasingly important share of the high positions of Islamic culture and of the liberal professions. They have flooded the administration, monopolized secular teaching, and make up the active element of the Neo-Destour. This last category of "new elites" has progressed with startling rapidity in the 1930's and has generally tended to replace the old families. It is this "new elite" that will be studied here.

This renewal of the elites is not an entirely new phenomenon in Tunisia. Long before the Protectorate, men of modest families acceded to the highest positions. The mamluks offer the most striking example of the renewal of the aristocracy through the mass, as the prince made his choice among his humblest subjects. But accession to fortune and honor in this way was still the exception, and the "parvenu" in turn became the head of a clan, a new "great family." What characterizes the present renewal of the leading class and gives it its originality are its intellectual and widespread aspects. It has occurred because of the value given to intellectuality in social leaders and also because of a general evolution of the indigenous society and the development of education. The result of institutions and customs it has spread irresistibly and uncontrollably.

The prelude to the present wave was the infiltration into administrative jobs of a few members of the lower bourgeoisie and the masses at the time of World War I. These early newcomers had been the recipients of free Sadiki schooling, whose doors they had forced by their exceptional abilities, aided by the fact that the administration was in great need of educated interpreters. They won the appreciation of the French authorities through their energy and activity and had most successful careers. . . . It was through the channel of interpreters in the Ministry of State and later through the French civil administration (none of whom come from the great families) that the new elite made its way into the corps of qaids . . . . The brilliant careers of that first wave of the new elite made a profound impression on the provincial populations from which they came, as well as on the old aristocracy of Tunis. The latter did not consider it beneath them to give their daughters in marriage to these civil servants, whose future looked bright indeed. . . . The lessons of these first successes were quickly learned by the small villages from which these bright young men had come. The small provincial bourgeoisie lived in a closed circle; the member families were related to one another, they observed, advised, and imitated each other. When a young man from Nabeul became an interpreter for the French civil administration, three of his close relatives followed his path. This imitation extended from one relative to the other, down to the lower classes.

This well-known phenomenon, which turns Auvergnats into Parisian coal-venders and Ghomrassen into Tunisian doughnut-vendors, also influences the evolution of the provincial petty bourgeoisie of Tunisia, even if less consistently. It explains why the petty bourgeoisie of the Sahel tend to choose administrative jobs, while those of Sfax or Djerba look more to trade or agriculture. It reveals the importance of the first examples of success in the attempts of the masses and the petty bourgeoisie to enter the high positions of the social structure.

The phenomenon spread rapidly after World War I. The new elite found work easily, which encouraged young men to follow their older brothers. The difficulties they met thereafter from the lack of job openings, compared to the enormous afflux of graduates, has troubled them (and there is no doubt that the effectiveness of the Destourian movement in recent years stems from this fact) but has not yet discouraged them.

The new social elite, born of the mass or petty bourgeoisie, is not entirely intellectual in origin. Some new elements — especially the veterans — have gotten administrative jobs purely as a favor. On the other hand, there is a class of parvenus who make their fortune in commerce, the crafts, or farming and then take their place in the social structure beside the old baldi families. Of the intellectuals, some have Qoranic education and others European schooling. It is important to distinguish these several elements, since their behavior is quite different.

After World War I, a "veterans' policy" similar to the "great families' policy" of the first decade of the Protectorate was instituted. But the veterans were mostly bedouins, since inhabitants of the large towns were exempt from military service, and they were able to accede only to lower positions: oudjak, spahi, police, sheikh, *amin,* with a few found among the qaids ... The parvenus in trade and agriculture play a more important role in the social structure, in the liberal professions, and especially in politics.

The renovation of the upper class by individuals of modest birth is a constant phenomenon; it has most certainly been aided by the economic upheaval of the country induced by contact with the modern world, but it was also present in many cases prior to the Protectorate. For example, the ben 'Ammar family, which in 1939 was at top of the ladder, with one of its member vice president of the Grand Council, descended from a man who made his fortune as a camel caravan driver and then in farming.... The examples of fortunes made since the Protectorate in commerce, the crafts, and agriculture are particularly numerous in Sfax and throughout the Sahel. In Sfax, the families who have built fortunes in olives are legion; they remain on their land and do not seem to be tempted by administrative posts or liberal professions. They make up a rich, independent bourgeoisie that lives apart. On the other hand, in the Sahel, the newly rich families push their children toward liberal professions and the administration. In Tunis, the new rich are almost all from the provinces and particularly from Djerba. The Djerbans have practically a monopoly of the grocery stores and now own most of the big trading houses. Despite the fact that it has been accepted in Tunis, the Djerban bourgeoisie seldom mixes with the baldi bourgeoisie.

"Intellectuals" make up a large percentage of the new elite, and it is notable that many rich traders' or farmers' sons receive advanced education that places them on the same level as the parvenu families. The new intellectual elite is divided into two very different classes: Zitounans and Gallicized (from Sadiki, secondary, and primary schools). The Zitouna University provides Qoranic teaching to about 3,000 students, most of them from the lower classes of the small villages. This deprived youth, tied to a rigorous program, lives and works in the hope of finding a job. Not satisfied with having won a large place in the teaching staff of the Zitouna and Shari'a, where little by little they are pushing out the old 'ulema families (55% of the posts are already in their hands), or with finding an open field on the *oukils* (60%), *mueddebs* (80%), and notaries (30%), they have pushed open the doors of the secular magistrature (40%) from the new Zitounan elite compared with 20% from the Gallicized petty bourgeoisie) and assiduously compete with the Gallicized intellectuals for all the administrative jobs. In this last branch, their success has been uneven; in the last examination for khalif's apprentice, they won only one-sixth of the available places, against two-thirds for the newly Gallicized elite, and they occupy only 10% of the posts in the State and Justice Ministries....

The new Zitounan elites have been unable to get into the official political structure, but they have taken a very active part in Destourian politics. Their traditionalist formation leads them more easily to the Old Destour; although they hold only one seat on the steering committee (made up mostly of sons of good families and Gallicized intellectuals), they fill 80% of the lower positions (most of the heads of cells are Zitounans). But they are also attracted by the dynamism of the Neo-Destour. Despite the fact that they are excluded from the steering committee and general staff [of the Neo-Destour] in Tunis, they make up more than one-half of the local cell leaders.

Despite the strenuous and generally successful efforts of the Zitounans to gain positions, many graduates of the Grand Mosque remain outside the organic social framework. Few students (about sixty per year) attain the higher degree of the *tatouia;* a larger number (over a hundred) receive the secondary diploma of the *tahcil,* and none leave the Mosque without at least the *al-ahlia* certificate. But only a few dozen out of each class find a job. The rest constitute a vegetating mass, a stillborn elite, that waits for its moment and in the meantime plays an amorphous and diffuse leadership role in society.

This jobless elite is not a monopoly of the Zitounans; it also contains the Gallicized, even if in lesser numbers: in each year, 60 to 100 secondary degrees, 10 to 20 graduates of the Sadiki, 100 to 120 French and Arabic diplomas, and 1,000 primary-school certificates. The Sadiki College plays a major role in forming the new intellectual elite. As the training ground for the civil service, it is the principal channel through which the new elite of humble origins has been able to accede to administrative posts. But the decrease in the number of available places in the administration drives them to look for other possibilities. Some go into teaching (20% of the professors in secular schools and the teachers in the Qoranic schools), others into liberal professions, such as medicine (75% of the physicians are of modest families graduated from Sadiki against 20% from "great families' " sons), pharmacy (20%), law (10%).

People from the lower classes and the petty bourgeoisie who were educated in high school go above all into teaching (70% of the Tunisian professors), administrative positions where Arabic is not required, and, especially in recent years, the liberal professions. The new elite whose basic education is in French (either primary or secondary), often complemented by education in Arabic language and literature at the higher level, successfully challenges Sadikis and *lycéens* for higher administrative posts (10% of the khalifas in the last examination, 10% of the secular judges). It has an overwhelming majority in the lower jobs (60% of the clerks and secretaries), is taking over the primary secular schools (100%), and makes up a large percentage of the staff in the Qoranic schools (50%). Finally, it finds jobs in the lower levels of the liberal professions (nurses, clerks, and so on), and in commerce and the crafts.

In the new Gallicized elite, there are even more types than in the new Zitounan elite, ranging from the lowest class to the petty bourgeoisie just below the baldi. There is no sharp demarcation line between the new elite of old families and the new elite of more modest extraction; one merges gradually into the other, and the two tend to resemble each other .... One difference is that elements of the new elite from popular origins tend to seek careers in France, while those who belong to the old bourgeoisie remain attached to their home towns.

The few members of the new elite who succeed in entering the official political structures are Gallicized (the Tlatlis, for example), as are those few who slipped into the Old Destour staff (the lawyer Jemail, the doctor Bar Milad, the publisher Chadli Kalladi), but they are rare in local cells, which are made up almost entirely of Zitounans. In the Neo-Destour, where there are no old families, the new Gallicized elite occupies an important place in the local cells (30%) and holds all the staff positions. Indeed, if the sons of the good families who joined the Destour are also considered part of the new intellectual elite because of their training, the movement's leaders are for the most part Gallicized (in the Old Destour, two Sadikis and two *lycéens* against three Zitounans, and in the Neo-Destour committee, three Sadikis, two *lycéens*, and only one Zitounan), while the heads of the local cells are mostly Zitounans. The new Gallicized therefore fill the leadership positions in the nationalist movement and the Zitounans are relegated to lower levels.

Yet this fact should not be overemphasized. The nationalist leadership only exploits and directs a current of complex feelings where the patriotic idea taught in [French] schools gives substance to an old undercurrent of Islamic xenophobia, embittered by contact with Western civilization. These feelings are stronger among the intellectual youth who received Qoranic or mixed education (Sadikis and Qoranic primary students) than among those of purely French training. Among the latter, there is greater loyalty than in the former, and it is, in short, the elite of Qoranic culture, disappointed at not having found jobs, who makes up the base of the Destour . . . .

Finally, the recent appearance of a new social structure should be mentioned: the labor unions, which tend to remove the indigenous proletariat from the influence of the traditional leaders. Labor unions were organized very rapidly because of the French political climate of 1936–37, through the action of French militants of the General Confederation of Labor (CGT), soon followed by some Neo-Destourian leaders who set up a Tunisian CGT. The promoters of the labor movement were able to organize only with the support of the new elite, who set up the unions, cultivated the natural leaders *[meneurs]* in the proletarian masses, and placed them at the head of the local unions, from where they infiltrated the top leadership . . . . A proletarian labor-union elite is gradually forming and is likely to constitute a new and distinct leadership group in the future.

CONCLUSIONS

The flood of new elites from the lower and middle classes rises continuously, gradually drowning the old families, even those who have learned to adapt to modern ways and to democratic institutions. Nearly 50% of the intellectual careers and 30% of the upper economic positions are already in the hands of these new elites. Although only a few enter the official political bodies, they are the driving force of nationalist politics.

It is foreseeable that this proportion will grow rapidly, so that the old families will soon fill only a small proportion of the leadership positions. As retirement eliminates members of the great families who entered the administration with government support, and as competitive recruiting examinations are extended, the petty bourgeoisie and then the lower-class elements will enter *en masse* into administrative positions. These same elements will also conquer the other liberal positions through their perseverance.

To have an idea, one only has to look at the present composition of the classes in the schools. In the Zitouna, the sons of good families presently enrolled could be counted on two hands. The great majority of the students are from the masses; the rest are from the petty bourgeoisie. They come from the Sahel (one-sixth), from all the little towns on the coast and in the oases, and also from the bedouin tribes; only one-fifth are from Tunis. In the Sadiki, at the beginning of the century, the terminal class was made up of fourteen sons of good families (one prince, five mamluks, one makhzen, seven baldi) and three from the petty bourgeoisie. In 1938, in the same class, there were only three sons of good families (one makhzen, two baldi) to twelve children of the petty bourgeoisie and even a few from the masses.

In Tunis high school, which previously was attended only by sons of rich families, the philosophy class of 1939 included ten sons of old families (one mamluk, one makhzen, two shorfa, six baldi) and ten children of the new elite (eight petty bourgeois, two lower class). In the *baccalauréat* class, the diminution of the old families was even more striking: they sent only three children (one makhzen, two shorfa), while the new elite had twenty children, of whom half were of modest origin. The invasion of the high school by petty bourgeois and mass elements has two causes: the new elite which has already "made it" has the means to send their children to the *lycée,* and the masses can obtain free tuition grants. In the 'Alaoui School, in the first class of primary school, the old families' children still numbered four compared to seven or eight from the masses. The same proportion appears in the provincial high schools, and in primary school the percentage of children from the bourgeoisie is tiny compared to the great number of children from the masses.

What will be the reaction of the sons of good families faced with this enormous popular competition? Many are already going into liberal professions or farming. Old maraboutic families, who own habous property and who up to now were content to collect their rent, now push their sons to exploit their farms with their own hands. The army, which in France was the refuge of the aristocracy, does not seem to attract the inhabitants of Tunis: only the mamluks find a traditional opportunity in the beylical guard. The renewal of trade and craft might save some baldi families, but most of the old Tunis families, the makhzen and even the 'ulema, seemed doomed. The provincial makhzen, on the other hand, will be saved because of its land.

What is the influence of the new elite over the mass? It will probably not enjoy the same prestige as the great families, which can still produce their effect on the tribes and even in the towns. But it might compensate for this inferiority through a better understanding of the feelings of the popular masses and through a stricter moral conduct. Presumably it will tend to apply increasingly democratic methods and will thus favor the national evolution of the country.

19

THE RULING CLASS IN MOROCCO

OCTAVE MARAIS

"Whoever tries to define an Eastern institution is struck by the sharp contrast with the meaning of the same term in the West. The fluent and the 'affective' are in opposition to the 'rule,' as is also the tendency to stretch terms out of shape."[1]

Whether in old or in present-day Morocco, the term "ruling class" has implications for which there is no exact equivalent either in the West or in the rest of the Arab world. In the West, the idea of a ruling class must be analyzed in the light of a certain conception of the state, the family, and patrimony inherited from our Roman past. In the Arab world, we arrive rapidly at a confusion of these notions and their underlying values. Behavioral models grounded on a sense of honor and challenge are closer to a civilization of pastoral nomads and constitute the common stock of Arabism. Moreover, in the East, reaching to the frontiers of Morocco, the military organization of Ottoman society imposed a rigid structure upon the Muslim world and spawned ruling castes that could maintain their domination only by refusing to integrate with the rest of the country.[2] European colonialism often resulted in the installation of a non-Muslim ruling class. But the original relations between rulers and ruled were hardly altered, and in any case, the countries, lacking a national elite, were too badly organized to be able to shake off their new yoke.

In Morocco, the state never had the military rigidity that a Turkish conquest might have imposed on it. The political organization inherited from Muslim Spain remained practically unchanged until the French Protectorate, undergoing a slow decline occasionally interrupted by the attempts of an energetic sultan, to impose reforms copied from Turkey or Europe. Moreover, in Morocco true ruling groups appeared within the nation although they were divided by rivalries and did not constitute a real force because of the absence of any centralized power.

At the end of the nineteenth century, foreign representatives often compared the social and political organization of Morocco to Europe of the Middle Ages. In fact, legitimacy in Morocco was more ambiguous, although it still depends to

Translated, by permission, from *Revue Française de Science Politique,* XIV, No. 4 (August, 1964), 709-37.

a great extent on a system of religious values. As in every Muslim society, the Qoran was the backbone of social and political organization. But its rules were subject to quite divergent interpretations, ranging from the mere acknowledgment of the spiritual (but not the temporal) power of the sultan to his absolute power in all domains. Before 1912, such an alternative coexisted in Morocco under the names of *bled as-siba* [dissident lands] and *bled al-makhzen* [government lands] and prevented the development of a genuine ruling class. The political and administrative fact of the Protectorate was then superimposed on this traditional organization without upsetting the old structures. To a large extent, Moroccan society of today has been modeled on a social organization inherited from pre-Protectorate Morocco, upon which modern political, economic, and administrative structures have been overlaid without effecting any deep transformation of society.

THE WEIGHT OF THE PAST

Before 1912, power was exercised within an apparently anarchic framework, within which, however, relations among the various groups achieved a kind of equilibrium. The term "ruling class" referred at that time to only a comparatively marginal part of the country, an urban, official Morocco in contact with the foreign powers.[3] The rest of the country by no means wallowed in anarchy, but the leaders could only occasionally attain a lasting degree of authority. After a time, the tribe would get rid of them and pass their fortunes and authority into the hands of other families. It was quite the reverse in the Morocco of the towns and central makhzen, Arab to the core, where a firmly established ruling class was made up of elements that finally joined together during the Protectorate period.

There were, first of all, the middle-class families descending from the Andalusian immigrants, who devoted themselves to handicrafts and trade in Fes, Tetuan, Meknes, and Sale. They were also the chief repositories of the Islamic culture and provided the members of the 'ulema. They controlled domestic trade, the commercialization of imports (cotton, fabrics, tea, sugar), whose consumption increased rapidly in the nineteenth century, and in exchange gathered the goods for export (grain, wool, skins). Fairly well informed of the world situation through their business relations, they feared for Morocco a state of affairs similar to that in Algeria, where the ruling class had been evicted by colonization. By the end of the nineteenth century, they occupied a leading position in the administration.

Another group was formed by the makhzen families, which often came from more recent stock than the urban bourgeoisie. They depended more upon the good will of the princes and often lived apart from the Arab *guish* tribes that had long kept the privilege of supplying the sultan with soldiers. To have some importance within that group, it was necessary to belong to a family that had been employed by the makhzen for several generations. The favor of the prince, however, could also rapidly raise to the highest position an individual whose low birth prevented him from ever being a political threat.[4] At the end of the nineteenth century, makhzen families still held many posts in the army and the government, but they had to share control of the central makhzen with elements of the urban middle class. On the other hand, they still provided most of the qaids in the tribes under the jurisdiction of the sultan. When the central authority was weak, the qaids tended to be chosen from the tribe they were to govern. Small local dynasties with far-reaching but precarious power thus came into existence. But the administered populations frequently threw off the yoke of a protection that had come to weigh too heavily on them. Often, too, the government dismissed and confiscated the possessions of qaids who became too powerful. (The alleged reason was usually corruption, an unavoidable evil encouraged by a system of government in which public offices were distributed to the highest bidder.)

Finally, among the members of the ruling class must be included individuals or families whose religious role was also political: the shorfa, found in urban society as well as in Berber tribes. One of their functions was precisely to act as a mediator between these two hostile societies. The shorfa are descendants of the Prophet, their lineage usually acknowledged by a *dahir*. This quality puts them in a kind of religious aristocracy whose prestige was sometimes even greater in the *siba* than in the traditional towns.[5] At the end of the nineteenth century one man, the sultan, whose authority was sometimes challenged, retained power, absolute by right although limited in its means. He was the subject of numerous intrigues. As he was a symbol of power, there were many who wished to govern through him. Should the sultan be too reticent, they would not hesitate to promote a rival for the highest office, the laws of succession being vague enough to make any sudden attack upon the throne possible. The means at the sovereign's disposal were so limited that bold attempts might be successful in a traditional society based on a strict but unstructured hierarchy.

Pre-Protectorate Morocco thus could not boast either a state structure or a well-established ruling class by European standards. Had those two elements existed, as a sort of "Young Turk" movement, the Protectorate could not have been established as it was. The outstanding fact of this period seems to be a tangled confusion of the various ruling groups together with the absence of any organization that might have enabled a strong-willed minority to impose its will on the whole country.

In the sixteenth century, there had been a widespread popular reaction to the first attempts at European penetration. This movement, led by the shorfa and uniting Berber tribes and the cities, ended with the elimination of the Sa'adi dynasty. The movement also imposed its austere morality on the whole country, checking the cultural and economic expansion of the bourgeois towns. A similar process seemed ready to function at the end of the nineteenth century. But at that time Europe appeared more powerful, and the Moroccan leaders from the makhzen and the cities were worried about the outcome of an opposition that would have exploited the religious and xenophobic feelings of the countryside, even though they often basically agreed with such reactions. There was, therefore, no force capable of unifying or modernizing the country. These various juxtaposed ruling groups were to be federated, as it were, by the Protectorate, which also made use of the absolute though powerless form of government to install a network of hierarchized command.

THE PROTECTORATE: OLD MEN IN NEW ROLES

Structural dualism was the Protectorate's principle of political and legal organization. From sultan to qaid, the old Moroccan state retained the appearance of absolute power inherited from the preceding period. But a parallel administrative hierarchy, running from resident general to indigenous affairs officers, exercised real and apparently unlimited power, through the convenient channel of the Moroccan authorities.

In the beginning, the system did not look like this caricature. From the Fassi bourgeoisie to a qaid such as Goundafi or a pasha like Glaoui, the old elites contributed to the pacification of the country, this being one of the elements of Lyautey's colonial policy.[6] But alongside the old structures of Moroccan society, consolidated by the existence of a strong and centralized power, the Protectorate set up a new modern structure controlling both the administration and the economy. The French ruling class in Morocco was characterized by deep contradictions and divergences. For some, membership in the ruling class was situated in a broader, French context, rather than simply in Morocco. Such was the case in the higher administration and, to some extent, in the large business concerns. Morocco was thus viewed as a necessary "provincial stage" in a brilliant career, or as one of the elements in the interplay of vast rivalries whose essential elements were to be found on another level.

The European ruling groups that were more closely bound to Morocco, such as the political administrators and the settlers, were divided in their view of the country's future. Some sought to install an enlightened despotism that, after a slow evolution, would arrive at broader Moroccan participation in the modern sector, under conditions similar to those in Tunisia or Egypt. Others worked to realign Morocco along the Algerian model and to establish their *de facto* preponderance on the legal basis of "co-sovereignty." Both of these attitudes turned out to be equally ill suited to the evolution of Moroccan society.

Since 1912, the evolution of the Moroccan ruling class has gone through two stages. In the first stage, ending about 1935, the ruling class remained much the same as when the Protectorate was first established. Marshal Lyautey had meant it to retain its role in the traditional sector, in politics and administration as well as in the economic field. The submission of dissident regions was most profitable to this class, which was thus free to spread its commercial influence, practice usury, exercise the functions of qadi or even qaid, and hold positions in the middle ranks of the Protectorate administration. But at the very time that their influence appeared to be spreading, their power was being undermined by the development of a modern sector from which they were carefully excluded. Ostracism was made easy by invoking European criteria of modern knowledge, which the Moroccans could not pretend to possess to the same degree as the colonizers. A theory of separate but equal development evolved, justified by the desire to respect the traditional structures of Moroccan society. The unavoidable consequence was a juxtaposition of two communities: a flourishing new one and another whose decadence soon provided further justification for the privileges of the first.

The Moroccan ruling class was slow to react. The men who had been in power before 1912 were little prepared to evaluate the development of the new community. They appreciated its outward qualities, its administrative efficiency, its guarantees of persons and property, and its technical facilities. They retained the appearance of the old power, though knowing full well that they were not capable of penetrating the new world of technology, but they tried to assure full membership for their sons by securing entry to and through the French schools that dispensed the new learning.[7]

This policy enabled a few members of the middle classes or sons of country notables to profit from a modern education and from an initiation in minor administrative responsibilities. The colonizers sometimes also favored a few children from among their servants or minor officials. The old ruling class thus succeeded in securing for their progeny a means of acceding to the new society. Such an opening remained limited, however, for by 1915, the number of the young Moroccans who had completed secondary education was estimated at about thousand.[8] The army, especially for young Moroccans from rural notable families, was another way of becoming part of modern society. World War II required heavy recruiting of officers. The Indochinese war kept up the flow. The Protectorate administration had subsequently made use of some of them as pashas or qaids, thus initiating a timid evolution toward sharing power with modern leaders who would accept a lasting French presence.

In another field, the urban middle class, with Fassis in the lead, began a conversion that led it to claim increasing responsibilities in the modern economic sector. Without giving up the part they had always played in commerce, they transferred the center of business from Fes to Casablanca. During the Depression and World War II, they became aware of the controls and restrictions imposed on the development of their activities by the public authorities. Whether in import licenses, building permits, or transport authorizations, their wishes for expansion were thwarted by strict, and sometimes even discriminatory, regulations. The danger increased when representatives of the dominant European interests started a campaign for legal measures to guarantee their lasting presence.

The Moroccan ruling class, which had accepted foreign protection in order to undertake modernization of the country, could have been satisfied with a gradual restoration of power to their hands; on no account could they acquiesce in a situation that legalized their permanent estrangement from public affairs. The mistakes of the administration and the international situation hastened the evolution of a conflict situation from which the present-day Moroccan leading class evolved.

THE RULING CLASS SINCE INDEPENDENCE:
CONTINUITY AND CONTRADICTION

The struggle for independence did not bring profound upheavals in the Moroccan ruling class. Launched from the first by the middle class and the king, in reaction to the threatening expansion of French interests, it relied on the world-wide movement that after 1945 caused the disintegration of the old colonial empires, and it tried to mobilize a large portion of French opinion on its behalf. The internal strategy of the nationalist movement did not turn to systematic violence, and most of what occurred was the result of Protectorate blunders. Thus, despite the latent crisis of 1945-53, the structures of Moroccan society were not upset. A slow evolution prompted the sons of the bourgeois

and even of the great qaidal families to become members of the Istiqlal, while
their fathers or uncles held important functions in the makhzen or were on good
terms with the Protectorate authorities. Repression, therefore, could not very
well be extended to the higher ranks of the nationalist movement without the
risk of alienating the traditional notables.

In 1953-55, the struggle hardened. The notables became more and more
involved in counterbalancing the ever more violent commitment of the youth to
the nationalist movement. Arrests and terrorism brought forth a new category of
leaders from the urban proletariat, for whom nationalist action was an extension
of the struggle against the political and economic structures of the Protectorate
but also against the pre-eminence of the traditional Moroccan elites. Both the
middle-class leaders of the nationalist movement and a liberal fraction of the
Protectorate administration acknowledged this danger, and soon came to an
agreement on the basis of political independence coupled with the maintenance
of the old economic structures. When the settlement of Aix-les-Bains was drawn
up in 1955, urban terrorism was checked by the weight of the rural resistance,
traditionalist and faithful to the throne.

The end of the Protectorate thus brought about a new substitution of roles:
this time the Moroccan ruling class succeeded in controlling at least part of the
modern sector, which would otherwise have been created without its
participation. The change was evident in the political field, where all power fell
into the hands of the middle classes, with the help of the Istiqlal. The short
duration of the struggle and the compromises of the settlement permitted
continued extensive technical assistance, which assured the Moroccan political
leaders an effective administrative unit and executive network. But the economic
system remained under European control, and the Moroccan middle class had
not as yet any marked intention of bringing about serious changes. It concentrated instead on its integration into the modern economic class, while retaining some forms of behavior that recalled the situation in Morocco before 1912.

At the same time, collusion and rivalries set up a sort of unstable equilibrium
between the former foreign rulers and the new political class. In the long run,
such a situation gave the impression of stagnation. Neither group deemed itself
capable of finding a solution to any problem of consequence, but each was busy
counteracting the efforts of the other. The result was, on the one hand, unrelated
initiatives that occasionally threatened the essential unity of the country, and,
on the other, a deplorable propensity for individuals to get the most out of the
situation in the shortest time, for want of the means to participate in a rapid
transformation of the structures.

Despite numerous superficial changes, the political class made up of
personalities arising from the higher ranks of the Istiqlal or chosen with the
approval of Mohammed V thus remains confined to a narrow circle. It seems to
have broken for good with the old ruling class of the Protectorate, but family
ties that had helped spread the influence of the young nationalist cadres in the
preceding period also prevent a too drastic purge.

The political class today includes politicians who hold positions in the
government, the parties and the trade unions, but it also includes men in senior
administrative positions. Members of parliament do not play an important part
as yet; if a few of them do so, it is because they also belong as individuals to one
of the preceding groups. The political class is small, less than a thousand, which

explains its vulnerability to the perturbations that have aroused public opinion since independence. Above all its divergencies, there is a kind of fellowship among the more prominent figures on the political stage that provides the tone of their actual relations. Those bonds, whose importance is hard to grasp, can be traced to family connections, to the common struggle against the Protectorate and in shared responsibilities in the Istiqlal movement, or to old school or university friendships in France that were formed too recently to be ignored. Until recently, rivalries and conflicts had not yet succeeded in obliterating the personal elements of solidarity among leaders. They can still be appealed to facilitate contacts or initiate reconciliations. Conversely, the same factor makes attempts at union difficult, because personal rivalries prevail rapidly over programmatic *rapprochements*.

The present study would be incomplete if it had parties and religious groups as its only subject, for there is also a king who has been able to retain and even enlarge upon his prerogatives since independence. Mohammed V returned from exile a national hero, and Istiqlal had to give way to a king who had personally conducted negotiations for independence. His power was restored to its pre-1912 dimensions, and the administration established by the Protectorate was transferred under his authority. Even as the king handed over management of large areas of government to the Istiqlal, he kept direct control of the army and the police. Thanks to his power of appointment, the political class found itself dependent on him. At first he avoided direct intervention and used his authority merely to counterbalance the influence of the dominant party. After 1960, Mohammed V and then Hassan II took over the actual management of government. Until January, 1963, however, they continued to share responsibility with the Istiqlal leaders, while placing in positions of command "king's men": former soldiers, dissident party politicians, minority party leaders, and a few members of the royal family. As long as there is a king, a single party is impossible except with his support. The Moroccan middle class supplies him with the executives he needs. He knows their ambitions and doubtless does not want to give them too much power. Indeed, the Istiqlal, like the Protectorate, was happy to maintain the prestige of the king in order to exert, under cover of his authority, a power that might be resisted by the country were it practiced alone. The National Union of Popular Forces (UNFP) later tried to make a ward of the king by propounding a theory of the monarchy that limited his role to that of a true incarnation of the popular will.[9]

For these reasons, the king has managed to ensure his freedom of action by playing off against one another the various elements of the ruling class who longed for his inheritance while using his prestige. To maintain his arbitrating position, he did not hesitate to commit himself more than was wished by some groups from the middle class. He was also tempted to try to keep all the elements that contributed to his authority, whether through religion or through the traditional relations between monarchy and political, and it would not be accurate to limit his influence to his official supporters.

The [Moroccan] ruling class may be divided into two groups: those who support an effective royal power, and those who do not. The first do not constitute a wholly coherent group. Most of them joined the Front for the Defense of the Constitutional Institutions (FDIC), created in March, 1963, to support the authority of the king and win the elections to the assemblies according to the December, 1962, constitution. Around a nucleus of government personalities, the Front included leaders of the Popular Movement ('Abdelkrim Khatib and Mahjoubi Ahardane), former leaders of the Democratic Istiqlal Party (PDI), Liberal Independents, former Istiqlalis who had long been known for their attachment to the throne (Mohammed Laghzaoui and Ahmed Bahnini), and even members of the royal family (Prince Moulay 'Ali). The party was created by the king's closest collaborator, Ahmed Reda Guedira, who was then practically deputy prime minister. The motto of the party was that of the state: "Our God, Our Country, Our King." But if the king allowed his supporters to act, he took good care not to sponsor the FDIC personally, so that he could disavow its leaders or at least arbitrate their differences.

United in opposition to the Istiqlal and the UNFP, the FDIC was spoiled by success. In May, 1964, a latent crisis broke out between former members of the Popular Movement and independents of various backgrounds who had founded the Socialist Democratic Party (PSD). Most ministers belonged to the PSD, including Prime Minister Bahnini, who was also party chairman, and Foreign Minister Guedira, secretary general and the guiding spirit of the party. The PSD leaders for the most part came from well-known middle-class families. But the Fassi bourgeoisie were fewer than those from Rabat, Sale, or Marrakesh, and the old makhzen families have more members than the commercial middle class. Some elements from the Fassi bourgeoisie, who, long since had broken with the Istiqlal, played an important role, however (Bahnini; Director of the Phosphate Office Laghzaoui; or Minister of Information Moulay Ahmed 'Alaoui). A great many members of the liberal professions, lawyers, doctors, businessmen, and civil servants hold top party positions. Most of them have had modern education on the French system either in Morocco or in France, and profess admiration for the French Fifth Republic and de Gaulle. They resemble the European nineteenth-century middle class in their desire for a liberalism restricted to the elite. They wanted closer economic ties with Europe; the Middle East, and also Algeria, they knew little and trusted less. In their hearts, they feel more inclined toward Senegal or the Ivory Coast in Africa than toward former members of the Casablanca Group [Egypt, Algeria, Guinea, Ghana, Mali]. They foresaw a slow evolution for their country with the help of Europe and without any upheaval in present social relations, which does not mean that they intended to share power with the European minority in Morocco. By means of Moroccanization, which they wanted to see take place not only in the administration but also in the private agricultural, industrial, and commercial sectors, they expected to recover the majority of functions still in European hands. The views of the group extended from the enlightened despotism of the young *dirigiste* technocrats to the unrestricted liberalism of the merchant, who wanted total freedom in his foreign business dealings. Unity of action with the Popular Movement was carried on in the upper spheres of government and in parliament under the conciliating authority of the king. There were many personal ties among leaders of both parties; for example, the interior minister, an active national leader of the PSD, was the brother of Dr. Khatib, president of the Popular Movement and of the House of Representatives.

In opposition to the economic and political tendencies of the PSD, the Popular Movement has stood for rural conservation. This tendency has been especially visible among large flock and landowners who still farm on the *khammes* system (a sharecropper system in which the farmer is paid one-fifth of the output). The greater number belong to the Berber families that supplied the qaids before 1912 and sometimes also during the Protectorate, which earned them the label of "feudals." As a highly structured rural middle class, they have not wanted to bear the cost of the necessary transformation of rural society through agrarian reform or political confiscation. Even though their traditional way of life has not always enabled them to get the most out of their property, it nevertheless has afforded them a prestige and influence they could not very well enjoy as modern farmers.

But in addition to the Berber rural notables, the Popular Movement included young political and administrative cadres, attracted by its anarchical opposition attitudes and also by the fact that the movement lacked modern men to fill party positions of executive responsibility that in the other parties are reserved for the political leaders of the independence generation. Competition with the PSD is limited to a contest of roles in the exercise of power, but it has not excluded an alliance among leaders cemented by unconditional allegiance to the monarchy. All trust the king, and him alone, to arbitrate the differences that arise between groups during the long and difficult period required to pull the country out of underdevelopment. When sacrifices are to be made, they are acceptable only if other groups — and particularly the commercial bourgeoisie from Fes — are not the prime beneficiaries.

Lasting resentments were roused by the Istiqlal after 1955, when it appeared to be seeking to appropriate the benefits of independence and extend its domination over the whole country. As a majority party, it strove for a unification of the country that others thought possible only under the king's authority. The failure of this attempt and the split of 1959 sapped the vitality of the party. However, it is not likely to continue in the opposition, for even though the Istiqlal does not easily give up its leading role in public affairs, it has nevertheless preferred to submit to the arbitration of the king than to see others question the bourgeois vocation to pre-eminence.

Most of the men who rose to power in 1955 belonged to Istiqlal. Mohammed V, sanctified by his active participation in the national movement, appeared more as an honorary party president than a rival power. In this way, his moderating influence was accepted, allowing the "Young Turks" to hold out for more progressive positions. The triumph of the Istiqlal was above all that of the upper middle class that led the party before independence. Most of them had a long nationalist past. Some of them belonged to the "old guard"[10] and militated in the first demonstrations of the party. Those who had a modern education (Balafrej, 'Abdeljalil, Lyazidi, Mohammed al-Fassi, 'Abdelkrim Benjelloun) served in the first governments. Those with a traditional education ('Allal al-Fassi and Boubker Kadiri) had to wait till the 1959 split to reach the front of the political stage again. If there is a majority of the more modern elements among the Istiqlal ministers, the members who held party posts of responsibility are usually products of the traditional education. Both groups, however, have a common tie: they belong to families of the commercial bourgeoisie of Fes. This character was already noticeable in the Istiqlal of the first years of independence, and it became predominant after the 1959 split. An important part of the Fassi middle class modernized its business and moved to Casablanca even before 1941. They expected to use their close ties with the political class to secure the favors of the state. Textile import licenses, public transport passes, state loans and markets, all have been normal sources of profits expected in return for the financial help they gave the party in the struggle for independence. Management positions in the administration have been bestowed according to a complicated system of influence in which family ties, party membership, and urban origins sometimes carried more weight than the personal qualifications of the candidate. Nearly all the young executives fresh from French schools and universities joined the Istiqlal after independence. As the party could not control the political levers because of the king's influence, they placed their men in posts of responsibility in the administration, so as to be fully prepared to get control of the machinery of the state should a crisis break out. For if they accept the king's supremacy for the time being, they have nevertheless the intention to achieve power as soon as possible. They looked upon the first stage of independence as a transitory period. Their tactics presupposed a solid party unity. But some groups inside the party could not accept middle-class immobilism. During the struggle for independence, young intellectuals with a socialist bent and modest urban origins (Mehdi ben Barka, or 'Abderrahim Bouabid) as well as trade-union leaders (Mahjoub ben Seddik, secretary general of the Moroccan Labor Union [UMT]) joined the old middle class militants. Each of these factions hoped to build party unity for its own benefit. Their rivalries led to the party split of January, 1959.

It is difficult, then, to characterize the political groups of the Istiqlal without taking into account this first stage in the story of the party. No doubt Istiqlal subsequently drew closer to the old guard and its leader, 'Allal al-Fassi. Yet it would be a mistake to restrict the political theories of the Istiqlal leaders to middle-class Muslim conservatism. The personality of al-Fassi, who exerts a determining influence on this group, cannot be reduced to such simple points. He alone shares some of the king's charismatic power, owing to his demagogic qualities and his career as a militant. The outstanding feature of his ideology has undoubtedly been his extreme nationalism and his deep sense of Muslim tradition. His concern for national independence and social justice based on the Qoran have led him toward socialism. His Islamic culture is broad, but he has been more interested in European culture than his ostensible disdain for it might let suppose. His *Self-Criticism,* translated in *al-Istiqlal* in 1957, and his articles show an extensive knowledge of the great Western current of thought, although he tends to be confused in his interpretation of them and seems bent chiefly on finding religious justifications for his attitude. In all this, Si 'Allal is representative of a large portion of the Moroccan middle class, which is undergoing deep transformation without wishing to give up its old traditions. The other leaders of the Istiqlal old guard hold views comparable to those of al-Fassi, even when they have received modern education (Lyazidi and 'Abdeljalil). Only younger leaders (Boucetta and Douiri) and a group of young men who span administration and political activity are actually pursuing objectives that differ substantially from the aims and methods of al-Fassi. Though they obviously hold him in veneration, they often are closer to the UNFP than to the other leaders of their party.

Most of the militants and cadres of Istiqlal have had traditional education. Thus, the party supervisors in the provinces have almost all been old 'ulema from the Qarawiyin University and have been closer to al-Fassi than to the leaders with a Western education. The problems of the Middle East, Arab unity, and the revival of Islam outweigh European affairs among their preoccupations. This attitude meets a sympathetic echo among the urban bourgeoisie, whose chief economic activity is directed toward importing and toward trade in manufactured articles, all demanding a high degree of liberalism.[11] The profits of such businesses are greater than those from investments at home. In recent years, however, a new source of investments, in the form of apartment houses, has arisen. The urban bourgeoisie has sometimes ventured into industry with important assistance from the government. More often, the purchase of farmland — through collusion with the administration when former colonial lands were involved — has contributed to the creation of a modern rural bourgeoisie in the coastal plains. Such a tendency is likely to increase in the future, but for the time being it is far from outweighing the most common traditional form of urban investment: cattle-raising in association with country people on communal lands. Such practice, however, bankrupts the country people, prevents the formation of a stable capital stock, and keeps up the opposition between town and country.

Investment has thus begun to present a growing interest for the urban middle class and to constitute the basis of a modern form of power, the accumulation of productive wealth. Yet wealth cannot be useful when so much of it is immobilized in the lavish expenditures necessary to achieve a large following. For, after all, the influence of an individual — or, rather, of a family — is measured more by the extent of his alliances or the number of persons beholden to him than by the size of his property.

Thus, in its general character, the group of the Istiqlal leaders has tended to be representative of the reactions of the Moroccan bourgeoisie or middle class. It is probable that, if other forces had not checked its expansion, it would have succeeded in securing supremacy after independence. The monarchy would have been preserved as a symbol and guarantee of authority imposed on the other social and ethnic group. If Istiqlal had had full control of the means of power, the kind of conflict that would have arisen inside the party, such as the 1959 split that gave birth to the UNFP, would have been solved by eliminating the minority.

The UNFP leaders are undoubtedly the most difficult to define. Nearly all of them are former Istiqlalis who entered the party after 1944. They come from more modest families than the Old Guard leaders and include many intellectuals with a modern education: lawyers, teachers, technicians, administrators, and students. Their estrangement from public affairs after 1960 has left gaps, because it is from this group that men with a clear notion of modern-state realities had been recruited. Their nationalism was often colored with Marxism during their days in French universities. Alert to the problems of economic development and aware of their country's lag, they sought to enforce the measures necessary to a transformation of the structures, which the other members of the ruling class thought advisable in theory but refused to put into practice.

They looked favorably on a one-party system and expected to be able to impose their views within the party. Coalition governments and compromises with the old guard and the palace were but transitional solutions in their opinion. They were persuaded that time was on their side and that they could carry the other leaders with them, or at least strengthen their own positions in the administration and the party. In fact, the stagnation of the first years of independence discredited them in the public's eyes nearly as much as the other leaders: victims of their own tactics, they were easily eliminated by their adversaries. They were unable to win the commanding positions that they sought, yet conditions had not deteriorated to the point where it was possible to persuade a greater number of people of the soundness of their opinions. Unable to apply their socialist program integrally, the UNFP ministers (especially 'Abderrahim Bouabid) practiced a policy of state planning.

They looked to the ben Bella government, the Syrian Ba'th, and Nasser for socialism and Arab unity. Their attitude toward Communism has been more ambiguous. In fact, the Communist Party was forbidden in Morocco under 'Abdullah Ibrahim's government; ever since, the opposition has maintained a certain tactical unity but with little benefit to the Communists. If the Istiqlal leans to the Arab East and the FDIC to Europe, the UNFP's position is rather difficult to define. Some leaders seem fascinated by the revival of the East, but most of them have had a French education and continue to receive their information in French. Their sympathies lie with French intellectuals and radicals who themselves are in opposition — with newspapers, such as *France-Observateur,* or movements, such as the Unified Socialist Party (PSU). The strength of the movement is not easy to estimate. Since they left the government in 1960, the UNFP leaders have concentrated on developing contacts with the Middle East and Algeria. They seem to expect little change from the evolution of Morocco, but put all their hopes in a revolutionary outbreak following the example, or even the intervention, of Algeria. The referendum of December, 1962, was a setback for them, but the communal elections of 1960 and the parliamentary elections of 1963 showed their strength in the large towns along the Atlantic coast. They have a particular constituency in urban, middle-class-cadres and young people with a modern education. An inherent discipline has enabled them to elect professors or lawyers whose names were scarcely known at the time in big cities over personalities from the Istiqlal or FDIC. They also hold the Souss region.

Thus, UNFP leaders appear as a petty-bourgeois and middle-class group clearly opposed to the political monopoly of the monarchy and the domination of upper bourgeoisie of the Istiqlal and the FDIC. They are growing in strength, but they are still far from being able to impose their program on the country by wholly democratic means. Their absence from the institutions of the state creates a vacuum that is not easily filled and doubtless drives their leaders to extremes, when they might otherwise be ready to come to terms with a regime in which the sovereign would still play a determinant role.

The Moroccan Labor Union (UMT) has supported the UNFP leaders. The union is an independent organization and its leaders ensure the local implantation of UNFP at the base. The leaders have never agreed to throw in their lot wholly with any political party, not even before the Istiqlal split. They are suspicious of leaders from the upper classes but at the same time are cautious of the UNFP leaders, whom they consider intellectuals without troops. They regard their own autonomy as the surest means of obtaining maximum advantages for the workers. As the most powerful organization in Morocco, their ambitions tends to go beyond the limits of labor demands into the political domain.

Resistance leaders from the nationalist struggle, often of humble birth, also support the UNFP, although many of them felt that they had been deprived of the fruits of victory after independence. Although they received material advantages as a reward for their role, they expected a greater place in government and they have accused the political parties of having monopolized power at their expense.

ADMINISTRATION, BUSINESS, AND CULTURE

Like the country itself, the civil servants are not a homogeneous body. High officials are appointed by royal decree after nomination by the competent minister and are released from their duties in the same way. They belong to the rural or urban-middle-class families that also dominate the political sector; often, they pass from one to the other. In 1955, the high administrative posts left vacant by the departure of the French were given to young men with university degrees, to former militants of the national movement, or even to minor officials of the French administration. Ever since, those who have been able to keep in the good graces of the successive governments, while lending a ready ear to the desires of the palace and keeping a sharp eye on the political fluctuations, have been able to remain in the forefront of the political stage.

The high officials who belong to the ruling class number three hundred at most. Among the nationalist militants who were appointed in large numbers after independence, only those who had a modern education remained, together with a few lesser former civil servants. Most of the higher Moroccan officials are young men, whose average age is about thirty-five. They usually carry out their responsibilities with spirit, often with ability, but they seldom have any fixity of purpose or sense of public service. They have ties of friendship and solidarity among themselves and also with the political class. They have vast responsibilities at an age when energy should not have already been spent in achieving a career; for many, the result is a desire for power that finds expression both in everyday life and in administrative empire-building. It is difficult to define their behavior, for it is a mixture of a youthful mentality, imitation of the old administration, and a desire to match the foreign accomplishments they discover in the course of their special missions all over the world. They are a picture of the new Morocco but are only a few years away from the weighty past of the country.

Except for the leaders of the army and the police, whose jobs give them a special position within the administration, high officials may be classified into three groups: administrative, financial, and technical. The Protectorate stressed authoritative administration, whose permanence enabled it to enforce its views upon the other services. The traditional sectors of the administrative authority — interior and justice — appear to be less important to the central administration. On the other hand, provincial governors have increased their power; their subordinates are appointed with their approval and often on their suggestion, they supervise the provincial services of the other ministries, and they play a determining role in elections for both local and national assemblies. Their origins are varied: five active senior officers, two former army officers, three former interior officials and one PDI leader who helped found UNFP, one doctor, one chief justice of an appeals court, one ex-leader of a rural union and member of an old Sharifian family, and, finally, two relatives of the king. Because of their political role, the governors depend more on the king than on the interior and other ministers. Several former governors have been appointed ministers, high commissioners, or directors of important services in the central administration.

The financiers are fewer in number, and they find greater scope for their activities in such public institutions as the National Bank, the National Bank for Economic Development (BNDE), the Joint Stock and Management Fund, and the Bureau of Industrial Studies and Participation (BEPI) than in the Finance Ministry. They have not yet played a leading role in a field where Moroccan politicians have been used to sharing their power chiefly with foreign technicians, and when there has not been sufficient latitude for decisions or sufficient means to permit coherent policy. Nevertheless, in the changes in government of November, 1963, two members from this group were appointed undersecretaries of state for economic and financial affairs.

The most prominent group is that of the pure technicians: Moroccan engineers (especially government, mining, and civil engineers) and agronomists, who head important administrative services and public institutions. They are the chief beneficiaries of state intervention in the economic field, which has become increasingly frequent since independence. They received their training in French schools and administrative services, and they have often preserved the traditions and rivalries of the schools and engineering corps. As they are less subject to political change, on account of their specialization, they favor an industrialization that could just as well be achieved by the UNFP leaders as by the king. Only the traditional commercial bourgeoisie has interests contrary to theirs and chafes under the restrictions of planned economy that they seek to impose. This body of technocrats is undoubtedly one of the most dynamic nuclei in the Moroccan administration, but its energy is sometimes spent at the expense of the state. A concern with efficiency does not always go hand in hand with a concern for the general interest. The result is a kind of administrative feudalism whose alliances could threaten the authority of the state.

A few French technical assistants continue to play more important roles than would appear from their official titles, in the shadow of Moroccan ministers and directors. They actually have more influence than control. Their presence is often offensive to Moroccan departmental heads, who chafe at seeing important responsibilities committed to foreigners and at receiving lower salaries than these technical assistants; the Moroccans then seek to raise their standard of living to the same level, which often leads to the corruption from which the administration suffers.

On the whole, the higher civil servants constitute an important sector, all the more because, through various devices (provincial autonomy, public agencies), they endeavor to capture the decision-making power of the politicians without incurring the same risks or the same responsibilities. They are a young group from the bourgeoisie with a modern training, whose desire for efficiency may incline them toward a radical program as much as toward a dynamic program backed by the king. Since they acceded to responsible posts at an early age, they will occupy the higher posts in the administrative hierarchy for a long time to come. Pressure from the lower grades should not be long in making itself felt, however, and might then bring a conservative reaction from the higher bureaucrats.

The army constitutes a privileged clan within the administration.[12] It is the chosen instrument of the king, who was appointed chief of staff while still crown prince. Morocco is by no means a military state, however, and is unlikely to become one unless the other means of government fail. The senior officers now on duty have all come from the French or Spanish armies. Many of them took part in World War II and the Indochina war. Most of them are of rural Berber origin and have had French training, graduating from the military academy of Dar al-Beida near Meknes after secondary schooling at the former Berber *collège* of Azrou; thus, both origins and education set them apart from the other members of the ruling class. Like their French counterparts, they consider politics a factor of disorder and do not look with any great favor on the Istiqlal leaders, who have too much of the urban middle class in them, or on those of the UNFP, who are too intellectual and antimilitary. Conversely, the military is suspect to these two groups because it used to be part of the French or Spanish army and because of the force it represents confronting the politicians' ambitions. Until then, however, the officers' attitude is characterized by a desire not to intervene in political life unless an emergency absolutely requires action. They are on no better terms with the politicians in power than with the opposition. They are faithful only to the throne and especially to the present king, who personally led the operations in Tarfaya, the Rif, and Agadir. Ever since, the army has been his favorite institution, and he often attempts to introduce his officers into the activities of the other fields, particularly the administration. They already provide a number of governors and agents in the regions of the country most difficult to govern, administer the National Promotion program, and build schools and communal centers. But they have practically no entry into the economic and technical sectors of the state's activities.

Within the Moroccan ruling class, the senior officers appear as a homogeneous body with a tradition, and constitute a formidable store of power. They do not seem to have ambitions of their own. But what is true of the senior officers of today might not be as true of those appointed after independence. There are fewer Berbers and more city sons in their ranks, and they have more contacts with political circles. They are harder to please because promotion is slower than in other administrative sectors, and are more committed in politics than are their seniors. A majority of the military still fit the classic image of the apolitical soldier, but politicized officers are beginning to appear among them, as in the Middle East. The day when they begin to take command of troop units, the military may begin to intervene in politics.

The police differ from the army in having no preindependence tradition. Laghzaoui, who belongs to the upper commercial bourgeoisie of Fes, organized the police after independence. He made it an effective and faithful instrument of the king, shying from publicity although probably less politicized than the army. The police are directed by an army officer. Its organization is similar to that of the French National Security, its senior officers for the greater part trained in the police school of Mont-Doré in France. Although they are closer in social origins to the other members of the ruling class than are the army officers, they tend to be distrusted by the bourgeoisie because of their surveillance functions.

Economic circles have been less affected by the evolution that has taken place since 1955 than any other sector of the ruling class. French preponderance remains strong, even though it may have had to assume a different shape. Settlers and commercial circles were the first to feel the effects of independence, and they consider their days in Morocco numbered. Only older men carry on their trade while trying to prepare for their reconversion to France. Moroccanization of this sector appears easy and inviting, since it allows an increase in the number of privileged people without danger. The examples of Algeria and Tunisia should accelerate the process.

Big business has resisted more successfully. It is true that the Bank of Paris and the Low Countries has lost control of the National Bank, the electric company, and the Moroccan railways, but the transfer was carried out under such conditions as to make it impossible to talk of spoliation. Since 1960, there has been an extension of the activities of the Deposit and Consignment Fund in Morocco; its provincial branches afford technical and management assistance for large projects carried out in association with Moroccan public agencies. Close cooperation has thus been set up between the French and Moroccan technical services.

The industrial sector that already existed in 1955 has remained in the hands of the French, but they can no longer intervene in economic life as they used to do before independence. They are always fearful that their actions will be criticized, and so are exceedingly respectful of the directives laid down by the Moroccan authorities. They support the king's government, but they also have some sympathy for the UNFP, whose protectionist tariff policy and labor-union moderation helped to bring about a business revival after independence. While retaining a commanding position, they have lost their fighting spirit. Some look only for maximum short-term profits from their investments, not hesitating to compromise their future, while others are liquidating their investments as best they can.

Independence thus entailed a decline both of bankers' capitalism and of the small and medium-sized business. The only firms to venture now on the Moroccan market are the big industrial firms that take advantage of protective tariffs to build a monopoly in one sector. Backed by the government, they set up assembly plants or industrial manufactures in cooperation with the Moroccan state capitalism. They are more interested in eliminating their market rivals and in the possibilities for rapid amortization than in the industrialization of the country. The Moroccan government is influenced more by these big businesses than by the firms established before 1955.

Foreigners, then, still play a preponderant role in the economic field, even if they can no longer control the decisions of the state. But the mere maintenance of the status quo has the effect of limiting the expansion of the Moroccan middle class. For various reasons, the Moroccan government has hesitated to change the situation too rapidly. At first, the satisfaction felt in recovering the external signs of sovereignty led to a disregard for the economy. Later, the fear of possible dislocation in a little-known field has limited the desire for intervention. Finally, bonds of solidarity have grown up between the former French leaders of agriculture, commerce, and industry and the members of the Moroccan middle class taking their first timid steps in the economic sector. Producers' associations and technical and professional committees have afforded a privileged meeting ground for these contacts. Moroccan representatives are thus in a better position to defend their professional interests in the eyes of the government. Behind them, the French leaders intervene unobtrusively. The campaign for Moroccan association with the Common Market is a typical example of such joint action.

The Moroccan business middle class, however, has not yet reached its full expansion. Its development in the industrial field is still timid and depends on government help. The choice area for its activity remains commerce and real estate speculation. Furthermore, the present interventionist system is not suited to the liberalism desired by the commercial sector. However, state orders and markets, on which they have a priority, make it possible for a few Moroccan firms to earn sizable profits. On the whole, therefore, their attitude is uncertain. On one hand, Moroccan businessmen would like to enter into partnership with foreigners in order to stand up better against state pressure and to maintain high technical standards in industry and commerce. On the other hand, they would like government support to eliminate foreigners and spread their influence over the whole sector, even if it results in a diminished capacity for production. If the first attitude was more common immediately after independence, the second has tended to replace it. The Moroccan middle class now feels ready with the help of the government, to take over the posts filled by the French, and is irritated by the obstacles of the present situation. Moreover, the state economic sector seems to be capable of assuming a truly leading role with the cooperation of upper middle class and the large foreign industrial or banking concerns. Far from being in competition with the private sector, the state has turned to be a help for venturesome initiatives. The main beneficiaries of such policy are the Fassi middle class of Casablanca and some businessmen who used to belong to UNFP. They are ready to buy back the foreign concerns cheaply and to launch new ones with the help of the government. But there are no private banks or large Moroccan industrial firms as yet. The economic power of the bourgeoisie still depends too much on import trade and speculation to be capable of suddenly changing direction to these investments, the risks of which they still leave to the state.

The subjection of the Moroccan ruling class to everything French is most remarkable in the cultural domain.[13] No Moroccan periodicals are as widely read by the elite as *Le Monde, L'Express, France-Observateur,* or *Le Canard Enchaîné,* all from Paris. The ruling class gets its information and thinks in French. All important decisions in politics and administration are made in that language. Legal texts are edited in French, even though the only authorized version is in Arabic. School programs still closely follow the French models, and more than 8,000 French teachers are teaching in Moroccan schools, from primary school to the university. Moreover, an important cultural mission, offering an education entirely on French standards, is besieged with requests for registration of children from the Moroccan ruling class, who want the French curriculum because it is considered to have special advantages. The principal French films, plays, and even Parisian music-hall stars all come to Morocco and perform for an audience that is half European and half Moroccan. On the whole, to have a French education on a secondary or university level is already a certificate of good social standing in Moroccan society. The same language, the same habits, the life in the same part of town, all constitute a very important element of solidarity. The French ruling class has no longer an important functional role to play in Morocco. It has, however, handed down a model of cultural behavior that has left its mark on Moroccan society. In the absence of a sudden reversal, the Moroccan ruling class in a few years will be very much like its French model, all the more so since numerous mixed marriages will have given birth to children for whom mixed culture will be one of the basic elements in their upbringing.

CONCLUSIONS

An examination of the different fields in which an elite could find scope for the exercise of decision-making power in a modern state has led to a compartmentalized and rationalized picture of the Moroccan ruling class. In fact, the present ruling groups, whether political, administrative, or technical, all come from the old ruling class and complement more than they oppose each other. Under the Protectorate, the first generation carried the traditional elites into the modern world, thus making way for the government and administration of today. Nowadays, the Moroccan middle class takes jealous care that its children get first-rate education in the schools of the French cultural mission, thus preserving future generations of technicians from the hazards of a policy of Arabization. In a few years, the majority of doctors and engineers will rise from this social group, thus making way for another change in the ruling class.

In retrospect, the most striking element for over half a century has been the continuity of the family network throughout an eventful national history. Indeed, the transmission of patrimony does not have the same character in Morocco that it has in countries under Roman law. Fortunes are quickly dissipated because of the large number of children in well-to-do families. But the name, the membership in a family, is a fortune in itself, often the only advantage a man can boast of to other members of the same social group. Such practice extends the influence of the family network already established in Morocco before 1912. Functional divisions matter less than a system of relationships dating back into the past. Thus, the separate ruling groups that had set themselves up within the bourgeoisies of the several cities now see their sphere of action expand to the national level. For the rural elites, ethnic solidarity produces the same effects. On these grounds, the common culture and education of the modern elite, building on these foundations, also create new situations that overstep functional boundaries. Indeed, members of the ruling class are easily interchangeable because of the absence of rigid structures.

Europeans and Jews, who in many ways share the life of this ruling class, cannot be considered dominant since they are accepted only insofar as they can support the activities of the Muslim Moroccan bourgeoisie, a group that undoubtedly wants to take over management of its own interests and the future of the country. For many, the king is still the supreme arbiter among groups and a connecting link with the masses; others want to see his role limited so that they may take direct control over coming social transformations. All are aware of the gap between them and the bulk of the country. Their urban origins, modern culture, European way of life, wealth and luxury, all constitute barriers that alienate the ruling class from the country and hamper the necessary contacts with traditionalist rural or urban proletarian groups. In 1912, a similar dissociation led the rulers to seek refuge in the Protectorate. They are today decided to assume their responsibilities, but they are reluctant to face the real problems. A search for external economic support makes it possible to delay choices whose consequences are hard to foresee. Such evasion before the difficulties and deficiencies of the country could be disastrous.[14] Should it fail, the ruling class may well be tempted to take advantage of its present situation to survive as a group. Other elements, who are less open to the external world but more imbued with Arab and Islamic culture, are preparing to succeed it. More widespread education with lower standards than those that benefited the present ruling class should stimulate the appearance of new social strata. Local administration and sometimes even political life are already the domain of younger elements educated in the country since independence. As a rule, they do not have the high cultural level of their elders, but they appear more representative of the country and its divisions. But numerous and violent conflicts are to be expected before a new modern ruling class can make itself accepted.

At present, the monarchy is the strongest link between the ruling class and the predominantly rural country. There is an interdependence between the king and the modern bourgeois elites that should make possible the necessary stages and mitigate momentary egoisms through a sense of the national continuity: In the absence of a single party, enlightened despotism is doubtless the best way for a country to evolve without a loss of unity.

Notes

1. Jacques Berque, "L'Univers politique des Arabes," *Encyclopédie Française*, 77-36-1.

2. See Henri de Montety, "Old Families and New Elites in Tunisia," pp. 171—80 in this reader.

3. See E. Michaux-Bellaire (ed.), "L'Organisme marocain," *Revue du Monde Musulman*, No. 9 (September, 1909) pp. 1-43.

4. See E. Aubin, *Le Maroc d'aujourd'hui* (Paris: Armand Colin, 1904), pp. 190 and 218.

5. E. Michaux-Bellaire, "La maison d'Ouezzane," and "Une Tentative de restauration Idrissite à Fes," *Revue du Monde Musulman*, No. 5 (May, 1908), pp. 23-98 and 393-424.

6. Dr. F. Weisberger, *Au Seuil du Maroc Moderne* (Rabat: La Porte 1947), pp. 310 ff., showing how Lyautey restored order in Fes after the 1912 riots through the help of the urban bourgeoisie.

7. As early as 1908, the grand vizir expressed the wish that the programs for Muslim colleges be identical to those in the French *lycées*, so as to allow young Moroccans to go on to higher studies. The Direction of Public Instruction for a long time tried to limit enrollment of young Moroccans to the *baccalauréat* by putting them in different programs. See R. Gaudefroy-Demonbeynes, *L'Oeuvre francaise en matière d'enseignement au Maroc* (Paris: Paul Geuther, 1928), p. 131.

8. See de Montety, *loc cit.*

9. See Ernest Gellner, "The Struggle for Morocco's past," pp. 37—49 in this reader.

10. Douglas E. Ashford, *Political Change in Morocco* (Princeton, N.J.: Princeton University Press, 1961), p. 219.

11. Marie Bousquet, "Les Rapports de la bourgeoisie et de la monarchie au Maroc," *Les Temps Modernes,* April, 1962, pp. 1483-92.

12. André Ammoun, "Les F.A.R. et le trone marocain," *Etudes Méditerranéennes,* No. 8 (November, 1960).

13. See Douglas E. Ashford, "Second- and Third-Generation Elites in the Maghrib," pp. 93–107 in this reader.

14. See the severe but justified judgment of the national bourgeoisie by Frantz Fanon, *The Wretched of the Earth* (New York: Grove Press, 1964), p. 113.

20

BUREAUCRATIC TRANSITION IN MOROCCO

JAMES R. SHUSTER

A recent excellent study of the political aspects of Middle Eastern social change[1] analyzes four principal "instruments of political modernization": the army, the political party, the trade union, and, finally, the civil bureaucracy. It is significant that the last-named instrument receives far less attention than the others, not because it is less important but simply because the bureaucratic-administrative aspect of political development has been relatively neglected by Western analysts. Although another recent publication[2] clearly recognizes this lack, not just in the Middle East but in the whole field of developing nations, and does a good deal to alleviate it, the fact remains that bureaucracy as an instrument of modernization has not been a favored focus for analysis. In the Middle East, where bureaucracy's role in modernization and social change has been of vital importance, only Morroe Berger among sociologists has chosen this traditional sociological field as a vehicle for his research.[3] It is not the purpose of this paper to develop reasons for the relative lack of concern with bureaucracy's role in development. Rather, our attention will be given to a case study involving three aspects of the topic: first, the importance of bureaucracy in developing Morocco; second, the problem of Moroccanization and its solutions; and third, the implications of these solutions for Morocco's future and for the place of bureaucracy in the Middle East's modernizing societies.

BUREAUCRATIC ATTRIBUTES AND MOROCCAN POLITICAL STRUCTURE

After obtaining her formal independence from France in 1956, Morocco was faced with the necessity of decision-making in both the value sphere and the instrumental realm. On the one hand, it was vital to decide on basic value-orientations and measures for coordination, continuity, and national solidarity. Such decisions involved the rejection of concepts like tribalism and overt secularization as being feudal or colonialist, and the acceptance of positive slogans such as independence, unity, and technical proficiency. On the other

Reprinted, by permission, from *Human Organization,* XXIV, No. 1 (1965), 53–58.

hand, Moroccan leaders had to make decisions and take action on the implementation of such values. Practical policies involved translating abstract sentiments like independence into feasible, systematic, and effective procedures. Also involved were allocative decisions concerning the mobilization and commitment of resources, both human and natural. In both these major areas, the value sphere and the instrumental but especially the latter, the Moroccan government bureaucracy played a preponderant role. The reasons will become clear after an examination of Morocco's politico-administrative structure and the characteristics of the government bureaucracy.

That bureaucracy possessed four attributes which gave it a major role in determining the direction of Moroccan policy. In general terms, they can be referred to as control, continuity, cohesion, and comprehensiveness.

Control means simply that the bureaucratic administration has been, and to a large extent still is, the effective government of Morocco. In the absence, until 1963, of any elected body of representatives who would be responsible to the people for the legislative process, the career civil servants and their appointed political leaders have enjoyed a monopoly of power. Both the elaboration and the implementation of policy lay in their hands. This is not to claim that there were no other power centers. The Moroccan monarchy is a potent force, combining traditional charismatic loyalties with an openly professed pledge to transform the country into a modern, democratically ruled nation. And the political parties vied strenuously behind the scenes to get their leaders into cabinet positions, although until elections were held and the assembly convened, there was no official political sphere in which they could operate and no institutionalized means whereby they could make legitimate their claims to popular support. In the intervening seven-year period the bureaucracy both proposed and disposed, and even today, as executive arm of the monarchy, it is still far from being subordinated to the legislature in the fashion that Western observers have come to expect. Political initiative and control has been, and largely still is, in the hands of bureaucratic administrative personnel.

The second attribute, continuity, is an important adjunct of the first. The bureaucratic-administrative aspect of government was the principal component of the French Protectorate era, from 1912 to 1956, and even after Morocco became independent the structure, methods, and general organization of the administration remained remarkably untouched by the shift in political status. Even in the pre-Protectorate era of Moroccan independence, the sultan's government of traditional mold leaned heavily to the executive side, and the administration was organized into a type of bureaucracy that was neither crude nor ineffective. Therefore, it can be argued that French control accented an already existing trend in Morocco and gave it form and substance by extending secular royal authority to the entire country and by transforming the traditional administrative organization into a full-fledged rational-legal Western bureaucracy. That basic form of administration has remained constant ever since, and although the regaining of independence brought extensive personnel changes, the structure, procedures, ideas, and even much of the training remained in essence similar to that introduced by the Protectorate. The "Moroccanization" of the administration will be examined below. What is important here is that, apart from the personalities of individual leaders, the bureaucracy has given Morocco the only continuous element in its political sphere.

Continuity stems in large measure from the cohesiveness of a bureaucratically organized administration. In a transitional situation where old ways of life are being challenged by vaguely defined modern alternatives, bureaucracy offers a systematic set of norms appealing to both traditional and modernizing values. The hierarchy of authority and extreme specialization of tasks appear normal to a culture where intensive specialization is basic (Carleton Coon's "mosaic society") and where authoritarian rule has long obtained. The modern aspect of the bureaucratic ethos is expressed in the explicitness of its regulations, the functional specificity of its role definitions, and the universalistic task-orientation of its selection criteria. Here the new employee can find freedom from traditional barriers and restrictions, provided of course he can obtain the skills and attributes valued by the new system. At the same time that he discovers the modernity of individually obtaining a well-defined position in a powerful organization actively engaged in leading and changing his own society, he also becomes aware of the bureaucracy's traditional appeal — a new kind of total organization offering a pseudo-kinship security and stability to its members. The bureaucracy tends to make of its members a real social grouping; the formal structure of the organization, its rules, the similarity of working conditions and economic rewards, all combine with the major norms of any bureaucracy — interdependence and loyalty to the system — to produce a special bureaucratic *esprit de corps* that is a force to be reckoned with in any social equation. Such a force may operate negatively to retard the attainment of national goals; interest in the development and welfare of the bureaucracy itself may take precedence over efficient task-performance in the minds of administrative employees. But any social structure that exercises control, possesses continuity, and incorporates powerful cohesion must be dealt with if an adequate analysis of forces working for and against change, in Morocco or elsewhere. And the more so when we consider bureaucracy's fourth attribute, comprehensiveness.

In brief, the Moroccan bureaucratic administration crosscuts all factions — political, ethnic, religious, regional — as well as all functions — planning, direction, and execution. Because of its essential task-orientation and rationalistic recruitment, the bureaucracy can include types of people (natives, foreigners, all social classes) who would be unable to fit into more particularistic organizations. Its only rival in comprehensiveness, the nationalist party, has no such institutionalized access to the key functions and important groups in the society. While attempting to be inclusive, the party is less well organized, and its recruitment methods take in factions whose only ties are common dislikes. The result in Morocco was an open split between the conservative and radical wings of the nationalist party, and even greater emphasis upon the bureaucracy as the sole structure in politics where persons of differing values could work together on necessary projects within a common organizational framework.

The four factors of control, continuity, cohesion, and comprehensiveness, however sketchily presented above, should serve to indicate the importance of the civil bureaucracy to independent Morocco's development into a viable modern nation. Our next task is to indicate how that bureaucracy became Moroccanized, transformed from a foreign element imposed by France into the keystone of the country's political structure.

STRUCTURAL AND ORGANIZATIONAL MEASURES FOR
INCORPORATION

The problem of Moroccanization is really that of institutionalizing the bureaucracy, and involves two aspects, the structural and the organizational. The structural aspect has to do with the functional independence and self-sufficiency of Moroccan society — whether or not it can meet the needs of a modern bureaucratic administration. The organizational aspect deals with the recruitment and training of Moroccan personnel — who fill administrative posts, and how they got there.

Morocco's administrative framework is a legacy of the French Protectorate. During the Protectorate era, it was linked much more closely to France's policies than to Morocco's needs. Strong overemphasis was placed on the control functions; administrative units like the police and the Interior Ministry were well developed. Coupled with the control emphasis was a heavy reliance on French institutions and organizations. Obvious lacks like policy-making bodies, foreign-relations units, and military forces were easily explained: their duties were performed by the appropriate French agencies. Even where Moroccan institutions were developed, as in education, the development was not extensive enough to provide an adequate base for self-sufficiency. Only an elite could be educated to take their place beside Frenchmen, and even most advanced education was in French schools and universities in France. Morocco was, in fact, a dependent society whose political institutions (and their educational infrastructure) were mere extensions of those in France. The task of an independent Morocco desirous of severing such ties was, and is, to provide administrative structures capable of performing all the necessary functions, including the function of preparing Moroccans to operate those structures. While this has meant that some units (like an engineering school and a foreign service) have had to be created out of whole cloth, the Protectorate did endow Morocco with at least the nucleus of advanced training institutions. The present University of Rabat is founded upon the former Institutes of Higher Muslim Studies and of Science. The school system in general is a vastly expanded version of the Protectorate-founded one. And, most important for Moroccanization's organizational aspect, there was founded in 1948 a special, educationally sound and potentially effective school, the Moroccan School of Administration. The basic difficulties in Moroccanization are no longer structural; the country is equipped with an administrative structure complete in all respects and with enough educational infrastructure to support the bulk of its requirements. In actual fact, however, for certain high-level jobs requiring special skills (such as physician or agricultural engineer) there is continued dependence on foreign, especially French, institutions. The continued existence of such structural dependence implies several things: one, that with the settlement of key political issues like independence there can be useful and cordial relations between the former controlling power and its ex-protégés; two, that a mark of political maturity and responsibility is the tempering of nationalist ideology with administrative rationality; three, that highly organized bureaucratic structures exhibit strong resistance to change, so that it is easier for administrators to continue a former system, even across political boundaries, than it is to come up with a viable alternative. It might even be suggested that wherever bureaucrats control the conduct of affairs, the prevailing mood will be one of sober and utilitarian preservation of whatever system exists. Political leaders are seduced by ideology, but bureaucratic administrators love regularity.

Organizationally, we find that Moroccanization has solved a number of its problems only to have those very solutions raise further questions. Under the Protectorate there was heavy dependence on French staff in top and second-level posts, and a French monopoly on the control jobs. Moroccans worked for the French administration in large numbers but were found almost exclusively in subordinate positions. This was the result of a kind of *de facto* segregation: recruitment standards were rigorously equal for both French and Moroccan candidates, but educational opportunities and motivational factors were not. And early attempts at deliberate recruitment of Moroccans took the form of creating low-level cadres for which Frenchmen were not eligible. After independence there was no longer a motivation problem, since the government was now viewed as "ours," not "theirs." The training problem, however, took on an even more serious aspect. Just at the time when French staff were leaving to take up secure positions in France, thereby creating vacancies, there was also a nationalist push for expansion of government services, particularly education. Without such expansion, long-term Moroccanization would be deprived of its vital training base, but short-term attempts to recruit Moroccans could not cope even with the vacancies, let alone the expansion. Nationalism notwithstanding, there was only one practical solution: French aid. The same situation prevailed in nonpolitical technical posts requiring considerable special training; until Moroccans could obtain this training, reliance had to be placed on the incumbents or on their French replacements. Why French aid? Frenchmen had the most interest in Morocco, both personal and national; there was no language difficulty; and the administrative system was totally French. While the question of French administrative assistance to Morocco deserves a separate study, it is noteworthy in passing that Moroccan objections were not usually to the use of new French employees but only to the retention of those who had served the Protectorate. In summation, independent Morocco continues to employ Frenchmen wherever Moroccans are lacking in numbers or skills. The other forces at work in Moroccanization help further to explain this.

One such factor is differential job attraction. The administrative generalist, with a liberal-arts background, is much more frequently found among Moroccan trainees than is the administrative specialist, even more so if we include technical positions like engineer. The vast majority of students at the Moroccan School of Administration take the general administration courses, even though there are three other options leading to equally good job opportunities.[4] Morocco, like all other nations, still faces the difficult job of channeling individual interests into social needs.

Another such factor is the bifurcation in skill levels. The mass of Moroccans possess few skills relevant to a bureaucratic administration, but a small number are extremely well trained. The result for Moroccanization is a kind of pincers movement: those who are well prepared go immediately to top-level positions, while the relatively low-skill posts at the bottom are easily filled. The middle-level cadres, the heart of any smoothly operating system, are left undermanned, and it is here that one finds a heavy reliance on foreign staff. The essential quality sought is not special training so much as it is experience with procedures and working familiarity with practical problems. And it is precisely these qualities that cannot be provided by any stepped-up Moroccanization scheme, however well run. One strong reason for non-Moroccanization in the middle cadres is that there is so much need, and room, at the top. Prerequisites for most jobs have been downgraded, meaning that candidates have in effect been upgraded. As a result, persons with what used to be middle-level skills now get top-level posts. For example, graduates of the Moroccan School of Administration now go to the top-level (A cadre, planning and direction) instead of, as formerly, to the second level (B cadre, management and application).[5] And Moroccans who are well prepared in needed specialties, such as medicine and engineering, do not stay even in the top bureaucratic jobs but move up to the political, ministerial level, often outside their specialty (physicians as ambassadors and ministers of education, for example). The positions of political leadership attract the truly skilled; middle range candidates move up to top bureaucratic jobs; low-level jobs are filled by low-skill persons permanently relegated to such positions; and the middle cadres are left to do as best they can, depending on French employees until recruitment stabilizes and the training facilities adjust to the present demands.

The structural changes, chiefly in education, aim at preparing the candidates to fit rational recruitment criteria. The actual recruitment procedures aim at devising reasonable criteria to fit the existing candidates. To accomplish this, the direct means has been to adjust the former standards downward. In general, school degrees needed for given positions were lowered one whole category, i.e., from university to secondary-school level, and so on. Likewise, access to qualifying examinations was eased, or the examinations even eliminated altogether. All such measures are perceived as temporary expedients, to last a maximum of five years. But the structural changes have had less effect than anticipated, and already some extensions to the temporary measures have been required. This time-extension is one matter, but the content-extension is much more important. Since the candidates for jobs are subject to less stringent criteria, there must be a means of supplementing their initial deficiencies in order to assure minimal performance levels. Each bureau where temporary recruitment criteria are operating uses special programs of in-service training to alleviate partially their new employees' lack of proper skills. Needs are so acute, and supervisory personnel capable of training recruits are in such short supply, that in practice the special training period becomes all too often a purely formal *rite de passage* instead of a true probation. An outline of possible recruitment schemes is not complex. Under optimal conditions one gives to well-prepared candidates a solid administrative training, with proficiency examinations, and the best of those who qualify, for example, graduates of the Ecole Nationale d'Administration at Paris, are hired. Or, one takes candidates with mediocre preparation and gives them a quality education, hiring those who obtain their diploma, for example, from the Moroccan School of Administration. Both of these possibilities occur before recruitment. A third logical possibility is to recruit without special regard for specific administrative skills but to depend on post-recruitment training and supervised performance. It is represented by Morocco's special in-service training, but this method is slow and inefficient unless there is a high ratio of supervisors to trainees, so that adequate performance levels are assured. Even though the operation of the Moroccan programs leaves much to be desired (supervisors are too few and busy to supervise), they are the only logical answer to the educational and experiential deficiencies of the present generation of administrative employees. The preparation given at the Moroccan School of Administration is unquestionably of better quality than in-service training, and it represents an important stage in the transition to a civil-service system truly institutionalized into the structure of Moroccan society. The process of gradual institutionalization, or Moroccanization, is showing results, but no program of large-scale social change ever accomplishes its objectives without strain or even disruption. The Moroccanization plans are exacting their social cost now and will exact it in future; our last task is to review some actual and probable sources of dysfunction and their implication for Morocco's future administration.

PRESENT AND POSSIBLE CONSEQUENCES OF MOROCCANIZATION

Despite the difficulties, Moroccanization has brought positive results. While there is still the dependency on France noted above, the bureaucracy is led by Moroccans, staffed in the vast majority of positions by Moroccans, and has functioned effectively in ruling the country for a lengthy period (since 1956) that has included serious crises: a bitter split in the main political party, the Istiqlal; regional revolts in Berber areas; a successful change of kings when Mohammed V, hero of the freedom movement, died and was succeeded by his son, Hassan II; and far from least, the battles of election campaigns in the country's first regional and national elections. The last point is especially crucial: power has been in the hands of men who were institutionally controlled by the bureaucratic structure. In a nation lacking national solidarity, where nepotism and favoritism have surrounded political decisions, whose citizens have had little experience of civic spirit, the bureaucracy can provide an institutional framework that helps to ensure responsible planning and direction by subjecting those in power to systematic, rationalized processes and relationships. A bureaucratic administration is not in itself a democratic organization, but it can play an important part in institutionalizing democratic government. Even in the United States, bureaucracy has provided examples and leadership to elective bodies in strengthening such elements of democracy as equal justice or fair and sensible criteria for participating in civic affairs. Not just in Morocco but in the entire Middle East, there is room for analysis of the contributions of bureaucracy to the establishment and maintenance of effective, orderly, responsible government.

There is also a less positive side to the Moroccanization program. One aspect of it has to do with short-term plans undermining long-range expectations. A kind of Gresham's Law of recruitment has begun to operate: direct recruitment by lowered criteria tends to drive out other means, particularly the Moroccan School of Administration. The first demands less of candidates, and the rewards are larger and immediate; the second, for similar eventual rewards, demands several years of hard work at a financial sacrifice, with the possibility of failure. The first method lowers standards, the second attempts to retain them. Recognition of the problem has brought attempts to suppress direct recruitment, but too many people are involved with this means to eliminate it now. The solution lies in tightening criteria, refusing to allow direct recruiting of school dropouts, and increasing the scale of rewards for those who present better credentials and training. A corollary difficulty is the conversion of intermediate educational goals into terminal ones. The secondary-school possibility of obtaining government jobs on the basis of secondary-school diplomas induces students to terminate their education at that point, instead of continuing on for an advanced degree. The eventual return to higher recruitment criteria is thereby impeded.

A second aspect is the effect that successful Moroccanization of personnel has on the administrative system. Reform of the civil service is a term employed frequently by its critics, by which they mean greater adaptation of the existing bureaucracy to the particular needs of Morocco. As noted above, there have been additions to the system imported from France, but few changes. The extra premium paid (and still paid) to Frenchmen was eliminated for Moroccan employees soon after independence; in 1957, salaries and family allowances were frozen; the latest proposal (May, 1964) was for a 20 per cent cut in pay. All these were attempts to transform an organization from one modeled on the scale of France to one fitted to the more modest Moroccan scale, but the last measure is the only one that will have major effect. Reform in general is supported only by nonbureaucrats; as more and more Moroccan personnel are recruited, increasing numbers of people develop a vested interest in keeping the existing system intact. Organizational success renders structural changes difficult.

Another form of vested interest may also develop. New personnel recruited under the eased regulations on entrance and advancement will very likely want to continue those regulations permanently. Slow economic growth and lack of opportunity in the private sector may continue to make government service attractive to future candidates, who will not wish their entry made more difficult. In a functional sense, one can entertain the notion that perhaps the original criteria were too high, unrealistically so, and that the use of different recruitment standards will result in a bureaucracy not so efficient on an absolute scale but quite capable of dealing with Morocco's present needs. One thing is certain: a return to the former standards, or their equivalents, will bring future difficulties within the system. Present employees, risen in rank by seniority at least, will have subordinates much better trained than they. Internal conflict can be expected. There will already have been advancement difficulties because the recruitment under the drive for Moroccanization takes place in waves, instead of the usual staggered entry into service under normal conditions of operation.

BUREAUCRACY'S ROLE IN DEVELOPMENT

In the final analysis, the crucial question for any bureaucratic system is its functional operating level: how well are the tasks performed? What is the nature of the system, and how well do its employees operate?

It seems clear that in many respects the Moroccan administration is still French, and that this particular form of bureaucracy may well prove to be one of France's most enduring legacies in Morocco. But it would be foolish to deny the effects of Moroccanization and the kinds of changes that they can be expected to bring. As education becomes increasingly Moroccan in character, and as Arabization (not yet very advanced) changes the language and the concepts of bureaucratic communication, the system will become less French.

Widespread education and the recruitment of personnel trained in the new schools will render the system less elitist, no longer a foreign element with Westernized employees but one whose workers and leaders will have closer ties to the Moroccan masses. At the same time, the formation and institutionalization of other power centers (such as parties, and the Assembly) will render the bureaucracy less powerful and will presage its eventual subordination to political organizations. As experience accumulates, there will be greater emphasis placed upon direct, effective action and less on grandiose plans, since administrative ability, like research ability, is only partly a matter of formal precepts. In addition, the new administrators will be less restricted by lack of specific skills and less handicapped by lack of breadth and the ability to take the long view. Finally the bureaucracy will tend to become less formalistic and self-concerned as the bureaucratic context of work becomes natural for Moroccans. And when it is no longer felt to be an alien element in the social fabric, it can become more flexible and adaptive to shifting needs. The growth of specialization and the accumulation of new knowledge place in doubt the continued use of strictly career civil servants. By using specialists from outside the bureaucracy proper, a far greater degree of administrative responsiveness can be had without commitment to an oversized corps of permanent government employees. However, development of this type of bureaucracy requires full development of other modern aspects of society — politics, business, education, and the free professions — to permit borrowing of personnel and efficient cross-utilization. Some indication of cracks in the too rigid structure of administrative recruitment has already appeared in the use of private contracts to evade the rules, thus hinting that even the revised procedures are not fully responding to the present needs of the system.

In an era when bureaucracies are attacked as enemies of democracy and political parties receive the limelight, Morocco provides a clear case of a new nation where bureaucracy has acted responsibly in directing the country on the path to modernization. This article suggests that such actions are not the result of powerful leadership personalities alone but are to a degree implicit in the structure of the bureaucracy itself. The Moroccanization of the bureaucratic administration has, and will continue to have, some serious dysfunctions, but the context of action also provides institutional safeguards during the period of transition. Studies of bureaucracy as both the instrument and the object of social change can provide further clues to the meaning of events in the Middle East's transitional societies.

Notes

1. Manfred Halpern, *The Politics of Social Change in the Middle East and North Africa* (Princeton, N.J.: Princeton University Press, 1963).

2. Joseph La Palombara (ed.), *Bureaucracy and Political Development* (Princeton, N.J.: Princeton University Press, 1963).

3. See his *Bureaucracy and Society in Modern Egypt: A Study of the Higher Civil Service* (Princeton, N.J.: Princeton University Press, 1957), and his article "Bureaucracy East and West," *Administrative Science Quarterly,* I (1957), 518–29.

4. The four course options, after a common initial year of study, are: General Administration; Social (labor problems, welfare, and so on); Economic and Financial; and Classical (having to do with traditional Muslim legal and social aspects).

5. There are four levels of cadres in the Moroccan civil service: A, B, C, and D. The C cadres (secondary) include duties involving skilled execution, such as clerks. The D cadres (subaltern) contain the lowest level of employees, with no particular skills or specialization.

21

THE ALGERIAN ARMY IN POLITICS

I. WILLIAM ZARTMAN

Politics in Algeria is revolutionary.[1] This means essentially five things:

1. There is no *legitimacy* outside of revolutionary symbols, groups, and policies.[2] The Revolution is invoked by any government seeking to legitimize its incumbency, to which the opposition responds by decrying the betrayal of the Revolution and by promising a return to it. Contenders for power come from among those who have participated in the revolutionary war, in combat or in prison, and who have thus established a mystical bond between themselves and the people through which the needs and desires of the mass are "known" and represented. Any political criteria for policies is couched in terms of bringing the fruits of the Revolution to the parts of the population most closely identified with it and represented by their spokesmen; although any precise definition of revolutionary expectations will probably be absent, they do include political positions as well as economic improvements, thus completing the circle.

Since legitimacy of this sort is basically unstable and does not derive from more durable sources, such as institutions or a history of satisfactions, governments so legitimized are continually in need of proving their right to rule and are inherently beleaguered and defensive.

2. The revolutionary war gave rise to a strong millennialist feeling, including immediate *expectations* for the fruits of the Revolution.[3] Those who participated in the war expected things to be better after it was over: in a typically ambiguous set of feelings, they expected to be rid of the disruptive and humiliating foreigner in order to return to their life undisturbed but also in order to benefit from social change and economic improvement. In addition, they expected an immediate inheritance of the visible goods of modern life in Algeria and accession to the newly vacated positions of power, prestige, and employment. The latter set of expectations was easier to achieve than the former,

This is a revised version of a paper originally presented at the Princeton University Conference on the Middle East, in 1965. The study is part of a project on "Revolution in Developing Countries" at the Center for International Studies of New York University; reprinted by permission. Other versions of the study have appeared in *L'Annuaire de l'Afrique du Nord,* 1967 (Paris: Centre National de la Recherche Scientifique, 1967), pp. 265–78, and Claude E. Welch, Jr., ed., *Soldier and State in Africa* (Evanston, Ill.: Northwestern University Press, 1970).

and in time conflicted with it. Visible goods were immediately inherited through the peasant land seizure that began in late 1962, was legalized by the March 1963 decrees, and has gradually been transformed into broad nationalization of agriculture and industry. Participants in the war occupied vacant positions, only to find — after a suitable period of enjoyment — that their deprivation under colonial rule and their experience in fighting the revolutionary war were not always useful when it came to running farms and factories (particularly in commercializing their products and maintaining their equipment) and to improving the lot of the people from positions of government and party leadership. Worse, those who participated in the war were told of their incompetence by other Algerians: urban ideologues and technocrats. The first sought an immediate stopgap in ideological explanations of current shortages and doctrinaire assurances of a clear road to future prosperity; divided between government and opposition, they were chased out by, then with, ben Bella. The second are more pragmatic and more useful to the effective running of a state mechanism, but their effectiveness is based on stable government and sufficient time, a point on which they are weaker than the ideologues.

The dilemma then remains: the expectations are high and immediate, two characteristics that are not propitious for their satisfaction; impatient reactions growing out of dissatisfaction create instability that retards effective government even more (and re-emphasizes the importance of the army).

3. If *power* in such a situation does not grow directly out of the barrel of a gun, it does grow out of the possession of a gun.[4] Politics has been escalated closer to violence as a result of war and political change. The military, by its structure as a disciplined body, by its command (and presumed monopoly) of force, by its composition as a national organization, and by its position as successor to the nationalist guerrillas, plays a predominant role in determining who rules and who revolts. The National People's Army (ANP) is in a poor position to rule by itself; its aims are limited, its numbers small, and the more accent it places on its nature as a professional army, the more its own legitimacy is contestable. However, it does feel that it has a mission as watchdog on the Revolution, a role that is minimal in "good times," that extends to intervention in the political process when the Revolution is not being carried out, and that is ambiguous in between. Because of this situation, factional splits within the ANP are of primary significance, and there is no question of a civilian-controlled, apolitical army existing in Algeria for some time. At the same time, the raw and ultimate nature of power in revolutionary Algeria means that no governmental change can take place against the army or without the army being involved. Its military nature makes the army the best organized and only truly national (that is, drawing from the entire population) group in the country; its organization gives it special interests to watch over and defend; its successor relation to the National Liberation Army (ALN) makes it the strongest political institution to grow out of the Revolution; and its past performance and beliefs (namely, Fanonism) shows it unafraid to use its power to defend the Revolution or its own interests. No other organization has these strengths; the only current competitor to the army is a part of it.

4. The *political system* is being redefined.[5] This poses a dual, and also somewhat incompatible, need. On the one hand, there is pressure for institutionalizing or state-building. New bodies and procedures must be

established to carry out governmental and political processes, that is, to make decisions on the allocation of goods and services in society and to establish channels for the integration of the population through political participation and identification. On the other hand, there is pressure for socializing or nation-building. The war and the Revolution excluded some segments of the population from the political system: collaborators, Messalistes, bourgeoisie, and profiteers. The war and the Revolution also consecrated the downtrodden, exploited mass as the reference point of the new political system. Since this mass is not a class, ethnic group, or region but is largely undifferentiated in political thought, and since the revolutionary situation creates pressures for rapid, assertive definition of the political system (there is not time to build consensus on precedent or demonstrative bases), such concepts as national unity and general will become important. Thus, every leader has to show that he represents all the people; plurality and divisions must be overcome or destroyed; opposition is treasonous and the work of enemies. The fact that the politization of Algerian society in a clandestine situation during the revolutionary war tended to focus action and identification on organizational, regional, functional, and personal fragments of the nationalist movement only increased the need to think in terms of national unity.

5. Criteria for entry into the *political class* are changing from wartime experience to technical competence. By far most numerous in the political class of the 1960's are the mujahidin, and since they joined the fight when young, they die off only slowly. Mujahidin are simply "those who fought," in the wilayas, external army, France, and so on, with any more precise identification difficult and perhaps unrewarding. More important is the fact that they know who they are, a fact that reinforces localistic politics and personal loyalties. The mujahidin form a sort of inchoate party or a political society-within-society, and they attempt to occupy all possible positions of power, both as their reward for their exertions *(jihad)* and as a base from which to enact programs to continue these rewards. The background of this group is generally rural, as is the focus of many of its demands; this point is also a basic source of alienation from the urban proletariat and the technicians. The mujahidin, however, have the legitimacy but not the skills – political or technical – to govern alone.

The technicians are far fewer, less coherent as an interest group, less clear in their leadership, and devoid of any mass organization behind them. They are better armed with skills, and their training and view of the needs of the state give them a sense of mission (but also sometimes a sense of right and personal enrichment as strong as those of the mujahidin). But they do not have the support or the legitimacy to govern by themselves.

Governing over this sort of dichotomized political class requires mediating leaders, or brokers,[6] who can combine skills and legitimacy to meet expectations. The brokers are more a role than a group, open to be filled by those who can reconcile the other two elements. Mujahidin or technicians may be political brokers, but in so acting they lose some of their former character as they seek to work with both elements. The brokers' base of power has none of the narrow, confraternal character of the two other elements; it is necessarily broader and "national," but also necessarily less direct. Their power derives from their ability to use and satisfy the political class and expectant mass in Algerian revolutionary society. Hence, the brokers are both necessary and vulnerable. They are dependent on the satisfaction of the other elements of the political class, neither of whom can themselves govern alone, but who can remove the incumbent brokers indirectly by withdrawing their support or directly by overthrowing them.

The army spans this class. Officers from the interior ALN who fought the guerrilla war often see the peacetime ANP as a means of watching over the Revolution and over the interests of those who fought for it. Another group of officers, however, came from the external ALN, which organized and trained on bases in Tunisia and Morocco during the war; their experience is in forming a regular army, not in guerrilla warfare, and some of them had French military service too. Their numbers are being slowly swelled by newly trained junior officers, many of whom share the same training experiences and a feeling of solidarity with technicians in the civil service. This group also considers its role as a watchdog over the Revolution, but a Revolution whose continual progress is assured by competent management; in addition, it is interested in developing a technically competent army and in watching over the interests of this army, as necessary, with the government.

Leaving aside the Provisional Executive and Provisional Government (GPRA) of 1962, Algeria has known two bodies of brokers: the ben Bella group and the Boumedienne (Oujda) group. The second, which is closer to both the mujahidin and the technicians (but especially to the technicians) than was the first, came to power because the first was unable to satisfy — and, in fact, threatened — the two basic elements of the Algerian political class. If there is a single line that can be discerned in the actions of Col. Houari Boumedienne[7] from 1962 through 1968, it is the following: interest in the specific task of running the army with like-minded members of the external ALN, through the encouragement of young professional officers (technicians) and the training of older officers (mujahidin) into professionals, and dedication to the general task of defending the Revolution. To accomplish this, Boumedienne and his political associates must be among the brokers, and the other (nonarmy) brokers must admit the same aims. Army officers need be placed in the civilian administration only to the extent necessary to protect these aims. When the professional control and development of the army are threatened by the government, however, the army must intervene actively to protect its interests and, secondarily, the interest of the Revolution, for the army is the microcosm of the political class (and hence of the Revolution) and has the means of deciding revolutionary politics. With the government in "sure" hands, the army officers can then return to the task of building up their own organization. Under this line of thought, the political and military roles of the army can be understood, even if not easily separated. Twice the army has installed a regime that is essentially civilian (although involving mujahidin); in both cases it acted to preserve its own group interests.

ORIGINS[8]

ANP officers are only an inchoate, heterogeneous group, coming from the wilayas, external ALN, and postwar recruitment, with backgrounds in urban or rural employment (or unemployment), *maquis*, French army, student life, and so on. Using a figure of 60,000 for ANP strength and an officer to troop ratio of 1 to 15 (a low normal ratio that seems realistic in view of ANP antecedents and recruiting), about 3,750 are officers. Since there seem to be not more than 10 colonels, no lieutenant colonels, and not more than 150 majors, the vast majority are junior officers, a higher proportion than in a classical army. There is no telling how many of these belong in the mujahidin category and how many are professionals (technicians), although it is safe to assume that those who have been "professionalized" through successful assimilation of modern training in military techniques and values will make up the largest group of subsequent promotions. Static, this dichotomy between mujahidin and professionals would already give rise to friction; since it is dynamic, in that the professionals are increasing and are trying to convert the mujahidin to their skills and views, and in that power will follow these shifts in the long run, friction is heightened. Such a view suggests that previous origins, ties, and experiences are of secondary importance.

The ANP has a popular base, drawing largely from the lower social strata: "sons of *fellahin* and sons of workers." But social origins are less important for the ANP than social change; the army is composed not of workers and *fellahin* but of their sons, whose present situation differs from their origins by their training, profession, and status.[9]

No *single* tie, experience, or origin is the key to the army's political action, and no constant *hierarchy* of ties can be established as a source of motivations. Moreover, no *combination* of past ties, experiences, and origins is sure to produce the same action, reaction, allegiance, or alliance in any two individuals. Any search for such simple motivations seems quite vain. By the same token, such restrictions are also applicable to the mujahidin-technician dichotomy. Useful and valid though it may be as an interpretive generalization, this dichotomy is not going to cover all cases nor, by the same token, will it be invalidated by the "professional" who allies with the "mujahidin" or vice versa. Finally, it may also be said that, all things being equal, similarities in ethnic or geographic origins, in war experiences or in educational "promotions," are all causes of friendships, debts, and solidarity feelings, and can be the basis for lasting ties, lasting enmities, or later appeals for alliances. These reflections may seem banal, but they are important to state, since they are often forgotten and often exceeded, and are about the maximum that can be posited on the political importance of social origins.

A major principle of the professional's military doctrine is to keep the army-people identity on the broad, abstract level of the "general will," and through military organization to minimize the detailed or particularist effects of social origins. "Part of the logic of military organization is to cut off the troops from civilian interests so that they will accept their officers' order unquestioningly."[10] Experience with the wilayas has clearly brought home the importance of this principle. ANP units are not organized on a regional basis. In times of crisis (after wilayist dissidence, after the 1965 coup), army units are shifted about the countryside; the expansion of the external ALN throughout the country in late 1962 was an early application of this idea. Officers from the same wilaya are scattered about and mingled with professional officers, who keep an eye on them. Training activities serve not only to professionalize the mujahidin but also to turn their loyalties from a region to a professional military establishment. The activities of the political commissariat — the publication of *al-Djeich,* the political and civic action training and indoctrination programs, the placing of political commissars in military units — aim at filling the same function.

All of these activities serve not only to strengthen the army as a national organization but also to increase the importance of the professional military against wilayist tendencies. Soldiers and officers are not "delegates" from their home regions, ethnic groups, or social classes to the army. When they go home, on leave for example, they return to their former origins, but as delegates of the army, in a new social status. Fraternization between the military and the population in areas where army units are stationed varies with geography. In the Sahara, the army is active in a civil-affairs program and invites local elements to barracks visits, to mess dinners, to local projects. But here the army's relations are strikingly similar to those of the special French Army officers assigned to the interior regions before independence (although, of course, now both the military and the population are Algerian). Around urban areas, the military are usually seen together; they are billeted apart from civilians; their activities are separate from civilian activities; and when the bridge is made (mess dinners in Algiers, visits to army farms and industries), it is done by permission and invitation. Even the criticism heard in Algeria of the well-off military helps to reinforce the army's separateness; part of the military's nature of an interest group is to remain a thing apart, to keep the privileges and maintain the *esprit* that are important to a modern professional army.

This divorce between social origins and military status has been remarkably successful considering the time passed since independence. In none of the prime instances of army dissidence (ou al-Hajj, Chaabani, ben Rejem, 'Azzedine, Zbiri) were the breakaway army leaders able to count on even a large percentage of their junior officers and troops. In each case, the government made a great point of announcing the junior officers who remained loyal to the ANP, and in each case, when the dissidence ended, the leader was surrounded by only a small group of followers. In the final showdown, in June, 1965, there were no known defections from the army to the former government, and army solidarity held during the military takeover. In 1967, there were no notable defections to the revolt from any military region (including Zbiri's old wilaya) except around Algiers.

There is an evident identity of military views between Boumedienne and the Oujda group, on the one hand, and the professionals or military technicians, on the other,[11] At the same time, as there is a need for the Boumedienne associates, as a brokerage group, to work with the mujahidin on the political level, there is also a need for Boumedienne and the professionals to work with the mujahidin with the army. To the extent that the mujahidin recognize the professionals' technical skills and the brokers' political skills, this working relationship is accepted. Thus, the three categories or elements, in the army as in the political class, are all kept in place by one another, by the need for one another's skills, and by a partial overlap of views and values. For all this interdependence among the three categories, the major present and potential split is based on the degree of social change or professionalization within the military leadership, buttressed by, but not dependent on, previous ties and backgrounds. The major factors that keep this split from reaching political proportions are the effectiveness of the brokerage groups and the success of organizational and training measures to create a coherent, reconverted, modern army — that is, the way in which the two original problems of control and reconversion will be handled. "Unprofessionalized," the army would fall prey to social and socially based political divisions that already exist within Algerian society. "Professionalized," it forms an important part of the new class of the nation, a means of personal modernization and rapid social advancement of its members. It is therefore in the interest of the army to maintain myths of national unity and popular identity while seeking to implement programs of modernization and social change among the military. In such a way, the army can become in reality what it is in theory: the spearhead of the Revolution. By the same token, its nature (and cohesion) as an interest group in politics is reinforced. However, in the process, "Revolution" becomes identified in technicians' terms of construction rather than in mujahidin's terms of consumption. Since construction is a slower, less immediately satisfying process than consumption, the army's role as an agent of control holding down dissatisfaction (including the dissatisfaction of mujahidin leaders in its midst) and hence as an active element in politics is enhanced.

POLITICAL CULTURE

It is possible to distinguish certain values that have been important to the professional leadership of the ANP. These can be divided into political and military values (with some overlap), since it has been seen that the army, no matter how "professional," still has a socio-political view of its socio-political position.

1. (A) *Identity with the people.* "The ANP will never let itself be cut off from the people, from whom it finds both its strength and its reason for being."[12] The use that ben Bella made of the army was sharply contrary to this image in Boumedienne's eyes, for in putting down dissidence, popular revolt, and unrest alike, the army became a repressive policy arm of the state, suspect in the people's eyes. "He [ben Bella] made us look like bloodthirsty men."[13] "The execution of this vile plot and this diabolical idea was to be reinforced on the political level by the denigration of the *junud* of the Army of Liberation by calling them 'militarists' and 'fascists.' In fact, our *junud* are simply the sons of *fellahin* and of workers who have fought to recover their lands and their factories. . . . I am not simply talking of the soldiers in general, the majority of whom are poor *fellahin* and workers who possess nothing; I am speaking of the officers, who should have the same doctrine and the same orientation as the Party and the country, that is, who should conform to the policies *[la politique]* of the country."[14] "We are not an army of mercenaries. We are above all militants, children of *fellahin* and workers, intellectuals and nationalists worthy of the name. . . . [We] are the people, [we] are the Revolution. . . . If [the army] rose up again to straighten out deviationism, . . . this cannot be called a military *coup d'état*. All they did was to assume their revolutionary responsibilities toward the people."[15]

(B) *The Revolution to them that made it.* The revolution should benefit those who made the sacrifice of participating in the seven-and-a-half year struggle. City boys inspired by foreign doctrines and late-comers alike are suspect, because they had not won the benefits they claimed and directed, because they were out of touch with the experience of those who had, and

because they took the available posts (as spoils and as positions from which to
distribute spoils) from those who merited them. "The great majority of the
people were separated from the party . . . with the help of . . . people who did
not participate once in the Revolution, or with foreign advisors, adventurers who
got certain organs of the Party in their pockets. . . . He [ben Bella] separated
and liquidated militants who had participated positively in the Revolution and
he permitted opportunist elements to accede to positions of responsibility and
to favor their own personal enrichment to the detriment of the people."[16] "The
militants and *junud* who were the basis of our country's glory and dignity did
not find their place because of the infiltration of foreigners and sideliners."[17]

Thus, the "people," as referred to in the previous tenet, is restricted to only
the "valid elements" of the population, the deprived masses by whom and in
whose name the revolution is defined. Outside elements of any kind are
suspect, except perhaps in a purely advisory or training function; although the
line is hard to draw clearly, there appears a strong nationalistic or xenophobic
bias, justified by criteria of participation in the Revolution. By extension, the
technicians' role is found between − but not separating − the mujahidin
leadership and the people, in a position to aid the former to increase or
distribute the benefits to the latter. In regard to the army, this go-it-alone
nationalism was early expressed by Boumedienne: "The army proved its
nationalism without waiting for that nationalism to be approved by New York
or Peking. The demagogues want to label our army; we say to these hypocrites:
don't play with fire."[18]

(C) *Unity is natural, division is an artificial counterrevolutionary trick;*
the Revolution built the nation, politics destroys it (and the Revolution). True
national unity arises naturally from the cooperation of national revolutionary
forces and their leaders but is disrupted by politicians who seek to divide these
forces in order to reign for selfish reasons. "No one man alone can incarnate
Algeria, the Revolution, and socialism all at the same time."[19] But collective
leadership is not necessarily divisive or competitive, since national unity is
incarnate in the right combination of recognized representatives of the people
and the Revolution.

"By stealthy methods of diversion and division, a large number of reactionary
and exploiting elements within the political and administrative machinery of the
country sow disorder and trouble in order to raise up the people against their
leaders and the revolutionary forces among them."[20] "Ben Bella wanted to raise
up some of us against others in order to climb on top of the heap."[21] "We made
blood flow and he made peace."[22]

The other side of this view is the conspiratorial image of history, a natural
outgrowth of both the revolutionary war and of the ben Bella period.
Frequently Boumedienne points out, "As long as there is a Revolution in this
country, a permanent danger will exist. The Revolution always has enemies.
There cannot be a Revolution without enemies and adversaries." [23] Hence,
counterrevolutionary elements are identifiable by their divisiveness. Factionalism
within the Revolutionary Council only tends to perpetuate this view, for it
shows that those who were thought to be trusted were in reality only divisive,
counterrevolutionary self-seekers. As Radio Algiers explained after the dismissal
of Ali Mahsas and Bashir Boumaza from the party, "Their participation in the
June 19 movement was in fact inspired by nefarious calculation on their part

and was based on ignoble thirst for power. Their defection abroad as a result of
the ministerial reshuffle affecting them confirms their opportunistic conception
of responsibility."[24]

(D) *A strong state structure must be built.* Incoherence, divisive polities,
and inefficiency are enemies not only of the Revolution but also of the proper
functioning of government institutions. The primary emphasis of Boumedienne
is on the state, not the nation. "One of the major cares of the Revolution is the
edification of a strong state, characterized by seriousness and the love of
organization."[25] "Wide awake, conscious of their responsibilities, and active
among the people, certain elements have given of their efforts and their leisure
time to build the Algerian state, to consolidate and reinforce the bases of the
Revolution."[26] Since the national unity is the outgrowth of the Revolution,
state-building, not nation-building, is the order of the day. Institutions must
build on the existing unity of revolutionary forces in society, represent these
forces, and channel their energies into creating a machinery that can meet their
needs.

On the surface, the emphasis of the view could be either on the technocratic
construction of institutions of economic development or the democratic
mobilization of political energies into greater participation in government. The
general accent on efficiency, economy, and effectiveness, however, combined
with the previous point, suggests a suspicion of politics, viewed not as the
natural interplay of a pluralistic society but as the divisive effect of self-seeking
politicians, and also suggests a greater role for technicians: economic, administrative, military. The ben Bella regime is criticized above all for confusion,
incoherence, extravagance; the new regime is to be one of order, efficiency,
assainissement, and good management. In this opposition of values, the army
and the other state institutions reinforce each other's roles, the army providing
leadership, vigilant order and protection, and the state effectively fulfilling the
other tasks of government so that the army can devote its attention to its own
training, equipment, and modernization.[27]

2. (A) *The Army's role as guardian of the Revolution gives it a primary
task of safeguarding its own group interests.* Since the army defends the
Revolution, the Revolution must maintain a place for the army among its
structures. "The Revolution will place all the necessary means at the disposal of
the army in order that it may fill the roles assigned to it: defend the integrity of
the fatherland and the acquisitions of our Revolution and our people."[28] "The
armed forces are the powerful shield and spearhead that protect the Revolution
from its enemies inside and outside. The armed forces are either with the
Revolution with all their heart, a situation that allows the reinforcement of the
force of the party and of all the militants, or they are far from the Revolution,
in which case all attempt to practice socialism is in vain."[29]

The army, in turn, must keep alive its relevance to the Revolution in order to
maintain its existence; this political necessity gives it political and other
nonmilitary roles. "The ANP, contrary to the classical concept, is not a force
living on the outskirts of society; it does not form a caste; it is not hardened by
years of tradition; it has been created and structured since the outbreak of the
Revolution and is composed of peasants and workers."[30] Yet, in fact, if it is not
quite a caste, the army *is* an interest group; it *has* been created, trained, and
structured into something more than just a band of workers and peasants; and

this fact is buttressed by the value that the ANP attaches to its own existence, justified in ideological terms as guardian and spearhead of the Revolution.

(B) *The army's primary military task is to build itself into a modern professional military force,* the first step necessary to its fulfillment of its other task of defending the Revolution within and without the state. "In modern warfare, an officer needs to have not only physical, psychological, and moral qualities, but also and especially technical, scientific, and even industrial skills. For the strength of a modern army lies today in its technical, scientific, and industrial strength. . . . Among other things, the Liberation War. . . taught our people, who at that time confronted one of the strongest armies in the world, that the courage and heroism so necessary to the combatant are nevertheless not sufficient in themselves to defeat an enemy clearly superior in numbers and armed with modern material and great firepower. . . . By its irreversible political choice and its international role, Algeria today needs a powerful modern army capable not only of defending its frontiers and guaranteeing its independence and its revolution, but also of discouraging and undoing all the maneuvers and attempts of its internal and external enemies by rapid, energetic, and effective action. . . . In the very heart of combat for national independence, the training of cadres became a self-evident necessity. . . . Born of the movement of revolutionary forces who were consolidating themselves, this imperative expanded, thanks to the will and realism of the Staff of the ALN, which throughout its entire existence and evolution gave itself the task of providing the ALN with the necessary cadres in all sectors."[31] This kind of language, written by the Political Commissariat of the ANP, indicates a remarkably strong point of view in the light of the guerrilla background of the ALN and the presence of large mujahidin forces within the army.

(C) As a military organization, *the army must have control over its own forces.* Any outside (political) influence opens up the dangers of division and rivalries. General-staff members, military-region commanders, unit commanders must be appointed by and responsible to the Defense Ministry;[32] in Algeria, this is military — not civilian — control of the army. The experience of Boumedienne since his appointment as chief of staff of the ALN in 1960 (and possibly before in the *maquis*) has graven this lesson into his political reflexes; on at least two occasions (July, 1962, and October, 1965), he alluded to the attempt of the GPRA to undercut his provisions in 1961, and his dismissal by the GPRA in 1962 made this lesson public.[33] "Ben Bella wanted to dissolve the Algerian Army of Liberation and put a party militia in its place."[34] This point, and the previous tenet of a professional army, strongly reinforce the state-building view. For all its close association with the people — and perhaps because this association already exists — the army needs to be formed as a *military* organization within a functioning state structure. Already the army is a more "national" and more coherent organization than the party; to place it under or replace it with the party is to suborn strength to weakness; it would deprive the army of its primary need for military improvement, while undermining its already acquired political strength.

(D) As national unity is important, so *the most important precondition of an effective army is military unity.* The value of unity reinforces the need for military control over the military; the operational and political lessons of unity among the military were indelibly burned on Boumedienne by the whole history of wilayism both before and after independence. "He took advantage of my trip to Moscow, which was to buy arms, to name Zbiri head of the general staff. Surprised, I understood that he thus wanted to divide the army."[35] "Conscious and continual acts of sabotage [were] undertaken against the unity of the revolutionary forces generally and against the national unity and unity of the National People's Army."[36] "The division of the army was an easy thing, but to unite it takes several years and maybe decades."[37]

Thus, unity, modernization, and military control are viewed as primary needs for an effective army, whose position in the Algerian polity is assured by identity with the people and the Revolution, by a functioning state structure in the hands of those who fought, and by revolutionary national unity. In values as well as in actions (which have and will reflect these values), the ANP leadership assumes the nation-building functions to be inherent in the revolutionary nature of Algerian polity and focuses its attention on the state-building functions. It is not stretching the point (nor is it surprising) to say that the ANP is, for army leadership, the model of the state-to-be: built on a revolutionary heritage, identity, and unity, the ANP is rapidly being modernized and institutionalized. The state should follow the example, avoid politics that destroy its revolutionary purpose and unity, and set up its own institutions for supplying the needs of those who brought about the Revolution.

This synthesis of coherent lines in professional army thought, largely through the words of Boumedienne (the only one outside of *al-Djeich* who speaks), should not be taken as a demonstration of logic and clarity at the source. First, there are many areas of incomprehension: Boumedienne has spoken of a state that will be under the control *(soumis)* of "the government and of men,"[38] and later announced that "ministers will be responsible before the council of ministers,"[39] a remark whose confusion is in the same tradition as his minister's declaration, after suitable emphasis on the painful processes of making decisions and chosing priorities, that the Algerian economic planning would "give prime emphasis to industry and agriculture."

Second, there is also a good deal of naïveté in the military man's view of politics. Perhaps the most prominent theme is that of deception: the army put its faith in ben Bella, and he deceived them, turning their values and actions against them to divide them. One gets a somewhat simplistic and evil view of politics, consistent with the views on national unity analyzed above, and one feels that these views are being expressed by people who have consistently been "had" and finally have enough of it. Once the Bad Man is removed, all will go better, if other divisive political forces are kept out of the political system. On the other hand, Boumedienne has grown tremendously in skill and sophistication since the 1967 Zbiri coup.

Third, some of these values are mutually inconsistent. What happens if "those who made it" are technically incapable of keeping the Revolution going? The answer for the army is clear: import (ex-French army officers), borrow (foreign advisors), and train (abroad as well as at home), using foreigners, foreign ideas, and late-comers. Efficiency over spoils, state (and army) over Revolution. The choice is doubtless wise; it is only mentioned to show that, as in any value system, choices and compromises have to be made and contradictions reconciled. Or again, what happens if the army is so close to "the people" that it begins to reflect its real divisions? The army is to reflect an abstract, simplistic "general will" view of the people, but not to fall prey to the political divisions that sunder national and military unity.

Finally, under the impact of need and experience, some of these values have changed, as suggested above. The most significant changes comes from the need to rely heavily on technicians (the "golden-egg tenders") to increase the construction aspect of the Revolution at the expense of mujahidin (the "goose killers"), with their view of the consumption aspects of Revolution, and to engage in politics as brokers to balance, encompass, and exclude factions within the collective leadership coalition.

These values — and the incomprehension, naïveté, inconsistency, and changes associated with them — can be subsumed under two categories of Algerian political culture with particular reference to the military. One is concerned with institutionalizing the Revolution, bureaucratizing the state, professionalizing and modernizing the army, controlling the party and national organizations, and rendering the operations of state and economy more efficient. This view, which we have called state-building and Mohammed Harbi has called "the bureaucratic revolution," can be associated generally with the Algerian technicians and with the ANP professionals. Output and allocation are decided at the top, in this view, and the technicians are the intermediaries between rulers and ruled. With its emphasis on technical and administrative skills, it would make social change or modernization the criterion for entry into the political class and is more interested in economic growth than redistribution.

The other is concerned with enjoying the Revolution, politicizing the state, controlling the army, mobilizing the party and national organizations, and rendering the operations of government and economy more accessible to a larger group of people. This view, which we have called nation-building and Harbi has called "the democratic revolution," can be associated with the mujahidin, inside and outside the army. Political organizations bring demands for allocation to the attention of the top, in this view, and the party brings together rulers and ruled. With its emphasis on past performance, it would make participation in the liberation struggle the criteria for membership in the political class, and it is more interested in spoils than in growth.

In the late 1960's, the army values taken as a whole reflect both points of view, because of the vested interests of its composite composition in their own criteria for membership in the political class. Both criteria are based on achievement, but one is closed, the other open. Since technical skills can be taught and technical students can be converted to state-building values; since the technicians are creating spoils while the mujahidin are only consuming them; and since the army's weight of authority, intervention, and control lends itself more to state- than to nation-building, the former view appears to be a prefiguration of the future Algerian military.

It also foreshadows a future shift in the Algerian political culture as a whole. The mujahidin cannot recruit; they can only bequeath their views and traditions (but not their criteria of membership) to populist-democratic elements in party and local assemblies. Although they were not notably successful in seizing this opportunity to use party structures under ben Bella, the advent of a new state-building regime has given them the occasion to perpetuate themselves in only slightly different form. But at the same time, the technicians can recruit, train, and increase their power. Optimally, this combination may produce a new Algerian political system in which democratic exercise at the base imposes demands on the government that technicians then fill. Unfortunately, such a horizontal division of a policy is rare and difficult to maintain. Continued strain between the two elements within the political class is more likely. In such a case, a brokerage group favorable to technicians and supported by the army is likely to use its authority to keep the populist successors of the mujahidin in their place. The dual nature of the political class will thus probably continue, but with the political culture of Algeria moving toward the state-building views of the technicians.

Notes

1. This study is based on interviews with Algerian political and military personnel and French and American diplomatic and military personnel in Algeria, as well as on research in current sources, notably *Le Monde* (Paris), *al-Djeich* (Algiers), *Jeune Afrique* (Tunis), *Maghreb* (Paris), *Annuaire de l'Afrique du Nord* (Aix-en-Provence), and others. Specific attribution is not given when so requested by the source or in establishing the general train of events.

2. See particularly Jean Leca, "Le Nationalism algérien depuis l'indépendance," in Louis-Jean Duclos (ed.), *Les nationalismes maghrébins,* Etude Maghrebine No. 7 (Paris: Fondation Nationale des Sciences Politiques, 1966), pp. 61—82; and Hisham B. Sharabi, *Nationalism and Revolution in the Arab World* (New York: Van Nostrand, 1966), especially pp. 82—92; Leonard Binder, *The Ideological Revolution in the Middle East* (New York: John Wiley, 1964), especially pp. 179—82; Donald E. Weatherbee, *Ideology in Indonesia,* Monograph Series No. 8 (New Haven, Conn.: Yale University Press, 1966), especially pp. 1—19.

3. Three has been much less attention devoted to this aspect of revolution, unfortunately. See, however, Herbert Feith, *The Decline of Constitutional Democracy in Indonesia* (Ithaca, N.Y.: Cornell University Press, 1962).

4. See Chalmers Johnson, *Revolutionary Change* (Boston: Little, Brown, 1966), especially pp. 7—14; Frantz Fanon, *The Wretched of the Earth* (New York: Grove Press, 1964), especially chap. ii.

5. See Samuel Huntington, "Political Development and Political Decay," *World Politics,* XVII, No. 3 (April, 1965), 386—430; James Heaphey, "The Organization of Egypt," *World Politics,* XVII, No. 2 (January, 1966), 177—93.

6. The term is used differently from the "horizontal" concept, as for example in Lucian Pye, "The Non-Western Political Process," in James N. Rosenau (ed.), *International Politics and Foreign Policy* (New York: Free Press, 1961), pp. 293—94, originally appearing in *Journal of Politics.*

7. Boumedienne was born in 1925 at Guelma (between Annaba and Constantine). He studied Arabic literature at the Zitouna (Tunis) and al-Azhar (Cairo). MTLD of Messali Hajj and schoolteacher in Guelma, he joined the FLN in Cairo in 1954. He entered wilaya V (Oran) from Morocco in 1955 and became wilaya V commander in 1957. Boumedienne was commandant of Western Algeria from Morocco in 1958. A member of the ALN General Staff and then Chief of Staff in 1960, he created the external ALN. Fired by the GPRA in 1962, he was made Defense Minister in the same year. He was a member of the FLN Central Committee and Political Bureau in 1964, and Chairman of the Revolutionary Council in 1965.

8. The following is not a political history of independent Algeria but an explanation of the military role in that history. For various treatments of independent Algerian politics, see David C. Gordon, *The Passing of French Algeria* (London and New York: Oxford University

Press, 1966); Arslan Humbaraci, *Algeria: The Revolution That Failed* (New York: Praeger Publishers, 1966); William H. Lewis, "Algeria Changes Course," *Africa Report,* X, No. 8 (November, 1965), and "Algeria Against Herself," *Africa Report,* XII, No. 9 (December, 1967); Gerard Chaliand, *L'Algérie est-elle socialiste?* (Paris: Maspero, 1965); Hervé Bourges, *L'Algérie à l'épreuve du pouvoir* (Paris: Grasset, 1967). The best articles on the Algerian army are by Jean Lacouture, "Anatomie d'une armée," *Le Monde,* July 14, 1965, and by Gerard Viratelle, "Le régime militaire algérien," *Revue Francaise d'Etudes Politiques Africaines,* No. 38 (February, 1969), pp. 63—78; see also *Le Monde,* June 20, 1965; David Wood, *The Armed Forces of African States,* Adelphi Papers No. 27 (London: Institute for Strategic Studies, 1966), p. 5; Daniel Guerin, "Un état dans un état: l'armée," *Combat,* January 25, 1964.

9. A good, if unsympathetic, commentary is presented by Daniel Guerin, *L'Algérie caporalisée?* (Paris: Centre d'Etudes Socialistes, 1965), p. 20.

10. Chalmers Johnson, *Revolution and the Political System* (Stanford, Calif.: The Hoover Institution, 1964), p. 19. The next two paragraphs (and scattered other material throughout the study) include information gathered through interviews inside and outside the ANP in Algeria in July, 1966 and 1969.

11. For a comparative note on the role of "technicians," see Herbert S. Dinerstein, "Soviet Policy in Latin America," *American Political Science Review,* LXI, No. 1 (March, 1967), 83.

12. Boumedienne speech, June 19, 1965.

13. Boumedienne to Mohammed Hassanein Haykal, *al-Ahram,* July 9, 1965.

14. Boumedienne speech, March 21, 1966.

15. Boumedienne to Haykal, *loc. cit.*

16. Boumedienne to Haykal, *al-Ahram,* October 8—10, 1965.

17. Boumedienne speech, June 19, 1966.

18. Boumedienne speech, June 6, 1963.

19. Boumedienne speech, June 19, 1965.

20. *Al-Djeich.* January 24, 1964; see also *Le Monde* January 25, 1964; *The New York Times.* January 27, 1964. The antecedent of the last word is not clear.

21. Boumedienne to Haykal, *al-Ahram,* July 2, 1965.

22. Boumedienne to Haykal, *al-Ahram,* October 8—10, 1965.

23. See, for example, Boumedienne speech, December 4, 1965.

24. Radio Algiers, October 29, 1966.

25. Boumedienne speech, July 12, 1965.

26. Boumedienne speech, December 4, 1965.

27. See *Le Monde Diplomatique,* special issue on Algeria 1965, pp. 1 and 9.

28. Boumedienne speech, February 5, 1966.

29. Boumedienne speech, March 21, 1966.

30. *Le Monde Diplomatique;* probably written by the Political Commissariat.

31. *ANP 1965,* special issue of *al-Djeich,* introduction to "Armor and Artillery" and "Infantry" sections, the former also in *Djeich Special 1954—1964,* pp. 21, 22, 30.

32. Note particularly the problems caused by the appointment of Colonel Tahar Zbiri to Chief of the General Staff, Colonel Mohammed Chaabani in wilaya VI, Colonel Bouhajar ben Haddou in wilaya V, and Major Sliman Hoffman to the armored unit.

33. See *La Nation Africaine* (Rabat), July 16, 1962.

34. Boumedienne to Haykal, *al-Ahram,* July 9, 1965.

35. Boumedienne to Haykal, *al-Ahram,* July 2, 1965.

36. Boumedienne to Haykal, *al-Ahram,* July 9, 1965.

37. Boumedienne speech, June 19, 1966.

38. Boumedienne speech, June 19, 1965.

39. Boumedienne speech, July 12, 1965.

FIVE

Forces and Institutions

In an era of nationalism, independence, and development, the political system is a major focus of analysis. There are many ways to approach the political system in order to understand the forces, relations, rules, and organs that compose it. Two broad approaches vie for primacy: the historical analysis, which seeks to penetrate cause and effect in a chronological sequence of events, and the conceptual analysis, which seeks to establish key categories and determine their roles, functions, relations, and effects on one another. Taken to extremes, either approach is sterile; both are needed for an understanding of reality.

Political systems generally involve four components: input functions of supports and demands, output functions of supplies and controls (and, or including, values), conversion functions that change the one into the other, and feedback. Political development involves increasing the capacity of the conversion functions to handle inputs and outputs. Developing systems involve increasing demands (including the demand for participation) and greater identification (including nationalism), increases that may be summarized as the integration of the population into the system. They also involve greater supplies of material and spiritual values, which may be termed the allocations of the system to its members. In simplest terms, the system is under pressure to set up regular ways (output) of meeting the increased pressures (input); since a few individuals cannot perform the job on an ad hoc basis over a long period of time, this increased capacity and regularization of conversion can be achieved durably only through institutionalization.

Useful though these ideas may be, they have neither been so widely adopted nor so narrowly refined as to be used by all analysts. As a result, the multifaceted approach still characterizes any collection of works on an area such as North Africa. Here we shall look at three major overlapping aspects of the political system: its recent evolution, its major force or institution, and its progress in integration through the use of elections. The allocation aspect — from the point of view of results and problems rather than as a process — is the subject of the following section.

The evolution of the Moroccan political system is treated by Stuart Schaar. His study chronicles the rise and fall of the parliamentary period whose preparation, installation, and dissolution (in several senses) characterized the first half-decade of the rule of Hassan II. The second half has been less eventful, as the monarchy continues to dominate and the potential competitive, or counterbalancing, forces — the parties — continue to develop their one notable characteristic, pluralism. The relationship between these two forces — the monarchy and the political parties — is the subject of the selection by I. William Zartman. Yet the monarch's desire for his people to participate in government and the parties' vigorous popular base have meant that Morocco has held the first free multiparty elections in North Africa. Paul Chambergeat, who had a role to play in their establishment, analyzes the electoral process and its results.

The Tunisian political system has had a different evolution and comprises different forces. Clement H. Moore analyzes the evolution of Tunisia's two main legitimizing forces, the charismatic leader and the single party. As Bourguiba moves toward the end of his career (and the end of an era in Tunisian politics), the single party remains the dominant institution; its relations with pluralism at a lower level — in the form of the active national organizations — continue to be an area of both conflict and promise. The past politics of pluralism and control are described in the selection by Edouard Meric. Tunisia's elections have been less competitive than those in Morocco, but they have a regularity unrivaled in the area. Professor Moore's study deals not only with the continuous nature of Tunisia's electoral experience but also with its degree of competition and its role in institutionalizing change at the local level.

Algeria's political system is, of course, unique. Legitimized by revolution, its leader consecrated by neither traditional nor modern charisma, its single party bereft of the organization and effectiveness of either the Istiqlal or the Socialist

Destour, the Algerian pluralistic system has been held together mainly by military control. The story of the single party and the military coup, which has been Algeria's mode of elite secession, is told by William H. Lewis. The story of the leader as a dominant characteristic of Arab politics — using ben Bella as the example — is related by P. J. Vatikiotis. Algeria's electoral experience was scarcely significant until 1967, when an innovation in the single-party system was introduced, allowing choice by providing two candidates for each seat. Working with the meager sources available, Nicole Grimaud analyzes the process and the (available) results.

Although major aspects of the three political systems have been covered in these selections, many more have been studied elsewhere, and still others remain to be analyzed in depth. Although there have been studies of the North African constitutions,[1] little work has been done on the political and social as well as the legal roles of the judicial systems. Even less work has been done on the parliamentary systems,[2] and in all three cases — Morocco's and Algeria's short-lived experiments and Tunisia's deceptively quiet perennial — there is material for much more study. Despite the good studies in preparation on Morocco, the limited degree of choice and contest in Tunisia, and the incomplete material on Algeria, electoral sociology remains an open field, and for those very reasons a challenging one. All of these areas for research involve institutionalization and participation, but it is in the field of allocation and decision-making that some of the most interesting work remains to be done by students of developing Maghribi political systems.

Notes

1. Good studies have been done by Louis Fougère in the *Annuaire de l'Afrique du Nord* on Morocco (1962, pp. 155–66) and on Algeria (1963, pp. 1–22). On Morocco, see also Maurice Duverger in *Le Monde,* November 30, 1962, and October 12, 1963; Willard Beling, in *Middle East Journal,* XVIII, No. 2 (Spring, 1964), 163–79; Jacques Robert, in *Le Monde,* November 24, 1962; the entire issue of *Confluent,* VIII, No. 27 (January, 1963); Ahmed Reda Guedira, in *Petit Marocain,* November 20, 1962; Charles Gallagher, in *American Universities Field Staff Reports,* 1963; and I. William Zartman, *Destiny of a Dynasty* (Columbia: University of South Carolina Press, 1964). On the 1970 constitution in Morocco, see Jacques Robert, in *Maghreb,* 41: 12–14 & 29–42 (September, 1970), and Maurice Duverger, in *Le Monde,* September 1970. On Algeria, see Raul Morodor, in *Revista de Estudias Políticas,* No. 133 (1964), pp. 111–28; François Borella, in *Revue Algérienne de Science Politique,* I, No. 1 (January, 1964), 51–80, and III, No. 1 (1965), 29–39. Two studies on Tunisia are by Victor Silvera, in *Revue Française de Science Politique,* No. 2 (1960), 380–94, and Charles Debbasch in *Revue Juridique et Politique d'Outre-Mer,* XV, No. 1 (1961), 145–55. Some work on the purely legal aspects of legal system has appeared in the *Annuaire de l'Afrique du Nord.* See also, however, John Waterbury, "Kingdom-Building and the control of the Opposition in Morocco: the Monarchial uses of Justice," *Government and Opposition,* V, No. 1 (1969), 54–66.

2. Rare studies were done for the *Annuaire de l'Afrique du Nord* in 1962 (Pierre Ebrard on Morocco, pp. . 35–80; Charles Debbasch on Tunisia, pp. 81–114; Anisse Salah-Bey, on Algeria, pp. 115–26), and in 1965 (Paul Chambergeat on Morocco, pp. 101–18).

22

KING HASSAN'S ALTERNATIVES

STUART SCHAAR

The unexpected result of the first nation-wide parliamentary elections ever held in Morocco raises an inevitable question: How stable is the palace-centered kingdom of Hassan II?

Most observers assumed that the royalist Front for the Defense of Constitutional Institutions (FDIC) would gain an overwhelming victory over the two opposition parties, the moderately conservative Istiqlal and the socialist-leaning National Union of Popular Forces (UNFP), thus automatically ensuring the king's continued dominance of the political scene. The resulting government, hand-picked by Hassan, would have no difficulty initiating those controversial policies he has known to favor — notably agrarian reform under palace auspices aimed at regrouping the peasants behind the monarchy, substitution of a regional development scheme for the defunct Five-Year Plan, establishment of ties with the European Common Market, and perhaps compromise on Moroccan claims to Mauritania. Instead, the disputed results (subject to judicial review) gave the royal Front a minority of sixty-nine seats, Istiqlal forty-three, UNFP twenty-eight, and Independents four.

The fragmentation of Moroccan political forces revealed by the 1963 elections had already begun before the country became independent in 1956. Although Istiqlal was still the predominant nationalist organization, power struggles within its ranks in 1953—56 had weakened its earlier monolithic structure. Much of the organized violence against the French, which reached its height after the exile of the sultan in 1953, was directed by terrorist groups acting independently of the "too moderate" Istiqlal. Istiqlal also lacked full control over the new quasi-political Moroccan Labor Union (UMT) — the largest autonomous labor union in Africa and the Arab world — created by Moroccan workers in 1955. Even during the pre-independence period, moreover, there were Moroccan officers within the French army — later integrated into the royal army and the administration — who disdained both the xenophobic, fundamentalist programs of the Istiqlal "old guard" and the revolutionary ideology of its younger intellectuals. Other splinter groups, some supported by French politicians and

Reprinted, by permission, from *Africa Report,* VIII (August, 1963) No. 8, pp. 7—12 and X (July, 1965), No. 7, pp. 6—14.

royal agents, were also evident at the Aix-les-Bains conference in August, 1955, which established the principle that Morocco would be free.

The sultan, long a popular religious leader and now a political hero, returned from exile in November, 1955. After protracted negotiations with the French, he was allowed to assume effective control of the administration and the Moroccan military forces. He quickly became the arbiter among the country's divided political elements as well.

In this new role, the sultan — soon to become King Mohammed V — viewed with decided misgiving the Istiqlal objective of creating a single-party system similar to that of the Neo-Destour in Tunisia. His doubts grew after Habib Bourguiba's *coup d'état* against the Tunisian bey in 1956. To forestall the consolidation of any such independent group capable of threatening the power of the Moroccan monarchy, he set upon a course of playing one set of leaders off against the other.

King Mohammed V was a shrewd politician steeped in the Arab tradition of cultivating and flattering one's adversaries. He customarily consulted political leaders to give them a sense of participation in decision-making, even though he often had no intention of following their advice. Discreetly aiding him in this complex game of divide and rule were Crown Prince (and Army Chief of Staff) Moulay Hassan, Police Chief Mohammed Laghzaoui (later a principal figure in the FDIC and the government's economic coordinator), and other loyal agents.

Hassan II, who succeeded Mohammed V upon the latter's sudden death on February 26, 1961, fully recognized the basic lesson of his father's reign: the key to the preservation of the monarchy in Morocco was for the king to become and remain the pivotal center of Morocco's disparate political forces (that is, to divide and rule). His tactical approach to his objective was strikingly different from Mohammed V's, however.

Unlike his father, Hassan is modern in outlook, deeply imbued with French culture, well educated, and debonair. He does not have the patience of Mohammed V or the temperament for protracted traditional niceties. He has many ideas of his own, and tends to act impulsively on them, sometimes without consulting at all. Nonetheless, confounding most political observers, Hassan consolidated his power rapidly. His unexpected political skill in taking command of the scene within days of his father's funeral revealed qualities that he developed while acting as Mohammed V's principal advisor, as army chief of staff, and as long-time royal troubleshooter. These qualities had been obscured for most observers by his reputation as a somewhat frivolous crown prince.

By the time Hassan ascended the throne, three political parties were jockeying for position. Berber leaders, loyal to the king, had formed the anti-Istiqlal Popular Movement in 1959, with palace support. Meanwhile, the Istiqlal itself had split into two wings in January, 1959, one of which became the UNFP in September. In part, this rift resulted from Mohammed V's discreet support of the "old guard" of the Istiqlal, whose position was being challenged by radical labor and ex-terrorist leaders. The radicals demanded that the party take steps to curtail the monarch's growing power, give them a greater share in party decision-making, and ultimately allow younger elements to control the Istiqlal organization.

In 1960, the monarchy was further strengthened — or, to be more precise, the opposition to Mohammed V's power position was weakened — when the powerful trade union, the UMT, which had allied with the UNFP in the 1959 Istiqlal split, adopted a more cautious political stance. Facing competition from a newly founded Istiqlal-oriented labor union, the General Union of Moroccan Workers (UGTM), aware of the growing political apathy among their own ranks, and fearful of the minister of labor's power, UMT leaders told UNFP militants they could not engage in pro-UNFP political activity within UMT cells, and adopted a lukewarm attitude toward politically inspired strikes.

Hassan rejected UNFP conditions for participation in his first government, organized in June, 1961. Instead, allied with Popular Movement and Istiqlal leaders, he concentrated on dividing the already weakened radical forces of the UNFP. At the same time, Minister of Interior Ahmed Reda Guedira cultivated UMT leaders to make certain that they did not waver in their new policy. This high-level fence-minding was essential, since over half of the administrative positions in the UNFP were held by UMT members.

As the December, 1962, constitutional referendum approached, the UNFP called for a boycott. The UMT leadership, on the horns of a dilemma, noted that the new constitution had grave deficiencies but nevertheless instructed its members to ignore the boycott call. Indeed, some section heads of the labor union, fearing reprisals against nonparticipants, advised workers to vote. Power struggles between UNFP and UMT leadership for control of the party organization further weakened the "radical" alliance at this crucial moment.

The attack on the UNFP during the referendum campaign was many pronged. New governors, unquestionably loyal to the monarchy, were assigned to administer provinces in which the UNFP was strong, for example, Agadir, Casablanca, and Rabat. An ex-UNFP leader, familiar with the party's weaknesses, was appointed minister of state for information. *Les Phares,* a Guedira-supported newspaper, attacked openly. It was not surprising that the UNFP boycott failed, giving Hassan's new constitution the decisive popular endorsement royal prestige required.

With the UNFP apparently safely robbed of its sting, Hassan turned his attention to the now strengthened Istiqlal party. While Istiqlal spokesmen had loyally campaigned for the constitution, they had also used the opportunity thus afforded them to appeal to the voters on radio and television and in countrywide tours at government expense to stress the particular achievements of the Istiqlal and its leaders. In addition, Istiqlal inspectors, who run the party's day-to-day activities, took advantage of the constitutional referendum to test their election machinery and pinpoint promising militants.

The king, who followed the campaign closely, apparently concluded that the Istiqlal would be even further strengthened at the expense of the palace if Istiqlal ministers remained in the government through another election. At the end of December, 1962, three Istiqlal ministers, who had defended the constitution vigorously during the referendum campaign (even against protests of a vocal minority in the Istiqlal national council) and fully expected to keep their portfolios until June, 1963, were stunned to learn that the king was about to shuffle them out of important ministries in the cabinet.

To make the most of a bad bargain, the three ministers resigned at the beginning of January, before the king had time to act, and Istiqlal party inspectors quickly and tactfully moved to rationalize Istiqlal's new position as an opposition party.

Some preparation of Istiqlalis for a change had already taken place. Throughout the autumn of 1962, I heard party inspectors remind members in local meeting that, despite Istiqlal's participation in the cabinet, the party could not really be responsible for government shortcomings, since it did not control such key ministries as Interior or Agriculture and was not involved in the direction of the royal cabinet. Moreover, when the ax fell, Istiqlal had a ready scapegoat on whom to blame the party's sudden departure from power: Guedira, who held all three of these "key" positions. Thus, Istiqlal's transition to the opposition was sufficiently cushioned that party unity was preserved for the parliamentary election campaign just ahead.

The idea of creating a royalist front opposed to established Moroccan parties had germinated for some time before the FDIC actually came into being in the spring of 1963. In an unpublished interview granted in October, 1961, Guedira stated quite frankly that he believed that one of the by-products of National Promotion (the large-scale WPA-style public-works program then being set in motion by the palace, with American assistance, under the direct supervision of the king and with the aid of Guedira's Ministries of Agriculture and Interior) would be the discovery, through its extensive rural organization, of new political elements capable of marshaling the peasants to a royalist party. It is noteworthy that army officers were employed as administrators in the initial stages of National Promotion, and that Istiqlal and UNFP leaders were given no important roles in the program.

In the same interview, Guedira said that the new king most certainly intended to carry out his father's pledge concerning the holding of elections, but observed that this would not be practicable in the immediate future because only the Istiqlal and the UNFP had organizations throughout the country. Aside from the intrinsic disadvantages of this situation for the palace, it was clear that any new rural-development program sponsored by the king without party participation would have been summarily rejected by these parties. Guedira said that he hoped it would be possible to hold elections by April, 1962, after a period of stability in which "a third force: new men, not warped by party interests" could have an opportunity to develop.

The realization of these hopes was, in fact, delayed a year beyond the original Guedira timetable. It was not until April 18, 1963, that the *Bulletin Officiel* announced that elections to the lower house would be held on May 17. . . .

Most well-informed Moroccans were taken by surprise, not only by the timing of the announcement but also by its substance. The original schedule, as set forth at the time of the constitutional referendum, called for the election of local municipal and communal councils and various consultative bodies (such as chambers of agriculture and chambers of commerce and industry, which are to channel advice and information to the government on agricultural and business matters) as the first stage. Instead, the government announced that parliamentary elections would be the first order of business. Since Istiqlal and UNFP had previously dominated local legislative bodies in Morocco, it was obvious that the Front would not find it easy to win control at this level.

The opposition quickly charged the palace with precipitating events in order to win a decisive victory in the parliament, and thus ensure victory in these other less certain elections on the strength of two landslides: the referendum and parliament. The vehicle created to achieve the parliamentary landslide — if, indeed, this was the intention — was the FDIC.

The FDIC, at base, is a fragile alliance combining the hastily organized, Berber-based Popular Movement, splinter-party militants, certain government administrators, and independent businessmen. Significantly, it also has the support of the national police and the sympathy of at least part of the army officer corps. What all of these elements have in common is loyalty to the king.

The FDIC's electoral objectives were to weaken the two established political parties, preserve the present character of the monarchical system, and establish the grounds for more certain governmental stability. The king has never been overtly involved in the Front, but his closest relatives, associates, and political advisers are active in its direction. The FDIC's organizational head is Guedira, who almost certainly laid the groundwork for the Front during his tours of rural areas as minister of agriculture. When he first publicly announced the FDIC's creation at a press conference on March 20, 1963, he cited the "totalitarian" and "dictatorial" character of certain Istiqlal and UNFP leaders as one of the reasons for the new party's existence.

The opening of the election campaign was scheduled for May 2, 1963, and was to last fifteen days. There was to be one ballot based on a simple-plurality, single-member constituency system. To ensure a parliament led by national leaders (rather than the local illiterates who predominated in the communal elections of 1960), candidates could sit for any constituency. This stipulation aided the UNFP and, to a lesser degree, the Front, many of whose candidates were national figures.

The scramble for candidates tested the skills of the various political organizations. Istiqlal and UNFP leaders had gained valuable experience in the techniques of mass mobilization during the struggle for independence and in both the communal council elections of 1960 and the constitutional referendum. Both parties sensed the crucial importance of these first parliamentary elections in Morocco's history: if the royalist party won a landslide, the future of political party life in Morocco would be very much in doubt. Despite this realization and some specific efforts by UNFP and Istiqlal conciliators, the two parties did not succeed in creating any significant alliance or even agreement on common candidates. . .

The Front's problems were much more complex. An expensive campaign organization, without antecedent, had to be created on short notice and by persons with far less practical experience on this score than either the rival Istiqlal or UNFP militants. Moreover, the Front's internal alliances were never strong enough to ensure a clear line of authority. Choosing candidates proved especially difficult. Disputes were so sharp among heterogeneous leaders and militants that close observers doubted the Front would ever survive the campaign. That it did suggests that the king may have intervened at some point to arbitrate differences.

Important leaders were quickly placed in "sure" electoral constituencies; the main difficulties arose over the choice of candidates for rural constituencies. Minister of National Defense Mahjoubi Ahardane, secretary general of the Popular Movement, drew on his familiarity with rural leaders from Morocco's often rebellious mountainous areas to put forth a slate of candidates. Minister of Interior Guedira, as the main representative of the provincial governors, asked their help in selecting likely candidates. Moroccan governors are in an excellent position to pressure voters, particularly in favor of a royal front: they control the distribution of local market and transportation licenses and have considerable leverage on indebted peasants (the majority of the population). The Aherdane and Guedira lists, for obvious reasons, did not always agree.

Underlying tensions between Berber rural dwellers and Arab urbanites added to the Front's difficulties. Indeed, a number of Popular Movement Berber candidates, already angry over the MP's alliance with Arab politicians, eventually broke with FDIC and ran on independent tickets in instances where they failed to win the Front's endorsement.

The king was clearly reluctant to tie himself too closely to any political group or to give Guedira full rein to employ all the resources at the palace's command during the campaign. Use of government-owned radio and television facilities by the Front was notably restricted, and no individual candidate was publicly endorsed by His Majesty. Was this because of the obligations such a direct alliance would entail or, more likely, because of the limitations a commitment would put on his future bargaining power? There can be no doubt that the king was fully informed on divisions within the Front as well as the greater efficiency of the Istiqlal organization and the well-coordinated activities and ideological pull of the UNFP.

The election campaign was virulent. Each of the protagonists attacked on personal issues designed to evoke responses among a largely illiterate population. At the last moment, the UMT abandoned its nonpartisan position and issued a somewhat ambiguous communiqué indicating that the labor movement now favored "progressive candidates." This shift had a curious history.

Early in the campaign, UMT had agreed to remain neutral in the election parley in exchange for government favor vis-à-vis the Istiqlali UGTM. When this agreement came to light — after a spectacular strike settlement in the iron mines of Eastern Morocco, arranged by the king's confidant, Mohammed Laghzaoui — local UMT militants rebelled in protest. To save the union's organizational unity, Secretary General Mahjoub ben Seddik made his hasty switch in support of "progressive candidates." This implicit endorsement of the UNFP slate, albeit late and equivocal, was an unexpected blow to the FDIC at a very important stage in the campaign. . . .

Meanwhile, Morocco's difficulties with its neighbors increased, putting new pressures on the king. The alliance that seemed to be developing between Algeria's Prime Minister Ahmed ben Bella and U.A.R. President Gamal Abd al-Nasser was not well received in Rabat's official circles, especially when it began to take on an antimonarchical character. During the spring, representatives of the Moroccan UNFP joined the Algerian FLN as observers at the Arab unity conference in Cairo, which produced a project for federal unity among Syria, Iraq, and Egypt; no official Moroccan delegation was present. UNFP newspapers openly cited the Egyptian and Algerian one-party republics as models suited to Morocco's needs, and several party leaders were known to be in close touch with Nasser and ben Bella.

Less than a week before the meeting of the Casablanca group powers was scheduled to convene at Marrakesh on May 8, President Nasser and Prime Minister ben Bella announced in separate messages to Hassan that they would not attend the conference. Quite clearly, neither of them wished to contribute to Hassan's electoral victory by being in Morocco as his guest a week before the parliamentary elections.

Moroccan radio and press had given much publicity to the imminent arrival of the Casablanca leaders for this important preparatory meeting before the opening of the summit conference at Addis Ababa, and its collapse was another serious blow to the beleaguered Hassan. When the coordinator of the Casablanca bloc, a FDIC candidate, resigned from his post shortly before the elections, the Casablanca group was already dead before its official burial at Addis.

Hassan's decision not to attend the Addis Ababa conference was also directly related to the elections. The opposition parties, already making capital of the collapse of the Casablanca bloc conference and related foreign-policy failures, would almost certainly exploit Hassan's participation in a meeting also attended by Mauritania's President Moktar Ould Daddah. Istiqlal leaders were particularly suspicious of a *rappochement* at the time, because two Mauritanian ex-ministers, long-time exiles in Morocco, had recently returned to their country. Weighing the issues, Hassan apparently decided that he could not risk the injection of another damaging foreign-policy issue in the election campaign.

In the wake of the elections, the king remains noncommittal and Morocco's political future uncertain. He replaced Guedira, one of Morocco's most frequently criticized political figures, as minister of interior by another loyal monarchist, but the FDIC leader remained as minister of agriculture and as director of the royal cabinet. Much of Guedira's time is being devoted to the reorganization of the Front on the basis of lessons learned.

The opposition parties, though more confident of their potential than before the elections, hesitate to attack the king directly. They are working hard, however, to build support to a point where direct engagement of the palace is feasible. There are some indications that they may become overconfident too soon and make demands or issue calls for popular demonstrations out of proportion to their power. . .

If he wishes to continue to rule Morocco's complex body politic, Hassan knows that he must continue to divide it into manageable segments or change his tactics completely and resort to open force against his adversaries. Having studiously avoided committing himself publicly to sponsorship of the FDIC, he is still in a position to make a sharp tactical shift without backing down on any open commitments. Several alternatives present themselves.

Disappointed with the UMT's hot-and-cold alliance with the government during the campaign, the king could — and, indeed, is reported to be taking steps to — encourage the development of a third labor movement under the leadership of an ex-UMT leader. Since the state is an important employer in Morocco, the king's support of a new union would unquestionably weaken both the UMT and the Istiqlal UGTM, and perhaps even preclude the unification of a "labor opposition."

Second, it is not to be ruled out that, after trial and error, he might drop the FDIC altogether, if he decides that it is too weak to balance against other factors in the Moroccan equation. (In this connection, it is significant that the Popular Movement is claiming fifty-four out of the sixty-nine seats won by the FDIC in the May balloting.) Once parliament opens, there still is even a faint chance the king might conclude that a new limited alliance with the UNFP on the left or the Istiqlal on the right would better serve his interests. However, the arrest of five prominent Istiqlalis on June 7 and 130 UNFP militants on July 17 — reportedly to prevent violence in connection with July 28 municipal and communal council elections — precludes the implementation of this policy in the near future . . . .

There is another possibility to be considered too. It can be argued that the king never intended that the FDIC should be more than a minority party and that he was not discomfited to see all major Moroccan politicians discredit themselves and each other through the violent personal attacks characteristic of the election campaign. The indispensability of a royal arbiter standing above the divided political scene was perhaps never more evident.

Even so, the king's surprise must have been great when he learned that the UNFP had won as many as twenty-eight seats — eight seats more than the highest estimates worked out by Guedira's advisors. The election results have made it necessary for the palace to re-evaluate the weight of the UNFP in the Moroccan balance of forces.

A card up Hassan's sleeve that is often forgotten is the generally royalist officer corps of the 30,000-man Moroccan Army. Although the army has never been directly involved in politics, many of its officers occupy key administrative positions (for instance, governor of Casablanca prefecture, chief of the national police, director of the king's military cabinet, and so on) and are familiar with the behind-the-scenes intrigue that characterizes the country's political life. Commandants, captains, and colonels, often of Berber origin, trained in the French army and now in their late thirties and early forties, are quick to contrast the army's efficiency with the untidiness of the usually Arab-dominated political ministries. Will they look with equanimity on parliamentary wrangling over the military budget or military policies?

The time could come, if the institution of a parliamentary system produces only prolonged governmental instability, that King Hassan might call on his officer corps and army-led police force to step in to end political wrangling. After Hassan became king, Morocco was divided into military regions, each administered by a trusted officer and equipped with mobile intervention units. More than a year ago, a score of dissatisfied young officers trained in France since independence — mainly of the rank of lieutenant — were permitted to resign from the armed forces. Some of them were known UNFP sympathizers. Their removal from the officers corps added to the homogeneity and discipline of the army behind the king.

The drastic step of calling the army into the political arena would doubtless be taken only as a temporary expedient, and on the assumption that (1) the king would remain as political arbiter and (2) the military would retire from the scene in favor of civilians as soon as the situation could be stabilized. To return armies to barracks once they undertake a political role is not always easy, however.

THE END OF THE CONSTITUTIONAL EXPERIMENT

In a dramatic move on June 7, 1965, after more than three months of crisis and several futile attempts to group together disparate political elements around a minimum program, King Hassan II of Morocco invoked his constitutional prerogatives, proclaimed a state of emergency, recessed parliament indefinitely, and dismissed the prime minister.[1] For the first time since the installation of a parliamentary regime in 1963, the thirty-six-year-old monarch assumed full responsibility over day-to-day operations of the government. Hassan thus adds head of government to his already impressive list of titles: head of state, commander in chief of the armed forces, and Imam, or religious leader of Morocco's nearly 13 million Muslims. . . .

This is not the first time in independent Morocco that the monarch has had to intervene openly in political processes and take over the reigns of government. Hassan's father, the venerated Mohammed V, acted as prime minister in the last years of his life. Hassan, then crown prince, became vice president of the Council of Ministers and filled the role of head of government in all but name, absorbing much of the political criticism that otherwise would have been directed at the head of state. . . .

With the first parliamentary elections under the new constitution in May, 1963, a new era was proclaimed. The king relinquished some of his powers to his prime minister, Ahmed Bahnini, who assumed office in November, 1963, and the new legislature immediately became the scene of a constant dialogue between opposing political tendencies. Ministerial decisions reflected a new sense of accountability to the parliament's main deliberative body, the Chamber of Representatives, where weekly interpellations provided the opposition with a public forum to pursue its watchdog role. If this was not exactly genuine parliamentary government, it was nonetheless an achievement in his direction paralleled by few of Morocco's Arab or African neighbors. Hassan took obvious pride in his constitutional innovations.

As 1964 drew to a close, however, the new system began to reveal its basic flaws. . . . Although the Istiqlal took its seats in the new chamber, it continued to challenge the legality of the body and to call for new elections. The ruling majority in the Chamber of Representatives, a fragile coalition of the PSD and the MP grouped together in the FDIC, barely survived the honeymoon period of elections and the distribution of ministerial portfolios. Tension between the partners mounted as their right to govern was challenged almost daily by opposition attacks questioning the very basis of their legitimacy: the disputed constitution and the parliamentary elections. Only three minor bills were passed by the parliament in the two and a half years it was in existence.

The riots in Casablanca at the end of March, in which a number of Moroccans were killed in a confrontation with the army and the police, opened still a new phase of the Moroccan political crisis. The demonstrations that precipitated the riots were initiated by secondary-school students protesting certain governmental educational policies, but the youngsters were clearly prodded to action by parents increasingly frustrated by the deteriorating economic and social situation. Violence ensued when the unemployed and slum youths, who daily fill the streets of Morocco's economic capital looking for something to do, joined forces with the students. In a passionate speech to the nation following the "March days," the king for the first time openly criticized the parliamentary deputies and questioned the utility of their continuing their "empty speeches" geared for newspaper consumption and ego satisfaction. In retrospect, this speech dealt the death blow to a dying parliamentary system.

Hassan was apparently deeply affected by the Casablanca riots. For the first time since independence (March, 1956), the policies of the sharifian throne were attacked directly by mass demonstrators in an urban setting. His first response was to reaffirm his power by ordering the execution of fourteen Moroccans previously condemned to death for secretly infiltrating across the Algerian border as part of a subversive armed guerrilla operation. After some reflection, he decided also to intensify the process of consultation with all political tendencies — a process that never really stops in Morocco — by moving to the level of outright negotiation with the opposition parties. On April 13, as a sign of good intent, he granted amnesty to all political prisoners incarcerated in Morocco, including UNFP leaders. At the same time, he extended an invitation to self-exiled UNFP leader Mehdi ben Barka to return home. In this way he fulfilled the major condition set by the National Union for opening negotiations.

All the political parties believed they stood to gain from consultations with the king at this time. The MP and the PSD expected to enlarge their ministerial representation in a new government. The Istiqlal, now ready to re-enter the government after having been separated from power for two and a half years, set new elections as their major prerequisite for participation. Those spokesmen for the UNFP willing to collaborate with the "traditional monarchy" led by 'Abderrahim Bouabid, demanded a fully responsible "homogeneous government" and a contract from the sovereign to allow this government to achieve set goals. Labor leaders of the Moroccan Labor Union were more adamant than their UNFP allies, demanding basic structural reforms before they would be willing to collaborate openly with the monarchy; 'Abdullah Ibrahim, a former prime minister, even failed to appear before a royal convocation of potential ministers. Everywhere that Hassan turned, he found that those with whom he sought to negotiate wanted to restrict his power as the price for national government.

The solution for which he finally opted appears to be only a tentative stopgap to allow time to work out a satisfactory political system that will stand the test of time. By proclaiming that he will revise the constitution, the king satisfied a major UNFP demand. By announcing that new elections will be held in the future, he holds the Istiqlal in suspense and undercuts their major talking point. At the same time, by retaining ten of twelve ministers of the previous government, he appeased his loyal supporters, the MP, the PSD, and the army. He also used the occasion to dismiss the minister of education, Youssef ben Abbes, whose educational policies sparked the Casablanca riots. The removal of Ahmed Bahnini as prime minister highlighted the break with an impossible and unworkable political situation.

King Hassan is thus again playing a familiar game of the Moroccan monarchy — keeping his opponents off balance in order to prevent a coalescence of forces sufficiently strong to threaten him. Though this is a tested legacy, it has some disadvantages, illustrated by the recent career of Ahmed Reda Guedira, the former minister of interior, FDIC leader, and long-time confidant and friend of the king. Guedira's handling of the 1963 legislative elections did not produce the results the king had anticipated. After the elections, Guedira was placed more and more on the defensive. His political rivals in the king's entourage stepped up their behind-the-scenes offensive against him, criticizing him for failure to use the Interior Ministry facilities more effectively to put across FDIC candidates. On his other flank, the Istiqlal attacked him publicly, using this as a convenient substitute scapegoat for direct attacks on the monarchy.

Guedira, a middle-of-the-road liberal in a West European sense, found himself out of step with the extremes at work in Morocco's political spectrum. A trained jurist of distinction, he could interpret a legislative text to its fullest extent, but he was unwilling to carry coercion beyond the borders of legality. The failure of his legalistic approach to his responsibilities as minister of interior in this crucial election left the door open for less moderate elements to have their say with the king. (The results of the July 28, 1963, municipal and communal council elections were thus more in keeping with what Guedira's opponents would have liked to see in the Assembly elections. The royal Front won over 85 per cent of these seats; the UNFP, Istiqlal, and the small unofficial Moroccan Communist Party all boycotted the polls.)

Troubles with the Popular Movement also added to Guedira's woes. After the May elections, the MP claimed the majority of seats won by the FDIC as their own. Guedira attempted to regroup FDIC deputies by founding the Socialist Democratic Party (PSD) on April 12, 1964. The new party included such important personalities as Ahmed Bahnini, prime minister until the June 1965 shake-up, former minister of information and present director of the royal cabinet Moulay Ahmed 'Alaoui, former minister of economy and finance Driss Slaoui, and Mohammed Laghzaoui, then director of Morocco's important state-run phosphate mining and marketing operation, but its creation did not succeed in solidifying the palace-oriented groups as a whole or in capitalizing on UNFP and Istiqlal weaknesses to become a grass-roots mass party. Guedira finally resigned from the government in August, 1964. Though he retained his parliamentary seat from Casablanca, and continues to devote his talents as journalist and organizer to the PSD, he is somewhat of a lone wolf, waiting for the day when the king will again need his services, ability, and energy for new purposes.

The once powerful Istiqlal has been relegated to a secondary position in the past two and a half years. Its impressive showing in the May 1963 legislative elections was a product of the party's highly centralized and efficient inspectorate system, which has long made it the fourth best organized structure in the country to reach the masses (excelled only by the administration, the army, and the police). Moreover, deep-rooted bonds of loyalty tie the Istiqlal's national and local leaders in almost every province of the kingdom. For many Moroccans in their forties and fifties, the era of the independence struggle represents the most important and exciting period of their lives. Well-trained party functionaries are able to fan these memories of the old Istiqlal, and to build their campaigns around the charge that other parties have jettisoned true nationalist goals. This approach not only brings out votes, but also the contributions needed to keep the party solvent over the short run.

Deprived of government portfolios since January, 1963, however, the Istiqlal has lost much of the patronage on which it depended for its mass political support. Although it can still rely on voluntary contributions to its treasury by old-time nationalists spread throughout the country, the party has been steadily losing its appeal among the younger generations. Treasury shortages have forced its French-language paper *La Nation* to operate in the red when not banned by the government; the weekly *al-Istiqlal* folded for several months, appeared again briefly at the beginning of 1965, and is now banned. Most local party cadres now must work without pay, and many adherents at local levels have been deserting to movements blessed with royal patronage or are losing interest in partisan politics altogether.

Since May, 1964, leaders have been attempting to re-establish working cells at the local level similar to those in existence during the campaign for in-dependence in the early 1950's. As part of a centralization drive, these local cells, though still responsible to regional inspectors, now have independent channels of communication with national headquarters. More recently, at the seventh Istiqlal Congress in February, 1965, four older members of the executive committee were replaced by the equivalent number of young, active, outspoken, and intelligent militants who have worked their way up in party ranks. This development was one of several recent indications that the leadership is serious about trying to reach an agreement on the left, and thus revamp the bases of Istiqlal's appeal. Certainly, Istiqlal President 'Allal al-Fassi is the first to admit that "every party out of power suffers." By 1965, any offer by the king for national union had to be considered seriously by Istiqlal leaders.

Morocco's other major opposition party, the UNFP, was created in 1959 as a result of a split in the Istiqlal. For all practical purposes, it has been in eclipse since July, 1963, when the government uncovered a "plot against the internal security of the state," charging that UNFP elements (including three of its major leaders, Mehdi ben Barka, Mohammed al-Basri, and 'Abderrahman Youssefi) were planning to assassinate the monarch and some immediate members of his retinue and ultimately invest the major cities of the kingdom.

The principal "victim" of the plot turned out to be the UNFP itself. More than 100 UNFP militants from all over Morocco were arrested on July 16, 1963, in a swoop on the union's central headquarters at Casablanca, where upper-echelon leaders of the party had gathered to decide whether to boycott the municipal and communal council elections scheduled for July 28. On the following day, the police rounded up hundreds of other militants in other cities. A few were released, such as 'Abderrahim Bouabid, a former vice president and minister of national economy. (Bouabid subsequently was quoted in the press as having said that the government intended that he should become the leader of a new "loyal opposition," but that he had declined to cooperate.) Ben Barka was in Cairo at this time, but was charged *in absentia.*

Of the 102 Moroccans affiliated with the UNFP who subsequently directly or indirectly stood trial, thirty-five were acquitted in March, 1964; eleven were condemned to death (including ben Barka and seven others who had escaped the country); and sixty-seven others received terms ranging from a few months in jail to life imprisonment. Two of the eight condemned to death *in absentia* returned to Morocco in June, 1964, only to be shot by the police in what still remains a mysterious encounter. After the killing, in August, the king commuted the death sentences of the three condemned men in custody, including Mohammed al-Basri, to life imprisonment. Youssefi was freed on a two-year suspended sentence.

Following the 1963 arrests, the UNFP central headquarters in Casablanca and some branches in other cities remained closed and under police guard until the end of 1964. Its major leaders were either imprisoned, in exile, or under careful surveillance. Party militants continued to meet informally in one another's homes, but there seemed to be little liaison between them and recognized UNFP leaders. Those acquitted by the court quickly resumed militant activity in their new roles as martyrs and are again busily organizing resistance to the regime, but the party remains only a shadow of its former self.

By the summer of 1964, all that remained active of the UNFP leadership in Morocco were a few deputies, such party spokesmen as Dr. 'Abdellatif Benjelloun, and Professor Mohammed Lahbabi, and a group of youthful journalists who carried on the union's propaganda efforts. Ben Barka, with two death counts on his head — the other was for statements he made during the Algerian border war calling on the Moroccans to revolt — was living in exile between Geneva, the Middle East, and Algiers.[2] Bouabid, whose stature was enhanced by his rejection of the palace olive branch at the time of the plot arrests, took shelter in Paris and boycotted parliament despite his election as a deputy; he did not return to Morocco until the fall of 1964. Youssefi was only semi-active in Casablanca, hampered in his work by ill health and police surveillance. Mahjoub ben Seddik, secretary general of the Moroccan Labor Union, and his ally, 'Abdullah Ibrahim, although still members of the UNFP executive committee, continued to take independent positions on many issues.

Perhaps the most significant but little publicized aspect of the entire 1963 plot affair was the role of the military. Although it is very difficult to check some of the facts, there were clear indications that army officers above the rank of lieutenant were implicated in the plot. Several military names came up repeatedly during the course of the trial. At least four of these officers disappeared from public view by the summer of 1964; about a dozen others were removed from positions of responsibility and were transferred to chief of staff headquarters in Rabat, where they have been employed in carefully supervised tasks. The air force hierarchy was also quietly shaken up shortly after the announcement of the plot. In today's Morocco, there is no equivocation in dealing with infractions of the unwritten rule that the involvement of military officers in any opposition political movement will not be sanctioned.

The plot momentarily slowed down but did not halt Hassan's development of the military as a pillar of his regime. Since he came to the throne in 1961, the king has shaped the army into a major support of the state and of his power position. After their show of strength against Algerian troops in the 1963 border war, army officers were appropriately decorated; more recently, they have received impressive salary increases, placing them well beyond the salary range of their peers in the civil administration. An increasing number of officers and ex-officers have been appointed as provincial governors or have been placed in local administrative positions as qaids under the direction of the minister of interior, General Mohammed Oufkir.[3] Even a minor military involvement in a subversive movement would be reason enough for Hassan to take vigorous counteraction, which may explain the severity of the response to the 1963 plot reports.

Parliamentary collaboration convinced at least the Istiqlal that a working agreement could be negotiated with the UNFP. No longer fearful of being challenged in a power struggle by the UNFP's now-weakened radicals and hopeful that the breach between the UMT and the UNFP was irreparable, the Istiqlal's president, 'Allal al-Fassi, decided he could risk a bid for outright consolidation of the two opposition groups. His reason was clear-cut: he needed the UNFP's ideological appeal to draw Morocco's youth to Istiqlal's banner.

Beginning in the summer of 1964, the Istiqlal put out feelers to the National Union concerning possible collaboration. Al-Fassi went to the point of publicly proposing union with the scissionists in the middle of October, 1964, which found a surprisingly favorable echo among the National Union of Moroccan Students (UNEM), a UNFP ally. By then, the antagonism generated by the five-year-old split between the Istiqlal and the UNFP had begun to wear off as representatives of the two parties became accustomed to sharing the same opposition benches in the National Assembly.

The UNFP was more cautious. Its leaders feared that amalgamation with the more conservative Istiqlal would cause their more radical adherents to bolt the party. Moreover, the UMT-UNFP relationship, though often strained to the point of near-rupture, had never reached the point of outright scission: the labor union leaders and UNFP differed on many tactical points, but they nevertheless shared several common ideological points of view. At moments of crisis, both groups recognized their common cause. Police action against the UNFP in the wake of the reported plot had weakened the party's organization, but it had also enhanced the National Union's martyr image and provoked the UMT leadership into renewed solidarity with their besieged political brethren.

Although the prospects of re-amalgamation of the Istiqlal and UNFP were thus never very bright, the fact that the possibility was even being discussed was enough to cause Hassan some disquiet. The 1963 legislative elections had given the two parties just short of a controlling majority, and the FDIC majority had long since lost its *élan* and internal cohesion. By late 1964, the king recognized that a new initiative was required.

ECONOMIC PRESSURES

Related to political unrest is the harsh fact that Morocco has thus far been unable to solve many of its economic problems since independence. A Three-Year Plan drawn up in 1964 died in birth, because the planners failed to collaborate with the Ministry of Finance and, therefore, schedules for allocating funds were meaningless. A new scheme produced by the Moroccan Planning Commission was approved in April, 1965, by the Chamber of Representatives, but in a vote marked by a UNFP walkout and unanimous Istiqlal opposition.

According to Planning Commission technicians, the new plan is primarily a checklist of resources and expenditures projected over the next three years. More venturesome schemes, such as the one drawn up by 'Abderrahim Bouabid for the years 1960–65, were set aside as "premature." This time each minister was given budgetary limits within which to draw up requests for submission to a central pool. It was only when final dispositions were settled that the plan was presented to representatives of business and finance for comments and criticism; labor unions were also invited, but boycotted the sessions on the grounds that the plan was "prefabricated."

The king instructed the Planning Commission to concentrate on three areas: agriculture, tourism, and the formation of technical personnel. He emphasized the importance of developing primary and secondary education and demanded that the commission work out a program for economic development within a regional framework. Hassan's option for regional planning would seem to be based on political rather than economic considerations. Regional planning schemes — as Americans are learning in the Johnsonian "Great Society" — are a useful means for the chief executive to demonstrate to all parts of a country that he is doing something for each citizen. Political populism requires a direct link between the ruler and the ruled. . . .

In the light of the Algerian border war of 1963, the continued strengthening of the Algerian armed forces, and especially now that the military has taken over power in Algeria, there is general agreement in Morocco that a strong, well-equipped army is an imperative. Money for this, as well as for expanded educational facilities, the Three-Year Plan, and even part of the day-to-day operations of government, will obviously require continued deficit financing and more foreign aid. . .

In Morocco, as in other newly independent African countries, leadership has been faced with the task of creating unfamiliar bonds of nationhood among a diverse citizenry accustomed to thinking in terms of local loyalties. Because of its size and geographic, ethnic, and political heterogeneity, Morocco's road was bound to be especially long and hard. The independence struggle alone proved insufficient for molding national unity and solidarity at a popular level, and irredentism was a most useful device for rallying the masses to national goals and symbols.

Although irredentism and soothing verbiage may be useful, perhaps even necessary, in solving short-run internal political problems in the first years after independence, those new nations that continue to concentrate indefinitely on political manipulation rather than economic and social development begin to travel on increasingly thin ice. In Morocco, there are some signs that the initial period of "verbal nation-building" may be giving way before the pressures of economic and social malaise. Today, unlike in the past, highly placed Moroccans close to King Hassan are warning him that Morocco's "honeymoon period" of postindependence must be stopped, and that all money and expertise Morocco can muster must be brought to bear against economic stagnation. But old ways die slowly, and it is still too early to predict whether Morocco will be able to close its opening chapter of nation-building by verbiage and open a new one better suited to realities.

Social unrest has clearly reached a new conjuncture point, and it would be a mistake to sweep all of this malaise under the all-encompassing carpet of "rapid social change." Corruption, always a part of any traditional political system, has now spread throughout the society, and nepotism, favoritism, and old-fashioned bakshish seem to have become increasingly institutionalized in the central administration. Newspapers and members of the elite no longer attempt to hide the phenomenon. Partly in reaction to this, nihilism has taken firm root among large segments of the Moroccan youth, especially in the cities. The word walo, colloquial Arabic's equivalent for the English word "nothing," is heard increasingly on the lips of Moroccan workers and youth when they are questioned about the effectiveness of their rulers. The Casablanca riots were but the first publicized manifestations of a new tension and impatience in Morocco, which were not vocalized in the early days of independence.

For the moment, this generalized discontent is not organized into a coherent force, and recent events in Algeria have sobered many budding revolutionaries. Most opposition leaders seem willing to sit tight for the moment, adding their bit to criticism of the regime in the hope that the nihilism they are helping nurture will eventually find extensive mass echoes. Such tactics, however, could backfire tomorrow and implicate those same politicians who are today sowing the seeds of nihilism. Meanwhile, most Moroccans, throughout the political spectrum, are waiting to see what the king will do now that he controls the reins of power. While he cannot possibly please all his friends and critics, his chief hope of holding off revolutionary change is to give priority attention to some kind of a strike at the roots of Morocco's social and economic crisis. . .

Notes

1. See Hassan II, "The Passage and Suspension of the Moroccan Constitution," pp.118–23 in this reader.

2. Soon afterward, in November 1965, ben Barka was kidnapped in Paris and disappeared, presumably murdered by the Moroccan Interior Ministry.

3. Oufkir in turn committed suicide in August 1972 when his role in the abortive Skirat coup of the previous year was disclosed during a second attempt to kill the king.

23

POLITICAL PLURALISM IN MOROCCO

I. WILLIAM ZARTMAN

"The Moroccan political system is unique in Africa, not only because Morocco is endowed with a monarchical regime but also because it is the only country to have tried and maintained a multiparty system since independence."

Societies are generally not monolithic or homogeneous; hence every political system must deal with the problem of pluralism in some way. But political systems tend to be organized hierarchically, with power and authority concentrated at the top. The confrontation of social pluralism and political concentration can well give rise to tensions, as centralized political structures deal with diversified social interests. Tensions are also likely to grow out of pluralism within the political structure itself as factions form on the bases of personalities, programs, and interests. Such factions can exist within a single organizational or institutional framework, or they can be reflected in competing parties, checking and balancing institutions, and separated powers. The single-party regime has often been noted as the usual way of containing these tensions and factions in developing countries, particularly in Africa, and the existence of so many African single-party regimes has led to efforts to discover the common elements behind the common phenomenon. The purpose of this study is not to challenge these explanations, but to look more broadly into the nature of interests, factions, and power in developing polities, suggesting a model of political development that puts both unipartism and political pluralism in their places. The question to be answered in relation to Morocco, then, becomes not: Why did the Istiqlal not become a single party? Or even: Why did not the divided nationalist movement unite? But rather: How have the inevitable pressures for pluralization affected the Moroccan political system?

Students of African politics have suggested that there is a typical sequence in the evolution of political organization in response to the challenge of political modernization.[2] The end of the colonial conquest and the beginning of the colonial pact was marked by a period of imitation, in which the newly formed and educated elite tried to show the colonizer that it was Westernized and to

Reprinted, by permission and in modified form, from *Government and Opposition: A Quarterly of Comparative Politics,* July-October, 1967.

stand before the traditional society as an example of the way to the modern world. This double purpose faced a double rejection, since the elite tended to lose contact with its own traditional society but still was not accepted on equal terms by the colonizer. The reaction to this double rejection was a dual reform movement: one regressed to seek the pure elements of traditional culture and to reform the local society along these lines while the other intensified its efforts to gain acceptance by pressuring the colonial rulers to grant reforms leading to equality, integration, and assimilation.[3] The regressive reaction undermined its own position by adopting modernistic methods in its reform of traditionalism, but it headed in the right direction by reaffirming its ties with the mass. The intensive reaction had a greater commitment to modernization, but its goal of assimilation was incompatible with the privileged position of the colonial overlay. Up to this point, nationalist political organization remained a reflection of fractional modernization in society but was as yet unable to create the necessary basis for political influence, that is, unable to generate power within the colonial system.

In the next stage — the dyarchy, the work of both reactions was undercut and replaced by the formation of a nationalist movement, which sought to create a rival political system and to overthrow the colonial system by wielding mass support, the one element of power left to it by colonial rule. In David Apter's terms,[4] the movement became — for the first time — both a dependent and an independent variable in the political process, depending on the structure of society for its leadership and followers but introducing its own means of generating power. Its goal, that of becoming "an intervening variable between the public and the government,"[5] now came into sight. Colonial opposition welded the nationalist movement into a united or unified organization, for if it were not (or as long as it was not) the colonial government could keep it weak by playing on its internal divisions. Thus, it approached independence as a representative of the vast majority of the population on the basis of a broad popular attachment to the single goal of independence, overriding divergent interests.

With the attainment of independence, which usually follows at this stage, the nationalist movement has been obliged to reverse its position: it no longer seeks to overthrow the old political system but to dominate the new one. Indeed, because of its united, popular nature, it is used to thinking of *itself* as the political system: sympathy with the movement, not citizenship, becomes equivalent to membership in the system. But the task of government poses new challenges to the movement and opens new alternative stages. The first tendency of the movement is to preserve its unity but to turn itself into a political party, with members instead of sympathizers. The presence of members, however, puts pressure on the party to aggregate their diverse interests instead of merely voicing their support for a single, undifferentiated goal. Although the underdeveloped nature of society may tend to keep these interests rather simple and few, the rise of expectations and the poverty of resources to satisfy them can rapidly lead to a sharpening and a multiplication of demands, and, not too long after, to either dissatisfaction or apathy bred of frustration. Thus, with membership comes pressure both for organization and control and for programs and policies, the former working for party unity and the latter putting strains on that unity. Ethnic, social, and geographic differences also tend to add further strains, as do ideological divergences and personal rivalries, although these must find an appeal in the interests of potential followers to be effective.

Thus, the attempt of the nationalist movement to adapt to the new situation brings strains which can lead to several results. If the political organization can aggregate and satisfy competing demands, if it can monopolize the means of control and coercion, if it can contain factionalism within its midst with a combination of carrots and sticks, the nationalist movement can turn into a nation-party at least as long as it can aggregate and allocate effectively.[6] If interest divergence is low, if enthusiasm gives way to apathy as the colonial enemy and the single goal disappear, if party organization atrophies, the single-party state can turn into a no-party state, at least until these conditions change.[7] If interests are not aggregated and demands not met, if enthusiasm gives way to dissatisfaction and becomes organized against the system, if there is no way of changing leaders or policies within the system, the party government can fall prey to revolution, until a new political system is established.[8] But if these conditions do not obtain, if alternative sources of authority are operative, if there is an effective (that is, legal and enforced) possibility of free political organization and electoral participation, a pluriparty system can emerge. Whether the political organizations are one or several, there continued vitality depends on their ability to support their role as an intervening variable in the political process with their roles as a variable dependent on the structure of society and independent in its generation of power.

Three qualifications should be placed on this model. First, the words "progression," "sequence," and "stages" should not be read to imply a strict and exclusive succession of events. Some of the pre-independence stages — notably the two reform reactions — can overlap, the lengths of periods can vary widely, and in exceptional cases the order and the relation to the independence-point may change (particularly if pre-independence elections bring in the need for an organized party); similarly, the reactions to independence can appear in varying order.[9] Second, the model is open ended and should be able to be extended by further studies in comparative politics and political sociology. Third, this analysis will be presented in terms of plural interests, in a rather broad sense. Admittedly, an explanation of politics in a country like Morocco could also be made in terms of regions or personalities, since both are real factors and both have a relation — geographic base and leadership role — to interest formation. Despite the accentuation of interests in this analysis, neither of these other elements are to be ignored for a full understanding of Moroccan politics. Neither by itself gives the broad and dynamic framework for understanding that interests provide.

MOROCCAN PLURALISM

This model can be compared with the Moroccan experience to find an answer to the initial question. It is the thesis of this paper that the single-party system is a natural but fleeting stage in political development; that Morocco's evolution into a pluriparty system is atypical only in the speed with which it occurred; that certain specifically Moroccan conditions — notably the existence of an independent institution of power and legitimacy, and secondarily the presence of a number of well-developed groups and interests — account for this acceleration; and that these conditions can be approximated in other developing political systems, particularly during the second generation after independence.

When Morocco became independent in 1956, its nationalist movement enjoyed the sympathy of the overwhelming majority of the population, under a leadership with roots in specific social groups.[10] The "old leaders," generally either modern or traditionally educated intellectuals coming from the old — mainly Fassi—bourgeoisie, primarily from the two categories of reform groups emerged from exile, deportation, or international lobbying to reassume direction of the movement. Another group was the makhzen associated with the palace and the protectorate government, at least up to 1953, when Sultan Mohammed V was exiled and many who formerly worked for him in civil service and local government resigned; when they returned they brought an essentially nonpartisan element of middle-class civil servants back into the political system. Within the nationalist movement was also a group of activist "younger leaders" who remained in Morocco before independence to organize resistance to the Protectorate, and some of whom were also jailed or under house arrest; they tended to come from new middle-class intellectual groups (that is, educated in secondary schools) and from proletarian groups, and had around them a large number of mostly urban "followers": students, workers, and unemployed. The most significant rural group in the nationalist movement was the Army of Liberation, based in specific (and largely Berber) tribal areas, mostly traditional in nature.

Political organizations cut across group lines: the overwhelming majority of the old leaders, young leaders, and followers were Istiqlalis; a few others were members of the Democratic Istiqlal (PDI) and, to an even smaller extent, the Moroccan Reforms (PRM) and Unity (PUM) parties in the Spanish zone. One small club in the makhzen was called the Liberal Independent Party, and another grouped mostly intellectuals into the Moroccan Communist Party. The Berber Army of Liberation group no longer had any organization by the end of 1956, and much of the rest of the countryside was only unevenly penetrated by the Istiqlal.

As was to be expected, the Istiqlal set about after the return of the sultan in November, 1955, to turn itself into a party and to convert the Moroccan political system into a single-party state. It launched a concerted recruiting campaign for members, particularly within the civil service, the police, and the army but also in the rural areas, to which little attention had previously been paid and which had often harbored animosity toward the Istiqlal. At the same time, the party also sought to destroy competing membership drives, particularly by the PDI and Liberal Independents in the towns.[11] It also began a campaign for a homogeneous (that is, all-Istiqlal) government. a claim that was supposed to be validated by the success of the Istiqlal membership drive and the failure of its opponents' drive.

By the end of two years of independence, the Istiqlal appeared to have reached its goals without exception. In May, 1958, a government of Istiqlalis and sympathizers was formed under party Secretary General Ahmed Balafrej. The Liberal Independents and the PDI had been squeezed out, the premiership had been taken over from a respected independent, the Defense Ministry was finally in Istiqlal hands. A Berber and palace-associated attempt at dissidence against the government had been quickly brought under control by the army. The three opposition parties and their press were lifeless; the first attempt in October, 1957, by the Berber group to constitute a new party was squelched with alacrity; one party in the ex-Spanish zone had affiliated with the Istiqlal and the other had melted away. Istiqlal infiltration of the civil service and police was well under way. Economic interests within the society — businessmen and artisans, landowners (large and small), labor — had been organized and their organizations dominated by the party. Yet, by the beginning of 1959, the Istiqlal had lost control of the government, the party and its functional auxiliaries had split, two new major parties had been authorized and organized, dissidence had again broken out in some mountain areas, new newspapers had appeared, and major political figures had left the Istiqlal to become independents. What had happened?

The most important factor lay in the fact that Morocco had an alternative source of legitimacy and power in the monarch, who was not dependent on any party but had his own sources of authority and popularity, and who in subtle ways opposed the concentration of rival power in any political organization and encouraged the creation of conditions wherein plural organizations could be formed.[12] Each of these characteristics bears separate investigation. Although the nationalist movement had created a dyarchy by the end of the 1940's, both political systems — protectorate and nationalist — looked on the sultanate as their apex. When the French deposed Mohammed V and replaced him with their puppet ben 'Arafa in 1953, they in fact handed over the legitimate sultan to the nationalists as the head of their system alone. Thus, in Morocco, membership in the system after independence was equated with allegiance to the king, not to a political organization. The king legitimized the independent Moroccan system, not only because of his traditional position as head of a historic dynasty and of the national religion but also because of his symbolic leadership of the nationalist struggle (albeit under the pressure of the nationalist movement) and his patronage of continuing modernization. Because of the important traditionalist roots in the nationalist movement and the decision of its leaders to militante under and for, not against, the symbolic leadership of the sultan, the movement gave up any chance of posing as an alternative legitimizer of the political system. Large numbers of civil servants, businessmen, and peasants remained directly loyal to the king, outside the reach of the Istiqlal.

While continuing to recognize and encourage the parties' allegiance to him, the king also set about developing ways of strengthening his own sources of support, and of weakening — without actually trying to destroy — the support of the parties when they threatened to become too strong. This meant reaffirming direct ties between people and palace and also meant balancing off the predominant organization — the Istiqlal — with strengthened rivals. Thus, the king appointed governors who were his personal representatives, kept the army directly and exclusively loyal to the throne through the crown prince as chief of staff, sought to set up nonparty elections, and kept channels of communication, interest articulation, and redress of grievances open between himself and constituent groups. Maintaining the power to appoint both his prime minister and his consultative councils, he imposed proportional formulas on cabinet and council memberships so that the Istiqlal, while predominant. was balanced both by PDI members and Liberal Independents (inflated beyond their popular strength) and by independents directly loyal to him. At the same time, he played a quasi-parliamentary game in the choice of his prime ministers by calling the candidate of the strongest faction in a governmental crisis to form the next government.[13] When (in 1958) this meant the creation of an Istiqlali government exclusive of other political organizations, he insisted on maintaining a key post (Interior) in non-Istiqlali hands and on including sufficient independents (four out of eleven) to ensure control over government policy. Through his representatives, through his own policy guidelines, through restraints and pressures on the government, and through his acceptance of minimal measures to undercut activists' demands for accelerated programs, the king was able to slow social change and foster political liberalization. The most important results were the activists' (mainly the young leaders') impatience with the more conservative party leadership's acquiescence to this moderation, and the passage of legislation allowing both the restive activists and the Berber Army of Liberation group to form new political organizations.

By 1959, the situation had changed in both subtle and dramatic ways. Instead of one predominant political organization that contained a number of interest groups and factions, organized Moroccan politics had been sorted out into interest parties. The old leaders and their followers in traditional cities and the central agricultural plain maintained control of the Istiqlal. The young leaders and their proletarian followers in the growing industrial cities (plus farmers and traders from the trans-Atlas Souss valley) became first the Confederated Istiqlal and then, with similar elements from the PDI, renamed themselves the National Union of Popular Forces (UNFP); during 1959 and half of 1960, this UNFP group formed the government, with the job of preparing local elections. The rural, Berber mountain group established the Popular Movement. Bourgeois intellectuals maintained the small Liberal Independent, Democratic Constitutional (ex-PDI), and Communist parties. The functionally and politically representative National Consultative Assembly was allowed to lapse;[14] the first nationwide elections, in May, 1960, for local councils, confirmed the regional and social clientele of the parties.

The more subtle change corresponding to this pluralization of parties was the reduction of party participation in government. The "UNFP government" of 1959–60 was chosen "in a personal capacity." An increasing number of leading nationalist figures regained their independence as nonpartisan, palace-oriented figures when the Istiqlal split. In the local elections, a quarter of the seats, particularly in the rural areas, were won by independents. After the elections, the "UNFP government" was replaced by a government of technicians (four members of parties — the UNFP refused to allow participation — were named as individuals and not as representatives of their political organizations) with the king as prime minister and the prince as acting premier. Not yet ready to put effective governing power in hands of an electoral majority without formal safeguards for the paramount position of the monarchy, the king tightened hold on the reins of government but promised a democratic, monarchial constitution by 1963 and then died.

Essentially, Mohammed V's tactics[15] in encouraging and maintaining pluralism had been to maintain his own predominance in position and power and to wear down the momentary challenge of a rising political organization by saddling it with the burdens of government. The tactics of Hassan II have been similar in their goal of maintaining pluralism but less formal in their methods.

Hassan has not saddled parties with authority but rather has kept them alive and competing only by offering the hope of participation, never fully realized, and has kept them weak by competition and control. The father practiced a sort of constitutional parliamentarianism without written constitution or elected parliament; the son has had a constitution and a parliament without any durable constitutionalism or parliamentarianism. From one point of view, it can be seen that Hassan is working under conditions more difficult (although of his own creation) than did his father. Under Mohammed V, all parties were working and waiting for the golden moment when a constitutional system with an elected parliament would be established.[16] Political effort — much of it constructive — was channeled into preparing for a new structure. As long as events seemed to be heading toward its creation, realistic hopes could be kept alive. When the moment came, however, it was scarcely golden; the letter of the constitution turned out to be filled with more democratic promise than the spirit of its application. In this situation, it has been much more difficult to keep the parties' hope alive, and it is tempting to draw the inference — however unsubstantiated — that all the crises befalling Morocco after 1962 were manufactured by the palace to avoid having to make the constitutional system work. Because of the problems in this situation that he created, Hassan has had to resort to political maneuvering to maintain the pluralistic political system, and to crisis management to maintain its stability. To Mohammed V, the problem was to encourage political pluralism by wearing the parties out with governing responsibility. For Hassan, who seeks to maintain political pluralism by wearing the parties out in opposition, the problem is to keep the parties in the political system without giving them any governing responsibility. These tactics demand more political skill and a more active political role for the king, but their long-range goal and merit are not very evident.

The first step in keeping the situation fluid was the constitution, promulgated after a referendum at the end of 1962. The constitution provided for a government responsible to king and parliament and specifically forbad a single-party state. Thereafter elections had to be held for national, local, and intermediate institutions, occupying attentions during most of 1963. Other crises arose in the form of plots uncovered in 1963 and 1964, and a border war with Algeria in late 1963; at least in the case of the plots, there is some doubt of their reality although there is no doubt of their use as an occasion to clip the wings of the opposition. When a riot broke out in Casablanca in March, 1965, the reality of the popular — and probably spontaneous — outburst was not in doubt, nor was the effectiveness of the police and army repression. Hassan used the occasion to blame and then suspend parliament, dismiss and take personal charge of the government, declare a state of emergency, and raise hopes for constitutional reform, new elections, and an opening to the left. While the UNFP opposition lived on its hopes, encouraged by discreet talks with the palace, the king himself enacted one of its prime policies, the nationalization of a large part of foreign commerce, and at the same time continued to encourage the separation of the major labor union from the political parties by granting new labor benefits.[17] In late 1965, a new crisis arose — again with no clear evidence as to how much the king himself was involved — when Mehdi ben Barka was kidnapped and probably assassinated, most likely by the minister of the interior. Whatever had been the hopes for the return of political parties to government before this latest crisis, they were sharply reduced.

If the situation changed under Mohammed V from factionalism within a predominant political organization to party pluralism, the lines of pluralism have become blurred under Hassan II. Two stages can be distinguished. In the first period, following the promulgation of the constitution, the king fostered further organizational pluralism by encouraging the palace-oriented independents and other groups to form their own party. Thus, the elections of 1963 were contested not only by the Istiqlal and the UNFP (until charges of plotting caused the two parties to boycott), but also by a new Front for the Defense of the Constitutional Institutions (FDIC), which grouped independents, Liberal Independents, and the Popular Movement, under royal patronage.[18] The instability of the new body was soon apparent: It was only an electoral alliance, too poorly organized to be called a party; its own unity lasted only as long as the elections themselves; and both the party and the king were somewhat restricted in their freedom of action by too close an association. Once the constitutional institutions were established with a tenuous FDIC majority, independents and Liberal Independents made a second attempt to form a political organization, in order to balance the Popular Movement within the FDIC. The resulting Socialist Democratic Party also proved ephemeral, for it never developed any grass-roots organization, and it lost control of the government when the state of emergency was declared.

Nevertheless, through their candidates and their voters, the parties in the 1963 elections showed the increased identification with distinguishable sectors and interests.[19] The Istiqlal drew its votes from traditional elements in older cities, small towns, and rural areas between the Atlas and the Rif, particularly in the Gharb, Doukkala, and Tadla farming areas and among the small town traders, artisans, and petty bourgeoisie. More than one-third of its successful candidates were farmers, one-quarter traders, and one-eighth teachers, whereas none came from the modern professions; more than one-quarter had only elementary Qoranic education, another quarter had only elementary modern education, and of more than one-quarter that had higher education, half came from the traditional school system. Generally, Istiqlal candidates tended to be older, traditionally educated figures; younger Istiqlalis were kept out of the running or were beaten, although youth does have great importance in party councils. Thus, the party represented a traditional, status quo (defensive) segment of small urban and rural population, under Fassi leadership.

The UNFP found its clientele in the proletariat (employed and unemployed) of coastal, modernizing cities from Tangier to Agadir (even though it was on cool terms with the UMT during the election) and in its peculiar fief in the Agadir-Souss region between the Atlas and anti-Atlas; it also attracted such lower civil servants as teachers and rural agents in the countryside, but their numbers were small. Its elected members were evenly divided among farmers, traders, modern professions (lawyers and doctors), and civil servants (mainly teachers); nearly half had higher modern education, although a third had only primary or secondary traditional schooling. Broadly, the party represented modern urban dissatisfaction (the Souss population being a large source of migrants and traders in UNFP towns, particularly in Casablanca).[20]

Some interpretation is necessary to separate Popular Movement clienteles from those of the PSD-to-be within the FDIC, but the differences are rather clear. Rather ironically, the Popular Movement brought most of the former *bled as-siba* or dissident region (minus the Souss) into the FDIC column, along with the Marrakesh region; the forty rural members of the FDIC group in parliament were generally all Popular Movement members, as were most of the forty-two FDIC members who had no more than primary education (twenty-eight of whom had only Qoranic schooling and seven of whom had none at all). The *siba* parallel is only partially paradoxical, however, for the party represents the dissatisfied traditionalists who inhabit the "disinherited" regions of the country; unlike their ancestors, they see redress of their grievances in effective attachment to the palace, but like the old *siba,* they react against the Fassi bourgeoisie (that is, today not the palace but the Istiqlal). The PSD appealed more to mixed elements in the towns, from unemployed to businessmen, ranging from those who benefit from the social services offered by local administrators to those who see their commercial interests defended by the palace. Although it is less accurate to group all this clientele together under one description, the PSD in general received its votes from urban populations touched by modernization and with interests to defend, the difficulty in generalization and the ability of the business interests to achieve direct access to the palace account to a large extent for the lack of cohesion of the short-lived party. Its deputies came mostly from the twenty-seven FDIC members who had modern education on the secondary level or higher (almost two-thirds of whom had a higher education diploma).

In the second period, the effects of downgrading the political organizations that began as early as 1960 have become apparent. First, the center of politics has shifted from the parties to the palace, where factions headed by the royal cabinet's director general, the interior minister and security chief, and the rather anonymous, technocratic ministers all maneuver to strengthen their positions (even more than their programs) close to the king. Rather than supplying political guidelines and checking and prodding the executants, as his father did, the young king takes a more active personal hand in policy decisions than ever before. Notable in this development is the increased importance of the army.

Since 1964, army officers have filled one or two government ministries as well as half the provincial governorships. The army played a hero's role in the Algerian War, and has been brought into greater prominence as a result of the frequent suspicion of plots, as well as the fear of another conflict with Algeria. The officers, in turn, tend to scorn the civilian government and parties for muffing diplomatic opportunities after the Algerian War and for making increased security measures necessary. While it is too early to say that there is a military-based regime, or that the military has become a political organization in its own right, or even that it is the client group of the interior minister, it is certain that the army has moved from a political to simply a nonpartisan position. With increased importance comes an increased awareness of its own interests — in terms of pay, equipment, activity. Already in negotiations with the left opposition (which ended with the ben Barka affair), the role of army officers in government was a point of discussion. When the military enters into competition with political organizations, it brings into play new elements of power that tend to change the rules of the game as well as the nature of the army. The decline of political parties as national, interest aggregating, and political recruiting organizations increases the possibility of the army's playing the same role.

Second, an increasing number of Morocco's leading political figures have withdrawn to the sidelines of politics, where they bide time, tend business, or mutter clandestinely. With ministerial positions being filled more and more with technocratic nonentities and party positions divorced from direct or constant influence on governmental programs, both the parties and the palace have lost some of their most notable figures. Many of these ex-politicians appear to have lost interest in politics, and only a small number seem to have been planning for a return. Similarly, many high and middle cadres have left government service, which they consider stiffling to initiative and efficiency, and have taken up less useful or even unrelated private jobs. The same phenomenon of apathy is evident on the popular level, where there has been a notable drop in organized political interest — not merely a change in focus from broad issues like independence to bread-and-butter problems but even a depolitization of the latter. The 1963 elections were understood by the majority of the electorate in terms of loyalty to the king and of local interests and attachments rather than as preparing for responsible national government.[21] The demonstration of March, 1965, is not a contradiction of this disinterest in national politics, but rather the other side of the same coin, for when organized political participation loses its effectiveness and hence its attraction, anomic outbursts become more likely as expressions of demands and dissatisfaction.

Third, the decline in political recruiting and organization has been reflected by increased use of pressure groups to represent various interests in society. Even the parties have sometimes shifted to operate as pressure groups, since their opportunities for institutional representation have been curtailed. Functional associations and political figures are consulted by the palace on specific measures, thus increasing the direct aggregative functions of the king himself, rather than having the parties serve as aggregators for several interests. A role as a pressure group, however, is a way of keeping the parties alive in a minimal existence. It also increases the possibility of payoffs, log-rolling. and dealing with the group representatives individually while reducing their ability to create broad and effective sources of power.

Fourth, the demotion of the parties to pressure groups for their client interests, the political maneuvering of the palace, and the ineffectiveness of the parties in their opposition role have naturally led to the further division of political organizations. Thus, the palace has succeeded in separating the UMT from the UNFP, leaving the latter with a greatly reduced clientele and placing the former in the role of simply a labor pressure group. This situation has further intensified the rivalry among the various leaders of the UNFP and weakened the party. Similarly, the Popular Movement has split into two factions, one in and one out of government. Only the Istiqlal has maintained its cohesion, thanks to its strong charismatic leadership and its long-standing organization.

There are three levels on which conclusions can be drawn: first, directly from the Moroccan experience; second, from comparisons with experiences in neighboring politics in the same North African culture area; and third, from comparison with broader notions of party development. Three lessons are evident directly from the Moroccan scene:

1. A political party, like any other alliance, tends to fall apart when its enemy is destroyed or when it is unable to attain power. When the nationalist

movement achieved its goal of independence, it was unable to make the transition from opposition to control of the political system and at the same time keep its component interests satisfied. Ironically, its very moment of triumph — the "homogeneous" government of 1958 — brought out the divergences among leaders and programs, based on needs and demands of clientele groups; like so many (other?) wartime alliances, the Istiqlal broke up in victory, unable to satisfy all its members with the booty (conceived of either in narrow terms of ministries or in broader terms of programs). Thereafter, in their time, the Istiqlal, UNFP, Popular Movement, and PSD have come to represent the four major interest groups in society: defensive (conservative) traditional, offensive (dissatisfied) modernist, offensive traditional, defensive modernist, respectively, depending on — in their own view — whether they had a stake in defending or changing the structure of society and polity. As time has gone on, even these political organizations have not been particularly successful in maintaining their internal cohesion; cut off from power (as organizations), they are nevertheless inhibited from turning their guns on the monarchy and making an enemy out of it.[22] In political terms, they no longer have very evident roles to play. Unable to function as an independent variable, they have lost effectiveness as an intervening variable between public and government, and are left only as a dependent variable, reflecting social pluralism.

2. Thus, in a political system, the pluralism of interests is the dominant factor in determining the pattern of political organizations when power is concentrated beyond their reach. The description given in the preceeding point is obviously not the whole picture; just at the moment of Istiqlal "victory," the hand of the throne reached down from on high, arrogating some of the ministries and directing the course of some of the programs. Whether or not the party would have split if the king had remained strictly neutral is an unanswerable question and one that opens up a number of conjectures, but the fact is that the king did enhance the conditions of the preceding point. Thereafter the palace role in Moroccan government increased, and even the king was unable to coalize the political parties into a National Unity government. The parties then became narrower interest parties and personal factions; they ceased to function as aggregators of interests, as this role was taken on more and more by the palace.

3. Alliances form among interest groups if they can achieve or create enough governing power to make a minimum coalition meaningful,[23] or if they find a new surmounting common interest in opposing the political system. The concept of a minimum coalition is meaningful only if its creation can accomplish something — the distribution of jobs or the enactment of programs. Minimum coalitions in a situation where power is distributed as it is in Morocco would be expected to involve the palace as well as the political organizations as members; thus, a governing coalition could be established by the king sharing his governing power with one party, as discussions with first the UNFP and then the Istiqlal have proposed. Otherwise, the only condition for forming a coalition would be the creation of an alternative (revolutionary) political system to challenge the monarchy. The reasons for this not taking place are simple: as long as the king gives parties a minimum, consultative role in the present formation of policy, and as long as he is able to keep alive their future hopes of governing, their interests as pressure groups are better served by playing the game than by challenging the system. Furthermore, and equally important, as long as the

king's security forces remain strong and loyal enough to show potential revolutionaries that they have no chance of success, the parties will continue to see their interests better served in the system than out. It is therefore important for the king to keep the parties minimally active as pressure groups, for if the king went to the point of totally destroying the parties and liberating their leaders from their clientele interests, he would decrease their stake in the system and increase their interest in destroying it. Yet basically, the only minimum winning "coalition" is the king alone.

On a second level, what can be learned from a comparison with other political systems in North Africa? Do similar situations exist in Algeria and Tunisia? In fact, perhaps contrary to appearances, both Tunisia and Algeria underwent similar crises after independence, although the outcome was different because of different political systems in each country. In Tunisia, where the labor movement the General Union of Tunisian Workers (UGTT), played a role similar to that of the Moroccan urban resistance in keeping the nationalist struggle alive before independence, the Neo-Destour Party faced its own threat of scission in 1957 on the part of Ahmed ben Salah and the UGTT, who wanted to form a socialist party. In Algeria, the National Liberation Front (FLN) and its component organs, the Provisional Government (GPRA), literally fell apart in the struggle for power that followed independence in 1962. But while such pluralism could be encouraged in Morocco, where the king could share power with the parties because his legitimacy was uncontested, in Tunisia, where power and legitimacy were created by Bourguiba and the party, pluralism was discouraged, and ben Salah was removed from the UGTT and then, together with his program, coopted into the government; and in Algeria, where power and legitimacy were both up for grabs, pluralism could never be totally eliminated even when power was finally concentrated in ben Bella's government. Thus both Tunisia and Algeria have faced the same challenges of scission in the moment of victory as did Morocco, although they have dealt with these challenges differently according to local political conditions. It may be added that Tunisia will doubtless meet a resurgence of the same tensions after the death of Bourguiba, and Boumedienne's regime is already having to deal with the same problems as did ben Bella.

Finally, how do the conclusions on Morocco, and on the rest of North Africa, compare with explanations of single-party regimes elsewhere in Africa? Comparisons will have to be summary. The absence of political pluralism in sub-Saharan regimes has been ascribed to a number of causes: "(1) the situation party leaders confronted at independence; (2) supportive or predisposing elements in traditional African society; (3) various aspects of the colonial legacy; and (4) the political culture of the new African elite."[24]

1. The heavy functional load and the ready availability of the party to perform these functions are the two characteristics of the postcolonial situation that appear to favor single-party regimes.[25] The unaggregable, nonexistent, or ethnic character of interests leads the party to formulate interests unilaterally; yet unaggregable or developing interests can also result in the appearance of separate interest groups, and especially so (but not only) when there is a legitimate, nonpartisan arbitrator. Parochialism and the weakness of national

communications lead the party to function as a common denominator of political socialization and communication and of national integration; yet the same characteristics may defeat these efforts and increase political pluralism, especially (but not only) when minimal functions of legitimization, allegiance, and identification are centered outside the party. Similarly, competitive forms of solidarity may be strong enough to defeat party efforts to bring political recruitment exclusively under its control. Thus, the postcolonial functional explanation appears to be theoretically ambiguous (which is by no means the same thing as "invalid"), although admittedly the ambiguity is increased by the presence of an independent center of power and legitimacy, and particularly in a historical kingdom with a good deal of development in some sectors of society.

2. Traditional factors, it is recognized,[26] are frequently sources of pluralism, although even this substantiating conclusion should be modified to note that an even greater source of pluralism is the coexistence of well-articulated and viable traditional and modern structures.

3. Colonial systems are also said to favor monopartism, particularly if they have weakened the traditional orders, governed through military or bureaucratic centralism, and granted the ruling party legitimacy by persecution or by elections.[27] Again, there is ambiguity. Colonial regimes can compromise traditional elites through collaboration, as in Tunisia and Morocco, and they can just as well enhance the prestige of traditional institutions by persecution, as in the case of the Moroccan sultanate. But neither legitimacy nor centralism are totally determined by the colonial policies, and the reactions to centralism can be pluralistic as well as monistic, just as the reactions to permission, collaboration, and persecution can all be legitimizing or compromising according to other variables. Morocco gives examples of both.

4. Finally it is suggested that the elitist, statist, nationalist political culture of new African elites favors single-party regimes, and the effect of these elements on the preceding factors is of importance.[28] It seems here that the crucial importance of the Moroccan monarchy is brought to light. For the monarchy acted as a focusing point for centralized government and nationalist legitimization and identity, as well as an alternative point of attachment for governmental elites, countering monopoly claims of the consolidating single party. In Tunisia, this condition is only being created by Bourguiba, whereas in Algeria, elitism and nationalism have not been monopolized by any functioning single party after independence, and even statism has been the source of conflicting views. "The one-party syndrome described in [these explanations] does not necessarily represent the end of the line in the political evolution of the new African states. Indeed, the triumph on one-party rule, the emergence of the dominant party as the political center of gravity immediately after independence may prove to be no more than a transitional phenomenon."[29] The "no-party state," the "party-state," and the "stable (or unstable) competitive party system" may well evolve. This study of Morocco has attempted to show that such alternatives, and particularly the last one, are highly likely when there is an alternative center of political gravity. It has also attempted to show, even in the absence of this condition, that the pluralism of society can be expected to increase as development proceeds, that crises of the single-party tend to take the form of pluralistic challenges, and that, in this, Morocco may not be atypical but simply ahead of the rest in African political development.

Notes

1. "Où en sont les partis politiques marocains?," *Maghreb,* No. 7 (1965), p. 19.
2. See, among others, James S. Coleman, "The Emergence of African Political Parties," in C. Grove Haines (ed.), *Africa Today* (Baltimore: Johns Hopkins Press, 1955), pp. 226-27; I. William Zartman, *Problems of New Power* (New York: Atherton Press, 1964), pp. 249-53; Charles Micaud, L. Carl Brown, and Clement Henry Moore, *Tunisia: The Politics of Modernization* (New York: Praeger Publishers, 1964), especially pp. 3-6; Clement H. Moore, *Tunisia Since Independence* (Berkeley: University of California Press, 1965).
3. On Morocco, see J. Abun-Nasr, "The Salafiyya Movement in Morocco," in Immanuel Wallerstein, *Social Change: The Colonial Situation* (New York: John Wiley, 1966), pp. 489-502; Robert Rezette, *Les Partis politiques marocains* (Paris: Armand Colin, 1955).
4. See David Apter, *The Politics of Modernization* (Chicago: University of Chicago Press, 1965), pp. 181-82.
5. *Ibid.* p. 181.
6. On integration and allocation functions, see I. William Zartman, "Morocco's Modernizing Monarchy," in John Mikhail (ed.), *Political Modernization in the Middle East and North Africa* (Princeton, N.J.; Princeton University Conference, 1966).
7. On the no-party state, see Immanuel Wallerstein, "Political Parties in Post-Independence Africa," in Joseph LaPalombara and Myron Weiner (eds.), *Political Parties and Political Development* (Princeton, N.J.: Princeton University Press, 1966).
8. On revolution, see Crane Brinton, *The Anatomy of Revolution* (New York: Prentice-Hall, 1952); Carl J. Friedrich (ed.), *Revolution* (New York: Atherton Press, 1966); Chalmers A. Johnson, *Revolutionary Change* (Boston: Little, Brown, 1966).
9. On the proper sequence of stages, see Micaud, Brown, and Moore, *op. cit.,* p. 5.
10. The following discussion follows the excellent article by Octave Marais, "The Ruling Class in Morocco," pp. 181–200 in this reader. See also André Adam, "Naissance et développement d'une classe moyenne au Maroc," *Bulletin Economique et Social du Maroc,* LXVIII, No. 4 (1955), 489-92; Marie Bousquet, "Les rapports de la bourgeoisie et de la monarchie au Maroc," *Les Temps Modernes,* April, 1962, pp. 1483-92.
11. See Douglas E. Ashford, *Political Change in Morocco* (Princeton, N.J.: Princeton University Press, 1961), pp. 302-33.
12. "The importance of the political party in providing legitimacy and stability in modernizing political systems varies inversely with the institutional inheritance of the system from traditional society." Samuel P. Huntington, "Political Development and Political Decay," *World Politics,* XVII, No. 3 (April, 1965), 424.
13. This process is spelled out in I. William Zartman, *Destiny of a Dynasty* (Columbia: University of South Carolina Press, 1964).
14. On the National Consultative Assembly, see, in addition to the above, Pierre Ebrard, "L'assemblée nationale consultative marocaine," in *Annuaire de l'Afrique du Nord, 1962* (Paris: Centre National de la Recherche Scientifique, 1964), pp. 35-81.
15. No one has ever been able to document the extent to which this tactic was conscious or planned rather than simply instinctive and informal.
16. See Jules and Jim Aubin, "Le Maroc en suspens," *Annuaire de l'Afrique du Nord, 1964* (Paris: Centre National de la Recherche Scientifique, 1966), p. 77.
17. The UMT declared its nonpartisan position in its January, 1963, congress, in exchange for palace support against the UGTM: the latter, Istiqlal-affiliated, is less effective in any role because of its smaller membership. Both unions, however, were reduced to pressure groups because of the need to defend workers' interests against the growing mass of unemployed.
18. A similar attempt, with the same participants (including the premier), was discussed in early 1958, before the formation of the "homogeneous" Istiqlal government, but failed because of Istiqlal strength and "king's men's" indecision; Octave Marais, "L'élection de la chambre des représentants du Maroc," *Annuaire de l'Afrique du Nord, 1963* (Paris: Centre Nationale de la Recherche Scientifique, 1965), p. 85.
19. Details taken from the careful analysis in *ibid.,* pp. 85-106, with some differences in interpretation on the nature of the Popular Movement.
20. See Robert Montagne, *et al, Naissance du proletariat marocain* (Paris: Peyronnet, n.d. [1951]).

21. Marais, *op. cit.,* p. 97.

22. There were threats to do so in the election campaign, however; see *ibid.* The plots of 1963-64, to the extent that they existed, also represented a momentary rise of those who considered challenging the political system.

23. On minimum coalitions, see William H. Riker, *The Theory of Political Coalitions* (New Haven, Conn.: Yale University Press, 1962).

24. James S. Coleman and Carl G. Rosberg, *Political Parties and National Integration in Tropical Africa* (Berkeley: University of California Press, 1964), p. 655.

25. *Ibid.,* pp. 655-58.

26. *Ibid.,* pp. 658-59.

27. *Ibid.,* pp. 659-61.

28. *Ibid.,* pp. 661 ff.

29. *Ibid.,* p. 672.

24

THE MOROCCAN COMMUNAL ELECTIONS

PAUL CHAMBERGEAT

... In his Speech from the Throne of November 15, 1959, the king announced that Morocco's first communal elections would take place in May,
1960.[1] Following this decision, a decree of November 17, 1959, opened
registration for thirty days, from November 25 to December 25. Another decree
on December 2, 1959, announcing communal redistricting, set up more than 800
communes averaging 10,000 inhabitants each. It also established the number of
councilors to be elected in each commune, varying from nine in rural communes
with fewer than 7,500 inhabitants, to fifty-one for Casablanca.

PREPARATIONS FOR THE ELECTION

Registration was first conducted by the local authorities, qaids, and pashas,
and then, at a level closer to the voters, by the *sheikhs* and *moqaddemin*. In
principle, registration was to be done in person, but in order to enable women to
vote, the Interior Ministry, agreed that they could be registered by their
husbands. (This was later to cause disappointment, since some husbands thought
that the same practice would be permitted at voting time.)

The political parties, unhappy with the voting system, did not show much
enthusiasm at the opening of registration. Furthermore, the Istiqlal and Popular
Movement expressed their lack of confidence in the government of 'Abdullah
Ibrahim, which, they said, was incapable of organizing an impartial vote. The
Popular Movement in particular apparently ordered systematic abstention for its
members in the north and east, for a while causing fears of renewed dissidence in
these regions. The results of the first five days were disastrous: barely 320,000
voters registered out of potential electorate estimated at nearly 5 million. Only
National Union of Popular Forces (UNFP) sympathizers showed any enthusiasm.

At the request of the Interior Ministry, the king appealed to his people to
register. Thereafter, a boycott became impossible, since it would look like
opposition to the sovereign; the Istiqlal and Popular Movement executive
committees then officially urged their followers to register and to encourage

Translated, by permission, from *Revue Française de Science Politique,* XI, No. 1 (March,
1961), 89-117.

others to do likewise. In the second week, 920,000 voters were registered and the parties organized to ensure that people registered under their banners. . . .

Even taking into account corrections in evaluating the electoral body, registration was higher than had been expected, thanks to the activities of the political parties and the local administration.[2] In the Western Rif, Middle Atlas, and pre-Sahara registration was very heavy. Most of Fes and Meknes provinces were also above the national average. But in Marrakesh and Taza, as well as some districts in Casablanca province, registration fell far below average. Registration appears to have been heavy where a political party was well implanted and light when the region was under the influence of several parties, which counterbalanced one another. At the end of the extended period on January 20, 4,127,000 voters were registered out of an electorate that turned out to be nearly 6 million (by the census figures of June, 1960), or about 70 per cent.[3] Following registration, a period was allotted for legal complaints to the courts. The small number of such claims — about 200 — showed that voters were generally satisfied with the operation and that irregularities were few. . . .[4]

The results of the final week for the filing of candidacies were as disappointing as the results of the first week of registration. For a while it was even thought that the elections would have to be postponed by decree, since the number of candidates was insufficient. Civil servants from the Interior Ministry were sent out to the provinces to stimulate local authorities, resolve eventual administration difficulties, and make a report on the operations. It soon became apparent that the delays did not indicate any lack of popular interest. On the contrary, in many districts the candidates took time to go out and meet their potential voters before filing their candidacy; some candidates also tried to obtain the nomination of tribal jema's before officially declaring their candidacy. No single candidacies resulted, but this kind of "primary election" did limit the competition to two or three. Local authorities were urged by the Interior Ministry to contact their populations through direct, active, and impartial propaganda to encourage candidacies in district's where there were none. Proclamations were read in the suqs to explain the meaning of the elections and elicit candidacies. In other places, the authorities had to limit the number of candidacies as much as possible because of administrative complications that might have occurred in making and counting the ballots. As a whole, where the political parties exercised real influence on the rural or urban population, the number of candidacies was limited. But rampant anarchy reigned in the regions where the parties were not well rooted, particularly in mountainous regions, where the population sometimes did not understand what filing was and thought the government was undertaking another round of registration. There were 47,000 candidates in about 10,200 districts, or an average of almost 5 candidates per seat. . . .

THE ELECTORAL CAMPAIGN

Political incidents (growing tension between the government and Prince Moulay Hassan, the discovery of a plot against the prince, arrests of "resistance" leaders) postponed the opening of the campaign. In Rabat and Casablanca, the Istiqlal and the UNFP waited until May 20 before organizing public meetings in stadiums and movie theaters. The national leader declarations had much more to do with general political problems than with programs at the municipality level . . . . More time was devoted to municipal problems during the many local meetings organized by the UNFP candidates, who presented a broad program for municipal socialism: schools, hospitals, and housing construction, eradication of shanty-towns. The Istiqlal campaign themes were built more around personalities: their "able and honest" candidates were contrasted with "drunk and corrupt" candidates, to whom it would be dangerous to hand the management of municipal affairs and a budget of several millions of dollars. . . .

Thus, two characteristics were evident in the electoral campaign. In Casablanca, Rabat, and the other cities, it grew into a general political confrontation between the dominant parties, in which Istiqlal posed as the party of the elites and the Moroccan Labor Union (UMT) generally used the political vocabulary of the European left. In the provinces, the electoral campaign was quiet but not without interest. The parties, the Istiqlal in particular, organized many meetings in the small towns that had no extensive means of propaganda. Often, a team from the nearby provincial capital held a meeting on market day. . . . Traditional means of propaganda were widely used, including discussion around a glass of mint tea or over a meal, but modern propaganda techniques, such as posters, were rare, largely because the majority of the people are illiterate.

A few days before the elections, the king broadcast a new appeal urging the people to vote. This initiative was very important, in that it gave a new impetus to the undecided voters. It also prevented some political groups from openly boycotting the elections for which they were not well prepared, for the official word had spread at one time that the elections would be postponed. Thus, after a very long preparatory period, whose weight fell mainly on the local administration, the material and psychological conditions were ready for making elections of May 29 a success.

ANALYSIS OF RESULTS

The elections went smoothly. The officials in charge had promised the king that there would be not more than 300 incidents in all Morocco. In reality, there was only one incident per province, which can be taken as a sign of maturity and self-discipline in the population. Everywhere, the vote took place in an atmosphere both festive and serious. A child, asked about a crowd in front of a polling place in Rabat, answered: "They are choosing the best."

Participation was exceptionally high. Out of 4 million registered voters, 3 millions (75%) voted. Electoral participation is rarely as high in developing countries; in India and Black Africa, it is generally about 50%. Abstentions were due to various reasons, some political, others sociological. In the first category were Nador and Alhucemas provinces, under military rule with political activities dependent on military authorization. The three Tetuan districts, with 31–45% abstention, fell into the same category. In the former Northern Zone, a bad economic situation and a feeling among the inhabitants of being misunderstood and left out by Rabat explains their reserve. In other regions, the reasons for abstention were as much sociological as political. Such was the case in some districts around Casablanca (Doukkala region), where the collapse of traditional structures and rural discontent (because of hardship imposed with the establishment of an irrigation network) was translated into a general rejection of all state interference. Elsewhere, the shortcomings of local administration explained the high abstention. The high rate of abstention in districts in Oujda, Taza, Ksar as-Souk, and Ouarzazat was primarily due to the difficulties encountered by nomadic shepherds in going with their families to the polling places. Abstentions were generally fewer in cities than in the countryside. Casablanca, Rabat, and Fes had only 20% abstention, which shows a high political awareness among the city-dwellers. . . .

In general, women also participated in the election in greater number in the towns than in the countryside. But we should not conclude that this meant total emancipation [of the city woman]. Most of the time, their participation and their vote were determined by their husbands or brothers, who were afraid of seeing the votes of their adversaries' wives or sisters determine the outcome of the election. . . .

Political analysis of the results is rendered difficult by the lack of official statistics. We have only the results published by the parties and in the newspapers, and these show only the number of seats won by the parties, not the number of votes each candidate received. . . .

The Istiqlal Party is the oldest and best organized Moroccan party,[5] despite its split on January 25, 1959. It won the largest number of seats, over 40% of elected candidates. The Istiqlal is particularly strong in the great plains of the north and in some districts of the Middle Atlas and Western Rif, where it won an absolute majority. Thus, success was due mostly to the backing of the rural bourgeoisie, organized into the Moroccan Agricultural Union (UMA). In the Berber-speaking regions of the Middle Atlas, Istiqlal influence was strongest among merchants, who were in constant touch with the great traditionalist cities of Fes and Meknes. It was they who, along with the Qoranic teachers, had introduced the party into the area under the Protectorate. They generally maintained their fidelity to the party, even if they did not always understand the 1959 split. The Istiqlal leaders from the countryside benefited from the divisions of their adversaries, whose effects were accentuated by the single-member system. They also knew how to use their connections and their clientele in the traditional sector to wage a limited but effective electoral campaign, inviting important members of the tribe or the fraction to dinner. . . . In the old traditionalist cities, such as Fes, Meknes, Sale, Larache, Taza, and as-Sawira, the Istiqlal also won an absolute majority on the councils. Here the party had the backing of the small craftsmen and commercial bourgeoisie organized in the Moroccan Union of Commerce, Crafts, and Industry (UMCIA). Economically, this group is much less dynamic than the UMA farmers, and it competes directly with the modern sector, which is still largely under foreign control.

The National Union of Popular Forces (UNFP) won absolute majority in the councils of the large industrialized towns, such as Casablanca, Rabat, Kenitra, Tangier, Safi, and in the southern countryside . . . . The seats won by the UNFP make up about 23%. In the modern cities, where the labor population is more cut off from its traditional roots without necessarily being integrated in the new social structures, the UNFP depended primarily on the dominant labor organization, the Moroccan Labor Union (UMT). The small and middle-class commercial bourgeoisie in the large towns generally made common cause with labor and backed the UNFP, as shown in the elections to the chambers of commerce.[6]

In the countryside, the UNFP had made agreements to abstain in favor of the Popular Movement, although they were not always respected because of local rivalries, sometimes of tribal origin (particularly in Khemisset). Two organizations brought their support: the "resistance" and the agricultural sections of the UMT. These sections are particularly strong in the work centers, a type of machine-tractors station set up to help modernize traditional agriculture. The "resistance" contains parts of the former Army of Liberation and urban resistants. This powerful and relatively unknown organization enjoys a prestige that is sometimes mixed with fear. Its backing is particularly important in Marrakesh, Agadir, and Ouarzazat provinces, where in order to prevent conflicts, local administrators have long been appointed with the unwritten agreement of the Army of Liberation. This tie has helped the UNFP make its influence felt. Another factor that favored the UNFP is the existence of a steady migration between these regions and the coastal cities. The workers and small traders who emigrated to Casablanca periodically return to their native villages and propagate new ideas. ... In the communes of the Ameul Valley (Tafraout), from which most of the Soussi grocers come, the victors were mostly from the UNFP. The Safi canneries, the Youssoufia phosphates, and the many lead, cobalt, and manganese plants of the Atlas and Anti-Atlas helped to give the UMT a hold in the rural communities. ...

As for the Popular Movement, its organization is practically nil. The party has close ties with traditional rural Morocco. Based on personal relations, using the tribal framework and its elites, it is less adapted to modern political ways than to the violent protests of the past *(siba),* even if the reasons for popular discontent that it exploits are of our time. ... It won its greatest success in Oujda, Taza, and Nador provinces and in the mountain districts of Beni Mellal province. Its total was estimated at 7% of the seats. ... The communes where the Popular Movement won a majority were mostly in the Berber-speaking regions, although — as noted above — not all Berber-speaking regions were controlled by the Popular Movement. ...

If in Rabat, Meknes, Fes, Taza, and Oujda provinces it was possible to identify to which party the candidates belonged, such a distinction was extremely difficult in other sectors. The winning candidates in the former Northern Zone did not fit into the framework of the two leading parties. Some councilmen would probably belong to the Popular Movement given the ties that exist between this party and 'Abdelkrim's former partisans. In Marrakesh and Agadir provinces, the sharp rivalry between Istiqlal and UNFP led many councilmen to stay away from these organizations and conceal their preferences for other tendencies.

GENERAL INTERPRETATIONS

In view of the uncertainty of the election results, it is not easy to draw precise political conclusions from them. However, some facts are certain: despite their peculiar character and the balloting used, the municipal elections did have a political overtone in the cities. As an indication, we can cite the frequent neglect of the individual candidate in favor of his party, and the use of ideological propaganda themes and of classifications such as "reactionaries" and "progressives." In the last analysis, since they were the only objective measures of the parties' strength, the elections could not but be political. The system of different colors for the ballots helped this politicization; instinctively, the parties found the means of fighting the fractioning favored by single member districts. Very soon the color of the ballot became more important than the candidate himself. In Casablanca, women wore veils dyed the color of the party they favored. . . .

In any case, party activities will be changed by communal elections. Their relations with the masses had previously been channeled through organizations with apolitical goals, such as labor unions or traders and farmers organizations. Lacking cadres, they naturally prefer to act through a small number of influential individuals within organizations whose members perform a leadership role in a milieu that has lost its traditional officials. The communal councilmen, who constitute new official rural elites, thus become the object of the attention of the political parties, and party activities are facilitated by the existence of a group of 10,000 people who are presently the only officials to represent the masses. The party leaders can then undertake a campaign of personal contacts with such a small group, with a good chance of success, since individual convictions do not always rest on solid ideological bases. The UNFP seems to have already undertaken such contacts with municipal council in the Chawia province.

It will be interesting to see whether the communal elections have effectively achieved their original goal of breaking up tribal structures. There is too little information to give a precise answer, but several polls have shown that many councilmen are former members of the judicial jema's of the Berber tribes or the communal councils set up under the Protectorate. In some regions, jema's of the *duar* handled the nominating process. Therefore, it would seem that in rural areas, perhaps with the exception of the modernized sector (in the plains), the tribal notables were integrated into the new administrative framework. The voting system favored their election. The tribal framework as such has been broken by the communal reform, but the old rural elites have kept their audience. There are indications that some notables who had been removed from official functions after independence, although without judicial sanctions, have been elected. If *sheikhs* and *moqaddemin* at the last minute had not been prevented from running, the traditional notables would have been even more numerous.

Notes

1. For the longer and earlier preparations, see Part I of the same article, *Revue Française de Science Politique,* XI, No. 1, 89-100. For other treatments of the 1960 elections, see Douglas E. Ashford, "Elections in Morocco: Progress or Confusion?" *Middle East Journal,* XV, No. 1 (Winter, 1961), 1-15; I. William Zartman, *Problems of New Power* (New York: Atherton Press, 1964), pp. 197-242, and L-J Duclos, Les Elections communales (Paris: Centre de Hautes Etudes Administratives sur l'Afrique et l'Asie Moderne 1961).

2. It seems that in the beginning the voter did not always grasp the meaning of his act. Many rumors circulated that a voter's card would enable the owner to get financial help, or that registration would be required by the authorities as an identity card, or that it would facilitate getting an administrative job.

3. Official estimates in January, 1960, set the electoral body at 4,590,000 giving a registration percentage of 86 per cent. The total was shown to be too low by the 1960 census.

4. The electoral lists confronted the administration with many difficulties. The lack of civil records and the changes in the spelling of names made for irregularities, but they should not be overestimated.

5. See Robert Rezette, *Les Partis politiques marocains* (Paris: Armand Collin, 1955).

6. The elections for chambers of commerce and industry on May 8 were a training ground for personnel in charge of organizing the communal elections. The vote of May 8 turned out to be of great political interest. Liberal qualifications for registration turned the election into a test of the reaction of the petite bourgeoisie; the parties quickly understood and intensified their propaganda at the very moment that they were neglecting the preparation of the communal elections. The results already gave an indication of what the results of the communal elections would be.

25

TUNISIA AFTER BOURGUIBA: LIBERALIZATION OR POLITICAL DEGENERATION?

CLEMENT HENRY MOORE

In the context of the Middle East and North Africa, it has been suggested that Tunisia, together with Turkey and Israel, illustrates a "liberal" pattern of political modernization.[1] Such an idea must inevitably come as a shock even to the most liberal and sympathetic observers of the contemporary Tunisian scene, if liberalism is to be taken seriously as a category of Western political thought. By all conventional definitions, Tunisia's personalistic regime is decidedly illiberal. Classic constitutional liberties have often been disregarded in Tunisia's bid to modernize — although possibly less so than in a number of new states. The courts in particular have often served as mechanisms for settling political scores with the regime's adversaries rather than as impartial instruments of justice.[2] Freedom of association does not exist in practice,[3] for no group is allowed to operate independently of the party or the government.

It is argued here, however, both that Tunisia's single-party regime has the potential to develop in a liberal direction and, more generally, that liberalization at a certain stage of political development may be an essential antidote to political degeneration. Implied in the analysis is a conception of political modernization or development (as opposed to degeneration), which first ought to be made explicit.

It may seem arbitrary even to isolate the political from the more general societal phenomena of modernization that first appeared in sixteenth-century Western Europe.[4] The growing body of current literature in American political science[5] tends to stress the instrumental aspects of political systems, so far as they are "modernizing," to solve problems. One author even goes so far as to distinguish modernizing from transitional systems by the former's revolutionary intentions.[6] But even if conceived strictly in terms of performance, political development requires national cohesion and mobilization — the expansion of the community's power resources — to increase the total impact of the political system upon society. Ultimately, in this view, political modernization is a

This paper was originally presented at the Princeton University Conference on "Political Modernization in the Near East and North Africa" in March, 1966; it is reprinted by permission.

process that is open-ended in time and subject only to the pragmatic appraisals of history; the only test of a modernizing system is its ability to cope with whatever demands are put upon it. Abstract liberal considerations would appear to be irrelevant (as Hegel foresaw) unless buttressed by a philosophy of history. Moreover, the contemporary realization that modernization in the new states presupposes political engineering for forging a new society clashes with the classic liberal assumption that political activity rests on a pre-existing social harmony.

But political modernization also involves, in addition to increases in political performance, the growth of new institutions.[7] The process of institutionalization is directly related to what some writers conceive to be the central problem of modernization, that of internally generated and self-sustaining change.[8] The level of institutionalization will determine a political system's capacity over time to generate new structures to meet new problems and thus, in Eisenstadt's words, "assure its own continuity in the face of continuous new demands and new forms of political organization."[9]

Institutionalization connotes, in David Easton's terminology, a process whereby structural legitimacy replaces or supplements legitimacy derived from an ideology or the prestige of an individual.[10] Actually, the concept is derived from organizational theory, where it describes how an organization may become infused with value, that is, valued for its own sake as well as for the functions it may perform.[11] But where one organization envelops the political process, as in operative single-party regimes, it seems plausible to equate institutionalization with legitimacy of a certain kind for the political system as a whole.

To develop into an institution, an organization must acquire an ideology of sorts,[12] form an elite to sustain the ideology and to provide future leadership, and generate "contending interest groups, clustering around various aspects of the organization's program and the values it represents, both inside the organization and among its external clients."[13] It is the latter condition that is particularly relevant to the process of institutionalization in a country like Tunisia, where the party has already fostered an ideology and an elite. This condition also points to the relevance of liberal constitutionalism for political modernization under a single-party regime.

If institutionalization requires contending interest groups, it follows that the party has to develop a framework of procedures for reconciling interests and groups and translating their demands into policy. As well as being an instrument for mobilizing and consolidating power for the sake of political performance, the party must tolerate and indeed encourage relatively autonomous groups that seek to influence policy. Its function then becomes the constitutional one of institutionalizing effective restraints upon the power of its own leaders who are the chief policy-makers. The party thereby endows the political system with legitimacy by virtue of the respect it engenders for its procedures for selecting leaders and making decisions, rather than by virtue of the support it mobilizes for particular leaders and decisions.

The reader at this point may well wish to object that American organizational theory, adapted to a climate where interest-group politics is the norm, should not be transplanted to less highly differentiated societies that reject American pluralist assumptions. It may, moreover, be difficult to imagine a pattern of political modernization that successfully and simultaneously advances both institutionalization and political performance. For interest groups in transitional societies tend to be diffuse in their objectives, highly politicized, opportunistic, ideological, and generally uncooperative and irresponsible, unless bribed or otherwise controlled by the government (or ruling party).[14] And such groups tend not only to block political performance but, rather than compromise, to assault the very procedures that institutionalization requires.[15]

A "liberal" pattern of political modernization, one in which institutionalization as well as the mobilization of political power occurs, is nevertheless conceivable though certainly not inevitable in one-party regimes. The model, to state it briefly, depends upon the timing of the emergence of certain types of interest groups and the elimination of other types. Contradicting the abstract liberal prescription of freedom of association, single-party regimes often eliminate or domesticate not only other political groups but also groups that appear to be functionally specific professional organizations, simply because these would otherwise serve as organizational weapons either for opponents of the regime or for cliques within the party attempting to convert themselves into organized factions. In the early stages of political consolidation, before power has been converted into policies having a wide impact upon the society, the demands of mobilization are strictly incompatible with institutionalization, because, in the absence of clearly defined policies, organized factions would inevitably bring into question whatever fragile consensus on policy had existed after the party attained independence. In the short run, while power is being mobilized and converted into policies, the party may even go into institutional decline, becoming the tame instrument of its leader, lest cliques crystallize into factions and paralyze policy-making.

But once the party has mobilized support for the policies its leaders succeed in imposing, differentiation between "politics" and professional interests may result. Only one issue, that of the succession, will be of burning concern to the party leadership, while heavy governmental intervention will elicit a great variety of functionally specific groups concerned primarily with technical issues of policy implementation. It is within such a climate that — and this is only a hypothesis — institutionalization might be compatible with sustained performance. The party would not sense any threats to its hegemony in the proliferation of functionally specific groups; indeed they would be a testimony of the widespread acceptance of its modernizing policies. But as political manager, the party would have to evolve procedures for aggregating the various interests. As the mobilized groups found it in their interest to work through party procedures, the party would be institutionalizing itself if, as an unintended consequence of its managerial role, cliques of party leaders found it necessary to compete for the support of these new groups on the "political" issue of the succession. Working through organized factions, the politicians would presumably also find it in their interest to respect the party's procedures, and these in time might perform the functions of a liberal constitution, by serving as a restraint on the exercise of power and as a guarantee for a competitive political process. Successions could be peacefully resolved because the party rather than an individual would be the prime source of the system's legitimacy.

The prospects of institutionalization seem brighter in Tunisia than in the other new African and Arab one-party states by virtue of the former's higher level of political performance. The Tunisian system has a substantial capacity for coherent policy-making as well as an administrative and political apparatus to implement its policies, and during ten years of independence the system has demonstrated its ability to cope with the demands put upon it. The Tunisian experience may therefore serve at least as a partial illustration of the pattern of political modernization discussed above, although it is by no means clear either that liberalizing tendencies at work today within the ruling party will ultimately prove successful or, more generally, that single-party systems can create, sustain, and make legitimate what amounts to a form of pluralistic competition.[16]

Tunisia's relative success as a modernizing political system is largely due to Habib Bourguiba, a statesman of the caliber of a Nehru, Ataturk, or de Gaulle (although Bourguiba's spiritual home is the liberal France of the Third Republic), and to his Destourian Socialist Party (PSD), which, founded in 1934,[17] is the oldest and one of the most organized parties in Africa and the Arab world. The main strength of the regime has been its ability to foster and sustain national cohesion — in other words, to marshal and expand the society's resources of political power. With the aid of his disciplined Destour, Bourguiba was able to avert a civil war with Salah ben Youssef, to erect an honest and relatively efficient administration, and to take bold political decisions to transform the fabric of Tunisian society in the confidence that they could be implemented. The abolition of polygamy and granting of equal rights to women in 1956, the consolidation of a unified and essentially secular mass-educational system in 1958, and the much needed abolition of certain archaic forms of land tenure[18] were not mean achievements in an essentially conservative Islamic society. Then, since 1962, Bourguiba has been able to channel the political passions originally aroused for the twenty-year independence struggle into a sustained effort of planned economic development. As *political* operations, the Three-Year Plan and now the Four-Year Plan have been remarkable successes, for the Destour has been able not only gently to smother all organized opposition but to steer the society's preoccupations to concrete goals. Today, such topics of conversation as Vietnam or the Congo are no longer of great interest to the Tunisian elite. Indeed, another of the Destour's achievements has been to silence pan-Arab demagogues and achieve a genuine consensus on foreign policy, without which Bourguiba's brave stand on the Palestine issue,[19] for instance, would have been inconceivable.

It can be argued that the national cohesion provided by the single-party regime was essential to Tunisia's very survival in the stormy years following its accession to self-government on June 3, 1955. But it is equally true that the country even then enjoyed a higher level of political integration than any other African country. For even apart from favorable geographical and historical factors (the concentration of half the population along a coastal plain endowed with excellent communications; six centuries of continuity as a political unit), Tunisia benefited from a unique colonial situation. French settlers, administrators, and educators were sufficiently numerous and influential to disrupt tribal and other traditional structures and prepare large sectors of the native population for the call of modern nationalism. In the course of the relatively bloodless struggle, the Destour was able not only to defeat the settlers but to displace the traditional bourgeoisie by mobilizing a new middle class.[20] The new leadership not only outdid the old elite in opposing alien Western domination but, thus assured of a national identity, it assimilated modern ideas and styles more wholeheartedly and creatively. Issues that have divided other Arab countries, such as relations with foreign reference groups, the role of Islam in modern society, and the problem of social justice, were in large measure already resolved by the Destour before independence. National cohesion was deep seated because it rested upon a common outlook shared by the modernizing elite, which, by birth and inclination, was in close contact with both the rural and urban populations of the coastal plain.

After France granted Tunisia home rule, however, the consolidation of the single-party regime was desperately needed to maintain this cohesion. The Destour and affiliated organizations grouped virtually all political participants (almost half of the active male population), and the old elite was both disorganized and discredited; but Salah ben Youssef, previously Bourguiba's leading collaborator in the Destour, turned against him and, encouraged by Cairo and other North African nationalist movements, split the party by his demands for immediate full independence. He enjoyed strong support in the party's Federation of Tunis[21] and also among conservative landowners and religious personalities to whom Bourguiba's French radical-socialist outlook was anathema. Even after he fled to Cairo and after the independent Tunisian government, with the help of the French army, eliminated his bands of terrorists and guerrillas,[22] ben Youssef alive[23] was a threat to the regime as long as a strong Algerian exile army was stationed on Tunisian soil. The requirement to help the Algerian revolution coupled with the need to remain on relatively good terms with France left Tunisia with little diplomatic leeway. Apart from a measure of international sympathy, internal cohesion was the country's only defense.

More positively, the cohesion sustained and augmented by the Destour in power is a precondition for the success of Bourguiba's distinctive approach to modernization. His vision of modern society requires an integral transformation of Tunisian social structures and the development of "new"[24] better-rounded individuals — people who not only perform an economic function but who have learned to live, love, and think like modern emancipated individuals.

The great transformation, as radical as any totalitarian blueprint, requires the sustained social engineering that only a highly organized state can provide. But Bourguiba breaks with the totalitarians not only in dismissing all hidebound ideologies but in rejecting their coercive methods. Bourguiba insists upon widespread active and reasoned agreement with his objectives, for he believes that individual conviction is the source of all lasting change. With the balance of Mediterranean man, however, he has too great a respect for the human personality ever to pass over the fine line that separates his brand of persuasion from the subtle Chinese techniques of brainwashing. If his humane methods can work in Tunisia, it is, in large part, because cohesion under the Destour reflects a genuine consensus of the Tunisian elite that is the product of thirty years of political activity. On the other hand, the party remains an essential instrument for reiterating Bourguiba's objectives to the people, re-enforcing the consensus, and sustaining the government's controversial policies and activities.

National cohesion for the sake of modernization, however, has dictated a sacrifice of liberal values that, in the long run, seems equally relevant to Tunisian development. In the Tunisian context the real issue is not whether one or more parties should exist. The Destour's only nationalist rival, another party bearing the same name, died of inertia shortly after independence. When the Tunisian Communist Party was banned in 1963, it had barely a thousand members and enjoyed little influence outside select student circles. In truth, Bourguiba's Destour had no competitors. Rather, the conflict between individual and group liberties on the one hand and national cohesion on the other has occurred within the Destour and its affiliated groups.

With an implacable logic that is startling in retrospect, Bourguiba, within three years of independence, succeeded in subordinating all other groups to the party, the party's federations to the fifteen-man Political Bureau, and the bureau to himself — while respecting democratic forms when necessary and maintaining the atmosphere of camaraderie and popular solidarity that the mass party had developed during its years of opposition. The utter ease with which he consolidated power was due less to any Machiavellian design than to the absence of crystallized groups within the party. Interests had not consolidated and individuals were aligned only to shifting cliques that cut across the organized paper framework.[25] In the interests of cohesion, Bourguiba only sought to avoid the hardening of cliques into antagonistic interest groups. His brilliant success should not be compared to that of a Stalin consolidating the dictatorship of the proletariat by liquidating all other forces.

In a somewhat mechanistic simplification of the fluid political reality, the writer discerns three potential groups that Bourguiba disarmed before they could crystallize as autonomous political forces. The groups can be identified more by the individuals who animated them than by any objective material or ideal interests, though of course the leaders tried to articulate interests. The most important of the groups was that of Taieb Mehiri, the minister of the interior until his death in 1965 at the age of forty-one. He was the protégé of Mongi Slim, the prestigious veteran who in 1959 seemed destined to succeed Bourguiba[26] but who meanwhile, until 1962, was kept abroad in high posts. Mehiri's power base was the party's Federation of Tunis, most of whose members had finally renounced ben Youssef when the latter broke with party orthodoxy. As the austere and impartial servant of Destour principle, Mehiri also commanded the respect and loyalty of party veterans from other regions, including the trade-unionist Ahmed Tlili, whose base was Gafsa. Mehiri stood for collective leadership by the party.

As one of his ministers, however, Mehiri could scarcely attempt openly to limit Bourguiba's power — especially after the latter, on July 25, 1957, had the popularly elected Constituent Assembly that the party controlled name him president of the republic, with full executive and legislative powers.[27] While Mehiri until his untimely death remained the one responsible Tunisian official who often dared to question important decisions of the president, he helplessly had to witness purges of close collaborators.[28] The party federations were suppressed in 1958; in their place, Bourguiba set up regional commissions under the direct authority of the Political Bureau; meanwhile, he had already placed a former student leader[29] in charge of the party apparatus to serve as a check on Mehiri.

The second and least important potential group was that of Mohammed Masmoudi, a man of Mehiri's age who in 1955 had served as minister of national economy and who later was Bourguiba's ambassador in Paris. The Masmoudi clique was never strong inside the party but assembled a number of enterprising young businessmen, including Bechir ben Yahmed, the minister of information and editor, in 1956, of *L'Action*, a weekly newspaper enjoying tacit party support. An exceedingly capable and trusted adviser to the president, Masmoudi represented the party's liberal Western face — the side that welcomed open discussion and an informed public opinion. While considered to be the most articulate organ of the party, *L'Action* did not hesitate to publish stories criticizing party and government officials.[30] But in the autumn of 1958, when the party, in the throes of reorganization, was especially sensitive to criticism, it withdrew its support of the paper and, with Bourguiba's blessings, dismissed Masmoudi from the Political Bureau. A few months later, he was pardoned and readmitted, but then, in 1961, Bourguiba again exiled him from political life[31] — this time for a full three years. The francophile Masmoudi had not only had the temerity privately to criticize Bourguiba's reckless policy of "liberating" the French naval base at Bizerte; the successor to *L'Action* editorialized about the vices of personal power.[32] Articulating nascent business interests, Masmoudi also objected to the authoritarian economic planning that Bourguiba had finally decided to endorse.

The third clique, that of the radical young intellectuals, was animated by Ahmed ben Salah, the secretary general in 1956 of the General Union of Tunisian Workers (UGTT) and [until 1969] minister of planning and finances. Slightly younger than Masmoudi and Mehiri, ben Salah had also been a Destour leader during his student days in Paris. Indeed, by background there was little to distinguish the three rivals. Each had studied at Tunisia's elite secondary school, Sadiki, and each had subsequently enrolled in universities in Paris. Though they became archrivals, Masmoudi and ben Salah came from equally modest families of neighboring villages in the Sahel. But whereas Mehiri made the party his career and Masmoudi business, ben Salah chose labor — partly because senior party officials had tethered the ambitious young graduate after he returned from France in 1948 to work in the party. As a *lycée* professor, ben Salah was able to join the teachers' union and, with the support of the party, he rapidly rose in the UGTT hierarchy. After the assassination of Ferhat Hached, the founder of the UGTT, the labor union lacked decisive leadership until ben Salah took over in 1954 with the party's blessing.

After independence, however, ben Salah, caring little for bread-and-butter trade unionism, brashly tried to use the UGTT as a power base from which to influence party policies. Tactically he advocated the organic fusion of party and trade union — a position that was quite logical, since virtually all of Hached's lieutenants who helped to form the UGTT had been party activists loaned him by the Destour.[33] In truth, no objective labor interests independent of the national interest articulated by the party had ever crystallized. But ben Salah made the strategic mistake of pushing too soon for socialist planning[34] — the content he wished to give the party policies once its goal of independence had been obtained.

Bourguiba easily got rid of ben Salah by allowing Masmoudi to engineer a split within the UGTT. Loyal party activists who were also veteran trade unionists were jealous of ben Salah's rapid rise to power and his utilization of the trade union for ideological rather than material objectives. Habib Achour in particular had been Hached's right-hand man in Sfax but was in prison when ben Salah was elected in 1954. With Masmoudi as his *eminence grise,* Achour broke away from the UGTT to form a rival trade-union movement. Then, in the interests of trade-union unity, Ahmed Tlili, Mehiri's close associate, was elected to replace ben Salah, who, outmaneuvered, prudently retired to await his recall as a minor minister a few months later. After five years, ben Salah had his revenge on Masmoudi when Bourguiba, having discovered the former to be an extremely energetic minister, made him the overlord of the Tunisian economy with full powers to carry out a more realistic version of the policies he had originally advocated. By 1961, however, ben Salah's authority depended entirely upon Bourguiba's; whatever trade-union support he had once enjoyed had been eroded by his years as minister of labor and social affairs, though a few loyal personal allies remained on the UGTT executive bureau.

Ben Salah was not the only politician, however, who tried to use the UGTT as a power base. In the late 1950's Tlili, although not a minister, was one of the four or five most influential men in Tunisia. In addition to being secretary general of the reunified UGTT, he was a member of the Political Bureau, treasurer of the party, and, most important, the unofficial liaison with the Algerians. Like ben Salah, Masmoudi, and Mehiri, Tlili had attended Sadiki; unlike them, he did not complete his studies but returned to Gafsa, where he organized the party federation and subsequently founded the regional union of the UGTT.[35] When it was time to replace ben Salah in the UGTT, Tlili, who was already assistant secretary general, was the logical candidate. His trade-union credentials were authentic and, unlike Habib Achour, he was a skillful politician and hence capable, like ben Salah, of blending UGTT and party interests. His strategy, however, was not, like his predecessor, to impose an economic policy upon the party, but rather, with Mehiri, to impose the collective leadership of the party upon Bourguiba; Tlili's aims, in short, were in the strictest sense political and bore even less direct relation to the professional interests of the proletariat than ben Salah's.

Just as Ferhat Hached once argued that the best defense of the workers lay in a tight alliance with the Destour against the colonial oppressor, Tlili could (though not publicly) argue that he was objectively best serving the interests of the proletariat by joining with the party — or at least some of its elements — in erecting institutional checks upon Bourguiba's personal power. Tlili's subsequent career illustrates the conflict existing in every new single-party state between limiting power for the sake of institutions and expanding it to further national cohesion for confronting new problems. Despite appearances, his career does not, as some American trade unionists may think,[36] represent a tragic confrontation between free trade unionism and a single-party monolith. Trade-union activity conceived as that of an autonomous interest group contending for influence in a stable political system has never existed in Tunisia, in part because there was no accepted forum in which interests might contend.[37] Bourguiba's dislocation of cliques before they could become coherent groups ensured that, far from becoming a monolith, the party became a faithful mirror to its demiurge — a formless energy in perpetual motion and barely distinguishable from the government except as a historical symbol of emancipation.

Until 1963, Tlili was able with the party's support to keep control of the UGTT, but within the union he was exposed to mounting pressures. At the congress in 1960, ben Salah's followers had astutely managed to elect two more of their clique (for a total of four out of nine) to the executive bureau by insisting before the election that Tlili be directly elected by the congress – a favor he could hardly refuse but that later prevented him from blocking the ben Salah candidates by threatening to withdraw from the elections. Virtually isolated in the executive bureau whenever Habib Achour and his ally cared to join forces with ben Salah's men, Tlili ruled the union with a minimum of consultation and, when challenged by his colleagues, retorted that he had been directly elected. He cut off the finances of regional unions that, like that of Sousse, were controlled by his adversaries. But it was mainly because of his pre-eminent position in the party that Tlili was able to maintain control of the UGTT – a large majority of the rank and file being Destour members little concerned with the clique policies that went on in the upper echelons of the trade union. At the same time, Tlili's influence within the party was largely based on his trade-union connections after his usefulness with the Algerians came to an end in 1960.

When Bourguiba appointed ben Salah minister of planning and finances in 1961, he also launched a political campaign to convince other Destour leaders of the need for rational economic planning. Tlili was the only member of the Political Bureau to be publicly out of step, though Mehiri and others were highly skeptical of ben Salah's ideological approach. Tlili continued as at the earlier UGTT congress to advocate flexible planning with modest and realistic objectives and let it be implied that ben Salah's objectives were neither modest nor realistic. In the rise of ben Salah, Tlili perhaps saw not only the political victory of a personal rival but the further erosion of the institutional strength of both party and trade union. But institutions could not block ben Salah once he had Bourguiba's full support. Though in free elections at the 1959 party congress ben Salah had failed to win a seat on the Political Bureau, Bourguiba coopted him – as he had many other bureau members in the past – late in 1961.

Probably at ben Salah's urging, the Political Bureau decided in 1962 to encourage the creation of professional cells. Though organized primarily on a geographic basis,[38] the party had occasionally assisted Hached by forming professional cells in enterprises and administrations where the UGTT was weak or needed more vigorous leadership for the independence struggle. The party weapon had also been used by Habib Achour against Ahmed ben Salah in 1956. Now it was to be used, as Bourguiba later explained, for furthering the "socialist" objectives of the minister of planning and finances. Though the Political Bureau assured the UGTT that the cells would not meddle with trade-union matters, a confusion of roles was inevitable. The party prudently relaxed its pressure in 1963, but meanwhile the trade union changed leadership.

Bourguiba withdrew his support of Tlili and pushed Habib Achour to the fore. The UGTT congress of March, 1963, was only too happy to defeat Tlili, who nevertheless put up a brave show in the face of pressure from above. Usually in Tunisia the leaders (though not the executive committees) of organizational unions are either elected unanimously or – it amounts to the same thing – appointed by a superior authority. The elections of the leader are prearranged and uncontested, because an atmosphere of consensus and harmony is required by the political culture, that is, by the popular sense of what is politically fitting. Tlili embarrassed the congress by insisting on being publicly defeated by Achour. The former was, of course, made a member of the nine-man executive bureau but was henceforth a marginal participant in domestic trade union matters.

Habib Achour, who had been awarded a place on the Political Bureau in 1957 for his assistance in eliminating ben Salah from the UGTT, had always nourished the ambition of becoming the leader of the trade union he had helped to found. Like his idol Ferhat Hached, he was of Kerkennah peasant stock, a strapping hulk of a man who, unlike Tlili and the others, had once been a manual laborer. His imposing stature and broad, weather-beaten face gave him the look of an authentic labor spokesman next to the diminuative white collar Destour politicians. Indeed, his line in the 1956 confrontation with ben Salah had been that the UGTT should keep out of politics, forbid its leaders from doubling government with trade-union responsibilities, and confine itself to voicing practical workers' grievances. It may seem curious that the least educated trade-union leader — for Achour had never gone beyond primary school — should voice a conception of trade unionism that was more "modern" than that of either ben Salah or Tlili. For Achour appeared to be the spokesman for a specialized and autonomous pressure group, the development of which might pave the way for a measure of pluralism as a counterweight to the cohesion orchestrated by Bourguiba and the Destour.

But appearances can be deceptive. Just as Tlili and Mehiri failed to capture the party, Habib Achour never succeeded in controlling the trade union. His pluralist theory therefore remained just as divorced from Tunisian political reality as the Tlili-Mehiri idea of institutionalizing party control of the presidency. Indeed, in the writer's opinion, Achour's idea was even more far-fetched: Tlili had judged correctly that, the trade union being weaker than the party, its autonomy as an institution presupposed that of the party.

Despite his old jealousy of ben Salah, Achour was ready in 1963 to cooperate with him and thus get Bourguiba's permission to displace Tlili and be elected secretary general of the UGTT. In his new position, however, his control of the union was even more precarious than that of Tlili had been. In the eyes of the Tlili forces, Achour, whatever his intentions, had objectively betrayed the UGTT. To gain Bourguiba's support, he had promised to "renovate" the trade union by replacing veteran (pro-Tlili) union officials with new "socialists" who would welcome economic planning with greater enthusiasm and spread the glad tidings to the rank and file. Achour, unfortunately a far less capable politician than Tlili, was forced by the weakness of his position to play even more of a double game than his predecessor.

It is impossible to judge precisely how strong each of the three factions that had contended for influence within the trade union movement really were. To the average member, even if he could identify the alignments, each clique was probably no better and no worse than the other. By the 1960's, the predominant mood in the UGTT seemed one of apathy, in part because the Destour government had satisfied many of its traditional grievances, in part because complacent trade-union officials did relatively little to suscitate or satisfy new demands. Occasional wildcat strikes were a sign of the UGTT's decadence.[39] The union's cadre, on the other hand, must have been very much aware of the infighting above. Achour probably had the loyalty of a third of this group —

mainly in his Sfax and Beja strongholds that had broken away from the UGTT in 1956. The rest of the cadre were loyal either to Tlili or — though many had been weeded out — to ben Salah.

To control this divided and disillusioned cadre, Habib Achour had to resort to Tlili's old methods of personal power. Despite lip service to autonomous trade unionism, he exercised his authority as a member of the Political Bureau to keep his trade-union comrades in line. In the interest of harmony, Tlili ceased to frequent the union headquarters, though he retained his seat on the executive bureau. For more than a year, Achour and the ben Salah forces maintained a shaky alliance; though the promised house cleaning of the UGTT fell short of ben Salah's expectations, the union became a champion of his Three-Year Plan.

The decision, in late September, 1964, to devalue the Tunisian dinar precipitated the breakup of the alliance and what remained of UGTT cohesion. In the Political Bureau, Achour had not criticized this necessary measure but, urged by some of his followers, he changed his tune at the meeting of the UGTT Executive Bureau that discussed the matter. Always eager to take a crack at ben Salah, Tlili temporarily rejoined Achour and, in a close vote, the bureau decided to support the devaluation only if workers were given higher wages to meet the expected rise in the cost of living. Though the UGTT quickly revised its position under party pressure, ben Salah was furious that it had dared to deviate from its mission of mobilizing the workers for planned austerity. He again pushed for a thorough house cleaning of the UGTT cadre and — now that the party, including leaders like Mehiri, was firmly committed to the plan — for tighter party control of the union.

At this juncture, it was probably already too late for Achour to join forces with Tlili, defer to the latter's political skill and ambitions, and bargain with the party to save the remnants of the UGTT's organization. Achour had no strategy. He refused to obey a written order of the Political Bureau to place the regional unions of the UGTT under the "supervision" of the party regional committees, but he agreed that the elections to renew the cadre of the UGTT be supervised by one union executive member and one Destour regional official. For a time in early 1965, these elections transpired relatively uneventfully — the predetermined outcomes often putting Achour's friends in power.

But then the party sharply accelerated the pace at which professional cells were being created and resorted to stronger tactics to wrest control of the locals from Achour. In his May Day, 1965, speech (censored in the press), he called for an extraordinary congress of the UGTT to confront the menace of party domination, but a few days later, resuming his role as Bourguiba's loyal militant, he agreed to hold off the congress in return for the president's guarantee of fair local union elections. By then, Bourguiba seems to have decided that the UGTT required a change of leadership though Achour might remain as a figurehead. The party and police continued blatantly to interfere in elections. By convenient coincidence, on June 7 an accident occurred that could be used as a pretext to get rid of Achour. A ferry boat belonging to one of his businesses caught fire and sank, resulting in the death of six tourists. Whether or not Achour was criminally responsible, a government case could be made that he was.[40] He was jailed for a month on charges of "forgery, the use of forgeries, and interfering with a judge in the performance of his duties." During this time, the UGTT administrative council was convened, and the party boss of Tunis told it what it had to do:

remove Achour and Tlili (who had jumped to the defense of his former rival) from the executive bureau and call an extraordinary congress.

It was hardly surprising that Bechir Bellagha, who had just resigned as governor of Tunis, was unanimously elected Achour's successor. He had acquired the reputation since 1956 of being a competent but authoritarian governor. Before independence, he had been leader of the powerful regional union of Tunis and, like Achour in Sfax, one of the founders of the UGTT as well as a party reliable. During the summer and autumn of 1965, the UGTT was finally "renewed" as Bourguiba and ben Salah had desired.

Immediately after Mehiri's funeral on June 30, Tlili fled Tunisia to foment opposition in international trade-union circles. Only two veterans of the Tlili-Achour era remained on the executive bureau, and only a third of the new federation's leaders were carry-overs of previous teams. One new executive member was ben Salah's *chef de cabinet,* but his old clique of followers does not appear to have directly profited from the reshuffle. Many of the new leaders are functionaries who are now combining party with trade-union responsibilities.

Under the new regime, the concrete material interests of Tunisian workers are likely to be satisfied as well or better than under the former UGTT leadership. The present incumbents enjoy the government's confidence and can already point to a general salary increase, the improvement of labor conditions in the mines, plans for a pension scheme that will include the private as well as the public sector, and promises of more housing and vacation colonies as signs of official solicitude for the laboring masses. But even as a myth — for it was never more — trade-union autonomy is extinct.

What in a liberal perspective must be deemed an inherent vice of single-party government, however, is also a cardinal virtue of Tunisian political development. By avoiding the crystallization of personal cliques into vested interests, whether they be in the name of labor, students, business, agriculture, or even the Destour, Bourguiba has not only safeguarded his own power from institutional limitations but kept the avenues of political mobility open. In developing countries, often rent by struggles between short-spanned political generations, mobility is essential to stability but usually cannot be achieved by institutional frameworks as in more stable societies. For frameworks tend to freeze the pattern of nascent interests unleashed by social change and thus to circumscribe their development and the careers of those who might represent them. If Tlili and Mehiri, for instance, had succeeded in consolidating the control of "their" party over Bourguiba, younger militants and the new administrative and technocratic elite might have been blocked. Large-scale economic planning under ben Salah would almost certainly not have been implemented.

Since 1964, as in other periods of Destour history, President Bourguiba has succeeded in promoting a new generation to positions of responsibility while persuading much of the old guard to share power. More than half of the governors, who, combining party and government roles, are the armature of Tunisia's decentralized order, have been changed since 1963. Some of them, unlike the veterans of independence, are university graduates who are highly qualified to encourage local initiative in the context of economic planning. Many of the elected party leaders in the provinces have similar backgrounds, unlike their predecessors, the bosses appointed by the Political Bureau before 1963.

Even the ninety-man parliament, though still pretty much a rubber stamp, was injected with new blood in 1964 and may play a more important role in the future. The personnel in the party's central headquarters has also been drastically rejuvenated – so much so that the disillusioned Tlili complained that the Destour was becoming a party of beatniks (*zazoa*).

Bourguiba keeps renewing his party by relatively gentle methods that are democratic in the sense that an overwhelming majority of the political cadre and people approves them. He wheedles and cajoles, lectures and threatens, and calculates his moves so as to achieve maximum consensus without letting himself be controlled by any formal body – be it parliament, the Political Bureau, his cabinet of ministers, or the triennial party congress. He accomplishes what in totalitarian countries requires the periodic purge of the party and the bureaucracy. The secret of his success is that he anticipates interests before they can be translated into cohesive groups that would have to be destroyed in the interest of national cohesion. Thus, the absence of pluralism in Tunisia, a vice by liberal standards, is an asset for Tunisia as long as it has Bourguiba.

But after Bourguiba? Though at the age of sixty-two he seems as active and enthusiastic as ever, the question inevitably occurs and points to the real dilemma of all new single-party states, each of which is ruled, albeit usually less competently, by an indispensable founder unchecked by the institutions he has created on paper. Unlike Solon, who departed, these leaders remain to make a mockery of rule by law of either constitution or party. But without the rule of law, without a measure of respect for institutions, an orderly succession poses insurmountable difficulties, as totalitarian countries have discovered.

Bourguiba is very conscious of the problem of his succession, though he may not be aware of all its implications.[41] The Destour Political Bureau, recently expanded to include fifty-six top-ranking party officials, ministers, governors, and members elected by the party congress, is to choose the man. Thus, the party, which is Tunisia's only possible source of legitimacy, will vest Bourguiba's heir with a fit title to rule. But there are probably no other Tunisians of Bourguiba's stature – none who could effectively imitate his personal methods of rule and get away with it. Cliques will therefore inevitably crystallize into groups contending for influence, and the future leader might be tempted to crush them – pushing Tunisia toward dictatorship – rather than arbitrating within the context of rules to which all parties could agree. It is for this reason that it would seem essential for Tunisia *now* to be developing the rules that might later help to avert political degeneration. The constitution seems virtually irrelevant in this context, for it is primarily an instrument for legalizing Bourguiba's personal power. If constitutionalism is to develop, it must be within the party. Like a Western constitution, the party might legitimize power and exercise institutionalized restraints upon it. But effective rules are not created *ex nihile;* either they develop as traditions in the political culture, like the idea of constitutional government in the West, or they are stillborn failures. No single leader can create them.

Tunisia's single-party regime does display constitutionalizing tendencies, although Islamic political culture – of which the Destour's faith, its historic sense of mission, is a reflection – has always opposed procedural restraints based on a separation of power. To discern these tendencies, one must look behind the Destour's monolithic façade at the new forces its cohesion is engendering. In place of the old *ijma'* (consensus) orchestrated for ideal political goals, the nation's attention has been shifted to more mundane matters. The change in goals implies a change in political style, because the new situation requires a new kind of political actor, more pragmatic, more attuned to technical problems than the heroes of independence. Though the translation of national cohesion into a consensus for economic planning hardly means that political problems are all solved – indeed, the opposite occurs; more problems become political – the political culture is likely to change under the impact of this new dimension of power. Already in Tunisia the emotional commitment of the political cadre to "Destour socialism," which was never deep, has given way to an attention to the concrete that is unknown in other Arab lands.

The planned economy has already had some structural impact upon the patterns of deliberations inside the party. Previously, the Destour, of course, always encouraged an intense level of participation of its political cadre. Periodic conferences and discussions at all levels are a party tradition, though after independence care was taken to prevent the rank and file from holding the leaders directly accountable, it instead being the cadre's function, apart from feeling the satisfactions of participation, to provide information that the leaders could use as they chose. What is new is not that leaders are any more accountable – for then the freezing of interests would occur – but that the pattern of consultation has become more elaborate and the level of discourse more sophisticated. Recently, for instance, the party assembled an open and representative gathering of civil servants and businessmen from the public and private sectors to discuss with ben Salah how the sectors should relate in a planned economy. In this and in subsequent meetings dealing with specific industries, the party is serving as a coordinator of discussions rather than as a decision-maker, since its officials lack the detailed technical expertise required for the latter role. The elaborate consultation[42] that occurs before the party ratifies economic plans illustrates a similar pattern. The government is also contemplating the creation of regional economic chambers to sharpen the contours of the consultative process. It is possibly significant, too, that while many Destour leaders blanch at the mention of "pressure groups" and "pluralism," they like the idea of professional groups expressing their concrete needs and interests. They apparently do not feel that "technical" discussions endanger the overriding goal of sustaining cohesion. Islam, of course, was never incompatible with flourishing corporations representing the various traditional trades of the cities.

Liberalization within the party naturally leaves much to be desired. Municipal elections remain single-list affairs when it would be natural – since cell leaders, like the regional coordination committees and a part of the Political Bureau, are elected from lists having half again as many candidates as places to fill – for the population to have comparable influence in choosing its spokesmen.[43] Deputies, too, are exclusively selected by the party and are supposed to represent the nation rather than their region. But the party under Bourguiba's animation is hardly a closed body; indeed, even the recent decision to make a distinction between members and militants has not been implemented. Moreover, if the party is sometimes rigid in its dealings with local populations, this is often, as in Msakken in 1964, because a well-trained local cadre is lacking – a deficiency that Tunisia's ambitious national education program among other things, by sending more schoolteachers who also serve as party officials to the villages, will help to remedy. It seems more significant that in the modern economic sectors the party is paradoxically impelled to be more liberal and open by the government's somewhat authoritarian economic planning. As the belt pinches, more consultation is needed and practiced to sustain the rational cohesion that in the last analysis, as long as Bourguiba's methods remain to sustain it, rests upon a genuine consensus.

But is consultation enough to induce consensus? The fascinating dilemma between cohesion and pluralism that is probably to be found in all new single-party regimes might conceivably be resolved, given the right timing and luck, with the succession crisis — at least in Tunisia. While the party will remain to orchestrate the abstract consensus on vague political principles — and thus serve to make the government the legitimate custodian of national mystique — the economic consultation behind the scenes may in time engender modern professional groups that cliques crystallizing into factions inside the party will have to represent. The party's deliberative structures, which exist on paper though they cannot control the man who framed them, might then be needed for resolving factional disputes, and, with this objective basis, take on a life of their own. The source of power, the party might succeed also in limiting the power of Bourguiba's successor — thus giving birth to constitutionalism in Tunisia. It may only be a straw in the wind, but literally "Destour socialism" in Arabic suggests constitutional participation.

Notes

1. This was the theme proposed by the organizers of the Princeton University Conference on "Political Modernization in the Near East and North Africa."

2. Clement H. Moore, *Tunisia Since Independence,* (Berkeley: University of California Press, 1965), pp. 80-81, 88-92.

3. *Ibid.,* p. 79. One application of the law of November 7, 1959, guaranteeing freedom of association under certain conditions, outlawed the Tunisia-U.S.S.R. Cultural Associations controlled by the Tunisian Communist Party. (*Tribune du Progrès,* No. 3 [February, 1961] and No. 5 [April, 1961].) The party itself was banned in 1963.

4. Although see the suggestive interpretation of Calvinism propounded by Michael Walzer, *The Revolution of the Saints: A Study in the Origins of Radical Politics* (Cambridge, Mass.: Harvard University Press, 1965). Political modernization might be said to have commenced when politics became "a kind of conscientious and continuous labor" resulting from the Calvinist theory of wordly activity.

5. For a general introduction to the various approaches to the study of political development, see Robert A. Packenham, "Approaches to the Study of Political Development," *World Politics,* XVII (October, 1964), 108-20; see also Lucian W. Pye, *Aspects of Political Development* (Boston: Little, Brown, 1966). For modified structural-functional approaches, see David E. Apter, *The Politics of Modernization* (Chicago: University of Chicago Press, 1965), and Gabriel A. Almond and James S. Coleman (eds.), *The Politics of the Developing Areas* (Princeton, N.J.: Princeton University Press, 1960), pp. 3-64. For an extension of this same approach, see Gabriel Almond, "A Developmental Approach to Political Systems," *World Politics,* XVII (January, 1965), 183-214. For a socio-demographic approach to this concept, see Karl W. Deutsch "Social Mobilization and Political Development," *American Political Science Review,* LX (September, 1961), 493-514.

6. Manfred Halpern, "The Revolution of Modernization in National and International Society," in Carl J. Friedrich (ed.), *Revolution* (New York: Atherton Press, 1966), pp. 178-214.

7. The most persuasive advocate of this view is Samuel P. Huntington, "Political Development and Political Decay," *World Politics,* XVII (April, 1965), 386-430.

8. See S. N. Eisenstadt, *Modernization: Growth and Diversity* (the Carnegie Faculty Seminar on Political and Administrative Development, Bloomington, Ind., 1963). See also the following articles by S. N. Eisenstadt: "Transformation of Social, Political and Cultural Orders in Modernization," *American Sociological Review,* XXX, No. 5 (October, 1965), 659-73; "Modernization and Conditions of Sustained Growth," *World Politics* (July, 1964), pp. 576-94; and "Social Change and Modernization in African Societies South of the Sahara," *Cahiers d'Etudes Africaines,* No. 5 (1965), p. 3.

9. S. N. Eisenstadt, *Modernization: Growth and Diversity, p.* 6.

10. See David Easton, *A Systems Analysis of Political Life* (New York: John Wiley, 1965), pp. 287 ff.

11. Philip Selznick, *Leadership in Administration: A Sociological Interpretation* (Evanston, Ill.: Row, Patterson, 1957), pp. 16 ff.

12. As should be clear from Sheldon Wolin's critique of organizational theory, however, administrative "ideologies" are hardly comparable to political ones. See his *Politics and Vision* (Boston: Little, Brown, 1960), pp. 419-29.

13. Ernst B. Haas, *Beyond the Nation-State* (Stanford, Calif. Stanford University Press, 1964), p. 95; and P. Selznick, *op. cit,* pp. 14-15.

14. For various approaches to the analysis of groups in the developing areas, see Lucien W. Pye, "The Non-Western Political Process," *Journal of Politics,* XX (1958), pp. 468-86. Myron Weiner, *The Politics of Scarcity: Public Pressure and Political Response in India* (Chicago: University of Chicago Press, 1962); and Fred W. Riggs, "The Theory of Developing Politics," *World Politics,* XVI (October, 1963), 147-71.

15. A pattern that may be typical of transitional societies is described by Stanley Hoffman, "Protest in Modern France," in Morton A. Kaplan (ed.), *The Revolution in World Politics* (New York and London: John Wiley, 1962), pp. 69-91.

16. To date, there are only two successful cases, that of Turkey, in which the single-party system was transformed into a two-party system, and that of Mexico, which has become an institutionalized dominant one-party regime. The Mexican case, which is more relevant to the present analysis, has been well documented in Robert E. Scott, *Mexican Government in Transition* (Urbana: University of Illinois Press, 1959).

17. In 1934, the founders, claiming to be the legitimate leaders of an older nationalist party, the Destour (Liberal Constitutional) Party, used its name while unofficially the new party known as the Neo-Destour until 1965, when the label "socialist" was added. For the best history of the party, see Roger Le Tourneau, *Evolution politique de l'Afrique du Nord Musulmane 1920-1961* (Paris: Armand Colin, 1962); see also Charles-André Julien, *L'Afrique du Nord en marche* (Paris: Julliard, 1952).

18. Public habous property was nationalized on May 31, 1956, while the hitherto inalienable private habous lands were divided among heirs and tenants as the result of a law promulgated on July 18, 1957.

19. During his tour of the Middle East in March, 1965, Bourguiba charged that the Palestine refugees were being used as political pawns by some of his brother Arab chiefs of state and suggested that they recognize Israel and negotiate with her on the basis of the 1948 U.N. resolution rather than delude themselves into believing they might "liberate" Palestine by their bellicose stances. On many occasions, Bourguiba has been able politically to afford stating unpleasant truths in public that other Arab leaders may think in private, because his party apparatus can, as during the Middle East tour, explain his positions to the public and effectively counter the Voice of the Arabs and other foreign propaganda.

20. The new middle class can perhaps most usefully be defined in the Tunisian colonial context not by its relations to the means of production but by its French education. As Henri de Montety shows in his paper on "Old Families and New Elites in Tunisia," reprinted on pp. 171—80 in this reader, one-half of the students admitted to Sadiki in 1939 were from the Sahel, while less than one-quarter were from the old Tunis mamluk and beldi families. The educated sons of small property-holders of the Sahel constituted the driving force behind the Neo-Destour.

21. In 1955, the party consisted of 325,000 members organized in 31 federations. The Federation of Tunis was the most important one by virtue of its numbers (approximately 60,000 members) and strategic location. For membership figures, inferred from the number of stamps sold by the party, see Destour Party, *National Congress of Sfax* (Arabic ed., 1956), pp. 57-58.

22. By the end of January, 1956, after ben Youssef had declared war on the Tunisian government, it was estimated that there were 600 Youssefist *fellaga.* Subsequently southern tribes joined the guerrilla "Army"; it was not until June that the last pockets of Youssefists were finally subdued.

23. Ben Youssef was assassinated on August 12, 1961, in a Frankfurt hotel room by Tunisian nationals; the German government never publicly revealed their identity, and the murder remains officially unsolved.

24. Editorials in the official party daily have occasionally stressed as one of the party's roles the creation of a "new" Destour socialist personality (for instance, see *L'Action,* April 7, 1965), but such aspirations are not enforced by totalitarian techniques of thought reform.

25. An elaborate framework of organized interest groups, known as "national organizations" was developed under the party's auspices before independence. The General Union of Tunisian Workers (UGTT) was founded in 1946 after efforts in the 1920's and 1930's to establish a national Tunisian trade union independent of French organizations had failed. The Tunisian Union of Craftsmen and Shopkeepers (UTAC, today UTICA) was also founded in 1946, while the General Union of Tunisian Farmers (UGTA, today UNAT) was launched in 1949. The students were organized by the party in the General Union of Tunisian Students (UGET) in 1953. For an analysis of the national organizations' role in contemporary Tunisian politics, see Clement Henry Moore, *op. cit.,* pp. 159 ff. For an excellent historical and contemporary analysis of the UGTT and the other North African trade unions, see Eqbal Ahmad, "Trade Unionism," in L. Carl Brown (ed.), *State and Society in Independent North Africa* (Washington, D.C.: Middle East Institute, 1968), pp. 146-91.

26. At the height of his fame as the Tunisian delegate to the United Nations, Mongi Slim was unanimously elected president of the party congress held in 1959. At that time he appeared to be at least as popular as Bourguiba, especially among party activists from Tunis. But in 1964, Bourguiba replaced him as foreign minister and limited him to largely honorific duties as his personal representative. With the rise of the younger generation (ben Salah, Bourguiba Junior, Masmoudi) Slim's chances to succeed Bourguiba diminished. For an analysis of cliques within the party that differs slightly from the one that follows below, see Douglas E. Ashford, "Neo-Destour Leadership and the 'Confiscated Revolution,'" *World Politics,* January, 1965, pp. 215-31.

27. Legislative powers were not explicitly accorded to the president of the republic, but Bourguiba confined the Constituent Assembly to drafting the constitution — a process that lasted almost two more years — while he maintained the right to promulgate all laws adopted by a cabinet council that was responsible only to himself.

28. Three high-ranking officials from the Federation of Tunis were suspended from the party in 1957, while a fourth, Azouz Rebai, who had given Mehiri his basic political training, lost his ministerial post. In 1960, the commandant of the National Guard, one of Mehiri's close collaborators, was removed and imprisoned on charges of corruption while the latter was vacationing outside the country.

29. Abdelmajid Chaker was also noteworthy for being the nephew of a famous party martyr and a native of Sfax, Tunisia's second city, where the party was especially weak.

30. See *L'Action,* issues of January 7, 1957; February 4, 1957; May 26, 1958; July 9, 1958; July 7, 1958; and especially September 8, 1958.

31. This time exile was total; Masmoudi was not even permitted to run for re-election as mayor of Mahdia in 1963.

32. See *Afrique-Action,* October 7, 1961. For an interesting, frank, but long-winded rebuttal, see *Le Petit Matin,* November 1-5, 1961, where the articles of a party propagandist are translated.

33. The better-known ones would include Ahmed Tlili, Habib Achour, and Bechir Bellagha.

34. In 1956, ben Salah was calling for the nationalization of all enterprises and a policy of economic planning based on the somewhat metaphysical economic "faith" of a progressist French economics professor. See General Union of Tunisian Workers, *Rapport Economique,* Sixth Congress, September, 1956.

35. Gafsa's phosphate mines made its regional union the third largest (after Tunis and Sfax) in the UGTT. Gafsa was also of political significance as a center of nationalist guerrilla activity in 1954 and of Youssefist violence in 1956.

36. See the article by Ahmed Tlili, "Tunisian Tragedy: Bourguiba Crushes Free Unions,"

AFL-CIO Free Trade Union News, September, 1965, pp. 4-6. The fact that this newspaper published the article suggests that the AFL-CIO was unreconciled to the party's takeover of the UGTT.

37. The National Constituent Assembly might have become such a forum, but ben Salah's efforts in 1956 to organize a UGTT pressure group were decisively defeated. The party could also conceivably have served as the forum, but the functioning of its institutions for organized deliberation, such as the congress and the national council, was severely curtailed. Between 1957 and 1962, the national council did not meet; between 1955 and 1965, the congress convened only once. The leaders simply disregarded the party statues.

38. The party's basic units are one thousand neighborhood or district cells. In rural areas, the district coincides with the lowest administrative subdivision, the *sheikhat,* a territorially defined unit.

39. There have been a number of strikes in recent years that were neither reported in the local Tunisian press nor organized by the UGTT leadership. See, for instance, *Alger Républicain,* January 18, 1963, and Ashford, *op. cit.,* p. 223; several years earlier these miners had gone on an unpublicized strike supported by Habib Achour until Mehiri made Tlili (secretary general at the time) recall his trade-union colleague.

40. On March 2, 1966, Habib Achour was found guilty of passing a bad check and neglecting to have all the necessary papers for his boat. The verdict astounded foreign observers, especially as the defense had produced persuasive evidence that the check was good. Achour was sentenced to six months in jail and a fine of 3,000 dinars ($6,000). For details about the domestication of the UGTT in 1965, see Eqbal Ahmad, *op. cit.,* pp. 185-90.

41. Recently Bourguiba raised the underlying problem, that of structural legitimacy: *"Si aujourd'hui la légitimité n'est pas en cause en raison de ma présence à la tête du parti et de l'état, en serait-il de même lorsque je disparaîtrai?"* See *Le Monde,* April 28, 1966.

42. The consultation has been codified by the decree of November 4, 1963, and the *arrêté* of June 5, 1964, outlining deliberation prior to the adoption of the Four-Year Plan.

43. The party's nominating procedures, however, were significantly liberalized for the 1966 municipal elections. Whereas the party commissioner, consulting sometimes with administrative officials, used to name the local candidates unilaterally, it is now the practice for the cell membership to nominate the party's slate subject to the approval of higher authorities. See *L'Action,* April 29, 1966.

26

THE DESTOURIAN SOCIALIST PARTY AND THE NATIONAL ORGANIZATIONS

EDOUARD MERIC

In his speech "Relations between State and Party," before a North African audience,[1] Mohammed Harbi, former editor of *Revolution Africaine,* a member of the central committee of the National Liberation Front (FLN), and one of the foremost proponents of socialist thought in Algeria, tried to demonstrate that party supremacy over the state was the only way to achieve socialism. After accusing parties in bourgeois parliamentary democracies of merging with the state machinery and of "managing it" for the benefit of a minority, he affirmed that "socialism cannot define itself only by nationalizing the means of production but must be a conscious organization of the people in all facets of their life." He passionately defended certain of the socialist dogmas and affirmed that, without them, the various "nationalized" socialisms were merely political artifices to maintain bourgeois privileges.

One can imagine that such statements, if taken up by the Tunisian opposition, could embarrass the Tunisian leaders. Such an evolution was quite the opposite of what the Neo-Destour advocated before it became the Destourian Socialist Party (PSD). The Neo-Destour has progressively relinquished its powers to the state. Its seventh congress, in 1964, marked the end of this evolution by merging administrative and political powers into the same hands.[2] The party has become nothing more than an extension of the administration, able to reinforce the organization of the "popular masses" and to ensure that laws, rules, directives, and slogans are executed.

But alongside the party and the state, Tunisia has four independent organizations,[3] born under the Protectorate for the defense of professional and economic interests. They are the Tunisian Union for Industry, Trade, and Crafts (UTICA), the General Union of Tunisian Students (UGET), the National Union of Tunisian Farmers (UNAT), and the General Union of Tunisian Labor (UGTT). From the beginning, these organizations, which are today called "national,"[4] have been dominated and led by Neo-Destourian nationalists and have played a vital role in both the open and the clandestine struggle against the Protectorate. They therefore had a claim to legitimacy that they might have been tempted to use for their own instead of national ends.

Translated, by permission, from *Maghreb*, No. 9 (June, 1965), pp. 19—25.

PROFESSIONAL ECONOMIC ORGANIZATIONS

UTICA was founded in 1946 by a Neo-Destourian militant, Ferdjani bel Hadj 'Ammar. It was originally a dissident branch of the Federation of Tunisian Small Traders and Craftsmen, a movement with Communist leanings, founded in 1945. (As early as that time the political [party] objectives prevailed over the purely professional [union] goals. Therefore, there is some logic in the maintenance of this relation.) The dissident organization took the name Union of Craftsmen's and Small Traders' Organizations in Tunisia.

At its first congress, in April, 1947, the organization became the Tunisian Union of Craftsmen and Shopkeepers (UTAC). Later, it took the name Tunisian Union for Industry and Commerce (UTIC), and finally, at its sixth congress in November, 1963, it was renamed the Tunisian Union for Industry, Commerce, and Crafts (UTICA). Bel Hadj 'Ammar was regularly elected president until August, 1964, when the president of the republic asked Ezzedine ben Achour, UTICA secretary general, permanently to take over the union leadership as a Destourian militant. A brief commentary accompanied the decision: "The Chief of State explained the importance with which he views the reform of commercial structures. To that end, he invested ben Achour with his confidence and authority that he will need for the task that must be accomplished in perfect harmony with the Secretary of State for Planning and Finances." The independence of UTICA was over.

UNAT was created in 1946 under the name the General Union of Tunisian Farmers, (UGTA), in order to organize the Tunisian farmers against the Protectorate and the French settlers. Led from the beginning, by the Neo-Destour, it continually obeyed its directives and gave it support.[5] But the interests that the UGTA defended, having to do with landownership, had political overtones. Its leaders were influential in the rural area. Its orientation was beylical and conservative. Its president, Tahar ben 'Ammar (who was to be the prime minister in charge of negotiating Tunisian internal autonomy from France), was a moderate. Its secretary general, Brahim 'Abdellah, supported Salah ben Youssef. The UGTA violently criticized the electoral law of January 6, 1956, written to favor the election of Neo-Destourian designated candidates. In a communiqué dated March 8, 1956, it affirmed that "the established electoral system is incompatible with the right of the voter to choose freely the candidate that seems to him to deserve his confidence. The electoral system, as well as the atmosphere that surrounds the elections, tends to remove UGTA affiliates and members from any control over the elections that could ensure their sincerity."[6]

It was the UGTA's last fight. Once the Youssefist subversion was crushed, the UGTA was dissolved and its secretary general arrested. From its ashes the Neo-Destour extracted the National Union of Tunisian Farmers (UNAT). Not much has been heard from it, and the name of its secretary general, Tahar Azaiz (president and director general of the Wine Office), is mentioned only in passing in the press.

STUDENTS' AND WORKERS' ORGANIZATIONS

UTICA and UNAT are organizations of proprietors. They are thus easy to dominate for a strong power who has radical means of reducing any opposition, since they are vulnerable through their means of production. They became docile tools of power once their reorganization was accomplished and their leaders imposed on them. The same is not true of UGET and UGTT. These organizations represent two social forces, the youth and the proletariat, and are aware of that fact. Many militants who rose to important positions in the state belonged to UGET or UGTT, fought in their ranks, participated in the building of the Destourian ideal, and defended the party's progressive orientation. It was therefore natural that they should maintain some sort of autonomy with regard to the Neo-Destour, and that at times they should take positions that were not the same as the party's. . . .

The General Union of Tunisian Students was created clandestinely in Tunis in 1952. In the UGTT, and especially through Ferhat Hached, the labor secretary general, it found the help necessary to begin. From the start, it took part in the nationalist struggle alongside the Neo-Destour. Its first success, on March 18, 1952, after the French roundup of Cape Bon, was the organization of a demonstration followed by strikes in all secondary and primary schools.[7]

The first national congress of UGET was held clandestinely in Paris on July 10–13, 1953, and the union remained clandestine until July, 1955, when its vice president, Abdel Jouad, a science student, and its secretary general, Kouiri, a medical student, tried to obtain legal recognition from the French authorities. Recognition was refused because the UGET had planned to include school-age children. At the third congress, which was finally held in Tunis on July 27, 1955, and succeeding ones, the organization and the "national and trade-union" orientation of the movement were defined. The governing body is the annual national congress of delegates, elected from the various "sections" *(corpos)*. The congress elects an administrative commission of twenty-seven members, which in turn designates a nine-man executive body. The sections and the *corpos* are grouped by region: Tunisia, Europe, Middle East. Each region is led by a committee elected by a general assembly of all UGET members in the region.

The UGET's orientation after its third congress was progressive. Like any student organization, it tried to maintain its independence from the party, but the regime, eager to bring together into a single bundle all the vital forces of the nation, and particularly the primary *elan* of the youth, increased its pressure and control, to the point of merging UGET will the Federation of Destourian Students (FNED), which it had created.

A power as pervasive as the Neo-Destour has strong means of control—material aid, indoctrination, organization — over a youth group with meager resources. The organization of Destourian youth began before independence, possibly under the influence of the fascist youth organizations that existed before 1939 among the Italian settlers in Tunisia. On June 1, 1955, the day of Bourguiba's return, the Europeans were startled by the number and discipline of the several youth movements, which came out of the shadows and helped the police and the army maintain order.

As soon as it acceded to power, the party and especially its president tried both to lead the youth and to follow it. A decree on June 21, 1956, created a Secretariat of State for Youth and Sports.[8] Another, on January 8, 1959, attached the direction of youth and sports to the presidency. Finally a third decree on February 24, 1961, established the Higher Youth Committee.

It is quite difficult to follow the organization of youth movements because of their apparent diversity and because their names do not always correspond to those of their leaders. It can be said that as soon as the Higher Youth Committee was created, the designs of the Tunisian leaders to extend their control over the national youth associations, and particularly UGET, became apparent. The committee is directed by high civil servants of the party. It watches very closely over the political education of the youth and appears to direct three movements: the National Union of School Children, the National Federation of Destourian Students, created to placate the UGET but to date without organic ties with it, and the Association of Pioneers of the Republic, composed of young civil servants and rural workers who intend to join the party.

In 1963, after the plot against Bourguiba of the preceding December and concurrently with the reorganization of the party, a decisive step was taken to control the student youth, in particular the UGET. Following a congress that gathered all youth organizations in Bir el-Bey in July, 1963, a new body — the Union of Tunisian Youth — was created for the purpose of training cadres. In each governorate, regional centers were organized, with schools to train regional leaders; growing out of this teaching, many conferences, seminars, and meetings were presided over by high civil servants from the Secretariat for Youth and often by the president himself.

Members of graduating classes, promoted outside the group of student organizations, have been subject to particular attention. A so-called orientation commission has guided student candidates in accordance with state needs and, one can imagine, with their attachment to the party. "The fact of pursuing higher education is not a privilege reserved to sons of wealthy families, but a social function," declared Secretary of State for National Education Mahmoud Messadi during an orientation seminar for high-school graduates in July, 1963. The leadership council of FNED, competitor of UGET, added fuel to the fire by asking the government to propose a law "that would give priority to putting Tunisian students at the service of the state."

Independent of these activities for organization and indoctrination, which are carried out faithfully and with a sincere desire to convince the youth (as if the Tunisian leaders, remembering their own youth, feared the thought that they might not have the support of young people), the authorities have strong means of pressure through the financial aid the state provides its students. The student is an investment; to be a student is already a social promotion. Scholarships are given not only to students who study abroad but to every student in Tunisia.[9] The size of the grant means "that the student starts at the top, he belongs to category A in the civil services, that of high figure generally responsible and in charge of more or less important services."[10]

But that is not all, Other important benefits are offered the regime's favorites: trips abroad, congresses, conferences, seminars, all of which abound in this age. Leaders of FNED and UGET, solid Destourian members, travel all around the world and are in fact high-ranking civil servants at the service of the state. Finally, and not least important, the student's loyalty to the party and his docility will ensure him, when the time comes, the job to which he aspires. An independent spirit will certainly keep him away.

It is therefore understandable from a moral as well as a material point of view, that the Tunisian student thinks twice before entering the ranks of the opposition. Nevertheless opposition exists, for it is characteristic of student youth throughout the world, and the Tunisian student is no exception to the rule.

THE OPPOSITION AND ITS COMPONENTS

The most serious opposition is in Paris, although on February 15, 1965, the government was shaken when, for the first time, a manifestation in the streets took place in Tunis; it involved 200 students who protested poor food in the university restaurant and the lack of heat in the dormitories.[11]

In 1961, when the Neo-Destour created its youth committee and tightened its control on the youth organizations, a minority who had wanted the union to remain independent from the party left UGET. This minority was at that time inspired by Tunisian Communist leaders. At the time of Patrice Lumumba's death, propaganda leaflets accused UGET of being stagnant and unrepresentative. In October, 1961, *Espoir,* a bulletin with Communist overtones, was distributed. "At the 1962 congress, the question of UGET's independence was raised anew. Two factions emerged: the Neo-Destourians, and the progressives who were against any form of satellization."[12]

In any case, according to newspaper accounts of the eleventh congress at le Kef on August 15–20, 1963, it appeared that peace had been restored between the Destourians and their opponents. The Charter of the Tunisian Student adopted by the congress was a veritable "creed" governing "the young intellectual's attitude toward life . . . for in it, he finds the reasons for commitment by accepting it philosophically as a way of life."[13] Secretary General Mokhtar Zannad, former secretary general of the European Federation, declared in an interview that "the minority faction has shown enough good will. At the end of the discussion, the final resolutions, including the charter and the individual statutes and rules, have been adopted almost unanimously. This same atmosphere also lasted during the election of the new administrative commission."

The congress excluded a dozen opposition members. The rest took part in the congress votes for fear of having their scholarships canceled or of being prevented from continuing their studies. Nevertheless, a number of students in secondary schools or in universities in Tunis, Paris, Strasbourg, Lyon, and Tours left UGET and considered organizing another union and later a political party of the opposition.

The hostility of the students, and not only those with Communist leanings, was disquieting to the government, which tightened its control over the students in Paris. According to Abdelmajid Chaker, political director of the party, the newly created National Union of Tunisian Youth was to "allow the party to integrate the students with the rest of the youth." This control met with serious difficulties in France because, in response to the Tunisian government attitude toward Frenchmen living in Tunisia, French authorization for new associations was not easy to obtain.

The non-Communist student opposition in the Paris section set up socialist study and action groups, which came to public notice at the end of 1963 with the publication of a review, *Perspectives.* Despite their opposition to the Destourian Socialist Party, the progressive students did not break with UGET, and twenty-four of them were delegates to the twelfth congress in Monastir on

August 17–24, 1964. In Paris, the progressives held two *corpos* and the Neo-Destourians the other two.[14]

Some of the students who were excluded or suspended in 1963 by the eleventh congress have been reintegrated into the movement. In a letter to the president of the twelfth congress, they wrote: "We affirm our unshakable attachment to our union and our sincere desire again to take up the struggle for a dynamic and effective UGET in the service of the well-being of our people alongside our student comrades, in full conformity with the decisions of our Congress and with the statutes of our union." The Communists on the other hand, in the issue of *Espoir* of January, 1965, again denounced government policies and the single party but approved the government plan to create agricultural cooperatives[15] and applauded the action taken against the rich landowners in Msakken.

This tip of the hat to the PSD by the Communist opposition and the reintegration of the progressive opposition, who did not hestitate to return to Tunisia to attend the congress, indicate that neither side will go too far. The opposition is reasonable, and the repression is moderate. The students ben Khadder, Smaoui, and Naccache were subjected to questioning because they distributed material that was forbidden on the national territory, but they were neither arrested or indicted.[16] The polemics of the opposition publications are rarely offensive. *Perspectives,* the progressive students' review, contains articles of real interest. The opposition is a minority, and the majority that combats it does so on equal terms, from the point of view of ideology, since the Destourian Socialist Party offers the students an ideal as inspiring for a nationalist as that of the opposition.

Nevertheless, the student opposition bothers the government. The regime knows perfectly well that its weak point is its inability to grant the same freedom of speech its members themselves enjoyed under the French. They fear that such freedom, if granted today, might degenerate into unrest tomorrow and jeopardize the progress already made. In gathering the students into a single Destourian movement, the government may well be looking for a way more to listen to and respond to student voices than to suppress them.

THE LABOR UNION

UGET causes the party some concern, but it is not yet a dangerous rival; students are no more than an emanation of the Destourian bourgeoisie. UGTT is another matter. It is certainly not the mass movement that its name might indicate, nor even, strictly speaking, a proletarian movement. It is a movement that defends the interests of workers and blue-collar employees who, as in Algeria and Morocco, have a relatively constant salary, supported by the development of agriculture, trade, and industry. The labor movement is powerful because its members are conscious of their rights and because their discontent could have an effect on the masses.

The Tunisian labor movement is the oldest in North Africa. In 1904, after workers' demands had caused serious troubles, the consultative organs of the Protectorate let it be known that they would like to see a labor union formed. In 1921, a series of railroad strikes caused the question to be raised again. The authorities felt helpless, since labor was being organized clandestinely. In 1924,

Tunisians entered the ranks of the central French union, the General Confederation of Labor (CGT). In September of that year, a strike broke out in the port of Tunis as Tunisian dockers demanded the same salaries as those of Marseilles. The CGT was not receptive. It was then that the real creator of the Tunisian labor movement appeared: Mohammed 'Ali.

Mohammed 'Ali, from El Hamma, a small village near Gabès, had led an adventurous life. During World War I, he had been Enver Pasha's chauffeur; after a stay in Germany, he returned to Tunisia in 1920. Bourguiba wrote of him: "Abandoning the high places he went to the workers ... and made a point of educating and organizing them."[17] In December, 1924, Mohammed 'Ali and his friends founded the Tunisian General Confederation of Labor (CUGTT), with the motto "Liberty in Unity." The movement was a great success. The Tunisian workers joined in mass in an enterprise that took their destiny into its hands and that kept away from the French and the Italians who, in comparison with the Tunisians, were privileged classes. In order to keep its national character, the CGTT maintained its distance from the CGT. Mohammed 'Ali, who had become very popular, traveled throughout the country and set up local unions. The French business community became suspicious and alerted the government, which succeeded in separating the Destourian nationalist movement from the labor-union activities of Mohammed 'Ali. Resident General Lucien Saint stated that consideration might be given the political demands of the party, provided it dissociated itself from the trade-union movement. A strike broke out, which the Destour disavowed. Mohammed 'Ali was arrested and condemned to exile. He took refuge in Saudi Arabia, where he once more became a bus driver; he died in an accident in 1932. That same year, the labor union received the right to exist legally in Tunisia. But it was only in 1936 that the Tunisian Confederation of Labor came out of its ashes, under the direction of a former Destourian militant, Belgacem Guenaoui, a worker who came from a village near Mohammed 'Ali's home town.

On March 2, 1937, a strike broke out in the phosphate mines of Metlaoui. The army intervened, killing and wounding strikers. A few days later, new incidents broke out in Mdilla: four were killed. The resident general took an opposite stand from 1926 and made promises to the CGTT if it would prevent the widening of the action into the political scene. Guenaoui finally agreed and declared that the CGTT would remain outside politics. But on April 8, 1938, following the arrest of some Neo-Destour members, a general strike was called. These large demonstrations ended with more dead and wounded. The CGTT was dissolved along with the Neo-Destour.

It was not until 1943 that the Tunisian labor movement regained life. The freedom to organize was established, and the French CGT went back to rebuilding its sections. It called on the Tunisian workers; with the encouragement of Ferhat Hached, a truck driver in a Sousse transport company, the Tunisian workers joined in mass. A year later, in 1944, Hached decided to create autonomous unions. The dockers were the first to organize, in Sfax. In each region, unions were created, banding together by locality. In March, 1945, at a congress in Tunis, Hached united these unions into a single national autonomous Trade Union Confederation, which, after the congress of June 20, 1945, became the General Union of Tunisian Workers (UGTT). Europeans were allowed in the union, but only Tunisians could direct it.

Until independence, the social struggle was identified with the political struggle, the latter overshadowing the former. But Hached soon became the real chief of Tunisian nationalism. Jean Lacouture wrote of him: "He is the strongest because the calmest, the least talkative, the most in control of himself. Today he is the kingpin of Tunisian nationalism, the activist master of the most disciplined troops, the best conceived doctrine, and of the strongest alliances. He maintains liaison with international left-wing opinion and indirectly with the United Nations."

In 1945, Hached asked the Communist-dominated World Federation of Trade Unions (WFTU) to admit the UGTT. But in January, 1946, the Tunisian CGT, to counteract the UGTT, obtained permission from the metropolitan federation to become an autonomous union, the Trade Union of Tunisian Workers (USTT), which was automatically admitted into the WFTU. The WFTU delayed its answer to the UGTT, hoping for a merger of the two unions and considering the UGTT a nationalist organization trying to play a political role instead of defending the rights of the workers. Nevertheless, on January 1, 1949, the WFTU admitted the UGTT. But Hached could not make himself heard in it and on January 23, 1950, for reasons that are still not clear, the UGTT Congress decided to break with the WFTU. On March 30, 1951, Hached spelled out UGTT's position on Communism and reaffirmed the national and democratic character of the movement. Against the advice of such labor leaders as Ahmed ben Salah, who later became secretary general, he entered into contact with the International Confederation of Free Trade Unions (ICFTU), founded in England in 1949 on Anglo-American initiative. Membership was granted in 1950, and Hached became ICFTU vice president a short time later.

In the following months, the UGTT's activities became increasingly political, as the Tunisian crisis entered its decisive phase. After Bourguiba's deportation and Salah ben Youssef's exile, Hached became the real leader of the Tunisian nationalist movement. He disturbed the Protectorate authorities by his friendship and contacts with the United States. He attended the annual meeting of the American Federation of Labor (AFL) in September, 1951, in San Francisco and went to Washington. On December 5, 1952, he was assassinated by a clandestine organization of advocates of continuing French rule, leaving behind a UGTT that was the most powerful labor organization in the Arab world.

The mission assigned to it by Hached meant continuous solidarity with the Neo-Destour. After his death, his successor, ben Salah, and his comrades maintained that solidarity. But it was a different matter after independence in March, 1956. Ahmed ben Salah dreamed of creating within the Neo-Destour a left-wing opposition based upon the UGTT that would have great prestige outside Tunisia, and he traveled to the United States to renew the confidence of the ICFTU. In March, 1956, at the time of Tunisia's declaration of independence, he wrote an article in which he recalled the activities of the UGTT over the decade and drew up the guidelines for the future role of the great national labor union. "Thanks to the sincere and powerful impetus given it by Ferhat Hached, the UGTT gave the struggle a decisive impulse. . . . Certainly the Destour was the party of the people, but rather than easily inflammable mobs the UGTT contributed organized masses, conscious of their rights. . . To be real the liberation will have to be a continual revolution of the political, economical and social institutions."[18]

At the Sfax congress of the Neo-Destour in November, 1955, M. Filali of the UGTT had presented vigorous motions asking for some form of socialism. At the UGTT congress of September, 1956 there appeared the desire to "turn independence into an overthrow of the regime and not a simple occupancy of the power."[19] The economic report presented by ben Salah gave a balanced analysis of the Tunisian situation and severely criticized Bourguiba's government. Bourguiba reacted, and through the intermediary of Habib Achour (Hached's friend and member of the administrative commission of the UGTT), encouraged a regional split that led, on October 20, 1956, to the creation of the Tunisian Workers Union (UTT). Ben Salah's position became difficult; he resigned on December 19, 1956, and the vice secretary of the Neo-Destour, Ahmed Tlili, was chosen secretary-general. Tlili came out in favor of total cooperation with the party. On April 16, 1957, the two unions reunited and the UTT disappeared into the UGTT. . .

The UGTT tends to be a Neo-Destourian organization specializing in labor questions. At the opening of its ninth congress, on March 27, 1963, Bourguiba reaffirmed the identity of thought between the union and the party. "Some are astonished at this cooperation. Some ill-informed people are shocked by what they call our labor class's lack of combativity. But this class will not fight the people who work for their own objectives."

Acknowledgment of union dependency on the party could not have been more clearly recognized: Tlili was removed and replaced by the old labor leader and member of the Neo-Destour Political Bureau, Achour, who had already appeared at the creation of the ephemeral UTT in 1956. But these measures did not prevent the UGTT from remaining a powerful force still able to show its independence with prudence. It did so at its national council on August 29-30, 1964, when it proclaimed "the need to practice a social policy that will assure greater purchasing power through a raise in salaries, already promised several times, its application in the shortest time possible, and its extension to all sectors."

The UGTT showed its independence especially after the freeze on salaries that followed the devaluation of the dinar on September 28, 1964. The next day, when the national organizations sent their traditional message of approval to the Head of state, the UGTT abstained. The following day, its administrative commission adopted a motion demanding "an immediate and equitable compensation and an austerity policy in all sectors and at all levels."

The government reaction was quick. A wave of telegrams sent from the "professional cells" denounced the UGTT's stand. The party attacked "suspect" elements within the central organization who were accused of having an old-fashioned view of labor-union duties and of seeking to sabotage the austerity program. Pressure was put on the Federation of Tunis to disavow the administration commission. The Political Bureau of the Neo-Destour met to discuss the problems and decided to call a meeting of the national council of the national union. On October 16, 1964, the UGTT national council met and bowed to the pressure by unanimously voting a motion of support, which contradicted the text adopted by administrative commission.

The party once more was the winner, but it was a close victory and the lesson was not lost. Since the docility of the leaders does not necessarily imply that of the militants, it was once more through the old maneuver of creating a rival organization that the UGTT was brought into line and the opposition broken. On November 4, 1963, at the time Tlili was removed, Taieb Mehiri, secretary of state for interior and vice secretary of the party, who had controlled the internal life of the party and country for more than a decade, had set up the first "professional cells" and defined their relations with the party and the existing labor organizations. Thereafter, it was mainly a question of developing these professional cells to the point where they could compete with the labor-union organizations, exactly as had been done with the Students Destourian Federation and the UGET .... [20]

If the UGTT and UGET merge into purely Destourian organizations, state control over the national organizations will be complete. The timid protest of UGET and UGTT would not be heard any more. In any case, they have become only minor elements in Tunisian political life. Political action in Tunisia does not spring from the masses. Tunisia is bourgeois, as Morocco is feudal and Algeria plebeian. The bourgeoisie holds the power, as it always has. As for the popular masses, observers agree about their passivity. They remain, however, to a great extent, the unknown factor in the Destourian regime, as in the one that preceded it.

Notes

1. See Mohammed Harbi, "The Party and The State," pp. 159—67 in this reader.

2. "The VII Congress," *Maghreb,* No. 7 (January-February, 1965), p. 26.

3. There is a fifth organization, the National Union of Tunisian Women (UNFT), set up after independence and tightly under the control of the administration.

4. See Ridah Abdallah, "Le Neo-Destour," *Revue Juridique et Politique d'Outre-Mer,* No. 4 (October-November 1963), p. 602.

5. *Ibid.*

6. Cited by Charles Debbasch in *Annuaire de l'Afrique du Nord,* 1962, (Paris: Centre National de Recherche Scientifique, 1963), p. 85.

7. See Ridah Abdallah, *L'Action,* October 16, 1964.

8. Since November 11, 1964, the secretary of state for youth, sports, and social affairs had been Mondher ben Ammar, former public health secretary of state; the direction of youth and sports is not mentioned any more.

9. Tunisian grants in Tunisia are around $76—$90 per month.

10. See *L'Action,* March 10, 12, 13, 1965, for articles by Fetah Ouali on the Tunisian student.

11. See *ibid.,* as well as Josette ben Brahem, *Le Monde,* May 13, 1965.

12. *Jeune Afrique,* January 17, 1963.

13. *L'Action,* October 16, 1964.

14. *Jeune Afrique,* January 17, 1965.

15. See Douglas E. Ashford, "Organization of Cooperatives and the Structure of Power in Tunisia," pp. 380—94 in this reader.

16. *Le Monde,* April 3, 1965.

17. Habib Bourguiba, *La Tunisie et la France* (Paris: Julliard, 1954), p. 380. See Henri de Montety, "Old Families and New Elites in Tunisia" pp. 171—80 in this reader.

18. "Prospect for the Tunisian Labor Movement," *Preuves,* No. 61 (March, 1956), pp. 26—28.

19. Ridah Abdallah, *op. cit.*

20. See *Jeune Afrique,* April 18, 1965. See also Clement Henry Moore, "Tunisia after Bourguiba: Liberalization or Political Degeneration?," pp. 267—284 in this reader.

27

POLITICS IN A TUNISIAN VILLAGE

CLEMENT HENRY MOORE

Single-party regimes, perhaps the wave of the future in Middle Eastern as well as African countries, have authoritarian overtones that are disagreeable to most Westerners. Even the apologist tends to regard such regimes as a poor second best for countries that are too "underdeveloped" to make representative institutions work. Some politicians have claimed, however, that one-party rule is authentically democratic in their national context. Unity, so they argue, accords better with indigenous values and traditions than the Western-style clash of parties. Whereas the Westerner demands competition, conceptualized issues, and mathematical majorities, one-party politics in many emergent nations are supposed to be the fruit of harmonious discussion and spontaneous agreement. "The elders sit under the big tree and talk until they agree."[1]

Though a politics of spontaneous conciliation hardly seems plausible at the national level in complex modern states, the process is conceivable in a village. I propose, therefore, to examine the politics of a village in Tunisia, a country ruled by one of the oldest and most firmly implanted of the new mass parties.[2] Quite appropriately, the ruling Neo-Destour Party organized municipal council elections [every 3 years after] 1957, but, after allowing local opposition lists in 1957, it permitted only one slate of candidates in each of the subsequent elections.[3] My question, then, is whether the representative forces of the village were actually conciliated and allowed a share of power, despite the absence of an organized opposition. If so, how are compromises reached?

THE VILLAGE OF HAMMAM-SOUSSE

Hammam-Sousse is not exactly typical of villages in the Tunisian Sahel, nor is the region, with a history of Mediterranean civilization going back to the Romans and Carthaginians, typical of Tunisia as a whole. But the densely populated Sahel — clusters of ancient villages and towns stretching amid olive groves along the forty-mile coastal axis of Sousse and Mahdia — constitutes Tunisia's national heartland. Here, at the center of the axis, the Neo-Destour

Reprinted, by permission, from *The Middle East Journal,* XVII (Autumn, 1963), 527–40.

Party was founded in 1934, and the educated sons of Sahel peasants provided much of the party's top leadership. After independence in 1956, as in other periods of consolidation of power in Tunisian history, the Sahel provided a pattern of stable village life that the new authorities tried to extend to other less civilized parts of the country. Thus, in important senses the Sahel, though including less than one-tenth of Tunisia's population, is the core of the Tunisian nation.

Similarly, Hammam-Sousse is a typical though not quite average Sahel village. Only four miles from Sousse — within easy commuting distance by donkey, bicycle, or bus — the village shared the impact of the colonial situation that transformed part of Sousse into a modern city. Yet, though partially a modern suburb housing a proletariat, it also retains many of the traditional characteristics of Sahel villages. Hammam-Sousse is really a dual society confronting the problems of social and political change which in lesser degree are affecting all of the neighboring villages.

During the French Protectorate (1881–1956), virtually no French farmers settled in the Sahel. No village took on the depressingly segregated aspect of the French farming villages of Algeria or northwest Tunisia, where European buildings formed the town center and miserable mud huts of Arab laborers cluttered the wrong side of town. But a few Tunisians who could afford it have built European-style homes to one side of Hammam-Sousse. To the external world the village presents the sparse façade of a few villas along the main highway between Sousse and Tunis. The hasty tourist notices only a (bilingual) signpost to indicate that these scattered modern buildings are part of a town. He may, however, perceive a rotary off to one side of the highway and then discover a narrow, winding street walled with traditional dwellings on both sides. Though two-way traffic would be risky, it is possible to drive up the winding street two hundred yards to a large open square: here is the center of Hammam-Sousse, where people can meet and drink coffee, buy or sell wheat or fish, register births and deaths, go to school or the post office, or visit party headquarters. The village is fortunate to have had such a center; many neighboring villages planned main squares only after independence. But otherwise the village could be any Sahel village. From the roof of the two-story school off the square, Hammam-Sousse's unplanned and crowded atmosphere becomes apparent. Only the minarets of the three village mosques stand out in the confusion of hundreds of courtyards, not meant to be seen, enclosed by flat anonymous dwellings skirted by a labyrinth of paths and blind alleys.

Though the mosques define the subcenters of three areas of town, Hammam-Sousse, unlike some of its more backward neighbors, is not divided into three extended family cliques. There are political rivalries, of course, but the village seems free of the rivalries of name and lineage that demarcated the factions of other villages. The relative absence of traditional family clique politics seems partly a gift of history and partly the result of the newly diversified village economy.

Unlike some of its neighbors of Roman or Punic origins that managed to survive the nomadic invasions of the eleventh and twelfth centuries, the village is of relatively recent date. In 1724, a European visitor observed only a few families, newly settled to take advantage of soil near the sea suitable for vegetable gardening.[4] The villagers have no sense of an exclusive, sacred origin;

there is no legend of any *murabit,* or holy man, who founded the village, though within the village and outlying area there are eight *zawiyas* or former centers of extinct religious orders. The villagers believe that they are all descended from sixteen families who founded the village two or three hundred years ago, but membership in such a family no longer seems to carry with it any political implications. Possibly the very diversity of family origins mitigated against the emergence of two or three stable family blocks that are still political forces in other villages claiming more exclusive family origins.

Though little more than a small community of vegetable gardeners two hundred years ago, Hammam-Sousse grew rapidly. Its population today is between 11,000 and 12,000, and it seems to be growing at the astounding rate of 3 per cent per year[5] The *sheikhat* — the village and its surrounding areas of cultivation exploited by the villagers — has one of the highest rural population densities in Tunisia — on the order of 600 inhabitants per square mile. Even before the establishment of the Protectorate, the villagers were in need of more land but could not take it at the expense of adjacent villages. Instead, they laid claim to a plot ten miles to the north, which they developed by planting 80,000 olive trees. To save it from arbitrary expropriation, they transformed it into a mixed habous[6] for the benefit of the village. Some villagers also habitually rented lands many miles from Hammam-Sousse. Another response to the population problem reflected a village spirit of innovation and initiative. When at the end of the nineteenth century the French director of an olive press imported new vegetable seeds to cater to a European clientele, the villagers at great cost removed stones and calcium deposits from their fields, to create better gardens integrated in a new market economy. The villagers also displayed initiative in 1938, when they divided up the village habous among 400 heirs.

Hammam-Sousse has few wealthy families. Though the cultivators do not all own their little gardens, the concentration of property is less than in most villages of the Sahel, which rely primarily on olive tree cultivation. The latter requires only seasonal labor, whereas gardening is a year-round occupation. Extra seasonal workers, often from transhumant tribes of the interior, are always needed to harvest the olives, whereas the gardener and his family may cultivate their land with a minimum of outside help. Moreover, with the development of nearby Sousse under the Protectorate, the poorer villagers had opportunities for employment that could be at least as lucrative as agrarian self-employment.

Hammam-Sousse grafted upon its traditional aspect a new function as a suburb housing urban workers. But the transition was neither startling nor revolutionary: Before European commerce and industry came to Sousse, it had always had a vegetable market and offered other employment opportunities for the village youth. Sousse, however, had been ingrown with traditional class distinctions that the new French employers ignored. Hardworking villagers trained for regular jobs and took their enhanced status as employees in the modern sector home to the village every evening. The atomized society of small families suggested by vegetable gardening was reinforced by the growth of a modern proletariat that continued, however, to live in the old village. Social change was inevitable, though it was a gradual process rather than conscious policy.[7]

With the Protectorate, of course, came new Franco-Arab schools hastening social change. They supplemented or replaced the local *kuttab,* the traditional primary school where pupils learned only to recite the Qoran. The Sahel villagers — so unlike their counterparts in Egypt[8] — were avid for the new learning dispensed by the colonial power. But since the French favored towns with old families that exercised influence in the traditional order, Hammam-Sousse acquired its new primary school only after World War I. It had just two classrooms. By World War II, demand for modern education was so great the villagers themselves raised the funds to build their own new schools — a private Qoranic school that combined the study of the Arabic language and religious culture with the modern French curriculum.[9] Starting with six classrooms and six school teachers in 1945, the new school had doubled in size three years later. Today, having been "donated" by the population to the national Ministry of Education, it handles twenty-one classes in relays, with thirty to forty pupils in each class. The boys of Hammam-Sousse are virtually all in school,[10] while the girls now have a recently constructed fourteen-class village school of their own. One or two old *kuttabs* survive only as a supplement to the modern program.

Secondary-school education came relatively more slowly to Hammam-Sousse. While roughly 300 boys and girls flock to the Sousse *lycées* today, the village has few educated adults. In the late 1930's only six students were working for traditionalist Zitouna high school diplomas, while less than a dozen pursued French or modern Franco-Arab secondary study programs. For financial reasons few completed their baccalaureate and in 1961 only one of the village's three French university graduates returned to Hammam-Sousse (he lives in one of the new villas). But though the educated elite was small, it served to bring the villagers into the Neo-Destour Party and thus make Hammam-Sousse an active part of the new Tunisian nation.[11]

PRE-INDEPENDENCE POLITICS

Nationalism in Hammam-Sousse seemed more the response to a paradoxical situation than the imposed figment of an intellectual imagination. In the context of social change stimulated by the colonial situation, official village politics were ridiculously anachronistic by the late 1930's when the Neo-Destour emerged as a nationwide force. Hammam-Sousse, like the typical Near Eastern village even today, experienced the "phenomenon of split authority" whereby "the lowest, village level, government official and the man whose word carries the most weight in the village are rarely one and the same person."[12] But with a difference: in Tunisia the phenomenon was one of alienation, a sense of grievance against an intensive colonial situation rather than one of mere isolation from central authority.

The sheikh, in theory elected, in practice appointed by the colonial authorities, was the absolute ruler of the village. The sheikh elected by the village notables prior to the Protectorate had been ousted in 1881 by the French for his lack of cooperation with the new regime. Collaborating with the French, a dynasty of father and son ruled the village for six decades, until 1942. After Rommel's Afrika Korps retreated and the Protectorate was restored, the authorities installed a new sheikh hated by the populace for his arrogance and immorality.

Shut out of the legal order, the villagers were susceptible to the nationalist politics of opposition. From roughly 1930, the symbols of the nationalist movement grafted themselves upon the village, to form its perspective in a new space and time. The space would be Tunisia, defined in relation to rival neighbors of the Sahel. Time, measuring the successes and disappointments of nationalist revolution, would elicit a new awareness in history as national progress.

First, a small group of respected members of the community formed a local committee in correspondence with the Old Destour Party. They discussed national problems among themselves, but the communiqués from Tunis provided no guide for action. Then when in 1934 the youthful Bourguiba organized a Destour congress to break away from the party's antiquarian leadership, three curious Destourian villagers attended the meeting as observers. Instilled with the young revolutionary's sense of purpose — for Bourguiba even then could project the forceful personality that made a nation — they returned and mustered twenty recruits to form a Neo-Destour branch. The lone survivor of the three pilgrims is an old man now who remains a weaver hunched all day long to his wooden loom. Bourguiba singles him out whenever he stops at Hammam-Sousse — once every year or two — to shake hands with the villagers. The weaver recalls being beaten up by orthodox Old Destour fanatics, for it was he who in 1934 had received the heretic Bourguiba in his home.

It was only after World War II that the Neo-Destour branch became supreme in the village. Propaganda tactics shunned by the older generation of nationalists paid off. In the *zawiya* just off the main square — a religious sanctuary that no French police could disturb — the party-trained activists and instilled them with the nationalist faith. The party also controlled the boy scouts, a high school student organization, and an association of graduates in the village. Then there was the village project. In 1945, Sheikh Bahri, the village scholar (with a Zitouna background), established the private Qoranic school. Very talkative but hardly a political revolutionary by temperament — he would have been more at ease, perhaps, in the circles of the Old Destour, but they were folding — Bahri cooperated with the Neo-Destour, which clandestinely helped him raise his funds. In 1948 he also became the imam, or preacher, in one of the village's three mosques — and thus a very substantial citizen in a culture that did not readily distinguish politics from religion. The party also attracted two younger men of substance, Kantawi Murjan and 'Abd al-Majid Bu-Ja'far, who returned to Hammam-Sousse in the early 1940's after completing, respectively, their Franco-Arab and Zitouna secondary studies. Murjan got involved with the party through heading the graduates' association, though as a well trained civil servant in the Protectorate's administration he could not identify himself openly with the party. Bu-Ja'far associated himself with Sheikh Bahri in the Qoranic school and in 1956 became an imam in another of the mosques.

In 1948, the party had its first tangible village success. By running a persistent campaign, the young secretary general, Yusuf Jidai, managed to pressure the authorities into dismissing the corrupt sheikh, one of his own cousins. Two years later — at a time when the French and the Neo-Destour were engaged in one of their periodic rounds of negotiation and compromise — the president of the party branch was elected sheikh of Hamman-Sousse. He was the grandson of the sheikh ousted by the French in 1881 — another man of substance whom the party had attracted and used.

When, in early 1952, negotiations with France were followed by two years of violence and repression, the shock troops of the Neo-Destour went underground. Some fifty village militants actively participated in the party's terrorist network, and the Neo-Destour assassinated three "collaborationist" villagers. The conspirators of the party were a varied group that included students and vagabonds, businessmen and fishermen, farmers and unskilled laborers. The most promising of the students, Hadi Baqqush, was arrested twice in 1952 but after months in prison was permitted to go to France to enter a university. One of his prison companions, 'Ajmi Dawas, was also an activist who, as an olive-oil producer, would not subsequently present the branch patronage problems. But most of the others were less well endowed. When in late 1954 the Neo-Destour was allowed to surface and have a share in the transitional government, the heroes of the revolution expected property or sinecures as rewards for their sacrifices. The branch was able to place a number in the public works administration, in which a fellow villager was a top administrator in Tunis. One of the village branch leaders was released from prison to become a prison guard. But even in 1961, the Neo-Destour was still distributing state lands to a few neglected veterans.

Some of them were not easy to satisfy. 'Ali Mani and his three brothers, fishermen before 1952, enjoyed shooting and joined a guerrilla band rather than give up their arms to the French when the trouble started. As it had for many of the *fallaga* — or "bandits," as the French called them — nationalism furnished the Mani brothers an excuse as well as a mission. Home from the wars in 1955, 'Ali Mani expected a hero's welcome. It soon became Bourguiba's policy to encourage these expectations, for he needed the sympathy of the *fallaga* veterans in the event of a showdown with Salah ben Youssef, his mutinous political lieutenant.[13] 'Ali Mani was included in the branch leadership and given a public works job. But the small job did not interest him and he had to be fired. The party then obtained for him a transport license and a loan to buy a small bus. But he overloaded the bus and got into trouble with the police, who no longer had to be indulgent after the Youssefist threat subsided. Forced to sell the bus, he became a small tradesman. Finally, in 1959, he bought an olive press and seemed to be settling down, but he and his brothers had already discredited the party branch and caused it to lose the municipal elections of 1957.

THE 1957 ELECTIONS

When Tunisia became independent in 1956, the Neo-Destour took complete control of the government. For the first time the national leaders and the natural leaders of the village shared a common political outlook and more than two decades of struggle in a common cause. The phenomenon of "split authority" seemed a thing of the past. Yusuf Jidai, the chief activist of the branch, left the village to take an important position in the new administration. He left the branch in the hands of the men of substance he had trained. On March 25, 1956, the village joined the rest of the nation in electing a Neo-Destour national assembly against a token opposition.

The spring of the following year, democracy came to Hamman-Sousse, one of ninety towns and villages selected to elect its own municipal council. The branch complacently drew up its list, which cemented the alliance between the worthy citizens and the ex-terrorists. Sheikh Bahri, Kantawi Murjan, and 'Abd al-Majid Bu Ja'far, were joined by such activists as the businessman, 'Ajmi Dawas, the prison guard, and the notorious 'Ali Mani. At the last moment, on the intervention of higher party authorities, Sheikh Bahri, though a branch leader, was crosed off the list for being too bossy and officious.

The popular president of the village sports club, who was a schoolteacher in Sousse, formed an opposition list grouping the remaining educated residents who, though sympathetic with the Neo-Destour, had never held office in the branch. Two of the schoolteachers on the independent list had been Bu Ja'far's classmates at Zitouna. Sheikh Bahri, on the other hand, loyally backed his friends on the party list.

The campaign, limited by law to two weeks, had bitter undercurrents. Only the Neo-Destour campaigned openly, in the cafés of the central square and at organized rallies. The branch argued that the party which had brought independence should govern the village. Perhaps alarmed that the Neo-Destour youth — ominously uniformed in red gym-suits — might break up a big meeting, the Independents held only one small public gathering, in a café off the square, forty-eight hours before the elections. But they campaigned vigorously from house to house — using tactics that the party politicians later claimed were "beneath the dignity of the Neo-Destour." They enlisted women to persuade other women — for this was the first time in Tunisia that women had the vote — and allegedly distributed candy to the children. What is more, they promised responsible local government freed from the expectations of the branch clique. A few months earlier one of 'Ali Mani's brothers had killed the village painter — a harmless gossip who ridiculed the exploits of 'Ali Mani — ostensibly because he was a supporter of Salah ben Youssef. For most of the peace-loving villagers, afraid of the returned heroes, the party's list had the horror of including the brother, objectionable in his own right, of a murderer.

The Independents won the election by a two-to-one majority. This is the only Tunisian election to date where the women's vote was probably decisive. One-third of the voters were women, and proportionately fewer women than men bothered to vote in the subsequent village election where there was only one list of candidates.[14] In, 1957, three Tunisian villages used the techniques of modern Western democracy not to disavow the Neo-Destour or independence but to replace a complacent clique with a new set of local leaders.

But two opposing sets of authority could not coexist in one village, either in Hammam-Sousse or elsewhere. Even as the village sports leader took office in the new municipality, the branch clique across the open square plotted his downfall. First there were the rumors about the Independents' undignified electoral tactics — with the implication that there had been some corruption. Then came the more serious charge that the elected incumbents across the street were subverting the authority of the party and even smearing the reputation of Yusuf Jidai, the former branch leader. The new municipality lasted only three months. One night the president was ambushed and beaten up. Then he decided, with prompt help from the Ministry of Education, to transfer to a school far from the Sousse area. Under special ordinance the governor of Sousse dissolved the municipality and placed the village under his administrative delegate. The new regime proved a fiasco when the secretary put in charge of the village administration was caught embezzling funds and had to be put in jail.

THE 1960 ELECTIONS

A new era of guided democracy began in the summer of 1959 when Hadi Baqqush, the promising student activist of the 1952 days, returned from France, his university studies successfully completed. Abroad he had become one of the party's best known younger leaders, as president of the Neo-Destour Federation of France. Unlike so many other young graduates who stayed in Tunis or became diplomats, he returned to his village and was appointed number two man in the party apparatus of the Sahel. Baqqush, a thin, shy-looking man, who seemed younger than his thirty years, had spent all his life in politics. He hardly had the air of a party hack — they are usually short and stocky, overly enthusiastic organization men — but could pass as a painter or philosopher. He was tall, slightly stooped, with an intensity that seemed more the cause than the effect of constantly squinting. His gestures like his thinking were collected but not conventional. He missed the student discussion of Paris cafés but never learned the French small talk of some of his more bourgeois colleagues. He seemed too honest to be a politician in the artificial and cynical Tunis milieu of young political climbers. His thinking followed the party line — the objectives of the new Tunisia were social welfare through economic planning and dignity for every individual — but without being confined complacently to its slogans.

Baqqush naturally headed the Neo-Destour list in the 1960 municipal elections. To avoid local bickering, the Sahel party leaders simply drew up all the lists for the village branches. Baqqush wisely omitted 'Ali Mani, though he included three or four others of the branch clique — Murjan, Bu Ja'far, the prison guard. . . . He also included his old prison companion, 'Ajmi Dawas, who had run in 1957 but was not otherwise identified with the in-group. Its leader, Sheikh Bahri, was again omitted. Bahri tried to have his revenge in the otherwise dull single-list elections. He copied the technique of spreading rumors among the women against Baqqush, whom he blamed for his omission from the list both times. But the votes for Baqqush were not significantly lower than those for the branch clique. (Results: Baqqush, 2,267, others 2,322–2,305) In protest against Bahri, an educated young *fonctionnaire,* who happened to be related to the village sheikh,[15] organized a small demonstration, which the police stopped. The youth strongly favored Baqqush against the gossiping old schoolteacher who still tried to control the branch behind the scenes. The young demonstrator bitterly recalls how one of his uncles, a schoolteacher like the evicted president of the municipality, had also been chased out of town. The branch in-group had not liked his independence as the village scout leader and so had spread rumors that he liked little boys.

Baqqush did more than set the new municipality's affairs in order. By conciliating everybody he resolved — at least for the time being — the conflict between the old and the new generation of which the demonstration had been a symptom. No sharp differences of attitude separated the two generations — even Sheikh Bahri, for example, advocated birth control and economic planning. The problem was rather to engineer ways for the young to share village responsibilities with the older men of substance, without alienating the latter, the people like Murjan and Bu Ja'far. At the annual branch elections of 1961, the executive committee was reduced from eight to five members, in accordance with new Neo-Destour policy in the Sahel. Deadwood was dropped — people like

Zamzam (sic!), a veteran activist who continued, however, to shuffle about in a faded blue uniform as the municipality's official errand boy. Four of the clique were elected. But when Baqqush cleverly decided not to run except as an honorary president, the path was open for a younger fifth man — one of Hadi's friends but not his first cousin as the clique had wanted. Through Baqqush and his protégé on the branch executive, other youths were encouraged to play a larger role. The one who fomented the disturbance against Sheikh Bahri became president of the village sports association, while others organized a drama group and a lending library for village students. Meanwhile Murjan remained president of the branch, and, cooperating with Baqqush and offering administrative skills, he also became Neo-Destour treasurer for the Sahel. Bu Ja'far, though he still looked to Sheikh Bahri for moral leadership, flexibly adapted himself to the new regime. Even Bahri continued to feel important as the preacher and director of the largest village school, though he was conspicuously silent during the 1961 branch elections.

VILLAGE POLITICS, CONFLICT AND CHANGE

By the early 1960's, it seemed that Hammam-Sousse had effected a remarkable evolution over the previous three decades. The scattered European villas along the main road, though still only a façade, seemed to augur its successful future as a suburb of the modern world. Grandiose plans that the municipality had charged an Italian city planner to draft — blueprints for a new town hall, a sports arena, a market, and a vast new residential section — were proudly displayed on the walls of the remodeled *zawiya* that had been converted into the village headquarters for party and municipality. The plans would perhaps not be implemented for another three decades, yet, adopted by the village's elected bodies, they expressed newly shared aspirations. Perhaps also they were a symbol of how far the village had already come. The *zawiya*, too, was a symbol of progress: the sacred sanctuary near the village square that had been a clandestine haven for Neo-Destour revolutionaries was now the seat of responsible village government, its newly whitewashed cupola bedecked with a Tunisian flag.

The Neo-Destour had performed a painless village revolution. It had resolved tensions between the activists and the more passive citizens and had succeeded in enlisting the support of the educated youth — yet without destroying the old basis of legitimacy personified by the men of substance. The long history of political education, too, suggested that politics had acquired meaning for the average citizen. When, as during the Bizerte crisis of 1961, for instance, the villagers gathered every evening on the main square to hear the party explain the latest developments, it is safe to assume that the citizens were comprehending, not simply appearing at a spectacle. The orators were people whom the village knew and had elected to office. Over thirty years of discussions and occasional armed conflict, the villagers had learned of the outside world, through the channel of the mass party.

Yet obviously the conciliation of rivals within the village did not occur spontaneously. A gifted leader, Hadi Baqqush, backed with all the prestige of the victorious Neo-Destour, had been needed to bridge the gap between generations that had almost destroyed the organized political fabric of the community.

Previously Jidai, too, had elicited the cooperation of the men of substance with an older generation of revolutionaries.

The distinctive facet of conciliation in Hammam-Sousse, however, was not so much the able leadership as the political style of the leader. Baqqush relied neither upon his party position nor upon his persuasiveness and superior education to produce cooperation. Personally he was more a listener than a talker, and, indeed, was appreciated in the village because everyone felt they could express their views to him. In engineering a consensus, he relied on a simple procedure that everyone understood and accepted as legitimate — voting.

Since the 1930's, the Neo-Destour branch had held annual elections to choose its leaders. Though conflicts concerned personalities more than issues, they could be resolved amicably at the ballot box, because within the party a sufficient degree of consensus already existed. Through the party and other similarly democratic associations, voting became a habit for most male villagers even before independence.

Naturally, a political engineer was needed if the voting was to achieve the right results. To resolve the conflict between generations after independence, all the representative forces, including the youth, had to be brought into the electoral process. By subtle gestures of support, Baqqush helped a younger man against those who had seniority in the branch. Clearly he did not rely on spontaneous discussion alone to perform the work of conciliation. Rather he used accepted procedures to arrive at a solution for a complicated problem of personalities Sheikh Bahri, who had also played the electoral game, had to abide by its results.

Under these circumstances the argument advanced by some one-party enthusiasts elsewhere, that unity is somehow natural if everyone is allowed to talk, seemed wishful thinking. Hammam-Sousse's intricate political pattern was certainly not the fruit of unstructured agreement. The mathematics of the electoral process were an intrinsic aspect of the pattern. Indeed, it seemed unfortunate that municipal elections, unlike elections within the party branch, became ritual gestures of village solidarity for prefabricated agreements.

It would be unwise, however, to draw the opposite conclusion that two or more competing parties are needed for village elections to be meaningful. Rather, the 1957 debacle in Hammam-Sousse suggested the dangers of the artificial division of a village into opposing electoral camps. Such expressions of differences did not help to resolve the conflicts of personalities that underlay them, but only exacerbated tensions. The Independents, capitalizing on the village's dislike of certain persons, naturally aroused the mistrust of the Neo-Destour. Local and national politics could not be compartmentalized as the Independents had desired, given their close relationship in recent village history. The intrusion of national politics on the local scene made cooperation between the party branch and an Independent municipality — so essential for the adequate functioning of the latter — an impossible task.

The way in which the conflict between generations was resolved in Hammam-Sousse possibly has more general significance. It suggests ·that elections can meaningfully arbitrate the claims of ambitious individuals for local power. Two factors accounted for the success of the branch elections in 1961. Firstly, broad consensus — the feeling of sharing in a common enterprise and an absence of serious divisive issues — pervaded the discussions of the branch assembly.

Secondly, Hadi Baqqush was there to provide democratic leadership, to exercise his influence sparingly but decisively. Did not similar conditions prevail in the village at large?

While only 108-odd party members attended the branch assembly in 1961, the whole village sympathized with the Neo-Destour, which had become an authentic national symbol. The party had grouped more than 500 members at independence, and even in 1961, after nationalist enthusiasm had worn off, the party had more than 200 full dues-paying members. The history of the village and that of the nationalist party were so intimately bound that – short of the formation one day of a rival national party from within the Neo-Destour – a politics of opposition within the village seemed inconceivable. All political rivalries in the village were personal matters having no basis in differences of policy either about national or local matters.

Within this context of consensus the party was to incorporate all individuals who desired to participate actively in village affairs. It therefore seemed fitting that the party devise the electoral lists for the municipality. But municipal elections could have been more meaningful – and elicited more voter participation – if they resembled branch elections in allowing the voter some genuine choice. In Hammam-Sousse as in most other villages, there were roughly twice as many candidates as offices to fill in the annual branch elections. Could not this practice, deeply rooted in Neo-Destour tradition, be usefully extended to the village as a whole?[16]

That such a question may be raised perhaps serves as an answer to my original set of questions. The representative forces of Hammam-Sousse were indeed conciliated and allowed an effective share of power, despite the absence after 1957 of local opposition. Conciliation was possible, however, because the Neo-Destour provided not only a form for spontaneous discussion but a set of procedures for selecting leaders and the political experience to make the procedures work. Whatever the solution to the problem of municipal elections, the party continued to provide mechanisms that had already helped Hammam-Sousse – and many similar villages – to resolve local differences, canalize youthful energies, and progress into the modern world, in intimate association with the new nation.

Notes

1. Quoted in Paul E. Sigmund (ed.), *The Ideologies of the Developing Nations* (rev. ed.; New York: Praeger Publishers, 1967), p. 294. Nyerere, who in this passage as in other writings has forcefully expressed the argument, was referring to a description of traditional African democracy. On another continent, Sukarno made much the same point in defense of "guided democracy." See *ibid.,* p. 96. Sékou Touré's *société communaucratique,* too, would appear to resemble Nyerere's "communitary" society. See Ruth Schachter Morgenthau, "African Socialism," in *Africa Report,* May, 1963.

2. It should be noted, however, that the Tunisians have not appealed to village tradition to justify single-party rule; solidarity is meant to be nationwide, and to create a modern society from the colonial legacy rather than to restore an idealized precolonial past. For more general studies of Tunisian politics, see Charles A. Micaud, Leon Carl Brown, and Clement

Henry Moore, *Tunisia: The Politics of Modernization* (New York: Praeger Publishers, 1964); C. F. Gallagher, "Tunisia," in Gwendolyn Carter (ed.), *African One-Party States* (Ithaca, N.Y.: Cornell University Press, 1962); pp. 11–86; Clement Henry Moore, "The Neo-Destour," *World Politics,* April, 1962, pp. 461–82.

3. But these mock elections were hardly satisfying to politically educated Tunisians, even when they were told, as in 1960 in at least one town, that their participation would enable them at subsequent elections to mark a protest (if necessary) by abstention! In 1963, the weekly *Jeune-Afrique* (May 13–19) ironically contrasted the home elections – in which the Neo-Destour was "preaching against the invisible and redoubtable adversary, abstention" – with the annual Tunisian student elections in Paris – in which the Neo-Destour lost to the leftist opposition in a closely fought contest.

4. See Jean Despois, *La Tunisie orientale: Sahel et base steppe* (Paris: Presses Universitaires de France, 1955), p. 180.

5. The population for the 1956 census was 9,419. According to the municipal secretary, 356 births were registered in 1960, as against 125 deaths. But this is not the whole story, for many children are born in Sousse and registered there, whereas few old villagers go to the hospital there to die. The secretary estimated that there had in fact been 500 births and 145 deaths in 1960. On the other hand, Tunisian economic planners estimate the country's annual population increase to be 2.1 per cent. See the Tunisian Government's *Perspectives Decennales de Développement 1962–71,* p. 22.

6. The habous was an institution sanctioned by religious custom whereby property becomes an endowment for religious or welfare purposes. As such, the property was inalienable, though the original owners and their heirs might still collect the income.

7. By 1961, village leaders estimated that roughly half of 'Hammam-Sousse's working population was employed in Sousse, though no formal statistics were available. According to the vice president of the municipal council, who was himself an executive in a big firm in Sousse, the village working force was occupied roughly as follows: 30 per cent were engaged in some form of agriculture, either as landowners or as tenants;. 15 per cent were daily laborers with no occupation; 35 per cent worked as clerks or petty officials in Sousse; 20 per cent were full-time manual laborers in Sousse.

8. Apparently most Egyptian villagers even in the early 1950's thought compulsory modern education to be a waste of time. They preferred the religious atmosphere of the *kuttab.* See Hamed Ammar, *Growing Up in an Egyptian Village* (London: Routledge and Kegan Paul, 1954), p. 216.

9. These modern Qoranic schools, of course, were not new in Tunisia. The first one had been launched privately in Tunis in 1906 and after World War I they spread, especially in the areas of the Sahel and Sfax. They combined the popular desire for modern education with the nationalist desire to perpetuate the country's Islamic heritage. That the quality of education compared favorably with that of the French schools was attested by the proportionately high number of Qoranic school graduates admitted to Tunisia's elite secondary school, Sadiki College.

10. The old Franco-Arab school takes an additional twelve classes.

11. The French educated elite could be easily counted in 1961. In addition to the three university graduates, six villagers, of whom three lived in Tunis, had terminated their secondary studies and were government administrators or technicians. Twelve others were studying in universities. Many more still studying in the Sousse *lycées* were expected to pursue university studies on generous government scholarship programs.

12. C.A.O. van Nieuwenhuijze, "The Near Eastern Village: A Profile," in *Middle East Journal,* Summer, 1962, p. 296. Many authors have commented on the lack of village integration into national life in this part of the world. A single-party regime with authentic roots, as in Tunisia, tends to overcome the problem.

13. In late 1955, ben Youssef tried to capture control of the party by making extremist Pan-Arab appeals to public opinion, impatient with Bourguiba's tactical compromises with France. He launched an armed uprising that Bourguiba only suppressed three months after independence with the help of French troops. Ben Youssef fled eventually to Cairo, where he was befriended by Nasser and some factions of the Algerian FLN. He was assassinated in Germany in August, 1961, under circumstances that remain obscure.

14. In 1957, out of 3,309 voting, Gallas received 2,215 votes while the top Neo-Destour man got only 1,199. (The apparent discrepancy is due to some voters choosing both men by

308

cross-list voting.) In 1960, 2,362 voted for the lone party list. Only 510 women voted, as compared to 1,146 in 1957.

15. The sheikh elected in 1950, now an old man, continued in office, but the new municipality performed many of his administrative functions.

16. I. Nicole Grimaud, "The Elections of February 5, 1967," pp. 340–343 in this reader.

28

TRADITION AND POLITICAL LEADERSHIP:
THE EXAMPLE OF ALGERIA

P. J. VATIKIOTIS

If this is the heyday of mass societies, popular revolutions, and protest movements against existing and pre-existing orders, the number of individuals who aspire to leadership because they essentially claim to represent the interests and welfare of whole nations has multiplied rapidly. Yet, because of the disruption of an old order upon whose rubble new states have arisen, those among them who accede to power must be able to lead a totally amorphous — often chaotic — mass society toward the achievement of a new order. In these circumstances, their claims tend to be all-embracing — in fact, totalitarian — in order for their leadership to become acceptable to everyone. Indeed, such leaders must affect not only political power and skill, but they must also ascribe attributes to their prowess which approximate to those of a potential saviour of a mass society.[1]

The claim to Arab leadership by the Sharif Husain of the Hijaz in 1916 derived in part from his religious office as protector of the holy Muslim shrines in Mecca and Madina, as well as from his alleged descent from the family of the Prophet.[2] Ibn Saud carved out a kingdom in the Arabian Desert (Najd) on the strength of his leadership of the Wahhabi puritan movement. In both cases, the leader appeared to be inspired — apart from the material help received from infidel powers — by the vision of an Arab-Islamic dominion, albeit vague in its territorial extensiveness or limits. In both instances, the leader claimed the ability to revive and strengthen the Arab Muslim community. The fact that today new and different leaders in Arab states claim the ability to found powerful realms by modern means does not imply that they eschew the revival or strengthening of an Islamic dominion. Actually, this leadership would be seriously disabled were they to do so. Whereas an Ibn Saud sought to purify and save the community of believers in Arabia from damnation by the imposition of his particular Wahhabi creed, certain contemporary revolutionary leaders in the Arab states propose to do the same for their fellow-Muslims via "modernization." Yet, in both cases, the relationship between the forceful ruler and the

Originally published in *Middle Eastern Studies,* II. (July 1966), No. 4; reprinted by permission of the publishers, Frank Cass & Company Limited, 67 Great Russell Street, London W.C. 1.

masses remains essentially Islamic in inspiration. To this relationship we now turn with a look at independent Algeria.

When considered part of the Muslim Arab world, Algeria in North Africa has differed in its evolution as an independent state from her sister countries in one significant respect: the Algerians fought a war of independence against France from 1954 to 1962. She also differs from them in another lasting respect, namely, the influence upon her of the particular Islamic nexus that developed in the Maghrib beginning in the eighth century. Islam in the Maghrib adapted itself to the tribal Berber peculiarities of that region, often erupting, from the twelfth to the nineteenth centuries, into puritan frontier movements.

Unlike Egypt, Saudi Arabia, and other Arab countries in the Middle East, the state of Algeria encompasses an ethnically fragmented society, the major division in which comprises a non-Arab Kabyle minority, constituting approximately 5 per cent of the total population. In terms of a significant political minority within its territory, Algeria is faced with a problem that could become similar (that is, as serious as) to that faced by Iraq in connection with the Kurds. But having fought a seven-and-a-half-years-long war of independence, in which the Kabyle minority was pre-eminently and effectively active, one might assume that Algeria has a greater chance than, say, Iraq or other neighboring Arab states of creating a more cohesive political community in which the masses — irrespective of ethnic or other differences — respond more readily and loyally to national leadership. . . .

Thus, unlike Egypt, where a nation of Egyptians historically and territorially defined has existed for many centuries, some Algerians at least had to discover a nation where none existed in their minds before that would permit them to work for the establishment of a sovereign territorial state. Even though for different reasons, both Egypt and Algeria manifest today the makings of mass-oriented political systems of the single-party variety, ruled by leaders whose legitimacy, to use a Weberian phrase, derives from both charismatic and traditional-religious sources. This suggests that leadership in both Egypt and Algeria is what is referred to here as claimant, that is, *za'amas;* and the leaders themselves are viewed by the public as *za'ims* who can lead the community in confrontation with the outside and alien — often inimical — world; a world whose material living standards are desired but the origins of which are disdained. In Algeria particularly, if one bears in mind the puritan Islamic background of the society, claimant leadership is more readily accommodated to a mahdistic, or messianic, tradition. And mahdism as such does not preclude the emergence of modern saviors. . . .[3]

But since this is not an essay on the question of Arab unity, one can only suggest two general premises upon which one can base a possible approach to political study in the Muslim Arab East and, in this case, Algeria. First, there is the proposition that Arabs today are aware of the fact that linguistically and culturally they partake of — if they do not belong to — a tradition deriving from a glorious Islamic civilization of the past. They, moreover, associate their pride in this civilization and its cultural heritage with a powerful Islamic Empire, as well as with powerful and politically successful lesser Islamic empires in the Middle East and North Africa — actually powerful Islamic rulers. Indeed, it is difficult for one to divorce this feeling for the past from the nationalist drive today for modernity and prestige. The loss of that power won and exercised by a past

Islamic Empire, or by lesser, though powerful, Islamic rulers is inevitably a source of both irritation and inspiration. To restore it now that outside power has been receding from the areas of the Muslim Arab East is a worthy task for any modern nationalist leader.

The restoration of power in the 1960s, however, requires the adoption of methods, techniques, and ideas whose origin lay outside Islam, or its cultural achievements, that is, outside the Islamic world. Bluntly, it means the borrowing and adaptation of alien constructs and organizations. Naturally, there is no reason why these methods should be denied to, or considered inappropriate for, a Muslim. Non-Muslim non-Europeans have done this. But when the Muslim himself insists upon a certain excellence for his cultural base, orientation, and achievement, the difficulty in such borrowing and adaptation is self-generated. Here one may suggest the second premise, namely, the study of Arab politics through a consideration of the problem of cultural identity. In Algeria, for instance, despite the relative pragmatism of its educated elite and national leadership, as well as its close proximity to Europe, this problem is most acute and academically fascinating.

One may even generalize about these two premises by saying that efforts to restore power and to recapture, through reformulation, an Arab Islamic cultural identity in the technological age are major political tasks of so-called modernization. And this task belongs primarily to the so-called revolutionary modernizing leaders, be they simply militant nationalists from any sector of society, or sophisticated intellectuals. But such generalization raises difficult epistemological and ontological questions, especially if one agrees that the foremost task of the academic student of politics is to explain phenomena of political significance and relevance, their working in the past, and their effect on the evolution of political systems today. Thus, what is meant by revolution? What is meant by the restoration of power? What is meant by the formulation of a cultural identity that is at one and the same time acceptable to the Islamic traditional-religious ethos on the one hand, and the minimum requirements of the modern industrial civilization on the other? Relevant to this essay is the fact that the meaning and direction of these questions appears at the moment to be politically determined, that is, by the national revolutionary leadership, and could conceivably be similarly decided in the future. Thus, the new goals to be achieved by the hoped-for modern political system are not only social, political, and economic, but are in a more complex fashion, cultural, and civilizational. The latter two goals could perhaps commit these societies into a civilizational confrontation with the outside world.

The French colonialism experienced by Algerians from 1830 to 1962 differs from any other colonial or European tutelage experience of the Arab Islamic societies in the Middle East. Briefly, French colonial policy in Algeria was one of literal colonization: the settling of Frenchmen (though actually mostly Corsicans, Maltese, Italians, and Spaniards) in Algeria — the so-called policy of *peuplement* — and the assimilation and integration of Algeria into metropolitan France. Economic, educational, and other policies aimed at transforming Algerians into Frenchmen. Without dwelling upon this matter at great length, one can fairly assert that French colonial policy succeeded in rendering the average Algerian French in speech only. As for transforming him into a Frenchman, not only did this policy fail, but it had serious repercussions culminating in a long and fierce war and ultimate Algerian independence.

In trying to make Algerians French-speaking – and only a minority of them became that – French colonial policy engendered a more complex problem, namely, that of illiteracy in Arabic. By deliberately quashing Arabic as the traditional language of the majority of Algerians, the French created a far more serious condition: the cultural eunuchism of Algerians, and their present dilemma regarding language and cultural identity. Consequently, the resentment against France was not merely political, but cultural too. This situation gave rise to even more complex problems after independence: that of communication between the traditional country-folk, who speak only the Algerian Arabic dialect, and the Kabyle minority, who speak their own Berber language. Both these groups, in turn, faced communication problems with the urban elites, who are almost totally French-speaking. Some would argue that the latter are French even in sentiment and, the intellectuals among them, French in thought also. ...

With the accession to power of ben Bella, aided by Colonel Boumedienne, it became clear that the *extérieur* would triumph politically over the *maquis*, a large proportion of whom were Kabyles. Moreover, the guerrilla commands, organized as they were into wilayas, could conceivably find it difficult to be loyal to leaders other than their regional commander. Despite the ability of ben Bella at the outset to impose public order and silence his critics and opponents, this fairly original sin of political steamrolling soon came back to plague Algerian politics in the form of a latent but fundamental rift in the Algerian political community. By October, 1963, it erupted into a brief armed uprising by the Kabyles in the Tizi-Ouzou and Boghni areas. This was the first defiance of, and open challenge to, the ben Bella order in Algeria.

Another interpretation of ben Bella's triumph so soon after independence is possible in terms of the domination by the militants of the political scene at the expense of the more liberal institutionally oriented Algerian leaders. Ben Bella after all, was prominent in the small but extremely militant Organisation Secrète (1950–51), which became impatient with the less extremist measures taken by national leaders in the struggle for independence. But he also reflects, as will be argued throughout this essay, given the traditional setting of Algerian society, the supremacy of the claimant, or za'im, mass-oriented militant leader over the more constrained intellectual type represented by the earlier nationalists in the country. The widening rift between these two elements came to the surface in Algeria with the resignation of Ferhat 'Abbas, president of the National Constituent Assembly, in August, 1963. His letter of resignation submitted to ben Bella on August 12, 1963, is, moreover, a historic document from which one may glean a definite pattern in the initial phases of the struggle for power in many of the new states. One thing in this connection is clear: those inclined to respect a certain political process roughly described as liberal or evolutionary and willing to compromise with a variety of groups in society are often anachronistic as serious contenders for power. The primacy of governmental action in the early stages of independent national state existence militates in favor of leaders who are activist nationalists, willing to subsume all interests and groups in society under strong personal rule, as well as willing to maintain a mixed traditional-modern establishment that can claim to reflect, but not necessarily represent, the will of the people.

The militant revolutionary leader has been acceptable in Algeria until recently to both the traditional masses and the more secular cadre of Algerian bureaucrats, army officers, professionals, students, and workers. Militant activism has been the common bond, so to speak, that united the traditionalists and secularists, as against the less militant attitude and ideas of those classical liberal nationalists who were gradually purged from the ranks of the ruling group in 1962–64. Their purge by the militants, led by ben Bella, was justifiable and acceptable to both the traditional masses and the secularists on the grounds that their classical liberalism rested upon, and derived from, such alien and therefore traditionally unacceptable notions as institutionalized power and representative processes of government. In fact, the crime of these liberals against the militant revolution was not just that their liberalism was of alien origin, but that some among them actually persisted in adhering to its precepts.

Essentially, the above is close to the concept of claimant, or *za'ama,* type of leadership proposed here. In the classical sense, however, one must be careful to insist that, according to the Islamic religious tradition of the sacred law, at least the ruler faced the obligation of justice toward the subjects and equity in his dealings through statecraft, or *siyasa;* that is, he was expected to conduct an equitable and just administration.[4] It is clear that in the Islamic tradition there is no theory of individual political rights of the variety known and demanded by the citizens of these new states. Nor was there any mechanism (that is, civil-political bodies, organizations, or institutions) by which a citizen could secure these rights and prevent their usurpation by the ruler. The ruler, on the other hand, like his subjects, was not above but under the sacred law, and was therefore accountable to its limitations as a believer, as well as to the limitations this law placed upon the exercise of his authority. In fact, there is no word in Arabic for the concept of a participant citizen of a polity, let alone a concept of an individual citizen's rights.[5]

Under these conditions, claimant leadership today in states like Algeria is acceptable even short of any legal-political limitations upon its power and authority, although other serious limitations upon its authority do exist and function. Moreover, representation, a conception alien to Islam, is unimportant to the mass of the population. Instead, consultation *(shura)* among a small group of advisers and assistants strictly loyal to the leader rather than to any system becomes of the essence, and remains within the traditional nexus that is acceptable to the society at large. In these circumstances, the institutionally-oriented leadership exemplified by, say, Ferhat 'Abbas could be logically accused of being antipopular and against the believers in the sense that it did not entertain too much faith in the masses *(al-sha'b).* It could furthermore be logically accused of being outside the pale of the tradition, since its insistence upon an institutional-representational base for a political system derived from a borrowed notion of non-Islamic origin. This, despite the possibility that what men like Ferhat 'Abbas may be against is the populistic nature of strong-man rule that eschews the firm institutionalization of a political process, or rules of the political game. This general situation, in turn, requires one to consider briefly the question of political modernization and political development.

Algeria, which is, to use modern jargon, emerging furiously, renders any systematic appraisal of its politics, of the evolution of a political system, and of future trends and patterns, difficult and sometimes misleading. Academic responsibility prescribes caution when studying the so-called new nations. One is also perforce skeptical about the potential of societies and their leaders who, under the general inspiration of nationalism, reach for goals they cannot achieve given the human and material resources at their disposal. The concept of political modernization used by social scientists today to explain the processes of evolution or revolution which new states undergo in trying to transform themselves from traditional or transitional to modern societies and polities is not a satisfactory one for many reasons. First, those social scientists who have attempted to identify — in fact, to enumerate — criteria that characterize modern societies, and through these, to posit commensurate criteria for modern polities, do so under the implicit assumption that political development and its ultimate result, political modernization, involve the creation and injection of preconditions and conditions that are neutral, that is, that are applicable everywhere, anytime. Such assumption inevitably renders political modernization a mechanistic concept.[6] Secondly, if by the term modern one means the existence of man in a technologically advanced industrial civilization, one obviously argues that political development and modernization for these traditional societies implies the aspiration and desire of their members to attain entry into this civilization. It appears, however, that this definition of modernity derives from a projection of the achievement of Western societies and civilization as representative of what is and, for some, what ought to be, desirable for all societies and states today — an arrogant projection at best, since it implies rather blasphemously the suggestion that Western civilization is permanent, eternal, and indestructible. Philosophically, this definition also suggests a linear conception of history, from Adam to the modern robot, so to speak. Thus, thirdly, modernization through development becomes a categorical imperative, though one that is void of prerequisites other than the neutrally mechanistic ones.

Such views of development and modernization present difficulties when employed to deal with Islamic societies. Logically and theoretically, but not necessarily pragmatically, Islam purports to provide a perfect arrangement for society through the revealed sacred law. How is the Muslim to develop from perfection? Obviously he could only degenerate from a perfect to an imperfect order — in this case, the so-called modern society and polity. In fact, one notes, on the other hand, that contemporary national leaders and rulers of states whose societies are overwhelmingly Muslim, aspire to the attainment of exactly this modernity. The question then arises: Are these leaders disregarding the Islamic base of society; are they adapting it to an essentially alien achievement because the latter is an efficacious instrument for the attainment of power? Or does the religious-traditional commitment make no difference in this matter? So that in this particular instance there is no difference between them and the Christian European whose imagination, nourishing itself from the riches of the pagan Graeco-Roman tradition, built a civilization so superior as to be desirable by all mankind without exception. One also observes that non-Christians have proved themselves most adept at learning the secrets and mechanisms of this civilization, as well as at grasping its complexities. Moreover, it is historical fact, not fancy, that rulers of Islamic states have been able in the past as they are able today to ride roughshod, cavalierly, forcefully, and effectively over Islamic sensibilities, beliefs, and institutions. Examples of this behavior range from Pakistan and Turkey to Egypt and the North African states. Hence the attitude of the militant Algerian nationalist intellectual today: *"Je m'en fous de l'Islam."*

One must therefore look elsewhere for the insistence by leaders upon the preservation of the Islamic ethos in these states, despite their aspiration to establish societies and polities whose premises derive from non-Islamic and, in fact, inimical sources. This, I submit, can be usefully done, if one could investigate the meaning of politics, government, citizenship and other concepts for the Muslims, as well as the relationship between the leaders and their communities, which, while basically Muslim, are trying to transform into modern ones with all that this condition implies. In doing this, they may alienate them from their Islamic belief as well as from their general socio-religious order. The leaders obviously cannot embark upon this task peacefully if they took a merely neutral mechanistic view of modernization. For modernity is not only empirically a real existential condition, but it also entails philosophical and ethical considerations, as well as explanations. Hence, the attempt by these leaders to articulate modernity within an Islamic nexus, that is, a commitment on their part to borrow from outside the pale but to retain the essentially Islamic orientation and character of the society to be. But this some may argue is crass causistry and humbug, which intelligent though lay people can .eventually detect. It is possible though that the basically traditional-religious nature of claimant leadership permits the approval, if not the support, of such adaptations by the public.

If by modernity, on the other hand, one means along with Ortega y Gasset,[7] the pre-eminence of mass man in society, who is essentially a parasite enjoying all the fruits (of civilization) produced by the efforts of the excellent few, then one sees no reason why Islamic societies should differ from any others. Mass man, in this instance, tends to be just as alienated from power as his counterpart elsewhere in the world, and leadership in a mass society becomes the ultimate arbiter of his political life. One must assume all the same that Islamic societies like the Algerian one have fought for the attainment of an independent state not purely for the purpose of remaining exclusively Muslim but also in order to create a modern (better?) society. But this implies improvement, that is, not only the rejection and ejection of French rule but the abandonment of traditional forms and structures in favor of new and different ones. It is exactly this task of pulling away from a previous order and existence toward a different one that belongs at the moment exclusively to the state and, more specifically, to its leadership.

The state must build a nation whose values, myths, and belief infrastructures — its very purposes — are different from those held by the traditional community and, in the case of Algeria, an Islamic community. This movement constitutes an activity, a process, that is so vital as not to be so easily assessed by the mere use of preconditions and criteria. For if the state is to lead this activity and supervise the process, it cannot rest after having asked the question: How can it, or should it, be done? It is forced to ask: What kind of society and nation can and must we build? It even asks: What kind of nation ought we to build, exactly because of the sensitive tradition from which it must perforce deviate in the actual building process.

The question then is: What kind of polity for Algeria? It entails both a necessity and a choice: What polity must Algeria have, and should have? The newly independent African south of the Sahara may be at an advantage over the Algerian insofar as he has no precolonial polity model to mesmerize him. Consequently, his choice from extant alternative models in East and West is freer and wider. The Algerian, on the other hand, finds himself on the horns of a dilemma between the Scylla of the Islamic ethic and the Charybdis of the industrial-technological revolution – the latter being the characteristic achievement of nineteenth- and twentieth-century Europe. He also observes that he must for the moment reject the political-philosophical base of this achievement, namely, liberal democracy. He must indeed defy and reject this social philosophical variant.

One should not infer from this that Islamic societies are not capable of absorbing, synthesizing, or accommodating alien ideas, including philosophical ones. Some may contend though that past experience is not encouraging, if one recalls the adaptation of Greek and Hellenistic philosophy by Islamic thinkers from the ninth to the twelfth century. They ended up either as mystics or as heretics, without any lasting effect upon the socio-political structure of the Islamic state.

I have argued elsewhere that, given the control by the forceful ruler and today the militant nationalist revolutionary leader over those who interpret and explain Islam, its tenets, and principles, it should follow that the traditional ethos is no obstacle to any and all modern permutations of it when these are necessary for change.[8] Clearly, then, there is no reason whatever for Islamic societies that have recently achieved statehood not to embark upon the road to modernity. But it is exactly this journey that requires delicate steering if the accommodation and transformation of the old to the new is going to be successful. Earlier attempts at evolutionary religious and social reform failed in almost every case. Only forceful leaders have attained a measure of success, although far short of the mark. Leaders today think that success comes not with a total rejection of the tradition of the past but with the use of an essentially traditional construct, the *za'ama,* or claimant leadership, which gives them an acceptable and total mandate to save the community. To lead an effective revolution, the leader must build from the traditional base. It is in this sense that ben Bella and Nasser are *za'ims.*

In the case of Algeria, the program of expanded religious instruction and Arabization is not so much a reflection of the leadership's faith in the efficacy of the Islamic tradition for the establishment of a modern polity as it is an attempt to wean Algerians from an alien language and culture, that is, French. By doing this, the leadership also hopes to give the Algerian an Arab national identity. But, one could ask, why not give him an Algerian identity whatever the language, French or Arab? That is, why not inculcate in him the kind of patriotism that derives from loyalty and allegiance to a socio-political system? After all, many Belgians speak French but are loyal to Belgium, not France. To consider these matters, one must look at the Algerian necessity for a new definition of culture and the role of the Islamic tradition in it on the one hand, and the program of Arabization that is inexorably connected with the former, on the other. Both these instruments of national-social mobilization can be best considered through a survey of the meaning of revolution expressed by the Algerian leaders and the means by which they propose to achieve its goals. This is important, because revolution in this case does not stop at the successful uprising against an existing order – French rule – but continues after independence in the form of a national campaign to set up a new order different from and often contrary to the pre-existing traditional one.

As long as the war of independence against the French was on, there was no need for Algerians to articulate the meaning of revolution. Independence brought to the surface the first divisions and conflict between the internal forces — the *maquis* — and the external group of revolutionary leaders. The outsiders, with the help of the army, won the first round in this conflict rather decisively during the first year of independence. But since July, 1963, there has been the urgent task of consolidating power. And this has entailed the dangerous process of selecting the cadres, the political apparatus, and the mobilization of society — especially the masses. Those in power had perforce to embark upon a definition of the meaning of revolution: a tricky proposition in itself for it unavoidably involves the ruling group in the task of programing. The latter, in turn, consists largely of choices among, and decisions upon, goals and methods — in fact, the total functions and the techniques of statecraft — for the achievement and maintenance of public order.

Given the high incidence of intellectuals (both armchair and activist) in Algeria, the above tasks were apt to evoke resentment and elicit criticism. The ruling group could either absorb, that is, appease the vociferous intellectuals by utilizing them in politically nonsensitive, tasks, or muzzle them. Until September, 1963, it had tergiversated between using some of them, and permitting others to let off steam. After October, 1963, it appears that the rulers could no longer afford the latter luxury and the tendency has been to attack and suppress them. And as many of the leading intellectuals also represented groups with political opposition potential, their demise was still more desirable, and convenient. Hence the elimination of 'Abbas, Khider, Boudiaf, Ahmed Francis, Boumendjel, Ferhat 'Abbas, and Ait Ahmed.

There could have been no articulation of revolutionary goals while such important groups as the Kabyles were opposed to the Arab ruling group; while the army reflected an uneasy relationship with the National Liberation Front (FLN); and while the intellectuals of both Right and Left were critical of the regime. A process of elimination had to precede the organization of the postindependence revolutionary apparatus in ben Bella's Algeria. Ben Bella survived this phase in Algerian politics, despite the brief but open armed challenge of the Kabyles led by Ait Ahmed in October, 1963, to his authority, and the border war with his royalist neighbor Morocco. one can now ask: What meaning to the Algerian revolution was ben Bella prescribing and how or why did he manage to communicate it to a nation that consists of a small minority of modernized Algerians concentrated in the cities and a vast majority of traditional Muslims in the countryside?

Like many other leaders in Afro-Asia ben Bella has often defined the revolution in sweeping — some would argue meaningless — terms. It is not easy to extract specific purposes and intentions from these definitions given the peculiar jargon that emerges with many of the so-called developing nations. Generally, for ben Bella, the popular democratic revolution is "the conscious edification of the nation in the cadres of the socialist principles," and seeks to create "power that is vested in the hands of the people." There is nothing new in the Algerian position that contends that armed conflict is succeeded by ideological combat, and that the struggle for national independence must be followed by a "democratic popular revolution."

The tasks set by the leader for the revolution are however revealing and confusing, at the same time. In the case of Algeria, the most urgent task of the revolution is to consolidate a nation that supports a socio-political system that is popular-democratic. The democratic characteristic is distinguished from the popular insofar as it relates directly to the establishment of new institutions that aim at the emancipation of man in "a socialist perspective" and in "a cadre of collectivization." The popular characteristic, so to speak, checks the democratic one insofar as it places the "collective expression of popular responsibility" above the liberty of the individual. And the democratic popular nation is to be embodied in and represented by a sovereign state that is strong by virtue of a "national economy" and a "national culture." It is with the political implications and significance of this "national culture" that we are mainly concerned here.

To the extent that the revolution must undermine, perhaps destroy, but definitely displace an old order, the revolutionary is presumably the younger Algerian, be he peasant, worker, soldier, or intellectual. As such, he is by nature against the older privileged class of Algerians, the so-called bourgeoisie. But the Algerian revolutionary must work within and under the guidance of the "conscientious avant-garde" — the FLN — which elaborates the social and political ideas that reflect the aspirations of the masses. The process is both directed and creative, in the sense that it is not haphazard or routinely bureaucratic on the one hand, nor circumscribed by any preconceived ideology on the other. Some Algerian regime intellectuals have referred to it rather snobbishly and pedantically as a "Bergsonian (in terms of a creative evolutionary process) ideological struggle." All this is necessary to the new definition of national culture, which in itself, the Algerians argue, is a necessity if the Revolution is to succeed.

The culture to be articulated and disseminated by the Algerian leadership must be national, revolutionary, and scientific. By national, the Algerians mean precisely Muslim-Arab, or the bringing-up of a new generation of Algerians whose national and official state language is Arabic, and whose national and official state religion is Islam. Both these characteristics, they argue further, are essential for a national culture and personality or identity. Hence the revolutionary commitment to an intensive nation-wide Arabization program — which in bitter fact is an alphabetization, or literacy, campaign. Briefly, this program proposes the Arabization of Algerian society through literacy campaigns in keeping with its historical and cultural Islamic character. But in order to look more closely at the question of a national culture and the problems it entails, it is well to survey the basic organization of official power in Algeria, and the role of the so-called elite of revolutionary cadres in it.

As head of state and government, and as secretary general of the FLN, President ben Bella controlled the Political Bureau, that is, the central apparatus of power and governing. This politbureau, in turn, kept a check upon — if it did not actually supervise — operations by and within the various government departments and the president's office, that is, the bureaucracy and the technicians. Its major tasks in domestic politics were: (1) The pulverization of all political activity outside the national organizations provided for and controlled by the FLN, including the armed forces;[9] (2) The integration of all associations and groups, such as the General Union of Algerian Workers (UGTA), the National Union of Algerian Students (UNEA), the mujahidin (veterans), religious groups, and others into the FLN revolutionary scheme under a system of political commissars; and (3) The mobilization of unorganized masses through the multifarious agencies of the FLN.

The FLN, then, has a unique function in Algerian politics and must plan the supreme role in the attainment of the revolution's goals. As the only party in the state it is the *organe moteur puissant,* which derives its force from the people in order to destroy old structures and substitute for them a new power exercised by the masses. It organizes the masses into cadres and educates them for the realization of the Revolution: socialism, Arabism, Pan-Africanism, and neutralism. It reflects the aspirations of the masses, for it is in constant communication with them. It alone can therefore elaborate and define the policy of the nation, and it alone must control its execution. The FLN is not, however, composed of all the masses. Instead, its membership is confined to those revolutionary elements in Algeria that are most conscientious, militant, and activist. The organization of its structure therefore is based on the principle of "democratic centralism." Neither a classical presidential nor a parliamentary system can guarantee the stability of a nation as revolutionary as Algeria, especially when its regime is based on the pre-eminence of a sovereign people. Only a single party – *parti unique* – can assume this task efficiently. That is, only the FLN, as the foremost revolutionary force of the republic, can guarantee this stability, and this by ensuring the conformity of the nation's policy to the orientation traced by the Revolution for all Algerians.

On these grounds, the necessity of the *parti unique* is firmly established. But to perpetuate this necessity in the minds of the masses requires in addition the elaboration of a mystique about it. As the *force agissante* of the nation, the FLN can be the only apparatus of the Revolution. Only the FLN can make the correct and right choice of solutions for the different problems facing the Algerian state. Even if a popular mandate were to entrust another national body with certain tasks, namely, the National Constituant Assembly of 1963, such body must be subordinated to the FLN, which represents *the only mandate from the people that is possible in Algeria.* No one, that is, can share in or detract from the power of the national leadership emanating from and centred in the FLN.[10]

In short then, the party is entrusted with the total transformation of Algerian society. All other associations, groups and institutions must comply with its blueprint and plan for the Revolution. Here one may return to our initial concern about the relationship between a traditional order and a projected modern polity. Are the various proposals of the single party – that is, in fact, of its leaders – acceptable to the representatives of tradition, and does it really make a difference what the traditionalists think? Logically, this new national culture and its institutions that the Revolution proposes to develop or build should concern the traditionalists, especially when, on the surface at least, they appear to accept, if not support, the regime.

Institution-building in Algeria has, so far, been rather perfunctory and only as an appendage and additional prop to the basic organization of power. Instead of regularizing such processes as legitimacy and consensus, the regime maintains them at an elusive, fluid state, so that the intermediary between the ruler and the masses never coalesces into concrete and discrete groups, legal or other rational mechanisms and devices. The "authoritative allocation of values" in independent Algeria so far, is monolithic in nature and pyramidal in structure. This is not to say that there are no other loci for the "authoritative allocation of values" in society, for this is where the traditional influences are still operative, and a determination of their relationship to central political authority could be significant.

Under these circumstances, and given the differences between Islam in the Maghrib and Islam in the Arab societies of the Middle East, the proposition that the *za'im* subsumes all public interests in his own person and program seems to hold.[11] This is essential in view of the unmistakable difference in outlook, political attitude, and response to power between the majority of traditional Arab and non-Arab Kabyle Algerians in the countryside on the one hand, and the Westernized Arabs and Kabyles in the cities on the other. The leader must appeal to both groups by projecting a public image which combines the characteristics of an Islamic *za'ama* with those of the modern revolutionary militant. Thus, to the first group he must appear as a mahdi and to the second as a charismatic leader. The difference between these two functions of leadership is that to the first group he must qualify as the defender of the faith and tradition; to the second group he should be the leader who can best undermine this tradition in favor of a modern order.

With regard to the FLN's revolutionary program, the traditionalists claim, for instance, that the constitution proposed in 1963 was flexible, that is, acceptable to Islam and especially Islamic sentiment. And this not because of its content but simply because ben Bella was an acceptable leader. He, in turn, was acceptable because he combined in his public personality the image of a country boy whose formal education was limited to a Qoranic school and the home environment of a pious Muslim family on the one hand, with a nebulous Islamic sentiment, though possibly not actual practice of the religion, on the other. Thus, the crisis of August, 1963, over the constitution, or the ben Bella—Ferhat 'Abbas controversy, reflected the adamant refusal by classical liberals and perhaps militant leftists of a constitution dictated by the FLN. It did not in any way concern the representatives of, or spokesmen for, tradition, namely, the religious groups, or the mass of the Muslim public. In sharp contrast to the classical liberals and leftists, the traditionalists viewed ben Bella as an essentially Muslim militant activist leading an essentially Muslim brotherhood, the FLN. In their minds, ben Bella was definitely not a Westernized intellectual.

One must not assume that there is an identifiable group, or leadership, that speaks for the tradition. The interests of the tradition are instead diffused through, and protected by, its representatives in the FLN, the army, the cabinet, the UNEA, the mujahidin, and the wilayas. So long as the leadership of the Algerian revolution supports a Ministry of Habous — religious trusts — that, in turn, maintains and supervises some 8,000 village and mosque schools *(kuttab)* in the country; seeks to establish a theological institute to train religious teachers and preachers; and adopts an Arabization program of public instruction, the traditionalist Algerian associates his interests with those of the leader of the Revolution, that is, of the Democratic Popular Republic of Algeria.

The Algerian revolutionary hardly conceived the *umma,* or Islamic community, as the collectivity of the Algerian nation in terms of classes and socio-economic or other groups. Significantly, neither did he understand it in the classical theological conception, that is, as the community of believers. Rather, the Algerian revolutionary viewed the *umma* as comprising the totality of the poorer traditional masses *(al-tabaqat al-basita)*. There has been therefore a dualism in the use and understanding of the term and concept *umma*. On the one hand, the Algerian man of religion — the preacher *(khatib)* — speaks from the pulpit of the Islamic community. On the other hand, the militant revolutionary, the FLN activist, the *maquis qaid,* the soldier, and the government official speak of the Algerian nation in a populist sense *(umma sha'biyya)*. Even in designating the "Father of Algerian Nationalism," the party devotee will choose Messali Hajj, the traditional Muslim will venerate 'Abd al-Hawid ben Badis, the westernized intellectual will name Ferhat 'Abbas, the plain nonpartisan, fanatic, intellectual will mumble about an "intellectual elite," and the militant revolutionary, especially if he is an ex-*maquis,* will pronounce the names of Amir Khaled and ben Rahal. What is curious and revealing is that, even though those who led the armed phase of the Algerian independence movement were, apart from their general subscription to an Islamic sentiment, inspired primarily by the notions of European nationalism — self-determination, independence, sovereign power — the general public seems to ascribe the success of the revolution to its inspiration from the Muslim Arab East rather than to Europe. Whatever the difference in attitude between traditional and secular Algerians, one observes that the ruler today, especially in his recruitment of the cadres for his apparatus of political control in the country, tends to observe local tradition. What Ferhat 'Abbas, in his classical liberal snobbishness, has referred to as the *République des camarades, des copains,* cuts, as invective goes, no ice in an Algerian state, where strong personal rule carries the sanction of tradition.

If modern Western-type legislation is inadequate for the attainment of revolutionary goals, neither would it be acceptable to the traditionalists. If, on the other hand, Islam and Islamic reform are also inadequate for the evolution of a modern society in Algeria, a complete break from it by any leader would be disquieting, if not convulsively disrupting. Thus, neither Islamic reform nor modernist processes alone are of much use. The building of new institutions that serve a modern existence without flagrantly slighting the tradition, and their stabilization can only be justified when proposed by a *za'im* in whose personality are fused the interests of all — Islam, the party, the army, the countryside, and the city. In this capacity there is no need for an identifiable coterie of leaders to speak for the tradition, as much as we saw that there was no reason for a similar coterie to speak for classical liberalism, and to exert influence upon the political establishment in their favor. The leader serves this function in society and alone plays this role for the nation. There is therefore no need to codify the intellectual content or power of any group in the state — traditional or other. Rationalism, permitted by Islam (but in this instance European rationalism) is utilized by the ruler in the service of the revolution and the administration of the government, but intellectualism in the classical European sense is neither appropriate nor permitted. The essence of intellectualism is uncompromising — almost merciless — questioning of given premises, and an irreverence toward tradition. It is even cynical; and cynicism is anathema to a revolution.

It was suggested earlier in this discussion that the nature of the ruler in Islamic society today — at least since the thirteenth century — permits him to interpret and accommodate the religious tradition in any way he deems necessary for the realization of the goals and objectives of power. This is most apt in the case of Algeria. The French, with their policy of referring to the *musulman* population in Algeria, activated and heightened the Algerian's own identification with Islam – the *sine qua non* of his exclusiveness from the French. In fact, only when this sentiment was exercised under repressive French measures during the early stages of the war of independence did the masses begin actively to support the rebels. Before, say, 1958, the mass of Algerians may have sympathized with the *maquis,* but were hardly implicated in the war themselves. Thus, in terms of loyalty to the revolutionary leadership as well as in terms of the latter's legitimate representation of national-communal rights against the French, consensus was implicit in this *musulman* identity. Islam, in the popular-local, not the theological, sense, served not only as a link between the leaders of resistance and revolution against France and the masses, but also became the motivating force – the sense of community – that ultimately pushed these masses forward, if not to participate actively in the fighting at least to integrate their support for the rebels.

Between the period of incipient nationalist endeavor in the 1920's and the outbreak of hostilities in 1954, there was extensive thinking among both the Islamic leaders and the western secular elite about what constituted a nationalist movement and related questions. To outline and define political notions and ideas for aspiring Algerians was a proper task of leadership and a legitimate part of the process of emancipation. But the revolutionary war obviously emphasized action – indeed, it established the primacy of action over thought and speculation. Interestingly enough this primacy of action appealed to traditionalists in the countryside and secularists in the city alike. Naturally, the hero of the traditionalist became the mujahid, the active warrior in the jihad, or holy war, whereas the hero for the secularist became the *maquis,* the resistance fighter against alien, and therefore unjust, rule. It is doubtful if the transformation of the Algerian independence movement from resistance to an all-out revolutionary war could have been accomplished in 1957–58 without the mobilization of this mass Islamic sentiment. Resistance to and rebellion against French rule in the major cities of Algeria was perhaps motivated by secular notions, including the cumulative influence of leftist ideas among Algerian workers and intellectuals who had long resided in France. The leadership of the revolution also, no doubt, based its program and action upon secular considerations. But it was the force of the religious tradition that eventually aroused the Algerian masses in the countryside and among the less educated groups in the cities to resistance. It was their passionate identification with the designation *musulman* in 1957–58 that marked the turning point from resistance to rebellion.

Activism then became the common variable uniting the secular revolutionary with the Muslim militant. It is not strange therefore that a nonintellectual leader who combines both variants of this activism should emerge as the ruler immediately after independence. Not only are intellectuals by definition incomprehensible and, thus, unacceptable to the tradition-bound masses, but they were already partly discredited with the transformation of the nationalist movement into a shooting war of independence. Moreover, the intellectualism of a moderate liberal, as was hinted at earlier, is much more difficult to reconcile with a tradition-oriented mass. Upon independence, therefore, the only possible leader was the type who could insist upon a national cultural identity based on Islam; yet an identity that was expanded to embrace revolutionary goals that presumably lead to modernity.

It is only fair to say that the above presentation of the relationship between tradition and desired revolution can be misleading without a consideration of the practical realities of the Algerian political setting. It is difficult for the outsider to gauge accurately the extent of the influence exerted by considerations of tradition upon ben Bella and his ruling group as against the influence exerted by secular militant revolutionaries, say the Left. To seek accuracy would be a futile and dubious academic exercise because it would really involve guessing, not intellectual effort. The closest parallel of such dubious academic exercise would be the various attempts made by students of group politics directly to relate the influence of a particular interest group upon a specific executive policy decision by a government, for example, the influence of a Zionist organization upon a specific policy decision by the White House. The trouble is that we can never know exactly all the other influences operative at the same time to assert without doubt a direct relationship.

Confusion in Algeria stems from the fact that while the regime encouraged the Islamic-Arab dimension of the national culture campaign – the Ministry of Habous, for instance, expanded the activities of Qoranic schools – it gave a free hand to the so-called radical, secular leftist group of ideologues in the propagation of a socialist revolutionary doctrine. This was particularly the case in the important presidential agency, the National Bureau for the Activation of the Socialist Sectors (BNASS). The latter, dominated by sundry exiled Trotskyites – among them Raptis of Greece and Loutfallah Soliman of Egypt – verbalized in popular fashion through Marxist terminology the basic aims and dogmas of the democratic popular revolution. To this group, *za'ama*-type leadership was logically unattractive and, in the final analysis, unacceptable. Organized labor, such as the UGTA, sympathized with this position and felt that a charismatic *za'im* is by definition anathema to political group existence.

Another source of confusion in Algeria was the subtle difference between the attitude to tradition of the educated Algerian, who has a more sophisticated and discriminating grasp of European culture and civilization, and that of his educated Arab brother in the Middle East. Despite the realities of the situation and the requirements of the moment, a *za'im* is not as easily rationalized by these elements in the Algerian population, let alone accepted. They manifest a greater understanding of the political processes necessary for a regularized relationship between authority and the public. It is for these and other reasons that measured scepticism about the Arabization program emanated from such groups. In direct opposition to the traditionalists, who consider Arabization essential to the fulfillment of the Algerian revolution, these secularists charged its exponents with unrealism. The bureaucrats, for example, argued that the cost of implementing the program with any measure of success is so staggering as to be beyond the means of Algeria. The secularists furthermore distrusted the Arabization program because of the infiltration possibilities into Algeria that it offers to quarrelsome Arab states via teacher aid, the supply of Arab textbooks, and so on. Yet no group could afford to reject the program off-hand, for two reasons. First, the program could not be dissociated from the prevailing cultural and religious sentiment. Second, it presented a forceful argument as a countermeasure to the fragmentation of Algerian society allegedly fostered for a long time by the French-inspired policy of "Berberization." For ben Bella, of course, Arabization was politically indispensable.

The Revolution was not, however, without its serious practical problems. One of the earliest for President ben Bella immediately upon the disbanding of the Provisional Government (GPRA) was the establishment and maintenance of public order. Directly related to the question of public order was the urgent need to provide the minimum requirements of a viable economy, to restore a functioning bureaucracy, and provide at least skeleton public services. Conditions became chaotic, for within a month of independence some 800,000 out of an estimated 1.2 million Europeans left the country. Having been responsible for most technical, educational, and public services, European personnel were not immediately replaceable by Algerians. The importation and re-importation of French personnel — especially technicians, teachers, and other experts — became, along with the need for funds, a necessity for a freshly independent, anti-French government. Schools, for example, were barely kept open, largely through the massive availability of French teachers. Moreover, none of these crises could have been weathered by the new government without massive French economic, financial, and technical assistance, and the presence of French troops in the country.

The return, or repatriation, of Algerian war refugees from Tunisia and Morocco presented for the government an immediate major rehabilitation problem. Many of these refugees had fled Algeria as small children (average age nine years) and had a bitter, albeit vague, recollection of the ravages of the war. Their bitterness could now be assuaged only by the ability of their national government to offer them a better life. Farmers whose villages and lands had been burnt or razed during the hostilities had to be grouped temporarily in centers scattered in the country; and this proved an enormously expensive operation. A group of some 300,000 veterans of the revolutionary war soon confronted the government with demands for jobs, housing, and other benefits. In addition to the veterans, a large number of war-widows and orphans constituted another major welfare problem for the government.[12]

These are only a few examples of the serious practical problems that faced the Algerian government in the summer of 1963. It is estimated that more than 2 million Algerians are unemployed. So far, many Algerians can still go to France for work. If this were to stop suddenly, the unemployment in the country would become oppressive. To provide a living and security for millions of Algerians is a human necessity. In the case of a so-called revolutionary one-party regime, it is also a political necessity. The *za'ama* of the leader — in fact, all his claims to save the nation — could hinge upon his performance in absorbing and resolving these difficulties.

Germaine Tillion, with her theory of "pauperization," may have come closer to the reality of the prospects of political development in Algeria, as well as in other states led by national revolutionary regimes.[13] What may happen is that a new privileged class — privileged, that is, by virtue of its proximity to a powerful claimant leader — will get farther removed from the masses, whose level of existence will not rise appreciably. And one might be left with the age-old political formula of "command-obey," the ruler and the ruled, the haves and the have nots. In the circumstances, another claimant leader may rise to lead the masses along the path of his formula for salvation, and so on, ad infinitum.

Most new nations have discovered that the real struggle for power begins on Independence Day.[14] Thus, when Algeria became independent in July, 1962, there were a number of qualified persons and groups to lead the new state. It is either to the credit of ben Bella, or to circumstances, or to both that he led for a while the Democratic and Popular Republic of Algeria. For one must consider that, first, ben Bella had been virtually out of the war of independence since his capture by the French in 1956. Second, he had no direct part in the Evian talks or in the resulting agreement. Yet within a few weeks after his release and independence of his country, he succeeded in ousting the members of the Provisional Government, many of whom had really fought for independence; attracted the support of the army commanded by Colonel Boumedienne; and drew up a list of acceptable nominees for the National Constituent Assembly. Within a year from that time, he strengthened the FLN by purging it of all possible antagonists, making it the only party permitted in the new state, as well as the apparatus for his power and control.

In its first year the Constituent Assembly still included potential competition to ben Bella, but by August, 1963, all opponents and critics had been eliminated, clearing the way for the subsequent referendum in September for the adoption of a new constitution. The latter was drawn up by the FLN and not, as one would expect, by the Constituent Assembly. Earlier that spring, the labor organizations of the UGTA were brought under control of the FLN, as was the UGEMA, the Federation of Algerian Students, during their congress in August, 1963. Presidential elections followed that gave ben Bella a five-year mandate as chief of state, head of government, chief of party and, as some caustic critics put it, "Mr. Algeria." The resentment he left behind along the ruthless path to power smoldered mainly below the surface. What was the secret, if any, of ben Bella's success? In this essay, the argument has been developed that there is no secret in the success of this kind of leadership that is typically appropriate to the Algerian environment. Yet, to consider this question further, one must, besides the conception of claimant leadership, emphasize a characteristic aspect of Algerian nationalism as it developed toward an independence movement that differs from the experience of many other Arab and African states.

Given the easy access to France, great numbers of Algerians, especially from the coastal districts and the Kabyle country, went there as workers. Many among them lived there for very long periods of time. Despite their relatively poor social and economic condition, their very presence in France gave them a practical awareness of the political. One could almost describe them as Muslim peasants, who came closest to being "proletarian." Another group of Muslim Algerians, probably coming from similar backgrounds, were afforded closer contact with the modern age as soldiers in the French Army. Still another class of Algerians, largely from the cities and possibly from higher economic status groups, also received intimate knowledge of Europe through study and long sojourns in France. These were the members of the liberal professions. So that the material for a revolutionary force and elite came from a cross-section of the Algerian population, not merely from notables, intellectuals, and rich businessmen. Without this wider and mixed group, an organized revolutionary war of long duration would have been most difficult, if not impossible.

These conditions in part explain the attitude of the revolutionaries in 1954–55 who, upon the start of hostilities against the French, defined two structures as basic to the Revolution. First, they declared the FLN as the only political organization in Algeria that represented and spoke for all Algerian nationalist groups. Second, they declared the National Liberation Army (ALN) as the sole military establishment responsible for the organization and coordination of underground activities against the French. Yet, it appears now that only the masses of militant Algerians accepted these two structures unconditionally. The so-called intellectuals among the Algerian nationalists never reconciled themselves to this arrangement. Moreover, after independence it was easier for the militant — and nonmilitant — masses to accept the command and rule of these two structures partly because of what the *za'im* claimed about their indispensability for the postindependence revolution. It is for these and other reasons that one must look at the evolution of the Algerian nationalist movement, and the relationship of the leader to the tradition-oriented masses within it.

An astute assessment of ben Bella by Jean Daniel, a writer for the French leftist paper *L'Express,* appeared in a July, 1962, issue of *The New Republic.* Daniel was perhaps correct in stating that ben Bella was not completely opportunistic or entirely cynical. The problem, as this writer sees it, is that far from being cynical ben Bella was apocalyptically messianic. Despite the fact that within a year after independence his leadership was contested by the *maquis,* the Kabyles, the trade unions, the intellectuals, and the students and, in 1964, by the Left, he was popular with the masses. To the vast mass of Algerians, especially the ones whose Islamic religious sentiment and tradition are still meaningful and unshaken by their brush with secular ideas, ben Bella was a popular *za'im* — the popular fighting hero captured by the French; the native son who suffered while languishing in French captivity. Did this *za'ama* help ben Bella to withstand the attacks from the rather articulate groups of Algerian proletarians, students, and intellectuals, or was his survival strictly due to his alliance with the army and to the massive French financial and other aid to his regime in its last two years? One cannot minimize either of the latter two sources of support. Yet one must recognize the leader's successful rapport with the masses, especially when ben Bella showed that he could eliminate his adversaries effectively without weakening his power and authority in the country. Ben Bella may have won the consensus of the Algerian masses to his claimant leadership by showing his mistrust of secular elements who can easily be associated in the minds of the tradition-oriented masses with alien non-Muslim ideas.[15]

To say that a leader like ben Bella was convinced of his charisma, his *za'ama,* is not enough. It may even be that the *baraka,* or blessing, that emanates from a Moroccan king next door, was outdone by the anointed leader in Algeria. But even though charisma and the "politics of the anointed" are forceful means in rallying and mobilizing the masses they are not sufficient for the governing of a state. In addition to these, ben Bella showed great organizing ability. In great measure this was due to the existence of a coterie of imaginative young men around him, whose average age was between thirty and forty, namely, Bouteflika, Hajj ben Ala, Hajj Smaine, and others. All of them seemed to believe, as ben Bella did, in the primacy of governmental action and in the idea that the state must pre-empt all political activity. The need, that is, for authoritarian structures was not apparently questioned by the elite of the revolution.

Daniel argued that there was no dictatorship in Algeria; that the country was not Egypt or Spain. He contended that the explanation of ben Bella's success lay in the realities of the Algerian revolution and supported this contention with the example of self-motivated agricultural workers who, on their own initiative, took over abandoned French farms. Whatever these "realities of the Algerian revolution" are, I have suggested here a set of conditions relating to leadership that one can argue as being inherent in Algerian society, that is, an Islamic society.

Malcolm Kerr has argued the proposition that the leadership of revolution in the Arab states subscribes to "radical notions of democracy."[16] The general trend of his argument at least is modeled after Talmon's conception of "totalitarian democracy." This kind of argument is useful in elaborating upon the more fundamental proposition that all revolutions that are based on the "sovereignty of the people" detract from the freedom of individuals and may clarify the movement for group liberation, recognition, and status. The argument is also useful for an interpretation of revolution in Europe but misleading when applied to an Islamic environment. Islamic society was, by virtue of its "first revolution" in the seventh century, committed to the realization of a strong state, not by any ideological or philosophical combat of a particular elite in it but by the militant action of a commander — a ruler — to whom allegiance and obedience by the believers is due as a matter of faith. He led the community of believers in this struggle — a struggle, moreover, that did not preclude in the past, and should not preclude in the future, militant combat.

Many writers on modern European political history have discussed the powerful psychological attachment of the masses to a leader in times of crisis. Some have described this condition as "caesaristic identification"; others as mass national mania over "conspiratorial theories of history," and so on. All of them, however, identified these conditions as symptoms of political alienation, largely because the emancipated Western man is not supposed to degenerate into mere cattle in a herd.[17] The Muslim, this essay has suggested — even our contemporary Muslim — does not consider this attachment of the masses to the forceful leader as alienation. This is a crucial and fundamental difference.

Notes

1. This essay was written in 1964. The army coup led by Colonel Boumedienne which ousted ben Bella from power in June 1965 is an indication of the extent to which the latter depended on his alliance with his army chief. On the other hand, reported demonstrations protesting his imprisonment and the stringent measures taken by Boumedienne to quash this display of support for ben Bella are an indication of the latter's popularity. It should be noted, however, that in states where the military remains the final arbiter of political power — where authority is not clearly distinguished from power — such popularity is, in a crisis, politically impotent.

2. Such claim to leadership, moreover, could not have been put forward by the Sharif Husain without the decision of British officials in the Middle East to support him to the

exclusion of other, perhaps equally worthy contenders, at the time, in return for his rebellion against the Ottoman state. See on this question, Elie Kedourie, *England and the Middle East* (London and New York: Oxford University Press, 1956), and "Cairo and Khartoum on the Arab Question, 1915–1918," *The Historical Journal*, VII, No. 2 (1964), 280–97.

3. On personalized power and an interesting interpretation of the *za'im*, see Hisham B. Sharabi, "Power and Leadership in the Arab World," *Orbis*, VII, No. 3 (Fall, 1963), 583–95.

4. On the term and concept *siyasa*, see Ibn-al-Muqaffa', *Al-adab al-saghir wa al-adab al-kabir* (Beirut, 1960); Ibn al-Tiqtaqa, *Al-Fakhri fi al-adab al-sultaniyya wa al-duwal al-islamiyya* (Cairo, 1899 and 1945) (English edition: *Al-Fakhri on the Systems of Government and the Moslem Dynasties*, trans. E. J. Whiting (London: Luzac, 1947); Ibn al-Furat, *Tarikh Ibn al-Furat*, Costi Zurayk (Beirut, 1936).

5. The Egyptian Ahmad Lutfi al-Sayyid (d. 1963) was an exception insofar as he attempted to construct and argue a concept of "civic virtue" and a viable political system based to some extent on the idea of reconciliation and compromise between individual and social interests *(al-maslaha al-'amma:* at times rendered the "public interest" and at others the "public good," depending on the context). See his *Muntakhabat (Selected Essays)* (Cairo, 1945); *Ta'ammulat fi al-siyasa wa al-adab wa alithima' (Reflections on Politics, Literature, and Society)* (Cairo, 1963).

6. See Gabriel Almond and James S. Coleman (eds.), *The Politics of the Developing Areas* (Princeton, N.J.: Princeton University Press, 1960). See also Robert E. Ward, "Political Modernization and Political Culture in Japan," *World Politics*, XV (July, 1963), 569–96. Leonard Binder, *Iran: Political Development in Changing Society* (Berkeley: University of California Press, 1962), is more careful with his attention to concepts and realities native to Iranian society, so that at certain points in his discussion he renders his interpretations more meaningful and plausible. But he undermines his ability to gauge theoretical concepts with reality by an oppressibly abstract theoretical framework, which is often both slippery and obscure. One of the stronger pleas for the relevant study of traditional forces in the "development" of new states appeared recently which significantly reveals the growing disillusionment with recent studies of political development. See Ann Ruth Willner, "The Underdeveloped Study of Political Development," *World Politics*, XVI, No. 3 (April, 1964), 468–82.

7. See his *The Revolt of the Masses* (New York: Mentot, 1961).

8. See P. J. Vatikiotis, "Islam and the Foreign Politic of Egypt," in J. H. Proctor (ed), *Islam and International Relations* (New York: Praèger, 1965), pp. 120–57.

9. Note that the army has had its own political bureau, which issued at least in 1963 a weekly political magazine *el-Djeich (The Army)* in Oran. The relationship – cordial or strained – between this politbureau and that of the FLN was very difficult to ascertain in 1963. But it indicates the inability of the FLN to exercise full control over the army.

10. Unfortunately, many of the cadres for the *parti unique* were not selected or recruited for any reasons of administrative competence or political ability but mainly for services rendered during the war of liberation. In the outlying areas of the country, especially in the eastern provinces, deteriorating economic conditions, from unemployment to abject poverty, do not endear the eagle-eyed ubiquitous party officials to the masses. Instead, as was shown recently – September-October 1964 – the public in these areas view these FLN militant minions as seekers of privilege and material gain. See especially the editorial columns of the Constantine newspaper *al-Nasr* for this widening gulf between the public and local FLN commissars.

11. In this connection, it would be interesting to inquire, for instance, into the influence – as distinguished from the power – of political leaders and rulers like the late Premier Nuri al-Sa'id of Iraq, and the late King Abdullah of Jordan.

12. One of the most heated debates in the National Constituent Assembly in August, 1963, took place over the so-called Algerian "GI Bill of Rights": who was a veteran *(mujahid),* and what benefits should the state grant him.

13. See her *Algeria: The Realities* (New York: Alfred A. Knopf, 1958).

14. A journalist, Brian Crozier, recently attempted to dramatize this problem in popular fashion with a book he called *Independence, The Morning After* (London: Oxford University Press, 1964).

15. The opposition from the Front of Socialist Forces (FFS), led by such men as Hocine Ait Ahmed and Boudiaf, against the ben Bella regime stiffened in 1964. Much of the support for the FFS came from the Kabyles. Yet, given the serious economic difficulties in

Algeria, especially unemployment, the FFS seemed to be recruiting active followers — or at least sympathetic listeners — from the unemployed masses demanding "work and bread." The outbursts in Oran and the Aurès in 1964 are a case in point. But even though one may conclude that there is a "socialist" force in Algeria that is opposed to the "socialism" of the state, the struggle for power remains very much one between two types of leaders, both of whom must depend for their success on their peculiar relationship with the masses. And this relationship is either traditionally perceived, as in the case of the Muslim Arab masses, or tribally determined, as in the case of the Kabyles.

16. "Arab Radical Notions of Democracy," St. Antony's Papers, No. 16, ed. Albert Hourani, *Middle Eastern Affairs,* No. 3 (London, 1963), pp. 9–40.

17. See, for example, Franz Neumann, *The Democratic and Authoritarian State* (Glencoe, Ill.: The Free Press, 1957); Erich Fromm, *Escape from Freedom* (New York: Holt, Rinehart, 1941); and others.

29

THE DECLINE OF ALGERIA'S FLN

WILLIAM H. LEWIS

The National Liberation Front (FLN), which served as both the embodiment and the engine of the Algerian liberation struggle during the period 1954–62, has fallen upon unhappy days. After independence was assured on July 5, 1962, the FLN lost its vaunted *élan,* its leadership fell into a demoralizing pattern of intramural rivalry, and the movement became deprived of its momentum and sense of purpose. In an age of one-party states, the FLN remains Algeria's *parti unique.* However, the Front's prestige has evaporated, and its national status has become largely symbolic.

The rise and decline of the FLN in considerable measure mirrors the painful process of social change in which Algeria has become enmeshed – as well as the dislocations, contradictions, and incompatibilities that more than seven years of conflict with France have produced. The June 19, 1965, *coup de main* by the army, under the direction of Colonel Houari Boumedienne, merely brought into public view the failure and bankruptcy of the *parti unique* as well as President Ahmed ben Bella, in coming to grips with the problems of change. As a result, the FLN's heroic image has become blurred, and Algeria remains a nation of parts waiting to be stitched together in a viable whole.

Maurice Duverger has observed that: "Just as men bear all their lives the mark of their childhood, so parties are profoundly influenced by their origins."[1] The FLN was born in a Kafkaesque world of plots and clandestinity, one characterized by authoritarian French administration, frustrated Muslim aspirations, and extreme factionalism within the existing hierarchies of nationalist leadership. Efforts at representative government under the terms of the 1947 Organic Statute for Algeria had been frustrated by *colon* maneuvers that resulted in the manufacture of tame Muslim majorities and the near exclusion of nationalists from municipal and other councils. Intimidation, harassment, and repression were also employed to cow more refractory Muslims. Rights to participation in the affairs of government clearly were to be measured out only to temporally faithful and politically safe aspirants.

The pre-1954 nationalist leadership failed to develop either a mass basis for political action or a coherent set of principles with which to meet the realities of

Reprinted, by permission, from *The Middle East Journal,* XX, No. 2 (Spring, 1966), 161–72.

French power. Ferhat 'Abbas, the product of a bourgeois background and French culture, had sought concessions through negotiation, compromise, mutual accommodation – and failed. His Democratic Union of the Algerian Manifesto, essentially representative of urban-middle-class groups, went into steady eclipse with its inability to secure a favorable hearing during sessions of the Second Constituent Assembly held in Paris in mid-1946. By contrast, 'Abbas' principal competitor, Messali Hajj, violently opposed his policy of integration with France, calling instead for total and immediate independence. The Messalist Movement for the Triumph of Democratic Liberties (MTLD) sought the support of working-class groups, rather than that of the new middle class and Algeria's slim number of professionals. The MTLD foundered, however, as a result of French repression, internal factionalism, and Messali's abrasive efforts to personalize leadership of the party rather than bolster existing collegial arrangements.[2]

The failure of the prewar nationalist leadership proved all the more glaring in the midst of the steady deterioration occurring within the Muslim sector of Algerian society. An ineluctable cycle of population growth, resultant pressure upon the land, land hunger, and limited agricultural credit was creating a rural *lumpenproletariat* of disinherited agriculturalists. Approximately 4.5 million Algerians became caught up in this cycle of *clochardisation* (pauperization).[3] For those seeking redress in the cities, life proved only slightly more rewarding. The overwhelming majority of Muslim Algerians, for example, were consigned in 1954 to the roles of casual day-laborers, an unskilled human reservoir for European-controlled commercial and other enterprises. At the onset of the liberation struggle, Algeria embraced three societies – the traditional, the transitional, and the modern. The traditional and transitional were the milieu of the Muslims, the modern the preserve of the Europeans.

The inability of the existing nationalist leadership to engage in more than political ritualizations produced a reaction of dissatisfaction and, finally, apathy within the Muslim community. As for the Messalist movement, influence increasingly tended to be based upon a corrosive calculus of personal relationships, with Messali himself unwilling to play any lesser role than that of *za'im*. The MTLD was fragmenting badly, losing its sense of direction.

The FLN was born as a reaction to these circumstances. Indeed, the outbreak of insurgency on November 1, 1954, has been only partially understood. Its immediate target was French power, but, even more crucially, the attacks marked a break with the previous generation of nationalist leadership. In its profoundest sense, the insurgent leaders also were rebelling against incompetence, the liberalism and moderation of "bourgeois" leadership, the doctrinaire pretensions of the Messalist intellectuals and the "cult of personality" being fostered by Messali himself. The leadership of the new force reflected less concern with political doctrine than with political action, channeling its energies into effective "revolutionism." What social conscience it embodied focused principally upon the people – their condition, well-being, and advancement.

The forerunner of the FLN, the Revolutionary Committee of Unity and Action (CRUA), was founded by nine chieftains[4] who accepted the principle of collegial leadership and responsibility. Based in Cairo, the CRUA established an underground network of approximately 500 commandos organized into five military operational zones (wilayas). In October, 1954, the CRUA redesignated itself the FLN.

Significantly, the leadership of the FLN sprang largely from two sources, the lower working classes of urban Algeria and the peasantry. However, at the outset, the rebellion was rural based, concentrated mainly in the Aurès and Kabylia mountain regions. Thus, at a second level of reality, the insurgency reflected a shift of nationalist orientation away from urban areas to the heartland of contemporary Algeria, the countryside.

WARTIME EXIGENCIES AND EVOLUTION

The course of the struggle between France and the FLN has been studied in sufficient depth elsewhere and, consequently, will not long detain us here. It is perhaps sufficient to note that hatred, cruelty, and hypocrisy belong to no single party, the excesses of war to no single combatant. All war is an atrocity. However, the Muslim community clearly suffered some massive shocks. More than 250,000 Algerians were killed and probably twice that number wounded; 2 million rural peasants were uprooted and placed in "resettlement" centers; billions of dollars in damage to farms and rural property generally was inflicted; more than 300,000 Algerians fled the country to settle temporarily as refugees in neighboring Morocco and Tunisia.

Within the FLN, the first flush of success soon gave way to a lengthy, enervating process of guerrilla warfare. The bulk of the indigenous population reacted with reserve to the emergence of the FLN, unhappy with nationalist exactions, fearful of retaliation for noncompliance, but equally anxiety ridden lest compliance engender French reprisals. (In the end, the French tendency to treat most Muslims as actual or potential enemies made double jeopardy an intolerable situation and led the bulk of Algerians to support the FLN either tacitly or openly.)

The old guard nationalist leadership reacted with stunned surprise to the FLN's emergence. During the first fourteen months of insurgency, the Algerian Communist Party, Association of 'Ulema and 'Abbas's UDMA viewed the FLN with neutral detachment. (Communist efforts at later infiltration failed; subsequent attempts to form its own *maquis* produced severe collisions with the FLN and a collapse of these endeavors.) The MTLD supporters of Messali, however, refused to endorse the FLN and engaged in a series of "café wars" with the latter in both Algiers and Paris. The effort ultimately failed, and Messali passed into political oblivion. By mid-1956, most of the erstwhile nationalist groups rallied to the FLN; in April, Ferhat 'Abbas escaped to Cairo, where he formally pledged fealty.

This shift of loyalties produced a severe internal crisis for the FLN. While its operational military arm, the National Liberation Army (ALN), gained in recruits and *élan,* the political apparatus was radically transformed. No longer could it function as a tightly interrelated coordinating body embracing field commanders and politico-military specialists. The sheer number of new recruits, their disparate origins and political persuasions, and the need to heal past animosities resulted in a profound metamorphosis. The FLN, in essence, became transformed from a Jacobin organization of closely-knit conspirators into a rambling, loose-jointed political movement embracing a wide range of activists, opportunists, and ideologues. Success in the field led inexorably to diffusion of power and dilution of standards.

Simultaneously, strains began to crystallize between military field commanders — under continuous pressure from the French — and their civilian counterparts. During the initial period of FLN insurgency, the close ties of political and military elements had produced a relatively smooth working relationship. Indeed, the external leadership frequently visited operational zones and, not infrequently, so-called "civilian" leaders assumed military commands in Algeria. However, the new non-military recruits proved less adventuresome, concerning themselves with diplomatic endeavors, propaganda campaigns and the formation of a government in exile. The death of some of the FLN founding fathers in the field, as well as the capture of ben Bella and four senior colleagues as the result of a French ruse in October 1956, simply widened the breach and alienated the ALN. After ben Bella's incarceration, civilian leadership passed slowly but inexorably into the hands of moderates such as Ferhat 'Abbas and Benyussef ben Khedda [who formed the Provisional Government of the Algerian Republic (GPRA)].

In an effort to shore up the organization and discipline of the FLN, the military leaders convened a "congress" in the Soumman region of the Kabylia during August, 1956. The conferees agreed on the need to develop more effective coordination of the civilian and military services through a collegial system of leadership. Full authority and control was invested in a thirty-four member National Council of the Algerian Revolution (CNRA). Executive responsibility was lodged in a five-man Committee of Coordination and Execution (CCE). The latter body was dominated by the internal military command, or wilayists.

These new bodies only briefly submerged the strains that were developing within the FLN, however. Indeed, the subsequent creation of a general staff with Colonel Boumedienne as its chief only exacerbated the situation. For, with the mounting effectiveness of the French in sealing off the Moroccan and Tunisian frontiers, deep fissures began to materialize within the Algerian military. In the years immediately prior to independence, Colonel Boumedienne succeeded in organizing an external army of 30,000 to 40,000 men in Morocco and Tunisia. Unable to cross the frontier as a result of French electrified barriers and fortifications, the external army became the primary beneficiary of Communist world arms and war matériel being supplied to the ALN. Ultimately, an imbalance developed between the wilayists and the external army — one that was deeply resented by harassed commanders in the field. By early 1962, on the eve of victory, the FLN had become a fragmented movement held together only by the common desire for independence for Algeria.

THE POSTWAR SORTING OUT PROCESS

The signing of the Evian Accords with France, in March, 1962, spelled the successful conclusion of one revolution and the continuation of a second, more profound struggle. Independence simply unleashed all the intrinsically fissiparous forces which had been accommodated within the FLN. There rapidly emerged divisions between such existing leaders as ben Khedda and the founding fathers (ben Bella and Khider), the wilayists and the external army, the external army and the government in exile, the negotiators of the Evian Accords and the Jacobin activists, Arabs and Berbers, Algerians in France and those lodged in the mother country. At issue were wartime misdemeanors, ideology, ethnic ties, loyalties to particular personalities, and competing perspectives on the nature of postindependence Algerian society. At stake was the locus of political power in this society. The absence of mutual trust and confidence meant that the competition would descend to the level of conflict where political survival would be involved.

Factionalism and deep-seated antagonism surfaced during the meeting of the FLN National Council at Tripoli (Libya) in June, 1962. An atmosphere of passion prevailed throughout the sessions and when it became clear that ben Bella commanded a clear majority of the council, the moderates under ben Khedda walked out. The Tripoli confabulations, nevertheless, are seminal because of the reform "program" which was fashioned. This "program" has come to be accepted as the hallowed guideline for political action by the FLN leadership. Its essential elements are as follows:

1.   The war of weapons is to be succeeded by ideological combat, one stressing the "construction" of a nation within the framework of socialist principles.

2.   The work of national reconstruction will embrace all Algerians; class interest will be suppressed. Algerian culture is to be revolutionary, national, and scientific.

3.   The leadership will foster an agrarian revolution in which the land will belong to those who work it. This will include the "modernization of agriculture."

4.   Ultimately, the FLN will sponsor the nationalization of credit, foreign trade, mineral resources, and resources of energy.

5.   To realize the social aspirations of the masses, the FLN dedicates itself to the progressive improvement in living standards, the elimination of illiteracy, acceleration of efforts to improve health conditions and emancipate women.

6.   In foreign affairs, the FLN is to be in the forefront of movements assisting in the liberation of colonial dependencies, fighting imperialism and striving for Arab and African unity.

Significantly, the Tripoli program defines the relationship between the party and the state as being somewhat akin to that of a horse and rider. The FLN clearly is to be the rider. It will establish the guidelines of policy and maintain firm control over the reins by assuring that the head of government and the majority of ministers are members of the FLN — and, by inference, accountable to the FLN's Political Bureau.

The 1963 constitution legitimizes the dominant position of the FLN within the state. For example, the FLN designates candidates for the National Assembly (Article 23), presumably under a list system. In addition, it is to elect the president of the republic (Article 34). The FLN, which is endorsed as Algeria's *parti unique* (Article 56), is to define national policy, "inspire the action of the state," and control the National Assembly and government (Article 59).

Ironically, however, the constitution merely enshrined a myth — the FLN had lost its revolutionary *élan* by late 1963; the party's supremacy was sacrificed on the altar of personal ambition.

Out of the welter of conflicting interests and groups, ben Bella, Khider, and Boumedienne emerged as the ruling *troika*. Ben Bella, however, was clearly the dominant personality, his rise to power the product of cool and calculated manipulation of forces and personalities. Having no direct control over the national groups operating in Algeria, ben Bella identified himself with those external elements which were likely to play a major postindependence role — army groups under Colonel Boumedienne's control, cliques concerned with planning a major reconstruction of Algerian society and elements favoring Arab unity. By not immediately endorsing the Evian Accords, he seemed to rebuff the GPRA leadership — a posture that endeared him to Boumedienne, the 'Abbas clique, and the Pan-Arabists. His instincts proved correct when, after June, 1962, it became clear that local wilaya commanders were not willing to accept GPRA authority, and that some actually were seeking to consolidate and perpetuate their local fiefs.

As a result, ben Bella rapidly came to be identified as Algeria's primary unifying symbol. Having formed a consortium with Colonel Boumedienne (whom, ben Khedda had attempted to depose as chief of staff of the ALN), ben Bella marched on Algiers in mid-1962 and, through a series of carefully staged maneuvers, assumed the mantle of prime minister. One year later he was overwhelmingly elected president under the new constitution, which gave him overriding powers.

Over the succeeding two years, ben Bella moved adeptly to consolidate his own position, often at the expense of admirers and supporters. One by one each of his erstwhile backers were pushed from the center of the political stage. Mohammed Khider, an important tactician, broke with the president over the role of the military; Hocine Ait Ahmed defected over doctrinal differences; Ferhat 'Abbas resigned as head of the National Assembly because of the government's authoritarian bent and flagrant violation of the Assembly's mandate. Belqasim Krim, ben Khedda, Boussouf, and Boudiaf also broke with their chief. In addition, ben Bella, through his constant political somersaults, alienated numerous other leaders, some of whom launched resistance movements in the more inaccessible reaches of central and eastern Algeria.

The consequences of these maneuvers proved disastrous for the FLN. Almost immediately, it was deprived of its most experienced and talented wartime leaders. Their defection led to the loss of considerable numbers of key personnel from the Kabylia region, Constantine, and Oran.

The exodus of 900,000 Europeans led to defections of other personnel for positions in the civil bureaucracy, local administration, and various ancillary services. While many retained membership within the FLN, their basic loyalties shifted to the new elites that crystallized within the vacuum created by the departure of Europeans. As members of new interest groups, their identity and ambitions tended to mesh with the "elite opportunism" of the civil bureaucracy. As a result, few grids of cooperation developed between the bureaucracy and the FLN, one of the salient goals of the Tripoli program.

Finally, divested of its best qualified personnel, FLN ranks became swollen with opportunists, claimants to prestige predicated upon war time exploits, and rural peasants anxious to secure full employment. An amorphous mass, on the whole, this membership was undisciplined, disorganized, and rarely paid dues. The political sorting-out process proved costly in terms of morale, *élan vital,* and prestige. The FLN remained an eclectic movement. It has yet to be transformed into a coherent, viable political party.

CURRENT EVIDENCE OF DECOMPOSITION

During the period June, 1962–June, 1965, the letter of the revolution, codified in the Tripoli Program, became separated from its spirit. The FLN no longer attracted a large following as new citadels of power arose in the army, labor unions, and the civil bureaucracy. The overwhelming majority of Algerians gave evidence of disillusionment, retreating often into sheer apathy, concerning themselves primarily with the pressing needs of food and work. The country's younger generation, unable to compete with war veterans for preferred positions within the FLN, sought escape to France or other forms of detachment from the schismatic politics of their elders.

Ben Bella's style of governance also did little to ensure confidence among a war-weary population. Born in an environment of peasant poverty and bred in an atmosphere of clandestine nationalist plotting, ben Bella proved a divisive rather than a unifying leader. Neither an intellectual nor inclined towards the theoretical, ben Bella engaged in forms of political narcissism that added to discontent. In addition, he increasingly surrounded himself with advisors of questionable competence. Often provoked to take unwise actions as a result of their counsel, he generated uncertainty and anxiety among the faithful. For example, he not infrequently repeated the allegations of a number of Marxist and Trotskyite advisors that the government and party apparatus was infiltrated by "counterrevolutionaries, incompetents, and bourgeois elements" bent upon the short-circuiting of the Algerian experiment in socialism. The by-product of these charges was the further demoralization of loyal and competent officials.

As might be expected, overlapping authority and jurisdictional responsibility created under the 1963 constitution added to the malaise, both for the FLN and government officialdom at local and regional levels. For instance, each official tended to be judged more in terms of his political loyalty and willingness to work with FLN organizations than his rapport with the local population or his skill as a coordinator of diverse services. The *functionnaire* was expected to share his duties with local FLN party representatives. (Moreover, to the extent that military commanders were required to cope with unstable security situations, the prefect was compelled to share his powers with the army.) This confused situation frequently produced a near paralysis of all three instrumentalities.

President ben Bella took official cognizance of these difficulties during the first national congress of the FLN, convened at Algiers in April, 1964. Bringing together 1,700 delegates, including army representatives, labor delegates, and workers from the "socialized sector," the congress was expected to sort out the differences among various competing groups within the ruling establishment. Speaking at the opening session, the president set forth FLN responsibilities in the following broad terms:

> We must edit and institute the laws of the state. We must react vigorously against formalism, the bureaucratic formalism of central administrations

against local administrations, and of administrations in general toward the administered. . . . [We] have three stages of urgency. First, to start with an initial reorganization of the communes through integration of the committees of socialist animation. . . . Secondly, to exercise a vigorous control of state organs. Thirdly, to create effective control on the level of the Political Bureau. . . . collecting all suggestions or criticism from the militants . . . which will make it possible to correct errors, to put an end to abuses of power . . . and to the ostracism of which authentically revolutionary militants are at times the victims.

Despite his call for the transformation of the FLN into a "driving force" to ensure the success of Algeria's "socialist revolution," ben Bella met with a severe rebuff by the assembled delegates, who overwhelmingly voted support for the preservation of traditional Islamic principles as guidelines for "socialism." Revolutionary ardor clearly was not the mood of the congress.

These setbacks led ben Bella and his advisors to cast about for appropriate models for developing the FLN into a viable political instrument. In addition to the inspiration provided by Cuba and the United Arab Republic, the president's Marxist coterie also sought to enlist his support for a conscious acceptance of the Soviet prototype. This would have involved the securing of Russian advisers (or, alternately, specialists from a West European organ such as the Italian Communist Party), the establishment of greater disciplinary controls, and the inculcation of Marxist doctrine among the rank and file. The approach, however, would fly in the face of the clearly expressed opposition of the 1964 congress delegates to "scientific socialism."

Ben Bella, in effect, was confronted with an exceedingly painful dilemma. Anxious to enlarge his base of support within the FLN, he had opened its ranks to widespread popular recruitment. However, his membership drive had ensnared personal supporters of essentially conservative outlooks. This mass mobilization approach was not yielding dividends. On the other hand, to transform the FLN into an élitist *apparat* along classical Communist lines would risk popular alienation and possible bloodshed. Realizing that the FLN was in disarray and increasingly ineffective politically, ben Bella decided upon the Communist model.

At the time of the 1964 congress, the FLN announced that its ranks comprised 153,000 militants and 620,000 associated members. They reportedly were organized into 17 federations, 109 *dairas,* and 1,112 *kasmas.* To cope with the establishment of needed discipline and *élan,* an ideological commission was formed under the control of the 80-member central committee. In addition, a purification committee was organized to inspect the credentials and reliability of FLN militants. Finally, political commissars were attached to each of the regional headquarters to oversee the orthodoxy and adherence of local leaders to the principles of Algeria's "socialist revolution."

Early in 1965, an FLN delegation sojourned to Moscow, under Communist Party of the Soviet Union (CPSU) auspices. After several days of negotiation, the ben Bella government announced that agreement had been reached to sponsor CPSU-FLN collaboration in the political realm, with a view to reorganizing the latter along communist lines. The regime apparently had decided to fly in the face of popular opinion. However, the political pendulum was soon to swing away from the president and his loyal supporters.

THE JUNE 19TH COUP AND ITS AFTERMATH

The postwar eclipse of the FLN tended to obscure the major structural shifts that were taking place in Algerian society. The disruptions of warfare had created a mobile mass, prepared to take advantage of whatever opportunities crystallized after the signing of the Evian Accords. With the mass exodus of European settlers, these opportunities assumed concrete form — vacancies suddenly materialized within the civil bureaucracy, the newly formed army commanded prestige and good salaries, labor federations required reasonably trained personnel, and schools were bereft of teachers. Within the crucible of crisis, Algeria's new elite was born.

By early 1965, it was apparent that the army constituted the principal citadel of material power among the elitist groups. Under Colonel Boumedienne, the ANP had "blocked" Morocco's claims against Algerian territory in the Sahara, contained the 1963–64 Kabylia insurrection, and faithfully served the administration in coping with the feudalist tendencies of the wilayists. In addition, the ANP had undergone a program of reorganization that moved it toward the goal of professional efficiency. Under the terms of an October, 1963, agreement, the Soviet Union was rearming the 50,000-man force, providing it with heavy armor and artillery, and making training billets available for approximately 1,000 Algerian cadets, technicians, and candidates for higher echelon posts. The ANP's control over the instruments of terror assured it a major position in the ben Bella regime.

The strains that produced the ben Bella–Boumedienne rupture were cumulative rather than sequential. Programmatically, the ANP had wished a more advanced role for itself in formulating and executing policy; ideologically, the army's officers tended to be more conservative than the president and his advisors; politically, the army preferred a collegial system of governing rather than the personalized, one-man approach of ben Bella; tactically, Boumedienne preferred to punish the "enemies of the state" rather than search for accommodation, which was the tactic of the chief of state. These considerations did not precipitate the June 19, 1965, *coup de main,* however. The main precipitant proved to be the efforts of presidential advisers to erode the power and influence of the ANP. During 1964, ben Bella agreed to assume personal control of the Ministry of Interior affairs — producing the resignation of Ahmed Medeghri, a Boumedienne supporter — and announced plans to form a People's Militia (an obvious counterpoise to the ANP) and to reshuffle the cabinet. By early 1965, the president made clear his desire to dispose of Foreign Minister 'Abd al-'Aziz Bouteflika, a Boumedienne protege. When the defense minister intervened in behalf of Bouteflika, the president apparently formulated plans for defenestrating the defense minister, some time after the final proceedings of the Afro-Asian conference (Bandung II), scheduled to convene in Algiers during the latter part of June.

Apprised of these plans, the defense minister moved during the early morning hours of June 19 to apprehend his adversary, with a small number of special troops (tank and commando) from Algiers garrison. With relative ease and virtually no bloodshed, the *coup de main* was swiftly executed, and ben Bella hurried into arrest. Algeria awoke later in the day to learn of these nocturnal events, surprised but without widespread visible resentment. In rapid succession, the cabinet pledged its support, followed by all elements of the army, and the Algiers federation of the FLN. With only a few notable exceptions, protest demonstrations failed to materialize throughout Algeria — mute testimony that ben Bella had failed to transform the FLN into a personally loyal instrumentality. . . .

In an effort to mitigate these fears, Colonel Boumedienne has retained the previous cabinet virtually *in toto* (although shifting several portfolios), brought a handful of civilian politicians into the Revolutionary Council formed in early July, and sought to convince several "fathers" of the 1954–62 revolution that their participation in government is essential. More crucially, perhaps, the new regime has moved carefully and with great prudence in reorganizing local administrative organs. While the People's Militia has been disbanded, no wholesale changes have occurred.

The FLN also is being approached with great circumspection. A five-man executive committee has been established to formulate plans for the reorganization of the party, pave the way for elections for a new party leadership, and plan a second national congress. Given the existing condition of the FLN, as well as the possibility that its erstwhile directors may seek to recoup their wartime influence, the executive committee is not expected to register rapid progress. Indeed, ultimately, the FLN may be disbanded or give way to a new mass organization that is sired by the present leadership. At present, the FLN clearly cannot serve as an effective instrument for consolidating the power and position of Algeria's "new" leadership.

Notes

1. Maurice Duverger, *Political Parties: Their Organization and Activity in the Modern State* (London: Methuen, 1954).

2. A subterranean arm of the MTLD, the Secret Organization (OS) was formed in 1947 to offset French repression. Its initial leader, Hocine Ait Ahmed, interestingly enough, was supplanted by Ahmed ben Bella a short time after the OS's formation.

3. Germaine Tillion, *Algeria: The Realities* (New York: Alfred A. Knopf, 1958).

4. Ben Bella, Mohammed Khider, Mustafa ben Boulaid, Murad Didouche, Larbi ben M'Hidi, Rabbah Bitat, Belqasim Krim, Hocine Ait Ahmed, and Mohammed Boudiaf.

30

THE ELECTIONS OF FEBRUARY 5, 1967

NICOLE GRIMAUD

Scheduled since the summer of 1966, the elections for the 676 communal councils were preceded by the establishment of party cells throughout the country, since the National Liberation Front (FLN) had been given the major responsibility for organizing the voting. In November and December, ward, departmental (regional), and then national commissions were appointed and installed to supervise the over-all operations. Each region was taken over by a member of the Revolutionary Council (Qaid Ahmed for Constantine, Mohand Ou al-Hajj for Aurès, for example, who supervised the preparations, directed the campaign, and then presided over the installation of the elected assemblies.

The candidates were selected by the party, the administration, and the national organizations according to established criteria: they were to be workers with no independent sources of income, militants serving the Revolution, citizens of proven competence and morality. The lists of candidates — twice as many as there were seats in each district — were sent to the voters a week before the elections. It is very difficult to know to what extent the population, which was supposed to be associated in the initial selection, did in fact participate in it, but it is likely that participation varied a good deal according to commune. Nevertheless, there were several cases where the party's list was discussed or altered by the people (Tlemcen and Blida). The electoral commissions charged with arbitration were made up of representatives of the party, local administration, army, veterans, and national organizations. The candidates were in fact appointed and had only a very limited role. They did not campaign and were often only presented to their electors during an official meeting. This anonymity was evidently more of a drawback in the big cities than in the small villages, where everyone knew one another.

Thus, the campaign was conducted by the *kasmas* (party sections) and national organizations, particularly the general Union of Algerian Labor (UGTA) and Women's Union (UNFA), although an important role was also played by the army. Because of the procedure followed, the campaign themes were almost totally devoted to the new institutions and the meaning of the communal

Translated, by permission, from "Réforme et élections communales en Algérie," *Maghreb*, No. 25 (March-April, 1967), pp. 8—10.

reform. Local problems were not discussed, although it is certain that had the candidates addressed themselves to problems of school construction or water supply the voters would have been more interested.

The means for campaigning were ample: meetings, press, television, films from the National Cinema Center, matchboxes, postmarks bearing slogans, and special civic-education courses on voting, which were given in the schools but were in fact aimed at the parents.

Everything was done to induce the Algerians into voting massively on February 5, 1967: registration lists were open as late as the day before elections; vote by absentee ballots and by proxy was authorized; a family mandate allowed one person to cast his vote for five members of his family; and election officials roamed the Saoura desert region to collect the nomads votes.

THE RESULTS

Six million citizens were called upon to elect 10,158 delegates to the popular assemblies. The elections took place without incident, and the government declared itself satisfied. Minister of the Interior Mohammed Medeghri estimated that between 70 and 80 per cent of the electorate participated.

Since departmental statistics have not been published, it is impossible to draw an electoral map of Algeria. It is also impossible to compare the results with those of the legislative elections of September 20, 1964, when participation was officially estimated at 85 per cent. There is only fragmentary information, since broadcasts of the results were stopped a few hours after the close of the balloting. The press nevertheless gave some final figures concerning electoral participation: Tindouf 92 per cent, Béchar 80.68 per cent, Oran 74.42 per cent, Tlemcen 68.71 per cent, Greater Algiers 62.41 per cent, and Algiers City 59.02 per cent. Interest in the elections was greater in the countryside, where voters are closer to their problems than in the cities. In Algiers, the list of results by districts indicates that abstentions were greater in the poorer districts: participation varied from 80.76 per cent in the third ward to 45.24 per cent in the second.[1] Finally, some observers mentioned that Kabylia did not vote in great numbers (it is a tradition); 50–54 per cent are said to have voted in Annaba.

The only complete results that are known were those proclaimed on February 7 at the courthouse of Oran: registered, 151,214; voting, 112,537 (74.42 per cent); valid votes, 56.313; blank votes, 56.224.[2] The results were given without comment, which is strange to say the least, since the number of blank ballots was almost the same as the valid votes.

It is particularly difficult to know whether Algerian émigrés in France, Switzerland, Belgium, and Germany voted. Their registration cards were sent through the consulates, but it does not appear that they massively returned their ballot to their native communes.

It would be interesting, too, to know the percentage of women who exercised their right to vote. The women's vote depended on the degree of traditionalism in their region, and was greatest in the cities and villages. Despite all the urging they received, however, Algerian women probably did not participate much in the election, although hasty conclusions should be avoided. Ghardaia is an example; one would have expected that in the fiercely conservative Mzab, the women would have abstained. But to elect the Ibadite candidates that they thought were not adequately represented in the lists in Ghardaia, 92 per cent of the women and 85 per cent of the men voted.

THE ELECTED COUNCILMEN

The names of the city councilmen were published in the press, but, given the present state of information, details are unfortunately unavailable. Only *La République*[3] published a picture of the candidates elected in Oran city, Saida city, Mostaganem, and Mascara — showing a majority of young men — and indicated their professions, the only precise information available.

	Oran City	Mostaganem	Mascara	Saida City
Civil servants	19	9	7	2
Shopkeepers	1	6	8	3
Teachers	5	4	1	8
Farmers	0	3	4	4
Labor officials	5	0	0	0
Business managers	3	0	2	1
Physicians and pharmacists	3	2	0	0
Party and national organization officials	2	1	0	0
Lawyers and notaries	1	0	1	0
Retired	0	1	0	1
Self-management directors	0	0	2	0
Craftsman	0	0	0	1
Women	0	0	0	1
Miscellaneous	4	3	4	0
Total	43	29	29	21

The above table shows the important place held by civil servants and shopkeepers in these assemblies. In Oran, the General Union of Algerian Workers (UGTA), beneficiary of a misunderstanding between the party and the prefectoral administration, won a real victory. But generally speaking, the elected representatives of the working class obtained only a small minority of the seats and are practically absent from the communal executive organs. On the other hand, it seems that an appreciable number of bourgeois or notables (particularly from liberal professions, civil servants, landowners, especially in the east) have been given a popular mandate and that the criterion of efficiency has often been preferred to that of militancy. But these are only general indications, and more work in electoral sociology needs to be done to fill in the missing details. Finally, the four ex-Frenchmen who took Algerian nationality after independence and became candidates were elected.

Despite the wish expressed in the high ranks of the National Union of Algerian Women (UNFA) to see many women involved in the councils, their candidates were few: 260, of whom 45 were elected.[4] The 6 women of Algiers who sought the votes of their constituents saw their courageous act rewarded, and one of them was named the vice president of the social affairs commission. On the other hand, the 3 candidates from Mostaganem lost. There too, more details are needed.

This first popular consultation since June 19, 1965, shows the desire of the Algerian government to hear the voice of the people and to convince them that their sense of both duty and interest should lead them to participate in the reconstruction of the state. In this, the government may not have been completely successful — does apathy, economic difficulty, or the call for boycott issued by all the opposition movements explain the abstentions and blank votes? But that does not hide the important fact that on the local level, new teams have been constituted to receive "on the job training" in performing the tasks that the central government will gradually hand over to them.

Notes

1. *El-Moudjahid,* February 7, 1967.
2 *La République,* February 8, and *El-Moudjahid,* February 9, 1967.
3. *La République,* February 8, 9, and 10, 1967.
4. *El-Moudjahid,* February 9, 1967.

31

LIBYA AND THE MILITARY REVOLUTION

JACQUES ROUMANI *

At the time of Libyan independence in 1951, a noted scholar of Libyan history observed that the emergence of the Kingdom of Libya ushered the country into a "new period of Arabization."[1] With independence, he felt, Libyan society would be increasingly drawn under the influence of the Arab East. Two decades later, the regime of King Idris, which ruled Libya until the military coup of September 1, 1969, is accused by its successors of having hindered this historical process in pursuit of particularistic, conservative goals in alliance with Western imperialism, to the detriment of the Arab nation and of the free development of Libyan society. The officers who set out to destroy the Senusi monarchy regard their intervention as a response to "the call demanding change and purification"; they see themselves as the liberators of the Libyan people from an oppressive past, "from the rule of the Turks to the tyranny of the Italians and the era of reaction, bribery, intercession, favoritism, treason and treachery."[2] Hence, the claim of the new Libyan leader, Colonel Mu'ammar al-Qadhdhafi, that "what happened on the first of September is a serious historical transformation."[3]

Couched in these terms, the Libyan "revolution" proclaimed by the September coup seems to echo its precedents in the Arab world and elsewhere. Its immediate causes, the nature and aims of the new regime, fall into the general pattern that has characterized military interventions in the Middle East since the countries of the area acquired independence. Like his predecessors in other parts of the Arab world, Colonel al-Qadhdhafi also declared that the "revolution" is "a natural phenomenon conforming to historical development."[4] Most observers would agree that the end of the Senusi monarchy was an element of certainty in the calculus of the political future of the country. Everyone knew that, for lack of leadership qualities, the crown prince and heir to the throne would not have been able to ensure the continuity of the regime, and a few might have anticipated the displacement of the seventy-nine-year-old monarch by voluntary abdication or through traditional palace intrigues. But the shattering of the

*I am grateful to I. William Zartman and to Manfred Halpern for comments on this paper. I am indebted above all to Professor Halpern for clarifying for me the dynamics of tradition and change in Middle Eastern societies. This chapter was written specially for this reader.

system of politics that sustained the monarchy by the sudden appearance of a radical military force was not expected in the Libyan context, not even by the closest sympathizers and allies of its cause.[5] The dissolution of the Senusi formula chosen eighteen years ago to create political order in Libya warrants an examination of the historic significance claimed for the event. For the seizure of power in Libya by the military, among all other groups, either can reintroduce a tradition of political competition by force or threat of force or can herald a new era in which progressive soldiers would become instrumental in organizing a political system possessing the capacity to cope with the divisions and problems of a society that will be increasingly experiencing uncontrolled transformation. Furthermore, as the September coup raises questions that are central to the nature and direction of the society's political future, an understanding of its meaning and promise must be anchored in the historical and social uniqueness of Libya.

Three broad historical patterns have repeatedly characterized internal political relationships in Libya through modern times. The dominant pattern has been one of renewed conflict among heterogeneous tribal and sedentary groups inhabiting the various parts of the territory. For hundreds of years, following the Islamic invasions of the seventh and eleventh centuries,[6] politics in Libya resembled the cyclical rise and fall of tribes and dynasties described by the fourteenth-century Arab thinker, ibn Khaldun.[7] The political process was a chronic struggle for power that posed a permanent challenge to any attempts at establishing direct and continuous authority. With the Ottoman conquest of 1555, Tripoli (on the western coast of Libya) began to emerge as a distinct political entity with claims to urban leadership supported by a small commercial role in the Mediterranean. Its evolving status led inevitably to a polarization of conflict between the sedentary coastal areas, which came under its influence, and the tribal hinterland.[8] The menace of tribal power as well as intertribal conflict persisted throughout the rule of the Karamanli dynasty (1711-1835) and the second Ottoman period (1835-1911). In efforts to establish some centralized control, the more effective Ottoman governors of the latter half of the nineteenth century chose to fight the tribes for twenty years in order to gain nominal authority over the Libyan hinterland.[9] Over half a century later, a vigorous tribal-led opposition to Italian colonial rule crumbled in Tripolitania under the weight of internecine warfare.

A second pattern that lingered to the very recent past, and that may be seen as complementary to the first, was the territory's susceptibility to strong external influences from the Mediterranean world, Egypt, and the Maghrib. Since its earliest history, the coasts of Libya came under the successive domination of Phoenicians, Carthaginians, Romans, Vandals, and Byzantines, followed by the Islamic invaders, the Tunisian Hafsids, the Spaniards, and the Ottomans. The fall of the Karamanli dynasty, which seized power from the Ottomans, was brought about in no small part by insistent financial and political pressures by subversive British and French consuls.[10] The outstanding feature of Ottoman policy in Libya since it regained power from the Karamanlis was an increasingly defensive posture against European encroachments. Following colonial rule, the independence of Libya was largely decided by the competing interests of the Great Powers and through the pressures of the Arab League.[11] Until oil discoveries began in 1959, Libya was greatly in debt to British, American, and U.N. support for its economic and political viability.

The third and most important historical pattern reflects the perennial failure of the various groups in Libya to translate their common historical experiences which molded them into a "historical-geographic entity distinct from neighboring countries" and gave them an "ethnic-political individuality"[12] — into a capacity to form a national community. Even the independence and loose federation that made the Libyan state in 1951 was largely the product of "compelling external circumstances."[13]

Paradoxically, the incapacity or unwillingness of the people of Libya to transcend these patterns and build linkages of collaboration on a system-wide basis was both reduced and exacerbated by political developments that initiated sustained efforts at establishing a common political framework. The earliest of these, the Karamanli dynasty, which remained in power for more than a century, succeeded in modifying, albeit briefly, the Ottoman system in Libya that kept rulers and ruled apart. The dynasty can be given credit for including local groups in the administration of the government while maintaining centralized personal control.[14] The founder of the dynasty, Ahmad Karamanli of mixed Turkish and local descent, made Arabic the official language of Tripoli and brought the city into cultural and political prominence, independent of Ottoman influence.[15] However, as the cohesiveness of the ruling family weakened, each of the various ethnic and tribal groups sought to appropriate the achievements of the dynastic founder, thereby breaking the balance of power that permitted the genesis of political order.[16]

Another development of an entirely different character had a much more profound impact in Cyrenaica. It was the rise of a revivalist Sufi *tariqa* (sect) founded by Muhammad ben Ali al-Senusi[17] around the middle of the nineteenth century, marking a revolutionary transformation in the political life of the hitherto stateless, marginal, and isolated Cyrenaican society. The Senusiya was correctly described as "an Islamic phenomenon, religious in its fundamentals, social in its effects and political in its consequences".[18] None of these qualities, which enabled the Senusi organization to give a corporate identity and a unique political personality to the Cyrenaicans, found response in Tripolitania. The reasons can be discovered in the social, cultural, and political conditions that obtained among the Cyrenaicans but not among the Tripolitanians. Of the greatest consequence was the fundamental difference between the structural and cultural uniformity of the Cyrenaican society and the heterogeneity of the Tripolitanian structure.[19] The former was a segmentary tribal system, pastoral and nomadic, in which political and social relations were governed by the concept of genealogy.[20] Segmentary structures consist of "a system of balanced opposition between tribes and tribal sections from the largest to the smallest divisions."[21] "Related and adjacent sections feel that they form a single and in certain circumstances a corporate unit in opposition to other and like units."[22] "Authority is distributed at every point of the tribal structure and political leadership is limited to situations in which a tribe or a segment of it acts corporately."[23] The supreme achievement of the Senusiya after securing acceptance on religious grounds, was to penetrate the Cyrenaican tribal structure by establishing its institutional base, the *zawiya*, within it. The *zawiyas*, centers of spiritual and socio-economic guidance administered by competent and deeply religious disciples, were "seeded in the crevasses between the tribes and tribal sections."[24] Its strategic location made the *zawiya* "a center for tribal unity as well as a center for the unity and control of the Order as a whole."[25] The political structure of the Cyrenaican tribal system was thus gradually transformed from a segmental to what may be described as a pyramidal-hierarchical type with the Senusi head at the apex. In Tripolitania, urban, sedentarized, and peasant elements tied to the land, mixed with nomadic and seminomadic tribes. Though also lacking a hierarchical authority system, Tripolitanian society was not receptive to one, because group cohesiveness was determined by particularistic political, economic, and territorial interests[26] and not by genealogical affiliations. Temporary and recurring solidarity ties, usually coalescing around a leader who personified the group's interests, and not structural principles, defined the political unit. A complex pattern of opposing forces in continual fragmentation resulted from volatile solidarity interests and prevented the system from achieving the equilibrium that was inherent in Cyrenaican society.[27]

Another major factor of political consequence which differentiated the two provinces was the relative isolation of Cyrenaica. The proliferation of religious orders in Tripolitania prevented the Senusiya from acquiring a strong following there; their absence in Cyrenaica made the charismatic appeal of the Senusi religious message the more powerful. Moreover, the bedouin of Cyrenaica, who held a tradition of veneration for saintly religious personalities, were even more strongly attracted to the Senusi goal of recreating the simple, austere life of early Islam. The combined effect of the religious and organizational powers of the Senusiya placed it in the position of a legitimate and effective arbitrator of tribal disputes, a function that gradually grew to embrace all the socio-economic, religious, and political needs of the tribes.[28] Had the Ottoman administration been functioning in Cyrenaica as it was in Tripolitania, the Senusiya would, necessarily, have limited its activities to religious practice. The reforms of the last quarter-century of Ottoman tutelage in Libya generated stronger ties of collaboration between the Turkish administration and indigenous elements in the capital of Tripolitania and in adjacent coastal areas. As a result, political and administrative institutions were strengthened (without, however, completely eliminating the tribal threat) to the benefit of social and economic development.[29] On the eastern side of Libya, the Sublime Porte recognized the *de facto* establishment of the simple but cohesive Senusi state, firmly rooted in the social structure of Cyrenaica.[30] On the eve of the colonial invasion in 1911, Tripolitania and Cyrenaica did not share a common political framework, except nominally through a formal Ottoman link. The two main provinces of Libya, subjected to different historical forces, had developed by the beginning of this century into similar but separate social systems sustaining a pattern of politics that divided them even further.

At this point, it might be pertinent to ask how, in the space of forty years, the divisive conditions described above were integrated into the new political system that emerged in 1951? More specifically, what made it possible for the Senusiya to transform its narrow-based organization into an Islamic monarchy for the whole of Libya? The answer lies in the political modifications imposed by the response of the Libyans to the colonial experience.

The Libyans did not effectively become part of a colonial system until after the first quarter of this century, and then for the brief span of a decade.[31] The impact of colonialism, limited to the coastal areas, was minimal, with no significant social or cultural consequences. "The two exclusive social organizations, the Italian colonial and bureaucratic and the tribal, functioned side by side with the most slight and occasional bureaucratic contact between them. For the most part, Italians and Bedouin lived as though the other did not exist."[32]

Yet the oppressive nature of colonial practices gave rise to an indigenous political response that is at the root of Libya's recent and present political process. In its oppositional encounter with European colonialism, Libyan society was compelled to define its very basic forces of conflict and collaboration, for continuity and change. It showed that the more threatening and direct the alien challenge the more likely the response to take the form of an integrative Islamic-oriented traditionalist reaction. As the Italian invasion appeared determined to perpetuate a regime of direct military rule, the Senusiya, under the leadership of Sayyid Ahmad al-Sharif, successfully mobilized the forces of the entire territory in a drive that defeated the modern Italian army and reduced its presence within a few coastal points.[33]

However, this historic genesis of Libyan unity soon created its own antithesis. For the tribal forces of the Tripolitanian hinterland, where the Senusiya found its most effective allies, responded to the leadership of Sayyid Ahmad al-Sharif on Islamic universalistic grounds. The Cyrenaican-based political organization of the Senusis was rejected in Tripolitania by the tribes which, having ridden the crest of victory, acquired a collective capacity in Tripolitania equivalent to that of the Sanusiya in Cyrenaica.[34] For the first time in Libyan history, tribal leaders dominated Tripolitania. Ramadan al-Shtewi al-Suehli, the most important of Tripolitania's tribal chiefs, and Sayyid Ahmad al-Sharif shared a common Pan-Islamic anti-European position in alliance with the Ottomans during their last confrontation with Europe. But Pan-Islamic ideology played a fundamentally different role in the politics of the two leaders. For the latter, it was an instrument of expansive goals. To the former, it served internal purposes of consolidation and legitimacy.[35] Thus, the Ottoman defeat and an earlier defeat of Senusi forces, when they attempted to support the Ottomans against the British in the Suez Canal,[36] compelled a reorientation of Senusi interests inward, to preserve the Cyrenaican political community they had created. To Ramadan al-Shtewi al-Suehli, a Pan-Islamic policy was the only possible path toward an integration of heterogeneous and hostile tribal and non tribal forces.

Thus, important political changes occurred in both societies after five years of colonial rule: A crucial change of leadership in the Senusiya[37] (after the defeat, Sayyid Ahmad al-Sharif transferred power to Sayyid Idris, the future monarch) implied the realization that the unique relationship of the Senusi organization to Cyrenaican society could not be extended to a different social structure;[38] a crucial change in the balance of power in Tripolitania created conditions for tribal chiefs to begin a cycle in which the struggle for supremacy was tempered by the Pan-Islamic formula (animated by continued Turkish activities in Libya)[39] which, in Tripolitania, was the only coherent alternative to colonial rule.

These important developments in the two societies continued to demonstrate that receptivity to change was greater in Tripolitania than in Senusi Cyrenaica. In fact, the outgrowth of this disposition was the dramatic emergence in Tripolitania of the first Arab republic, in 1918;[40] in Cyrenaica, after prolonged negotiations for a *modus vivendi*, the Senusiya was officially recognized by the Italians as a dependent Amirate.[41] However, these were nontransforming changes. For, although the greater the complexity and heterogeneity of a tribal-based society, the greater its receptivity to change, it may well be that this disposition is inversely proportional to its capacity to create and sustain stable political authority and institutions and effectively to adopt change. The simpler and more homogeneous a society, the lesser its disposition to change but the greater its capacity to effect change.[42] Whereas the Tripolitanian Republic collapsed because it never transcended its weaknesses (it was correctly described as a "confederacy" of tribes),[43] the Senusiya under the leadership of Sayyid Idris developed a political position that identified it as the only available opposition to colonial rule. In 1922, Tripolitanian chiefs had no choice but to seek refuge in the Senusi alternative to colonial subjection.[44] The socio-political resiliency of the Senusiya survived the devastating blows of the Fascist colonial regime even when its leader repaired to exile in Egypt. Armed resistance was carried on in the name of the Senusiya for almost the entire duration of the colonial period under the leadership of Umar al-Mukhtar, the representative of the exiled Sayyid Idris.

The enduring strength of the Senusi regime was nevertheless again a source of conflict with Tripolitanians when the opportunity for independence seemed real.[45] Sanusi interests supported by Great Britain in gratitude for their active help during World War II, dictated a separatist preference when the political leaders of the more urbanized and more populated Tripolitania demanded the creation of a state that would reflect their own nationalist, unitary, and Pan-Arab political tendencies (an enlargement of the earlier republic) and their numerical and economic strengths.[46] As a requisite for independence, a compromise emerged in the form of a Senusi constitutional monarchy over a federated Libya, encompassing Cyrenaica, Tripolitania, and Fezzan. In this new attempt at Libyan unity, the greatest assets of the Senusiya were again, as during World War I, symbols of legitimacy, power and a potential instrument for unity. To the new Senusi monarchy, the costs involved the repetition of an unsuccessful experiment to absorb groups and forces outside its own system which flourished best in isolation. The political reality of an independent United Kingdom of Libya required of the Senusi system an ever increasing adaptation to a wider role for building a viable nation and state out of a context of heterogeneity and socio-political cleavages; but, in addition, the beginning of new conditions, symptomatic of economic and social change, demanded a parallel but much more profound adaptation. The abrupt but bloodless coup d'etat symbolizes the fact that the kingdom of Idris al-Senusi failed to institutionalize its political goods while attempting to fulfill the first task. The lesson that the authors of the coup claim to have gained is that the failure of the monarch was due to his insufficient recognition or understanding of the decisive importance of the second task.

Most of the theoretical writings on the role of the military in the new nations[47] attribute the cause of military interventions to the weakness or absence of civilian institutions, a low level of public support for the regime, the government, or the system and to the corresponding strength of a conscious, cohesive, disciplined, and technocratic military class. While to some degree all of these factors have been present in the Libyan case including the "crisis of modernization," a general analysis in these terms would be difficult for lack of sufficient and reliable information and in view of the short period that elapsed since the coup took place. A theoretical construct, would, therefore, tend to obscure the value of the particular Libyan conditions and might prejudge this preliminary analysis of military rule in Libya. For the Senusi monarchy was beset by fundamental dilemmas, on which the present military regime is advantaged by the fact that it can only approach them on an entirely new basis. Political stability in Libya's federated structure, "which virtually led to the establishment of four governments, four parliaments and four administrative bodies,"[48] was inherently a function of the monarch's ability to shift governmental leadership to reflect the balance between particularistic, often tribal interests. The effective discharge of this function depended, in turn, on maintaining the role of the monarchic system as the only mechanism for the representation as well as reconciliation of conflicting interests. The monarchy could not tolerate organized political parties, which, in its view, would only strengthen particularistic loyalties.[49] Continuity of this type of stability was the necessary price that the Libyan political system had to pay in order to develop a national consciousness, which for Libyans was not a natural by-product of independence, and in order to allow the experiment of "democratic Western institutions" to cement unity among Muslim Arabs drawn together for the avoidance of conflict rather than as a result of common identity and interests.

Within the brief span of a decade the integrative capacities of the monarchy were severely taxed for political and social innovation under the stress of the unexpected but inevitable consequences of an oil-led economic revolution.[50] The king was required to exercise his position as a source of power and legitimacy for the unaccomplished task of unity, at the same time as new centrifugal forces demanded reform for which his kind of power and legitimacy would no longer be adequate. In an attempt to put an end to traditional provincial and local rivalries, and palace-cabinet-parliament conflicts, the federal system was replaced by a unitary state.[51] Nevertheless, in addition to traditional cleavages, new tensions arising out of economic and social dislocations, aggravated by high economic expectations, were fomenting persistent though inarticulate demands for regular channels of political participation. To the frustration of labor[52] and other forces that were not allowed to organize were added the vociferous demands of the younger Libyans, the would-be intelligentsia, and those on salaried income, the "outs" in Libyan politics.[53]

This amalgam of interests and demands found a common emotional expression in Pan-Arab nationalistic sentiments, kindled by the ana-chronistic presence of foreign bases and the ambivalent attitude of the regime toward the cause of the Arab nation.[54] "Arabism," observed P.J. Vatikiotis in his study of the rise of the Free Officers in Egypt, "seems to be a sentiment which develops most rapidly in areas where 'revolutionary change' is fomented or is imminent."[55] In Libya, this sentiment, which, grounded in the colonial past of Tripolitanians, had always been an instrument for popularizing opposition to the Senusi regime, was reinforced at each outburst of unresolved social and political issues. In its various forms, nationalist Pan-Arab ideology was vaguely beginning to manifest itself not merely as a sentiment but as the alternative to the monarchy,[56] whereas it was viewed by the regime and its supporters as a threat to the fragile foundations of nation-building.

Major cabinet shakeups reflected the trend of crisis. In the first place, the rate of cabinet changes and reshuffles was high. Between 1951 and 1961, there were seven cabinet changes, an average of one change every twenty months, and only two cabinet crises.[57] Between 1961 and 1963, there were four cabinet reshuffles under the same prime minister, but there were six cabinet changes between 1963 and 1969 and three major political crises.[58] Under the premiership of Muhammad Fekini, serious disturbances sparked by student demonstrations broke out in 1964 over Libya's passive role in Arab affairs. The crisis was exacerbated by tensions between a reform-minded administration, which attempted to contain the more flagrant aspects of an incipient corruption, and conservative opposition. It led to a generalized demonstration of anti-Senusi forces but it also forced the resignation of Dr. Fekini.[59] On its heels came the call from Cairo for liquidation of foreign bases in Libya causing an uproar within the government and parliament. In a sign of disapproval and helplessness, the king offered to abdicate.[60] The 1967 war produced another violent expression of dissent with the regime over its failure to join revolutionary Arabs in assailing the West and in rushing support to the beleagured Arab armies.[61] The impatience of nontraditional elements with the character of the country's political system found concrete manifestation in open subversion, both internally and externally inspired.[62] Finally, the profound weaknesses of the Senusi monarchy and its ultimate inability to cope with the problems of the society were demonstrated in the appointment, in late 1967, and dismissal of a young prime minister, 'Abd al-Hamid al-Bakkush, who was intended to satisfy the "outs" in Libyan politics without alienating the interests of tribal forces, powerful families, the oil-rich bourgeoisie, and the higher echelons of politicians and bureaucrats. "Enthusiastically endorsed by university students, youthful technocrats both in and out of government and the emerging professional class,"[63] al-Bakkush lasted in office for ten months.

Thus, it becomes abundantly clear that the king's concept of reform operated within the narrow limits of the existing framework of political relations. Under pressure, the monarch sought to extend his mediating role to the new groups, which demanded instead responsive leadership and a new order in conformity with the trend in the progressive Arab world. Since the king understood that the challenge was aimed at the monarchy itself, he opened his own path to reform in economic and social development and, to a lesser extent, in foreign affairs.[64] But the cautious pace of the king was incongruous with the rapid spread of discontinuous change. All the instruments in the power of the monarchy, including the incipient repressive arm of police and security forces, could not bridge the distance between the polarized forces of Libya. The society thus entered what is known as "the praetorian phase," characterized by "the absence of effective political institutions capable of mediating, refining, and moderating group political action," where "social forces confront each other nakedly,"[65] and invite intervention, usually by the most powerful.

It is not known for how long or to what extent junior officers of the Libyan Army had been developing their own analysis of the political conditions of the country before deciding to intervene. Elements of the army may have been planning attempted coups since the major disorders of 1964, and, undoubtedly, there was always the influence and example of military rule elsewhere in the Arab world, particularly in neighboring Egypt. However, the "disposition to intervene"[66] could not possibly have emerged out of the small size of the army, its inexperience, or its doubtful discipline and cohesiveness, but did emerge from its consciousness of these deficiencies and its resentment of the aggrandizement and elite status of the well-trained, rival police corps and the regional Defense Force of Cyrenaica.[67] Above all other factors, the general malaise of political corruption and stalemate of the country offered the opportunity for change, and the military, who gained new sympathy for their agitation during the 1967 June war,[68] decided to seize the moment before a palace coup could mature.[69] The Libyan case proves again "the determinative influence which a small military force could exercise in a situation in which countervailing institutions or power groups are absent,"[70] or when one institution intended to be countervailing, i.e. the Cyrenaica Defense Force, could be rapidly neutralized. The coup of the young officers was initially received with a mixture of concern, apathy, and jubilation, but not with resistance, not even from royalist strongholds; it was planned and executed by officers of "humble origins"[71] without the knowledge or collaboration of civilian groups. Its success depended exclusively on the skill of the few army units directly involved.

From its inception, the regime of the Free Unionist Officers (as they chose to be identified) represented itself not as a junta with the limited purpose of cleansing the political system, but as a revolutionary force sharing the ideas and interests of all progressive groups in Libya and in the Arab world, in the name of which it would guide the nation to its destiny; "the revolution is a popular revolution and what happened on the first of September is as far as could be from being a military coup."[72] "There are no civilians in the Revolutionary Command Council (RCC) because the officers truly have the conscience to represent better than anyone else the demands of the Libyan people."[73] "The RCC guides the country. The . . . government is the executive organ."[74] Clearly, these declarations implied the subordination of civilian authority to military rule. To give them legitimacy, the RCC constructed its revolutionary ideology for universal acceptance among all sectors of the society. By espousing a combination of radical Islamic and Arab nationalist commitments, the RCC sought to present itself in the image of the precedents of both Tripolitanian Pan-Islamism and the religious austerity and Islamic drive of the Senusiya before the rise of Sayyid Idris.[75] A decidedly anti-Western posture aimed at reviving memories of an oppressive colonial past helped create a sentiment of identity with the "liberators." For the younger and more modern groups, this sort of Islamic fundamentalism (exemplified by a rigid application of religious tenets and the banning of any trace of European cultural influence) was tempered by an aggressive Arab policy aiming at bringing Libya to the center of the "Battle of Destiny" and to the forefront of Arab unity and Arab socialism.[76] Thus, the regime of Colonel al-Qadhdhafi, exploiting the latent power of an anti-Senusi tradition in Tripolitania (whence he and possibly the other "revolutionaries" originate), created with stunning swiftness the semblance of a new political formula; perhaps of greater long-term significance, it prescribed the "natural" conclusion of a religious-political force in the modern history of Islam, which survived the upheavals of a crucial century (mid-nineteenth century to mid-twentieth century) for the Middle East and yielded only before the poorly understood complexities of the modern age.

By the first anniversary of the "revolution" (September 1, 1970), the RCC had proven itself a master-provider of "the most attractive political remedy in the Middle East."[77] It had removed the British and American bases, nationalized foreign banks, Libyanized every aspect of economic, cultural, and social life that could be handled by Libyans, expelled the Italian community of 30,000 to erase the consequences of the colonial past, and established new terms with the powerful oil companies that concentrated control over prices, production, and revenues in the hands of the government; it lent its strongest support to the Palestinian cause and other liberation movements and demonstrated its strong political and economic linkages to the UAR by inviting its technical experts to replace foreign assistance in economic development.[78] With these policies, Libya cast its choice to become overnight an integral part of the political, economic, and cultural life of the Arab East.[79] No comparable innovation has occurred until now in the economic and social fields, where for many months a deterioration has set in. "The revolution has a tendency to forget about the everyday life of the people and neglect the economy,"[80] wrote a sympathetic observer after witnessing the discontent that followed a virtual freeze of economic activity. It seems that, upon reflection, the military regime chose to follow the major policies of its predecessors with greater vigor, pragmatism,[81] and increased expenditures, but with no ideological restructuring. During the same period, however, the political moves of the regime can be at best classified as falling into the pattern of the "non-political model of nation-building"[82] that assumes that the popular revolution is identical with popular government. Spectacular success in the foreign field appears to be viewed almost as a substitute for the necessity to replace the old with a new political framework that will guide the changing structure of the society in a coherent direction.

The record of sixteen months of military rule in Libya contains strong indications of the intended permanence of this regime and vague promises of the sharing of power with civilian groups or institutions. In the first place, even the government, the executive organ of the policy-making RCC, gradually passed to a controlling majority of military officers.[83] The resignation (January, 1970) of the first prime minister, a civilian, was followed by the dismissal a few months later of a key minister, Salah Busair, an experienced politician who had long been an enemy of the deposed regime. Secondly, potential rivals within the RCC were eliminated under the pretext of a countercoup.[84] "The enemies are individuals and this does not mean that there is a counter-revolution,"[85] Colonel al-Qadhdhafi explained. The regime's instruments of control appear to be based on the skillful use of the mob and the threat of mob violence, on neutralizing the former police forces and on a security apparatus that received the direct support, if not the actual participation of interested external elements.[86] Through these, the regime can hope to hold its monopoly of power within the armed forces and to prevent the rise of civilian or tribal opposition, which had also manifested itself in an attempted "CIA-supported" counter coup.[87] The objective needs, especially for social and political integration, of a heterogenous and divided society, have been appeased by the promise of a supranational federal association with three other revolutionary Arab regimes[88] and by the vague references to the future establishment of a popular organization that will link revolutionary leaders with "the popular vanguard . . . of conscious active groups."[89]

So far, the links between rulers and ruled have been limited to the build-up of a personal, charismatic leadership whose policies are legitimized by the simple endorsement of organized popular rallies. The institutionalization of military rule was ushered in by the acclamation of Colonel al-Qadhdhafi for President of the Libyan Arab Republic[90] by spontaneous popular forces (January 27, 1971) and by the conspicuous demonstration of newly acquired military might.[91] These latest acts evoke the possibility that the regime may be oriented toward a form of direct military rule dominated by one man. However, as the regime penetrates all levels of government and administration, it finds that it needs the alliance of civilian groups, especially among the bureaucracy. Whether this alliance will mature into a stable and constructive working relationship between the military and the groups it claims to represent will depend on whether "army leadership . . . can transcend the political and social divisions of the country *sufficiently* to act as its vanguard."[92] Until then, the majority of the population, the unorganized masses with no specific political interests or social consciousness, will probably tolerate any new power as long as it does not interfere too much — as it did for centuries before the coup and before the advent of the Senusis.

Notes

1. Ettore Rossi, "Il Regno Unito della Libia," *Oriente Moderno,* XXXI, Nos. 10-12 (October-December, 1951), 176.

2. From the Proclamation of The Republic, September 1, 1969. "The Libyan Revolution in the Words of Its Leaders," *Middle East Journal,* XXIV, No. 2 (Spring, 1970), 203.

3. *Ibid.,* p. 216. From an address in Tripoli on October 16, 1969, by Col. Mu'ammar al-Qadhdhafi.

4. From the opening speech of Col. al-Qadhdhafi at a Revolutionary Intellectual Seminar held in Tripoli on May 8, 1970. *Arab Report and Record,* May 1-15, 1970, p. 269. The notion that the intervention of the army is inevitable in the present context of Arab politics is subject to a wide-ranging, serious scrutiny by Eliezer Be'eri, *Army Officers in Arab Politics and Society* (New York: Praeger Publishers, 1970).

5. "Who had ever believed that a revolution would break out in Libya?" asked Muhammad Hassanein Heikal in a report from Libya a few days after the coup took place. He added: "I can say with confidence that there was not an Arab government or an Arab political party or any group from among the active groups in the wide spectrum of Arab politics which was not taken by complete surprise with what happened in Libya. Anyone who claims otherwise should be lying to himself before lying to the truth and to history." "Report from Libya," *al-Ahram,* September 6, 1969, pp. 1, 3. "The West reacted with shock and surprise to the September 1 coup in Libya. . . . Neither the well-entrenched American and British intelligence nor the various police forces of King Idris anticipated an armed insurrection, much less its success," wrote Eric Rouleau in *Africa Report,* November, 1969, p. 24. A recent study of Libya, critical of its traditional policies, fails even to mention the military as a potential source of change. See Sami Hakim, *Haqiqat Libya* (Cairo, 1968).

6. The first Islamic invasions of Libya were part of the westward thrust of the nascent Arab empire, and their impact was slow and uneven. They were met by a prolonged resistance of autochthonous settlers. The Islamization and ethnolinguistic Arabization of the territory were given a decisive impetus four centuries later by the invasion of the Banu Hilal and Banu Sulaym tribes, which originated in the Arabian peninsula but were in Egypt prior to the invasion. In Libya, this process was more complete in Cyrenaica than in Tripolitania,

where Berber elements continued to persist. For reference on the history and consequences of these invasions, see Enrico De Agostini, *Le Popolazioni della Tripolitania* (Tripoli, 1917), pp. x-xix; Xavier De Planhol, *Les Fondements Géographiques de l'Histoire de l'Islam* (Paris, 1968), pp. 132, 152, 159; Ettore Rossi, *Storia di Tripoli e della Tripolitania* (Rome, 1968), pp. 23-64, but especially pp. 57-59; and al-Tahir Ahmad al-Zawi, *Tarikh al-Fath al-Arabi fi Libya* (Cairo, 1954).

7. Ibn Khaldun, *The Muqaddimah: An Introduction to History,* ed. Franz Rosenthal, I (Princeton, N.J.: Princeton University Press, 1968), 273-310, 313-55.

8. "The authority of Tripoli was never securely and continuously consolidated in the hinterland, which existed in a state of autonomy or better, of bedouin and nomadic anarchy." Ettore Rossi, "Considerazioni Generali sulla Storia della Libia Durante il Dominio degli Arabo-Berberi e dei Turchi," *Atti del Primo Congresso di Studi Coloniali* (Florence, April 8-12, 1931).

9. See L. Charles Fearud, *Annales Tripolitaines* (Paris, 1927), pp. 373-440, and Enrico De Leone, *La Colonizzazione dell' Africa del Nord* (Padua, 1960), pp. 251-312.

10. An account of the immediate causes of the fall of the Karamanli dynasty is given in a documented study by Ismail Chemali, "Documenti Inediti sulla Caduta dei Caramanli," *Rivista delle Colonie Italiane,* VIII, Anno IV, Nos. 2-3 (February-March, 1930).

11. The following works give differing viewpoints on the role of external forces in the question of Libyan independence: Benjamin Rivlin, *The United Nations and The Italian Colonies,* (New York: Carnegie Endowment for International Peace, 1950); Sami Hakim, *Istiqlal Libya bayn Jam'iyat al-Duwal al-Arabiyah wal-Umam al-Muttahidah,* (Cairo, 1965); Adrian Pelt, *Libyan Independence and the United Nations: A Case of Planned Decolonization* (New Haven, Conn.: Yale University Press, 1970); Nicola Ziadeh, *Libya, Sanat 1948* (Beirut, 1966).

12. Ettore Rossi, "Storia della Libia dalla Conquista Araba al 1911," *Libia, Rivista Trimestrale di Studi Libici,* Anno II, No. 1, January-March, 1954), 42.

13. Majid Khadduri, *Modern Libya, A Study in Political Development* (Baltimore, Md.: Johns Hopkins Press, 1963), p. 109. The author also noted, "Rarely in the life of a nation did external forces prove to be so helpful in overcoming centrifugal forces." *Ibid.,* p. 111.

14. The system of government of the Karamanli dynasty is described in: Rodolfo Micacchi, *La Tripolitania sotto il Dominio dei Karamanli* (Rome, 1964); N. Slousch, "La Tripolitanie sous la Domination des Karamanlis," *Revue du Monde Musulman,* IV (1908), 58-84, 212-32, 433-53; Teobaldo Filesi, "La Reggenza di Tripoli," *Africa* (Rome, May, 1968), pp. 233-44; Robert Mantran, "Tarih Arastirmalari Dergisi," *Ankara Universitesi,* Dil ve Tarihlografya Fakultesi Tarih Arastirmalari Enstitusu, II (1964); Ettore Rossi, *Storia di Tripoli,* pp. 259-94.

15. Ettore Rossi, *Storia di Tripoli,* pp. 234-35.

16. *Ibid.,* pp. 259-94; Feraud, *op. cit.,* 305-71; Chemali, *op. cit.*

17. Although there is no one single comprehensive study spanning the development of the Senusiya to our day, the following sources are by far the best: Ahmad Sidqi al-Dujani, *al-Harakah al-Sanusiyah* (Cairo, 1967); Alfonso Nallino, *Scritti Editi Ed Inediti,* II (Rome, 1940); Muhammad Fuad Shukri, *al-Sanusiyah Din wa-Dawlah* (Cairo, 1948); E. E. Evans-Pritchard, *The Sanusi of Cyrenaica* (London: Oxford University Press, 1949); al-Tayyib 'ibn Idris al-Ashab, *al-Sanusi al-Kabir* (Cairo, n. d.); Fernando Valenzi, "La Senussia in Cirenaica e il Suo Patrimonio," *Rivista delle Colonie Italiane* (1932).

18. B. Ducati, "Lo Stato Senussita," *Rassegna Italiana,* (February, 1928), p. 175.

19. The origins of the sociological differences between the two populations can be traced to the tribal invasions of the eleventh century, which, as mentioned in Note 6, had a lesser impact on Tripolitania, whose population remained akin to other societies in the Maghrib, than in Cyrenaica. The population of Cyrenaica *"détient sans doute le record absolu d'une bédouinisation poussée jusqu'au littoral."* (Xavier De Planhol, *op. cit.,* p. 152.) The excellent ethnographic studies of Enrico De Agostini (1917 and 1922) stated that in Tripolitania "of the total indigenous population . . . the real sedentary . . . are without doubt a strong majority" *(Le Popolazioni della Tripolitania,* p. 18); whereas the Cyrenaicans have "common characteristics and the general physiognomy of the nomadic people." *(Le Popolazioni della Cirenaica,* p. 33).

These findings are further confirmed in later studies by Y. T. Toni, "The Population of Cyrenaica," *Tijdschrift voor Economische en Sociale Geografie* (January, 1958), pp. 1-11. This author states in another study ("Social Mobility and Relative Stability Among the

Bedouin in Cyrenaica," *Bulletin de la Société Géographie d'Egypte*, XXXVI [1963], 113-36) that "In Cyrenaica a high degree of cultural uniformity exists" (p. 113) and "By its way of social organization, the sedentary bedouin belongs culturally to the nomadic population rather than to the peasant or urban one" (p. 134). Even in Cyrenaica's major city, Benghazi, "tribal influence is very strong and in constant opposition to the immigrants from the West that constitute the urban core" (Hadi M. R. Bulugma, *The Urban Geography of Benghazi* [unpublished Ph.D. thesis, Department of Geography, University of Durham, England, September, 1964]. Further on Cyrenaica, see the works of the anthropologist E. L. Peters, especially *The Sociology of the Bedouin of Cyrenaica* (unpublished Ph.D. thesis, Lincoln College, Oxford University, 1950).

It is worth noting that the sociological differences underlie a major source of tensions between the Cyrenaicans and the Tripolitanians: "The Arabs of Cyrenaica and above all the bedouin nomads consider the nomads of Tripolitania as a heterogenous mixture of different tribes and places, socially inferior to them; they, therefore, consider themselves to be the stronger and the more noble and it is not possible that they follow them," (From a memorandum presented to the Ministry of Colonies by a notable from Benghazi who was a close adviser to the Senusi, dated January 11, 1918.) Source: The Archives of the former Ministry of Italian Africa, Ministry of Foreign Affairs, Studies Section, Rome.

20. See Enzo Savarese, *Le Terre della Cirenaica*, Part 2 (Benghazi, 1928), esp. p. 38.

21. Evans-Pritchard, *op. cit.*, p. 59.

22. E. E. Evans-Pritchard, "The Tribes and Their Divisions," *A Handbook on Cyrenaica*, Part 7 (Benghazi: British Military Administration, 1945), p. 2.

23. Evans-Pritchard, *The Sanusi of Cyrenaica*, p. 59. For a clear review of political relationships in segmentary societies, see Lloyd Fallers, "Political Sociology and the Anthropological Study of African Politics," in Richard Bendix (ed.), *State and Society: A Reader in Comparative Sociology* (Boston: Little Brown, 1968), pp. 73-86.

24. Evans-Pritchard, *The Sanusi of Cyrenaica*, p. 73.

25. D. C. Cumming, "The Modern History of Cyrenaica," *A Handbook on Cyrenaica*, Part 5 (Benghazi: British Military Administration, 1945), p. 20.

26. On the evolution of private, nontribal territorial and economic interests, see K. S. Machlachlan, *A Geographical Study of the Coastal Zone Between Homs and Misurata: A Geography of Economic Growth* (unpublished Ph.D. thesis in four volumes, Department of Geography, University of Durham, England, 1961), p. 240; and J.A.N. Brehony, *A Geographical Study of the Jebel Tarhuna* (unpublished Ph.D. thesis, I and II, Department of Geography, University of Durham, England), pp. 226-329.

27. For an analysis of the concept of "equilibrium" that applies to tribal societies like Cyrenaica's, see Max Gluckman, *Politics, Law and Ritual in Tribal Society* (Chicago: Aldine, 1965), pp. 279-85.

28. See Enrico Insabato, "Notes on the Sanusiyah," *Africa* (Rome, 1950-51), p. 199; Evans-Pritchard, *The Sanusi of Cyrenaica*, p. 83; Emilio Canevari, *Zauie ed Ichuan Senussiti della Tripolitania* (Tripoli, 1917), p. 20.

29. On internal developments in Tripolitania during the last two decades of Ottoman rule, see Edmonde Bernet, *En Tripolitanie* (Paris, 1912); Henry Marchand, "La Tripolitanie—Une Colonie Turque," in *Renseignements Coloniaux et Documents*, published by the Comité de l'Afrique Française et le Comité du Maroc (Paris, 1908), pp. 249-51; N. Slousch, "Turkish-Indigenous Relations," *Revue du Monde Musulman* (Paris, 1907), p. 367; Ernesto Queirolo, "Municipal Government Under the Turks" (Italian), in *La Rinascita della Tripolitania* (Milan, 1926), pp. 399-408; Henri Froidevaux, "L'Oeuvre Civilisatrice des Turcs en Tripolitanie (1910-11)," *Questions Diplomatiques et Coloniales*, CXXXIV (Paris, n. d.); De Leone, *op. cit.*, pp. 347-67. For developments in Cyrenaica during the same period, see Olinto Marinelli (ed.), *La Cirenaica, Geografica, Economica, Politica* (Milan, 1922).

30. E. E. Evans-Pritchard, *The Sanusi of Cyrenaica*, p. 99. Also, see a correspondence between Turkish governors in Cyrenaica and Constantinople, in a booklet entitled *Relazioni fra Turchi e Senussi* (Benghazi, 1912).

31. The Italian invasion of Libya began in 1911, but the country was entirely pacified only in 1932. The colonial regime collapsed with the defeat of Italy in World War II.

32. E. E. Evans-Pritchard, "Italy and the Bedouin in Cyrenaica," *African Affairs* (January, 1946), p. 21.

33. The history of the Italian defeat in Libya by indigenous forces is documented in a five-volume confidential report, *The Rebellion in Tripolitania in the Year 1915*,

Confidential Series No. 8, Ministry of Colonies (Rome, 1915-16). For shorter studies, see G. Fornari, *Gli Italiani nel Sud Libico* (Rome, 1941), and, by the same author, "The Sanusiyah in Tripolitania," *Rassegna Italiana* (1950), p. 171. See also Corrado Zoli, "La Riconquista della Tripolitania," *Politica,* XIII, No. 39 (December 31, 1922), pp. 325-42.

34. Fornari, *Rassegna Italiana,* p. 172.

35. al-Tahir Ahmad al-Zawi, *Jihad al-Abtal fi Tarablus al-Gharb* (Cairo, 1950), pp. 158-91.

36. Shukri, *op. cit.,* pp. 147-70, and Evans-Pritchard, *The Sanusi of Cyrenaica,* p. 124.

37. The transfer of power occurred smoothly, but the legitimacy of Sayyid Idris as the Head of the Senusiy remained a matter of controversy within the Senusi family. The assassination, in 1954, of Ibrahim Shalhi, the king's most trusted adviser, was apparently motivated by the unfulfilled power aspirations of members of Sayyid Ahmad al-Sharif's family. The event prompted an unusual pronouncement by the king asserting his rightful claim to the throne. "Memoirs of King Idris: A Definitive Clarification of the Political History of Libya," *al-Zaman,* January 27, 1955.

38. The Senusi representative in Cyrenaica, Sayyid Safi al-Din (a cousin of Sayyid Idris), proved incapable of organizing or governing the Tripolitanians, many of whom resented the authority of a Senusi; they refused to pay taxes he levied and contested his right to distribute public offices. Al-Zawi explains that the Senusis, sheltered in their own system, did not know how "to interact with other types of people." *(Jihad al-Abtal,* pp. 181-83.)

39. The most thorough account of Turkish activities in Libya until 1918 is available in an unpublished Ph.D. thesis by Philip Hedrick Stoddard, *"The Ottoman Government and the Arabs, 1911-1918: A Preliminary Study of the Teskilat-I* Makhsusa" (Department of Oriental Studies, Princeton University, Princeton, N.J., 1963). See especially Chapter III.

40. The best published account of the rise and fall of the Tripolitania republic is in al-Zawi, *Jihad al-Abtal,* pp. 222-64. Another good account from an opposing view is in Ottone Gabelli, *La Tripolitania dalla Fine della Guerra Mondiale all'Avvento del Fascismo,* II (Rome, 1937).

41. See cited general works on the Senusiya, but also Fabrizio Serra, *Italia e Senussia* (Milan, 1933), and Bruno Aglietti, "La Confraternita Senussita," *Oriente Moderno,* XXVI (January-June, 1946).

42. These are preliminary conclusions of part of the author's thesis on change in Libya under colonial rule.

43. Quoted from Shekib Arslan, "On the Present Situation in Islam," in al-Zawi, *Jihad al-Abtal,* p. 217.

44. At a meeting in Sirte, Tripolitania leaders agreed to request the Italian authorities to extend the Senusi Amirate that they had granted for Cyrenaica to Tripolitania. The decision was a political maneuver to obtain refuge under the Senusi umbrella, in view of the impending Italian preparations to crush the weakening resistance in Tripolitania. In an earlier conference in Gharian, in 1920, the Tripolitanians opted for a Muslim Amir to replace the defunct republic, but they did not specify who the Amir would be. See al-Zawi, *Jihad al-Abtal,* pp. 304-7. Both assemblies of Tripolitanian chiefs were called at the instigation of Abdulrrahman Azzam, who had counseled the Tripolitanians and mediated their disputes since 1916. Thus, these decisions cannot be regarded as a genuine expression of Tripolitanian unity with the Senusiya.

45. During the twenty-two years of exile of Sayyid Idris in Egypt, the conditions that made Tripolitanians seek a Senusi Amirate over their territory had "evaporated." See Sami Hakim, *Haquqat Libya,* p. 11.

46. The working of such compromise is the subject of Adrian Pelt's account, *Libyan Independence and the United Nations: A Case of Planned Decolonization.* He is quoted as having stated, in connection with the issue over the method by which the Libyan National Assembly was established to draft a constitution, "What has happened up to now in Libya, whether one does or does not like it . . . is the result of a carefully worked out compromise among the Libyans of the three territories. To upset this compromise . . . would have the most serious political consequences . . . one must even take into account the possibility of a breakdown of the Libyan unity which has so far been achieved." (Khadduri, *op. cit.,* pp. 153-54.)

47. For recent reviews of the subject in general, see Robert E. Dowse, "The Military and Political Development," in Colin Leys (ed.), *Politics and Change in Developing Countries* (New York and London: Cambridge University Press, 1969). On the Middle East in

particular, see Amos Perlmutter, "The Arab Military Elite," *World Politics,* XXII (January, 1970), 269-300. On the impact of military rule, see Eric A. Nordlinger, "Soldiers in Mufti: The Impact of Military Rule Upon Economic and Social Change in the Non-Western States," *APSR,* LXIV, No. 4 (December, 1970), pp. 1131-48.

48. Khadduri, *op. cit.,* p. 320.

49. *Ibid.,* pp. 84-88, and Nicola Ziadeh, *Libya, Sanat 1948,* pp. 57-63.

50. Following are some of the recent studies on aspects of social change in Libya: Ragaei, El Mallakh, "The Economics of Rapid Growth: Libya," *Middle East Journal,* XXIII, No. 3 (Summer, 1969); Pierre Marthelot, "Les Ressources Pétrolières et l'Evolution Sociale et Economique de la Libye," *Etudes,* No. 8-9 (Brussels: Centre pour l'Etude des Problèmes du Monde Musulman Contemporain), pp. 53-61; and, in the same issue, Robert Marchal, "Urbanization Problems in Libya with Special Reference to Cyrenaica," pp. 41-52; Robert S. Harrison, "Migrants in the City of Tripoli, Libya," *The Geographical Review* (July, 1967); J. D. Farrell, "Libya Strikes It Rich," and Robert Wylie Brown, "Libya's Rural Sector," *Africa Report* (April, 1967); Jamil Hilal, *Family, Marriage and Social Change in Some Libyan Villages* (unpublished master's thesis, University of Durham, England, 1969).

51. The federal system was abolished on April 27, 1964.

52. For a profile of Libyan labor issues, see John Norman, *Labor and Politics in Libya and Arab North Africa* (New York: Twayne, 1965); F. G. Thomas, "The Libyan Oil Worker," pp. 439—49 in this reader; N. A. Arsharuni, "The Position of the Working Class in Libya," Nardui Azzi i Afriki, I (1964), pp. 37-43.

53. For a brief synthesis of the position of these groups, see Rouleau, *Africa Report,* p. 25. Also the sources mentioned above in Note 50.

54. These sentiments broke out in the open from time to time following the rhythm of crises in the Arab world. Thus, there were disturbances in 1956 over the possibility that the British might have used their bases in Libya against Egypt. (See Majid Khadduri, *op. cit.,* p. 273). In 1964, student-led disturbances broke out again, protesting the king's absence from the Arab summit conference held in Cairo in January of the same year. A vivid description of the riots is given in Agnes N. Keith, *Children of Allah* (Boston: Little Brown, 1965), Chaps. 41-43.

55. P. J. Vatikiotis, *The Egyptian Army in Politics: Pattern for New Nations?* (Bloomington: Indiana University Press, 1961), p. 203.

56. M. Khadduri, *op. cit.,* p. 330. See, also, Hisham Sharabi, "Libya's Pattern of Growth", *Current History,* XLIV (January, 1963), 45. Both authors note that there was strong Baathist sentiment in Libya among the educated groups. In a subversion trial (see Note 62 below) held in January, 1968, the main charge against the accused was "the formation, between 1960 and 1967, of a political organization based in Beirut" *(Arab Report and Record* [January 16-31, 1968], p. 21), which was identified as the Arab Nationalist Movement. Those sentenced included the general secretary of the Libyan Oil Workers' Union and the head of the banned Libyan Student Organization. (*Arab Report and Record* [February 16-29, 1968], p. 48.)

57. Khadduri, *op. cit.,* p. 202.

58. *Middle East and North Africa, 1970-1971* (London: Europa Publications), p. 478.

59. See Note 54, and Sami Hakim, *Haqiqat Libya,* pp. 299-301.

60. Keith, *op. cit.,* pp. 422-24; John Wright, *Libya* (New York: Praeger Publishers, 1969).

61. *Arab Report and Record* (June 16-30, 1967), pp. 212-13; *ibid.* (August 16-31, 1967), pp. 275-76; "La Republique Arabe Libyenne," *Notes et Etudes Documentaires, Nos. 3740-41* (Paris: Secretariat Général du Gouvernment, Direction de la Documentation [November 27, 1970]; Anthony Thwaite, *The Deserts of Hesperides: An Experience of Libya* (New York: Roy, 1969), Chapter 9.

62. *Arab Report and Record (January 16-31, 1968), p. 21; ibid.* (February 1-15, 1968) p. 35; *ibid.* (February 16-29, 1968), p. 48.

63. William H. Lewis, "Libya, The End of Monarchy," *Current History* (January, 1970), p. 36.

64. For a brief review of the king's accomplishments, see Rouleau, *op. cit.,* p. 25; Wright, *op. cit.,* pp. 264-77; *Africa Report* (April, 1967). Seventy per cent of oil revenues were marked for economic development, particularly in the agricultural sector. A $1-billion housing scheme was launched by the king to alleviate shortages for workers and low-income groups. See *Mashru Idris Lil-Iskan,* by Muhammad 'Abdallah A'nan (Beirut, 1967). In

foreign policy, discussions began in 1964 for the evacuation of the Wheelus Field and for the complete withdrawal of British garrisons. The regime also gave considerable support to the Palestinian cause and, after the 1967 Khartoum conference, became one of the principal financial supporters of the U.A.R. and Jordan.

65. Samuel Huntington, *Political Order in Changing Societies* (New Haven, Conn.: Yale University Press, 1968), p. 196.

66. The concept was elaborated by S. E. Finer, *The Man on Horseback: The Role of the Military in Politics* (New York: Praeger Publishers, 1962), pp. 23-71.

67. As J. C. Hurewitz has pointed out, "King Idris dragged his feet in developing a regular army." *(Middle East Politics: The Military Dimension* [New York: Praeger Publishers, 1969], p. 236.) The Libyan army counted fewer than 7,000 members before the coup, whereas the Cyrenaica Defense Force and auxiliary mobile police units (al-Quwwah al-Mutaharrikah) numbered 15,000. The latter, an outgrowth of the Libyan Arab Force that the Senusi organized to help the British forces in the Libyan desert during World War II, and in which Tripolitanians did not participate, was trained by the British and well equipped. "The weapons which should have belonged to the army were in the hands of the police, and the weapons which should have belonged to the police were the only weapons that the army possessed," the Libyan interlocutor (a member of the Revolutionary Command Council [RCC]) explained to Hassanein Heykal soon after the coup. *(al-Ahram,* September 6, 1969, p. 4.) See also "La Libye Entre en Revolution," *Jeune Afrique,* No. 454 (September 16-22, 1969).

68. It was reported that in protest against the nonrevolutionary positions of the regime during the 1967 war, some army units deserted to the U.A.R. *(Arab Report and Record* [August 16-31, 1967], p. 275). In the Heykal report *(al-Ahram,* September 12, 1969, p. 3), officers of the RCC said that they attempted but failed to reach Egypt.

69. Reliable sources indicated that a palace coup led by the king's closest advisers, the Shalhis, was being prepared just prior to the military takeover. *(Notes et Etudes Documentaires,* p. 14.) The details of the palace conspiracy are given by Zachariah Nil, *al-Ahram,* September 14, 1969, p. 3, and John K. Cooley, "Made-in-Libya Power Seizure Surprises Arab Observers," *The Christian Science Monitor,* October 25, 1969.

70. James Coleman and Belman Brice, Jr., "The Role of the Military in Subsaharan Africa," in J. J. Johnson (ed.), *The Role of the Military in Underdeveloped Countries* (Princeton, N.J.: Princeton University Press, 1962), p. 399.

71. Although the social background of these officers in not known, there are hints that they belong to rural Libya: "We are not propertied people . . . The parents of many of us live in huts. My parents still live in a tent in the Sirte area." From Col. al-Qadhdhafi interview, "The Libyan Revolution in the Words of Its Leaders," *Middle East Journal,* p. 204.

72. *Ibid.*

73. *Ibid.*

74. *Ibid.,* p. 205

75. In the proclamation of the Republic on September 1, 1969, Col. al-Qadhdhafi addressed himself to supporters in the following terms: "O you who witnessed the holy war of 'Umar al-Mukhtar for Libya, Arabism, and Islam. O you who fought the good fight with Ahmad al-Sharif." *Ibid.,* p. 203.

76. Speech of al-Qadhdhafi in Benghazi on the occasion of the visit of the U.A.R.'s President Gamal Abd al-Nasser. Special Publication of the Ministry of Defense, *The Great Encounter* (December 25-30, 1969), pp. 24-27.

77. This refers to the charismatic leadership of army officers; its limits and potential are analyzed by Manfred Halpern in *The Politics of Social Change in the Middle East and North Africa* (Princeton, N.J.: Princeton University Press, 1963), p. 273. See also Charles E. Brown, "The Libyan Revolution Sorts Itself Out," *Africa Report* (December, 1969), p. 13.

78. *Notes et Etudes Documentaires,* pp. 16-22; Francis Hope, "The Tripoli Hillbillies," *The New Statesman,* May 22, 1970, pp. 727-29; "Tunisia-Libya-Malta, No. 2, 1970," *The Economist Intelligence Unit,* April, 1970, p. 11.

79. The Maghrib Economic Conference due to be held on March 10, 1970, was canceled after Libya withdrew its participation. *(The New York Times,* March 11, 1970.) See also, "Libye: Non au Maghreb," *Jeune Afrique,* October 20, 1970, pp. 49-50.

80. Charles E. Brown, *op. cit.,* p. 15.

81. Development policies have been strengthened and reorganized since September, 1969. Changes in emphasis but not in content distinguish the present from past economic

policies. In agriculture, resettlement and irrigation are underlined. Allocations for agricultural development in 1970-71 are now expected to reach $140 million, compared to $36 million in the previous year. In industry, large-scale projects in many areas of development would be carried out by the public sector, while small-scale industries and trade would be left to the private sector as before. In the oil sector, it should be remembered that, since 1968, new oil concessions have been granted under partnership arrangements between a government-owned Libyan corporation (LIPETCO) and foreign oil companies. The new regime can be credited so far only with obtaining new favorable terms on prices and revenues. Finally, development expenditures are budgeted for 1970-71 at about $560 million, almost double the level in 1969-70. For details, see *Libyan Arab Republic, Recent Economic Development,* Tripoli, Government Printing, 1970.

82. It is too early to predict whether this approach will materialize into a system of action resembling the Egyptian pattern, which is analyzed by James Heaphey in "The Organization of Egypt: Inadequacies of a Non-Political Model for Nation-Building," *World Politics,* XVIII, No. 2 (January, 1966), pp. 177-93. For the moment, the concept should be understood in the Libyan context only as an orientation of the new regime toward politics: "No partisanship after today . . . There will be no labor unions . . . There may be certain labor organizations but only for *ordinary administrative duties* . . . We do not accept intermediaries between the revolution and its working forces." From Col. al-Qadhdhafi interview, *Middle East Journal,* pp. 206-7.

Change and Environment

Although the relationship between the
various types of development has not
been precisely identified and formulated,
there is little doubt that it is present;
similarly, general notions of political and
social development have proved useful for
understanding North Africa, even though
the concepts themselves have not been
defined beyond controversy.[1] Three
overlapping aspects of the development
process — symptoms or indicators rather
than equivalent measures — are education, urbanization, and industrialization.
Although none of these is properly
political, they all tie into the political

development process at two points: all three must be the result of government concern and considered allocation of scarce resources (the output side of the political process), all three help increase both the desire and the capacity for popular participation in politics (the input side).

But the net of interrelations does not end there. Any change of the type associated with development is a response to a problem and, in meeting the problem, creates new ones. The idea of a single leap from a traditional level of stability to a modern one is absurd, but no more so than the notion of a slow, smooth improvement in which tensions, dysfunctions, and contradictions are husked off one by one until the perfected inner core of individual or collective man appears. The bumpy road of development doubtless by its very nature presents a more unfavorable balance of problem-solving and problem-raising than do other phases in the life of a society. Not only are more problems (tensions, dysfunctions, contradictions) created than solved, but — even more important — these new problems are of a very different nature. Education, urbanization, and industrialization are considered "good things," even though the unemployed high-school graduate, the urban slum-dweller, and the alienated worker may be "worse off" than they were in their traditional condition. What makes these transitional beings "better off" is that the new problems created by their position in the midst of the development process help move the society to a more complex level of problem-solving.

Complexity is a characteristic of development, whether it manifests itself in political pluralism, social diversification, or economic differentiation, and there is a continual interaction between social and political change and the framework within which it operates. The selections presented here examine various milieus in which change is occurring. Although they are not parallel presentations of interaction between change and its environment, they are all concerned with typical aspects of change in North Africa: the problems change solves, the problems it creates, and the way it has been induced and confronted.

Education is the central problem facing all the North African countries. But it is the pride of Tunisia, which took advantage of its heritage of high-quality education and, after independence, put considerable emphasis on developing its human resources. L. Carl Brown reports on the strains, progress, and implications of education in that country.

In the economic field, Tunisia's greatest innovation is probably the rural cooperative system, which sought to provide the same difficult mixture of initiative, organization, and unity in agriculture as does educational reform, in its way. Douglas E. Ashford, in his study of the Tunisian cooperatives, shows that underlying the problem of rationalized agricultural production is a problem of adjusting political structures to the results of economic and social development measures; his article foreshadows the radical change in cooperatives that accompanied ben Salah's removal in 1969. Keith B. Griffin gives a comprehensive and detailed analysis of agricultural development in Algeria, which is experimenting with the self-managed farm. The sharp division of colonial and traditional agriculture and the sudden evacuation of the modern sector left a heritage of problems for the new state, but the spontaneous takeover and the later state organization of the modern sector have created greater — and, it is to be hoped, productive — challenges for Algerian structures, production, and manpower.

The process of urbanization involves both the formation of new urban complexes and the expansion of extant agglomerations. In North Africa, as elsewhere, towns grow out of the focusing of human activities on one spot, activities that include transportation, communication, and commerce. The rural market (suq) in the Maghrib is both a predominant phenomenon in itself and a stage in the urbanization process, as the study by Marvin Mikesell shows. The massive expansion of the existing cities is another aspect of the urbanization process. "Urbanization" is perhaps too crude a word, for the new city-dweller in the shanty-town is never really urbanized; he is simply uprooted from his rural context. Yet he does adapt to the new milieu effectively in some, if not in all, ways. The article by Robert and Claudine Descloitres and J. C. Reverdy, although written before Algerian independence, is a classic description of a North African shanty-town. A look at the other end of the process is presented by Frederick C. Thomas, Jr. The oil worker drains out of the marginal milieus in the Libyan (and Algerian and Tunisian) interior, yet problems of labor market, turnover, training, and sudden inflation cause new tensions. As they are resolved, a fuller life with more goods and services (and more complex values) for the individual is created. Some people, however, choose to stay behind, "occupying" the largest territory in North Africa, without regard to boundary or nationality. Yet as Robert Capot-Rey, the leading authority on the Sahara, shows, even the desert responds to social change.

The last two selections, which deal with the urban milieu, look to the future. (Future prospects in agriculture are discussed in Keith B. Griffin's article.) Algeria has again been the most imaginative of the North African countries in responding to the radically changed status of its industrial sector. It has shifted from handicrafts to industry (as has all the Maghrib), from foreign to domestic ownership (as has much of North Africa), but also, unlike the rest of the area, from management to worker control. For the moment, the new problems are greater than the old ones, but the challenges for the economic, social, and political development of the workers' civic sense, social consciousness, participatory and management skills, and economic expertise are all immense. The late Damien Helie weighs these pros and cons. The final section is a regional, projective view. Written by United Nations experts, it examines the possibility — indeed, the necessity — for economic cooperation in North Africa as the basis for significant economic expansion. It provides a realistic base for the idealistic notion of unity, and a detailed foundation for the hopes for development in the region. The cooperative approach offers the opportunity not only for combating underdevelopment but also for harmonizing newly liberated political energies.

There is a wide-open field for those who wish to study the efforts of the developing North African states as they meet, create, and respond to the problems of change. A growing number of sound studies based on cross-national demographic and economic information are an important contribution.[2] It would be an endless task to list the challenges for further study. A few significant areas can be cited, only as an indication of the possibilities. There is a growing need for in-depth studies of experiments in self-management. Studies are also needed of business: the process of social and economic change from artisan to industry, from trader to commercial firm, from hoarder or lender to banker. Although there are a few studies of North African villages, rural anthropology, and tribal structure,[3] there is room for many more. Perhaps the most striking lack is the total absence of work on social change in the medina, the traditional North African city.[4]

Notes

1. See Manfred Halpern, *The Politics of Social Change in the Middle East and North Africa* (Princeton, N.J.: Princeton University Press, 1963); Douglas E. Ashford, *Political Change in Morocco* (Princeton, N.J.: Princeton University Press, 1961); Douglas E. Ashford, *National Development and Local Reform* (Princeton, N.J.: Princeton University Press, 1967); I. William Zartman, *Problems of New Power* (New York: Atherton Press, 1964); I. William Zartman, *Destiny of a Dynasty* (Columbia: University of South Carolina Press, 1964); I. William Zartman, *Government and Politics in Northern Africa* (New York: Praeger Publishers, 1963); Charles Micaud, L. Carl Brown, and Clement Henry Moore, *Tunisia: The Politics of Modernization* (Praeger Publishers, 1964); Clement Henry Moore, *Tunisia Since Independence* (Berkeley: University of California Press, 1965); Lars Rudebeck, *Party and People* (New York: Praeger Publishers, 1969) Samir Amin, *Le Maghreb moderne* (Paris: Minuit, 1970).

2. Amor Benyoussef, *Populations du Maghreb et communauté économique à quatre* (Paris: Société d'Edition et d'enseignement Supérieur, 1967); Werner Plum, *Sozialer Wandel im Maghreb* (Hanover: Verlag für Literatur und Zeitgeschehen, 1967); André Tiano, *Le Maghreb entre les mythes* (Paris: Presses Universitaires de France, 1967); Samir Amnir, *L'économie du Maghrib,* 2 vols. (Paris: Minuit, 1966).

3. Bernard G. Hoffman, *The Structure of Traditional Moroccan Society* (The Hague: Mouton, 1967); Pierre Bardin, *La Vie d'un douar* (The Hague: Mouton, 1965); Pierre Moreau, *Le Pays des Nefzaouas* (Tunis: Bascone & Muscat, 1947); Pierre Bourdieu, *The Algerians* (Boston: Beacon Press, 1963), to name a very few. See the bibliographies in the appendix and also Camille Lacoste, *Bibliographie éthnologique de la Grande Kabylie* (The Hague: Mouton, 1962).

4. On the pre-independence period, see particularly the work of Roger Le Tourneau, including *Les villes musulmanes de l'Afrique du Nord* (Alger: La Maison des Livres, 1957); *Fes avant le protectorat* (Casablanca: Société Marocaine de Librairie et d'Edition, 1949), *Fez in the Age of the Merenides* (Norman: University of Oklahoma Press, 1961); "Social Change in the Muslim Cities of North Africa," *The American Journal of Sociology,* LX, No. 6 (May, 1955), 527-35; and the only comprehensive review of cities in independent North Africa, "Implications of Rapid Urbanization," in L. Carl Brown (ed), *State and Society in Independent North Africa* (Washington, D.C.: The Middle East Institute, 1966), pp. 123-45.

32

TUNISIA: EDUCATION, "CULTURAL UNITY," AND THE FUTURE

L. CARL BROWN

It is a sacred principle of general pedagogy — the necessity of safeguarding the cultural unity of a country. This is a corollary of the idea we developed earlier: education is social integration. If the society is a living reality, one and indivisible, then the culture will be so as well, and the pedagogical system must be a harmonious whole given the task of not letting the unity of the whole be placed in peril. To ignore the principle of cultural unity is . . . . to sow the seeds of discord and — another unavoidable consequence — to place it in peril of death."

These lines appeared in 1947 in an Arabic-language review, *al-Mabahith*. The author, Mahmoud Messadi, then a Tunisian professor at the newly created (November, 1945) Institut des Hautes Etudes, went on to contrast this ideal with the "virtually tripartite culture" existing in Tunisia with its three separate and unrelated systems of education.

Some eleven years later, the author of that article received the chance and the challenge to put his ideas to the test, for, in May, 1958, Mahmoud Messadi became minister of education.

M. Messadi's "sacred principle" of cultural unity was not to be resolved simply by reshuffling existing educational facilities. Equally important, and probably of greater political urgency, was the basic task of greatly increasing the total school attendance. At the time of independence in 1956, roughly 180,000 Muslim students between the ages of six and fourteen attended primary schools. This represented only 22 per cent of the total in this age group. The enrollment in secondary education was about 16,000 or 3 per cent of the total number of Tunisians between the ages of fifteen and twenty. Even this low figure gives a somewhat distorted and overly optimistic view of the true picture facing the new Tunisian state. For only by dint of a fairly impressive effort in the last ten years of their Protectorate had the French attained this modest level of school attendance. In 1947 (at the time of Messadi's article cited above), only one-half of that proportion were in school — 11 per cent of the total Muslim Tunisians of primary-school age and 1.5 per cent of those in the secondary-school age group.

Reprinted, by permission, from the report of L. Carl Brown to the Institute for Current World Affairs report of December 1, 1960.

From this dual legacy — the lack of a uniform system of education and the abysmal numerical inadequacy of that which did exist — several important considerations arise. First, as with so many newly independent countries, the new government and administration is led by an extremely small elite possessing the educational qualifications deemed necessary to govern a modern state.

Further, with the achievement of independence, this small ruling elite must move abruptly from agitation to implementation, from planning (and promising) to day-to-day operations. It suddenly finds itself free in two different senses — free for the first time of outside control, but also virtually free of past experience upon which to base important administrative decisions. Every action in such a situation is a precedent; even the decision to make no change in the old Protectorate system involves discussion and soul-searching unknown to routine, settled bureaucracy. And the impulse to change, to exert one's own personality, to prove that independence means more than a simple change of government — must necessarily be strong in such circumstances.

Finally, since so few Tunisians have had the chance to receive any education in the past, there exists a great gap in the cadres (a favorite word of the planners in the Ministry of Education) necessary to run a modern state and economy. As a result, graduates of the intensified educational program will quickly assume important positions, and in little over a decade the results of the present program will be felt in all sectors of the society. For example, the current plans would call for an increase in intermediate- and secondary-school enrollment from approximately 21,000 in 1959 to 130,000 in 1969. This seems modest enough even for a small country with a population of about 4 million, but absolute figures are misleading in education-starved countries like Tunisia. It is perhaps more valid to note that for every one student now enrolled in secondary or intermediate education there will be seven in 1969. The small "ruling elite" will have increased itself in roughly the same proportion in that brief span.

In short, it is not too much to suggest that the large question of what will be the future political-cultural orientation of Tunisia will be determined less by reactions to Great Power maneuvers, by the relations with Abd al-Nasser and the Eastern Arab world, or even by the resolution of the Algerian question, than by the results of the programs now being advanced by M. Messadi and a few hundred like-minded persons in the Tunisian educational system. It cannot be stressed too much that this very small group now has the initiative. The government is popular. Groups that might be inclined to oppose are (for reasons to be noted later) both discredited and lacking leadership and/or firm orientation. The chance for a "guided social revolution" comparable in its results if not its methods to that of Ataturk's Turkey is available to the government presided over so ably today by President Habib Bourguiba. However, it must be recognized that this government — this small ruling elite — "represents" Tunisia only in a sense acceptable to Edmund Burke. Having the confidence of the masses now, they have the intention of imposing by persuasion their own idea of what should make up the proper "cultural unity" of their country. A big order, and if they should falter after some three or five years, much of what now seems to typify the new Tunisia could quickly change. If, however, enough *élan* and efficiency can be generated and maintained for about a decade, then a better-prepared and more broadly based ruling group could, in fact, maintain and perpetuate the social revolution being worked out by today's leadership.

Before describing the major points in the present educational program, a few remarks are in order to show just what the Tunisians inherited in this field when independence came in 1956. Many Western writers are inclined to state boldly that modernization in Tunisia began with the French Protectorate in 1881. This is not quite accurate. Instead, the pattern seems to be more in line with that of Egypt and the Ottoman Empire at that same period. Tunisia, as these other countries, had begun to feel the influence of a physically superior Western culture and had, while still maintaining some independence. begun its first tentative steps to synthesize Western thought and technology into its existing Islamic culture. However, the combination of internal inefficiency and outside aggression would not permit the realization of such changes from within. Still, the establishment of the French Protectorate in Tunisia, like the British occupation of Egypt in the following year, can be considered more justly the continuation and intensification of modernization, rather than its beginning.

The main features of the pre-Protectorate phase of modernization in Tunisia are linked with the reforming zeal of one Khayr al-Din Pasha, a mamluk of Circassian origin whose various services for the beys of Tunis included that of prime minister from 1873 to 1877. His plans for adapting Western technology to the Islamic heritage are best symbolized and realized in the Sadiki *collège* (in the French sense, a secondary school) founded in 1875 and still in existence. . . .

The immediate impact of the French Protectorate in the field of native education was negligible. The French authorities, concerned with the embarrassing number of Italians in Tunisia, concentrated on schemes for French colonization. The idea of spreading French culture among the *indigènes* hardly existed. Nor was this inconsistent with the mentality of the times. This was, after all, the classic period of imperialism, and the concept of "mission" or "stewardship," even where active, did not automatically embrace the social services taken almost for granted seventy years later. It might be noted that the total number of Algerian Muslim children in primary school in 1892, after sixty years of French control, was only 11,409.

The French legacy in education can most readily be explained in terms of the three-way educational system deplored by Messadi. There was, first, French education integrated completely into the system of metropolitan France. In 1954, the next to last year of the Protectorate, roughly one student in four in the completely French system was a Tunisian Muslim (and nearly half of the 59,281 students were French).

Second was the "assimilated" system, called in the primary grades "Franco-Arab." (For secondary, it was usually termed "modern," or the "Sadiki type.") For the same year, 1954, nearly all of the 125,859 students were Tunisian Muslims. In the Franco-Arab schools the language of instruction was divided between French and Arabic on a roughly two-thirds to one-third basis. The schools were avowedly lower in standards than the French schools (where no Arabic was taught), but to compensate, the Tunisian Muslim was able to get some training in his native language and culture. The third major category, the Zitouna type of education, was left virtually untouched by the French authorities. Some Tunisians might want to see in this both a Machiavellian policy of divide (into divergent educational systems) and rule, and a desire to foster the obsolete segment of Tunisian education so the Tunisian will not "catch up" with the European. The truth seems to be much simpler. The French had their hands full with their own plans in other fields, and there seemed to be every justification for taking a stand in principle against interfering in religious matters. If this policy also gave some marginal short-run political benefits, *tant mieux*. As a result, the Zitouna complex was marked by two major trends during the Protectorate: (a) sporadic, but never quite successful, attempts at reform from within (usually the student body, such as in the 1920's, and 1940's, leading even to a student strike in 1947 based on demands for better physical facilities. foreign-language instruction, and equal job opportunities for Zitouna graduates; and (b) a rather impressive growth in total enrollment. The number in attendance at Zitouna is estimated to have increased almost tenfold from 1931 to 1951. . . .

A hybrid type of primary school not mentioned in Messadi's three-way classification deserves mention. This was the "modern Qoranic school" designed to modernize the traditional *kuttab* system by adopting many of the techniques of modern pedagogy while at the same time maintaining Arabic as the language of instruction and continuing full emphasis on Islamic studies. This type of school, which resulted from native Tunisian efforts solely (as will be seen later), remained basically private in character to the end, being financed by private subscriptions and habous funds to which in later years was added some governmental assistance and supervision. At the end of the Protectorate period, these schools had a total enrollment of 35,000, or about one student for every four in the governmental Franco-Arab primary school.

The social result of this complicated and diverse educational system was (1) a level of school attendance and a standard of performance among the European community comparing favorably with metropolitan France; (2) an almost equally good record among the Tunisian Jewish community[1] educated also almost exclusively in the French schools; and finally (3) a modern education available to only a handful of Tunisian Muslims who made up over 90 per cent of the total population.

During this period, the Tunisian Muslim who wanted a thoroughly modern education but who did not relish the thought of becoming one of Marshall Lyautey's "100 million Frenchmen," found his ideal in the Sadiki *collège* — which, in fact, set the pattern for modern Tunisian education (as opposed to French education in Tunisia).

Reserved for Tunisian Muslims, most of whom entered by competitive examination, this single school with a total student population never rising far above 700 served as the training ground for the indigenous Tunisian leadership from the turn of the century to the present day. Its alumni include President Bourguiba and eight of the eleven members of the [1960] cabinet. Two other cabinet members who were not students at Sadiki later taught there. One must continually make a few mental adjustments and recall the paucity of modern education available to Tunisians during all of this long period in order to appreciate fully how one small secondary school could exert that much influence and serve as the focus for so much intellectual and political activity. It is perhaps helpful in this respect to draw comparisons with the early, formative years of the American University of Beirut or with Gordon Memorial College in Khartoum, Sudan.

If the Sadiki *collège* represented an attempt to bring some of Tunisian and Arabic culture into modern, Westernized education, then the Khalduniya represented a parallel attempt to blend some modern methods and subjects into the Zitouna education. The Khalduniya, taking its name from the famous fourteenth-century Arab historian ibn Khaldun, was established in 1895 by a few reform-minded Tunisian Muslims for the purpose of giving Zitouna students some background in modern studies. Finding little official response from the Zitouna leadership, the Khalduniya (which, interestingly, did get the warm support of the French Resident, René Millet) was obliged to give off-hour instruction in foreign languages and modern studies on a completely voluntary basis to interested Zitouna students. . . .

These, then, were the main lines inherited by the new Tunisian government in 1956 after seventy-five years of the French Protectorate and a pre-Protectorate generation of cautious beginnings in modernization: not much education of any kind; and then, to compound the problem, the existence of a French school-system peopled by Europeans and a handful of Tunisians; the Sadiki-type assimilated and "Franco-Arab" schools; and the archaic Zitouna system, whose prestige had declined, possibly beyond redemption.

In its first two years of independence, the Tunisian government moved energetically but cautiously. Impressive increases in school attendance were recorded, but education continued basically within the existing framework. This was a wise policy. The obvious reaction in the first flush of independence would have been to propose changes too sweeping for existing personnel and facilities; and at the same time, what might have seemed to outsiders as radical and somewhat irresponsible policies would have discouraged foreign teachers who will be needed in increasing numbers for at least another decade.

Again, that great exception — Zitouna. To describe the first two years as cautious might seem a poor joke to a Muslim traditionalist, for radical changes were made in the Zitouna system in April, 1956. All of the old annexes of the Zitouna Mosque were integrated into the secondary system of national education. The university mosque itself became a public institution with a "civic personality" under a sheikh rector who is nominated by decree and responsible to the minister of education. The university mosque teaches two major categories of studies: Arabic language and literature, and juridicial and religious sciences. In short, Zitouna is no longer a "system," and the remaining university mosque is under considerable pressure to become a modern *faculté* within the new Tunisian University. However, the teaching staff of Zitouna and, in general, the religious leadership of similar background had fallen into such low esteem that changes that might have caused no end of conflict in other Arab or Islamic countries went into effect in Tunisia with hardly a murmur of protest.

This state of affairs deserves a few explanatory remarks, since it is essential background to an understanding of the cultural outlook of today's leadership in Tunisia. The decline in status of the religious group can be traced in Tunisia to three interrelated factors:

1. As is the case in large measure in most other Arabic and Islamic countries, the religious leadership remains in the hands of a rigid orthodoxy who do not have the capacity and who by training would abhor the attempt to "rethink" and adjust their theology to the daily problems of the modern world. This group have, in short, forfeited that role vital to any "clergy" — that of being the conscience of the community, often somewhat behind the times, possibly at

times even a bit ahead, but at least in touch with and talking the same language of those in the community worried about and trying to adjust the actual to the ideal.

2. The religious leadership further had the bad luck to get itself identified with the old Destour and forces opposing the Neo-Destour, and even in some cases they were linked with the French that is, the Sheikh al-Islam was on the committee under whose patronage the Eucharistic Congress at Carthage was held in 1931, and Islamic *fatwas* [advisory judgments] were never lacking to condone or pave the way for any change in French policy). Here the contrast with the eastern part of the Arab world is striking. The Muslim Brethren might well be accused of obscurantism, of a myopic view of the real world in addition to many other shortcomings, but their "nationalist" record of consistent opposition to the foreign occupying power was always beyond reproach. Even the "complaisant" 'ulema of the era of British and French dominion in that part of the world always managed to maintain some force, bargaining power, and respect vis-à-vis the ruling infidels.

3. Finally (and this is both a result and extension of the above two factors), the vicious circle of declining job opportunities to Zitouna graduates in the modern age leading to declining prestige and thus the impossibility of inducing the better qualified candidates to consider a Zitouna education virtually eliminated the chance that the university mosque could reform itself. As a perceptive observer noted of these students in 1951, they "are no longer those of a century ago. The sons of good families (not excepting those of the 'ulema), the children of the bourgeoisie and even of urban workers move *en masse* toward modern education. . . . What remains to people the Grand Mosque and its annexes? Those who have not been able to find a place in the modern schools or who have not done well (about a thousand holders of the *certificat d'études* who have not gained places in the secondary schools and who do not want technical education), and the bedouin who still have faith in the value of Zitouna diplomas. In sum, the frustrated students, intellectually and materially."[2]

Zitouna is rapidly withering on the vine. Since the forced retirement of its last rector — Tahar ben Ashur, who refused to condone Bourguiba's proposal that the *jihad* (holy war) against poverty justified breaking the Muslim fast in the month of Ramadan, no steps have been taken to appoint a new one; and the considerable inefficiency and disorganization always endemic with Zitouna is now compounded by that arising from despair and disillusion. The government line fixed on several occasions by Bourguiba is to praise Zitouna for the role it played in resistance to Frenchification by preserving the Arabic and Islamic heritage, but to follow this praise with the observation that resistance is no longer needed, as independence has been achieved. Zitouna is now *dépassé*. Among the aims of independence, according to the official "L'Enseignement en Tunisie" in *La Documentation Tunisienne,* was to begin the unification of the *general outmoded* Zitounian education with the general education, first administratively and then culturally [italics added].

How could anything approaching the old system be revived, assuming some revolutionary change in policy in the next few years? Of the many Zitouna annexes that used to give the traditional equivalent of a secondary-school preparation for later entry into the university mosque, there remains only the ibn Khaldun school (even the name is significant), designed to let students who began their traditional studies before the changes finish their studies in something resembling the old way. The school with a population of 1,800 in 1959 was down to 1,350 in 1960, and expects to close its doors in another four. The remarks of this school's director might serve to epitomize the "line" or, better, the last-ditch stand of the diminishing traditionalists. With considerable circumspection and after persistent prodding, he ventured to me the following summary: no one disputes the goal of unification in education, although there are some who would like to see greater emphasis given religious studies in the new unified education. The "nationalization" of the Zitouna is acceptable since it is — unlike al-Azhar — and has always been a national Tunisian institution (or at most a Maghribi institution) serving the needs of this area. He was a little more revealing of what were probably his real sentiments in urging me to see many people from all sides (and not just those in official positions) in order to get a proper perspective of the Tunisian views on this subject of education. He also expressed the desire to see more Tunisian students study in the eastern Arab world as well as more professors from those countries come to Tunisia to teach.

By 1958, the time was ripe for an ambitious long-range educational program. The Zitouna problem was virtually out of the way; two years of independent government had given the new leaders a chance to know intimately the problems and prospects; and enough time had lapsed since independence to avoid the stigma of having taken precipitate, unplanned action.

These first two years also showed that yeoman efforts along the previous lines would not be enough. As with so many newly independent countries (the almost overwhelming combination of an underdeveloped economy making for limited budgetary possibilities, a high rate of natural increase in population, and a woefully low level of literacy and education as a starting point), Tunisia found it had to run hard even to stand still and keep its present low proportion of educated to total population. With a birthrate of 41 per 1,000, Tunisia could expect an average annual increase of about 15,000 primary-school-age children (six to fourteen). Thus, an annual increase in school attendance of 15,000 would be essential merely to maintain the present low standard. Over and above this annual demand loomed the challenge of some 530,000 children of primary-school age (or two out of every three in 1958) deprived of any chance to get an education. That is to say, with an annual increase of primary-school attendance of 20,000 (which would be for 1958 an impressive 8 per cent increase), it would require approximately 106 years to achieve universal *primary* education in Tunisia. This, it should be stressed, is to consider *only* primary education.

The government's attempt to increase school enrollment without changing in substance the system inherited from the days of the Protectorate (excepting the Zitouna system already noted) had been impressive. In two years, the total primary-school population had risen from over 180,000 to 265,000. Unfortunately, there was no chance of maintaining this rate of increase or of even approaching it under the existing system. The needed annual increase in teachers would not be available for over a decade, and the point of saturation had been reached in the prospect of recruiting foreign (almost all French) teachers.

In addition, the government could not continue to ignore its *idée fixe* of a unified educational system, and to the extent that one postponed that goal while increasing school attendance one merely compounded the problem.

It was time for a breakthrough by mid-1958. After a committee of education experts guided by Mahmoud Messadi had worked out the main line, President Bourguiba announced the ten-year educational reform at the commencement exercises of Sadiki *collège* in June, 1958. With his usual good sense of the proper gesture at the right time, the president had chosen as the site for announcing the government's plan the very school that he himself had entered just fifty years earlier.

Universal primary education was to be achieved in ten years, after which time it would become compulsory. This average annual increase in primary-school enrollment of just over 50,000 would be achieved, *inter alia,* by two dramatic revisions that may well be long argued and possibly even deplored by many a pedagogue, but that to this writer seem just the right balance of realism and idealism: (1) For the first two years of school, there will be two shifts of students, each attending for one-half day, or a total of fifteen hours of instruction per week. (2) The seventh year of primary education will be eliminated. By these measures alone, the potential primary-school enrollment can be increased almost 30 per cent, but these innovations are joined with an intensive program of accelerated school-building and teacher recruitment.

In a sense, these two measures can be viewed as the sacrifice (in possible total over-all efficiency) deemed necessary to make the goal of universal primary education feasible. When one considers the dangerous possibilities inherent in any society having a small educated minority shoulder to shoulder with a vast majority completely unlettered, the choice seems obvious. It was essential that a large number of people who had lived until that time on the vague promise of better days when and if independent, now be given a stake in society by seeing their children obtain a modern education. From another viewpoint, to be blunt, Tunisia is (as is almost every newly independent country) in greater need of two mediocre doctors than of one good one — and the same holds true right down the line of professions and crafts.

As for the vexing question of language of instruction, the reform took a line that, while giving Arabic a slight primacy, seems at the same time to commit Tunisia to a practical bilingualism of Arabic and French. The first two years of instruction are given solely in Arabic, but after that time French predominates.

In secondary education, the language of instruction (barring one or two exceptions, such as the ibn Khaldun school mentioned above) is just as it was under the Protectorate — French in everything except the teaching of Arabic language, "civic and religious studies" (one hour per week for the first three years), and the study of Islamic thought (not taken by most students). In short, a little under one-third of the total secondary instruction is given in Arabic. Tunisian officials, understandably, soft-pedal this fact, which the shortage of trained Arabic-speaking teachers makes inevitable, in the short run at least. Every possible detail concerning the language of instruction in primary school (where a great change has been made) is available, but one will look in vain for any such breakdown in official publications dealing with secondary education. It was also somewhat frustrating trying to get a true picture of this situation from ministry officials, and only *chef de cabinet* Tayib Triki was finally willing to offer a blunt, direct answer. He insisted that the ultimate goal was 100 per cent education in Arabic, but he would not even hazard a guess of what the ratio of the two languages of instruction might be at the end of the ten-year reform program in 1969.

So much for the language problem. Secondary education itself is now of two types: either an intermediate education lasting only three years or a preparatory education of six years' duration. The former is designed to give a more practical and "trade-school" training to those who will not be going on to higher studies, while the latter follows the traditional preparatory-school pattern — with, however, considerably greater emphasis on the natural sciences. Competitive exams at the end of the primary education decide which type secondary education (if either) the student will enter. The separation of the secondary sheep from the intermediate goats at the tender age of thirteen or fourteen seems a little harsh, but the principle is recognized that a student who later does especially well in intermediate education can be considered for transfer to the secondary. In any case, the Tunisian problem is such at this juncture that it must be tackled by a sort of statistical morality without too much concern for occasional individual hardships. Also, the real personal hardship is felt by those students who barely fail to get in either type of secondary school; for even at the end of the ten-year reform program, only one out of every three primary-school graduates will be able to continue in either terminal intermediate or secondary education. The policy must be to "save the maximum number of potential intellectuals, recognizing that for a time many will go unschooled."[3]

The six-year secondary education offers three options to the students, to be chosen at the end of the first three years: (a) a general course of studies, (b) technical (mainly aiming toward engineering), and (c) commercial and economic studies. It is planned that the proportion of students taking each option should be, respectively, 50 per cent, 30 per cent, and 20 per cent. This sharp move away from classical and liberal-arts studies, the early specialization, and the planned heavy increase in graduates with considerable technical knowledge is bold indeed for a country with Tunisia's present economic development. Whatever else can be said, there should be no shortage of candidates to carry out this new approach — of 200 students recently applying for government scholarships, 63 per cent expressed a preference for higher studies in the natural sciences. Only 20 per cent opted for law, and 17 per cent for letters.

Created also with the reform program was an Office Pedagogique (Diwan al Tarbiya). In addition to all the tasks that the name might imply (assist in working out a uniform curriculum, publish a journal keeping instructors up to date on problems and new developments in education, and so on), this office has the assignment of supervising the writing and publication of appropriate textbooks. At the time of independence, Tunisian education relied mainly on foreign textbooks — all French for instruction given in French; Egyptian or Lebanese for instruction in Arabic. Obviously an educational declaration of independence from both sources is an important ultimate aim for the Tunisian leadership, but an excess of zeal in such a program could easily lead to a rapid decline in standards. This has been avoided to date. Most of the Office Pedagogique books published thus far are either selections of texts for use in teaching Arabic and French or history and geography books closely following previously used texts. The very fact that Tunisia needs to free itself from both French and Egyptian textbook domination probably facilitated the middle way.

(It is interesting to speculate how much pressure would exist for more Arabic teachers and textbooks from Egypt if Abd al-Nasser had taken a more subtle line in relations with Tunisia in the last four years.)

The publication of native textbooks reaps other benefits for a country straining every budgetary nerve to finance an intensive educational program. The Office Pedagogique books will be published and distributed directly by the ministry to students without the intermediary of the bookdealers. As a result, foreign books now costing \$3—\$6 will be replaced by books costing about 50 cents. The government should be able to put to other uses the roughly 45,000 dinars (one dinar equals \$2.40) used [in 1959] to provide textbooks for poor students, and, in human terms, scores of family crises over how to pay for Ahmad's or Fatima's books will be solved. Having been in the various bookshops of Tunis at the time of the return to school, I lived with this problem while waiting my own turn in the queue. It was touching to see small children (boys and girls) handing over in return for bright, new French and Egyptian textbooks sums of money that might well represent more than a week's wages to their father, or even (not unlikely with chronic underemployment) the diminishing savings of a family having no one gainfully employed at the moment. One example will serve for all. An illiterate workman whose clothes indicated his peasant origins came into the al-Najah bookshop (located just a few yards from the Zitouna Mosque) clutching in his hand a grubby piece of lined paper on which was written (by someone else, of course) the name of a textbook. The bookdealer with the deftness of a bartender reached without looking to pick a book from the shelves behind him, flicked it on the counter, and barked out with the arrogance of a gendarme, *"dinar wa nus"* (\$3.60). The workman, astounded, fell automatically into the only world of trade he knew — the bargaining of the suq. "Surely the gentleman was joking . . . an impossible asking price . . . or perhaps you have something similar for less?" It was all over. The bookdealer had already given the universal Arabic sign of negative — the head tossed back quickly with an accompanying click of the tongue — the book was back on the shelf, and several small schoolchildren were eagerly swarming into the workman's place to make their purchases. (The workman's son may eventually have been one of those to receive a free book after his teacher had ascertained by a rough, informal "means test" that the family could not afford the purchase, but it is likely that the father, after consulting with friends or with passers-by who would listen, spent every available franc to buy the book, fearing that without this "amulet" his son might not be able to stay in school.)

The education reform, it has been stressed repeatedly, has as its keynote national and cultural unity, and this idea of unity extends to both the sexes. There is great concern to achieve eventual universal education for both boys and girls, and as late as his press conference in September of [1960] Messadi, while taking pride in the increases in school attendance, went on to deplore the fact that only 27 per cent of the girls of primary-school age (as against 57 per cent of the boys) were attending school. He pledged increased efforts to close this gap. Nor is this window-dressing. The Bourguiba government is dedicated to the idea of bringing Tunisian Muslim women into full participation in society, and the president himself, as a top leader of the National Union of Tunisian Women once said, "is the first feminist."

At the peak of the educational pyramid will be the University of Tunis (officially in existence since March, 1960). Up to the present time, this university is little more than a regrouping of various existing institutions under one administration, for example Institut des Hautes Etudes, Zitouna Mosque/University (embracing only the "higher" studies and not the secondary studies now "nationalized," as already noted), the Ecole Normale Superieure, and so on. In fact, most of these institutions remain at their old locations, and many of the other aspects of unification have yet to be completed. In one sense, it is recognized in principle that the real growth of the university can and should only be realized as the products of the present primary and secondary reform reach college age (only after 1964). Still, there has been an impressive advance in university attendance since independence. The Institut de Hautes Etudes (the nucleus of the new university — all other branches such as the Ecole Normale the Agricultural School, and so on, being specialized departments) numbered in 1956 only 362 Tunisian Muslims (24 of whom were women). By the school year 1959-60, the number of Muslim Tunisians had jumped to 955 men and 146 women. Even more impressive was the change in emphasis to natural sciences (which enrolled less than a quarter of the 212 students in 1952 and more than half of the 1,084 students in 1959).

Even with this impressive increase, Tunisians getting their higher education abroad exceed the locally educated by about three to two. There were in 1959 an estimated 1,500 Tunisians pursuing higher studies in France and about 100 in Iraq and Lebanon. This should be compared with the situation in 1956, when there were some 500 in France and about 200 in the Near East . . . .

In any case, the University of Tunis will grow — according to present plans — in stages consistent with the remainder of the reform program, and the inspiration will not come from the East. The following statement, taken from an official Ministry of Education report entitled "Study of the Creation of the Tunisian University" seems almost to go out of its way to make that point clear:

> The example of certain young universities created in the last forty years in various countries formerly dependent or underdeveloped, notably in the countries of the Arab Near East, demonstrates that a University which is not sufficiently concerned with research rapidly becomes a teaching institution, the level of which approaches some sort of complementary secondary education.

Two years have now passed since the beginning of the ten-year educational reform. How does performance compare with the plan? Statistically things look good, although not quite up to the mark set. The proposed primary enrollments for 1959-60 and 1960-61 were respectively 373,000 and 428,000. In 1959-60, the actual enrollment was only 362,000, and the expected 1960-61 enrollment (statistics are not yet available) will be in the neighborhood of 412,000. At this rate, the aim of universal primary education would probably not be reached for at least twelve instead of ten years. However, this is hardly a severe criticism if the upward spiral can be maintained if only at a slightly reduced rate. The terminal intermediate- and secondary-education enrollment, on the other hand, are both slightly ahead of plan.

As for the budgetary possibilities of such a program, one is loose in a field of variables. Some points are clear. By Gladstonian principles of financing, the plan is unfeasible. Involved is an estimated increase in the annual budget from $21,360,000 in 1959-60 to $58,320,000 in 1968-69 — not to mention a building program of over $122 million over the ten-year period. Education already absorbs 17 per cent of the total budget. Implementation will in any case require a considerable amount of foreign aid — more, perhaps, than the Tunisians would like to think, or admit. But essentially the educational reform is linked intimately with hopeful plans for rapid economic development. "A policy of reduced or slow school attendance implies a choice of underdevelopment or at least a resigned attitude toward a permanent protraction of economic and social underdevelopment. . . . [But the opposite policy can] help carry out successfully any plan of transformation of the economic and social structure of the nation."[4] Educational reform and economic development — each depends on the other. If the latter fails, no politically conceivable amount of foreign aid could make up the budgetary deficit; and, in any case, the increasing number of trained cadres could not be absorbed in the lagging economy. If educational reform falls short of the mark, the economic plans fail for lack of necessary trained personnel. . . .

A word more about foreign aid. United States economic aid to Tunisia in the field of education was in its third year in 1960, and the average expenditure about $2-3 million per year, or a total to date of approximately $7 million (including expenditure to be made the remainder of this fiscal year). This aid has gone almost exclusively for assistance in the construction and equipment of schools, especially technical secondary schools. U.S. officials have (wisely, I think) shunned heavy commitments in other fields of education both to avoid the introduction of yet another educational system (and language, in many cases) when the national theme here is "cultural unity" and also to keep on good terms with the French, who are hypersensitive about others' efforts in their former Protectorate.

Assuming U.S. aid in the same ratio for the full ten-year period, the total value of our aid in implementing the ten-year program would be in the neighborhood of $23 million. Since the estimated credits for new construction and equipment in the Tunisian ten-year reform program amount to $122.5 million — $31 million for primary education, $16 million for terminal intermediate education, $74 million for secondary education — roughly one dollar out of every five for the total construction program would come — if the present situation were projected — from U.S. aid. This is to leave out of account completely the planned $2.5 million U.S. aid for construction and equipment of part of Tunisian University. Comparison here is not possible for the Tunisians have not prepared budget estimates.

American aid, involving mainly credits, is potentially expendable. It is, in other words, politically possible that some other state or group of states might be willing to offer the same amount of aid; but the French aid, in the short run at least, is absolutely vital not only to realization of future goals but even to the maintenance of present levels. This aid takes the form of just under 1,300 teachers. By terms of a cultural and technical cooperation agreement signed between Tunisia and France in April, 1959 (superseding an earlier agreement and giving somewhat better terms to Tunisia), the French government not only aids the Tunisian Ministry of Education in recruiting needed personnel in France but also pays approximately 40 per cent of the total salary and allowances granted teachers so recruited. Since the total average payment (salary and allowances) to French teachers in Tunisia amounts to about 38 per cent above the total average payment to teachers in metropolitan France, it works out that the government of Tunisia is able to recruit French teachers at prevailing French salary scales, while the French government makes up the difference entailed by transportation, additional allowances, or in effect in the bonus payment, which makes the arrangement sufficiently attractive to bring in the required numbers.

In short, for the school year 1959-60 there were (in addition to forty-four French teachers in higher education): 212 in secondary schools, or about 1 for every 5 native Tunisians; 94 in technical schools, or 1 for every 8 native Tunisians; 928 in primary schools, or about 1 for every 7 native Tunisians.

In addition to the 1,300 French teachers in the Tunisian national school system there are over 1,400 teaching in the remaining French schools in Tunisia. However, these teachers also make a real contribution to Tunisia's education needs – giving primary and secondary education to some 8,000 Tunisian Muslims and 6,500 Tunisian Jews, as well as to 19,600 children with French citizenship. Thus, 42 per cent of the pupils attending these totally French-staffed and French-financed schools are Tunisian citizens.[5]

Even this number of French teachers must be increased if enrollment goals are to be met, and for this school year the Tunisian government was seeking an additional 750. Only in the latter years of the reform program can Tunisia begin to think of a gradual replacement of French by trained native Tunisian teachers. This state of affairs is one of the many which must be considered in understanding the Bourguiba policy vis-à-vis France in spite of the many sources of friction – Algeria, the 1958 bombing of Sakiet Sidi Yusif, the Bizerte naval base, etc.

So much for the question of statistics, budget, and foreign aid in appraising the progress to date. Of more importance really is the question: What sort of new Tunisian is being produced by this education? What are the ingredients making up this greatly prized "cultural unity" that independence has presumably made possible?

Certain trends can be picked up from the lists of studies themselves. We have seen an almost equal division of instruction between Arabic and French in the primary grades, and virtually no change from the Protectorate days as regards the language of instruction in the secondary schools. This is, of course, in large part dictated by necessity. One must rely on French-speaking teachers for several years to come. However, what conclusions are to be drawn from the fact that "Qoranic and moral studies" in primary education average one hour per week, as against a weekly average of three hours for arithmetic, seven-and-one-half hours for Arabic language, and five hours for French?

In secondary education, the teaching of French language and literature will take only slightly less time of the total schedule than Arabic language and literature. Again, is it harsh reality or conscious choice? The necessity of continuing to teach many subjects in French is not disputed, but doesn't this continued emphasis on the teaching of French language and literature (an average of five hours out of thirty per week for the first four years, as against an average of six for Arabic) involve a more deliberate choice?

Official publications have often noted the need to re-integrate Islamic philosophy into independent Tunisia's educational system. The official program

for secondary education lists in a single fascicule the subject "Philosophy and
the Study of Islamic Thought." This sounds intriguing — a synthesis of Western
philosophy and traditional Islamic studies? No, the title is confusing. They are
two completely different subjects taught in the last year of general secondary
education according to the following schedule:

Hours per week
(*total of 30*)

Degree Program	Modern Letters	Classical Letters	Science	Math	Normale
Philosophy	7	7	4	4	5
Study of Islamic Thought	2	3	1	1	2

Further, lest one have the idea that perhaps some Zitouna thinking has been
able to carve out for itself a small niche in the new, unified secondary education,
note should be taken of the following remark explaining the general aims of the
program (translated from the Arabic — the program for Islamic thought covers
ten pages in Arabic; that for philosophy twenty-two pages in French):

> In a word, the methods to be relied upon in teaching Islamic thought should
> be those employed in what is today called the study of religious thought from
> the sociological point of view (*sociologie religieuse*). This is the method that
> attempts to go beyond the investigation of any given *Weltanschauung* (*aqliya*)
> to discover the substantive factors that determined its various viewpoints just
> as they determined the solutions and the problems arising from that very
> *Weltanschauung* in any given age. This [method] in short, calls not for simply
> receiving and believing but for thought, investigation, and criticism.

We have also noted the genuine effort being made to give equal educational
opportunities to both sexes, and this new mentality seems to be striking roots.
In a recent lecture on modern Tunisian literature, there was only one poem cited
by the speaker which drew guffaws and catcalls from the audience (about
three-fourths students) — that written in the early 1930's by a conservative
exhorting women to remain true to their religion by keeping their veils and
habits of seclusion.

What then will be the final result of this cultural unity? This much seems
certain. The present leadership is genuinely devoted to a modern, secular,
Western cultural outlook in a manner exceeding in boldness the various
modernist movements found in any other part of the Arab world. This does not
mean any necessary political francophilia or pro-Westernism. It is rather the
modernism of Sartre and Sputnik — of the rights of man and of successful
five-year plans. The rejection of the Arab East also goes deeper than the existing
troubles with the U.A.R. Basically, the Arab East has not made a very impressive
showing, and no amount of appealing to a common heritage can obscure this to
the Tunisians.

Much of what seems to be developing wins the support of us Westerners
(naturally enough, since the aims overlap so many of our own cultural values) —
the goal of universal primary education with all it implies of social responsibility,
female emancipation, the moderation and good sense of bilingualism and

apparent biculturalism, the increased emphasis on natural sciences and the attempt to build a better material world. . . . However, small ruling groups trying to change too quickly the most basic tenets of their society have often come to grief at what seemed to be the height of their influence. If the present government, now so firmly established, should for any reason begin to lose some of that popularity, is it not especially vulnerable to the charge of being too Western — too much opposed to the "good old values" of Islam and Arabic culture? One can imagine what a demagogue from the religious right might make of the following fact: the Student magazine *Jeunesse* asked students of the Ecole Normale Superieure if they had a personal problem concerning the existence of God. Of those answering the questionnaire, 47 per cent admitted to a problem. Of the remaining 53 per cent to whom this question caused no doubts, 8 per cent believed God exists, 45 per cent believed He does not exist.

Perhaps this is just a flash in the pan — a sort of freak like the celebrated Oxford Union decision not to fight for king and country, but it is serious enough to cause concern. One can only hope fervently that the many noble aims of this Tunisian guided social revolution are achieved and that while striking out against the false god of *immobilisme* and religious obscurantism, the Tunisian rulers will nevertheless strive to build on the foundation of what is best in their own cultural heritage.

Notes

1. The Tunisian Jewish community is an interesting subject of study deserving more attention than can be given here. There is almost no Zionism among Tunisian Jews, and, on the other hand, Tunisian official governmental policy is one of thoroughgoing racial and religious toleration. Public sentiment is not far behind this official policy. There is no more anti-Jewish sentiment than exists in certain quarters in our own country. This happy state of affairs for an Arab country is, deservedly, fairly well known. It is even more extraordinary in the light of recent history, for the large majority of Tunisian Jews welcomed the French Protectorate and adopted French language and culture. Many can no longer speak Arabic, and as many as could took French citizenship. As noted, Tunisian Jews were educated almost exclusively in French schools: even the schools of the Alliance Israelite had a completely French curriculum, with the sole difference of an additional program of Hebraic studies. These schools, under the Protectorate, were largely financed by the Tunisian government. They are now in the process of being "nationalized" (that is, open to all students and with the same curriculum as in other public schools), a source of muted discontent among Tunisian Jews.

2. Henri de Montety, "Révolution moderniste à l'Université ez-Zitouna," *L'Afrique et L'Asie,* No. 13 (1951).

3. "L'Enseignement Tunisien à la veille de la réforme," *L'Action,* July 15, 1958.

4. From the Ministry's announcement of the reform plan, entitled *Perspective Decennale de Scolarisation.*

5. According to M. Teyssier, Director of the Mission Universitaire et Culturelle Francaise en Tunisie, in 1960 there were over 3,000 French teachers in Tunisia (the difference being the increase for 1960-61 for which statistics are not yet available), 6,000 in Morocco, and only 3,000 in the rest of the world, including all of the former French colonies in Africa. This gives an interesting indication of the importance France attaches to North Africa.

33

ORGANIZATION OF COOPERATIVES
AND THE STRUCTURE OF POWER IN TUNISIA

DOUGLAS E. ASHFORD

Development analysts of all varieties seem to agree that the most difficult issue confronting the emergent nation in the next decade will be the mobilization of the rural population. In country after country, we find political leaders and technicians grappling with the problem of integrating into the new society a rural mass that often constitutes three-fourths of the total population. Because of the pressing questions of food production, population control, and savings for investment, rural mobilization is perhaps most often seen as an economic problem. The purpose of this article is to underscore some of the political dimensions of rural development, particularly those appearing in the single-party state. On a per capita basis, Tunisia has become one of the largest aid-receiving countries in the world, and her experience will undoubtedly strongly influence the thinking of other African countries as well as other single-party states in developing areas.

Although the analyst is not likely to disregard the political instrument in the implementation of social change, the political problems of development are considerably more complex than simply estimating feasibility. Indeed, if feasibility were the only political criteria, the United States would be withdrawing assistance from countries like Nigeria and India in order to concentrate on more effective governments such as the United Arab Republic. But political development involves more than a reasonably stable decision-making apparatus or even a foreign policy responding to American international interests. The political structure of the developing country is not independent of social change, nor does the existence of agreement among the elite in the developing country guarantee that they will be able to transform this very limited form of consensus into a political system relevant to a rapidly mobilizing society. Where such an effort is being made on a large scale, as is the case for Tunisia, a serious attempt should be made to identify the nature of the political tensions.

There are at least two components in the political analysis of a developmental problem. The first is to establish the way in which the elite's desires to remain in power have influenced decisions about development. In my view, this is

Reprinted, by permission, from *The Journal of Developing Areas,* I (April, 1967), 317–32.

relatively easy to do, although surprisingly little comparative research has been done on political constraints in different governments among the developing countries.[1] The second aspect of politics and development is much more difficult to study, for it involves predicting in what form, if any, the existing decision-making apparatus will survive. This step involves a fundamental divergence of opinion among developmental analysts, because there are two distinct methods of making such a prediction. One can devise a model of the more complex society and see whether the requirements of the existing government can be met, or one can simply project these requirements as constraints on any major developmental program.[2] Despite some remarkable advances in the analysis of political development, it is doubtful if we have at our disposal either a model of complex society sufficiently refined, or an account of the social impact of new programs reliable enough, to make predictions in either fashion.

An objection to both these alternatives is that they do not permit the analyst to take into account what might be called structural change. The magnitude of the transformation anticipated in the developing country involves something similar to economies of scale. Modern society is not more productive simply because its members are individually more educated and more highly skilled, but also because their interaction is patterned by new organizational and group structures, which are difficult to state in models of society. Modern government even may operate under constraints similar to those of any government in a developing country, but the constraints themselves take on new forms and are expressed in different ways. The inquiry into the rural development programs of Tunisia, centering on the rapid expansion of cooperatives, will enable us to identify some of these structural problems within the context of the single-party government.

There are both empirical and analytical advantages in focusing such an effort on a single-party government – the single-party government operates under constraints that are more specific and more severe than those found in most developing countries. Not only does the government possess a remarkable capacity to enforce sanctions, but it can apply coercion selectively and in graduated amounts with great skill. Regardless of whether one is more interested in the relations of new patterns of social differentiation to government, or the way in which constraints on decision-making may persist, political change is easier to observe. The conditions are empirically specific in the sense that the single-party organization itself tends to coincide with the pattern of power in the society. In fact, the single-party state can be looked upon as an organizational device to identify and incorporate new sources of influence in the society.[3] To a much greater extent than in other regimes of the developing areas, the single party is concerned with political socialization and political recruitment. In addition, the constraints are much more severe. The sudden rise and fall of members of the elite is one manifestation of the narrow margin of tolerance for political expression, not to mention the curious cycle of redemption for the fallen figures. The very notion of the single party, of course, makes possible the exercise of power in this way and produces a political structure whose modification is readily observed. The problem, then, becomes one of seeing how Tunisia's rural development effort appears to relate to a political system operating within very specific and severe limitations.

EMERGENCE OF THE TUNISIAN COOPERATIVE SYSTEM

The Tunisian cooperative organization can be viewed as the logical outcome of an intensive development program begun in 1961. Tunisian officials are perfectly accurate in describing cooperatives as the "movement (which) responds best to the objectives of our economy and social beliefs, and adapts itself perfectly to our circumstances and means."[4] Before looking more closely at the cooperative organization, it is helpful to trace the emergence of the present structure and the political forces that have made the cooperative an attractive developmental device.

The Destourian Socialist Party (PSD) has been in firm control of the country since independence in 1956, but has nevertheless had to deal with an array of opinions and crises over the past decade. While it would be unfair to accuse President Bourguiba and the Tunisian leaders of resisting pressures for social change, it is also clear that they postponed making a substantial commitment to rapid development until they were sure that the party could withstand the strains and tensions of massive change. The point is made not to question the wisdom of the party hierarchy but only to establish the fact that a political organization in many respects the most advanced in Africa found it desirable to wait, and that the pace of change in Tunisia until the early 1960's was no greater, for example, than in the much more conservative Moroccan monarchy.[5]

The turning point came in 1961, on the eve of Algerian independence. By this time the Tunisian elite had begun to realize that they would never escape the tutelage of France unless they had firm control of their economic and social development. Moreover, North African leaders anticipated that Algerian independence would create an aggressive modernizer and a thoroughly socialist regime in their midst. There was no way of knowing at that time that Algeria would succumb to the maladies of independence, but both the Moroccan and Tunisian governments were acutely aware that five years of independence for their peoples had been made possible by the Algerian struggle. Algeria had already mobilized its "disinherited" population in the course of the revolution, while the rural populations of Morocco and Tunisia remained largely detached from modern political forces.

With encouragement from the United States, the Tunisian government prepared a Ten-Year Plan for 1962-71 and unleashed the full force of the party organization to explain it to the people. The details of this campaign are not essential, but it should be noted that Bourguiba encountered resistance in many quarters of historical party strength, particularly in the cities and the central coastal plains or Sahel region. Although the plan did not provide organizational details, it was clear to the predominantly middle-class supporters of the PSD that the proposed redistribution of new income placed severe limits on how much they might benefit from development; the party had been run by the bourgeoisie, but the plan promised more for the workers and rural laborers. Local and regional party militants had already experienced a substantial reduction of their powers in the party congress of 1958, when party committees had been replaced by centrally designated deputies. The plan's notation that a General Commission for Regional Development would be appointed in Tunis and that a regional planning commission would supervise planning in each province[6] quite reasonably appeared as a new parallel hierarchy to a party that had already largely escaped the influence of the Destourian elder leaders.

The background of the cooperative system would not be complete without noting the role of Ahmed ben Salah in the Tunisian mobilization effort. A vigorous and imaginative leader, ben Salah had fallen from power immediately after independence when he attempted to use the trade unions (General Union of Tunisian Workers [UGTT] as the vehicle for advancing his socialist ideas. During his penance as secretary of state for public health, he provided Tunisia with a medical-care program that surpasses that of any African country, and laid the groundwork for a comprehensive social security scheme. Ben Salah's antipathy for the merchant was well known, and he frequently stressed the importance of completely overhauling the commercial structure of Tunisia, on which hundreds of Tunisian middle-class families depended.[7] When he was appointed secretary of state for planning and finance in 1961, everyone knew that his organizational skill would focus on a new structure for the mobilization of Tunisian resources. The structure was the cooperative.

COOPERATIVE STRUCTURE

The structure for the Tunisian co-ops did not, of course, arrive on the scene full blown but was the product of events and problems affecting the country's development program. However, the over-all organization as it existed in 1965 will be outlined in order to acquaint the reader with the full scope of the organization and to facilitate an explanation of the political considerations that shaped the final scheme.

The cooperative system is organized under ben Salah's superministry, which has control of the financial resources and technical studies made prior to the establishment of cooperatives. A director of cooperation was established in the ministry in July, 1962.[8] Under his supervision a Regional Union of Cooperatives (URC) had been established under the governor of each of Tunisia's thirteen provinces by the end of 1963.[9] Each URC is basically a managerial device for the coordination of all co-ops in the province. It will supervise accounting and finances, provide a channel for subsidies and loans from the central government, and act as the provincial policy-making group for all co-ops in the province.

Two observations should be made at this point. Contrary to the prevailing philosophy in co-ops in modern nations, the Tunisian cooperative structure was organized from the top down. Moreover, the cooperatives were not viewed as products of voluntary, cumulative efforts at the local level, but were to be products of carefully coordinated and planned action by the political and administrative hierarchy. No agrument is made more forcefully by Tunisian officials than the absolute necessity for a technical study prior to the consideration of any new co-op. Beneath the governor, whose powers are often described as greater than those of a minister, are marshaled all the forces of the single-party state. There is, first, a director of the URC, invariably a party militant, often a member of the young, ambitious group of technicians who have arrived on the scene since independence. The director has formidable support, for in addition to specialized sections on cooperatives for agriculture, consumption, credit, construction, and a number of additional activities, he is in direct liaison with the party and its "national organizations." Beneath him there is a president of the regional commission for agricultural cooperation, where the delicate task of mobilizing the farmer, farm worker, and rural unemployed is focused. The commission includes the director of the URC, two representatives of the provincial committee of coordination of the party,[10] two representatives of the national organization of farmers (National Union of Tunisian Farmers), and two representatives of the secretary of state for planning — an inspector and an agricultural engineer. The second component is perhaps most important, though not stressed by Tunisian officials. The president of the party's regional coordination committee is directly and independently present in all cooperative activity.

The model statutes of the URC reveal a central conflict of cooperative activity in Tunisia, to which the analysis will return.[11] The statutes give highly detailed instructions for the accounting practices to be followed, even chastising the provincial officials for regarding accounting as an "onerous formality." This caution is followed by an equally strong circular insisting that there must be full participation in the URC. The general assembly of subscribers to the URC must meet quarterly and the administrative council of the URC is not to take over the full management of the cooperative. The experience of co-ops in modern nations has, of course, greatly disappointed those who saw them as an instrument for encouraging local participation and expression. Nevertheless, ben Salah has repeatedly stressed that "democratic participation constitutes the fundamental character of the cooperative enterprise" and that the *prise de conscience* among the co-op members is a primary goal of the organization. The reconciliation of the demand for financial control and active participation is perhaps the central political issue in the Tunisian cooperative scheme, and cannot be fully explored without consideration of the general characteristics of the political system as a whole.

With minor variations, the overlapping organization of co-ops, party, and administration at the provincial level coincides with similar structures at the local level. Again under direction of the central ministry, regional plans are being designed for the entire countryside. These plans, prepared in most cases by French agencies under contract, are complete for most of the northern and central coastal provinces. The Regional Union of Development (URD) was established by law on November 4, 1963, as the vehicle for all cooperative activity within the technically defined regions. The region generally conforms to the local administrative unit — the *sheikhat* — and to the area encompassed by the local party cell. By the end of 1964, 134 URD's had been organized and the entire country is to be included in comparable regional cooperatives by the end of the ten-year planning projection. The initiation and management of all co-ops operating at the regional level, which includes most agricultural co-ops for production, is under the supervision of a URD.

The URD is composed of local co-ops of one of four standard forms, also carefully outlined by model statutes provided by the ministry. There are, first, agricultural production co-ops, whose various subordinate types will be described later. There are also consumer, credit, and specialized co-ops. The specialized co-ops include such activities as construction, handicrafts, wine storage, olive-oil marketing, and are usually under a supervisory co-op at the provincial level. Marketing co-ops for the major agricultural exports — olive oil, wine, citrus fruit, and dates — have existed for some time, and their activities are now coordinated with the various provincial and regional co-ops. The organization of co-ops does not follow the same sequence in all provinces. In the north, emphasis has been placed on agricultural production co-ops; in the central plains, stress has been placed on creating service cooperatives among olive-oil producers; an initial effort to create credit cooperatives was concentrated in the Cap Bon area; in parts of the north, experiments are beginning with regional co-ops to service the cooperative farms with seed, machinery repairs, and crop storage; the program to replace merchants with consumer co-ops generally begins in the major regional towns and then spreads to small outlets in villages and on larger production co-ops.

The basic organization of the co-ops is complemented with several enabling laws, and a long sequence of land tenure legislation that goes well back into the protectorate period. Two pieces of legislation govern the conditions under which cooperatives at various levels may be organized. The over-all impact of this legislation is to make certain that no cooperative can be organized unless it fits within the URC-URD scheme and the requirements of the national development plan. These stipulations are laid down for agriculture in a law of May 27, 1963, which establishes the three basic forms of production cooperatives and the form for all agricultural service cooperatives.[12] Each co-op is to have a general assembly and administrative council following the lines of the higher-echelon co-ops. Another law of December 28, 1964, governs the conversion or expansion of any type of co-op. The import of this legislation is, quite simply, to bring the entire cooperative structure under complete and detailed governmental control.

COOPERATIVE FUNCTIONING UNDER SINGLE-PARTY GOVERNMENT

Because this essay is primarily concerned with the relationship of the cooperative structure to the single-party government, more detailed attention will be given to the most delicate aspect of the growing co-op organization. Like most developing countries, about three-fourths of the Tunisian population of roughly 4.5 million people gain their living from agriculture.[13] The agricultural population is, then, slightly more than 3 million people having an active population of about 1.5 million. At least a quarter of a million of these farmers fall within a Muslim sharecropping system known as *khammes,* giving the farmer about one-fifth of his produce. The remainder run the full range of landowners, from large absentee landlords to small independent farmers and farm workers. From a political viewpoint, the problem is how this population can be made more productive while maintaining a single-party government. (The hierarchical structural created for the cooperatives responds admirably to this requirement.)

The political nature of the problem should not be minimized, although it is easily ignored by both Tunisian and foreign technicians, who, for very good reasons, see the mobilization of the countryside as an economic and technological issue. The best refutation of this convenient detachment from the full reality of the co-op scheme comes from the highest Tunisian leaders themselves, who constantly place the developmental goals of the cooperatives on the same plane with the necessity of social advancement and full participation. In the Four-Year Plan (1965-68), for example, human development is given first importance and participation is considered "indispensable" if each cooperator is to understand his role in collective action. The relevant qualification is, however, that the government essentially adopts the Western mode of thinking and immediately follows this statement with an acknowledgement that most

Tunisians lack both the financial and technical means to engage in such action.[14] Operating on Western premises, it is to be expected that Western conclusions will follow. The neglected condition is, of course, that Tunisia has and intends to continue a power structure suited to the single-party state.

The problem of increasing production under such a power structure can be attacked at two levels: the response of the individual farmer or peasant and the future of the political regime whose capacity to accommodate more complex organizations is being tested. From the perspective of the individual farmer the conditions of rural life have always been precarious. This is doubly true in a semi-arid country whose pattern of agriculture is heavily oriented to the needs of the former colonial rule. One only need survey the political influence wielded by the farm bloc in any industrial nation to see how effectively the farmer has exercised power that is vastly disproportionate to his popular or economic strength. Once the farmer is mobilized within the political system he places heavy demands on the society, dictated in part by his essential and high-risk profession. He tends to protect his interests effectively, if necessary by violence or by the simple expedient of depriving society of nourishment. Possibly more than any other figure in society, the farmer lives by the very touchstone of politics, survival itself. The Tunisian leaders are certainly not unaware of historical experience. The sensitivity of the single-party system makes rural mobilization an exceedingly delicate political issue. In brief, the transformation of the isolated, impoverished peasant into a more productive, active citizen may indeed be the most difficult political hurdle encountered by any single-party government.

Agriculture is by its very nature a diverse and localized activity. The differences in soils, rainfall, crop patterns, and harvesting necessitate individual judgment. The farmer in the developing country has of course found a minimal but reliable level of subsistence farming, which in itself often represents remarkable adaptation to his environment. The development process demands that he incur additional risk in order to become a more productive farmer. In every society this risk is shared by the entire population, the *modus vivendi* being worked out in the political system. The Tunisian government has already been forced to recognize the diversity of agriculture. From a second perspective the cooperative structure can be looked upon as its attempt to reconcile the single party's need for uniformity and predictability with the inescapable uncertainties of farming. The cooperative structure provides a single hierarchy to shape these conditions to the single-party structure. The fundamental political diversification of labor and skill in the modernization of rural society. Before exploring this argument further, it may be helpful to examine the extent to which the cooperative structure has already been modified to meet Tunisia's agricultural needs.

The agricultural production co-ops are adjusted to the three major components of the rural economy (see Table 1). The northern regions were developed by the French into large commercial wheat farms. The Three-Year Plan (1962-64) envisaged 200 production co-ops organized to cultivate 100,000 hectares of the one and a half million hectares of arable land in the north, with a third of the total amount to be eventually cultivated under co-ops. By the end of 1963, 97 production co-ops had been started including some 114,000 hectares; by the end of 1964 there were nearly 200 such co-ops.[15] These co-ops are for

TABLE 1

GEOGRAPHICAL DISTRIBUTION OF CO-OPS AND CO-OP MEMBERSHIP,
December 31, 1964

	Agriculture and fishing		Handicrafts and Small Industries		Consumer and Credit		Total	
	Co-ops	Membership	Co-ops	Membership	Co-ops	Membership	Co-ops	Membership
Tunis	32	8,338	31	2,285	16	8,916	79	19,539
Bizerte	10	959	9	595	3	316	22	1,870
Beja	61	3,940	1	121	4	760	66	4,821
Souk el Arba	23	1,801	1	46	4	1,881	28	3,728
Le Kef	71	3,919	6	286	5	2,302	82	6,507
Kasserine	4	3,531	3	623	–	–	7	4,154
Gafsa	12	2,082	7	463	1	83	20	2,628
Medenine	4	326	10	364	4	433	18	1,123
Gabes	9	1,9015	2	108	1	284	12	2,297
Sfax	5	2,388	11	1,306	3	1,097	19	4,791
Kairouan	15	1,861	10	541	31	8,040	56	10,442
Sousse	124	36,669[a]	39	3,432	15	2,090	178	42,191
Nabeul	19	3,615[a]	8	723	8	4,558[b]	35	8,896
Total	389	71,334[c]	138	10,893	95	30,760[d]	622	112,987

SOURCE: Figures provided by the Cooperative Section, Secretary of State for Plans and the National Economy, Government of Tunisia.

[a]In all cases except Sousse and Nabeul the co-ops are for production. In Sousse there are 18 service co-ops with 35,784 members and in Nabeul 19 service co-ops with 3,615 members.

[b]The only case of credit co-ops as part of pilot project, including the entire figure given for Nabeul (Cap Bon).

[c]In only four provinces were there fishing co-ops, the most important being Sfax with 2 co-ops and 1,848 members and Sousse with 6 co-ops and 885 members. The portion of the total in fishing is 11 co-ops with 2,889 members.

[d]Column includes 9 co-ops with 3,597 members who were unclassified.

the most part centered on old *colon* farms that have been nationalized and have been reconstituted as co-ops with the former agricultural laborers designated co-op members. Approximately half the land, however, has come from private landowners who hold parcels peripheral to or within the co-op.[16] Although some praiseworthy efforts have been made to involve the workers in the actual management of these farms, generations of day labor have reduced their concerns to the same time perspective, and the co-ops have not yet achieved a level of production that might convince them otherwise. The regional managers estimate that about half are operating on a profitable basis, but it is next to impossible to sort out the foundations for such a judgment given the government subsidies to higher echelons of the co-op organization and rudimentary bookkeeping at the local co-op level. In inspecting co-op records, it was not uncommon to find unpaid bills that were two years old. The goal of the northern co-ops, like that of agricultural co-ops throughout the country, is to provide the members with a minimum annual income of 250 dinars (about $500) by 1972.

In the central regions of the interior, agriculture is extremely precarious and the land has only been removed from collective ownership since independence.[17] Of the 2 million hectares that might be brought under cultivation, 600,000 are destined to become *cooperatives de polyculture et de mise en valeur.* By 1965, the government had achieved nearly half this goal in co-ops centering on the Enfida, Sidi Bouzid, Souassis, and Maknassi regions. The first two each had about twenty co-ops in operation and the latter regions about ten. The organization of co-ops in the central part of the country is a slow and costly process, even where, as in the case of Enfida, the government is building on the remnants of a colonial plantation.[18] The human impact is likely to come even more slowly than in the north, and for the moment the co-op appears to most members to be a form of public relief. The acreage brought under irrigation is rigidly supervised and productive, but still much to small to bring substantial change to the area.

The third type of agricultural cooperative is for service, and functions in many regions to manage machinery, supplies, and marketing. Its most important application, and politically the most controversial aspect of the entire co-op scheme, has been to organize the independent olive farmers of the Sahel, or central coastal plains. From Nabeul to Sousse are located the ancient olive orchards that have been the backbone of purely Tunisian agriculture. The region has been a major source of political support for the party outside the cities since the 1930's. By the end of 1964, some 35,000 olive farmers in Sousse province had been organized into over a hundred service co-ops (see Table 1). The transformation came as a shock to the relatively well-off, middle-class farmers of the Sahel, and in one town, M'Saken, there was a rebellion.[19] The agricultural problem was equally pressing. Some 5 million of the 9 million trees in the region are estimated to be yielding too small a harvest to justify cultivation. A massive program of root and limb pruning, fertilization, and cultivation has begun, and about 2 per cent of the worst trees will be removed each year.[20] As a test of the persuasiveness of the cooperative scheme, the experience in the politically articulate province of Sousse is not encouraging. There is a certain irony that the historical party supporters were to find the full force of the single party's political and administrative machinery turned against them under the pressure for rapid development.

Through the cooperative structure, the single-party government has an instrument to reach every village and every farmer in Tunisia. Even the small independent landowner will be incorporated into the specialized, regional service co-ops for agriculture. Although the large landowner generally became involved with the party years ago and his family frequently holds high political and administrative posts, he too will feel the impact of the new organizations. These observations are not intended to minimize the achievements of the Tunisian government, nor to denigrate the motives of her leaders. However, the cooperative structure has clearly become a useful device to manage the mobilization of the countryside. An estimate by Tunisian officials from Table 1 indicates that almost 12 per cent of the active population in rural Tunisia was enrolled in co-ops in 1965. The structure coincides with the political and administrative machinery of the party and local party notables and militants are chosen to initiate and supervise co-ops. Though leaders are aware of the need to have general and active participation in co-op management, priority is assigned to economic viability and political reliability.

POLITICAL AND DEVELOPMENT "MIX" EFFECTIVENESS

Having arrived at the point where the political meaning of development programs can be identified, the question can be raised whether the "mix" of the political and development components of rural development seems likely to work effectively beyond the limits of the Ten-Year Plan. More simply, how long will the present realistic and convenient assumption by the Tunisian leaders that political differences are subordinate in the cooperative organization hold true? At what point in the mobilization of rural resources will the assumption of automatic reconciliation of political and developmental demands no longer hold? Is the single-party regime likely to place arbitrary limits on development in order to sustain the requirements of party harmony? These questions are especially important for American officials to ask themselves, for unlike earlier European colonial powers, our country has generally operated on the maxim of automatic reconciliation of local and national interests and of the unavoidable benefits to be derived from material progress.[21] American assistance officials and the national elite in the recipient nation agree that political factors should not enter into development, but for directly opposed reasons.

The response to these questions is, first, that it is indeed naïve to divorce power considerations from development. There is no doubt that Tunisia's enthusiasm for cooperatives is the result of policy decisions made to enhance the single-party system. In May, 1964, the Tunisian government nationalized over 45,000 hectares of foreign-owned land.[22] About a fourth was cultivated by French companies, and the remainder was divided among French and Italian farmers. These farms were among the richest and best developed in the country and operated by 2,000 experienced farmers. The cooperative was the country's only means of keeping these farms in production unless the government were to opt for wholly state-owned farms on the Soviet model. In fact, the present situation is a combination of the two types of farms because a large portion of the nationalized land has remained in the hands of the Office des Terres Dominales, partly cultivated by day laborers under state supervision and partly rented to wealthy Tunisians. Neither alternative is politically feasible for Tunisia, and the cooperative became the solution, meeting for time being at least, both political and developmental needs.

There are no precise figures on the overlap of party and co-op office-holding, but it is clear that little mobilization of the Tunisian countryside will take place without party clearance. In the 1964 congress of the PSD the party was brought more closely in line with administrative divisions, and the governor was made the supreme figure in provincial party organization. Each provincial region now has a regional coordination committee to which the governor appoints appropriate union representatives, professional and regional officials, and his own appointees.[23] In effect, he regulates all party and developmental activities. The regional and provincial co-op organization has no way to express its differences above the governor's position, and it is unlikely that differences below this level are encouraged.

An even more distinctly political consideration relates to the co-ops as a result of disagreements between the labor union and the party. Without going into the complex history of the relation between the Destourian Socialist Party and the UGTT, it can be noted that the unions were uncomfortable with wage restraints and organizational limits placed on the unions since the developmental effort began in the early 1960's. When the secretary general of the UGTT was removed in 1963, his successor encountered the same problems and left office in the summer of 1965, and the government and party then took full control of the unions. The UGTT had started co-ops in Tunisia, operating some of the most profitable cooperatives in construction, fishing, and importing.[24] More important, the rural mobilization posed the threat of a labor organization among rural farm workers, thereby destroying the neat hierarchy of party and cooperatives and possibly extending the rivalry of the party and unions in the cities to the entire country. The decision of the party congress in 1964 to organize professional cells not only undercut the unions in the expanding modern sector of the economy but also barred the way for union organization in the rural areas. The official policy thus not only incorporated the resources of the UGTT co-ops within the government's program but also helped eliminate a major critic of the single party.

The problems of land nationalization and trade-union control illustrate the political constraints on the cooperative program generated by the single-party system. They have had similar effects in that both policies created pressure to organize co-ops rapidly and sensitized political leadership to the political potential of co-ops in controlling the countryside. Whether or not a more diverse hierarchical structure would have led to more rapid development will never be known. The party's decisions have transformed the political question into a new form: How much social diversity can be tolerated within a single hierarchy? The critical role assigned to co-ops in Tunisian economic planning cannot be understood without taking into consideration the power structure of the single-party state. Essentially, the conflict is the classical political problem of reconciling "rational" expert opinion with the diffuse and uncertain aspects of political control. The problem becomes especially acute in developing countries where large numbers of persons are being recruited into the political system in short time periods, and where substantial resources are being used in ways that are not easily manipulated by the government once the facilities and funds are made available.

The conflict takes place at two levels. There is, first, the organizational dilemma of reconciling the expert's view with the need to generate popular support and sympathy. The Tunisian co-op scheme has illustrated how expertise can become a rationalization for hierarchical control and careful centralization. The organizational costs, however, are quite explicit. Popular participation in the co-op is simply postponed. Individual advancement in the co-op structure depends heavily on party reliability and service. The cooperative structure must be standardized and strictly enforced by making financial support contingent on meeting the demands of government. Such constraints are not excessive while the cooperative structure is small, but as the development effort produces a structure of the size anticipated in Tunisian planning, the impact of the political system will be increasingly in evidence. The organizational problem is also cumulative. The extreme priority given to expertise in the Tunisian co-op scheme means that resolution of differences may be more and more difficult as the entire co-op organization is constrained by administrative and political requirements.[25]

The conflict is similar at the level of national politics, though clearly more difficult to assess and to observe. In the single-party system, particularly as it has evolved in the African states committed to rapid development, there is a great temptation to accept the more easily calculated (and therefore more "rational"?) judgments of experts where developmental programs involve political uncertainty. In the single-party state, there is no discussion once decisions have been made and there are no institutional devices for publicly reconsidering policy decisions, although this must obviously take place among the elite in the light of experience. The tendency to identify expertise with political judgment becomes less relevant the more complex the society becomes. The diffusion of skills, resources, and institutions makes the calculation of policy alternatives more difficult rather than simpler, thus the control established for Tunisia's rural mobilization may in time become a handicap rather than an advantage. The single-party system must therefore be carefully observed to see how, in effect, the system itself can be modified as it succeeds in its developmental goals.

As stated in the introduction to this essay, there is a deceptive similarity between the demands of development and the power structure of the single-party state in early stages of development. For very different reasons, both the Western adviser and the political leader find precise organizational control desirable, although the national leader is often less naïve than the adviser. Bourguiba did not hesitate to sacrifice the 2,000 skilled farmers from abroad when the system could no longer justify the obstacles they created for development. Neither could he tolerate the growing cooperative organization of the trade unions once it became the potential foundation for effective opposition to the single-party regime. These departures from the dictates of expertise suggest that the Tunisian single party has not lost its capacity to adapt to radical change and may one day remove the political constraints placed on the cooperatives.

Notes

1. Perhaps the strongest impetus for this kind of research has been the recent concern with development administration. However, few of these efforts have been comparative. For an effort in this direction, see Douglas E. Ashford, *National Development and Local Reform* (Princeton, N.J.: Princeton University Press, 1966).

2. The model-based approach prevails among sociologists and stresses new patterns of social differentiation. The conclusions are often pessimistic, as illustrated in Fred Rigg's observations about negative development in Joseph La Polombara (ed.), *Bureaucracy and Political Development* (Princeton, N.J.: Princeton University Press, 1963), pp. 120-67. The decisional framework often comes close to an elitist view of government, and often stresses the essential hierarchical aspects of social change. See, for example, David Apter, *The Political Kingdom of Uganda* (Princeton, N.J.: Princeton University Press, 1961), especially

pp. 20-28. In fact, of course, division of labor and hierarchy are inextricably mixed in any society, and changes in either dimension must be related to structural characteristics of the society in question. Perhaps the most effective presentation of this viewpoint, which inspires much of what will be said about Tunisian development in this article, is S. N. Eisenstadt's *Modernization, Growth, and Diversity* (Bloomington, Ind.: Carnegie Faculty Seminar Reprint, 1963).

3. See Douglas E. Ashford, *The Elusiveness of Power: The African Single Party State* (Ithaca, N.Y.: Cornell University Center for International Studies, 1965). For more detail on the Tunisian party's organization, see Clement Henry Moore, *Tunisia Since Independence; The Dynamics of One-Party Government* (Berkeley: University of California, Press, 1965).

4. "La Coopération," *Plan Quadriennal* (1965-68) (mimeo.; Tunis: Secretary of State of Plans and the National Economy, 1965), Sec. V, p. 1. See also the speech by Ahmed ben Salah, "La coopération dans notre socialisme," *La Voie coopérative,* I (November-December, 1963), 14-16.

5. Perhaps the most dramatic illustration is the purely symbolic attachment to national planning that characterized both countries until the early 1960's. See Douglas E. Ashford, *Morocco and Tunisia: Politics and Planning* (Syracuse, N.Y.: Syracuse University Press, 1965).

6. *Perspective Décennale* (1962-71) (mimeo.; Tunis: Secretary of State of Plans and the National Economy, 1961), p. 106.

7. As UGTT secretary general after independence, the merchants were his *bête noire,* and as the nation's chief planner he made little effort to conceal his hostility. See, for example, the *Plan Quadriennal,* p. 7, on "eliminating the numerous intermediaries" between the consumer and the producer.

8. Moncef Guen, "Le Mouvement coopératif Tunisien: problèmes et perspectives," *La Voie Coopérative,* I (November-December, 1963), 24. This article and Guen's book, *La Coopération et l'état en Tunisie* (Tunis: Edition de l'U.G.T.T., 1964), provides more detail on the several governmental organizations involved in various cooperative activities prior to centralization in the superministry.

9. A table giving the dates of establishment appears in *La Voie Coopérative,* I (November-December, 1963), 26. Financial estimates are unreliable without details on costing practices, but the *Rapport d'Exécution du Plan Triennal* (1962-64) (Tunis: Secretary of State of Plans and the National Economy, 1965), notes in chap. IV that 280,000 dinars (about half a million dollars) were spent on studies for cooperatives and that 455,000 dinars were extended in credit to initiate URD's in 1964.

10. After six years of very tight party control under the *délégués,* the party congress of 1964 decided to revive local committees. Most observers agree that only pliable militants were accepted in the new local organization, and that the interlude has been used to install new local leaders. See *Jeune Afrique,* November 1, 1964, and *Maghreb Digest* (January-February, 1965), pp. 28-29.

11. Two prototype documents have been prepared for use in the establishment of each URC: *Les Unions régionales de coopératives: recueil de documents, relatifs àl' organisation administrative et au personnel* and *Les Unions régionales de coopératives: normalisation des methodes comptables et Tenue des livres* (mimeo; Tunis: Secretary of State of Plans and the National Economy [n.d.]). Although conflicting with the figures cited in note 9, government officials claim that by mid-1964 there were 384 co-ops organized under the UEC plan with a capital of 8 million dinars (about $16 million). Of this amount, about 6 million dinars were subscribed by co-op members.

12. The basic law on agricultural co-ops is Law No. 63-19 of May 27, 1963 (4 moharrem 1383), on cooperation in the agricultural section *(Journal Officiel de la République Tunisienne,* May 28-31, 1963, pp. 748-53). For additional details on the early administrative structure for Tunisian agriculture, see M. Callens, "Cinq années d'action administrative dans le domaine agricole," *I.B.L.A.,* XXV (1962), 111-34.

13. A new census is underway in Tunis and the population is expected to be about 4.5 million. A summary of the agricultural manpower situation and also, land tenure patterns appears in *Le production agricole de Tunisie* (Tunis: Secretary of State for Information, December 5, 1959). One of the major problems of Tunisian planning has been that until recently they were dependent on statistics collected in the last years of French rule.

14. *Plan Quadriennal,* pp. 1-3.

15. See *Plan Quadriennal,* p. 6, and "Agriculture," *Rapport d' Exécution,* Sec. I, p. 1. See also "Les unités cooperatives de production du Nord-Tunisien," *Maghreb,* May-June, 1964, pp. 28-30, and July-August, 1964, pp. 25-27.

16. The co-op legislation enables the government to purchase or rent land falling within the area designated as a production co-op. The very beneficial effect is, of course, to reduce parceling and to create viable farms. The unfortunate effect has been to discourage a number of capable private Tunisian farmers, whose skill is badly needed. In the summer of 1965, officials were discussing a new scheme to encourage capable Tunisian farmers to work on units of 50 hectares, which would naturally be serviced by the same co-ops organized to care for the production co-ops. The profit-sharing plan does offer some consolation to the landowner who contributes land. Ten per cent of profits go to reserves, 25 per cent to workers in proportion to days of work during the year (in addition to their daily wage of 200 millimes, or about 25 cents), 20 per cent to repay loans, and 45 per cent to co-op members in proportion to the amount of land they have contributed to the co-op.

17. The handling of collective land represents one of the more substantial reverses in official policy. A law of September 28, 1957, made collective land immune to all forms of alienation. A law of June 4, 1964, transformed over 2 million hectares of collective land into private holdings and enabled the government to recognize as owners those peasants who worked on the co-ops. Some may call this socialism, but the principle comes straight from Locke.

18. The Enfida project has a history worthy of notation. The tract of some 50,000 hectares was given to an Ottoman official by the sultan in the mid-nineteenth century. The official sold his land to a French company, which was in the process of selling the land back to the Tunisians. The 1964 uprising was forcefully repressed. See *Jeune Afrique,* January 3, 1965.

19. The interlocking of the local elite in the Sahel and the entire government is a complex and fascinating study. See Clement Henry Moore, "Politics in a Tunisian Village," pp. 296—308 in this reader.

20. The fact that the Sahel farmers retain private title to their land rather than being incorporated into the production co-ops indicates their political influence. The nature of olive culture makes their problem particularly acute. A tree requires fifteen years to begin bearing fruit and root-pruning sharply curtails yields for seven years. The neglect of the Sahel orchards is dramatically revealed by comparing yields with newer orchards around Sfax to the south. The Sahel trees produce ten to twelve kilos of olive oil while the Sfax trees yield thirty or more kilos. (Interview, Director of URC, Sousse, July 2, 1965.)

21. Although I have made this point in other writings on North Africa, it perhaps bears repeating that our principles of operation in foreign assistance appear more Marxian than those of the socialists. The philosophy of technical assistance as the keystone to development, which dominated our foreign-aid program until recently, also lends itself to this interpretation.

22. See *The New York Times,* May 14, 1964, and *Le Monde,* May 13, 1964, for more details. The fact that land nationalization occurred after the decision to emphasize co-ops would constitute a contradiction only if both policies were historically independent. In fact, the government had been negotiating with France for years on the recovery of *colon* land and the results were not impressive. Costly as co-ops are to establish, they had even less chance of becoming economically viable, and thereby fulfilling the party's goals for development, if the richest lands were completely excluded. The government had already learned this in pilot co-ops begun on the fringes of the Enfida estate on marginal lands.

23. "Le VIIème congress, les élections, les remaniements," *Maghrêb,* January-February, 1965, pp. 26-30; and "The Destourian Socialist Party and the National Organizations," pp. 287—97 in this reader.

24. The UGTT operated a variety of specialized co-ops that were very successful. The construction co-ops found in nearly every provincial center were UGTT co-ops, now under government control. In Tunis, the unions ran a chain of retail fish-stores in connection with their cooperatively owned fishing fleet. The fleet of taxis in Tunis constituted a profitable UGTT co-op. The incident that forced Habib Achour from office in 1965 involved the management of a cooperatively owned excursion line of the UGTT. The technicality used by government in order to sue the union was hardly more serious than a thousand favors extracted in the overlapping power structure every day. See *Jeune Afrique,* April 18, 1965, and *The New York Times,* July 6, 1965.

25. French authority on rural Tunisia mentioned this rigidity in the co-op schemes several years ago. Noting the standardization of practices and procedures, he questions "whether the anticipated policy will be sufficiently consistent and continuous to permit the passage from a stage of state decision-making to that of real collaboration between the base and the summit through channels of assemblies, discussion, and democratic councils." Jean Poncet, *Paysages et problèmes ruraux en Tunisie* (Paris: Presses Universitaires de France, 1963), pp. 371-72.

34

ALGERIAN AGRICULTURE IN TRANSITION

KEITH B. GRIFFIN

THE ROLE OF AGRICULTURE IN THE ECONOMY

In terms of its contribution to national income, the balance of payments, and employment, agriculture is by far the most important activity in the Algerian economy. Over 25 per cent of domestic production is generated in this sector; a large proportion of all exports are agricultural products; and approximately 70 per cent of the population lives in rural areas.

It is not only in this static sense, however, that agriculture dominates the economy. Algeria's experiment with socialism began in the agricultural sector when landless laborers spontaneously occupied and started managing the estates abandoned by the departing French *colons*. Only later was the principle of *autogestion* (self-management) extended to the small and rather primitive nationalized industrial establishments. The dynamic impulse behind the postindependence revolution was and continues to be the modern, socialist, agricultural sector. Thus, an understanding of Algerian agriculture is essential to understanding Algeria.

The table below summarizes what is believed to have been the evolution of gross domestic production from 1959 to 1963. Unfortunately, the data on national income are not very reliable. The latest available information is a preliminary estimate for 1959; anything referring to more recent periods is a mere guess and extrapolation.

National Income

(in million constant dinars)*	1959	1963
Agriculture	2,750	2,200
Industry and public works	2,750	2,400
Services	5,500	3,800
Total	11,000	8,400

*The dinar became Algeria's monetary unit on April 10, 1964; it is at par with the French new franc.

SOURCE: L.J. Zimmerman, *Report on Industrialization in Algeria.* See also *Tableaux de l'Economie Algerienne* (Algiers: General Statistical Service, 1960). Others have estimated the value of Services to be only 2,000 m. D.A. in 1963.

Reprinted, by permission, from *Bulletin of the Oxford University Institute of Economics and Statistics, XXVII,* No. 4 (November, 1965), 229–52.

The above table seems to imply that national income declined about 23.5 per cent after Algeria obtained her independence. The greatest drop was in the "services" category, which declined 30 per cent. This category, however, includes French military expenditures in Algeria, and the sharp reduction in these expenditures had very little effect upon the standard of living of the Algerian population. There were, of course, some domestic multiplier effects of military spending, but most of this leaked abroad in the form of imports from France. Thus if one wants an indication of the "real" changes in national income the decline in "services" must, in large part, be excluded.

On this basis it would appear that the "revised" national income declined between 10 and 15 per cent. A large part of this decline was due to a drop of 20 per cent in the value of agricultural production. This reduction of agricultural output and value, as we shall see later in detail, occured almost exclusively in the socialist sector. Unhappily, the production problems in this sector have not been solved completely and a further decline in output is possible.

The decline in the value of agricultural production — due partly to a decline in production and partly to marketing difficulties — has not been reflected in an equal decline in income of the Algerian, that is, Muslim, population. The brunt of the impact was absorbed by redistributing income from the French *colons* to the new Algerian privileged class, the permanent workers on the socialist farms. This was rather easy to do, since there were only 22,000 French exploitations and these accounted for approximately 60 per cent of gross agricultural revenue. Thus in spite of a general decline in output, it was possible for most Algerians to remain at least no worse off and for certain elements of the population — especially the permanent workers, urban salaried personnel, and the armed forces — to increase their per capita income and consumption. This process cannot continue indefinitely, however, without incurring the danger that the nation's capital will be consumed. . . .

Seventy per cent of the Algerian population lives in rural areas and 60 per cent of the population obtains a livelihood directly from agricultural activities. The overwhelming proportion of these 6 million people are engaged in the traditional sector where, under primitive conditions, a pastoral life is combined with subsistence wheat farming. In contrast, no more than 200,000 people are permanently employed in the modern sector. The amount of rural unemployment and underemployment is staggering. This will be discussed in detail later.

LAND TENURE AND FARM MANAGEMENT

Before Algeria obtained her independence there were 22,037 agricultural exploitations encompassing 2,726,700 hectares that belonged to non-Muslims, that is, to French settlers. Virtually all of these farms have now been nationalized and these comprise the socialist sector of the agricultural economy. The socialist sector plus a few private Muslim holdings constitute the modern agricultural sector of the economy. (It is anticipated that the private holdings in the modern sector will be reorganized under a further agrarian law.)

Production in the modern sector was almost exclusively vegetable and almost exclusively for the market. Only 5 per cent of the output could be attributed to animal production and less than 3 per cent to autoconsumption. The major crops were wine (which represented 5 per cent of total cultivable land and 50 per cent of the value of output of this sector), fruit, vegetables, and wheat.

As the table below shows, management of these modern estates was extremely efficient and highly profitable. Profit per hectare was almost 400 dinars. Taxes absorbed no more than 4 per cent of net revenue and profits (after taxes) were equal to 65 per cent of gross revenue. The 22,000 European settlers completely dominated the 630,000 Muslim agricultural producers. The Europeans accounted for 60 per cent of gross agricultural revenue; their profits alone were 54 per cent of total net agricultural revenue.[1] Perhaps even more striking, the profits of this minority — which represented less than 4 per cent of the agricultural population — were equivalent to at least 12 to 15 per cent of the national income. These are the estates which now have been nationalized and — with the possible exception of oil revenues — it is from them, and them alone, that Algeria can obtain the domestic savings necessary to ensure her rapid development. The socialist sector represents the most important (potential) source of savings. It is absolutely essential that the decline in efficiency in this sector be minimized and that as large a proportion as possible of the surplus be extracted.

Agricultural Revenue of European Exploitations, 1957
(*in million dinars*)

Gross revenue		1,649
Current expenses		528
Material	186	
Services	55	
Salaries and social charges	287	
Net revenue		1,121
Taxes	45	
other revenue, i.e., profits	1,076	

SOURCE: *Tableaux de l'Economie Algérienne*, 1960.

The process of nationalization occurred in three stages. The first took place in July and August, 1962, shortly after Algeria obtained her independence. The French *colons* farthest from the coast, in regions relatively sparsely populated by Europeans, abandoned their estates. These *bien vacants* promptly and spontaneously were occupied by the Algerian workers in an attempt to safeguard their employment and income, and in this way the motivating force of the Algerian revolution — *autogestion* — was born.

In this first stage approximately 950,000 hectares were incorporated into the socialist sector. This land roughly was distributed among the various product groups as follows:

Cereals	750,000 ha.
Vineyards	100,000 ha.
Fruit trees	25,000 ha.
Market gardening	16,000 ha.
Other	59,000 ha.
Total	950,000 ha.

As seen from the table, most of the newly socialized land (approximately 80 per cent) was devoted to cereals. In fact, almost all of the cereal lands belonging to

Europeans had been nationalized by July. In addition, the first stage included less than one-third of all the vineyards (the less productive third) and less than one-half of the citrus-fruit production.

In order to avoid chaos in the countryside, and to regain control over the revolution, the government ratified the spontaneous action of the workers in the famous decrees of March 18, 22, and 28, 1963. At the same time, the government introduced the second stage of the agrarian reform by expropriating the largest French estates (Germain, Bourgeaud, and the like). This added another 600,000 hectares to the socialist sector. An additional 200,000 or more hectares were incorporated into the sector by transferring and reorganizing the CAPER (Caisse d'accession à la propriété et à l'exploitation rurales) lands.

No further nationalizations took place until October 7, 1963. On that date the remaining 1 million hectares in French hands were expropriated. (This occurred during the Moroccan and Kabyle crises and probably represented a bid by the president for increased political support.) Included in this last stage were the remaining two-thirds — and the most productive — of the vineyards, plus the remaining half — and again the most productive — of the citrus orchards.

Thus, in the short space of fifteen months the agrarian reform, which started spontaneously on the abandoned estates in the wheat-growing regions and ended as conscious policy with the expropriation of the vineyards, absorbed slightly over 2.7 million of the richest and best-farmed land in the country. This land, almost literally overnight, was converted from a system of colonial production based on private property to socialist production based on worker management. It is no exaggeration to say that the success of the Algerian revolution depends upon the success of the agrarian reform, that is, upon the success of *autogestion.*

The decree referring to the management of socialist enterprises was published March 22, 1963. The socialist sector has been reorganized into approximately 3,000 self-managing units (*unités d'autogestion*) whose average size, with wide variations, approach 1,000 hectares. The permanent workers of each *unité* — as opposed to the seasonal workers — are organized into a workers' assembly. The assembly then elects a workers' council, which, in turn, elects a management committee.

The management committee is directed by a president. In addition, a technical director is appointed by the National Office for the Agrarian Reform (ONRA) to assist the president and his committee. The appointment of the director is subject to the approval of the community council on *autogestion,* which is composed of the presidents of the various management committees, plus a representative of the party, the unions, the army, and the administrative authorities of the community. In theory, the director is under the authority of the president, although the functions of the two offices are not clearly specified, and in practice the director is quite independent. This is especially true as regards production. ONRA is responsible for organizing production and allocating output quotas (in terms of hectares) among the various farms. The director, as their agent, is responsible for implementing this policy. In the event of a conflict between ONRA and a self-managed farm, the director could veto the president's wishes. In practice, such open conflicts are rare, but there frequently seems to be some tension between the president and the director — a tension that occasionally is increased because the director is considered a "young upstart with no practical experience" and the president is viewed as "old, ignorant, and conservative."

There are at present several organizational problems on the socialist estates:

1. Many of the French farms were consolidated and regrouped into estates which approach 1,000 hectares in size. From the point of view of worker psychology, these are too big. The individual feels no identification with his farm; he believes his contribution makes no difference to the income or profitability of the *unité*. As a result, petty thievery plus a lack of initiative and enthusiasm are rampant. Although it might be difficult to correct this deficiency on the existing estates, this relationship between the size of the farm and individual initiative should be considered in the planned extensions of the agrarian reform.

2. Related to this is the problem of monetary incentives. The minimum wage in the socialist sector, namely 7 dinars per day, has been set too high, and as a result the workers have little incentive to contribute additional effort and increase their income through a share of the profits. Ideally, the minimum wage should be set very low so that the workers virtually would be forced to increase their productivity, maximize profits, and thereby supplement their wages.

3. According to the March decrees, only the permanent workers participate in the profit-sharing arrangements; the seasonal workers are unorganized and receive no share of the surplus. This sharp division of the work force into two classes has created resentment among the underprivileged laborers, has led to some friction on the farms, and has undermined the spirit of cooperation necessary to make the socialist revolution a success. It would seem appropriate therefore, that the decrees be altered so that all laborers participate in the distribution of profits, perhaps in accordance with the number of days actually worked.

4. At the end of the early stages of nationalization there were 1,500 *unités d' autogestion*. The directors of these estates were obtained by transferring monitors attached to the Sociétés Agricoles de Prévoyance (SAP) — who were credit and extension officials — from the traditional to the socialist sector. This, in one blow, completely destroyed the extension service. Unfortunately, there were only 1,200 of these monitors, and of this number, only 400 had experienced as much as a year of training. Thus, Algeria began her experiment of *autogestion* with a severe shortage of trained personnel. Today the shortage is even more severe, as the number of *unités* has doubled without a parallel increase in farm managers-bookkeepers. In some regions, one director may be responsible for as many as five socialist estates. This situation is the logical consequence of moving too rapidly and not coordinating the agrarian reform with a massive training program.

The traditional sector is composed roughly of 630,000 *fellahin* who eke out a living on 7,349,000 hectares of infertile and rather badly eroded land. Most of these *fellahin* — approximately 438,000 — have holdings of less than ten hectares. Since the average family has five or six members, the amount of land per capita is less than two hectares. In any given year, however, half of this land will be in fallow. Thus, a family will have to maintain itself on the income from less than one hectare per person of productive land plus an additional amount derived from livestock-grazing on the fallow ground. Pressure on the land is increasing rapidly, as the population is estimated to be growing at an annual rate of nearly 3 per cent. Current estimates indicate that per capita income in this sector is between $40 and $60.

Over 80 per cent of all animal production takes place in the traditional sector and, in fact, livestock normally represent over 40 per cent of gross revenue in this sector. Mixed flocks of sheep and goats are most common, and particularly among the nomads and in the high plateaus they are the major source of life. The most important crops are cereals, especially hard wheat. These are grown using primitive dry-farming techniques in a two year, wheat-fallow cycle. The average yield is 5.2 quintals per hectare. Somewhat over 40 per cent of all production is for autoconsumption, although it varies between crops and from one year to another.

In the event that the year's output is sufficient to cover all the *fellah's* needs — subsistence, seeds, and storage — the "surplus" will be sold and used to enlarge the family flock. This form of investment, when aggregated over the entire community, is almost completely illusory as, especially in the dry and overgrazed regions of the country, an increase in the number of livestock is likely to accelerate the process of erosion without noticeably increasing the peasant's income. There is a pressing need to introduce controlled grazing and improved breeding techniques. This cannot be done, however, as long as the *fellah* is in a subsistence economy and remains outside the market mechanism. As long as survival is the dominant factor of his life, the peasant will make no attempt to maximize income but rather will try to maximize security. From this point of view, his preference for an old ram and two tough but scrawny goats over, say, a well-bred but market-oriented sheep is not irrational but is the logical consequence of the social and economic institutions under which he lives.

In the traditional sector, the nomadic and sedentary ways of life are not competitive but on the contrary are complementary. It is not uncommon for a cereal producer to entrust his flock of ewes to a nomad. In return for an advance in wheat and barley, the nomad will take the *fellah's* flock with him when he moves south toward the Sahara in October. When he returns in the spring, seven months later, the *fellah* will be given half the lambs and wool produced by his sheep, and the nomad will be entitled to graze his flock on the *fellah's* land until the following fall. Thus, each partner provides an essential service to the other: the *fellah* grants credit and pasture rights; the nomad guards the combined flocks.

The equilibrium of social and economic forces described above has now been destroyed; the causes are three:

1. As mentioned above, population pressure on the land is growing rapidly. In the absence of improved techniques of production this (a) is leading to increased underemployment in agriculture; (b) is accentuating the natural attraction of the cities by pushing the younger and more dynamic people off the land into the urban areas where they become openly unemployed; (c) is creating additional problems of erosion by forcing the *fellah* to clear all possible land for increasingly unproductive cereal cultivation; and (d) is exerting strong downward pressure on the already extremely low per capita income of the sector.

2. Normal cultivation in the traditional sector was completely disrupted during the war. The French, for purely military purposes, relocated vast numbers

of the population in so-called regroupment centers. It is estimated that anywhere from 2 million to as much as half of the agricultural population were affected. *Fellahin* and their families were transferred miles from their property, placed in artificially created villages, and left to manage as best they could. As a consequence, a lot of land has gone out of cultivation. Little or nothing was done, or is being done, to increase the economic viability of the regroupment centres, as psychologically they were very similar to concentration camps. Of course, there has been a movement back to the prewar properties, but the demoralization, the enforced absence, and the destruction of capital — such as watering points and houses — are such that the peasants' roots in the soil have been ruptured.

3. These difficulties have been aggravated by the wholesale theft and destruction of livestock that took place during the war. Half the goats, 70 per cent of the cattle, and 40 per cent of the sheep were slaughtered; in some regions the proportions were much higher. This liquidation of the *fellah*'s capital and the nomad's only source of livelihood has profoundly altered economic activity in the traditional sector. Pastoral occupations have been greatly reduced.[2] Nomadism has declined, and with it the great routes across the Sahara have begun to fade into memory. Many nomads have been forced to settle permanently in the oases along the fringe of the desert. There they lose their self-respect and swell the ranks of the unemployed.

Unfortunately, very little can be done immediately to transform the traditional sector. The socialist sector, for reasons given above, must receive first priority. There are, however, measures in two directions that can relieve distress and increase the development potential of the *bled*.

The purpose of these policies would be to increase the capacity of the traditional sector to absorb capital. At present, the productivity of any large investment scheme would be seriously prejudiced by the lack of certain social overhead facilities and the acute shortage of trained personnel. As a first step, the vast amount of unemployed labor available in this sector immediately should be mobilized in a labor intensive public works program systematically directed away from roadworks toward anti-erosion measures and *petite hydraulique* [one-man irrigation schemes, as opposed to industrial dams].

As a second step, a "policy package" should be prepared that includes provision for an extension service, credit facilities, a mass program of rural education, and the evolution of cooperatives from a land reform. The four components of this package are interdependent: Agricultural credit is worthless unless it is accompanied by an extension service. Extension and credit facilities are much more effective if they complement a program of general agricultural education. The injection of knowledge (education plus extension) and capital (credit) is much more fruitful if the land is exploited in a rational way. Land cannot be exploited rationally in the traditional sector until tenure rights are reformed[3] and the *fellahin* are grouped into cooperatives. The creation of cooperatives, however, will not be successful unless credit and extension services exist and unless the *fellahin* have received both technical and general civic education. Thus, the premature creation of cooperatives would be extremely dangerous. On the other hand, once the complementary services exist, the formation of cooperatives could contribute to a large and prompt increase in productivity in this sector.

PRODUCTION

Almost all cultivation in Algeria is done in the three northern regions — in the Constantinois, Algerois, and Oranie. This area includes approximately 29.5 million hectares, or which 6.7 million represent cultivable land. Since about 3 million hectares are annually in fallow, only 3.7 million hectares — or 12.5 per cent of the land surface — are actually cultivated. The land is divided between the two sectors roughly as follows:

	Socialist Sector	Traditional Sector	Total
	(in million hectares)		
Arable land	2.7	4.0	6.7
Cultivated land	1.7	2.0	3.7
Fallow	1.0	2.0	3.0

About 15 million hectares are subject to erosion, and it is estimated that each year 40,000 hectares are lost. This is a rate of over 100 hectares per day. For this reason, all types of erosion control, reforestation programs, and comprehensive schemes for rural renovation are extraordinarily important. The entire future of the *bled* depends upon them.

Short-run changes in output, however, depend in large part upon the amount of rainfall. Generally speaking, the average annual rainfall on the coast is about 500 millimeters. The amount increases as one moves east from Oran (360 mm.) to Algiers (700 mm.) and Constantine (550 mm.). In the high plateau, the average is about 300 millimeters per year and decreases sharply as one moves farther south. The rains are concentrated in the late fall and winter and are highly variable from one year to another. As a result, Algeria's agriculture is vulnerable to both the timing of the rains and their quantity. Fortunately, for the past two years the weather has been unusually favorable. This has prevented an otherwise disastrous decline in production and given the country precious time to become organized.

We do not have exact information about the amount of land under irrigation. It appears that there are about 250,000 irrigable hectares, that is, land equipped or partially equipped for irrigation, but little more than half this amount is actually irrigated. Most of the irrigated land is located in the coastal plains, where it plays an essential role in the modern sector, although its impact is nil for the vast majority of the population.

The eight major irrigation works provide water for one-third of the total irrigated land. Water for the remaining two-thirds comes from some 200 small irrigation facilities scattered throughout the country. As the table below shows the amount of unutilized irrigation potential is distressingly high: only 40 per cent of the capacity of the major works is being used.

		Irrigation Works	
		Major	Minor
Irrigable land	250,000 ha.	100,000 ha.	150,000 ha.
Irrigated land	130,000 ha.	40,000 ha.	90,000 ha.
Unutilized potential	48%	60%	40%

In the future, emphasis should shift away from major irrigated works, although dams presently under construction should be completed. Large dams are very expensive (historically, average cost per irrigable hectare is three times higher for *grande hydraulique* than for *petite et moyenne hydraulique,* namely 7,500 dinars versus 2,500 dinars), and they fill up rapidly. At the present rate of soil erosion some of the dams, for example Ksab, are lasting little longer than ten years. Additional effort should be concentrated immediately on using more fully the existing capacity of the major works and expanding small-scale irrigation facilities. *Petite hydraulique* is a particularly attractive investment because (1) these facilities can be constructed very cheaply by mobilizing unemployed labor in a rural public works program; (2) they can be constructed quickly during the dead season; and (3) their capacity utilization is much higher than the major irrigation projects. Of course, just as with any other agricultural investment, small-scale irrigation projects will be ineffective unless credit and extension facilities also are provided.

In terms of land, surface cereals are by far the most important crop grown in Algeria, but in terms of value of output — which on the average exceeds 2,200 million dinars — wine is twice as important. Next in importance comes citrus fruit, followed by vegetables and — way in the rear — industrial crops, notably tobacco and cotton. This is shown in the table below:

	Cultivated Surface (in hectares)	Per Cent of Value of Plant Production (Average, 1951-57)
Cereals	3,100,000	24.0
Wine	350,000	51.0
Vegetables	160,000	10.1
Fruit	60,000	12.0
Industrial crops	·25,000	2.9

In spite of the extraordinarily good weather the country has enjoyed for the last two years, agricultural output has begun to decline. Wine production — which historically has averaged 15 to 16 million hectoliters per annum, and with the favorable weather should have been 17 million in 1963 — is estimated to have been only 12.6 million hectoliters. Some people guess that only 9.5 million hectoliters were of marketable quality, but it is more likely that the correct figure is closer to 11 million. Of this amount, approximately 8 million were produced in the then private sector and about 3 million in the socialist sector. This represents roughly a 20 per cent decline in the output of the private sector (which can be explained by the uncertainty associated with the policy of nationalization) and a decline of perhaps as much as 50 per cent in the socialist sector. A continuation of this tendency on the newly nationalized farms would be very serious as it would undermine Algeria's capacity for capital accumulation.

According to the official data, there has been no decline in citrus-fruit production. Average annual output was 3.5 million quintals before independence as compared with the 1963 harvest of 4 million quintals. There was, however, a decline in the marketable quantity — due to an increase of on-farm consumption — and a sharp decline in quality.

As wine and citrus fruits are the most important commodities produced in the socialist sector, their movements can be taken as a general index of agricultural output in this sector. One then has an impression that the lack of trained Algerian personnel in combination with the exodus of the Europeans, the nationalization of the land, and the reorganization of the modern sector into "people's farms" has had a fairly strong negative impact on the quantity and quality of agricultural production. This impression is confirmed by partial evidence indicating production of noncitrus fruits, for example, apricots and plums, and vegetables, for example, tomatoes and carrots. also has declined sharply. Exports of vegetables declined from 1.8 million quintals in 1961-62 to 1.1 million in 1962-63. Nonetheless, one has the impression — particularly if training were accelerated — that the "production problem" in the socialist sector gradually could be, and perhaps is being, solved. In the future, the major difficulty is likely to be marketing, including processing and transformation.

Cereal production in the traditional sector was not affected by the revolutionary changes that occurred in the modern sector. Thanks to the abundant and timely rainfall, the 1964 output — and especially the harvest of hard wheat — was exceptional. Production was 2.4 million tons and about 2 million tons were harvested. Of the latter, half was delivered to be marketed. The remainder was used to replenish peasants' stocks.

The table below summarizes recent output data for the three major agricultural commodities. Due to the unreliability of the data no attempt has been made to include additional crops or to provide more complete information.

Gross Agricultural Production

	1960	*1961*	*1962*	*1963*
Wine (hl.)	18,600,000	15,650,000	13,000,000	12,750,000
Citrus fruits (qls.)	3,980,000	3,680,000	3,780,000	4,000,000
Cereals (qls.)	8,472,000	22,263,550	24,446,000	19,207,000
Hard wheat	4,804,000	11,757,000	14,618,000	12,416,000
Soft wheat	1,475,000	3,301,550	3,360,000	2,730,000
Barley	2,008,000	6,900,000	6,150,000	3,714,000
Oats	185,000	305,000	318,000	347,000

SOURCE: *1960-63: Revue du Plan et des Etudes Economiques,* special issue: "Situation Economique en 1963." The 1963-64 data on cereal production are estimates prepared by the Ministry of Agriculture one month before the harvest.

Meat and animal products normally account for slightly more than one-fifth of gross agricultural revenue. Most of this is produced in the traditional sector and represents a significant proportion of the *fellah*'s income. During the war, however, about half of the herds were destroyed, so that today animal production is considerably below its normal average. In the absence of an accurate livestock census — or even an aerial survey — it is impossible to indicate exactly the size of the existing herds. Nonetheless, the official revue of the Ministry of Agriculture has published the following figures:

	1963 Estimates	*Normal Average*
Sheep	4,000,000	6,500,000
Goats	1,500,000	3,000,000
Cattle	300,000	1,000,000

SOURCE: R. Khaoukha, "Notre Elevage," in *L'Algerie Agricole,* N.O., p. 27.

The existing flocks seldom are homogeneous, usually are a mixture of sheep and goats with an occasional cow, and include a large number of very low-yielding animals. In spite of the reduction of herds, the pasture is only mediocre — in both a qualitative and quantitative sense — and nothing has been done to improve it. Almost all the small-scale irrigation facilities are in a bad state of repair, and most hydraulic resources and scarcely utilized. . . .

UNEMPLOYMENT AND WAGES

Although no accurate estimates of under- and unemployment exist, there can be no doubt that the number of workers without work is extremely high. In economic terms this means, first, a resource for development is not being utilized, and second, insofar as the unemployed consist of workers with some skills, unemployment causes a deterioration of these resources through nonuse. The failure to use skills and large-scale unemployment is creating and will continue to create social and political difficulties which cannot be ignored.

According to the table presented earlier, the active population is about 4,175,000. Of this amount, 1.5 million people — or almost 40 per cent — are located in the cities and rural villages. A reasonable guess is that only one-third of the active labor force is employed in the cities, and only one-sixth in the villages. In other words, slightly over two-thirds of the nonagricultural active population may be without work.

It is more difficult to estimate un- and under-employment among the agricultural population. To do so, two important assumptions have been made that appear to be supported by fragmentary evidence:

1. In the traditional sector, the average member of the active population works 60 of a possible 250 days a year.

2. In the modern sector, the average seasonal worker is employed 100 out of a possible 250 days.

Using these rules of thumb the following "guesstimate" of un- and underemployment can be made:

Unemployment and Underemployment of the Active Labor Force

Sector	Underemployed Persons	Equivalent Man-Years
Urban population	800,000	800,000
Rural population	2,725,000	2,071,000
Nonagricultural	250,000	250,000
Agricultural	2,475,000	1,821,000
Traditional sector	2,100,000	1,596,000
Modern sector	375,000	225,000
Total	3,525,000	2,871,000

The above table indicates that about 3.5 million people — or 84 per cent of the active population — are estimated to be unemployed or severely underemployed. It appears that 68 per cent of the theoretically available man-years are unoccupied.[4]

No attempt has been made to estimate the extent of self-employment, although it must be quite high. Hence the figures in the above table quite likely overstate the number of jobless workers. This means that from a socio-political point of view the problems may not be as grave as the figures indicate, although unemployment would be extremely serious even if the estimates were reduced by 50 per cent. From an economic point of view, however, the proliferation of self-employed people is not likely to be very meaningful, as their impact upon output and income will be marginal. It is obvious that if more employment opportunities were offered to these people, more work would be forthcoming.

Of the 3,525,000 workers without full-time jobs, fully 2,475,000, or 75 per cent, are subjected to seasonal unemployment. Almost all of this is located in the traditional sector, where it has become a way of life. To mobilize these workers for economic development, it will be necessary to design a "policy package" comprising at least four items: a mass training program; changed techniques of production, for example increased use of irrigation; changed composition of output (a) within the agricultural sector, and (b) between agriculture and industry; a program of rural public works.

Although it is clear that financial resources are not the chief restraint to an expansion of output, industrial employment could be increased somewhat if the present tight-credit policy were relaxed. The concern of the Central Bank with inflation appears to be premature and excessive. It is evident that the Algerian inflation is not due to an over-all excess of demand and therefore cannot be combated by a general reduction of the money supply.[5]

A policy of credit expansion, on the other hand, would not be effective unless it were complemented by a large program of industrial training, as the lack of technicians is, without a doubt, the major bottleneck. The fastest way to remove this bottleneck would be to organize the training program around accelerated courses. These courses would concentrate, first, on retaining formerly skilled workers who had become de-skilled through enforced idleness; second, on upgrading existing technical personnel; and third, on the longer task of producing new technicians and managers out of inexperienced recruits.

	Official Estimates	*Our Estimates*
Available man-years	2,200,000	4,175,000
Employment	1,280,000	1,304,000
Unemployment	920,000	2,871,000

Note: The explanation of the difference lies in the official definition of the "active population," namely, men between the ages of 15 and 55. Arguing from such a narrow base the government concludes that 45 per cent of the active population are not fully employed and 17 per cent are completely unemployed. However, if one assumes the active population is composed of (a) half the boys between the ages of 10 and 15; (b) all men between 15 and 60; and (c) half the women between 15 and 60, then the results will come very close to our estimates.

As a third step, the composition of industrial investment should be altered to favor the reactivation of the *biens vacants*. A quick increase in output and employment could be obtained by investing relatively small amounts in equipment for the abandoned manufacturing establishments. In the long run, industrial employment should be increased by raising the rate of investment. This means that taxation and wage policies will have to be designed to extract as much of the surplus as possible from the most efficient production units.

Permanent agricultural employment in the modern sector could be increased by providing strong tax incentives to shift to more labor-intensive techniques of production. That is, there should be — over a certain range — an inverse relationship between the contribution of the *unités d'autogestion* to the national employment fund and the amount of permanent employment per (homogeneous) land unit.

Increased output and employment in the traditional sector ultimately depend upon the existence of trained personnel. Most of the unemployed in this sector are totally unskilled and, hence, are unemployable. For this reason, the implementation of a mass program of agricultural training should have top priority.

The techniques of production and the composition of agricultural output should be changed. Irrigation facilities — both small- and large-scale — should be extended and used more fully where possible. This would enable production to shift from the relatively capital-intensive cultivation of wheat to more labor-intensive crops grown on irrigated land.

The quickest way to mobilize the unemployed for productive activity in the agricultural sector is through a program of rural public works. This program should be divided into two separate but related schemes:

1. Projects — such as the construction of small irrigation and drainage works (earth dams and ditches); repairing war-damaged wells, or the construction from local materials of schools, community centers, infirmaries, hospitals, or houses — which would be of particular and immediate benefit to local communities could be organized around local work groups. More specifically: (a) the villagers could select the projects to be undertaken and the work could be organized by the party on a volunteer basis; or (b) each adult could be liable for a given number of days' work or an equivalent tax; or (c) the work and the selection of the projects could be channelled through cooperatives.

2. Those projects — such as large reforestation programs, terracing of hillsides, construction of major dams, irrigation canals and pipes — which are of national importance and/or require heavy equipment and supervision by skilled engineers could be constructed by laborers of a national development corps. The corps would conscript young adults and incorporate them for a year into a paramilitary organization whose functions would be: (a) to provide labor for the construction of major public works; (b) to give its members employment and teach them useful skills and work discipline; and (c) to provide a basic education in literacy for its members.

The public-works scheme outlined above could be financed in large part with surplus food available from the United Nations' World Food Program and the United States' Agency for International Development (AID). It is indeed sad that, because of Algerian prejudice against this type of assistance and the reluctance of some workers to accept payment entirely in kind, more productive use has not been made of these opportunities.

TRAINING

The provision of trained agricultural manpower should have an absolute priority over any other development project in Algeria. The success of everything else — schemes to increase employment, regional development plans, the creation of credit and cooperative institutions — depends upon the prior or simultaneous existence of technical and administrative personnel, particularly at the lower and medium levels. This was recognized by the government in its 1964 investment budget. Top priority was given to agricultural education, and — in addition to current operating expenditures and the costs of projects already begun — 27 million dinars were allocated to new training programs.

The Government's Intermediate Program. The Ministry of Agriculture recently has prepared an estimate of manpower needs for the nest five years. The requirements for administrative and technical personnel are broken down into four categories which, in order of increasing specialization, are as follows: monitors, technical agents, technical assistants, and agricultural engineers. Separate estimates have been made of the needs of the socialist and cooperative farms for specialized workers.

Manpower Requirements, 1965–69

	Personnel	Teachers
Technical and administrative services	8,405	240
Monitors	3,250	60
Technical agents	3,000	50
Technical assistants	1,400	70
Agricultural engineers	755	60
Socialist and cooperative farms	28,400	290
Farm managers	2,600	50
Accountants	4,500	25
Tractor drivers	12,000	60
Mechanics	1,000	90
Workers specialized in tree crops, vineyards, or irrigation	5,500	30
Animal husbandry	2,400	30
Food-processing specialists	400	5

SOURCE: Ministry of Agriculture, *Enseignement et Formation Professionnelle Agricoles, Elements de Base.*

The specialized workers for the socialist and cooperative farms are to be trained in accelerated courses located in sixty different teaching establishments. Seventeen centers already exist and fourteen new ones are being financed by the European Development Fund. This means that another twenty-nine will have to be financed and constructed.

Technical and administrative personnel are to be trained in an entirely separate educational system that will include 240 teachers located in thirty-nine different educational establishments. The emphasis in this system is on quality.

The monitors and technical agents, for example, are even more highly trained than under the French. Entry requirements are rigid, and a great deal of stress is placed on general literary (classical) education. As a result (a) the teaching process is rather slow, and (b) the system is highly compartmentalized.

As presently designed, the program for agricultural education suffers from two deficiencies:

1. It is too difficult for a capable person in the classical system to advance from one educational category to another. For example, a monitor could become an engineer only after eight additional years of agricultural education plus several years of experience.

2. No provision at all has been made for the products of the accelerated courses to advance by moving into the classical system. Thus, for example, an ambitious, capable but, perhaps, barely literate person who was trained in an accelerated course as an irrigation specialist never could become, say, a monitor. This complete separation of the accelerated from the classical systems incurs the danger that two classes will be created: one undertrained and neglected, the other literate, educated, and privileged.

These two deficiencies easily could be corrected by introducing increased vertical mobility within the classical system and horizontal mobility between the two systems. At the moment the classical system does little more than tap the general educational stream at various levels and channel the output flow to the several specialized agricultural schools. All that need be done to complete the system is (1) allow the graduates of any one agricultural school to attend the next school in the hierarchy, and (2) give credit for, say, the first year of agricultural training. This would accelerate vertical mobility — in terms of time required to advance through the system — by 33 to 50 per cent.

Similarly, the isolation of the unorthodox (accelerated) system could be eliminated by (1) establishing a hierarchy of accelerated courses that would gradually upgrade the participants in these courses, and (2) allowing the best products of this system to attend schools in the classical system.

ADMINISTRATIVE ORGANIZATION FOR AGRICULTURAL PLANNING

With her independence Algeria inherited a French colonial administrative structure that was excessively cumbrous even by French standards, and that was poorly suited to administer a planned socialist revolution. During the past two years, nearly 1 million Frenchmen, including about 70 per cent of the administrative personnel, have abandoned the country, and as a result the initially inappropriate government administration has sharply deteriorated. Reform of the civil service and administration, therefore, has a top priority.

At the moment, and within this general context of an inappropriate and deteriorated administration, the virtual impossibility of effective comprehensive agricultural planning is particularly clear. Administrative arrangements within the Ministry of Agriculture are extremely unstable and chaotic. This is both to be expected and, because of the tremendous importance of agriculture to the nation, regretted. More than any other sector of the economy, agriculture is undergoing a revolution. Managerial methods, the techniques of production, the composition of output, and marketing facilities all are undergoing radical changes.

Algeria's privileged position in the French market is disappearing. Hence, it has become necessary to develop the domestic market and find new export markets. This in turn has required a change in the composition of output and the creation of new marketing institutions, notably ONACO and the Office des Cereales. Unfortunately, the Minister of Agriculture has not been given sufficient voice in these new institutions, and hence he cannot have firm control over agricultural revenue and the direction of planning. This lack of authority and control by the ministry over essential activities in the agricultural sector is then translated into a lack of coordination between the plan and the ministry.

Coordination between the Ministry of Agriculture and the other technical ministries has completely collapsed. For example, the Ministry of Social Affairs has been allocated $15 million to finance public-works employment projects. The ministry, however, is unable to use these funds because it has neither the experience nor the technicians necessary to manage soil-conservation schemes. The Ministry of Agriculture, on the other hand, has the experience (the AID project comes under their jurisdiction; the forestry division is quite familiar with rural-renovation programs), the responsibility, and the technicians, but so far has only been able to obtain $1 million. As a result of this confusion, it is quite likely that no new massive programs to reduce unemployment will be implemented.

The administrative and planning difficulties described in the above paragraphs are further hampered by the acute shortage of organizational and executive ability. For the moment, this shortage is unavoidable. The best that can be done is to utilize such abilities as exist in the most efficient manner possible — by eliminating duplication of effort and enforcing coordination.

1. It should be clearly established that the plan is responsible for formulating general policy guide-lines for the agricultural sector and coordinating the policies and activities of the various technical ministries.

2. The various chefs de service of the Ministry of Agriculture should participate actively in the planning process, and especially should be responsible for providing data and informed opinions about their particular areas of operation on a systematic basis.

3. The Bureau d'Etudes of the Ministry of Agriculture should be responsible for designing specific projects for implementation. The projects should reflect policies and priorities indicated by the plan as well as the technical possibilities indicated by the several departments of the ministry.

4. The relevant department or service should be responsible for implementing projects in the field of their competence. Only where projects clearly are interministerial and fall within the competence of no particular ministry, for example, multipurpose regional development schemes, should the plan be directly responsible for implementation.

The minister of agriculture should be ultimately responsible for — or have a very strong voice in — the activity of all the other independent agencies dealing with specific agricultural problems. Anything that goes on in the agricultural sector of the economy — be it rural education, marketing, agricultural credit, or a reafforestation program — must receive his approval. It has become quite clear that a dispersion of authority and responsibility has led either to inefficiency or to inactivity.

Under present conditions, it would be extremely difficult, if not impossible, to prepare and implement a comprehensive plan for development. The basic requirements for such an exercise are missing.

1. The necessary statistical information either does not exist or, in some cases, is dispersed among the various ministries and has not been centralized and presented in a useful form; not even national income data are available.

2. A complete planning organization and the people, for example, economists, necessary to staff such an organization are not yet available. There is no national advisory council attached to the plan that can represent and reconcile the interests of the various sectors of the economy. Nor are there any regional planning offices capable of supervising regional development efforts and determining future needs. At the moment, there are only a few overworked officials in Algiers trying desperately to keep the economy moving from day to day.

3. There are no technicians to implement a plan. This is the chief bottleneck.

Hence, Algeria must not be excessively ambitious in its desire to plan, as this will only lead to failure. A serious failure at this stage would most likely create a reaction discrediting not only the idea of planning but, almost certainly, the officials responsible for formulating the plan. It should be remembered that it was several years after the Russian Revolution before the Soviets were able to prepare their first Five-Year Plan.

In the Three-Year Plan now being considered, Algeria ought to concentrate (a) on removing the major bottlenecks to planning, investment, and growth; (b) on coordinating policies; and (c) on enumerating priorities and formulating a development strategy.

There is no doubt that the major bottleneck in Algeria is the acute shortage of trained personnel at all levels. It is absolutely essential, therefore, that a general plan or program of agricultural training be elaborated as soon as possible. This program should reflect the priorities of the chosen strategy of development and should concentrate on producing technicians of various types as soon and as cheaply as possible. A complete break with the French classical system is essential.

Two major tactical decisions are (i) the regional allocation of investment, and (ii) the investment sequence. It is our opinion that (a) investment should not be dispersed but, on the contrary, concentrated regionally; and (b) investment should be located in the region where the increment to investment is highest. (In technical terms, this would be the region where the product of the marginal propensity to save and the productivity of investment is the highest.) On this basis, it would appear that the best strategy for Algeria is to concentrate capital formation — not necessarily effort — in selected regions of the socialist sector, for example the Cheliff or the Plain of Annaba. Insofar as possible, investment should be organized in sequences, so that the resulting increases in output from each component of the sequence would, in large part, finance the next step. The choice of tactics of investment would determine the ease with which the surplus could be extracted from the producers.

Investment in the socialist sector should be oriented toward increasing the capacity utilization of the existing major irrigation facilities. It is a tragedy that, in a country where water is the ultimate bottleneck to increased production, only 50 per cent of the existing capacity is being utilized. An expansion of irrigation will require a simultaneous emphasis on agricultural education. Farm managers, credit officials, and a whole series of technicians will have to be trained. New crops and methods of production will have to be introduced to ensure that the facilities are used efficiently. One should not allow, for example, vineyards, olive orchards, or cereals to be irrigated.

As the socialist sector is the only one potentially capable of producing a large surplus and generating savings for investment in other sectors, it is essential that factor prices and taxation policies – including land rent – be reformed so as to achieve maximum benefit. Wages should be set as near as possible to their opportunity cost. An unskilled worker, in theory, probably should receive no more than 4 dinars a day. Expenditures on agricultural machinery should be economized whenever possible. Perhaps more emphasis should be placed on providing good repair shops and using rebuilt equipment rather than buying new tractors. This would have the advantage of producing more employment in Algeria and reducing the heavy pressure on the balance of payments.

It is urgent that guaranteed marketing and new distribution arrangements be organized as soon as possible. Algeria's export possibilities are particularly uncertain at the moment. One suspects that for the period of the pre-plan, France will continue to absorb approximately the same volume of agricultural exports as she did last year, although wine sales will probably decrease somewhat. If this assumption is correct, the planners will have three years to reconvert some of the vineyards, develop new exports, and find new customers. In the meantime, it might be wise to emphasize import substitution in the new production plans. There are a great many possibilities – for example, sugar, textiles, milk and other dairy products, processed foods, and footwear – and the reduced uncertainty associated with producing for the domestic market should be a factor stimulating output.

Work should begin on transforming the traditional sector and integrating it more closely into the modern economy. The way to do this is to mobilize the unemployed for investment in infrastructure – including reafforestation and *renovation rurale* – and directly productive activities. Great emphasis should be placed on repairing facilities damaged during the war and expanding small scale irrigation works. *Petite hydraulique* should be a particularly attractive investment because these facilities (i) can be constructed cheaply, (ii) can provide additional employment, (iii) can be completed quickly, and (iv) are more likely to be used at their full capacity. A program of rural public works probably is the only way of quickly integrating the two sectors, reducing the amount of fallow ground, and enabling the *fellah* to shift from cereals to more valuable crops.

For maximum effectiveness, such a program should be complemented by a "policy package" that, in order of priority, includes provision for mass technical and civic education, agricultural extension, and credit services. Once such services are provided, it will be possible to complete the transformation of the traditional sector by establishing multipurpose cooperatives. It must be stressed, however, that the creation of cooperatives should be the last step of an evolutionary process. A premature institutional reform will only court disaster.

Efforts in the traditional sector should be concentrated within the context of a regional plan so as to internalize external economics and appropriate complementary relationships. This will increase the productivity of effort and accelerate the process of integration. It should be possible under a regional plan to start cooperatives at the end of the pre-plan period, say 1966-67. On the basis of this experience, cooperatives could be extended to the rest of the country during the first Five-Year Plan, beginning in 1968. By that time all the necessary complementary services should be available and it should even be possible in the traditional sector to establish local food-processing industries.

The target of the Three-Year Plan should be to increase income and output to its pre-independence level. Per capita income will be lower, of course, as the population will have grown in the meantime. (The authorities should begin seriously to consider policies to control the rate of increase of the population.) Income will continue to decline throughout 1964 and probably will be below 8 billion dinars, say 7.8 billion (in 1959 prices). If we consider "real" income (that is, excluding military imports) in 1959 to have been approximately 10 billion dinars, Algeria will have to increase her output by 2.2 billion dinars, or by 28 per cent, to return to the same level. To achieve this goal the country will have to grow at an average annual compound rate of almost 9 per cent during the pre-plan period. The growth rate, of course, will not be constant throughout the period but will accelerate as the economy gathers momentum. One hypothetical pattern might be as follows:

Year	Output (in billion dinars)	Increase in Output	Development Expenditure*	Productivity of Development Expenditure	Rate of Growth
0	7.8				
1	8.1	.3	1.50	.200	3.85
2	8.8	.7	1.65	.425	8.62
3	10.0	1.2	2.00	.600	13.62
Total		2.2	5.15	.426	8.69

*It is assumed that

$$\frac{\text{Development expenditure}}{\text{Output}} = .5$$

Note: At present the domestic savings rate is almost zero, and it is likely to remain so unless a tax reform is introduced.

This target would be difficult to achieve, but it is not impossible. It can be realized only if the investment program is strictly coordinated with policies for implementation and the provision of trained personnel.

It should be noted that the high postulated rate of growth depends less dramatically upon the large volume of resources. Algeria is beginning her development effort with an extraordinarily good infrastructure and a large volume of unutilized resources. The latter include (i) 50 per cent of the irrigation water; (ii) at least 30 per cent of industrial capacity and 50 per cent of transport and power facilities; (iii) a minimum of 2 million people unemployed; and (iv) inefficient use of land, with about 3 million hectares in fallow. The task of the pre-plan should be to mobilize these resources by injecting a minimum of capital investment and concentrating on mass training. The yields from such a program would be unusually high.

Notes

1. It must be recognized, however, that the profits of the *colons* were rather heavily subsidized both on the input side (power and irrigation water) and in the privileged prices granted to Algerian produce in the French market.

2. A further contributory factor to the decline of nomadism was the prohibition of access to the Sahara by the French during the war.

3. Tenure rights in the traditional sector are ill defined, but in principle they are subject to the Qoranic laws pertaining to individual *(melk)* or collective *(arch)* property.

4. Our estimates of the extent of unemployment differ widely from the official estimates, although the global figures on employment are practically identical. (The official estimate can be found in *Revue du Plan et des Etudes Economiques,* special issue, "Situation Economique en 1963.") This can be seen in the table below.

5. The urban middle class is living considerably beyond its income and is consuming the nation's capital. The new bourgeoisie lives in a *bien vacant* and — at the time of writing, in June, 1964 — pays no rent, gas, or electricity bills; his salary is spent almost entirely on food, imported clothing, and automobiles. In such a situation, an anti-inflation policy would not consist in reducing liquidity but in increasing taxation, collecting bills, and prohibiting imports.

35

THE ROLE OF TRIBAL MARKETS IN MOROCCO

MARVIN W. MIKESELL

Western observers in Morocco are astonished by the juxtaposition of modern urban districts and deeply rural tribal territories. The gleaming, up-to-date buildings of Morocco's European quarters remind one of California rather than of France. Casablanca bears a strong resemblance to Los Angeles and its suburbs, Rabat could be San Diego. Oujda has the aspect of Fresno or Bakersfield. It is possible to travel for weeks in Morocco and never leave excellent highways. But in the areas of European influence one is never far from the "real Morocco," where tribal authority is still dominant and the goals of life are independence and self-sufficiency. The generalization is often made that the tribal territories are evolving from a medieval to a modern way of life, but such comparison does not do justice to the magnitude of the change. The economic and social environment of tribal Morocco more closely resembles that in northern Europe at the time of earliest Roman conquest. In recent years Morocco has been struggling with problems that were resolved in the West more than a thousand years ago.

The clearest expression of this "split personality" is an abrupt transition from urban to rural settlement. In the Western world we are accustomed to think of towns as links between these two modes of life. In Morocco, such links are hard to find. Between one city and another are only villages, hamlets, or isolated farmsteads. Towns of the Western type are of very recent origin, and most of them are in areas where European influence has been strong. The almost total absence of towns in Morocco can be explained by the presence of a special instrument of trade — the weekly market, or suq (plural, aswaq). These markets are held in the open, at predetermined sites which are deserted during the rest of the week. In each tribal area, one or more sites are reserved as market places and are named according to the day of the week on which the market is held. On the morning of the appointed day, streams of people converge on the market place. After a few hours of brisk trading, the market begins to break up, and by nightfall the site is empty again.

The deeply rural Northern Zone of Morocco (until April, 1956, controlled by the Spanish as a "protectorate") is an excellent area in which to study the

Reprinted, by permission, from the *Geographical Review*, XLVIII (1958) 494-511; copyright by the American Geographical Society of New York.

traditional role of the suq. This zone, like the large area of Berber speech in the High, Middle, and Anti-Atlas, has suffered little from the obscuring effects of foreign influence. The Arabs, who first entered Morocco at the end of the seventh century, had small interest in the highlands. European colonists, largely concerned with mechanized agriculture, also preferred lands of gentle relief. All the mountain tribes have embraced Islam, some have learned to speak Arabic, and a few have adopted the Singer sewing machine. But it is only in the last two decades that their traditions of independence and self-sufficiency have been seriously disturbed.

TIME AND PLACE

Maps of Morocco show more than a thousand markets. Their presence is indicated by the following names:[1] *El had* (Sunday), *Et tnine* (Monday), *Et tleta* (Tuesday), *El arba'* (Wednesday), *El khemis* (Thursday), *El jema'* (Friday), *Es sebt* (Saturday). For political as well as economic reasons each tribe holds at least one suq of its own, and a complete cycle of markets may be maintained. Six markets, for example, are held by the numerous Rifian tribe of the Beni Ouriaghel.[2] The ideal location permits any member of the sponsoring tribe to visit the market and return home in a single day. This stipulation can be satisfied even when the distance is as much as twenty or thirty miles, for the Moroccans are great walkers, and on market day no one wants to remain at home. The suq is much more than a market in the economic sense; it is also a social and political assembly of great importance in tribal life. Market day is the time for legal transactions and all manner of negotiations. By nightfall, tribal authorities have resolved most of the problems of the week. Since the suq serves as a clearinghouse for gossip and news, its attraction is overpowering. The *qadi* (Qoranic judge) of the tribe of the Beni Seddat once granted a divorce to a woman whose husband had refused to allow her to visit the suq. On market days in the Senhaja mountains, the writer has seen people wading barefooted through snow.

Physical factors are of primary importance in the selection of market sites. The critical requirement is a reliable water supply. In the moist highlands of Jebala and Rhomara, each tribe possesses dozens of potential market sites, but in the Rif perennial streams are rare, and the chief markets are located where there are springs or wells. Markets are often placed close to a religious sanctuary or shrine (*murabit*), since the site is protected by sacred authority, and malediction (*tagat*) falls on anyone who disturbs the peace. This was a major consideration a generation ago when Morocco was rent by tribal warfare and markets were turbulent assemblies of armed men.[3]

Two types of market are distinguishable. The more influential is the local suq. Markets of this type draw a few hundred people from a radius of ten or twelve miles. Their main function is to serve as foci of commerce for dispersed but sedentary populations engaged in subsistence agriculture. Differences of slope, exposure, and soil permit some specialization, but no community specializes to the point of dependence on others for staple foods. One village may try to increase its flocks beyond the level of need or, if its land is wooded, may make pitchforks or plows. Another village may have a surplus of eggs or an overabundance of fruit. In spring, cereal stocks are low, and there is a brisk trade in raisins and dried figs. The local suq also serves as a place of deposit for sugar, salt, cooking oil, and kerosene — the primary commodities that must be brought in from outside.

The second type of suq, the regional market, draws a larger number of people from a radius of as much as twenty miles. Markets of this type are located at the convergence of major communication lines and on the frontiers of complementary production zones. Moroccans make a distinction between *bled seguia,* where crops can be grown under irrigation, and *bled bour,* where only dry farming is possible. The larger markets are usually on the frontiers of these two zones. The Wednesday market at Targuist, on the eastern edge of the mountains of Senhaja es-Sghair, enjoys this combination of advantages.

The sole transportation artery between the humid Rhomara and the semi-arid Rif passes nearby. Targuist is also the apex of two tracks over northern Morocco mountainous spine. From the irrigated terraces of the highlands come summer crops of maize, beans, squash, and *kif* (hashish). In the drier but warmer Rif, there is in normal years a surplus of winter wheat and barley, nuts, fruit, and olive oil. The mountain tribes bring planks of cedar and pine, and the Rifian tribes make baskets, hats, and matting from cane, palmetto fibers, and esparto grass. The mountain tribe of Tarhzout specializes in tanning and leather work, which can be exchanged for pottery manufactured in the Rif.

EXAMPLES OF LOCAL AND REGIONAL MARKETS

Let us consider two markets celebrated on the same day. El-Had Beni Bou Nsar (Sunday [market] of the sons of the father of Nsar) is a local suq that attracts about 300 people from a narrow zone extending along the flanks of a deep valley cut by the Oued el Had (Sunday stream). This is an area of subsistence agriculture. The slopes are steep and the soils stony and thin, but a few streams are perennial, and a variety of crops can be grown under irrigation during the dry summer to supplement the winter crops of barley and rye. The suq is reached by a track from Targuist, and when this is not blocked by snow or mud, a small bus filled with merchants comes to the market. They set up tents or booths and display rolls of cotton cloth, soap, sugar, salt, tea, and a variety of other goods ranging from fertility charms to ball-point pens. Artisans repair shoes and make charcoal braziers from scrap iron. There may be a truckload of fish from Alhucemas and possibly a travelling medicine man.

By noon, all who are coming to the market have arrived. The suq is at its peak, "a vociferating, seething mass of human beings, quadrupeds and feathered things."[4] The women exchange gossip as well as their special property — eggs, poultry, bread, and fruit. The men gather apart and besides settling the important tribal business haggle over the prices of tea, oil, sugar, and meat. Everyone has a turn with the itinerant peddlers, but few purchase anything; for in this area of subsistence economy, each family guards its currency for a marriage or some other special event. A rough system of quarters (*rahba*) is recognized, and week after week the same goods are found at the same place. Butchers and blacksmiths work a short distance away from the rest of the group. When there is a load of fish, fires are kindled and part of the purchase is consumed on the spot. But most people are satisfied with a simple meal of barley bread and dried fruit. By mid-afternoon the load of fish has been sold, and those who live close to the road — sometimes more than fifty people —

crowd on the truck for a ride. The bus stays as long as the merchants feel that there is a chance for a sale, but by nightfall the suq is abandoned and the market bus is stirring up giant clouds of dust.

Each market has four main functions: (1) distribution of local products; (2) exchange of rural surplus for urban goods; (3) circulation of articles such as pottery and millstones from special places within the country; and (4) dissemination of foreign imports. The larger, regional, markets differ from the smaller, local, markets in a greater emphasis on the last two functions. A good example of the regional type is El had Jebel Arruit, located close to the ports of Melilla and Nador. In addition to the simple goods offered at Had Beni Bou Nsar, this market boasts toy balloons, firecrackers (for use on wedding days), and a myriad of other commodities of national and international origin. On a representative day at Jebel Arruit one can see cotton cloth from England, canvas shoes from Spain, flashlights and padlocks from Japan, political posters from Egypt, and spices of many varieties, mostly from India. More than a thousand people gather here on market day. Four buses bring merchants from Melilla and Nador. Trucks also come from these cities and from Alhucemas and Oujda. This suq is large enough to require the services of professional weighers and criers.[5] But at nightfall the market place is deserted, and there is little to suggest that this suq was large and the other one small. The largest trade at both markets is in the simple necessities of rural life, such as sugar, salt, and kerosene.

UNIQUENESS OF THE SUQ

This system of trade has no counterpart at present in the Western world. The uniqueness of the suq derives from the fact that it is regarded as an institution, an event, and not as a feature of settlement. Merchants and peasants meet on neutral ground during a time of truce. For more than a thousand years, merchants in the Occident have occupied fixed positions and encouraged dispersed rural populations to come to them. Three rural trading institutions have been prominent in Europe,[6] and none of them corresponds to the suq. The general commodity fairs of medieval times, such as those founded by the counts of Champagne, were annual or semi-annual events designed to encourage wholesale exchange. Livestock fairs began either as specialized derivatives of general commodity fairs or as expressions of more ancient commercial contacts between pastoral peoples and entrepreneurs based in towns. The periodic village markets, still to be found in most of Europe, show a closer functional resemblance to the suq. But as early as the twelfth century, rural markets in Europe had concrete expression as *bourg, Marktflecken,* or *market town.* Furthermore, these were imposed institutions with "market rights" and "market days" assigned by decree. In order to find a counterpart in Europe of the Moroccan suq, one must look beyond the Middle and Dark Ages to pagan times. Then, in northern Europe at least, "market" meant periodic assembly and not necessarily a feature of settlement.[7]

Open-air markets of the Moroccan type represent an attempt to reconcile desires for security and for commercial exchange. But this system of trade can be effective only among populations of sedentary habit and dispersed settlement. Where settlement is dense, as in the Nile Valley, or widely dispersed and nomadic, as in the pre-Saharan steppe, other arrangements for trading must be made. Another prerequisite is that communications must not be too elaborate; for when transportation facilities evolve to a Western standard, markets of this type tend to lose their ephemeralness and change into trading towns.

Where are these prerequisites satisfied? And where are recurrent markets to be found? Carleton S. Coon[8] considers that the right conditions for the existence of a "staggered series of weekly markets" are found in North Africa and along the Caspian shore of Iran. In reality, markets of this type are scattered over an area extending from Morocco to the Philippines. Patterns of rural trade in Ethiopia are similar.[9] Stanley[10] found market places on the banks of the Congo, where all was "animation and eager chatter" until noon, when they became "silent again and untenanted, a prey to gloom and shade." Weekly markets play an important role in the economy of rural India.[11] The West Bengal *hat,* for example, functions almost exactly like the suq, and a similar comparison can be made between Moroccan markets and the village fairs of Szechwan.[12] As in most problems of culture history, it is a question of independent invention versus diffusion. Is a pattern of trade with rotating weekly markets sufficiently complex to suggest origin in one culture area? Or are we dealing with a system of exchange that could have evolved spontaneously wherever conditions of settlement and livelihood were appropriate? It may be noted that annual and weekly trade fairs also exist in parts of Latin America, and that the weekly fairs, at least, probably trace to pre-Columbian time.[13]

NEGATIVE ROLE IN URBAN EVOLUTION

Fortunately, ignorance of cause, in this case, does not preclude consideration of effect. The successful functioning of the suq in Morocco has had an arresting effect on urban evolution. These markets serve as links between cities and the rural countryside and render trading towns unnecessary. Indeed, there is no equivalent in Maghribi Arabic of the word "town." From *medina,* "city," the Moroccan vocabulary turns to *dechra,* "village," *douar,* "hamlet," and *azib,* "farmstead."

How could cities have evolved in Morocco without leaving traces of intermediate stages of urbanization? The answer is that Moroccan cities did not evolve as trading centers for the rural countryside; they were established by decree. The Moroccan city is an imposed entity, foreign to tribal life. Some cities trace their origin to Roman time, others began during the period of Arab conquest, still others were founded by the Europeans. No Moroccan city is truly native. It is not surprising, therefore, that cities should be found only in the lowlands, where alien authority was easy to establish and maintain. In the highlands Berber ideals of political independence and economic self-sufficiency acted as a check against urbanization.[14]

Intimate relations between city and hinterland are difficult to establish when urban institutions are imposed by alien authorities. Cities thus established become parasites, drawing support from the rural countryside but offering little in exchange. The peasant population continues to look to its local markets for satisfaction of basic needs. Fes, located in a rich agricultural area and renowned for the high quality of its crafts, is the only Moroccan city intimately related to its hinterland. But the nucleus of the Fes bourgeosie is formed by descendants of

Arab immigrants from Spain, whose pronunciation of Arabic is often unintelligible to tribesmen living a few miles away.

Illustrations can be taken from the Northern Zone. The ports of Ceuta and Melilla were used by the Portuguese and Spanish as bases of colonial and military activity and even today are governed as integral parts of Spain (*plazas de soberanía.*) Larache and Arcila also reflect Iberian influence. Tetuan began as a military fort designed to protect the government route between Tangier and Fes. In the sixteenth century it was a focus of immigration for Muslims and Jews who were being expelled from Spain. Chauen, established in 1471 as a base for campaigns against the Portuguese, served also as a refuge for Andalusian Moors. Alcazarquivir (Ksar el-Kebir) served a similar function in the eleventh century. Tangier has been the headquarters of a whole series of foreign interests – Carthaginian, Roman, Portuguese, Spanish, English, and, lately, even "international." Most of the Moroccan residents of Tangier are immigrants from the Rif, who have little in common with the Jebalan tribesmen of the nearby hills.[15] There are only two other settlements in the Northern Zone that deserve to be called town, Alhucemas and Nador, and they owe their origin to the establishment of the Spanish protectorate.

The same pattern exists in the French zone. Casablanca, Kenitra, and the mining communities of Khouribga and Youssoufia reflect European planning and investment. The name of Casablanca's tiny ancestor, Anfa, is no longer remembered; Moroccans know their bustling economic capital as Dar el-Beida, which also means "white house." The important native cities likewise began as planned communities. Oujda, Rabat, Salé, and Marrakesh owe their origin to governmental decree. Taza and Meknes began as military outposts. Even the maritime trading centers of Al-Jadida, Safi, as-Sawira, and Agadir were established as centers of political control. The economic function of these cities was a consequence of their urban function rather than a cause.[16]

RECENT TRENDS

At the beginning of the twentieth century there was not a single kilometer of road in Morocco suitable for wheeled vehicles. In fact, the only vehicles known were decorative carriages used by the sultan for ceremonies. The French, realizing the need for good communications if they were to pacify the country and remain in power, promptly began work on an extensive network of roads. The Spanish made similar, though less successful, efforts in their zone. In 1955, there were 10,000 kilometers of primary or secondary roads (mostly macadam) and 35,000 kilometers of tracks open to buses and trucks during the dry season.[17] With the advent of roads and motorized transport, the traditional role of the suq began to change. The markets located on natural communication routes grew in size and influence, whereas the more isolated markets either remained local or simply faded away. Elderly Moroccans everywhere speak of markets unknown to their children. The site of an abandoned market can be established by suq terminology in a local place name; for example, a name such as *Bab et-tleta* (Tuesday Pass) or *Ain et-tleta* (Tuesday Spring) in areas where no Tuesday market remains.

Before the establishment of the European protectorates, not only were communications primitive but they were disrupted by tribal warfare. One of the main themes of Moroccan history is the distinction between *bled al-makhzen* (the land of government) and *bled as-siba* (the land of dissidence). The *bled as-siba* corresponded to the Rif and the Atlas Mountains, where communications were difficult to establish and maintain. Travel was possible only under the approval and protection of local authorities. Since intertribal feuds were common, long-range travel involved great risk. Merchants and travelers assembled in the cities until they were numerous enough to pay for protection. In parts of the Rif the tradition of market truce broke down, and a special system of woman's markets had to be established so that noncombatant members of the feuding tribes could carry on a rudimentary trade.

Primitive communications and tribal strife not only prevented the evolution of towns; they even discouraged the growth of the regional suq. The modern trend has been different. The more accessible markets have grown in size, and some have evolved into permanent establishments. In short, the suq, which for centuries acted as a substitute for the trading town, is now evolving into the very thing it had militated against.[18] This trend ceases to be paradoxical when it is viewed against the background of Morocco's expanding network of roads.

The changes that have taken place at Tleta Ketama are indicative of this trend. Thirty years ago this was a local suq patronized mainly by members of a single tribe. Today the market easily qualifies as a regional suq. During the warm months of spring and summer, more than a thousand people assemble here. Today's market has one advantage over its predecessor — it is reached by a road. The presence of the road does not mean that the market is more accessible to the tribesmen who gather there, but it does mean that the site is more accessible to merchants from Targuist, Alhucemas, and Tetuan. Before the road was completed, the suq was no more attractive than several others in the area. Now everyone who possibly can goes there, even if it means neglect of markets closer to home. The simple charms of the local suq lose their appeal when larger markets with a wider range of goods are accessible.

The principal expression of the new trend is the overcrowded market bus. These buses carry a simple notation in Arabic script, *aswaq* (markets), which is perfectly understood by the merchants and shoppers who board a bus at its terminal or flag one on the road. On Monday they are going to *suq et-tnine,* on Tuesday to *suq et-tleta,* and so on through the week.

The circulation from Targuist, in northern Morocco, is representative of the whole country. Two buses of 1935 vintage start from here. On Monday, one goes to the market of the Beni Hadifa and the other to the market of the Beni Ammart. On Tuesday, they both go to the mountain suq at Ketama. Wednesday is market day at Targuist, and not enough bus tickets can be sold to justify a trip. On Thursday, the buses go back into the mountains to the small market at Isagan (Spanish, Llano Amarillo). Friday is a day of rest, and the buses again stay at their base.[19] On Saturday, there is a large market at Imzuren, in the territory of the Beni Ouriaghel. On Sunday the attraction is the small suq of the Beni Bou Nsar, described above. There is not a single kilometer of surfaced road in this whole area, and by American standards the buses are long overdue for the junkyard. Yet day after day, year after year, they lumber on.

The buses are also used by tribesmen who take advantage of the market circulation to get close to their homes. Most villages in Morocco are within a day's walk of a bus route at least once in the week. But most of the tickets are sold to merchants who follow the complete circuit to sell their array of goods. The prices current at Targuist give an idea of the weekly volume of trade. Each round trip costs about one dollar. In order to recover this investment, pay for his goods, and make a small profit, the itinerant merchant must earn about twenty dollars during the week. By Western standards this seems a small sum. But it must be remembered that rural Morocco is still a region of subsistence agriculture, and that barter usually has priority over cash transactions. By Moroccan standards, the Targuist merchants are doing well.

The influx of a larger number of people from farther away necessitates a more elaborate establishment at the market place. Inns are necessary, and also permanent storehouses and shops. Some structures were built by the Europeans. The officers of Affaires Indigénes in the French zone and of Asuntos Indígenas in the area of Spanish influence functioned as overseers of the native government, and this function required that they be present on market day. The practical procedure was to establish headquarters at the larger markets, and this led to the erection of buildings to serve as offices and dwelling places. Walls and gates were added, since the suq was the best place to collect taxes. At the larger markets the services of veterinarians and physicians were provided, and they too needed places of consultation and residence. As often as not the suq also served as headquarters of a military detachment. Almost all the regional markets now have structures built by Europeans, and many of the local markets have been enhanced in some way. A few markets have been moved from their original locations or shifted from one day to another. For example, the market at Targuist was moved from the valley of the Oued Rhis to the center of a small garrison town built by the Spanish after the end of Abd el-Krim's rebellion.[20] These innovations seem likely to persist. The local officials of the Moroccan government function independently of the old tribal authorities, and for the most part they have simply taken over the offices and houses used by the Europeans before Moroccan independence.

As a result of these trends, many markets now have an appearance of permanence and solidity. In time trading may be spread throughout the week. Merchants may elect to stay out instead of moving their goods from place to place. Perhaps the shifting suq will continue as an instrument of barter, and permanent markets will develop as centers of retail trade. It is not yet possible to predict the outcome of these trends. In fact, it cannot be taken for granted that they will persist. The principal cause of change has been Morocco's expanding network of roads, and it remains to be seen whether the new government will be able to continue this work. Here is the key to the problem; for it seems to be a principle of economic geography that improvement of communications encourages centralization of trading facilities.

Notes

1. In the preparation of this paper, special use was made of sheets of the "Carte de reconnaissance," 1:100,000, published by the Institut Géographique National (Annexe du Maroc), Rabat, 1936-.

2. For additional information on markets in the Rif, see D.M. Hart, "An Ethnographic Survey of the Riffian Tribe of Aith Wuryaghil," *Tamuda,* II (1954), 51-86.

3. The elaborate precautions taken to ensure order at markets are described in Robert Montagne, *Les Berbères et le Makhzen dans le sud de Maroc: essai sur la transformation politique des Berbères sédentaires (groupe Chleuh)* (Paris: Alcan, 1930). pp. 251-53;

4. This colorful phrase, written by Budgett Meakin at the turn of the century, is just as applicable to the markets of today.(*The Moors: A Comprehensive Description* [London and New York: Sonnenschein, 1902], p. 172).

5. The Riffian term for such people is *imazilen*, "shameless ones." Shyness and reserve are cardinal virtues to the dignified Rifi. Market criers, musicians, dancers, and others who display themselves in public are members of outcaste groups.

6. See André Allix, "The Geography of Fairs: Illustrated by Old-World Examples," *Geographical Revue*, XII, no. 12 (1922), 532-69.

7. See R. E. Dickinson's discussions of this topic in *The West European City: A Geographical Interpretation* (London: Routledge and Kegan Paul, 1951), pp. 311-15, and *Germany: A General and Regional Geography* (London: Methuen, 1953), pp. 156-69.

8. *Caravan: The Story of the Middle East* (New York: Holt, Rinehart, 1951), pp. 171-90.

9. F. J. Simoons, "The Peoples and Economy of Begemder and Semyen, Ethiopia" (unpublished Ph.D. dissertation, University of California, Berkeley, 1957), pp. 484-527.

10. H. M. Stanley, *Through the Dark Continent* (2 vols.; New York, 1878), II, 167-68.

11. The literature on Indian markets is rich. See especially C. D. Deshpande, "Market Villages and Periodic Fairs of Bombay Karnatak," *Indian Geographical Journal*, XVI (1941), 327-39.

12. J. E. Spencer, "The Szechwan Village Fair," *Economic Geography*, XVI (1940), 48-58.

13. The best accounts of rural markets in Latin America known to the writer are G. M. Wrigley, "Fairs of the Central Andes," *Geographical Review*, VII (1919), 65-80; and G. M. Foster, "The Folk Economy of Rural Mexico, with Special Reference to Marketing," *Journal of Marketing*, XIII (1948), 153-62.

14. This statement echoes Walter Fogg's remarks in "Villages and *Suqs* in the High Atlas Mountains of Morocco," *Scottish Geographical Magazine*, LI (1935), 144-51.

15. D. M. Hart, "Notes on the Rifian Community of Tangier," *Middle East Journal*, XI (1957), 153-62.

16. See Fernand Joly, *et al., Géographie du Maroc* (Paris: Delagrave, 1949), p. 113.

17. These figures are from the Michelin guide to Morocco, 1954-55 ed., p. 27.

18. The best illustrations of evolution from country market to trading towns are Settat and Souk el-Arba du Rharb, both in the French zone. For an interesting historical sketch of Settat and a discussion of many other aspects of urban evolution in Morocco, see Konrad Wiche, "Marokkanische Stadttypen," in *Festschrift zur Hundertjahrfeier der Geographischen Gesellschaft in Wien* (Vienna, 1957), pp. 485-527.

19. There is no Qoranic sanction for the designation of Friday as a day of rest. The religious importance of this day derives from the fact that the imam preaches in the mosque on Friday, and the prayer of that day is the most important of the week. In recent years the idea of a "weekend" extending from Thursday evening to Saturday morning has gained wide acceptance in the Muslim world. In Morocco, at least, the idea of a workless Friday also has political overtones.

20. Changes of this nature are described in detail in two papers by Walter Fogg: "The Economic Revolution in the Countryside of French Morocco," *Journal of the Royal African Society*, XXXV (1936), 123-39; and "Changes in the Lay-Out, Characteristics, and Functions of a Moroccan Tribal Market, Consequent on European Control," *Man*, XLI (1941), 104-8.

36

URBAN ORGANIZATION AND SOCIAL STRUCTURE IN ALGERIA

R. DESCLOITRES, C. DESCLOITRES, AND J. C. REVERDY

... If independence is a struggle against individual or collective alienation in order to arrive at popular participation in national reconstruction, it presupposes first of all an integration of citizens into local collectivities. In the cities of many developing countries, this condition is not fulfilled; an urban minority born of the nationalist struggle creates juridical institutions which can perhaps conform to the structures of the groups from which this minority comes, but which do not fit the masses, formerly of the countryside, who now populate the suburbs and surroundings of the large cities.

Will Algeria escape this danger? Will the urban organization of Oran, Algiers, and Constantine at least partially express the social structure of the hundreds of thousands of men who inhabit the slums? We cannot answer; we can only pose the problem in order to analyze it from a sociological point of view, showing the alternatives that are available.

To this end, we will first draw a schematic picture of the urban phenomenon in Algeria, showing the relation between urbanization and slums, and the consequences. Particular attention will be given to the marginal situation of the slum populations in the urban framework. Then we will analyze the slum social structures that have sprung from those of the original urban groups and are incompatible with the present urban structures. To illustrate the relation between organization and structures and the city-slum duality, we will describe an abortive attempt at organization in an Algerian slum. In conclusion, we will try to show several alternatives based on our studies and experiences in Algeria.

The reader may be surprised that we did not pay attention to indications of the war (development of consciousness, political life, mass action, and so on). We made our choice deliberately: in addition to the operative difficulties inherent in studying a society that is undergoing the sharp crises of clandestine action, not enough time has passed to give the perspective and detachment necessary for social history. The Algerian drama has certainly given rise to "effervescent, innovating and creative" collective conduct (to quote Georges Gurvitch); a scientific study of this phase of social reality remains to be undertaken if we are to get beyond the present hagiographic stage. We prefer to limit our examination to older, more established behavior.

Translated, by permission, from *Civilisations*, XII, No. 2 (1962), 211-30.

SHANTY-TOWNS BETWEEN CITY AND COUNTRY

The big city in Algeria has long since lost the appearance that colonization gave it for several decades. The old saturated Muslim *cité* gradually overflowed into the European quarter next door; while the colonial *cité* transformed itself into a vast industrial and commercial metropolis, the massive arrival of Muslims from the *bled* swelled the suburbs beyond measure. Today, two cities make up each urban agglomeration: the modern city, a prosperous reflection of the Europe that created it, and the city of the new arrivals, who are less and less able to find a home in it.[1]

The process of urbanization in North Africa has had practically the same results as it had in nineteenth-century Europe or twentieth-century Asia, Latin America, and Black Africa; sections of Paris and Berlin, refugee camps in Jerusalem and Karachi, Latin American *favelas,* African tin-can shanties — all the unusual urban forms incarnate the juxtaposition of two worlds. Algeria is called upon to face problems common to all developing and rapidly urbanizing countries, but her problems are doubly aggravated: the opposition between modern city and neo-urbanites is reinforced by the tension of ethnic differences. The war has precipitated migratory movements toward the city since 1954, to the point of a veritable exodus.

Between 1886 and 1960, the rate of urbanization in Algeria[2] increased from 14 per cent to 32 per cent. This movement, which began in Algiers and Oran, spread to Bône (Annaba) and Constantine about 1930, and after 1954 reached such secondary centers as Sidi-Bel-Abbes. In 1962; these five cities with more than 100,000 inhabitants each, contained more than half the urban population of Algeria; between 1954 and 1960, they received more than 60 per cent of the new city-dwellers. Their rate of growth during the last ten years is close to that of classic mushroom towns: Algiers, for example, grew from 470,000 to 870,000 between the censuses of 1948 and 1960.

The qualitative change is no less striking than the quantitative, for cities like Algiers, Oran, and Annaba, which have always been the European fief of Algeria, owe their extraordinary growth to Muslim immigration. Their European population has scarcely increased since 1926, but their Muslim population has grown in wildly unforeseen proportions. Algiers is the best example: 73,000 Muslims in 1926, 225,000 in 1948, 293,000 in 1954, 558,000 in 1960. This evolution, which after 1954 reached the secondary towns of the interiors as well as the coast, has every chance of continuing. Not only must the *bled,* with its natural population growth, inevitably continue to supply the big cities with its population overflow, but most of the present occupants of the regroupment centers and the workers, called back from France will also move to the cities.

Thus, two basic aspects of urban growth in the new Algeria appear: the cities, European constructions above all, are today populated by Muslims (16 per cent in Algiers, 50 per cent in Oran and 70 per cent in Annaba), and the Muslim population is 27 per cent urbanized, representing three-quarters of the total urban population. . . .

The causes of the rapid urbanization of Algeria and the "Islamization" of its cities are too deep and too complex to be developed here in detail. For half a century, the progressive impoverishment of the *bled* — due to geographic and economic as well as demographic factors — and the disintegration of traditional structures gradually gave free rein to the attraction of the cities. The migratory waves, which had shown a certain regularity up to 1930, expanded, multiplied, and changed into a rural disinherited landslide toward the urban zones and, above all, toward the coastal cities, where the European presence and accomplishments seemed to guarantee a better way of life. Algiers, the administrative, commercial, and industrial capital, was the obvious center of attraction.

The tragedy is dryly summarized by a general description that is applicable to present-day Algeria: "The invasion of the cities by rural misery is today the basic characteristic of economically underdeveloped countries."[3] There lies the drama of urban Algeria and, indeed, of the entire country. While their departure has in no way improved living conditions in the *bled*, where the population — far from diminishing — continues to grow, the country folk who invaded the cities have only brought with them their own emptiness and have set up the tramp life that is so typical of the third world.

Deprived, in every sense of the word, the neo-urbanites find none of the things they came to the cities to seek; underemployment and housing crises have long plagued all Algerian cities. Thus, in Algiers, where most secondary and tertiary activity is concentrated, 15,000 Muslims were officially listed as underemployed in 1948 and 18,000 in 1954. Four-fifths of the lodgings occupied by Muslims in 1954 were overcrowded. There is thus reason to believe that the 200,000 Muslims who came to Algiers between 1934 and 1960 remained for the most part without employment or lodging. The exceptional efforts of industrialization and construction undertaken at the cost of thousands of dollars during the late 1950's (and unfortunately undermined by the effect of the war) were not commensurate with the demand. The Constantine Plan of 1959 provided for only 20,000 new jobs in all Algeria over eight years to absorb urban unemployment; at the beginning of 1961, investments planned by authorized industrial enterprises represented only 37 per cent of the projected total, and investments actually made were only 12 per cent of those expected.[4]

First undetected, then flagrant, and finally overwhelming, the consequences of this nonintegration of immigrants are visible in all Algerian cities: in the hollow of the ravine, on the steepest slopes or on their edges, in all the empty and bypassed by construction the slum shacks mingle together, hug each other, and proliferate. From a few houses to a huge urban slum of 10,000 inhabitants or more, they literally lay siege to the city, crying their misery at its gates. *In 1954, one out of three Muslims in Algiers lived in a slum;* ten years later, the number was probably one out of two.

Slums first appeared about 1930, at the time when the process of Islamizing Algerian cities also began.[5] Although their presence worried municipal authorities from the start, it did not give rise to an administrative policy until after World War II, when the former current of immigration turned into a tidal wave and provoked a terrifying multiplication in the number and size of slums. The astonishing vitality of these new urban forms stood up year after year against the most energetic decisions and achievements. Paradoxically, the absorption of the slums by the municipalities led to their administrative takeover and, by that very act, to their durability; in fact, they were installed on municipal land for the praiseworthy purpose of resettling the occupants as soon as the construction of new housing would permit. Such a policy was not a monopoly of Algeria but also was followed in Casablanca, Tunis, the medina of Dakar, and in Ciudad de Dios in Lima, Peru.[6]

While the slums spread out over unconstructed zones — around cemeteries, along former ramparts — the construction programs proved notoriously insufficient. The continuously increasing arrival of new immigrants made even the most farsighted predictions obsolete, and the measures taken encouraged further emigration from the countryside. In the Kasbah of Algiers, the average housing density reached four people per room in 1954. The transient relocation centers did not lose their inhabitants, and every slum shack emptied of its occupants was immediately filled by others.

Unable to house their immigrants, the big cities of Algeria are even less capable of finding them employment. The economy was founded long ago on the needs of a European majority and it owes the greater part of its prosperity to trade with metropolitan France; only recently has it been oriented toward the creation of jobs. It is now generally admitted that, in developing countries, industrialization is not necessarily the cause of the social problems of urbanization but, on the contrary, can permit their solution. Until recent years, however, the secondary activities of the Algerian cities were carried out for the most part by small and medium-sized business, essentially for the production or transformation of consumer goods; most of their income was devoted to tertiary activities carried out principally by Europeans.

Nothing was less propitious than these structures for the integration of hundreds of thousands of rural inhabitants totally devoid of capital and professional training or even of elementary education. The army of immigrants brought nothing but useless hands to the cities of the "haves." Muslims who had come to the city earlier and had found their place as laborers, workers, or lesser employees in construction, transportation, and trade, where they held a large proportion of the jobs, appeared highly privileged in the eyes of the new arrivals. At best, the latter could find only the little jobs of the underemployed. This doomed in advance any battle for housing undertaken for them, because the uncertainty of their income made the payment of rent — no matter how modest — impossible.

Thus it was in the slums, the drain for the joint privations of country and city, that the urban crisis inevitably crystallized. There, deprivation is king; it appears in many forms, most of them unknown in the [modern] city nearby. There is no common measure between these piles of shacks and even the most disinherited Muslim quarter. Brick, tile, and cement give way to sheet metal and old boards, to reeds and dry mud. Streets cannot be built without demolishing many homes; an undergrowth of shacks permits only winding paths. Gutters take the place of sewers, and garbage is carried out on the backs of donkeys. Urban services do not come into the slums except as a few public spigots to fill individual receptacles; the slum is saved from total darkness only by the dim glow of the lights from the neighboring town. Schools, hospitals, dispensaries, stadiums — everything the urban complex offers to its inhabitants is far away, serving others. Retail trade is carried out by a few shopkeepers from their shacks, where all their stocks are kept. News from the city is brought by the few men and women who have the good fortune to work there, or who go there to buy.

Only the sources of income of the slum tie it in some slight way to the city, but by placing it in a situation of dependence without allowing it to participate in the essential activities of the city. In Nador-Scala, for example, a relatively old (1955) Algiers slum of 4,000 people at the foot of the new city of Diar-el-Mahsoul, half the active population were underemployed, working mainly as market workers, maids, and day-laborers. Among the several hundred men with a more or less stable job, several tens of qualified workers and dockhands had a choice place compared to the more numerous laborers in building-trades and commerce. Humble as they were, these jobs allowed daily contact with the realities of another world that, from the slums, seemed a mirage.

Economic dependence, but also social dependence. The city, which tolerates the slum without accepting it, pays not only its salary but also its services, when the interested parties make the proper requests. Many families could not live without some welfare, pension, or retirement payments. New city-dwellers become welfare cases, cause the creation of social agencies that tend them, and as a result feel their inadapted condition all the more. Living in the city and by the city, they remain as foreign as the inhabitants of the *bled*.

RURAL ARRIVALS AT URBAN DOORS

Even more than the difficulties of settlement and subsistence, a meager place in the urban social system makes the immigrant a stranger, even if he has been in the city for several years. He is a marginal man. He does not participate in the enlarged groups of the new city, he does not assume the numerous and diversified social roles that characterize the urbanites: citizens, administered population, or members of voluntary associations. It is from this triple point of view that we will examine his marginal situation.

In order to appreciate the degree of participation of slum inhabitants in communal public life, we must first understand the administration of local communities in Algeria. Until 1956,[7] the Algerian communal organization comprised two types:

1. Fully autonomous communes, so called because they were governed by the law of April 5, 1885, which applied to French communes. They were administered by a mayor and a city council elected by a double college: three-fifths of the councilors by the first college, almost entirely European, and two-fifths of the councilors by the second college, representing the Muslim population.

2. Mixed communes, whose vast territory was often larger than a French department, were governed by civil administrators (civil servants) assisted by elected representatives.

Algiers, a fully autonomous commune, was governed, after the municipal elections of 1953, as a "Chevalier municipality"[8] where a loyal and effective collaboration took place between European and Muslim councilors. Conditions were therefore apparently favorable enough to permit new city-dwellers to participate in the management of local matters. In fact, no such thing occurred. For example, few of the men in Nador-Scala exercised the right to vote. "I don't get involved in politics," was the reason generally given for abstention. For the new urbanites, most of whom came from mixed communes, the management of "public affairs" was always seen as the job of the administration. Governing the big city did not concern them. Their behavior was completely different with respect to the elections of the *jema'* (council) of the *duar* (village); despite the distance and the time involved, everyone followed the public life of the *duar* attentively, gave his advice and encouragement by letter (often written by a scribe), offered his bit to a "party," even went into debt to be able to return home to participate personally in political affairs.

Politically, the new urbanite remained a countryman attentive to village affairs, indifferent to the management of urban matters which interested — he thought — only others: people with houses and jobs, who lived outside the shanty-town and whom one met "downtown," where there were streets, shop windows, and lights. Withdrawn within his limited group, the urban immigrant is now aware of belonging to a larger group that comprises all the newcomers who live on the fringes of urban society. Thus, protest behavior, which could give rise to political action on the communal level, does not.[9]

Yet it must not be thought that the immigrant is politically passive. His civic sense in his original society is alive. But there he is acting within a social group that is his own and is well structured, if poorly organized; urban political life, on the other hand, is expressed through diverse organizations built on the social structures of the city and therefore foreign to the new urbanites.

Not exercising his civic rights[10] and not considering himself a member of urban society, the shanty-town dweller cannot even be considered a consumer of the public services of the urban collectivity. There is a relation between the two facts. It has been seen that one of the characteristics of the shanty-town is their absence of collective equipment: no streets, no sewers, little electricity, and so on. One might think that public services (administrative, social, educational) would be wide open to immigrants who should benefit as much, if not more, than others from the support of urban institutions. Such is not the case. If the rights of all are theoretically equal, in fact the ways of enjoying these rights make them inoperative for many.

One must first be aware of the possibilities and, to do so, have a notion of the possible. How can a sick man with a cough know that he can have a free X-ray in a dispensary if he does not know of the existence of X-rays and their relation to his cough? Many similar examples could be given.

After awareness come other obstacles: to knock at the door presupposes knowing on which door to knock, and thus an understanding (difficult to acquire) of the intricate ways of urban administration. Such ways are mysterious to any rural inhabitant, especially when he is illiterate and does not speak the language of the administration. Words float around for a long time before they fall into place: "social worker," "welfare," "social service," "social center," and so on.[11]

Once the path has been found, the adventure has only begun. Face to face with the representatives of the bureaucratic, paper-bound society, the former shepherd Kabyle mountaineer undergoes a ritual whose meaning escapes him — identity card, family book, residence certificate, birth certificate. The man who comes from a society where ritual formulas govern the subtle code of social relationships discovers a secular world where the spoken gives way to the written word. How can he find his way? The administrative formulas are usually totally foreign to the problems of the shanty-town dweller. How is he to prove that he has lived in the town for at least six months so that he can benefit from welfare assistance? If he lives in a shack he has no rent receipt and no gas or electricity statement. To get one, he has to turn to other municipal services, and so on. In sum, the obstacles are piled so high that even when he is informed, the new urbanite is scarcely able to profit from the benefits society offers him in principle. He is no better integrated into the city administratively than he is politically.

Given this fact, it is all the more striking to note that in Algeria there are few native associations comparable to the secondary groups in Black Africa, veritable havens for the detribalized population in the native quarters of colonial cities.[12] There is nothing like the many legal or clandestine sports or recreation societies, friendship associations, and cultural clubs, found in the large cities of Black Africa.

Certainly the use of associations is explained by the "uprootedness and availability" that is characteristic of immigrants. But if the shanty-town dweller is indeed uprooted, his availability is low. L. Wirth has said that "it is largely through voluntary groups, with their economic educational, religious, recreative, and cultural objectives, that the city-dweller expresses and develops his personality." But such a situation implies, as a precondition, the substitution of secondary for primary relationships and thus a marked weakening of domestic structures and their adaption to or integration into urban life. In the shanty-towns of Algeria, such conditions are not present. The original family group transplanted into an urban milieu is highly defensive, and its members seek *partial* integration into the city but refuse the clutches of an urban society born of European intervention.

Voluntary groups of all kinds are not lacking in the large Algerian cities, but the new urbanites have no place in them. Even the nationalist political parties, products of a more or less "Western" organization, do little recruiting among the new arrivals, whose social models do not agree with the foreign-organized superstructures. Labor leaders are also rare in the shanty-towns; they are found instead among men who are well integrated in the urban economy, such as dockers, and who enjoy an exceptional social professional status in a society where unemployment, underemployment, and "odd jobs" are common.

RURAL STRUCTURES IN AN URBAN SETTING

Located on the outskirts of town, the shanty-town is not just an economic framework peopled by chance. It is a social group, structured if not organized, whose members are not outcast, banned, or ostracized city dwellers but people who came from somewhere else. Side by side with the Western city, the shanty-town bears witness to a different society, integral in its own right: rural Algeria. Here, where partial manifestations of so-called patriarchal and pre-Islamic societies persist, the essential base is the often extensive domestic group. Although its political function has been lessened by the "municipalization" of the tribe, the domestic group still remains pre-eminent, to the point of absorbing other types of groups. The persistence of social models alone is not sufficient to explain the reconstitution of this type of structure in the shanty-town. For this reconstruction to be possible, it must be favored by the conditions of immigration.

Each well-defined region of emigration generally has its corresponding settlement or settlements in the large Algerian cities. A tribe or a fraction of a tribe can constitute a source of intense emigration, while nearby groups may be losing none of their members to the cities. Just as each Kabyle village that sends immigrants to France has its "own" section or street in Paris, so each tribe has one or two shanty-towns in the big city. Thus, for example, the Oulad Amara, a tribe of the Saharan Atlas, had 650 members in the shanty-town of Nador-Scala, compared with 2,900 people who remained at home.

Although he is uncertain of finding work in the city, the emigrant usually knows, when he leaves home, where he is going and with which relative he will live. The inhabitants of the *duar*, members of the faction or of the family that have lived longest in the shanty-town (some from as early as the 1930's) greet, guide, house, and orient the new emigrant. The extended family ties, characteristic of agnatic groups, in principle assure room and board to every arrival, at least for the first weeks. Are they not paternal cousins or descendents of the eponymic ancestor? For them, the home is enlarged or divided, or, if that is not possible, a place is found somewhere in the thick conglomeration of shacks. The real adventure of emigration only begins after the welcome. . . .

These patterns of emigration are common to all the inhabitants of the shanty-town, without geographic variation. They would not lead to the structuring of the shanty-town, however, if the domestic group was not maintained through the exodus. Geographic indications show family emigration. One indicator is the balance between sexes: 100 men to 100 women at Nador-Scala. This equality is all the more remarkable when it is compared with the imbalance of the sexes in most of the Black African cities' immigrant quarters. Bachelors — men or women — are rare, despite a stereotype that claims that they make up most of the migrants. The couples in the shanty-town were married before their departure, and when they left home most of them had one, two, or even three children. This family emigration produces an age pyramid that is broad at the base and balanced on both sides.

Further analysis, based on interviews with heads of families, shows that the phenomenon is not limited to couples and their children. Often it is the whole domestic group — a full segment of the extended family — that emigrates. Thus, in addition to the case of the son or the married brother who brings his wife and children to join the father and the grandfather who left before them, there are frequent cases of group departures. Two to four married families — a father and his two sons, or four brothers — emigrate as they have always lived: together.

Thus, a continuous current carries more or less large segments of the original groups toward the city, increasing during the bad years of drought and want, slightly decreasing during the few good years. It takes only a few years for several dozen domestic groups belonging to the same tribe and often comprising several hundred members to come together again in the same shanty-town. For example, nearly half of the inhabitants of Nador-Scala come from six tribes:

	Nador-Scala	Tribe
Oulad Amara (Saharan Atlas)	644	2,900
Oulad Ameur (Saharan Atlas)	423	7,018
Ouennougha (Tell Atlas)	393	13,992
Oumelakhoua (Saharan Atlas)	176	14,371
Bitham (Hodna)	156	3,085
Beni Maoush (Lesser Kabylia)	130	7,041

The spacing of the arrivals, the diversity of geographic origins, and the rapid diminution of free space constitute obstacles to the regrouping of members of the same tribe in the shanty-town. The difficulty is increased by the urban authorities, who forbid the construction of new shacks. So severe are these constraints that luck alone seems to determine settlement, and the old tribal solidarity loses its morphological base.

Yet, at the end of a long road that has tested the patience and ingenuity of the whole group, the impossible reunion takes place with striking precision. Obviously the spatial differentiation is not airtight. It is found at the level of tribal groups that are traditionally linked either by a mythical ancestor – like the numerous tribes founded by Sidi Nail and his sons – or by political and economic alliances – like the Ouennougha confederation formed by three tribes in the last century. Thus, the population of Nador-Scala is divided into three distinct areas; the first two contain the tribal groups mentioned above, and the third includes members of the tribes of the Guergour mountains in Lesser Kabylia. Spacial delimitation is just as rigorous inside each of these areas, with each tribe occupying a specific location. Lesser separations become more permeable; only the best-represented tribal factions preserve a relative isolation.

This regrouping of original tribal members within the shanty-town is not the same thing as a simple home-town group based on ethnic affinities or regional links and traditions. A deeper sociological analysis shows that its form is derived from the structures of the original tribe. To understand these urban structures, it is worthwhile to recall the rural ones briefly.

The tribe is a federation of large domestic groups. On the pattern of these groups, a tribal organization is based on kinship. All the members of the tribe call themselves "maternal cousins," even though this group does not have the family character of the domestic group. The alliances from which it results are both hidden and sanctioned by the myth of a common ancestor cement the organic union of the different constituent groups. If its model and its justification are found in filiation, the tribe, a pluralistic society, by this very fact experiences internal tensions that continually threaten its existence. The subordination of domestic groups is not easily achieved. For the power of kinship tribes is such that it strongly limits the adherence of the members of domestic groups to a larger group founded on the same principle. It is in its struggle against foreign forces – neighboring tribes – that the tribe overcomes its internal contradictions and reinforces and maintains its cohesion. This situation explains the character of the *jema'* of the tribe, an assembly of elders whose functions concern, above all, "external affairs" (in the words of E. Doutte), that is to say, relations with other tribes, alliances, and the conditions of group survival: grazing, transit, and watering rights, and so on.

Since they represent only a part of the tribe and since the total society of which the shanty-town is a part is radically different from the traditional society that nurtured it, emigrant groups are not restructured entirely on the model just described. Starting with this model, they create a type of structure that, although marked by its origins, already has its own originality and authenticity.

The different large domestic groups that federate to make a tribe do not participate in equal measure in the movement of emigration. At Nador-Scala, only two of the five fractions that make up the Oulad Amara – Oulad Lakhdar and Oulad Ali ben Amara – were strongly represented. Similarly, the domestic groups that belong to these two factions did not always emigrate in the same proportions, and few among them were totally transplanted into the shanty-town. In such conditions it is highly improbable that the *jema'* of the tribe be reconstituted in the shanty-town.

Faced with new forces whose different origins made them all the more formidable, the tribal regrouping — unlike the original tribe — is not able to surmount its internal contradictions, and therefore its cohesion weakens. The hierarchal domestic group, structured with such difficulty within the original group, is brought into question and overthrown. Economic equality is the rule in the shanty-town: here the proud "son of the big tent," owner of many flocks, does not rub elbows with the humble shepherd or the inferior farmer. Here are only poor people, all without possessions, all seeking work and food.

Roles and social status also change hands. The learned old man is still respected; the title "sheikh" translates the veneration and affection bestowed on this matter of knowledge and model of religiousness. Consideration mixed with envy is still accorded to the man who formerly owned several hundred head of cattle, but his advice is no longer asked and, worse yet, he might not even be listened to when he gives his opinion. The most affluent head of the family, whose company is most welcome and whose urban language and different clothing is awkwardly imitated, is the oldest inhabitant of the shanty-town.

Over a period of twenty years, he has succeeded in creating the most spacious and most solid quarters. Perhaps his work does not indicate a rapid rise in the professional hierarchy of the city, but it is stable and lucrative. He has social security, family subsidies, and the right to paid vacations, all of which increase his prestige. He speaks French correctly, and if he himself has hardly had access to Western culture, he intends his children to have at least a primary, if not a junior high school, education. He allows them to buy magazines and regularly gives them money for the movies. In learning how to move through the new world of the urban metropolis without too many incidents, he has also learned how to get something from it. If his attempts to get a European-type house have been unsuccessful, he at least knows on which door to knock and what forms to fill out. In appearance, the respect owed to elders has not varied. However, subtle compromises and interceptable changes in consideration have focused on a new type of "elder," the man relatively well adapted to urban life.

At the end of the process of destructuring and restructuring, it is the domestic group, to a large extent liberated from the counterbalancing effects of the tribe, that appears the most structured and the most capable of aiding its members to bear or attenuate the tensions of city life. Furthermore, the weakening of the myth of the common ancestor, to the point of its being outmoded, strengthens immediate family ties within the domestic groups. The strength of ties of real filiation is maintained despite variations of type and dimension.

By that very fact, the eminent position of the father or the older brother of the group is consolidated. From the double hierarchy that coexists in the tribe — hierarchy of families and hierarchy of brothers within the family — only the later remains, reinforced by the corollary hierarchy of wives. From the very beginning, first the men and then the women initiate the child in the rules of etiquette that govern relations among members of the family. Whatever his age, every member of the group will take into account the fact that behavior his peers consider normal may appear to his elders to show a lack of respect. There is a long list of prohibitions that cannot be transgressed without shame or dishonor. Even when he becomes the head of his own family, even when he is old, a son will not smoke, discuss subjects that could be considered dirty, or make jokes before his father. He will try not to be in the café or in the public bath at the same time as his father, and if he finds him there, he will leave discretely. The same careful formalism, the same reserve, governs relations between elder and younger brother, between the wife of the oldest brother and the wife of the youngest or the younger sisters.

The autonomy of the individual is limited by the strictness and inflexibility of collective control and also by the type of community life of the domestic group. In the shanty-town, the "big house" of the family is the vigorous morphological expression of this community life. Made up of independent rooms opening onto a single courtyard and enclosed by a wall, it attests to the permanence of a cultural model that is foreign to the modern city but common to the rural Maghrib. Each has his place in conformity with the rules of precedence governing domestic relations. There are no common facilities, each married family has its functional autonomy. The wife prepares her family's meals and takes care of its needs. The location of the rooms, the direction of the doors, the installation of interior separations, all assure the married family a minimum of privacy and above all permit the respect of a collective *savoir-vivre*. In the big house there is no family communism but rather, as noted, community of living. The courtyard is the permanent meeting place; the youngest children play there under the watchful eye of one of the wives of the household, solidarity appears spontaneously, mutual help ties daily life together, and collective meals and celebrations take place on holidays.

The multifunctional character of the community of life of the domestic family is widespread. In addition to its own family functions, it performs many other functions ordinarily carried out by urban organizations. The group acts as a sort of social-security system that, if rudimentary, is highly diversified and covers the risks of unemployment, sickness, and old age. Shopping is generally combined, especially for food. Purchases made by the head of the group are divided among the different families, so that each one is assured of subsistence, whatever his resources at the moment. Mutual aid is shown even more strongly within the family by gifts and loans of money from more successful to poorer brothers. The same is true of the good name of the entire family.

When the head of the family considers that it is time to retire or when illness or weakness limit his activities, he is cared for by his sons and his brothers according to the code of honor. Like an employment service that "pushes" its clients, the lucky job-holder will try to help his relatives, either by finding them jobs with his employer or by taking them on as assistants paid from his own pocket. This explains the large number of relatives or members of the same *duwar* who work in the same shop or factory. For example, nearly all the men of Nador-Scala from Bitham work in the abattoirs. The Oulad Amara are for the most part stevedores in the markets.

This mutual aid, so abundant within the family and more diffuse within larger groups, is effective. The ties of tribal solidarity have outlasted the upheavals of emigration, and even though the men of the shanty-town forget (or never knew) the geneological fiction that united their fathers, they know that an appeal to mutual aid is never in vain. Furthermore, although the tribal structures are weakened they still persist. Tribal intermarriage, for example, is faithfully respected; whether it is their first or second marriage, the men of the shanty-town marry women of the same origin as their own.

But relations between the shanty-town and the home country are not limited to temporary visits for the purpose of marrying or remarrying. A continuing relation is established between the two milieus. There are always reasons for a visit: the harvest, the search for physical healing or spiritual comfort at the sanctuary of the local saint who can cure body and soul, pilgrimages and votive festivals, or simple family visits. On these occasions, there is a wide exchange of news: The smallest doings and happenings of city and country are reported from one relative to another. Despite the distance, the original society continues to govern the life of the exiles to a large extent. In this way the vigorous social control exercised by the shanty-town is reinforced; the infrequency of juvenile delinquency and of prostitution is a striking example, among others. A symbol of this cohesion is the modest mosque of Nador-Scala, built with local contributions. The community of belief solidifies the community of life.

The protection that the group brings to its members extends to all domains. The harsh conditions of urban life and the precarious resources offered by the city are felt equally by all, to be sure, but group-belonging in a strongly structured society gives them a different color. Supported by the network of collective mutual aid, the individual does not feel the insecurity born of solitude. He is not the miserable immigrant or the pitiful vagabond that we think. His fears, his disappointments, and his failures are softened and even absorbed by the community. No matter how far he travels in his search for work, he never escapes his family group. Although the city-dweller sees this man as an isolated wanderer, in fact he carries his ties with him. Wherever he goes, whatever he does, he remains somebody's son, brother, or cousin, and his place in the hierarchy of the social group dictates his daily conduct.

Because he is taken in hand by a multifunctional group, the availability of the man of the shanty-town for participation in other groups is considerably limited, which explains in part his lack of participation in urban life. The tensions created by his passage from a traditional to an urban milieu are reduced, and the disadvantages of his marginal situation are largely compensated for. It is through the partial reconstruction of his former milieu that his adaptation to the city is effected, but his integration into urban society now depends on the latter's response.

NADOR-SCALA: A CASE STUDY

It has been seen that the social structures of the shanty-town are incompatible with those of the city, and any attempt to organize the one along the lines of the other appears doomed to failure. The case of Nador-Scala may serve as an example.

Toward the end of 1953, several of the older inhabitants of Nador-Scala took the initiative of forming an association, the Committee for the Defense of the Interests of the Quarter, similar to those already organized in Algiers. The Committee had the proper papers and was registered. A systematic recruiting campaign was begun. About one-third of the heads of the families — some two hundred – joined and paid the small dues necessary to cover operating costs. They met in a shop and elected an administrative council, composed of a president, two vice presidents, secretary, treasurer, their deputies, and eleven assessors. Membership cards were printed, filled out, and stamped.

Even before the recruiting campaign had begun, the founders of the committee had drawn up a program for the improvement of the shanty-town. The program was adopted in a public meeting and sent to the mayor, accompanied by a request for the desired improvements, essentially in the infrastructure: paved roads, public lighting, sewers, running water. More ambitious but no less justified was the request for the construction of a dispensary near the shanty-town and the creation of a park or children's playground. In making these requests, the committee stayed strictly within the limits of the legal powers conferred by its statute and by administrative custom: to note needs and shortcomings so that they could be met in the interest of the collectivity. These requests included no systematic criticism or unwarranted demand. The official response was that the execution of the work requested depended on the closing of the complex of Diar-el-Mahsoul, a large construction project nearby.

Thereafter, the enthusiasm that had been raised by the expectations fell abruptly. Attendance dropped off at the meetings, whose usefulness was no longer evident; worse yet, the inhabitants began systematically to deprecate the founders of the committee. The accusations – often innocent but sometimes also malicious – were too complex to report here, but they included lack of seriousness and industriousness, absence of a fighting spirit, ostentatiousness, and, most serious, embezzlement. Soon nothing was left of the association but a list of names and several packs of membership cards. One might wonder what the future of the committee would have been had the dialogue with the city authorities continued. What is significant is that, after the first attempt, no new demands were presented. The leaders' lack of cohesion, exacerbated by poor participation of the members, killed the association.

In addition to the local factors, there were other reasons for the failure of the association, some of them peculiar to the shanty-town and others growing out of its relation to the urban society. In the shanty-town, the domestic group was the most structured. Based on reinforced multifunctional kinship, its predominance is "absorbing," in the word of Gurvitch. This community is based on passive social forms and is not favorable to organization. Moreover, the rigidity of the shanty-town's social hierarchy left individuals "unavailable," and the spectrum of social roles that they could play was limited. They did not have the latitude to participate in associations.

On the other hand, the structures of the shanty-town and the city were also incompatible. In no way could the shanty-town be considered a "quarter" of the city; it merely existed "alongside" the town. The committee of the quarter was of urban origin and represented a foreign type of organization. The maintenance of its cohesion, its continuity, and the success of its action obliged its members to play characteristic urban roles. Only the founders were able to do so. The most active of them, the man who played a major role in creating the committee, had been in the city longest; because he was relatively young, literate in French as well as in Arabic, acquainted with the city, and well aware of the workings of its institutions, it would seem that with the help and participation of all he could have brought some of the requests to fruition. Few of the members really had the freedom or the capacity to take on the new, multiple roles inherent in such an enterprise. Since the first efforts were not successful, the antagonism between city and slum — the former represented by the group of founders — rapidly increased, causing widespread bitterness.

INDEPENDENCE AND SOCIAL STRUCTURES

The accession of Algeria to independence provides an opportunity to take stock of the situation inherited from colonial times.[13] Too often, thinking about the new situation is conditioned by the dichotomous approach (colonial power — colonized people) dating from the former era. In fact, "the forces now unleashed are only — despite all appearances — the antithesis of the preceding phase."[14] True, decolonization can be influenced by relations — or the lack of them — with the former metropole. The transfer of political power, however, means a radical rearrangement of the whole social structure rather than an "institutional" break; there is a challenge to the social hierarchy, for the change in political sovereignty also leads to a change in social sovereignty. There should, therefore, be a re-examination of social relations prior to the setting up of any new political or administrative superstructure.

It is essential that a policy of city planning be established to incorporate the submerged mass of shanty-town dwellers into the community. This can be done either individually or collectively. In the first case, the pressure of public authorities, party, unions, and youth organizations may bring about a speedier adaptation of the individual; but at the risk of destroying mechanisms that safeguard his mental stability before others are available, and of doing away with an elementary system of social security before the public authorities are ready to step in. In the second case, the structure of existing groups is respected in the process of integration: *the new set-up must not only take account of social structures but must actually derive from them, so that "basic" links unite the organization at the deepest levels of social life.* Juridical forms — too often an exclusive preoccupation — are not enough; what is important is to ensure that "the graft takes."

The desire to harmonize structures and organized superstructures arises from sociological necessity; it does not imply any value judgments or reformist intentions. Collective integration may be slower, but the strength and dynamism of social mechanisms are best judged by their adherence to and ability to promote the development of underlying structures. It may also be supposed that a developing society stands to gain from the limitation of those tensions that it generates.

Decisions taken at the critical time may well decide the fate of Algeria's cities. Looking beyond the present bloody crisis into a doubtful future, the sociologist speculates without taking sides. He may at least hope that his remarks will not have been made in vain.

Notes

1. See Jacques Selosse, "Contribution to the Study of Moroccan Attitudes," pp. 65—73 in this reader: also Jacques Berque, *North Africa Between The Wars* (New York: Praeger Publishers, 1968).

2. See the statistical appendix in this reader.

3. *Report on the World Social Situation* (New York: United Nations, 1957), pp. 124—25.

4. *Tableaux de l'économie algérienne* (Algiers: General Statistical Service, 1960), p. 73; and *Rapport sur l'activité' de l' administration en Algérie au cours de l'Année 1960* (Algiers: Delegation General in Algeria, 1961), p. 202.

5. See R. and C. Descloitres and J. C. Reverdy, *L'Algérie des Bidonvilles — le Tiers Monde dan la cité* (Paris: Mouton, 1961).

6. *Etude internationale des programmes d'action sociale* (New York: United Nations, 1959), p. 207.

7. Decree of June 28, 1956, abolishing mixed communes.

8. The mayor, Jacques Chevalier, was a member of the Mendès-France government in 1954 and a "liberal," that is, in the political vocabulary of the time, a pro-Muslim, hostile to a policy of "pacification." The Muslim Councilors were nationalists (MTLD-UDMA) and many later held important positions in the FLN.

9. Which were limited by the two-college system and also by electoral fraud and pressure.

10. See Frantz Fanon, "The North African Syndrome," pp. 74—82 in this reader.

11. See *Aspects sociaux de l'industrialisation et de l'urbanisation en Afrique au sud de Sahara* (New York: UNESCO, 1956), pp. 393—542.

12. See Marvin Mikesell, "The Role of Tribal Markets in Morocco," pp. 415—23 in this reader.

13. A concerted government effort, aided by the European exodus that left much urban housing vacant, resulted in the formal "abolition" of shanty-town in June, 1964. This concluding summary is based on the English résumé that appeared with the original article.

14. See Jacques Berque, "Medinas, villeneuves et bidonvilles," *Les Cahiers de Tunisie,* No. 42 (1959), pp. 21—22.

37

THE LIBYAN OIL WORKER

FREDERIC C. THOMAS, JR.

The impact of the oil boom is most readily apparent in the cities of Tripoli and Benghazi. Here the oil companies have their offices and workshops and employ large staffs. New hotels are being built, and other businesses have grown as a result of petroleum activity. Purchasing power is concentrated here, and the sharp rise of prices, particularly in the case of goods and services consumed by foreigners and the wealthier Libyans, is most strongly felt. And here the mushrooming shanty-towns are bleak reminders that there are some social problems that the discovery of oil will not by itself solve.

By contrast, the rural economy, except for a few large farms run mainly by non-Libyans, appears to be relatively unaffected by the surge of business activity. To the casual observer, life outside the cities continues to follow the traditional pattern and provide a comforting element of stability. However, a closer look reveals that important and fundamental changes are taking place in the rural areas.

In the Fezzan some villages are all but deserted. Only the aged, the women, and the children remain. The manually operated wells have been abandoned, and sand has reclaimed the once productive gardens. In the Shati Valley the young palms are not watered even though an estimated 4 million gallons of artesian water are lost daily due to run-off and evaporation.

In the mountains behind Tripoli the movement, mainly of young people, away from agriculture has been encouraged by two years of drought. An elaborate system of terraces and irrigation canals has been neglected, and the men, some with their families, have gone either to Tripoli or to the district headquarters where they idly pass the time awaiting a grain distribution or possibly a job with an oil company.

Even in the more favored coastal belt, where standing water is found and intensive cultivation is possible, much good land is unworked. The boundary walls go unrepaired, and the goats and sheep cross over to graze at will.

In a country where less than 1 per cent of the total land area is suitable for settled cultivation and yet must support a majority of the population, such waste of the arable land and limited water resources is difficult to excuse. It

Reprinted, by permission, from *Middle East Journal,* X (1956), 264—76.

means increased dependence on imported foods. It means a permanent loss of skills that, however primitive, have sustained the people in their unyielding environment and should continue to do so until gradually improvements can be introduced and accepted. Also, the movement away from the land means inevitably the severing of community ties. The kinship bonds of the village and the tribe have been the basis of social security in the past and are the surest foundation for rural self-help and development in the future.

PETROLEUM FIELD OPERATIONS AND THE RURAL EXODUS

The exodus from the land is not a new phenomenon. It began during the Italian occupation when some of the best lands were confiscated and the farmer was left with the choice of becoming a landless farm worker, and unskilled urban laborer, or a shepherd on the barren edges of the desert. Libyans found employment on the Italian concessions and estates, with the army, and on the roads and other public works. During the war, thousands were employed in the mechanical repair shops, and with independence a whole range of new opportunities for wage employment opened up, mainly with the government as policemen, drivers, post-office workers, watchmen, messengers, and so forth. More recently, it has been the oil companies and the contractors working for them who have furnished the Libyan farmer with the alternative employment he is seeking. For most of the rural population, their first contact with the oil industry is when an exploration party moves into the district and hires some labor from the village. The farmer who has only a few animals may entrust them to his brother or near kinsman and go to work. But after a while he usually quits the job, or the party moves to another district and he is laid off. He returns to his village, but rarely does he go back to farming, especially if his land has not been worked during his absence. Instead of embarking on the major task of repairing the irrigation channels, rebuilding fences, and breaking up the soil, he waits for a while and then looks for another job. If another oil party comes into the area, he may be in luck; if not, he may consider going to Tripoli or Benghazi to obtain work.

This is the current pattern, and to this extent the oil companies have contributed to the movement away from the land. They offer opportunity to the farmer or shepherd who is dissatisfied or hard-pressed, or to his son or to the laborer who works for him, diverting them from agriculture and starting the process of estrangement from the environment that they have known. . . .

THE ATTRACTIONS OF OILFIELD WORK

From the point of view of the Libyan, working with an oil company or a contractor in the desert has a number of attractions. First and foremost, of course, are the wages. This is a subject in which there is unflagging interest, a topic for endless comparisons and discussion. The starting rate is 35 piasters for an eight-hour work day, and the unskilled laborer can soon advance to 42 or even 50 piasters, almost twice the amount that the farm laborer is paid for a ten- or eleven-hour day (100 piasters equal one Libyan pound, or approximately $2.90). Besides, the oil worker is given bedding and shares a tent with four or five of his fellow workers. Usually they are from the same village and work on the same shift.

The oil worker in the desert receives three meals a day. His minimum daily ration, prescribed by the Labor Department, is invariably exceeded. It includes cheese, butter, potatoes, canned fruit, and other comparative luxuries. More important, he is entitled to 250 grams of mutton every day and always receives more, whereas formerly he could rarely afford meat and then usually bought the cheaper varieties, such as dried beef and camel meat. In addition to this, each week he is issued a tin of tunafish or sardines, a large tin of evaporated milk, tea, sugar, and some boxes of biscuits. Most of the tea and sugar is consumed in his tent in the company of his fellow workers. The rest of his rations, however, are taken back to his village and often sold.

Of course, there is a tendency to exaggerate the importance of food to people who are accustomed to austerity. The ordinary Libyan laborer is not used to three "square" meals a day nor to the variety of foods and cooking that the European needs to stimulate his appetite. Food for him, on the other hand, is more than a means of filling the stomach and warding off hunger. The meal that is taken together with family or friends has ritual significance, and the food must be prepared according to custom. It is, therefore, not entirely fair to say, when noting the quantity of food, that the workers in a modern oil camp have never before eaten better than they do now. However, they appreciate the savings when meals are provided for them on the job. Casual workers, employed within a short distance of their homes, will live at the oil camp if they can enjoy the savings, if not the amenities, that this entails.

The accumulation of rest days that can be spent in their villages is another attraction of desert work. Under the Libyan labor code, every worker is entitled to a regular weekly rest day with pay. Since it is usual in desert operations to work a seven-day week, rest days are accumulated and taken at one time. The schedule of rest days depends for the most part on the nature of the operation and the availability of transport. A drilling rig operates continuously, and work is divided between shifts. If the shifts are rotated each week, three shifts work while one shift is on its day off, resulting in a generous schedule of rest days.

If the drilling site is located far from the village or oasis where labor has been hired, transport becomes the main factor in scheduling rest days, for the vehicles are needed to haul fresh water and other camp requirements. It is a matter of logistics in desert operations that vehicles be used for the dual purpose of transporting workers at the time of scheduled water runs. Likewise, the rest days of employees whose homes are in Tripoli and Benghazi must be arranged with reference to available airplane space, because, in addition to passengers, the aircraft carries fresh fruit, vegetables, meat, and other perishables, as well as emergency spare parts.

Consequently, the Libyan oil worker can look forward to an accumulation of rest days, at least a week's vacation for every five weeks on the job. Especially for the younger Libyans, whether married or not, this arrangement is ideal. It satisfies the somewhat conflicting desires to get out from under family authority and still return periodically to their families and the surroundings that are familiar to them.

THE SELECTION OF WORKERS

The provincial authorities have discouraged employers from transferring unskilled labor from one province to another or even from one district to another. Therefore, such labor is usually hired in the actual district in which operations are taking place. The object of this is to stimulate the local economy by spreading the benefits of oil-industry employment. Field hiring is also to the employers' advantage because of the impracticability of transporting large numbers of workers to and from the cities or returning them to distant villages outside the district or the province for their rest days.

When the seismic or drilling party moves to a new area, the party chief hires the casual labor he needs through the district commissioner *(mutasarif)* or sub-district head *(mudir)*. In the case of a drilling rig, from thirty to sixty workers may be needed, depending upon the size of the rig, and a seismic party often requires as many as eighty locally hired workers. At the other end of the scale, a waterwell rig may require eight or nine.

In theory at least, the local authority divides the total requirement among the sub-districts or the principal sheikhs of the tribes, as the case may be. If time allows, the sheikhs go out among their people and further subdivide their quotas among the main fractions *(biyut)* and important lineages (*'aylat*) of the tribes. This is the same procedure that in theory applies when the government calls for labor for work on the roads or other public works.

In practice, however, the system breaks down. There are never enough jobs to fill to necessitate the procedure operating in its classic form. Also, there are always a number of unemployed already congregated at the district head-quarters, and the *mudirs* and sheikhs need go no further to find deserving candidates for the job openings. (Nevertheless, an effort is made to distribute the opportunities among the various tribal groups, and the fact that everyone present knows each other's kinship affiliation guards against excessive partiality toward any single group.) When the call is for a few workers and it is impossible to divide the number, a few of the most needy or most persistent are chosen by the *mudir* for the jobs.

The *mudir* is also obliged to find work for his poorer relatives. Such nepotism is a function of kinship as much as it is an accepted prerogative of authority in customary Arab society. On the other hand, although the *mudir* is an appointed official, his tenure partly depends upon the backing of his people; so he must be fair in distributing jobs among the various opposing segments of the community. Later he can extend his influence by interceding in worker disputes that arise on the job. Sometimes he will even ask that a relative or local dignitary loyal to him be hired for the sole purpose of keeping discipline and arbitrating disputes in the oil camp.

Increasing numbers of job-seekers nowadays possess chits, papers, and letters of reference showing some previous work experience. Such documents are highly prized. Kept in the wallet, displayed to every passing European who may be a potential employer, they become so soiled and dog-eared as to be practically illegible. However, they give the possessor an edge over the less sophisticated applicants and further influence the selection process. The *mudir* will often assemble a greater number of candidates than is needed to fill the openings and leave the final choice to the employer. In this way final selection is largely based on previous experience (besides an intelligent appearance and physical fitness for the job), and the *mudir* does not offend any group.

The sedentary farmers and farm laborers are more likely to seek work than are the nomads. This may be due to the inherent conservatism of the nomad or a prejudice on his part against manual labor. Also, the *mudir* is in closer contact with (and more dependent upon) the sedentary people under his jurisdiction and may tend to favor them when selecting workers.

The nomad who only owns a few sheep and goats and perhaps a camel may go to work in the oil fields, entrusting his animals to his kinsmen. And the sheikhs will choose from nearby encampments those "who have no sheep" when notified that a company is hiring. However, for the nomad such employment is temporary. It is the means of earning money to buy more animals and does not indicate a desire to change his occupation permanently. Near the town of Sirte, for example, where the nomads congregate to receive relief grain, tribesmen will hire out with oil companies only until there is rain and the grazing improves, at which time they return to their encampments.

As regards the age of workers, the strenuous work in some oilfield operations, particularly drilling, favors younger men. But there are also camp kitchen positions which can be filled by older persons. Few workers are certain of their age, and some are hard put even to make a guess. The following, however, are the ages that were claimed by the Libyan personnel on one drilling rig:

Age:	18-19	20-24	25-29	30-34	35-39	40-44
Number:	7	12	20	8	6	2

Age:	45-49	50-54	55-59	60-64	65-69 (Total: 57)
Number:	1	0	0	0	1

There are a number of other factors that determine who will go to work in the oilfields. Some men will leave their families and go away to work only if a brother, that is, a real brother, remains behind to assume responsibility for the family's care. For this purpose an uncle will not do. Animals can be left with more distant kinsmen and in some areas with a professional shepherd (who is paid a flat monthly rate per head plus a small gift of food and tobacco). While the worker is away his land will either be used by his family, or a neighbor, or left idle. In return for the free use of the land, a neighbor will agree to water the young palm trees and fig trees, the produce of which belongs to the owner when he returns.

TURNOVER OF LABOR

Several factors, some already mentioned, contribute to the high labor turnover in desert operations. There is the government requirement that unskilled labor be hired in the district in which operations are taking place. This usually means terminating at least 50 per cent of the work force when the job is finished and operations are shifted elsewhere. Of course, the good worker may be promoted to a semiskilled or skilled position, in which case he can be transferred to work in another district. But then the problem arises of transporting him to his village for his days off. This may entail a round trip of several hundred miles over rough desert track.

Thus, in the more remote desert areas, it is practical that even semiskilled labor come from the nearest oasis where fresh water is obtained. Alternatively, the workers must be picked up at some point along the route of access to the work site or from coastal towns through which supply trucks pass going to and from Tripoli.

In short, the shifting nature of desert oil exploration and the formidable problems of logistics necessitate field hiring and a high labor turnover. This has an adverse effect on the continuity and efficiency of operations and requires the training of new men at each new location. The unsettling effect on the individual who has adjusted to the working conditions and wishes to continue is obvious. If he is skilled, his only alternative is to make Tripoli or Benghazi his base. Then he is provided air travel to the city. But that means separation from his family and his village.

The rate of turnover varies depending upon the type of operations. It is highest in the case of waterwell crews and survey parties that move camp every week or two and often over great distances. Rarely in such cases are unskilled workers employed for more than the four-week period within which they can be laid off without receiving vacation credit or termination indemnities. (Because of this, employers are sometimes accused of taking advantage of the provision in order to avoid paying these indemnities.)

Labor turnover in a seismic party is also very high because of location moves every few months. When the move is to another district, most of the field hired workers are laid off. Some good workers will be retained if they are willing to make their own transportation arrangements for returning to their villages. This is a stopgap measure that seldom works out. They soon resign, hoping to get another job closer to home.

CHANGING ATTITUDES REGARDING EMPLOYMENT

The Libyan is accustomed to this type of temporary employment. In agriculture seasonal unemployment is expected, for example between the time of sowing and harvest or the maturing of one crop and the next. Also, the practice of some form of shifting cultivation results in extended periods of semi-employment. Plowing is done in the fall, at the time of the first rains, after which there is little work for the men to do except for watering the livestock at the wells. The spring harvest only requires about two months of work before the long days of summer begin, to be spent largely in conversation, games, and semi-idleness.

Periods of relative inactivity are just as much a part of the life of the oasis cultivator. If he can, he employs an ex-slave or poor relative to do the harder tasks, such as working at the well and maintaining the irrigation channels, and in return will give him a third or half of the crop. Much of the harvesting of alfalfa, sorghum, and vegetables is done by the women. Only the collection of dates is a time of general activity.

Other work is also seasonal or temporary in nature. Libyans employed in the tuna industry work only two or three months in the summer and then must find another employment. The sponge fisher goes out only when the sea is calm. Many road-maintenance workers and dock workers are employed on a temporary basis.

For many Libyans, this insecurity is the life they know and have adjusted to in a land where drought can wipe out an entire crop and kill as much as 60 per cent of one's flock. The Arab plows in parts of Cyrenaica where the chances of a harvest are one in four, and in Tripolitania he sows barley within the walls of reservoirs despite the near certainty that the next flood will destroy the crop. This is not fatalism. It is adjustment to the harsh realities of the environment.

However, a new awareness of being unemployed or unprofitably employed is beginning to emerge. This is largely due to the attractive wages that are now being paid. In the past, paid labor was regarded as undignified, the rewards small, and was undertaken only when circumstances required it. Now the rewards are not only greater, but wage labor offers the Libyan freedom from the uncertainties of agriculture (for which he has little enthusiasm in any case) and even a certain amount of prestige. It enables him to marry earlier, to provide for his family and help his relatives, and to act generously toward his friends.

The spread of education and improvement in communications have also contributed significantly to this change. From schooling come new values, especially the importance of individual effort rather than reliance on the community and on faith, and also the responsibility of the individual for self-improvement. There is a general awakening to new ideas, and new symbols of success — radios, bicycles, and wristwatches — have come into fashion.

This new awareness has prompted many persons, who before would have taken for granted a perpetual state of semi-idleness, to look for work during the agricultural slack season. Boys from the mountain villages come to Tripoli to get jobs as house servants and gardeners. They plan to return home after a few months in order to work in the olive groves and cultivation, but many of them stay on. The poorer nomads get jobs with an oil company or a mine-clearing crew until the lambing season or until grazing improves. Oasis dwellers obtain temporary employment until the time of the date harvest, when they return home.

Some go to great lengths to get a job. They leave their families and travel long distance, wait patiently around the *mudiriya* or at some road junction where the oil convoys stop. Yet, they often quit a job at the slightest provocation — a small argument or fight, the "poor quality of the food" at the camp, or because they were not issued new work gloves or clean overalls. Or the worker simply does not bother to report back to work after his days off.

This apparent contradiction stems partly from a basic conflict of values. The job offers much that is attractive and desirable but it also presupposes acceptance of certain values that the worker finds new and strange. The job stresses the importance of time and punctuality, whereas the only schedule the cultivator or nomad knows is that which is prescribed by nature and the needs of his crops and his animals and which ultimately is the will of God. Also, the Puritan notion that hard work is intrinsically good is meaningless to the Arab, who considers manual labor as something that is undertaken only out of necessity. Equally foreign to him is the idea that the individual should strive to gain greater responsibility and rise above his fellow men. For him such competition is not a behavioral value. Everyone who conforms to the rules of society and religion and, above all else, is loyal to his kin will get his just rewards. Related to this, moreover, is the view that authority does not stem from those qualities which the job stresses — skill, experience, and achievement — but from lineage and wealth. It is not earned by hard work, but is either inherent or superimposed by force. He has never experienced the need for a work hierarchy and the discipline that is essential in an industrial undertaking.

These are the conflicts that confront the Libyan worker who is new on the job and require on his part major adjustments. Such adjustments take time. (Unfortunately, his immediate responses are apt to be interpreted by his boss as lack of ambition or appreciation, ignorance, and laziness.)

The fact of the matter also is that the job is still regarded by the ordinary Libyan worker as a temporary condition which provides little real security. The only positive security in the long run comes from his kinsmen: those who were perhaps instrumental in getting him the job in the first place, who take care of his animals and his trees when he goes off to work, are responsible for his family while he is away and who help him out when he has no work. He may face conflicts in his responsibilities to his employer and the demands which his job makes on him, but there is no question in his mind as to his obligations to his relatives. For example, tradition rules that he must support a relative without asking the cause in the case of a fight. He is similarly obligated to attend a wedding or a funeral, although it may mean great inconvenience.

THE TRAINING OF FIELD HIRED LABOR

Training is generally regarded as the obvious means of developing a skilled, job-oriented, and stable work force. Employers hope that training on the job will inculcate a sense of pride in work, a spirit of competition now lacking, and perhaps even a degree of company loyalty.

Irrespective of these long-term objectives, training becomes a practical necessity in desert operations. The employer cannot provide transportation for more than a few skilled employees and must rely, therefore, on field hired labor to do many jobs of a semi-skilled nature. He must make maximum use of those "casuals" who exhibit intelligence and a willingness to learn by training them to fill more responsible positions.

As an inducement promotion usually entails a very substantial increase in earnings. An unskilled laborer on a seismic crew may be promoted to an assistant driller within a year — a jump from 35 piasters to L£1,200 in his base salary. A messboy receiving 40 piasters a day may become an assistant cook at twice the salary in even less time if he shows ambition and an opening occurs. In this he has an advantage in being from the local village, for the workers usually prefer to have their meals prepared by one of their own people. When he is promoted he is classified as a skilled employee and can remain with the camp when it moves. As already mentioned, the principal difficulty which then arises is transporting the employee to and from his place of origin on his days off, which often results in losing the newly trained worker.

Training efforts are also frustrated by an apparent unwillingness on the part of some Libyans to learn a new job without receiving an increase in salary first. This characteristic continually baffles Americans and Europeans, who tend to place more emphasis on job responsibility and view a higher salary as concomitant or attribute of higher status rather than a prerequisite for improvement.

To take an example: When he is first employed in a drilling operation the casual laborer is put to work moving sacks of cement, digging ditches, cleaning up debris, and doing other menial tasks. Soon, however, a replacement is needed to work on the floor of the drilling rig and the casual laborer is given the job with an automatic increase in his day rate. His more experienced co-workers help him learn the routine of handling the heavy tools, and very soon he becomes a part of a coordinated team. Training in the routine responsibilities of the job is a relatively simple process, and the time gap between the pay increase and full qualification is comparatively short. However, the next step up the promotion ladder — to the job of derrickman — is a much bigger one. The job requires considerable skill and involves a number of independent responsibilities. Not only is the task of training correspondingly greater, but there is no certainty that the trainee will qualify for the job. But not appreciating the implications of his new assignment, the worker selected to try his hand at it reacts with an impatience that frustrates the training process. Once he has climbed up to his perch high in the derrick and has mastered the raw fundamentals of the new job, he demands a derrickman's full rate of pay. The only recourse that is then open to his boss, if he is to train a Libyan in the job, is to settle on some intermediate rate. This means bargaining (which Americans usually abhor) because the worker expects assurances as to the period of training. These cannot be given, since the time element depends largely on the individual's ability and progress.

The implication here is that in a highly technical operation, such as oilwell drilling, many Libyan workers do not yet ascribe any particular status to those positions that are within their reach. Unlike the truckdriver, whose "profession" is clearly defined and respected, the derrickman is doing a job that, in the complexity, dirt, and confusion of oilwell drilling, is, on the surface, indistinguishable from the jobs of other workers. The only factor making his job more desirable is the higher wage it carries. The job is then defined strictly in monetary terms rather than in reference to the skills it requires and responsibilities it entails.

PROSPECTS FOR THE FUTURE

The number of Libyans working in the oil industry will no doubt continue to increase during the next few years as exploration and development proceed simultaneously and new concession holders begin operations. Then it will level off and may decline somewhat. The World Bank mission has estimated that the industry will eventually provide direct employment to 20,000 workers at the very most, or about 5 per cent of Libya's total force.[1] It would seem that this figure is high. In Saudi Arabia, for example, only 12,000 nationals are employed in the oil industry. Of course, Libyans will find work in fertilizer and other industries which use petroleum as a raw material, but such industries are also comparatively small employers of labor.

We have seen, however, that the impact of oil employment in Libyan society cannot be measured simply in terms of the number of workers involved. Because of the nature of operations and the high rate of labor turnover, probably more than twice the number presently employed have at some time worked in petroleum exploration. This experience has had an unsettling effect on the individuals directly involved as well as on the rural communities from which they come.

The adjustments are striking: almost overnight oasis cultivators and desert herdsmen have become part of a complex industrial undertaking. Libyans have moved from the hoe and the adze of their subsistence economy to mastery of technical skills and familiarity with elaborate machinery. A quick intelligence and natural aptitude have equipped them to deal with the demands of the job and the novelties of oil camp life. A simple analysis of the problems involved tends to overlook the real drama of this change.

The adjustment, however is far from complete: acceptance of a new discipline and new values requires greater continuity of employment than the oil industry provides. Also, as we have seen, the Libyan worker reacts to the job in a traditional way. He is apt to approach it in an offhand manner and quit on impulse. When he leaves or is terminated, he returns to his village and, rather than go back to working the land, lives off his earnings and looks for another job.

In the village, cultivation is neglected. The people are idle and dependent on the remittances of others. When there is oil activity nearby, there are indications of prosperity: shops are put up and roads improved; there is traffic and commerce. The people have more money than before, and they say that times are better. But despite appearances, the community has lost much of its former productive capacity and has become, in some cases, little more than a hiring center and water-supply point for the oil companies operating in the vicinity. Uncertain that the boom will last, the villagers charge exorbitant prices for a sheep, a barrel of water, or a young palm which has been run over accidentally by an oil truck. A progressively hardening attitude toward outsiders conceals the innate dignity, humor, and sense of hospitality of the inhabitants.

What can be expected in the near future? With time and exposure to the new working conditions, the Libyan worker may value his job more highly and take greater pride in it. If this happens on a wide scale, jobs will fill up and there will be less turnover. It will become increasingly difficult for the cultivator, the shepherd, and the semi-employed to find the type of temporary employment they now seek.

While this reevaluation is taking place, changes in the nature of operations should also encourage the emergence of a more stable work force. The exploration phase will draw to a close, and operations will settle down within more restricted limits. Certain concessions will be written off as non-prospective, and attention will focus on those areas where oil has been discovered in commercial quantities. Emphasis will be on the drilling of development wells, the construction of gathering and field storage systems, the laying of pipelines, and the building of permanent installations. Labor for these works will be drawn from the vicinity, and there will be fewer terminations because of location changes.

Greater continuity of employment should facilitate training efforts and encourage specialization. Competition and the acceptance of industrial norms will become necessary for promotion. Salaries will probably be more closely related to skills and responsibilities than is now the case and, in general, job security will have a higher place in the scale of values of the workers.

When cultivators can no longer look to industry as a source of temporary employment, they should see it instead as an assured and growing market for the food which they can produce. Each drilling camp, for example, requires some 500 pounds of fresh vegetables, 200 pounds of fruit, and 800 pounds of meat, poultry, and fish a week, all of which now comes from Tripoli. In the future the local producer should supply some of this demand in addition to the growing demand in the oasis itself. Thus, it may be possible, with proper planning and incentives, for agriculture to benefit from developments that thus far have had a disruptive effect on the rural economy.

Note

1. International Bank for Reconstruction and Development, *The Economic Development of Libya* (Baltimore: Johns Hopkins Press, 1960), p. 62.

38

THE STATE OF NOMADISM
IN THE SAHARA

R. CAPOT-REY

In the Sahara, as in most hot deserts and their surrounding steppes, animal husbandry has so far been the main source of livelihood. True, cultivation is not unknown and certain palm groves are so thickly planted as to recall the richest agricultural lands; but such cultivation is necessarily restricted to limited areas, which the geographer Strabo compared to islets lost in the vast expanse of ocean. Outside these, man can survive only by the extensive exploitation of natural pastures, living as a parasite on his flocks and herds. Human existence necessarily becomes nomadic; in other words, men and animals must move from place to place, whether periodically or not.

NOMADISM AND THE SAHARAN ENVIRONMENT

Nomadism is the product of the climatic and botanical characteristics of the Sahara environment: sparse vegetation; interruption of plant growth by drought and, in one part of the Sahara, by winter cold; seasonal drying-up of springs, pools, and other natural watering places.

The basic factor then is the special nature of the desert vegetation: this extremely poor steppe has the lowest number of species in the world outside the polar regions, and its vegetation is very scattered, mainly comprising clumps of gramineous plants, succulents, and thorny bushes; as a rule, there are no plants of high nutritive value, whether crucifers or legumes, nor are there any trees apart from a few scattered acacias. In such an environment, if animals were kept for long periods in one place, they would simply ruin the pasture and die of hunger. Unless one can store fodder — and the very nature of the low, woody vegetation precludes this — or create artificial meadows (impossible without irrigation), there is no alternative to a continual change of pasture and hence continual moving about.

In their wild state, the herbivorous animals wander according to the condition of the grazing lands: the hordes of antelopes that normally keep to the thorny bush country on the edge of the Sudan appear in the heart of the desert as soon

Reprinted, by permission, from *The Problems of the Arid Zone* (Paris: UNESCO, 1962), pp. 301–10.

as a rainfall has brought out the *acheb*. Then, too, there is the need for water. In the cold season, the camels can go for more than a month without drinking, the sheep only drink every four or five days; in the hot season, the thirsty animals move toward the wells and pools. Finally, other shifts are due to the herbivorous animals' need to vary their diet and at certain times to consume salt, sodium chloride, or, if the worst comes to the worst, sodium carbonate (natron), whether in solid or liquid, mineral or vegetable form.

Migration, spontaneous in the case of wild animals, has become controlled with domestication, but the pattern remains the same, the one abiding rule being to follow the rain, to seek out fresh pastures. It is not uncommon in the regions on the edge of the desert for these migrations to have a seasonal character, as in the zone nearest to the Mediterranean it rains mostly during the cold season, and south of the Tropic [of Cancer] mostly in summer; in the center of the desert, rainfall has nothing to do with the season and camps are moved as storms occur and patches of green appear. This difference is well illustrated by the contrast between the regular migrations of the Arbaa of southern Algeria toward the Tell at the beginning of spring and the haphazard migrations of the Regueibat of northern Mauritania. Finally, at the limit of the southern Sahara, the spreading out of the herds and flocks when the pools are full coincides with the lure of the salt springs south of the Air, a fact that leads to an increase in the migrations of the Tuareg of the Niger and the Peuls Bororos who, for the rest of the year, are restricted by the abundance of the grazing to relatively limited areas.

Nomadism is not only a way of life, it is also a form of social organization based on ties of family and allegiance; for example, families gathered in clans, groups, or tribes who claim a common ancestor, recognize a sort of collective ownership of the pasture lands and even of the land and, in case of danger, accept the authority of a chief, even if they resume their freedom once the threat is past. Nomadism has always been linked, if not with insecurity (against which mobility and dispersion are not always an adequate protection) at least with the absence or impotence of the central power. Though the nomadic tribes have sometimes been regimented, incorporated into a state like the Sherifian Empire or had their lot linked to a Muslim brotherhood like that of the Senusi, the history of the Maghrib shows that nomadism only flourishes in a climate of liberty bordering on anarchy.

Within each ethnic group is a hierarchy of tribes and, within each tribe, a hierarchy of classes, both having a historical or ethnic basis. The highest rank is held by the descendants of the Arab invaders from Morocco or the Seguiet al-Hamra and often also to the descendants of venerated figures of the past. The hierarchy is very pronounced among the Moors, where it controls the distribution of professional activities, less clear-cut among the Arabs on account of the rival claims of the *Shorfa* and the Mrabtin, and, among the Tuareg, is reduced to the sovereignty of the Imochrar tribes over the Imrad tribes. It vanishes completely among the Toubou, where even the poorest clans refuse to pay tribute to the strongest. Even among the Toubou, however, we find the two lower classes that exist elsewhere — the former slaves *(egré,* corresponding to the Arab *'abid* and the Tuareg *iklan)* and the freedmen *(kamadja,* corresponding to the *haratin* or *bella).* Although they comprise distinct endogamous ethnic groups, these people live in a state of symbiosis with the nomads, as "hewers of wood and drawers of water." From this viewpoint, the organization of nomadic society seems to constitute an attempt to counteract by a division of labor the insecurity and the absence of public services.

Hence, while the natural conditions have remained the same, historical circumstances have caused the number of pastoralists to vary and have modified the ratio between the strength of the nomads and that of the fixed population. This ratio cannot be established in respect of the past but the present position is shown in the following table.

Territory	Total Population Within the Sahara	Nomads
Algerian Sahara	539,000	202,000
Morocco	500,000	100,000
Mauritania	600,000	150,000
Spanish Sahara	50,000	30,000
Mali	100,000	30,000
Niger	250,000	150,000
Chad	50,000	45,000
Tunisia	400,000	30,000
Libya	1,091,000	255,000
Egypt	150,000	23,000
Sudan	1,000,000	200,000

The figures in this table are very approximate and can only give a rough idea of the numbers involved. Nevertheless, they indicate that there are over 1 million individuals in the world's largest desert who live wholly or mainly from animal husbandry. In the north, these nomads are concentrated in Cyrenaica, in southern Algeria and southern Morocco; in the west, they are concentrated in Mauritania; in the south, on the edge of the Sahelian zone. It is estimated that there are three head of livestock per inhabitant in the north, while in the Sahara zone of Mauritania, the Sudan, Niger, and Chad, the official estimate is six, and the real figure is probably twice that. On the other hand, in the most typical regions of the Sahara, the rocky plateaus of the Ahaggar, the sandy *regs* of Ténéré, the *ergs* and *serirs* of Libya, there are either no herds or they only appear during brief periods, and it may be said that most of the Sahara nomads keep away from the desert as much as possible. This fact makes it all the more necessary to see how they live.

TRADITIONAL ECONOMY AND LIVING STANDARDS

In the traditional Sahara economy, the herd or flock is primarily a form of capital that automatically increases in a good year and, in a lengthy drought, is saved by its mobility. Additionally, it constitutes a means of subsistence by providing milk, butter, and cheese, together with various raw materials for home crafts, among them leather, wool, and hair. Meat is not a particularly important item in the list, since the nomad only kills his animals on special occasions, such as the arrival of a guest or the holding of a religious festival. Generally speaking, milk itself is not enough to feed a nomadic family; some of the Regueibat *friq* in the remote Iguidi or Maqteïr can live for months on milk and nothing else, but the diet of most of the Sahara nomads, unlike that of their Asian counterparts, is partly vegetable, and the barter or sale of livestock enables them to obtain the items they need. Hence, the nomads have long been accustomed to take their surplus animals to market, either at the oases — in spite of the fact that the oasis-dwellers have an extremely limited purchasing power — or outside the desert at sort of market fairs, like the Dra *moussem,* which are regularly attended by farmers and stockbreeders.

The Sahara pastoralists can be classified, according to the type of livestock they own, into shepherds, goatherds, camel-herds, and cowherds, though the first two categories also keep camels to carry their tents and themselves.

Sheep are mainly raised on the northern border. They can stand the hard winter conditions and put up with the thin grazing of the desert steppes. Far from harming them, the long treks keep them in good condition; but they need to drink every second day during the hot season, and hence they must have a choice of pasture lands within a radius of under twenty miles of a watering point (this being an average trek for a sheep in transhumance). It is for this reason that certain southern Algerian tribes go in *achaba* [pasture] in the high plains of the Tell, even as far as the settled area. This practice dates from the Middle Ages and only came to an end with the outbreak of the [war for independence]. Sheep were formerly raised essentially for their wool, but for the past fifty years the tent crafts that used wool have been on the wane and nowadays sheep-raising is directed toward meat production.

Goats, as hardy as the sheep, are more agile and can put up equally well with the rocks with their few scattered thorn bushes as with the plains dotted with acacias, whose pods they devour with relish. They do not give as much milk as sheep, and their meat is not as good, but their hides are put to a variety of uses in the camps.

As a rule, their needs exclude cattle from the desert zone: they are big eaters, drink deeply, and are poor travelers. As a result, they hardly move outside the Sahelian zone except to stock up with salt on the southern edge of the Sahara. Stockbreeding as practiced by the Tuareg of the Niger bears a closer resemblance to that practiced by the Peuls than to that of the Ahaggar Tuareg.

Camels have an advantage over other domestic animals in that they can go for a long time without drinking, even in the hot season. This makes it possible to disperse them over a wider area and make maximum use of the desert vegetation even when there are no nearby watering points. Every second year, the female camels provide between five and nine pints of milk per day. Camel meat, although commonly eaten in the oases, is always considered inferior to beef; but, on the other hand, the camel is superior as a mount and pack animal and, for a long time, for some tribes hiring out their camels was the only source of revenue.

Until the motor car appeared on the scene, camel caravans provided the sole means of travel and transport along tracks that, apart from occasional wells, were devoid of any sort of facilities. These caravans offered a double source of revenue to the nomads, from the hire of the animals and their owners and from the protection afforded to merchants by the tribes at fixed rates.

It is difficult to estimate the size of such income since the extent of the traffic varied greatly according to the epoch and the region. During the epoch of ibn Battouta, in the middle of the fourteenth century, the transport of gold and slaves offered a handsome return, but this had unquestionably fallen considerably four centuries later when the caravans brought nothing but leather and ostrich feathers from the Sudan. Even so, a caravan that reached Tindouf from Timbuktu in 1887 was still carrying more than 1 million francs worth of merchandise. During the nineteenth century, the European penetration of southern Algeria and, later, the Niger took place; at the same time, protection was given to the merchants by the Sennusi who settled in Kufra in 1890; as a result, trans-Saharan trade inclined toward Libya. Less than a century later, the great trans-Saharan caravans had ceased to exist. Nevertheless, regional trade continued, especially in the border areas. In 1903, the caravans of northern Oran set off in winter to pick up dates from Gourara. A single trip, lasting two months, provided each of those taking part with a profit that enabled him to pay his taxes and purchase a certain quantity of spices, in addition to supplying him with enough dates for the year. In the southern Sahara, the *azalay* (salt caravans) of Idjil, Taoudenni, or Bilma, involving thousands of animals at a time, produced an annual profit of more than 100 million francs, almost all of which went to the nomads.

As a general rule, the picking of wild produce and cultivation must be added to the two main sources of livelihood, animal husbandry and transport. Poor as the natural vegetation of the desert may be, it nonetheless provides the desert-dwellers with berries, seeds, and roots of various edible species. In the central Sahara, it is enough for the rain to cause the *taouit (Aizoou canariense)* to flower and bear, for the upper part of the Ahaggar to be invaded by whole families, both nomads and settlers, anxious to harvest the seeds. The same influx takes place in the *wadi* when the waters have swelled the ears of *drinn* and *mrokba*. Among the Toubou of the Borkou and the Ennedi, a small wild gramineous plant, the *kreb (Urochloa helopus)* is picked at the end of the rainy season, providing a sufficient attraction to draw off the floating population of the Ounianga palm groves. The *terfas* (a sort of truffle) and broom-rape are everywhere sought after by shepherds.

However, these are only the garnishings and, apart from milk, the nomad depends essentially on cultivation for the bulk of his diet. The word "cultivation" may sound incongruous as it appears so inconsistent with nomadism. Is there not a hadith, wrongly attributed to the Qoran, which denounces work with the "plow of ignominy?" The plow, in fact, is only a symbol, and the nomad's attitude to work on the land is more subtle. He detests, it is true, the idea of working a field each year, since this would mean forfeiting his freedom and paying rent to a proprietor or tribute to a ruler; but he is not averse to sowing a basin that has been flooded by a chance rainfall or even to building a small dam so as to divert the water to a part of the *wadi* it has not already reached. If another rainfall should occur at the right time, he will be able, with luck, to harvest 100 for 1. This gambler's farming is very widespread in the *daya* of southern Algeria, the *madher* of southern Morocco, and the *grara* of Mauritania; in Libya, where the tribes have much more space, cultivation is limited only by the quantity of seed and the number of plowing teams the nomad has.[1] On the other hand, such temporary fields are not found in the central Sahara, where rainfalls are irregular and violent, nor in the southern Sahara, where all the millet is brought from farther south by caravan.

Regular cultivation, that is, tying oneself down to the same piece of ground in order to wrest a yearly harvest from it, remains alien to the nomad, at least as far as the farming itself is concerned: this is left to colored sharecroppers, the *haratin,* who are only entitled to a proportion of the harvest — usually, one-fifth; the remainder goes to the owners, who either sell it or keep it for family consumption. It is relatively unusual for a peasant tenure to have succeeded in establishing itself, as at M'zab, Souf, and in southern Tunisia, free of all obligation to the nomads. In Mauritanian Adrar, northern Fezzan, at Kaouar and Borkou, the nomads more often than not own one-quarter or one-third of the palm groves — 39 per cent of the productive palms at el-Goléa (1956), 26 per cent at Ouargla (1945), 28 per cent at Borkou (1957) — and over half if the seminomads are included. Even if the nomads are not actually owners of the palm groves, they accord them protection by virtue of written agreements, some of which are centuries old. In these circumstances, the return to the oasis for the date harvest becomes a major event interrupting the pastoral migrations, a sort of annual fair that, for a few weeks, brings together men who are scattered throughout the rest of the year.

The nomads' profits from the palm groves vary from one district to another and are very inequitably distributed between the different classes of nomadic society: and this makes it difficult to make a general appraisal of the living standards of that society. However, two surveys, in the northern and southern Sahara respectively, carried out at a time when the traditional way of life had already been deeply affected, revealed in both cases that the nomads' living standards were higher than those of the sedentary population. At Laghouat, in 1955, a nomad family budget showed an income of 53–54 francs and 1,776–1,797 calories per person per day, against 28–46 francs and 1,349–1,770 calories for the sedentary folk. The average annual income of a nomad family was estimated at 115,323 francs against 106,754 francs for a farming family.[2] At Borkou, in 1955, the nomads had 500 grams of dates, 180 grams of millet, and 4 liters of milk per person per day, together with a sufficient sum of money to pay taxes, buy one or two articles of clothing, and drink a certain amount of tea. The settlers, on the other hand, had only 400 grams of dates, 400 grams of millet, very little milk, and 12 francs per day in cash.[3]

Although the hazards of the climate can hardly be disregarded in a country where the lean years are more common than the fat ones, it seems quite certain that, outside the central Sahara where the Tuareg and the Tedas have always lived on the hunger line, nomadism, at least until about 1925, satisfied the very modest wants of those who practiced it.

RECENT CHANGES AND THE NOMADIC CRISIS

The political and economic changes that have occurred in the Sahara over the last half century have upset the balance between the pastoral peoples and the desert environment.

Whether directly or indirectly, they are a consequence of the European penetration. The conquerors have either imposed a new order in which the social organization peculiar to nomadism has no place, or they have introduced methods of transport and trade that the native inhabitants would have adopted less speedily and in different forms if left to their own financial and technical resources. Except in the Spanish Sahara, the Europeans, despite their intention to preserve things as they were, despite their determination not to upset the established order, nevertheless occasioned a general disruption. In this sense, it can be said that the taking of Laghouat in 1852, of In Salah in 1900, and of Tindouf in 1934 were turning points in the history of Saharan nomadism.

Pacification immediately freed the pastoralists from their fear of the hostile neighboring tribes. Just as the town-dwellers destroy the city walls and move on to the plains as soon as danger is over, so the nomads spread out into regions that were hitherto forbidden to them. The Regueibat Lagouacem entered the Iguidi; the Ahaggar Tuareg, driven from the Tidikelt and the borders of the Arab world, found some compensation in the plains of the Niger. Elsewhere, the Ksourian people bought camels and temporarily abandoned their palm trees. On the whole, the first result seems clearly to have been that greater distances were traveled and the area of nomadism widened.

But this initial effect was not lasting. Animal husbandry soon lost ground as a result of the progress of cultivation on the edge of the desert, where the nomads were in the habit of seeking out pasture land to supplement their income. In Algeria, the tendency was especially early as a result of the colonization of the upper plains of Constantine and Sersou; subsequently, it appeared in Tunisia and Morocco, and, more recently, Niger, where the growing of millet and ground nuts is fast increasing in the Hausa country.[4] The nomadic area is being nibbled away at both ends.

Pacification deprived the nomads of all excuse for inflicting their expensive protection on the others; the "brotherhood tax" became a useless imposition now that the sedentary population and (indignity of indignities!) the nomads, too, paid state taxes. The dues that the warrior or aristocratic tribes levied on subject tribes have vanished or are in the process of vanishing. In Mauritania, the *horma* were bought up between the two world wars. In 1945, at Borkou, a simple administrative decision ended the feudal system: the nomads' rights over the palm groves already in existence were confirmed, but they lost all rights over new plantations: henceforward, anybody is free to turn vacant land into a garden and can cultivate and harvest without paying anything whatever. Even where the old system was maintained — for example, in the Ahaggar — the nomads' share of the harvest was reduced from four-fifths to one-half, and tribute shrank to the dimension of a mere gift. This was no more than a wound to the nomads' self-esteem, if you like, but such wounds often hurt the lords of the desert more than the loss of money; and, in any case, it represented an initial blow at their rank.

At the same time, the main source of revenue from transport suffered a disastrous decline. Motor vehicles appeared in the Sahara in 1925, and it was at once clear that caravan transport could not compete with trucks, at least on the great trans-Saharan routes. Such regional caravans as were maintained in the most difficult or most distant areas were reduced to transporting merchandise of limited value, such as ordinary dates and firewood. In the southern Sahara, only salt continues to provide employment for the camel traffic, which handles some 8,000–10,000 tons per year. In turn, however, this is threatened by the European salt imported via the Gulf of Guinea: a load of Amadror salt which could be exchanged for six loads of millet in 1946 was only worth two in 1955.

Along with the trucks appeared another and more dangerous rival, one that was virtually nonexistent in the old economy of the desert: the tradesman. Today the Moorish, Chaamba, Mozabite, and Fezzan tradesmen have reached out as far as Tropical Africa. With cash and letters of exchange they despise barter, sell on credit, make loans on harvests and, ultimately, hold all the desert peoples in their grasp. Whole groups, such as the Tuareg and the Toubou, have been ousted from commercial dealings in this way to the advantage of richer or more enterprising groups.

Motor transport in the Sahara has so far been limited by the cost of petrol and the bad state of the tracks. The working of the oil fields in the Algerian Sahara and Libya should make possible (and, indeed, has already made possible) more intense motor traffic, which will lead to the complete disappearance of the caravans in all those parts of the desert covered by trucks.

In addition to these political and economic factors there are the new social conditions. As we have already seen, the traditional society was founded on a hierarchy of classes. This was sapped at its base by the loss of the slaves and freedmen who supplied the herders. No move affected the Tuareg of the Niger so deeply as the liberation of the Negroes. "That is the supreme reason for our hatred," said a chief of the rebel Tuareg in 1916. Why, it might be asked, did the dispossessed owners not attempt to replace the slaves by paid herdsmen? Such a question would be to betray an ignorance of how hard it goes against the grain to pay someone hitherto always regarded as (to use the official euphemism) "a born servant." The question likewise leaves out of account that wages in cash have no place in the traditional pastoral economy: a nomad who does not sell his animals and hires them out less and less would be hard put to it to pay the wages of a herdsman.

Nomadic society simultaneously lost its governing class, its elite of honest stockbreeders or reformed plunderers. The administration recruits chieftains on a basis that leaves nomadism out of consideration: it pays them but it degrades them by making them officials with the job of rounding up statute-laborers, the sick and truant schoolchildren and, above all, collecting taxes. Left to their own devices by their bureaucratized chieftains, the bulk of the small stockbreeders tend to drift aimlessly. Since the feeling of solidarity has been weakened by security, everyone pitches his tent where he feels inclined: the most common type of settlement, the Regueibat *friq* or the Gorane *ferik,* comprises half-a-dozen tents. Within these minute camps mutual assistance still exists for the watching or watering of herds and flocks, but the nomads now leave such community jobs as the maintenance of wells to the authorities. Finally, nothing has been found to replace the "verbal newspaper" of the caravans that took the place of a weather report: in a world where contacts among people are ever increasing, the nomad paradoxically finds himself more and more isolated.

Thus, there was, at one and the same time, a loss of prestige, a reduction of employment, and a fall in income, the latter made all the more serious by the emergence of new needs (for instance, for tea and sugar) as a result of contact with the Europeans and increase in population. Although the birthrate among the nomads is lower than that of the sedentary folk, the increase in population following a long period of peace such as we have had was enough to make the nomads feel cramped on pasture lands, which, though extensive, are not expandable.

The reaction of the nomads to these various causes of decline has differed according to the benefit which they could reckon on from cultivation. On the edge of the steppes or at the foot of predesert mountains, the itinerant cultivation

already practiced has become general. Each household returns each year to work
the same site, if necessary cutting short the pastoral migration; land is no longer
redistributed at intervals: with the agreement of the *jema'* it can even be sold
— a development that indicates a move toward individual ownership. This
cultivation of flooded lowlands, however, is too uncertain to guarantee the
livelihood of a whole family and families therefore split in two, one section
staying to look after the flocks and living mainly on milk, the other pitching
camp at least six months out of the year near the fields under cultivation. Thus
we have the seminomadism of the tablelands of Algeria and southern Tunisia,
which nowadays is tending to spread everywhere in the northern Sahara, from
the Atlantic to the delta of the Nile. Throughout northern Libya, the nomads
have fields in the *oudianes* and palms and olive trees near the villages.

No further progress can be made so long as cultivation cannot fall back on
permanent irrigation. But modern techniques such as dams, wind-driven pumps,
and artesian wells offer the prospect of more extensive irrigation: the lack of
water is less and less of an obstacle to increased cultivation. The pastoralist can
henceforward settle at an oasis: no longer obliged to roam with his animals, he
counts among the sedentary people practicing transhumance of their flocks and
herds. This system is still not widely used in the central and southern Sahara,
where the cases are few in number and where diet is based on milk, but it is
spreading in regions where plantations can be established on a dry-farming basis
(Souf, Borkou) or on the edge of irrigated zones (Ziban, Oued Righ).

Although he may be settled at an oasis, the pastoralist leaves his capital —
and, what is more, often his heart — in the desert. Every spring, full of joy, he
sets off to revictual his herdsman, to go on a diet of milk, or merely to breathe
the pure Sahara air, which Arab poetry, in the accents of Rousseau, contrasts
with the reek of the cities. This feeling must not be underestimated, even if there
is a literary element and a measure of convention involved.

These returns to the desert are only possible if the former nomad has kept a
flock; and it often happens that the flocks are destroyed by some weather
calamity. It only needs a slightly excessive cold spell in winter that prevents the
grass from growing or failure of the spring rains to bring out the *acheb* (as
happened in Libya during the "terrible years" 1917–18 and 1947–48) and the
ewes miscarry, the lambs die like flies, and our nomad is as poor as Job. He does
not even have to lose all his animals: With less than two camels to a tent, it
becomes impossible to transport the tents, and the nomad has no alternative but
to settle down at the nearest well. The spectacle of tattered tents on the edge of
the palm groves is a sign that the "proletarianization" of the pastoralists is an
accomplished fact.

But the inability to shift tents is only a beginning. Once the nomad has found
work at the oasis, he builds a house (on the same lines as a tent, incidentally)
with a sheep-pen in front. At first, these conglomerations of scattered houses
have no form, then the village takes shape, streets and water-troughs appear, and
within one or two generations the nomad, at least as far as his environment is
concerned, is transformed into a town-dweller.

Definite settling therefore comes about either progressively, following on the
decay of the traditional way of life with a transitional period of seminomadism
or organized migration, or abruptly, as a result of some disaster that has
decimated the flocks or finally robbed the nomad's poor income of its value.

The process is quickened when building and drilling starts up — this is due not so much to the changes brought about in pastoral habits (as far as water is concerned, the results are mostly advantageous) as to the contrast between living standards. Since work began at Hassi Messaoud the number of houses built in the outlying quarters of Ouargla during a year has more than doubled; the curve for the last thirty years is parabolic-shaped.[5]

The settling of the nomads did not begin yesterday and is not restricted to the Sahara. The history of the Semitic peoples contains other examples, beginning with the settling of the Hebrews in the Promised Land. Without going farther than the French Sahara, there is the example of the Zenatas, nomadic Berbers at the time of ibn Khaldun (fourteenth century), and today, farmers at the Gourara oases; or the Trouds, descendants of the Hilalian Berbers who invaded North Africa in the twelfth century, and some of whom are today settled in the Souf. Coming closer to our time, the Chaamba of Metlili, at first established near a Berber ksar, have replaced the original population and are largely settled. The oasis of el-Goléa is the product of a combination of a core of Zenatas, migrants from Touat and the Gourara and the Chaamba families who began cultivating the land when the artesian wells were sunk. The same is true of most of the oases that comprise, along with the old settlers, a more or less substantial proportion of former nomads.

Until recently, however, settling was an occasional phenomenon, connected with various particular circumstances that could be altered by the return of more favorable weather conditions; the pendulum had not stopped swinging, and it was reasonable to suspect that the swing was a consequence of climatic variations and hence subject to an age-old law of the desert.

Since the end of World War II, the movement has taken on a very different aspect. It now affects whole tribes, such as the Mekhadma of Ouargla (4,300 individuals), closely studied by Prohuza, who have lost nine-tenths of their flocks, and sections of tribes considered as the most nomadic, such as the Chaamba. Nor have those peoples among whom nomadism was at its most prosperous been spared. For example, since 1958, the Goranes of Borkou, traditionally camel-breeders and owners of palm groves, have been building houses and making gardens in the groves. There have been various reasons for this: a series of dry years, competition from imported European salt, lower prices for camels (sometimes as low as the price of cattle), a snobbish contempt for matting tents, and a desire to imitate the chieftains who have built houses near the administrative center. One of the most essentially nomadic peoples of the Sahara, a people who lived exclusively from camel-breeding and from caravans and who never even went in for occasional farming (a permanent temptation for the northern pastoralist), is in the process of becoming, at the very least, seminomadic.

It would be going too far to affirm that all the Sahara nomads are affected by present trends. The northern Tuareg, Ahaggar or Ajjer, may provide a few workmen for the Edjeleh sities but have still not reached the point of building houses or keeping gardens. Among the southern Tuareg, settling is restricted to the tribes with the strongest Negro strain on the edge of the Sahelian region. The Tedas, who have never been counted among the true nomads but who have always been seminomadic palm-grove owners, apparently have no yearning to give up their migratory habits. Some Moorish chieftains have purchased building lots at the new capital of Nouakchott, but the tribe still lives in its tents. Among the Regueibat, despite the upsetting of the traditional pattern, the vitality of nomadism remains intact: the practice of lending livestock *(mniha)* offsets the disadvantages of the growing individualism; cultivable lands are still owned collectively; the amount of tea and sugar sold at the Tindouf market (mainly to nomads) was between two and three times larger in 1958 than it had been in 1950.

Nevertheless, even if the Atlantic and southern Sahara are holding out quite well, it would appear that elsewhere the contagion is irresistible. Previously linked to prevailing circumstances and always subject to relapses, settling is now tending to become general and irreversible.

RANGE AND LIMITS OF SETTLING

The establishment of a settled dwelling-place or, as the Italians put it, "stabilization," is not the end of the evolution that is bringing the nomads into modern society; these new villagers lack the qualities that make a peasant class — love for the earth, farming experience, permanent presence on the plantations, a wealth of effort only equaled by the shortage of financial resources. It took thousands of years for Egypt to melt together its Arab and Libyan invaders in the crucible of the Nile;[6] no such assimilation can take place in the western Sahara, where the process began later and where the village communities are themselves on the decline. As result, there is a lag between the arrival of the nomads, no longer grouped in tribes, and their integration in the new social frameworks, between the increasing number of settlers and the agricultural production figures, which remain stationary (grain, vegetables) or are continually decreasing (dates).

It will perhaps be urged that this is only a difficult period to be endured and that, once their settled status is established, the ex-nomads will enjoy living standards far higher than those they had before. It is noteworthy that all the Saharan authorities since Rome — Turkish, French, Italian, and Egyptian (only excepting the Spanish) — have encouraged settlement. The authorities are always influenced by financial considerations; but a man who, more than any other, was indifferent to such concerns, Father de Foucauld, also believed that "education and teaching are incompatible with the nomadic life." The Soviet authorities are of the same opinion — hence the policy of "denomadization" adopted by the U.S.S.R. in the steppes of the Caspian and central Asia, a policy that has led either to total settlement (through the development of irrigated prairies) or a combination of cultivation and organized migrations, the latter being entrusted to brigades of herdsmen. Instead of the old Yourtes camps, visitors are now shown neat villages, with schools, laboratories, and hospitals — in a word, all the instruments of social progress. "The end of nomadism is identified, in many people's minds, with access to modern history, democracy, and economic improvements."[7]

Such results, however, have not sufficed to convince those with an affection for the nomadic way of life and the values which it represents. Here are a people perfectly adapted to the natural environment, not only physically, through the sharpness of their senses, the sureness of their instincts, the speed of their reflexes, but also by their social organization and their sense of honor; and simply in order to obtain workmen for the oil fields, it is planned to transform these lordly people who command our respect by the dignity of their attitude and the wisdom of their rare utterances into a rabble seeking jobs or doles. Those Europeans who know them best — M. Monod, Colonel Chapelle, Commandant de Fraguier, to mention only the French — are outraged by the notion.

Put in this way, the problem may never be solved, since standards of happiness are now universal and there will always be the lean dogs who prefer freedom to fleshpots. But is it really necessary to give a summary ruling on the issue and settle the future of the nomads without reference to them? There are three prime reasons why we cannot envisage the rapid settlement of the 1.2 million nomads who live in the Sahara. The first is that they are spread through regions where there is a rocky outcrop or where rock is close to the surface, thus prohibiting any sinking of artesian wells, except in such areas as the Tanezrouft; the only available water tables are in the alluvial tracts of the *wadis* or in primary sandstone having a limited porosity and could never keep up the flow (100 liters per second per well) needed today for the installation of an irrigated cultivation area.

The second reason is that the oil and mining sites alone cannot absorb much labor. An oil company's requirements are more or less proportionate to the number of drills in operation; once drilling is completed, manpower needs are reduced to a handful; an undertaking that stops spreading, even if in full operation, stops taking on hands. The opening up of oil fields undoubtedly encourages building, transport, and trade, but until the Saharan economy becomes more diversified and the secondary and tertiary sectors are represented in the cases, it would be idle to hope that the curve of employment will follow that of the urban population.

Finally, the complete disappearance of nomadism would not only leave human beings without employment but would leave the steppes unused since, with our present means, they cannot be utilized in any other way. This would mean a definite loss of food supplies. The income from livestock in the French Sahara has been officially estimated at 1,363 million old francs.[8] Even taking this figure for what it is, namely a rough estimate, we have no right to sacrifice this income, to let a region that feeds a million individuals return to the desert, at a time when a third of mankind is suffering from hunger.

If we take this empirical view, which leaves aside any question of values and concentrates wholly on geographical contingencies, we must recognize that the problem does not arise everywhere in the same way and that we should differentiate between countries where the nomads are drawn by the prospect of wages to the workings of the irrigated regions and get rid of their flocks and those where nomadism or seminomadism still retains some chance of survival.

Governmental action has been most frequent in the first case, either preceding and to some extent bringing about settlement or aimed at mitigating its effects. Whenever drilling is begun with a view to resettling a specific number of nomad families on irrigated land, it usually attracts double the number: quite often, in such cases, the authorities find they have started something they cannot control.

Egypt is the first example to come to mind. In this country where the bedouin has always been looked at more or less askance and where, since the time of the pharaohs, the assimilation of the nomads has been a continuing thread in the national history, the government every now and then feels it necessary to start things off again. Since the war, the main efforts have been made in the Western Desert, more especially in the Wadi el-Natrun Depression. A project now under way aims at putting nomads through a training course as paid workers on a state farm and then settling them on reclaimed land, planted with fruit trees.[9]

A Tunisian experiment is even further advanced. This was begun immediately after the war in the old palm groves of Tozeur and Kebili and has now extended to the edge of the Eastern Erg. The sinking of artesian wells has made it possible for settlers from among the poorest villagers or the Merazig nomads to be supplied with large quantities of water, without unduly affecting the springs that in each village are the monopoly of a few big families. Not long ago, a French officer praised the admirable spirit of the associations of collective interest, which have been set up in the vicinity of the wells,[10] a fact that seems to indicate that the nomads have no objection to integration within a community that is genuinely open to them.

The Algerian Sahara can point to a number of similar experiments, for example at Ouargla, where the settlement of the Beni Thour began with the first cased wells; at el-Golea, where the artesian wells, to use the expression of the Chaamba themselves, ought to be like "the copper rings or the rein used to lead the camels"; but these were individual cases of settlement, and their timing contributed to their success. The mass descent on the oases that has been taking place for the last fifteen years has made a general policy necessary; an instrument for such a policy was thought to have been found in the Rural Improvement Sectors (SAR). An SAR is a relatively large piece of land, irrigated by artesian wells and developed for the production of dates, cereals, and artificial fodder. To begin with, the SAR operates as a pilot farm with paid workers; when the trees bear, the plantation will be divided up and the various lots allocated to the *haratin* or to settled nomads.

It is still too early to give an opinion on this experiment, which, in most cases, has not yet reached the most important social phase — apportionment of the land. However, the yields so far obtained from the pilot farms seem to prove that it is possible to effect a rapid increase in agricultural income — specialists claiming that it can be quadrupled within twenty-five years. The SAR system has the additional advantage of tightening the bonds of solidarity and mutual assistance, which have been weakened by the changeover to a sedentary life, since the SAR is due to become a production and marketing cooperative like certain Israeli *kibbutzim*.

But the resettlement of nomads in such conditions is an expensive business: it cost 17,000 new francs per family just to sink wells and develop and plant the land, and 23,000 new francs if the house is included. There can be no question of doing as much for all the Algerian nomads; even if it were technically possible, the whole OCRS budget would be insufficient for the task. Moreover, the cash income derives mainly from the sale of dates, and for some years past these have been fetching a poor price, and there is no improvement in sight. Finally, however much better the income from agriculture in the SAR may be, it is still markedly lower than what unskilled laborers earn on the various sites. In other words, young people will never be attracted to agriculture as long as they can find other work. At best, the SAR will act as a steadying force in an economy that has tended to get out of control since the discovery of oil but that is at the mercy of any slowdown in drilling. To sum up, in spite of the theoretical security provided by the artesian wells, in spite of the concern displayed by all governments, the future of those nomads who have finally broken with the pastoral existence is far from being secure, owing to the disproportion between needs and means.

Elsewhere, fortunately, nomadism is holding its own. Obviously, there is a change of form, a drift toward seminomadism and transhumance, which, perhaps wrongly, we look on as a sign of decadence; the vitality of these hybrid modes of existence, in Libya for example, demonstrates that a seminomad is not a nomad in decline. But the role of the authorities in such cases is no longer to facilitate the transformation, to hasten settlement, but to maintain the balance that has spontaneously come about between animal husbandry and cultivation. Three types of action can be envisaged for this purpose.

The first should work toward restoration of natural pasture lands and a more rational exploitation. So far, nothing, or almost nothing, has been done to enrich desert flora and vegetation, although experiments with *saxaoul* in central Asia, with *Kochia* in Egypt, and with spineless cacti in southern Morocco indicate that it is possible either to regenerate the natural plant populations or to introduce new plants, at least in the sub-desert regions. Elsewhere it is possible to facilitate the return of natural vegetation, which has been impoverished by the temporary excess of flocks arriving in the area after a rainfall; this is done by regulating the movements of flocks and imposing a rotation between favored sectors. An official rainfall bulletin, broadcast by radio, could usefully replace the *khbar* passed on by word of mouth. The creation of areas in which grazing was forbidden would be a first step toward constituting natural reserves that would attenuate the severity of the climatic and botanical environment without seriously intruding on the nomads' living space. As motor vehicles destroy the last clumps of grass spared by camels and men, it becomes increasingly urgent to promote the regeneration of desert vegetation elsewhere. Might it not be well if UNESCO's Advisory Committee on Arid Zone Research were to add its voice to those of certain scientists and the International Union for the Protection of Nature? *Vox clamantis in deserto.*

As stated at the beginning of this study, nomadism is linked to a certain type of land tenure. This is so true that an Egyptian author recently wrote that "landholding is considered to be the determining factor in the process of establishing sedentary life in the desert." Conversely, some sort of collective ownership is essential to the cohesion of the nomadic group. Wherever animal husbandry is still active, therefore, steps must be taken against the monopoly of tribal lands by individuals, the communal status of pasture lands must be preserved, and, in the case of arable land, there must be a return to collective redistribution. In this regard, there is no conflict between agronomical and social considerations, for there is no advantage in consolidating private ownership where, because of the absence of permanent irrigation, it cannot ensure yearly crops; the growing of grain in the *oudiane,* as practiced in northern Libya, is justified as a supplement to animal husbandry, not because it sustains an autonomous way of life.

Other steps of a commercial nature could ensure for the nomads the equivalent of the cash income that they formerly derived from caravan transport. These consist primarily in opening markets in the heart of the desert or on its outskirts. In recent years, the demand for camel meat has benefited from the wage-earner's increased buying power; above a certain level, there is a preference for beef, which will limit the potential market demand for camel meat. On the other hand, the creation of urban centers in the oil fields opens new prospects for sheep from the Saharan steppe region and for cattle from the Sahelian zone, since these can be carried by truck from the Niger and the Chad to Edjeleh. Thus pastoral economy, ruined by the disappearance of camel transport, may recover through the regular delivery of livestock to the markets.

A great number of nomads will doubtless settle in the next few years. Others will remain faithful to the tent, the pastoral migrations and the periodic cultivation. As long as they thereby obtain an adequate income and their nomadic outlook is revitalized, that can only be of benefit to the community.

So far, nomadism may have been linked with the absence of public service and with class inequality; that is not to say that it cannot prosper in an egalitarian and organized state, always subject to the condition that the state accords the pastoral communities full freedom of movement. Nor is it necessary for a pastoral society to be backward and illiterate: whether in respect of crafts or pure culture, the civilization that developed among the tents of Mauritania need envy nothing in the civilization of the oases: the fact that the Moors were the first of the Saharan peoples to acquire a national consciousness is rather an indication of a more advanced development.

Notes

1. O. J. Wheatley, *Report on Agriculture in Libya*, United Nations Mission to Libya Report Series No. 6 (New York: United Nations, 1952).

2. H. Merlet, "Enquête sur le revenue de la population de la commune mixte de Laghouat," *Trav. I.R.S.*, XV (first semester, 1957).

3. Le Rouvreur, *Rapport économique sur le district du Borkou en 1955*, Budget types (1955).

4. J. Dresch, "Les transformations du Sahel nigérien," *Acta geographica*, 1959.

5. Madeleine Brigol, "L'Habitat des nomades sédentarisés à Ouargla," *Trav. I.R.S.*, XVI (second semester, 1957).

6. Mohammed Awad, "The Assimilation of Nomads in Egypt," *Geographic Revue*, XL, No. 245 (1954).

7. Jacques Berque, "Nomades et nomadisme en zone aride: introduction," *Revue Internationale des Sciences Sociales Unesco*, XI, No. 4 (1959), 510.

8. A. Calcat, "Etat actuel et possibilités de l'agriculture saharienne," *Trav. I.R.S.*, XVIII (first and second semesters, 1959).

9. A. M. Abou Zeid, "La sédentarisation des nomades dans le désert occidental d'Egypte," *Revue Internationale des Sciences Sociales Unesco*, XI, No. 4 (1959), 578.

10. Gaillard, "Quelques aspects du problème de l'eau dans les oasis," *Les Cahiers de Tunisie*, No. 20 (first and second semesters, 1957), pp. 17–18.

39

INDUSTRIAL SELF-MANAGEMENT IN ALGERIA

DAMIEN HELIE

Throughout the independence struggle, Algerian political leaders continually emphasized values that gave a theoretical base to the rejection of foreign domination: "solidarity of the national community, the right of the people to self-determination." Nationalist ideology is in fact indispensable for mobilizing popular masses in a war of liberation. Once independence is obtained, however, nationalism no longer suffices as an ideology, because new tasks far more complicated than making war face the leaders, who want to direct their country toward development and modernization and enable it to catch up with other industrialized countries. A nationalist ideology does not provide an answer to all these problems.

The temptation then becomes great for the political leaders of newly independent, underdeveloped countries to embrace socialism, especially since that word can be applied to very different realities. "Algerian socialism" may be interpreted in many ways. In fact, it is made up of many unrelated elements, not all of them compatible. Different political groups also make different interpretations. "Socialism" could thus perhaps be defined as the result of a tension between two poles, with the result varying in time and depending on the social groups holding political power.

The first pole is the Marxist idea of socialism, generally referred to as "scientific." The Marxist influence in Algeria is quite strong, particularly in the vocabulary of the press and the leaders' speeches, in the proclaimed ideas, and in a certain number of decisions taken and effectively applied (state control of a large segment of the means of production, the single party). Its influence goes far beyond the number of actual Marxists, which is small. Marxism is found diffused throughout public opinion rather than in a single coherent doctrine. Its spread is explained mainly through the example of the socialist countries' economic achievements, for in Algeria Marxism is above all considered as a technique of development. It is from this point of view that Adam Ulam has said that "at the crucial point of transition from a pre-industrial society to a modern, at least partly industrialized state, Marxism becomes in a sense the natural ideology of that society and the most alluring solution to its problems."[1]

This article, based on a survey of self-managed industries, was written especially for this reader.

The second pole of Algerian socialism is "specific," or Arabo-Muslim. This trend of thought is equally important and has deep roots. It is by proclaiming themselves Arabs and Muslims that the Algerians have succeeded in founding a positive common denominator (compared to the negative definition that they had to make vis-à-vis the colonizer). They have re-evaluated their religion, history, and traditional society, and some have even gone to the point of saying that to realize socialism one has only to follow Islam, to return to the sources of the religion.[2] "Specific socialism" represents a synthesis between two contradictory demands: on the one hand, adherence to the values of the industrial world, and on the other, fidelity to traditional values. Up to now, Algerian socialism has been far more colored by "specific" than by Marxist socialism.

The ideological importance of self-management derives from the fact that it is the first concrete realization of Algerian socialism. Self-management has undoubtedly been created in a very pragmatic way by a government confronted with the problem of "abandoned property" in the agricultural and industrial sector, property left behind by its former European owners. But self-management was above all considered as a means to socialism. At first, self-management was mainly an attempt to salvage the Algerian economy: the decrees of March, 1963, were only applicable to abandoned lands or industries. But in October, 1963, it was transformed into a political choice, for on that date the government decided to complete the "Operation Vacant Lands" by totally liquidating colonial landholdings and by nationalizing a number of industries.

There is a contradiction between self-management in practice and self-management as an ideology. As an ideology, it is viewed as a way toward socialism, a method for economic development, an abstract idea that does not have to become concrete to exist. Self-management has become a value in itself, to the point where it is now synonymous with "socialism." One must admit that the government has paid far more attention to self-management as socialism than to the self-managed industries themselves. A study of the political forces behind self-management, and of their system of ideas as expressed in the Algerian press, will help to clarify the role that self-management has had in Algerian political life since 1962.

The most convinced partisan of self-management is the General Union of Algerian Workers (UGTA), whose business it is to represent the workers. The second group behind self-management is made of the left wing of the National Liberation Front (FLN) and the administration, two components that often overlap. The Charter of Algiers, published in April, 1964, at the end of the first congress of the FLN, ratified the self-management system in these words:

> Self-management expresses the will of the working class to emerge on the politico-economic scene and become a ruling force. On the economic level, self-management has imposed the necessity of extending agrarian reform and nationalization, both in agriculture and in industry, and of reorganizing internal and external trade as well as the banking system. On the political level, it puts relations among state, party, labor union, and people in a new light, implying a continual development of the democratic nature of all these institutions in their relations with the masses.

Self-management, the embodiment of "specific socialism," is considered by its partisans as the spontaneous work of the Algerian people. The vocabulary used indicates the point of view:[3]

1. The "bourgeoisie" is the enemy of self-management and socialism, although no precise identification is given to the term.

2. "Bureaucracy" is a threat to self-management and is used to explain any difficulties that arise.

3. "Self-management" is considered capable of ending the alienation of the workers by giving them the responsibility of managing the industries.

The concepts used by supporters of self-management serve a useful function, but they refer more to mythology than to reality. The place given to self-management in the press is a good indicator of its importance from the ideological point of view. A considerable number of articles on the subject appeared in the Algerian press after independence. *Révolution Africaine,* the organ of the Algerian Left, is a good example: in fourty-five issues in 1964, there were seventy articles devoted to socialism and self-management, forty of which were directly related to self-management. The June 19, 1965, movement that overthrew ben Bella bitterly criticized the over-all policy of the preceding government, and its economic policies in particular, but it did not dare to question socialism or self-management, the basic options of the defunct regime. In February, 1966, it launched a huge propaganda campaign in favor of self-management. On the ideological level, therefore, the new regime did not bring about a radically different orientation.

The role of ideology is to provide the essential values that are to be the bases for political action. These values are used to obtain the people's cooperation, which is indispensable for the exercise of power. That ideology can be used for hiding social contradictions is a well-known fact since Marx. Algeria is no exception, for since independence a socially privileged bureaucracy has entrenched itself in the name of an officially egalitarian socialism. Ideology therefore returns to politics and on that level, self-management has had as its main purpose the mobilization of the popular masses.

Self-management has been used by the group in power as a tool to discredit the regime's adversaries. The first independent government was under particular pressure to appear radical because it was vigorously contested from its formation to its overthrow. Self-management was an excellent propaganda tool for supporters of the new regime. The industrial self-management congress organized by the FLN in March, 1964, was a typical example. Officially, the congress was to draw up a preliminary balance sheet and to have the workers and managers of industries make decisions to remedy the shortcomings of the industrial self-management sector. In fact, the objective was to have party decisions and government policies approved, and particularly to win the political support of workers in self-managed plants, but certainly not to have them participate in the decision-making process concerning these self-managed industries.

In independent Algeria, self-management has been of great political importance, because it constitutes one of the principal slogans of the government and incarnates socialism, the fundamental option of the regime.

THE INDUSTRIAL SELF-MANAGEMENT SECTOR

In 1962, the Algerian economy was in bad shape. The flight of most Europeans, who were the country's cadres, and the systematic sabotage by right-wing groups, had almost completely disorganized economic life. It was only little by little that the state of anarchy disappeared and the situation returned to normal. Nevertheless, the fact remained that the richest part of the population, the prime consumers of industrial products, had left. At least a partial reconversion of the economic structures was necessary.

The negative consequences of the European exodus could only be met by state action. Yet, to date, public development programs, still incomplete, have not brought about an effective economic recovery. The activity of the various industrial sectors has fallen off considerably (between 10% and 75%). Even in the most active sectors, such as the textile industry, where new units are being added, the existing plants have not found sufficient demand in the local market. The abnormally high selling-prices caused by the increases in salaries after independence also affected the market. As markets for industrial products dwindled, the supply of raw materials became uncertain. Algeria is dependent on external sources of supply, and especially on France, because of the ties established during colonization. With independence, the commercial circuits disintegrated; as a result, commercial delays have lengthened unreasonably and the financial conditions have become extremely difficult. On the financial level, the system was profoundly disorganized. In 1962, bank deposits dropped considerably (40%); credit became expensive and difficult to obtain for self-managed plants, whose juridical status was only just defined and did not fit within the framework of previous legislation.

Despite all the official declarations about socialism, there has been no break with the past in the government's economic policy: Algeria remains a dependent country without essential industries, and a capitalistic country with its prices set by the free market. Any authentic development plan is still in the drafting stage, the government being satisfied with an annual development budget. The self-managed plants, socialist in principle, are therefore not part of a general framework. They suffer from competition from private enterprise and are in contact with institutions, such as the government administration and banks, which are accustomed to working with private business and not with new entities with little security.

At the administrative level, the European exodus was unsettling, affecting the quality of administrative personnel on both the central and the local levels. The colonial administration had not prepared the Algerians to administrate themselves, and services were disorganized for lack of competent personnel. These gaps can doubtless be filled in a relatively short time, since the problem is a technical one. More important is the fact that the colonial machine itself was put back into operation, insofar as possible after independence. It is difficult to believe that it is capable of dealing with the new problems that are arising. Under colonial rule, the administration's objective was to maintain order; its new goal must be to promote economic development.

The present Algerian administration is a heavy and ineffective instrument where formalism and irresponsibility reign. It has inherited the drawbacks of the French administration and has also invented new ones. A considerable increase in its numbers has not been marked by growing productivity. In fact, decisions that were formerly made directly by lower civil servants are now made at the highest levels because of the intrusion of political problems into the administrative domain. Only high-level civil servants with political power are able to make decisions for which they are responsible. Under these conditions, it would be surprising if decisions were made rapidly. This poor administrative organization considerably hinders the development of industry.

The roadblocks to normal business operation are therefore so numerous that in the case of an enterprise in a critical situation, it is impossible to separate management problems from external economic factors. Since there is no basis for valid comparison, there is no way to judge the economic efficiency of an industrial self-managed plant. It is therefore impossible to evaluate self-management on a purely economic basis.

Statistical sources concerning the self-managed industries sector are few and unreliable. To date, no complete census of self-managed industries has been made, and information is therefore scattered. Moreover, the sector changes constantly since, month after month, industries that had previously been private are brought into either the self-managed or nationalized sectors. As for the evolution in the size of the self-managed sector, the wave of confiscation of industries to bring them under self-management was practically limited to 1963. Until the end of that year, abandoned enterprises or industries whose activity was not judged sufficient were handed over to the workers, headed by a self-management committee that they elected. After that date, official policy changed, and no more private plants were brought under self-management: confiscated industries were nationalized.

In general, given the low level of industrialization, Algerian enterprises are small, a characteristic that is even more marked in the self-managed sector, which has inherited a large number of marginal enterprises of minor economic interest that have often been maintained or reactivated for reasons of social policy. All abandoned industries have not been reopened, however; 200—300 out of 700 remained closed. Small plants are numerous in the self-managed sector: 45% of these enterprises are craftsmen's shops. Middle-sized industries employing more than twenty workers are few: forty-five in Algiers region, twenty-two in the Oranais, twelve in the Constantinois. Large enterprises are even fewer: fewer than five plants employ more than one hundred workers. The self-management sector makes up only a small part of all Algerian industry. Algerian industry, excluding public works and construction, employs 60,000 workers; the self-management sector employs only 25% of this industrial manpower.

Technical and administrative cadres in the self-managed industries usually left at the same time as the managers. The situation was further complicated by the fact that not only the white-collar workers but also the blue-collar workers, foremen, and skilled workers were Europeans and also left. On the administrative level, competent managers are rare, and trained accountants are often lacking. The personnel is generally composed of a very small number of managers or skilled workers and an overly large number of poorly trained or unskilled laborers.

Independence was followed by a general rise in salaries, about 30% in the self-management sector. Administrative control was only slowly established and brought an end to salary raises decided by the workers themselves. The major problem is that the self-managed sector cannot offer the same salaries as private enterprise and that an equalization of salaries in the two sectors, as demanded by the Industrial Self-Management Congress of March, 1964, was not easily feasible.

In general, production has declined badly. The industries most affected pose serious questions of reconversion that are difficult to resolve because of the government's political preoccupations: to close a particular plant would be considered an admission of defeat, so the government often prefers to use artificial means to keep open plants that would otherwise go bankrupt. Yet the administration has not effectively supported the self-managed sector and has not provided it with the help it needs to function rationally on the economic level. State action has been characterized by slowness both in the promulgation of legislation and in the establishment of the organisms necessary to make the self-managed sector succeed.

It is striking that, despite the political importance of the self-management idea, the party has shown so little interest in the self-managed sector. There never have been any party cells in the plants, but only a few scattered militants. The party apparatus almost never intervenes in the life of the plants; it does not play the directing and encouraging role that it should. The activity of the UGTA has also been minimal. One reason for this quasi-abstention is that the labor union is a general staff whose militants still have to be mobilized. The Algerian labor movement was not well organized before independence, and its members were few. There is a striking contrast between the world of politicians who talk ideology and politics, and that of workers in the factories, who talk salaries and everyday problems. Everything happens as if there were no communication between the top and the lower social levels, as if the people involved did not even speak the same language.

FUNCTIONING OF THE SELF-MANAGEMENT ORGANIZATION

The essential action set into motion by the March decrees was the conferring of the management of abandoned properties to the workers of these plants and farms, to be organized as follows:

1. The general assembly of the workers holds the decision-making power in the enterprise concerning the adoption of the industrial development plan and the annual equipment, production, and sales programs, the establishment of regulations governing the organization of labor, the division of responsibility, and the adoption of the final accounts. The assembly was to meet at least once every three months, with each member having a vote by secret ballot.

2. The workers' council was to be the executive organ elected by the general assembly.

3. The self-management committee was to be chosen from the workers council and to be in charge of everyday business. The committee president, elected from among its members, was to direct business operations.

4. The director was to be the state representative in the enterprise. His relations with the committee president were not specified, and no hierarchy of relations was established between the two.

These texts show the government's desire to bring about a "workers' democracy" within the plants. The basic decisions are to be taken by the workers, each of whom is entitled to vote. The distrust of bureaucracy is apparent in the provisions that at least two-thirds of the workers' council and self-management committee members are to be workers directly employed in production and that the organs of management must be renewed by one-third every year. Self-management also has the purpose of eliminating salaried labor as such. The workers collectively become entrepreneurs with capital furnished by the state (former abandoned property) and have the right to divide among themselves a percentage of the profits earned in their enterprise.

Elections for workers's council and self-management committee are organized by the authorities (administration, party, labor union). The number of candidates is one and one-half to two times the number of posts available. However, the workers are not represented by an official organism, party, or labor union. This absence of interference in the elections is quite remarkable in a country where the single party aspires to mobilize and direct all facets of national life. Generally those who agree to run and are elected by their comrades are professionally the best qualified and the senior workers in the enterprise. The criterion for selection of the leaders is solely technical; hence, the technical and the elected hierarchy tend to coincide. Indeed, elections may seem useless, since they only confirm an authority structure that already exists on its own. In fact, power in the enterprises is in the hands of a few qualified men who have accepted responsibility and who cannot be replaced, even if the rules set by legislation are respected.

The periodic meetings of the general assemblies and workers' councils are usually orderly. But it is not at this level that decisions concerning the plant's activity are made. These meetings are held to explain current operations to the workers and occasionally to ask their approval of a decision taken by the self-management committee. The leaders call these meetings and speak to the workers, who limit their participation to requests for salary raises or bonuses. All decision-making powers are in the hands of the self-management committees; the workers' councils have become inactive, and the general assemblies limit themselves to electing the leaders.

The general assemblies and the workers' councils therefore play a very limited role in the activity of the plants. All decisions are made at the management level. The dual position of the managers is not conducive to a rapid solution of the conflicts or tensions that occur between labor and management. These conflicts, which rarely appear in the open but are more often latent, are good indicators of the shortcomings of the self-management system.

The principal labor demands concern wages. The workers want to maximize their gains and tend to judge their enterprise solely on the basis of the salary they receive. Other tensions come from the wage scale. The wage levels themselves have not been altered, but there has been much movement within the old levels, many workers having been promoted without any rational selection agreeable to all. The elected members of the self-management committees often grant themselves privileges, but the workers only accept inequality when it is justified by ability. Rare are the workers who agree with their own position on the wage scale. A tendency to a egalitarianism also poses complex problems, particularly because it is an upward egalitarianism: the workers want as much as those at the top but rarely as little as those at the bottom. In fact, every workers' demand has something to do with wages. This simple fact is striking in industries that are theoretically managed by the workers' body. The leaders have a different point of view: they blame the workers (often rightly) for their lack of discipline and productivity.

Conflicts inside the self-managed plant rarely become acute since there is no organized action to mobilize the workers. Generally they are personal frictions without serious consequences. Short strikes can take place, however, as the expression of anarchic demands outside the framework of the self-management institutions. On these occasions, the workers act as if the self-management organization did not exist. The latent conflicts, which remain unresolved, indicate problems in the functioning of self-management organizations and an inability to maintain liaison between workers and managers. The workers do not use the procedures that the legislation offers them, and they do not react effectively when the consultation process is not respected.

The operating problems of self-management do not arise from a lack of respect for legislation, since the workers generally are not aware of it. Conflicts and tensions arise because the established organization of the plant has disappeared and been replaced by ineffectual organs of management in which the workers do not really participate. This lack of participation is characteristic of the industrial self-management sector. The workers do not know the legislation on self-management and are unaware of their rights. Apart from their wage problems, they participate little in the meetings since they do not have the background necessary to tackle the current problems. Still, at the time when the first industries were open to self-management, in 1963, there was some enthusiasm — a form of worker participation — for the goals promoted by the advocates of self-management. The workers kept watch over the plants before their reopening, to prevent dismantling. They often agreed to forego their first pay check to make the reopening of the plant possible. But these actions were often the work of a small number of employees and could be explained as much by the desire not to see their source of income disappear as by a real spirit of participation. It is only the few professionally qualified workers and the senior employees in the plant who participate in management. Only at the blue-collar level are the workers able to take part in plant management.

In Algeria, given the economic and political conditions that obtained after independence and the small size of the enterprises, no plant has enough qualified leaders and workers to make the normal functions of the self-management organs possible — through a real participation of all the workers in the enterprise.

ATTITUDES OF THE WORKERS

An analysis of workers' reactions toward their own problems — either toward plant difficulties or toward self-management and the state — shows two types of responses. A first group of workers — the majority — reacts only in terms of its direct concerns, for example, salaries or plant discipline. This group does not feel any responsibility for the plant and does not participate in its management. The second group — much smaller — reacts on the basis of its view of the plant's role, or even of socialism. It is made up for the most part of skilled workers and managers. The problems the industry faces are generally met with indifference. It is the skilled workers who usually have a coherent view of these problems and who are aware of the general problems of material life. They are conscious of the objective difficulties confronting them and, if they themselves do not have the means to cope with the situation, they are at least able to analyze it.

Most workers favor self-management, but only as the existing system established after independence and after the European exodus; self-management is not judged abstractly, as a new way of management, but concretely, in terms of the situation in the industry in which they work. Self-management meant work, employment stability, a raise, the end of production norms – these, together with the idea of independence, made a complex of positive values. But self-management is not understood as the management of the plants by the body of its employees.

The analysis of the attitudes toward self-management is confirmed by the attitudes of the workers toward the state. In fact, most of the workers would like to see their plant controlled by the state, which would mean purely and simply the abolition of all workers' representative bodies. The workers are not bothered at all by this possibility, to the extent that they are conscious of the extremely limited role played by the different assemblies and that they feel powerless before the problems that they have to solve to make their plant work. The workers hope that the state would control management properly, and the leaders think that in this way anarchy would disappear. Each group sees in state control the solution to its particular problems.

If left to themselves by the administration, the labor union, and the party, the workers in self-managed plants would clearly seek to hand over to the state the responsibilities entrusted to them by the March, 1963, decree. Confronted with more difficulties than with means to resolve them, they see only one solution – state intervention.

CONCLUSION

Industrial self-management is an idea that twice failed. On the one hand, it has remained limited to a small sector and did not benefit either from a massive and necessary influx of leaders or from support by the administration, which really never was enthusiastic about the self-managed sector. Its growing period was 1963, but in 1964, government policy changed, and confiscated industries were given over to national companies, which meant the end of worker participation in the management of the enterprise. The government thus chose to put a rapid end to the experiment and prevent it from growing. Confusion was maintained by grouping together self-managed industries and nationalized companies under the term "socialist sector."

On the other hand, in the limited sector that was handed to them, and where the administration could not be accused of crushing self-management under an all powerful bureaucracy, the workers, unprepared for that kind of work, could not face up to the challenge and did not take the occasion to participate in the management of their industry.

The failure of industrial self-management, linked to the workers' inability to take their future into their own hands, poses the problem of survival for the Algerian working class. If class consciousness is considered a necessary prerequisite to the existence of a social class, then a working class as such does not exist in Algeria. This conclusion then poses a fundamental political problem for underdeveloped countries: is socialism possible without a working class? If by socialism is meant "scientific socialism," the first step of the Algerian experiment suggests that the answer is no.

The working class is in fact the only class that has both an interest in rapid transformation of the economy and the capability to develop a coherent ideology that could mobilize the population and promote economic development. Nothing prevents the petty bourgeoisie of the underdeveloped countries from satisfying themselves with the fiscal exploitation of the country, since they do not depend on industrial activity for their income. A "Potemkin socialism" can serve as an ideological screen and do away with the real effort required to bring about development.

That is perhaps the real reason behind all the arguments about "specific" socialism. The petty bourgeoisie is not opposed to development, which means consumer goods from the industrialized West, but since it has the means — at least for the moment — to acquire them without making the effort necessary for industrialization, it hesitates to adopt efficient means of transforming the economy and advocates "the specific" to cover up its rejection of socialism. At the present time, there is little evidence of social forces capable of changing a policy that can only bring economic stagnation and political demobilization.

Notes

1. Adam Ulam, *The Unfinished Revolution* (New York: Random House, 1950), p. 10.
2. See Raymond Vallin, "Muslim Socialism in Algeria," pp. 50—64 in this reader.
3. See I. William Zartman, "The Algerian Army in Politics," pp. 211—24 in this reader.

40

INDUSTRIAL COORDINATION IN ALGERIA, LIBYA, MOROCCO, AND TUNISIA

A. F. EWING ET AL.

A United Nations Economic Commission for Africa [ECA] mission visited Algeria, Libya, Morocco, and Tunisia from January 2 to 28, 1964. . . .

The principal objective has been to assess in concrete terms the possibilities of industrial development over the next decade or so in the North African countries covered, with the primary emphasis on projects serving more than one country, and to make suggestions for continuing cooperation to this end among the countries concerned. From this it follows that particular emphasis has been given to industries the minimum economic scale of output of which is beyond the probable market available in any of the individual countries concerned. . . . Underlying the mission's work have been two basic economic principles: specialization between countries and the economies of scale.

In some of the industrial sectors examined the kind of cooperation required is evident; in others there is a choice, and it is for the countries concerned to make decisions. Among the main conclusions are the following:

A coordinated energy policy is essential. . . . There would be great advantage if Algeria, on the basis of its abundant natural gas resources, were to supply electric power, not only for its own purposes, but also to its neighbors. . . .

There is a strong case for a coordinated policy of mineral surveying and development and joint action, particularly between Algeria and Morocco.

The sub-region is very well endowed in phosphates, and Algeria, Morocco, and Tunisia can all export on the world market phosphate fertilizers. There would, however, be great advantage in setting up one ammonia plant to serve the whole sub-region. . . .

Coordination of production of iron and steel in the sub-region is imperative. Tunisia has already embarked on the installation of an integrated plant . . . too small to be economical. Morocco is contemplating the laying down of a small rerolling works to meet her own requirements. Algeria is building a relatively large integrated works. Coordination of rolling programs is essential. . . .

There are great possibilities of developing metal working, mechanical engineering, electrical engineering, and assembly work in the sub-region, pro-

Reprint of a mission of the United Nations Economic Commission for Africa, February 5, 1965 (U.N. Document E/CN. 14/248); abridged and reprinted by permission.

vided again there is detailed dovetailing of production programs. Morocco in
particular has well developed facilities in this field. Much benefit would result
from a joint [Algero-Tunisian] program in the Annaba—Menzel Bourguiba
area. . . .

Apart from the basic chemicals required for the production of fertilizers,
where sub-regional cooperation is required, the main possibility lies in the
development in Algeria, on the basis of natural gas, of petrochemical industries
which should serve not only the Maghrib but other African countries, and could
indeed also compete in world markets. There are immediate possibilities of
producing synthetic rubber and also the raw material for a growing range of
plastics.

There is probably scope for one, but only one, factory producing flat glass for
the sub-region.

The sub-region is well endowed with cement-making facilities, production is
increasing, and before long there will be little or no need to resort to imports.
There is, however, scope for cooperation in developing cement production in the
Annaba—Menzel Bourguiba area.

There is much scope for increasing production of a wide variety of textiles
with a view to import substitution. Looked at from a sub-regional point of view
the immediate possibility is the development of one factory to produce rayon
for the whole Maghrib market.

The report indicates that it would seem essential at an early date for an
agreement to be reached at an appropriate level between the four countries to
establish a series of expert committees to examine and make specific proposals
for coordination of production sector by sector. These arrangements might well
be followed by institutions working on a more permanent basis. . . .

INDUSTRIALIZATION AND THE ECONOMIC DEVELOPMENT
OF THE MAGHRIB

. . . The dual nature of the Maghrib economy should be recalled, that is, division
in two distinct and unrelated sectors: the modern sector with large farms,
mining, industry, banking, trade, and all the ancillary services necessary in a
modern economy, and a traditional sector where agriculture and stock-breeding is
archaic, with handicraft production and small traders. Some figures can be given
as illustrations. The traditional sector comprises 70% of the population and its
contribution to gross domestic product (GDP) is of the order of 30%. Living
conditions are wretched; the average income per head can be put at about
$60.

The major task now facing the Maghrib governments is, therefore, the
improvement of the traditional sector of the economy. The priority given to
agrarian problems in development plans is understandable. Some discussion of
the relations between the development of the traditional sector and industrialization is necessary and a number of points can be made.

In the first place, only if this sector is developed can there be, in the long run,
a sufficient market for industrial products. The considerable potential demand
for fertilizers and agricultural machinery can assure outlets for phosphates and
the engineering industries. If the traditional sector enjoyed the same income as
its modern counterpart consumption of textiles could be tripled.

In the immediate future, however, such perspectives cannot be envisaged. To develop industry in the next ten to fifteen years, the only road open is the enlargement of national markets for basic industry as is shown in this report. One exception, however, is the possibility of governments through state orders taking direct action in the traditional sector (for example, fertilizers).

Overpopulation in the traditional sector, spilling over into the towns, can be a considerable handicap to industrialization. Although, in the long run, the unemployment problem can be solved only through the setting up of a powerful industrial sector, it would be a serious mistake to underestimate the time required to do this and to try therefore in the next ten years to embark on the setting up of industries in the towns with a view to reducing unemployment. In this connection, the Tunisian policy of laying down works for the unemployed, with the task of improving the traditional sector, has made sufficient progress to warrant being edited as an example, given the availability of finance. It seems clear that only labor-intensive rural development can resolve the unemployment problem in the coming years. It would be disastrous from the point of view of building up basic industry in the Maghrib to give priority to the creation of new jobs rather than the search for economic efficiency and higher productivity.

It was the modern agricultural sector that has been in the past the driving force in the development of the economy, in the same way as attempts are now being made to get the traditional sector to play a similar part. The modern agricultural sector, which has shown the way toward high levels of technique, has the defect of being oriented (especially in Tunisia and Algeria) toward products complementary to those of Europe, within the framework of a colonial economy that now belongs to the past. The reorientation of this sector, already well underway in Algeria and Tunisia, may run the risk during a transitional period — which, it is to be hoped, will not last more than a few years — of leading to time lags in economic growth. It cannot be expected, therefore, that an expansion of the market for industrial goods can be found in the growth of this sector. This argument is additional to that deduced from the analysis of the traditional sector. It is necessary to look elsewhere than to agriculture to find the stimulus for industrial development in coming years. The coordination of industrial-development plans, with a view to enlarging national markets, is thus seen to be not only necessary in the long run but particularly opportune in the immediate future.

Analysis of external trade opens up in its turn a useful field for reflection concerning its relationship to the industrialization process. Except in the case of Morocco, where imports of equipment goods are about one-third less than during the 1950's, it can be seen that in recent years there has been a marked development of imports of such products. In Algeria, they doubled between 1956 and 1960 following investment in the Saharan oil fields and the industrialization program within the framework of the Constantine plan. Imports of equipment have been at record levels in Libya since 1957, following the discovery of oil. In Tunisia, the index of imports of equipment for the period 1957–61 is 150 compared with the period before independence, as a consequence of the industrialization program.

So far as imports of consumption goods are concerned, there is also an upward tendency from 53% in 1960 to 66% in 1961 in Algeria, from 48 per cent to 51 per cent in Tunisia, and from 45 per cent to 62 per cent in Morocco during the same period. Two conclusions can be drawn — first, there are great possibilities for industrialization in the three countries through import substitution — textiles, shoes, plastics, and so on. These possibilities are being taken advantage of in the industrial plans in the course of execution in Algeria, Morocco, and Tunisia, a policy which should be encouraged. Second, such an approach will not be wholly successful without some discipline on the part of consumers, who are bound to see some falling off in the range of products offered and often in their quality. In any case, as can be seen clearly in the assembly of motor vehicles, it would be of little value to the economy to produce such goods on the basis of imported components. On the contrary, the task is to set up in North Africa factories capable of producing such components. Another example is textiles, where the objectives should be not only spinning and weaving but also the manufacture of looms. Industrialization will not make much progress, and, indeed, has already been slowed down in Morocco, which is well ahead in this field, if it is based wholly on consumer goods. Once again, therefore, this points to the need for a larger market on a North African scale, which alone is able to provide semi-finished products and equipment required for the transforming of industries.

Exports are based essentially on five products: oil, phosphates, wine, citrus fruits, and olive oil. Oil and natural gas are available in sufficient quantities to solve the balance-of-payment problems of Algeria and Libya, which showed a deficit in the past. Two points should be made. One is that if the Maghrib economies are to obtain the foreign exchange necessary to buy equipment for industrialization, the only possible policy is at one and the same time to export petroleum products to the maximum possible extent and to develop the internal market. Secondly, the importance of upgrading exports, for instance, triple super-phosphate or ammonium phosphate rather than phosphate rock, cannot be overstressed. It is essential to emphasize, however, that this process of working up raw material must be on the basis of costs competitive in export markets. Attention is drawn in this report to some serious problems in this field, for example, manufacture of ammonia, esparto pulp, etc.

In general, it can be said that the development of industry in North Africa also requires a carefully coordinated commercial policy vis-à-vis other countries. Some exports to Europe will need to decrease (wine, cereals, and so on). New outlets will have to be found for some commodities (citrus fruit, olive oil, petrol, natural gas, phosphates). Such new markets may be found within the framework of an African common market. At the same time, imports should be encouraged that promote, not hinder, industrialization.

It is not easy to obtain from past experience even recent indications of the likely future economic growth in the Maghrib within the framework of a policy of industrialization. First, long periods are required to establish average growth rates in economies where climatic conditions cause considerable fluctuation in agricultural production. Thus, a bad harvest in 1961 was sufficient to cause a fall in the GDP of the countries of the Maghrib. Second, despite what may appear to be said in the ample literature now available on development problems, it is in the long-term only that industrial investment demonstrates its value, at least in the early stages of the industrialization process. The essential reason is that, at the start, productivity of both labor and capital is low (workers lack experience, there are difficulties in maintaining machinery, scales of operation are too low, and so on).

Nevertheless, the past is quite encouraging. It is useful to recall that in a number of areas there is already considerable experience of industrialization in North Africa. The real problem, if a high rate of industrial growth is to be maintained, will be to maintain technical staff and to make a major effort to train labor. In Tunisia, the rate of growth of GDP, which was 2.5 per cent for 1950–59, seems to have risen to 4.4 per cent in 1959–61. In Algeria, the rate of growth of GDP was 9.7 per cent during the period 1953–58. This figure should be corrected to make allowance for a number of artificial factors (considerable growth of military and administrative expenditures). Once these factors are eliminated, there still remains a high figure: 6.8 per cent a year. In Morocco, the rate of growth of 5 per cent during the industrial boom in the 1950's has not subsequently been surpassed.

The total GDP per head in 1960 was $130 in Libya, $160 in Morocco, $175 in Tunisia, and, after allowing for the elimination of military and administrative expenditures, $220 in Algeria.

As to the likely future trend of GDP, it seems that a growth rate of 5 per cent, based on an average of several hypotheses, is not unreasonable for the period 1964–70. If such a growth rate is obtained, it would seem reasonable to expect in the subsequent period up to 1980 the take-off of the Maghrib economy, that is to say, the stage of development where self-sustaining growth can be based principally on national savings.

The hypotheses underlying a growth rate of 5 per cent are as follows: from the side of output, it is assumed that expansion of agricultural production will be limited by changes in the agrarian structure, and that investment in the industrial sector will not yet have borne all its fruits. From the point of view of expenditure, a limited growth of consumption per head is assumed, together with a policy of investment in the production sectors of the economy at a rate of about twice that of the GDP, that is, an annual rate of increase in capital formation of from 8 to 10 per cent. . . .

Summing up, the conditions precedent to economic growth in the coming years would seem to be a policy of relative austerity in consumption, large-scale utilization of labor for the development of agriculture, and a considerable industrialization effort based on the coordination of industrial plans and an enlargement of domestic markets, especially for intermediate products and industrial equipment.

INDUSTRIAL DEVELOPMENT: LARGE-SCALE INDUSTRIES

. . . In this sub-region of Africa there is no need to advocate the development of large-scale modern industries, since this is already the policy of the governments concerned. The need for industrial coordination between the North African countries as a necessary condition for the effective development of large scale industry is also widely recognized. . . .

In applying the principle of economies of scale, account has been taken of the trend of technological advance, which in some industries now makes possible economically small-scale production at less capital cost than is current practice in the industrially advanced countries. Production at lower scales of output than those envisaged is often, of course, technically possible but at higher, sometimes substantially higher, cost. This is the essence of the case for an agreed pattern of industrial coordination and established arrangements to keep the whole scheme under constant review.

One further general point should be made. The industries that are most likely to be successful are those based on local natural resources, which in the sub-region as a whole are relatively abundant. Furthermore, even industries of this kind will frequently require protection, at least for some time to come. There are, of course, exceptions such as Tunisia's olive-oil and super-phosphates industries, which are profitable yet operate solely for export. Industries based largely on imported raw materials are likely to be justified only when producing for the internal market and if their productivity is at least 50% of similar undertakings in developed countries. Otherwise they will require such high protection as to price themselves out of the domestic market, or, alternatively, heavy government subsidies. Examples are the sugar refinery in Tunisia, safety-match manufacture in Libya, and several North African assembly plants. . . .

The total energy resources of the Maghrib are very substantial. With industrial development, energy consumption will increase rapidly within the area but energy exports will remain the most important single source of foreign exchange for many years to come. Nearly all the known energy resources are accounted for by the big reserves of oil and natural gas in Libya and Algeria, which are only in the first stage of development. Minor occurrences are also found in Morocco and Tunisia. North Africa's crude-oil resources may be estimated at present as representing 5% of the total world reserves. The corresponding figure for natural gas is about 10%. Considering the fact that the region accounts for less than 1% of the world population, it may be deduced that a considerable proportion of the Maghrib's energy resources can be absorbed by other regions without any prejudice to the Maghrib's own industrial development. . . .

Apart from foreign-exchange earnings and government revenues, the petroleum industry provides other direct and indirect benefits to the Libyan economy. It is estimated that more than 12,000 persons are directly employed in the oil industry, of whom about 9,000 are Libyans. Many of the Libyan employees are receiving technical training from the oil companies.

Libyan crude-oil production is at present obtained from four main producing fields in Cyrenaica. The oldest is in Zelten, which, together with the Raguba field, feeds a pipe-line to the port of Marsa el-Brega at a daily rate of 350,000 barrels. The Dahra and Waha fields are linked by pipeline to the port of Es-Sider, where over 200,000 barrels of crude oil are being shipped. The next producing field will be concession 65 in southern Cyrenaica, from which the production will be piped over 580 kilometers to the coast.

Petroleum development in Western Tripolitania could play an important role in future industrial cooperation between Libya and Tunisia. A number of producing wells have been drilled in this area: they will remain tapped until a sufficient volume has been established to justify production, piping, and port facilities. The oil in the part of the country comes from older formations than in the Sirtica area, and the structures are smaller. There are a few wells with high gas/oil ratio, but only two, both in Western Tripolitania, can be considered true dry-gas wells. . . .

The country's first oil refinery at Marsa el-Brega is currently being tested. This 5.5 million-plant is designed to meet Libyan requirements for some basic petroleum products: only regular gasoline, premium gasoline, kerosene, diesel oil, and heavy fuel oil. The refinery has a capacity of 350,000 tons per year. Such a small-scale plant is relatively inefficient, since it cannot extract the same variety of products as refineries treating several million tons per year.

Tunisia has no natural gas except for a small deposit on Cap Bon, which barely meets the capital's domestic requirements; the output is 6 to 7 million cubic meters per year. . . . Tunisia's potential need for natural gas is about 100 million cubic meters, including every conceivable industrial use: this would only account for a fraction of the minimum volume required for special pipelines from one of the known fields in Libya or the Sahara. It would therefore be in Tunisia's interest if a transmission line for export could be laid either through her territory or close enough so that her requirements could be met by a take-off from the main pipeline.[1]

The Bizerta oil refinery's . . . output capacity is 1 million tons per year, but the production target for the first year's operation is 650,000 tons, of which 450,000 are destined for the domestic market and the remainder to stockpiling. The crude-oil supply is being obtained from Iraq, since that material best meets the various proportions of refinery products required by the domestic market.

Algeria's total oil and gas reserves are not yet fully known: as in Libya, new discoveries continue to be made. At present, the main producing fields are in the Hassi Messaoud region and in the eastern Sahara, south of the Tunisian border. The crude-oil production in 1963 amounted to about 24 million tons, which were evacuated by the two existing pipelines to Bejaia and La Skhirra respectively. These lines are now approaching their total carrying capacity estimated at 31 million tons per year, and the construction of the third pipeline for crude oil is therefore being planned. Algerian crude is a light oil that breaks down mainly into gasolines and fuel oils. It has not the complete range of petroleum products of crude oil found, for example, in Iraq or Venezuela.

The new al-Harrache refinery near Algiers . . . has a rated capacity of 2 million tons, while the country's present consumption of oil-refinery products is about 900,000 tons. Like her neighbors, Algeria will have excess refinery capacity for some years to come. Nevertheless, a second large refinery on the coast is being considered at present. A field refinery of 200,000 tons per year capacity is operated at Hassi Messaoud in the Sahara. This plant could meet economically the immediate needs of the population centers of Tamanrasset, Gao, and Agades, about 1,600 kilometers to the south.

Algeria's gas production amounted to over 400 million cubic meters in 1963. This represents a small fraction of the country's known potential output. The only field in production at present is that of Hassi R'Mel, where the reserves are estimated at several hundred million tons and which is connected to the coast by a gas pipeline. Starting 1964, some 2 billion cubic meters of gas, equivalent to about 1 million tons, will be exported in the form of liquid methane. This method of shipping natural gas may take the place of the different direct pipeline projects across the Mediterranean into the heart of the European market.

The various fields of the eastern Sahara have not yet been exploited. Numerous deposits are known between Gassi Touil and Edjeleh, and their total reserves are believed to be nearly equal to those of Hassi R'Mel.

Algeria's huge reserves of natural gas cannot be made available at once and directly to her neighbors. A primary pipeline transmission over several hundred kilometers costs about $100,000 per kilometer length; the minimum amount of gas to justify such a pipeline is 1–2 million cubic meters per day. Neither Morocco nor Tunisia could account for more than one-third of this figure, even if all possible projects are taken into consideration.

The Algerian authorities are planning a gas pipeline from the eastern Sahara fields to a Mediterranean port where the gas could be converted into liquid methane for export. It would be to the advantage of both Algeria and Tunisia if the port of La Skhirra were choosen for that purpose. Compared with Annaba, the line would be about 300 kilometers shorter. It would also make natural gas available at low cost in the Sfax-Gabes region, where several large industrial projects are being planned by the Tunisian authorities.

Morocco's known oil and gas reserves are limited to two small fields with an annual production of 150,000 tons and total reserves of about 2 million tons. The output is treated by the old established refinery of Sidi Kassem. The second refinery in the country is a recent installation at Mohammedia, with a capacity of 1.2 million tons per year. This plant works on imported crude; the present output is 800,000 tons, which is sufficient for the internal market. Morocco has therefore a total refining capacity of about 1.5 million tons, which will not be fully utilized for some years.

Future tar and asphalt production at the Mohammedia plant is being studied. The project envisages an output capacity of 50,000 tons per year. The actual domestic requirements are about 30,00 tons per year, and the surplus might find a ready market in Algeria where the crude oil is not suitable for the manufacture of bituminous products. . . .

Morocco has substantial reserves of fossil fuel in the form of anthracite. The Jerada deposit is at present the most important producer in North Africa. Its annual production is approximately 400,000 tons. The coal has a considerable amount of fines and no coking qualities. Production costs are increasing, while export outlets are dwindling as hydrocarbon fuels replace coal as a source of energy. A limited amount of the unsalable fines is consumed in Morocco by cement and thermal power plants. The Jerada operation is not economical and has to be subsidized.

Electric-power generation in North Africa is based on the transformation of two sources of energy: water and fossil fuels. Until quite recently, the development of hydroelectric power was given priority; it could not only be combined with irrigation projects but was also more economical in the long run than thermal power which depended on imported fuels, expect in Morocco. . . . Fuel oil will be available at the national refineries in increasing quantities. However, the vast reserves of natural gas represent the most obvious material for electric-power generation. Gas is a clean fuel that is easily handled. It is a most economical source of energy, provided its transformation into electrical power is effected within reasonable distance from its production.

Libya's power generation and distribution facilities are still very limited, since no substantial industrial demand has been developed as yet. Generating plants based on the country's own resources have recently been installed in the oil fields for field operations. They are powered by natural gas from the gas-oil separation plants. A new 25-milliwatt (MW) power plant at Marsa el-Brega uses fuel oil from the refinery. It has just been started up and will service the port, and also the Zelten and Raguba fields.

Tunisia has limited hydroelectric energy resources. Thermal power provides three-quarters of the present consumption. Additional thermal plants are planned for the necessary increase of the generating capacity. The present cost of electricity production is 12 mills per kilowatt-hour (KWh) at the Tunis plant, the biggest in the country. Industrial consumers pay 20 mills per unit. It has been estimated that the projected 50-MW power plant at Gabes would be able to furnish electrical power at 12 mills per KWh to the future chemical industry to be located in that region. Such power costs are a serious handicap for large-scale industries and will delay Tunisia's industrial development. . . . It would seem preferable not to contemplate atomic-power generation in southern Tunisia for the present. . . . If natural gas becomes available in southern Tunisia by the installation of a transmission line for export, then a gas-driven power plant is a feasible project. It should, however, be remembered that the investment costs for a pipeline are about ten times those of an electrical transmission line of the same length.

Algeria's electric-power output potential is almost 2,700 gigawatt-hours (GWh), including 520 GWh which are being installed at present. The 1963 consumption amounted to about 1,000 GWh or less than half of the possible production. This country has therefore a large power surplus.

The northern provinces are well covered by a distribution network. Large plants are operating near the Moroccan border in Oran, where the installation of an additional 60-MW unit is scheduled, and near the Tunisian border at Annaba. Because of cheap natural gas, electric power can be generated in Algeria at little more than half the cost prevailing in the neighboring countries. The present sales price . . . corresponds to an electric-power generating cost of 5 mills per unit.

Morocco's main source of energy is hydroelectric power. This has been developed in combination with irrigation schemes. The installed generating capacity exceeds 300 MW. The hydroelectric power output is dependent upon rainfall; its guaranteed annual minimum is 800 GWh, though the present annual average is around 900 GWh, which represents 90% of the country's total consumption. The thermal power stations have a total generating capacity of 400 GWh. One quarter of this amount is being used at present, most of the existing plants being on a standby basis. . . .

The industrial consumer rate is 12 mills per KWh. This figure is high in view of Morocco's advanced stage of industrial development. It is difficult to evaluate the actual generating costs, in which bookkeeping plays a predominant part: the hydroelectric installations are linked with irrigation projects drawing varying amounts of water. The division of amortization charges for the required civil engineering work is not clear-cut and obviously effects the unit cost of generated power. Furthermore, Morocco has as yet few large scale consumers who use power at a steady rate. As in other developing countries the network has to cope with peak loads out of all proportion to the normal rate of consumption, and this also increases the over-all generating costs.

With a normal growth in consumption, extra generating capacity will be required after 1965 to meet peak demands. It is estimated that the power consumption in 1967 will exceed 1,500 million KWh and may approach 2,000 million by 1970. Immediate projects include a new thermal power unit of 60 MW at Casablanca, which is estimated to cost $14 million, and a smaller hydroelectric plant of 60 GWh capacity, which is now being built. . . .

The utilization of Algeria's output capacity on a sub-regional basis would result in substantial savings in each of the three countries. This can be illustrated by rough estimates, based on available information. Morocco's projected new power unit of 60 MW at Casablanca will cost $14 million and add about 300 GWh to the network. This has to be compared with the alternative capital investment of $2 million required for a link between the Algerian and Moroccan networks. It is difficult to give an exact estimate at this stage of the cost difference between Algerian power experts and Moroccan national production; the latter is probably 9–10 mills per KWh, whereas Algerian power imported into the country should cost 6–7 mills per unit. On the basis of 300 GWh, the estimated difference of 3 mills per KWh would reduce Morocco's annual power bill by $900,000.

Tunisia's new La Goulette plant of 50 MW will have an installation cost of $15 million and produce about 250 GWh. A similar plant is being considered for southern Tunisia. There are no known estimates of the cost of repairing the two existing lines that link the Tunisian and Algerian networks. The expense is unlikely to exceed $1 million. Tunisia's electric power production costs have been given as 12 mills per unit. While allowing for lower production costs with new units, there will still be a difference of at least 3 mills per unit, compared with the cost of Algerian power delivered to the Tunisian network. The annual saving would therefore amount to $750,000.

The prospective export of 500–600 GWh per year by Algeria would considerably increase the utilization factor of that country's existing power plants. This alone would result in decreased operation charges and overhead expenses per unit of power used and would therefore be an economic advantage to Algeria.

The above estimate gives an indication of the benefits to be derived by all three countries if there were a joint policy in the field of electric energy. It would result in the virtual elimination of multi-million-dollar capital investment and would also enable an annual saving of $500,000 to $1 million in each of the three countries.

MINERAL EXTRACTION AND PROCESSING

Tunisian lead mines produce at present some 2,000 tons of concentrates per month. The Djebel Hallouf smelter in western Tunisia takes the local production of about 500 tons per month. The remainder is treated by the Megrine foundry in Tunis; this is a modern plant working at half of its rated 3,000 tons per month capacity. In 1962, the resulting operating loss was reported as over $10,000 per month. The plant could break even with an additional 500 tons. This could be effected by diverting the Djebel Hallouf production to Megrine. . . .

Zinc concentrates are being produced and exported at the rate of 8,000 tons per year. This quantity is too small for local smelting. Algeria, on the other hand, produces seven times as much, and this makes zinc smelting in Algeria a distinct possibility. If this were undertaken, the treatment of Tunisian ore might be envisaged. The economics would depend on the rail transport charges. These might be greatly reduced if eastern Algeria's lead concentrates, about 4,000 tons per year, were carried as return freight across the border to the Megrine smelter.

Morocco is a significant producer of lead and zinc ores. The present rate of production is 100,000 tons of lead concentrates averaging 70% metal, and 60,000 tons per year of zinc concentrates, representing 35,000 tons of metal. A substantial part of the production is from small and medium-size workings, dispersed along the Atlas mountains, which ship their concentrates directly for export through the nearest port. The Oued el-Heimer smelter near Oujda treats the lead ore from the two most important mines in the country — Bou Beker and Touissit, which work a lead-zinc deposit extending across the border into Algeria. The smelter has an output capacity of about 18,000 tons of metal per year, which accounts for about two-thirds of the present mine production. These two mines also account for almost the entire zinc ore production in Morocco.

Algeria's production of lead and zinc concentrates in 1963 is reported as 11,574 and 56,135 tons respectively. The two mines extracting the deposit on the Moroccan border shipped 7,100 tons of lead and 48,500 tons of zinc mineral. No detailed reserve tonnage figures could be obtained, but it is generally agreed that this geological formation contains rather more ore on the Algerian than on the Moroccan side.... In 1963, the four mines on both sides of the border produced 99,000 tons of zinc concentrates, containing about 60,000 tons of metal. This production was obtained notwithstanding stoppages due to border troubles. A tonnage of this order would seem to justify the installation of a zinc smelter, provided a sufficient tonnage of ore reserves can be proved, ensuring at least twenty years of output at the present rate....

The pooling of mining and concentrating facilities would be of mutual benefit to both countries. By treating the area as one product and ignoring the political frontier, it would be possible to plan a long-term annual production rate of not less than 50,000 tons of zinc, and 15–20,000 tons of lead, and over 20,000 kilograms of silver. An over-all exploration program might prove sufficient ore reserves to consider zinc metal production. If such a smelter were located on Algerian territory, cheap energy and suitable port facilities would be available, for instance, Ghazaouet, or possibly Oran....

The most important industrial projects in the three countries are based on fertilizer manufacture. At first sight these projects appear to be directly competitive. However, the world market for certain phosphate fertilizers is large enough to warrant more than one producer-exporter in the Maghrib, where there are favorable conditions for low-cost manufacture. Each country should base its immediate production schedule on the available natural resources. Under these conditions the three big country projects would become complementary and establish the Maghrib as a major fertilizer manufacturer.

The outstanding industrial project in Morocco is a fertilizer plant based on the country's phosphate rock resources. Production and export of phosphate rock is the most important item of the country's economy and provides the largest source of income, about $90 million for 8 million tons. Morocco is the second largest producer in the world of the essential mineral in the manufacture of phosphates. It has the largest known reserves of high-grade rock, about 20 billion tons, ideally located at about 100 kilometers from the ports of Casablanca and Safi. The mining industry's labor force is 12,500.

The Safi project is well planned, and its execution has been laid out in several stages. The first step is scheduled for completion in 1965. It envisages a plant for the manufacture of 200,000 tons of triple superphosphate and 150,000 tons of diammonium phosphate a year. This project is based on the importation of liquid ammonium at the rate of 52,000 tons per year. The required sulphuric oil will be manufactured by roasting about 500,000 tons of cupreous pyrrhotite from the Kettara mine near Marrakesh. The establishment of these facilities will require an investment cost of $52 million. Export will present no difficulty, since there is a great demand for this kind of fertilizer. The domestic market may absorb about 5 per cent of production. The next step contemplated is the manufacture of ammonia and ammonium nitrate. It is estimated that Moroccan agriculture could usefully employ 36,000 tons per year of this fertilizer by 1970, which would require 16,000 tons of ammonia. Another phase of the Safi project at present under study is the extraction of copper from the pyrrhotite sinter. This would produce 2,700 tons of copper metal and an iron sinter called "purple iron," with a high iron content and almost free from impurities.

Algerian phosphate production has been based for many years on the Kouif deposit south of Annaba. The annual rate was around 400,000 tons, of which the country's superphosphate factories received about one-quarter, while the balance was exported. With the progressive extraction of the Kouif deposit, the Djebel Onk mine further south has been developed to take its place but preparations have fallen behind schedule. The reserves are 140 million tons of low-grade ore that has to be concentrated prior to shipping. For the time being, extraction will continue at Kouif at a rate of 70,000 tons per year, to meet the needs of the fertilizer plants that work exclusively for the domestic market. There are three such plants, located at Oran, Algiers, and Skikda, which manufacture a total of about 100,000 tons of superphosphate and composite fertilizers. . . .

Algeria's almost inexhaustible reserves of natural gas recommend the manufacture of ammonia and nitrogen fertilizers. Such a project [has been constructed at] for the coastal town of Arzew, east of Oran. The country's present requirements for 26% nitrogen fertilizer are estimated at 100,000 tons annually and may approximate 170,000 tons by 1970. The latter amount requires almost 60,000 tons of ammonia. An Algerian plant of economical size and using natural gas at the realistic figure of 60 cents per cubic meter could sell liquid ammonia at about $40 *f.o.b.* This would be a very competitive price in the present world market. The plant would also be an economical manufacturer of nitrogen fertilizers both for the domestic market and for export.

Phosphate rock has been Tunisia's most valuable mineral resource for many years. Its BPL content of 65% has to compete with production from Morocco (70–75), Senegal (90–83) and Togo (80+). Phosphate rock can be processed into different types of fertilizers, and this is being carried out at present by three plants in Tunisia. One small plant in Tunis produces superphosphate from the Kalaa-Djerda rock. Another factory in Sfax converts a small tonnage from the Gafsa field into hyperphosphate. The most important operation is the S.I.A.P.E. plant, also at Sfax, which produces sulphuric acid, phosphoric acid and triple superphosphate. Its present output capacity is close to 150,000 tons per year but an increase to 200,000 is projected for 1965. A second plant of 150,000 tons per year capacity and using the same process is scheduled for production in 1965.

The most important industrial project in Tunisia is the creation of a chemical industry at Gabes to produce initially synthetic ammonia, diammonium phosphate and ammonium nitrate. The annual production of these two fertilizers is projected at 200,000 and 50,000 tons, respectively. It is intended to produce the required ammonia by a 200 tons per day cracking and synthesis plant. In the absence of natural gas, the raw material for hydrogen manufacture would be naphtha; the Bizerta refinery or the La Skhirra pipeline have been mentioned as possible sources of supply. The total capital investment for the "Industries Chimiques Maghrebiennes" at Gabes has been estimated from $35 to $40 million. This includes a 14-MW power plant with seawater cooling. The

Gabes location might present a problem for the chemical plant's sweet-water requirements, and a water demineralization plant would increase the capital investment and production costs. . . .

The second stage would be the industrial development of the Gabes region. This would be greatly facilitated if a gas pipeline for export purposes is laid from an eastern Sahara field to the port of La Skhirra. Alternatively, sufficient gas reserves might be developed in the frontier region of western Tripolitania to justify a small pipeline across the border. In that case, Libyan interests would probably be willing to participate. The natural gas would be an economic fuel for the proposed 50-MW power plant at Gabes, which could produce simultaneously and at low cost several thousand cubic meters of demineralized seawater per day.

The Zarsis potash deposit southeast of Gabes has been known for many years and was not considered to be of economic interest. It was always known to contain bromine, potash, and magnesium chloride, but the tonnage was considered insignificant. A recent geophysical survey has yielded new information that indicates very substantial reserves. This will have to be clarified by drilling before chemical industries can be planned in detail. . . .

The economics of synthetic-ammonia manufacture make it advisable to construct a plant producing not less than 150,000 tons per year and using natural gas as the source of hydrogen. The estimated combined ammonia requirements of the three countries in the immediate future are of this order, that is, 50–60,000 tons per year in Algeria, 30–40,000 tons per year in Morocco, and 60,000 tons per year in Tunisia. The Moroccan Safi plant envisages a 35,000 tons per year ammonia plant using fuel oil or naphtha at an investment cost of $10 million. Tunisia's project includes the manufacture of 60,000 tons per year of ammonia, which is also based on haphtha. It is estimated that the cost of ammonia from these two undersized plants will exceed $60 per ton.

The Maghrib's immediate demands could be met most economically from a single ammonia-manufacturing plant, with an output of not less than 150,000 tons per year and working with low-cost natural gas. The investment cost would be $25–30 million, compared with about $40 million required for the three smaller plants with a similar total output. Production costs would be reduced by 5–10 per ton of ammonia, which represents a combined total annual saving of about $1 million for the three interested countries. Such a plant would also be in a favorable position to manufacture nitrate fertilizers on a sufficient scale to meet the present needs of the sub-region.

Libya's most promising mineral source, apart from oil and gas, is potash. Three main deposits are known. The Marada Carnallite deposit has been partially explored in the past. An incomplete Italian survey estimated the visible reserves of 1.6 million tons of 40 per cent K_2O and 7.5 million tons of $MgCl_2$. The salt flats cover 150 square kilometers. In 1939, the Italians produced and exported 21,000 tons of potash salts containing 40–50 per cent K_2O. An exploration concession was given in 1962 by the government of Libya to the U.S. Cabeen Exploration Company, joined by Homestake Mining Company. It may be possible that this deposit could export chloride of potash refined to 80–90 per cent KCl and having a value of around $70 per ton. Such a product would find a ready market as fertilizer in neighboring countries.

The Pisada deposit is located west of Tripoli, near the harbor of Zuara. It covers fifty square kilometers. The salts are mainly halite near the surface.

Possibly enriched zones of magnesium and potassium salts occur in depth, but this would have to be established by systematic drilling. The Idir deposits occur west of Brac in the Fezzan province and cover an area of about twenty square kilometers. Samples of the crystalline crust show a comparatively high potash content. This deposit merits further study. It should be remembered, however, that any final product would have to stand high transportation costs from this remote area. It might be possible to ship refined potash to neighboring Tunisia or Algeria.

Tunisia has in hand the setting up of a small integrated iron and steelworks in the Menzel Bourguiba region. Foundations are being put in and the equipment in the course of manufacture abroad. The object of this work is to draw upon domestic ores, one of which is difficult to sell, having an iron content of 49–52% and high arsenic; the other has an iron content of 54%. The works will comprise a blast furnace with a capacity of 220 tons per day, capable of being pushed to 300 tons. . . . Coke will be imported. In addition, there will be agglomeration facilities with a capacity of 500 tons per day; a mixer and refiner; two LD converters of 250 tons capacity; oxygen-making; two continuous casting installations to produce 90-by-90-millimeter billets; gas production; and one rolling mill, together with wire drawing.

Production is expected to start in October 1965. At the first stage, capacity will be 70,000 tons. The finished products will be reinforcement rods of 3–20 millimeter small sections and wire rods. The investment at the first stage of $15 million. The employment created will be 800, of which 700 are process workers. At the second stage, a doubling of output is envisaged, with the rolling of flat products.

The scale of output envisaged, even at the end of the second stage and in terms of all phases of the industry, is such as to make high production costs inevitable. At the blast-furnace such cost is broadly proportional to surface area, while capacity is proportional to volume, at the steel-making stage, costs decrease for the same reason, together with heat economies; and at the rolling stage, they decrease, because the larger the unit of material rolled the greater the output. In general, the so-called 0.6 rule applies, for example, if the capacity of the plant increased by 10% the cost of the plant increased only by 6%. Similarly, an increase of 10% in capacity reduces cost per unit by 4%. Again, broadly speaking, it has been shown that if the index of production cost of finished steel, including rolling and labor costs, is 100 for a capacity of 200,000 tons, it is 80 at 400,000 tons and 65 at 800,000 tons. . . .

Morocco envisaged as a first step a small electric steelworks based on scrap with a capacity of the order of 70–80,000 tons, rolling reinforcing rods, small sections, wire rods for wire-drawing and nail-manufacturing already installed, as well as galvanized wire for the manufacture of wire netting, and so on. The capacity will correspond to internal requirements in 1970.

Algeria has a small steelworks. There is no production of iron, but through an open hearth and scrap, billets are produced and rolled into reinforcing rods and small sections. The open hearth has a capacity of 30,000 tons per year, and there is a rolling mill with a capacity of 35–40,000 tons per year. . . .

The major project at Annaba, the detailed study of which is almost completed, is for the building of an integrated iron- and steelworks with a capacity of 450,000 tons of crude steel per year. The first step is iron and steel production; foundations are in the course of being finished. The equipment has been ordered abroad and is in the course of being constructed. This plant will have sintering facilities; a blast furnace using oil injection and therefore with a low coke rate and with a capacity of 1,200 tons pig iron per day; and an LD converter. The capital cost at present prices up to this stage of production is of the order of $47 million. A rough estimate of the total capital cost at present prices through the finishing stage is of the order of $185 million. Provision has been made to double capacity throughout at a later stage, at an estimated cost, at current prices, of a further $95 million. Even in terms of the first stage of the plant, the cost of billets would be fully competitive on ex-work basis with European costs. . . .

Detailed estimates of the volume and pattern of probable finish-steel consumption in North Africa in 1970 and later years have not yet been made. Average consumption of steel in the four years in 1959–61 was 610,000 tons. By 1970, total steel demand is estimated to rise to 1,650,000 tons, of which indirect consumption would account for 460,000 tons and direct 1,190,000 tons. The present product pattern is approximately 40% or more of bars, rods, and sections, 15% of flats, and more than 30% of tubes. A new product pattern is bound to emerge. . . .

The investment cost of the Annaba plant in Algeria on a half-million-ton basis and including rolling and finishing, the first stage of the Moroccan plant and the first stage of the Tunisian plant, together with an allowance for a tin-plate works serving the sub-region, but not counting any other iron- and steel-making facilities, including tube-making, is of the order of $235 million. Of this sum, perhaps $70 million have already been committed at Annaba and in Tunisia. Without an agreement in North Africa for a coordinated program of iron and steel production, much of what has already been committed may well prove to have been wasted; the remainder of the investment required is unlikely to be forthcoming. The consequence on the development of metal transforming and mechanical engineering in the Maghrib will be evident. . . .

In Tunisia, the primary metal transformation sector is developed little, if at all, but the plan provides for several projects. In Morocco, this sector is relatively developed, especially drawing of annealed coil or blank nail wire, boiler-works, iron and steel constructional works. Current needs are covered, and the potential is very high. Projects for longitudinal welded tubing (small sizes) and helicoidal (large diameters up to 1,400 mm) are also in the process of being realized. Existing equipment, plus that in process, will cover needs through 1970. Morocco possesses several iron and steel foundries with sufficient capacity to cover needs for the next five years. Algeria is also well equipped in this sector, having in action two gas-pipe factories, . . . one lightweight tubing factory, . . . one longitudinal and . . . one helicoidal welded tubing factory for large diameters, . . . [and] Boiler-works and iron and steel coundries. . . . Tunisian plans, together with the important potential and its current development in Morocco and Algeria, render coordination among the three countries indispensable. Moreover, both Algeria and Morocco possess very important railway rolling-stock works, either of which has a productive capacity sufficient to cover the Maghrib's needs. There, too, cooperation between the two countries would seem desirable for an eventual division of the range of products or to make production complementary. . . .

In Morocco, industrialization efforts undertaken have oriented some concerns toward production of certain semidurable goods — such as oil stoves, electric hot-water accumulators, locksmithery, small farm tools, other industrial accessories, conveyor-belt rollers, mining machinery parts, equipment for crushers, grinders, or the cement industry.

The setting up of automobile assembly lines has made it possible for a large number of these enterprises to find full employment and in many cases to invest in machinery and tooling for the mass production of mechanical parts for such vehicle assembly on a satisfactory economic and quality basis. This equipment is important in mechanical and subsidiary industries (boiler-work, woodwork, electrical equipment, refractory materials, control fittings, and so on). Its availability has made it possible for local industries to participate to a significant extent in the construction of new industries when large industrial complexes such as SOMACA, General Tire, Sucrerie du Beht, Complexe Chimique de Safi, and Industrie Textile were launched.

Until very recently, Tunisia had little possibility along these lines. However, the dockyard at Menzel Bourguiba, referred to later, has a potential for heavy industry through its basic equipment. Lacking precise information, it would seem at first glance that in Algeria, this type of mechanical industry has less possibility than in Morocco.

It goes without saying that coordination among the Maghrib countries will allow rapid development of this branch by way of specialization, the only avenue leading to large scale production in assembly industries. A large number of assembly industries present great possibilities for subcontracting: assembly of private cars, utility vehicles, small and large lorries, tractors — both road and tracklaying — textile equipment (needs in the Maghrib for cotton or fibrane weaving looms alone, during the next five years, run into several thousands). Highly developed coordination in the choice of types and range is indispensable to the success of such an industrialization program, owing to the large size of the series needed to lower the cost price and to the required quality and interchangeability of the parts produced. . . .

North Africa currently consumes annually 130,000 metric tons of paper and board, or 4.5 kilograms per head. This compares with 60 kilograms per head in Western Europe. Estimated consumption in the four countries here studied is as follows:

Average Consumption, 1960—62
(in thousands of metric tons)

	Newsprint	Other Paper and Paper Board	Total	Production
Algeria	23	41	64	63
Libya	1	1	2	
Morocco	4	41	45	69
Tunisia	2	17	19	27
Total	30	100	130	159
1970 estimate	60	180	240	

There are now seventeen pulp and/or paper plants in North Africa, aggregating 97,000 tons capacity of paper pulp and 103,000 tons of paper and board capacity. However, many of these are relatively small, nonintegrated, paper and board mills. Paper production is based mainly on eucalyptus and esparto, with some imported long-fiber pulp. . . .

Esparto has long been known as a paper-making material, and for many years baled and dried esparto grass was an important export for North Africa to Europe. . . . Esparto occurs naturally in all the North African countries, and given proper harvesting, a continuous supply can be maintained. If harvesting is careless, so that the grass is pulled up by the roots, not only is sustained supply affected, but soil-conservation problems arise. This seems to have happened in parts of Libya. It is natural that attention should be concentrated on esparto in North Africa, since this is one of the region's most important reserves of fiber. Moreover, during the harvesting season — normally about three months — it affords remunerative occupation to underemployed rural labor. . . .

Since eucalyptus and esparto comprise the region's main fibrous resources, it is evident that North Africa must continue to supplement its own reserves by imports of either long-fiber pulps or of those grades of paper that require a high long-fiber furnish. This severely limits the extent to which the region can hope to become self-sufficient in paper and board — even when it is conceded that technological progress has made it possible to use a higher proportion of short-fiber pulps in the finish of many grades of paper. . . . Recent studies have shown that . . . there has now arisen in Europe (and in North America) a very considerable excess of pulp and paper capacity in relation to current demand. This excess is likely to endure until toward the end of the present decade. . . .

The second fact is that Europe's pulp deficit will be first and foremost for coniferous long-fiber pulps, since many West European countries still have ample reserves of short fiber (for instance, temperate hardwoods) that can be turned to account. Moreover, there is one important fiber source — the cheapest available — that can serve as the basis for a considerable further expansion of capacity for paper board and some grades of paper. This is waste paper.

This does not necessarily rule out the possibility of establishing mills in North Africa to export short-fiber pulp to Europe. The final test lies in the relative costs of producing short-fiber pulps in Europe and in North Africa. But a number of considerations have to be borne in mind. Scale economies are very pronounced in pulp manufacture; capital costs per annual ton, for well-known reasons, tend to be somewhat higher in North Africa than in Europe; and the cost of other production factors — power, water, chemicals — may also be higher.

For these reasons, it is important that any new export-oriented plants established in North Africa be rigorously scrutinized from the standpoint of their economic viability if misinvestment is to be averted. Moreover, given the special marketing conditions that are likely to apply in the next few years, there is a strong case for reviewing pending and potential projects from the point of view of their timing, lest new supplies vastly exceed what the market can be expected to absorb. Provided these conditions are observed, it is quite possible that North Africa's fibrous reserves could eventually make a significant contribution toward the region's exchange earnings. . . .

The textile industry is normally one of the first to be laid down in a country on the way to development. Given large internal requirements, this is an industry that can develop smoothly on the basis of domestic markets. North African coordination has a part to play in the period of development of domestic industries and in the exchange of raw materials, semifinished, and finished products. The real coordination effort, however, given the growing equipment requirements, should be toward the standardization of the equipment used, so that advantage can be taken of present and potential construction facilities in North Africa. Possibilities of producing synthetic fibers can also give rise to coordinated efforts to produce equipment and to meeting the growing needs of the fibers themselves (both artificial and synthetic).

Libya produces textiles on a limited scale. . . . Tunisia has set up a national textile office with the responsibility of promoting the development of the industry. Its program is ambitious but corresponds to the real needs of the internal market. . . . Algeria imports cotton textiles to the value of 600–700 million new francs. . . . The textile industry is insufficiently developed and it has not been possible to obtain yet a sufficiently clear picture to draw up a precise program of requirements. . . . The textile industry in Morocco is well developed in all branches: cotton-spinning, combed and carded wool, weaving of cotton, fibrane, wool, rayon, nylon, embroidery, dyeing, printing, and so on. Consumption per capita is rising sharply. The increase in 1963 was 8% higher than in 1962. The differences between requirements and domestic production is covered by imports. An investment program, private and semipublic, is in the course of being executed, covering 1,500 looms in the next two years.

From the foregoing, it can be seen that one aspect of cooperation in the Maghrib could be partial manufacture under license of textile equipment. Furthermore, requirements of artificial fiber would justify the setting up of fibrane-rayon production based on the ample availability of strong-fiber cellulose pulp produced from eucalyptus at the Sidi Yahya works. Given that from 30,000 tons per year viable production can be envisaged, the natural location of such a works should be as near as possible to the pulp and therefore in the Kenitra region, which has port facilities and where the supply of water and evacuation of waste give rise to no problems.

Note

1. A large oilfield at el-Borma astride the Algero-Tunisian border has since been discovered and tapped.

Appendix A:

A Statistical Summary of the Contemporary
Maghrib

The following tables are designed to
provide up-to-date informational sum-
maries in a readily accessible form to
supplement the preceding articles. The
statistical information is relatively accurate, although the precision of figures
is often misleading in social matters.
Where possible, spaced time series figures
have been given to illustrate important
aspects of social change and development. In many cases, the tables are
presented to update figures given in
earlier articles, so that the reasoning and
flow of the articles could be left undisturbed as written.

TABLE 1

LAND USE

(in thousands of square kilometers)[a]

	Morocco	Algeria	Tunisia	Libya
Total area	445.0	2,381.7	164.1	1,760.5
Meadow and pasture	76.5	343.8	56.5	11.4
Forest	53.5	30.5	8.4	0.5
Arable land	78.6	67.8	43.3	23.8
Cultivated land	50.0	40.0	40.0	10.0
Former colonial land	10.3[b]	27.3[b]	8.5[b]	3.1[b]

SOURCES:*Food and Agriculture Organization Production Yearbook 1967, p. 6. Maghreb,* No. 18 (November 1966), p. 70. Libyan 1960 Agricultural Census. Enrico deLeone, *La Colonizzazione del Africa del Nord* (Padua: CEDAM, 1960), II, 562-65.

[a]1,000 square kilometers = 10,000 hectares
[b]Divided among the following number of former colonial owners: Morocco, 5,000; Algeria, 22,000; Tunisia, 4,000; and Libya, 6,000.

TABLE 2

MUSLIM LANDOWNERSHIP

(in thousands)

	Morocco		Algeria		Tunisia	
	No. of Owners	No. of Hectares	No. of Owners	No.of Hectares	No. of Owners	No. of Hectares
0-1 ha	446	238	106	37		
1-4 ha	439	945				
0-5 ha					133	307
4-8 ha	137	815				
5-10 ha					73	512
1-10 ha			333	1,341		
8-15 ha	60	685				
15-20 ha	9	173				
10-20 ha					64	888
20-50 ha					42	1,304
10-50 ha			167	3,186	(106)	(2,192)
20+ha	15	535				
50-100 ha			17	1,096	8	562
100+ha			8	1,689	5	1,449
Total	1,106	3,391	631	7,349	325	5,022

SOURCE: André Tiano, *Le Maghreb entre les mythes* (Paris: Presses Universitaires de France, 1967), p. 281.

TABLES 3

POPULATION GROWTH, 1935-75

(in thousands)

YEAR	Morocco	Algeria	Tunisia	Libya
1935-36	7,040[a]	7,234[a]	2,538[a]	849
1956	10,396	9,962	3,783	1,171
1960	11,626[a]	10,784	4,168	1,325
1966	12,820	12,093[a]	4,458[a]	1,682
1970 (estimated)	15,379[a]	13,300	4,644	1,940
1975 (projected)	18,226	15,500	6,543	2,324

SOURCES: Amor Benyoussef, *Populations du Maghreb et Communauté économique à Quatre* (Paris: SEDES, 1967), pp. 93, 370. *United Nations Statistical Yearbook 1965*, pp. 80-82. *United Nations Demographic Yearbook 1961*, pp. 126-28. *United Nations Demographic Yearbook 1967*, pp. 124-25. *Libyan Statistical Abstract 1966*, p. 3. *League of Nations Monthly Bulletin of Statistics 1939, no. 20.*

[a]Census figure (censuses prior to 1960 were incomplete). Libyan census was made in 1964. Third Moroccan census was taken in 1970.

TABLE 4

POPULATION GROWTH RATES AND DENSITY

	Morocco	Algeria	Tunisia	Libya
Annual rate of growth	3.2%	3.1%	2.9%	2.8%
Cumulative rate of growth, 1958-62	12.0%	8.4%	5.6%	7.6%
Years required for population to double	23	23	29	27
Population density per square kilometer	30	5	27	1
Population density per arable square kilometer	170	167	102	64

SOURCES: *Economic Commission for Africa Demographic Handbook for Africa 1968*, p.18. Georges Sabagh, "The Demography of the Middle East," *Middle East Studies Association Bulletin,* IV, No. 2 (May, 1970).

TABLE 5

PERCENTAGE OF AGE DISTRIBUTION, 1966

Age	Morocco	Algeria	Tunisia	Libya
0-9 years	34	34	31	34
10-19 years	23	22	21	18
20-39 years	27	24	27	28
40-65 years	14	15	18	16
Over 65 years	3	5	4	5

SOURCES: *Economic Commission for Africa Demographic Handbook for Africa 1968,* p. 26.

TABLE 6

PERCENTAGE OF MUSLIM POPULATION LIVING IN TOWNS, 1954, 1960, and 1966

	Morocco			Algeria		
	Over 100,000	Over 20,000	Over 10,000	Over 100,000	Over 20,000	Over 10,000
1954	16.5	23.6	25.2	12.3	18.0	20.4
1960	18.9	23.7	26.5	16.4	21.6	26.8
1966	19.4	n.a.	n.a.	13.4	26.5	32.0

	Tunisia			Libya		
	Over 100,000	Over 20,000	Over 10,000	Over 100,000	Over 20,000	Over 10,000
1954	10.8[a]	20.7[a]	26.6[a]	11.9	18.3	30.0
1960	10.6	21.9	n.a.	n.a.	n.a.	n.a.
1966	10.4	22.9	30.1	22.5[b]	22.5[b]	24.5[b]

Sources: Samir Amin, *L'Economie du Maghreb* (Paris: Minuit, 1966), I, 28. *United Nations Demographic Yearbook 1967,* p. 140. Algerian census. *Economic Commission for Africa Demographic Handbook for Africa 1968,* pp. 39, 45.

n.a.: not available

[a] Figures for 1956.
[b] Figures for 1964.

TABLE 7

CITIES OF OVER 100,000 POPULATION, 1954 and 1966

(in thousands)

Rank City in 1966		Morocco		Algeria		Tunisia		Libya	
		1951	1966	1954	1966	1956	1966	1954	1967
1	Casablanca	682	1,120						
2	Algiers			525	943				
3	Tunis					410	642		
4	Oran			299	328				
5	Rabat	156	276						
6	Marrakesh	215	275						
7	Fes	179	255						
8	Constantine			150	253				
9	Tripoli							140	205
10	Meknes	140	200						
11	Annaba (Bone)			114	152				
12	Tangier	165	135						
13	Oujda	81	125						
14	Benghazi							50	113

SOURCES: Werner Plum, *Sozialer Wandel im Maghreb* (Hanover: Verlag fur Literatur und Zeilgeschehen, 1967), p. 268. *United National Demographic Yearbook 1967*, pp. 206-7. *Economic Commission for Africa Demographic Handbook for Africa 1968*, pp. 44 ff.

TABLE 8

MINORITY POPULATIONS, VARIOUS YEARS, 1952-68

(in thousands)[a]

Year	Minority	Morocco	Algeria	Tunisia	Libya
1952	Jews	255 (2.7)	140 (1.5)	105 (2.9)	35 (3.5)[b]
1955	Foreign	450 (4.4)	984 (10.0)	155 (6.5)	47 (4.3)
1961	Foreign	365 (3.1)	1,040 (9.7)	110 (2.6)	n.a.
1963	Foreign	295 (2.3)	140 (1.3)	68 (1.6)	49 (3.1)
1963	Jews	130 (1.1)	5 (0.0)	30 (0.7)	4 (0.2)
1966	Foreign	150 (1.1)	81 (0.7)	30 (0.7)	n.a.
1966	Jews	100 (0.8)	1 (0.0)	15 (0.3)	n.a.
1968	Jews	50 (0.4)	1 (0.0)	8 (0.2)	.3 (.0)
1960	Berber-Speaking	(35)	(18)	(5)	(5)

SOURCES: Werner Plum, *Sozialer Wandel im Maghreb* (Hanover: Verlag fur Literature und Zeitgeschehen, 1967,) pp. 29-30. *Maghreb,* No. 27 (May 1968), pp. 24-36. Samir Amin, *L'Economie du Maghreb* (Paris: Minuit, 1966), I, 23, 25, 27.

n.a.: not available

[a]Figures in parentheses represent percentage of total population.

[b]Figures for 1948.

TABLE 9

SCHOOL POPULATION, 1966

(in thousands)[a]

School Level	Morocco	Algeria	Tunisia	Libya
Primary (age 6-12)	1,124 (42)	1,332 (57)	734 (83)	195 (78)
Secondary (age 13-19) (including technical)	211 (11)	116 (8)	104 (18)	28 (16)
Higher (age 20-24) (including specialized)	9	10	10	2
Total	1,344	1,458	848	225

SOURCES: *Moroccan Five-Year Plan II*, pp. 582-84. *Algerian Report to UNESCO Conference on Public Education 1966*, p. 14, *1968*, pp. 22-23. *Tunisian Annuaire Statistique*, 15:39. *Libyan Statistical Abstract 1966*, p. 57. *International Yearbook of Education, 1967*, pp. 513-14, 518, 528, *Moroccan Report to UNESCO Conference 1966*, pp. 12-14. *UNESCO Statistical Yearbook 1969*, pp. 70-77.

[a]Figures in parentheses represent percentage of eligible age group.

TABLE 10

PERCENTAGE OF FEMALES IN TOTAL SCHOOL POPULATION, 1966

School Level	Morocco	Algeria	Tunisia	Libya
Primary	29	38	35	28
Secondary (including technical)	27	30	28	14
Higher (including specialized)	11	16	19	8

SOURCES: Same as Table 9.

TABLE 11

UNIVERSITY DISCIPLINARY SPECIALIZATION, 1966[a]

Discipline	Morocco	Algeria	Tunisia	Libya
Law and social sciences	2,382	2,340	1,165	789
Philosophy and letters	1,357	2,304	1,307	893
Science and medicine	1,461	4,666	1,129	537
Teachers' college	1,875	320	652	112

SOURCES: Same as Table 9.

[a]Including Islamic higher education.

TABLE 12

DISTRIBUTION OF THE LABOR FORCE, 1960-66

(in per cent)

	Morocco[a]	Algeria[b]	Tunisia[c]	Libya[d]
Active population	24	15	28	30
Agricultural sector	62	70	57	42
Industrial sector	13	10	22	20
Service sector	25	20	21	38

SOURCES: André Tiano, *Le Maghreb entre les mythes* (Paris: Presses Universitaires de France, 1967), pp. 110-17. *Libyan Statistical Abstract 1966,* pp. 10-17.

[a]First figure for the year 1960, subsequent figures for 1965.

[b]All figures for the year 1966.

[c]All figures for the year 1964.

[d]First figure for the year 1966, subsequent figures for 1964.

TABLE 13

MILITARY PERSONNEL AND DEFENSE BUDGETS, 1967

(in thousands)

	Morocco	Algeria	Tunisia	Libya
Army	45.0	50.0	13.0	7.0
Air Force	2.6	3.5	1.0	.8
Navy	1.4	1.5	.5	.2
Gendarmery	3.0	8.0	5.0	—
Police	14.0	30.0	3.0	12.0
Defense budget[a]	$63	$106	$16	$27
Defense budget as percentage of GNP	2.4%	4%	1.7%	2.3%

SOURCE: American Universities Field Staff Reports, XIII, No. 9 (May, 1967), 24.

[a]In millions.

TABLE 14

GROSS AND PER CAPITA NATIONAL PRODUCT, 1957 and 1966

	Morocco		Algeria		Tunisia		Libya	
	1957	1966	1957	1966	1957	1966	1957	1966
Gross national product (in millions of $US)	1441	2600	1807	2700	662	935	68	1200
Per capita national product (in $US)	142	193	178	225	173	208	60	750

SOURCE: American Universities Field Staff Reports, XIII, No. 9 (May, 1967), 24.

TABLE 15

FOREIGN TRADE, 1962 and 1966

(in millions of dollars)

Exports and Imports	Morocco		Algeria		Tunisia		Libya	
	1962	1966	1962	1966	1962	2966	1962	1966
Total exports	345.3	428.5	733.5	758.3	115.7	140.6	141.1	995.0
Total imports	429.7	478.0	784.7	676.4	216.1	249.9	205.7	404.5
Exports to developed areas	275.5	338.8	720.6	728.5	99.1	104.5	138.6	985.9
Imports from developed areas	335.0	360.2	725.8	648.9	194.1	197.2	187.6	338.8
Exports to first partner[a]	135.4	196.5	592.0	507.2	61.3	48.6	16.4 / 26.1	331.5 / 113.3
Imports from first partner[b]	183.0	192.9	619.1	480.8	113.4	86.0	49.5	111.9
Exports to less developed areas	35.5	23.0	12.9	29.8	7.6	20.3	2.2	8.9
Imports from less developed areas	33.3	52.8	58.9	27.5	10.8	25.1	11.7	34.8

SOURCE: United Nations Annual Direction of Trade (IMF-IBRD), 1962-1966.

[a]France (For Morocco, Algeria, Tunisia) or Germany and Italy (for Libya)
[b]France (for Morocco, Algeria, Tunisia) or Italy (for Libya)

TABLE 16

GOVERNMENT BUDGETS, 1966 and 1970

(in millions of dollars)

Expenses and Revenues	Morocco		Algeria		Tunisia		Libya	
	1966	1970	1966	1970	1966	1970	1966	1970
Operating expenses	$433	$587	$640	$889	$176	$295	$252	$512
Development expenses	162	445	453	1,347	91	137	272	560
Tax revenues (excl. oil)	289	534	495	728	137	215	101	n.a.
Nontax revenues	260	458	41	262	130	n.a.	35	n.a.
Oil revenues	0	0	140	267	0	n.a.	390	700

SOURCES: André Tiano, *Le développement économique du Maghreb* (Paris: Presses Universitaires de France, 1968), pp. 113, 117, 119. *Annuaire de l'Afrique du Nord 1967* (Paris: CNRS, 1968), pp. 541-45. *Maghrcb*, no. 38 (March 1970), pp. 11-20, and no. 40 (July 1970), pp. 12-13.

n.a.: not available

TABLE 17

CONSUMER PRICE INDEX, 1958-68

Country	1958	1959	1960	1961	1962	1963	1964	1965	1966	1967	1968	1969	1970
Morocco	83.4	83.7	88.4	90	94.5	100.0	104.1	107.6	106.5	105.7	106.2	109.3	111.0
Algeria	84.1	92.3	96.9	100.0	103.9	n.a. ∠100.0	105.4	103.1	103.5	n.a.	n.a.	n.a.
Tunisia	105.7	102.6	99.9	104.1 ∠97.4	100.0	104.2	111.1	115.4	118.8	121.7	126.8	128.0
Libya	n.a.	n.a.	n.a.	n.a.	n.a.	n.a. ∠100.0	105.8	114.3	118.5	123.6	134.2	132.9

SOURCE: *International Labor Organization Yearbook of Labor Statistics 1968*, pp. 648-49, and *ibid. 1971*, pp. 549-554.

n.a.: not available

∠ indicates new index

TABLE 18

ELECTRICITY PRODUCTION, 1953, 1960, and 1968

(in millions of kilowatt hours)

Year	Morocco	Algeria	Tunisia	Libya
1953	780	771	203	50
1960	1,012	1,325	316	105
1968	1,538	1,305	680	274

SOURCE: *United Nations Statistical Yearbook 1969*, pp. 337-344.

Note: Morocco, Algeria, and Libya include public usage only. Tunisia includes about 20 per cent override of self-consumed industrial electricity.

TABLE 19

OIL PRODUCTION AND RESERVES

(in millions of metric tons)

	Morocco	Algeria	Tunisia	Libya
Production in 1950	.1	.1	—	—
Production in 1964	.1	26.5	—	41.5
Production in 1966	.1	33.2	.5	72.3
Production in 1970	.1	47.3	4.1	161.7
Published proven reserves in 1969 (and percentage of world total)	.1 (-)	1096 (1.7)	69 (.01)	4795　(7.2)

SOURCE: *Middle East and North Africa 1967-68,* (London: Europa, 1967), p. 51, and *ibid., 1970-1971*, p. 55.

TABLE 20

REFINING CAPACITY, 1960 and 1966

(in thousands of metric tons)

Year	Morocco	Algeria	Tunisia	Libya
1960	150	—	—	—
1969	1,650	2,300	1,000	795

SOURCE: Same as Table 19.

TABLE 21

DUES-PAYING MEMBERSHIP OF POLITICAL PARTIES AND LABOR UNIONS

(in thousands)

	Morocco		Algeria		Tunisia		Libya	
	1956	1965	1956	1965	1956	1965	1951	1965
Political party or parties	2,000	50[a]	30	330	500	400	10-100[a]	0
Labor union or unions	300	250	80	120	110	80	2	37

SOURCES: Eqbal Ahmed, *Labor and Politics in North Africa* (Princeton, N.J.: Princeton University Press, pending). Lars Rudebeck, *Party and People* (New York: Praeger Publishers, 1970), p. 199. Clement Henry Moore, *Tunisia Since Independence* (Berkeley: University of California Press, 1965), p. 113. Douglas E. Ashford, *Political Change in Morocco* (Princeton, N.J.: Princeton University Press, 1961), p. 246. Nicola Ziadeh, *Libya—1948 (Official Documents)* (Beirut: American University of Beirut, 1966), pp. 60-63, 158-60. Michael K. Clark, *Algeria in Turmoil: A History of the Rebellion* (New York: Praeger Publishers, 1959), p. 299.

[a] Estimate

TABLE 22

PARTICIPATION IN ALL ELECTIONS, 1952-69

	Number of Registered Voters (in thousands)	Percentage of Registered Voters Voting	Number of Candates Per Seat	Results
Morocco				
Communal Councils (May 29, 1960)	4,172	71	5	Istiqlal 40% of seats, UNFP 25%
Constitution (December 7, 1962)	4,655	84	—	95% in favor
House of Representatives (May 17, 1963[a]	4,785	73	n.a.	FDIC 34%, Istiqlal 30%, UNFP 22%
Communal Councils (July 23, 1963)	4,818	76	2	FDIC landslide, others boycott
Communal Councils (October 3, 1969)	(4,800)	80	2	Independents landslide

	Number of Registered Voters (in thousands)	Percentage of Registered Voters Voting	Number of Candates Per Seat	Results
Constitution (July 24, 1970)	4,847	93	–	99% in favor
House of Representatives (August 28, 1970)	4,853	85	3	independents' landslide, others boycott.
Constitution (March 1, 1972)	4,864	93	–	99% in favor bot higged.
Algeria				
Independence (July 1, 1962)	6,562	91	–	99% in favor
Constituent Assembly (September 20, 1962)	6,328	82	1	98% in favor
Constitution (September 8, 1963)	6,392	83	–	97% in favor
President (September 19, 1963)	6,581	89	1	98% in favor
National Assembly (September 20, 1964)[b]	6,248	82	1	98% in favor
Communal Councils (February 5, 1967)	5,200	70	2	Choice among FLN candidates
Provincial Councils (May 25, 1969)	5,735	72	2	Choice among FLN candidates
Communal councils (February 14, 1971)	(6,000)	76	2	Choice Among FLN candidates
Tunisia				
Constituent Assembly (March 25, 1956)	726	83	1	National Front 97%
Municipal Councils (May 5, 1957)	372	78	1.5	Neo-Destour landslide
President and National Assembly (November 8, 1959)	1,100	92	1	Bourguiba 99%, Neo-Destour, 98%
Municipal Councils (May 15, 1960)	438	84	1	No contest
Municipal Councils (May 12, 1963)	514	85	1	Half incumbents
President and National Assembly (November 8, 1964)	1,302	97	1	Bourguiba 99%
Municipal Councils (May 15, 1960)	438	84	1	No contest
Municipal Councils (May 12, 1963)	514	85	1	Malf incumbents
President and National Assembly (November 8, 1964)	1,302	97	1	Bourginba 99%
Municipal Councils (May 15, 1966)	588	91	1	One-third incumbents
Municipal Councils (May, 4, 1969)	691	91	1	No contest
President and National Assembly (November 2, 1969)	1,453	95	1	Bourguiba and PSD 99%

	Number of Registered Voters (in thousands)	Percentage of Registered Voters Voting	Number of Candates Per Seat	Results
Libya				
National Assembly (January 19-February 7, 1952)	n.a.	n.a.	n.a.	NCP won Tripoli, Indepents rest
National Assembly (January 7, 1956)	n.a.	n.a.	2	One-third contested, no parties
National Assembly (January 17, 1960)	n.a.	n.a.	3	Seven-eighths contested, no parties
National Assembly (October 10, 1964)c	(600)	70	2	Two-thirds contested, no parties, fraud, women voted
National Assembly (May 8, 1965)d	n.a.	n.a.	3	Five-sixths contested, no parties

aNational Assembly dissolved, June 7, 1965.

bNational Assembly dissolved, June 19, 1965.

cNational Assembly dissolved, February 3, 1965.

dNational Assembly dissolved, May 8, 1969.

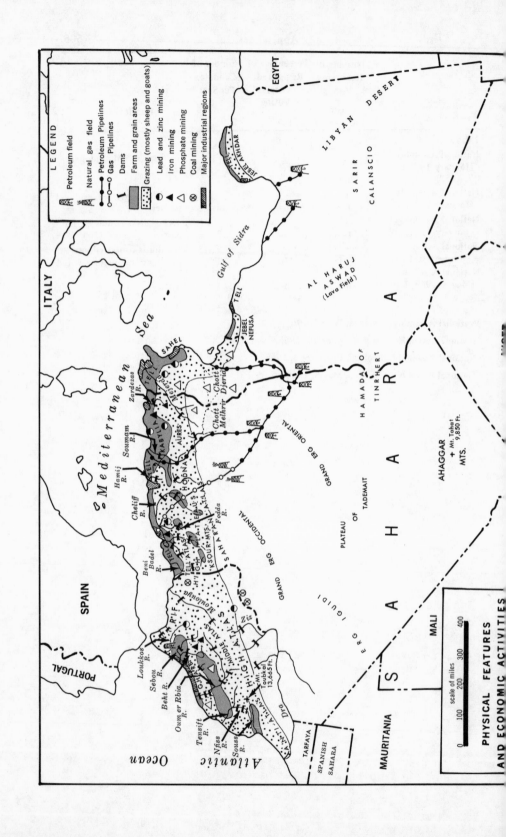

PHYSICAL FEATURES
AND ECONOMIC ACTIVITIES

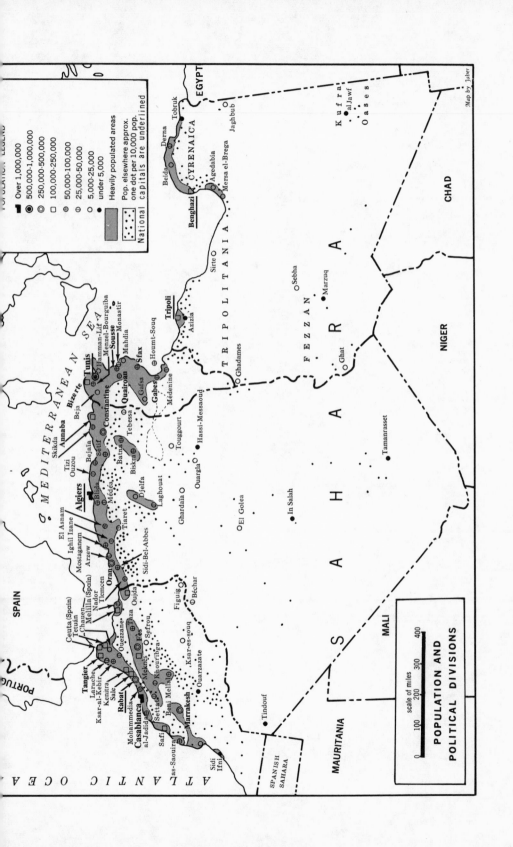

POPULATION LEGEND

Over 1,000,000
500,000-1,000,000
250,000-500,000
100,000-250,000
50,000-100,000
25,000-50,000
5,000-25,000
under 5,000
Heavily populated areas

Pop. elsewhere approx.
one dot per 10,000 pop.
capitals are underlined
National capitals are underlined

**POPULATION AND
POLITICAL DIVISIONS**

scale of miles
0   100   200   300   400

Map by Tuber

BIBLIOGRAPHY

Topical bibliographical evaluations have been given in the introduction to each section, and references are included in the footnotes to the articles reprinted; most of these will not be repeated here. The following essay focuses instead on the region and its component states. It does not include works devoted primarily to pre-independence history, nor fiction.

THE MAGHRIB

The best book on the region since independence is Clement Henry Moore, *Politics in North Africa* (Boston: Little, Brown, 1970). The study combines a modified systemic approach to comparative politics, building on the work of Gabriel Almond, with a sensitive understanding of the culture and dynamics of the region. A work with greater breadth and diversity but inevitably less internal coherence is L. Carl Brown (ed.), *State and Society in Independent North Africa* (Washington, D.C.: Middle East Institute, 1966); a considerable amount of information and several unique studies by Berque, Le Tourneau and others are found in this collection. Charles Gallagher, *The United States and North Africa* (Cambridge, Mass.: Harvard University Press, 1963), although it has little to do with the United States, is a sound and sensitive synthesis, less analytical than Moore's but somewhat more oriented toward cultural aspects. David Gordon, *North Africa's French Legacy 1954-1962* (Cambridge, Mass.: Harvard University Press, 1964), is a small gem that shows deep understanding of the Maghribi soul, torn between what is modern and French and what is Arabo-Muslim and traditional. The latest work of Samir Amin, *Le Maghreb moderne* (Paris: Minuit, 1970), is an important contribution that argues the evolutionary similarity of the three countries.

The best survey of contemporary history, which combines dispassionate scholarship with long personal acquaintance with the region, is Roger Le Tourneau, *L'évolution politique de l'Afrique du Nord Musulmane, 1920-1961*

(Paris: Armand Colin, 1062); there is nothing in English to equal it. Jacques Berque, *French North Africa: The Maghreb Between Two World Wars* (New York: Praeger Publishers, 1967), offers more social detail but covers a shorter period. Nevill Barbour (ed.), *A Survey of Northwest Africa — The Maghrib* (2d ed.; London and New York: Oxford University Press, 1962), now a history, treats segments of the area and its fringes in detail but has a rather encyclopedic approach to the rest; the original edition of the book, published in 1959, was the first English-language work on the region. The first work to come from the new American wave of scholarship on the Maghrib was Lorna Hahn, *North Africa: Nationalism to Nationhood* (Washington, D.C.: Public Affairs Press, 1960); it is still valuable, particularly on the nationalist period, despite errors. Richard M. Brace, *Morocco, Algeria, Tunisia* (Englewood Cliffs, N.J.: Prentice-Hall, 1964), is thin, inaccurate, and not recommended. A fine German-language work that compares well with Le Tourneau in comprehension and insight, although it covers a shorter period of time, is Wilhelm Fernau, *Arabischer Westen* (Stuttgart: Schwab, 1959). A shorter but valuable conceptual work is Jean-Louis Duclos, *et al., Les nationalismes maghrébins* (Paris: Fondation Nationale des Sciences Politiques, 1966).

Three works treat the political development of the Maghrib within a larger context. Manfred Halpern, *The Politics of Social Change in the Middle East and North Africa* (Princeton, N.J.: Princeton University Press, 1963), is organized around the concept of social forces; I. William Zartman, *Government and Politics in Northern Africa* (New York: Praeger Publishers, 1963), is based on a comparison of national units; J.C. Hurewitz, *Middle East Politics: The Military Dimension* (New York: Praeger Publishers, 1969), focuses on military organization by type and by country. Douglas E. Ashford, *National Development and Local Reform* (Princeton, N.J.: Princeton University Press, 1967), provides an incisive comparison of the approach to local politics in two North African countries (Morocco and Tunisia), as well as in Pakistan.

Four excellent studies approaching development from the socio-economic point of view appeared at approximately the same time, and each has such a broad command of the data that a choice among them is difficult. They are Samir Amin, *L'économie du Maghreb* (2 vols.; Paris: Minuit, 1966); Amor Benyoussef, *Populations du Maghreb et communauté économique à quatre* (Paris: SEDES, 1967); Werner Plum, *Sozialer Wandel im Maghreb* (Hanover: Verlag für Literatur und Zeitgeschehen, 1967); and André Tiano, *Le Maghreb entre les mythes* (Paris: Presses Universitaires de France, 1967). Shorter treatments are André Tiano, *Le développement économique du Maghreb* (Paris: Presses Universitaires de France, 1968), and René Galissot, *L'économie de l'Afrique du Nord* (Paris: Presses Universitaires de France, 1961). Two valuable symposia on specific problems of economic development are *Industrialisation au Maghreb* (Paris: Maspero, 1963), and *Reforme agraire au Maghreb* (Paris: Maspero, 1964). Gregori Lazarev and Jacques Dubois, *Institutions et développement agricole du Maghreb* (Paris: Presses Universitaires de France, 1967), is a more useful contribution to the debate on rural change in North Africa than is the more legalistic Jean-Maurice Verdier, *et al., Structures foncières et développement rural au Maghreb* (Paris: Presses Universitaires de France, 1968); the first work does not include a chapter on Tunisia, however. On a rather unique segment of the North African population — the Berbers —

two books are recommended, in addition to more specific works cited under the individual countries: the older, shorter summary by G. H. Bosquet, *Les Berberes* (Paris: Presses Universitaires de France, 1956), and the excellent new collection edited by Charles Micaud and Ernest Gellner, *Arabs and Berbers in North Africa: A Study of Ethnic Group Relations* (Boston: Heath Lexington, 1973). Finally, socio-economic development is approached from the point of view of human and physical geography in the best of the rare geographies of the region, Jean Despois, *L'Afrique du Nord* (Paris: Presses Universitaires de France, 1958), and *Géographie de l'Afrique du Nord* (Paris: Payot, 1967).

No review of the literature would be complete without special mention of the *Annuaire de l'Afrique du Nord* (Paris: CNRS,yearly since 1962), which has published increasingly sophisticated and penetrating articles on North African society, polity, and economy, filling many of the gaps left by books and journal articles. The other essential publication for any student of the Maghrib is *Maghreb* (Documentation française, bimonthly), which is more reportorial but also more up to date. The journal's "predecessor" was *Confluent* (Rabat, monthly), which was more a journal of opinion and less reportorial; the latter function was filled by *Maghreb (Labor) Digest* (University of Southern California, bimonthly), now also defunct.

MOROCCO

Probably the single best study of Morocco is the latest: John Waterbury, *The Commander of the Faithful* (New York: Columbia University Press, 1970), a richly informed work that interprets Moroccan politics in the light of historical segmentary patterns of interaction with the monarchy. Douglas E. Ashford, *Political Change in Morocco* (Princeton, N.J.: Princeton University Press, 1961), the first developmental study of a North African country, offers an extensive cross-sectional portrayal of Morocco before the 1960 single-party split. I. William Zartman, *Destiny of a Dynasty* (Columbia: University of South Carolina Press, 1964), covers the period to the constitutional elections of 1963 but focuses on institutionalization. I. William Zartman, *Problems of New Power* (New York: Atherton Press, 1964), is one of the few books on the developing world to deal with the policy process, output, and decision-making, in this case during the five-year independent reign of Mohammed V, but it suffers from the absence of an explicit theoretical framework. Finally, among the recommended general works, Jean and Simone Lacouture, *Le Maroc à l'épreuve* (Paris: Seuil, 1958), is an example of European journalism at its very best; for all its outdatedness, it remains one of the most insightful and comprehensive works on independent Morocco. An important, if uneven, forward-looking political statement by a Moroccan is Mohammed Lahbabi, *Les annees 80 de notre jeunesse* (Casablanca: Editions Maghrebines, 1970). Among the weaker general works, Jacques Robert, *La monarchie marocaine* (Paris: Librairie Générale de Droit et de Jurisprudence, 1962), is dry and legalistic; Lorna Hahn and Mark I. Cohen, *Morocco: Old Land, New Nation* (New York: Praeger Publishers, 1966), is contentious and contradictory; and Rom Landau, *Morocco Independent Under Mohammed the Fifth* (London: George Allen & Unwin, 1961), is well intentioned but unsophisticated. Two more popularized versions of Moroccan history and current events are Nevill Barbour, *Morocco* (New York: Walker, 1965), and Vincent Monteil, *Morocco* (New York: Viking Press, 1964).

Without going into colonial or precolonial history, there are excellent works on the nationalist background to independence that help to make independent politics understandable. Robert Rezette, *Les partis politiques marocains* (Paris: Armand Colin, 1955), Albert Ayache, *Le Maroc: Bilan d'une colonisation* (Paris: Editions Sociales, 1956), Stephane Bernard, *The Franco-Moroccan Conflict, 1943-1956* (New Haven, Conn.: Yale University Press, 1968), an abridged, one-volume edition of the three-volume French work (Brussels: Institute de Sociologie, 1963), Ladislav Cerych, *Européens et Marocains 1930-1956* (Bruges: de Tempel, 1964), and John P. Halstead, *The Origins and Rise of Moroccan Nationalism* (Cambridge, Mass.: Harvard Middle East Center, 1967), all have sound data and good analysis. Paul Buttin, *Le drame du Maroc* (Paris: Cerf, 1955), is one of the best French liberal views of the events; 'Allal al-Fassi, *The Independence Movement in Arab North Africa* (Washington, D.C.: American Council of Learned Societies, 1954), speaks for the Istiqlal. Arguments for the legal bases of the Moroccan monarchy may be found in Jacques Bonjean, *L'unité de l' Empire chérifien* (Paris: Librairie Générale de Droit et de Jurisprudence, 1955), and Mohammed Lahbabi, *Le gouvernement marocain à l'aube du XXe siècle* (Rabat: Editions Techniques Nord-Africaines, 1958); both books are serious and readable.

The most comprehensive economic treatment of Morocco is John W. Beyen *et al., The Economic Development of Morocco* (Baltimore, Md.: Johns Hopkins Press, 1966), which is more digestible than its origins as a World Bank mission report might indicate. Charles F. Stewart, *The Economy of Morocco, 1912-1962* (Cambridge, Mass.: Harvard University Press, 1964), and André Tiano, *La politique économique et financière du Maroc indépendant* (Paris: Presses Universitaires de France, 1963), are both sound; the former is largely historical (focusing on the Protectorate), the latter much more critical. Both characteristics are combined in an important specialized work by 'Abdel'aziz Belal, *L'investissement au Maroc (1912-1964) et ses enseignements en matière de développement économique* (Paris: Mouton, 1968), in which the author goes well beyond the limits of his Marxist origins. Two other critical works by Moroccan economists are Fathallah Oualalou, *L'assistance économique face an développement économique du Maroc* (Casablanca: Editions Maghrébines, 1969) and Abdelhadi Benamor, *Intermediation financiérse et développement économique du Maroc* (Casablanca: Editions Maghrébines, 1970). Two studies of economic planning are informative but somewhat brief and technical: Douglas E. Ashford, *Morocco-Tunisia: Politics and Planning* (Syracuse, N.Y.: Syracuse University Press, 1965), and Albert Waterson, *Planning in Morocco* (Baltimore, Md.: Johns Hopkins Press, 1962). Mention should also be made of *Entwicklung und Entwicklungs politik in Marokko: Zusammenfassung der Ergebnisse und Empfehlungen, ausgerichtet nach Prioritäten* (Bonn: Forschungsinstitut für Wirtschaftsfragen der Entwicklungsländer, 1967).

It is striking that most of the writing on political philosophy coming out of North Africa is Moroccan. In addition to the bibliographies of Mehdi ben Barka's and 'Allal al-Fassi's works, given in the introduction to chapter three, above, Mohammed 'Abdel'aziz Lahbabi, *Le personnalisme musulman* (Paris: Presses Universitaires de France, 1964), and 'Abdallah Laroui, *L'ideologie arabe contemporaine* (Paris: Maspero, 1967) should be noted; the latter will remain important long into the future.

It is in the fields of sociology and anthropology that quality studies have most frequently appeared, a legacy of both the strength and the limitations of the colonial period. Three classic works that date from the colonial era are necessary to an understanding of social reality in Morocco today: Robert Montagne, *Les Berbères et le Makhzen dans le Sud du Maroc* (Paris: Alcan, 1930); Robert Montagne (ed.), *La Naissance du proletariat marocain* (Paris: Peyronnet [1951]; and Jacques Berque, *Structures sociales du haut Atlas* (Paris: Presses Universitaires de France, 1955). Three Frenchmen who remained in Morocco have continued this tradition in exhaustive studies: Jean LeCoz, *Le Rharb: fellahs et colons* (Rabat: Association des Sciences de l'Homme, 1968); Julien Couleau, *La Paysannerie marocaine* (Paris: CNRS, 1968); and Daniel Noin, *La population rurale du Maroc* (Paris: PUF, 1971). In English there are the meticulous conceptual studies of Ernest Gellner, *Saints of the Atlas* (Chicago: University of Chicago Press, 1970) [Zawia Ahansal]. B.G. Hoffman, *The Structure of Traditional Moroccan Society* (Paris: Mouton, 1967), attempts to aggregate Moroccan ethnological work in a background volume, but the result — although instructive — is uneven and often misleading. A small masterpiece, for reasons of both method and content, is Clifford Geertz, *Islam Observed: Religious Development in Morocco and Indonesia* (New Haven, Conn.: Yale University Press, 1968), an artful portrayal of the sociology of religion. A unique factual account of urban administration is Katherine Marshall Johnson, *Urban Government for the Prefecture of Casablanca* (New York: Praeger Publishers, 1970).

Five Moroccan periodicals provide important data and articles on the social sciences: the *Revue de Géographie Marocaine* (Rabat, quarterly),the *Bulletin Economique et Social du Maroc* (Rabat, quarterly), *the Annales Marocaines de Sociologie* (Rabat, annual), *Hesperis-Tamuda* (Rabat, quarterly, replacing the two separate journals after 1960), and the more popular *Lamalif* (Rabat, monthly). The *Bulletin* has also published an important collection, *Etudes sociologiques sur le Maroc* (Rabat: BESM, 1972), edited by Abdelkebir Khatih.

ALGERIA

Algeria has proven to be a difficult society to grasp, although many have risen to the challenge, some with notable success. Three works are outstanding: David Gordon, *The Passing of French Algeria* (London and New York: Oxford University Press, 1966), is an admirable presentation of the forces and ideas behind Algerian politics from the pre-revolutionary period to the fall of ben Bella; David and Marina Ottoway, *Algeria: The Making of a Socialist Revolution* (Berkeley: University of California Press, 1969), is a more reportorial account of politics and policies through the crucial first three years of the Boumedienne period. William B. Quandt, *Revolution and Political Leadership: Algeria 1954-1968* (Cambridge, Mass.: MIT Press, 1969), brings the study of Algerian elites closer to disciplinary theory than does almost any other book on this aspect of North Africa, thus raising the level of analytical debate; but it shows in spots that such analysis requires a greater distance from its data than do less conceptual interpretations. Arslan Humbaraci, *Algeria: A Revolution That Failed* (New York: Praeger Publishers, 1966), on the other hand, is bereft of concept or criteria and is of uneven reportorial — even anecdotal — value. Joachim Joesten, *The New Algeria* (Chicago: Follett, 1964), while informative, is neither very profound nor very analytical. In a class by itself is Pierre Bourdieu, *The*

Algerians (Boston: Beacon Press, 1962); although this is not a political work and does not deal with independent Algeria, it provides a sensitive and comprehensive sociological analysis of component Algerian populations that is basic to an understanding of the country today.

Three sympathetic left-wing French studies from the ben Bella period offer valuable insights into and appreciations of Algerian political life. The best of these is Gérard Chaliand, *L'Algérie est-elle socialiste?* (Paris: Maspero, 1964); Hervé Bourges, *L'Algérie à l'épreuve du pouvoir* (Paris: Grasset, 1967), goes more deeply into presidential politics; Claude Estier, *Pour l'Algérie* (Paris: Maspero, 1964), is also useful. Also valuable but more critical from the left are A. P. Lentin, *Le dernier quart d'heure* (Paris: Juillard, 1964), and Daniel Guerin, *L'Algérie qui se cherche* (Paris: Présence Africaine, 1964). More academic in their analysis of the problems of newly independent Algeria are the collections edited by Francois Perroux, *L'Algérie de demain* (Paris: Presses Universitaires de France, 1962), and *Problèmes de l'Algérie indépendante* (Paris: Presses Universitaires de France, 1963); these volumes cover economy and society as well as the political system. Of two notably critical works, the left-wing approach, Daniel Guerin, *L'Algérie caporalisée* (Paris: Centre d'Etudes Socialistes, 1965), is interesting and insightful; the right-wing work, François Buy, *La République algérienne démocratique et populaire* (Paris: Librairie Française, 1965), merely longs for the "good old days." Finally, a detailed and dispassionate analysis of the struggle for power in late 1962 deserves special attention: Jean-Claude Douence, *La mise en place des institutions algériennes* (Paris: Fondation Nationale des Sciences Politiques, 1964). In the same series, a specialized study of an aspect of Algerian government stands out as a model of multiple-approach analysis of developing government and decision-making (and also of good writing): E. J. Lapassat, *La Justice en Algérie* (Paris: Fondation National des Sciences Politiques, 1968).

There have been some general works on Algeria by Algerians. A few memoirs and political statements — such as those of Hocine Ait Ahmed, *La Guerre et l'après-guerre* (Paris: Minuit, 1964), and Mohammed Boudiaf, *Ou va l'Algérie?* (Paris: Etoile, 1964) — touch on postwar events and hopes. The attempts at more organized description have generally been somewhat dry and legalistic; Abderrahmane Remili, *Les institutions administratives algériennes* (Algiers: SNED, 1967), is sound and useful, but Missoum Sbih, *La fonction publique* (Paris: Hachette, 1968), is limited. A valuable but more specialized study, based on surveys among self-management workers, is Mourad Benachenhou, *Problèmes sociologiques de l'autogestion agricole dans le Mitidja* (Algiers: SNED, 1970); of equal interest is Tami Tidafi, *L'agriculture algérienne et ses perspectives* (Paris: Maspero, 1969), which covers problems and policies. The Algerian attempt to rectify the colonial view of the national past contributes to historiography as well as to history; the subject is treated with verve by Mostefa Lacheraf, *L'Algérie: nation et société* (Paris: Maspero, 1965), and Mohammed Salhi, *Décoloniser l'histoire* (Paris: Maspero, 1967). Algerians have also contributed two items to the important debate on their education system: Abdallah Mazouni, *Culture et enseignement en Algérie et en Maghreb* (Paris: Maspero, 1969) and Abdelmaleh Sayad's chapter in Robert Castel and J.C. Passeron, *Education, développement et démocratie* (Paris: Mouton, 1967).

There is great diversity among sociological studies on Algeria. There have been fewer tribal monographs on Algeria than on its neighbors, although the latest, Auguste Cauneille, *Les Chaanba* (Paris: CNRS, 1968), is a comprehensive treatment of an important nomadic Saharan confederation whose ways have been changed by oil. A more significant focus of investigation for revolutionary Algeria is the uprooted villager, whether he had been moved to a resettlement center during the war for independence, had migrated to the city in hope of a better life, or had remained in his traditional home while conditions changed around him. Resettlement is the subject of two good studies: Michel Cornaton, *Les regroupements de la colonisation en Algérie* (Paris: Editions Ouvrières, 1967), and Xavier de Planhol, *Nouveaux villages algériens* (Paris: Presses Universitaires de France, 1961). Urban migration deserves more attention, since it is a continuing problem; it has only been studied in the colonial period, by Pierre Bourdieu, *et al.*, *Travail et Travailleurs en Algérie* (Paris: Mouton, 1963), and R. and C. Descloitres and J. Reverdy, *L'Algérie des bidonvilles* (Paris: Mouton, 1961). Traditional agriculture in disruption is well portrayed by Pierre Bourdieu and Abdelmalek Sayad, *Le déracinement* (Paris: Minuit, 1964); this should be supplemented by the comprehensive study of colonial farm labor by Michel Launay, *Paysans algériens* (Paris: Seuil, 1963). A unique psychological study of villages is Horace Miner and George de Vos, *Oasis and Casbah* (Ann Arbor: University of Michigan Press, 1960).

Self-management has received considerable attention, although the success of the experiment still remains unclear. Thomas L. Blair, *'The Land to Those Who Work it'* (Garden City: Doubleday, 1970) is a fine study of the movement and its context. A good collection that examines detailed aspects of communal administration as well as agricultural and industrial self-management is Francois d'Arcy, *et al.*, *Essais sur l'économie de L'Algérie nouvelle* (Paris: Presses Universitaires de France, 1965). Another useful communal study is Robert Descloitres and R. Cornet, *Commune et société rurale en Algérie* (Aix en Provence: CASHA, 1968). Other good studies of rural self-management (in addition to those of ben Achenhou and Lazarev, mentioned above) are Michel Raptis, "Dossier de l'autogestion en Algérie," *Autogestion*, October, 1967; Philipps Foster and Herbert Steiner, *The Structure of Algerian Socialized Agriculture* (College Park: University of Maryland Agricultural Economics Department, 1964); and Jean Teillac, *Autogestion en Algérie* (Paris: Peyronnet, 1965). The complex topic of Algerian workers in France is well treated in Georges Mauco, *Les étrangers en France* (Paris: colin, 1930), Andrée Michal, *Les travailleurs algériens en France* (Paris: CNRS, 1957), and Madeleine Trebous, *Migration and Development: The Case of Algeria* (Paris:: (Paris: OECD, 1970).

The status of women is a topic (and problem) that has drawn special attention in Algeria. The subject is examined from many sides in David Gordon, *Women of Algeria* (Cambridge, Mass.: Harvard Middle East Center, 1968). One of a number of Algerian women's views on the subject comes from Fadela Mrabet, *La Femme algérienne* and *Les Algeriénnes* (Paris: Maspero, 1969).

It would require a separate bibliography to evaluate the works on the revolutionary war. Most complete are Yves Courriére, *Les fils de la Toussaint* (Paris: Fayard, 1968), *L'heure des colonels* (Paris: Fayard, 1970), and *Les feux du desespoir* (Paris: Fayard, 1971). The best accounts in English are Edward Behr, *The Algerian Problem* (New York: W.W. Norton, 1962), and Joseph Kraft,

The Struggle for Algeria (Garden City, N.Y.: Doubleday, 1961). Mohammed Bedjaoui, *Law and the Algerian Revolution* (Brussels: International Lawyers Committee, 1961), is a useful source book on the FLN-ALN organization. Two informative English-language works on opposite sides of the war are Michael K. Clark, *Algeria in Turmoil: A History of the Rebellion* (New York: Praeger Publishers, 1959), and Joan Gillespie, *Algeria: Rebellion and Revolution* (New York: Praeger Publishers, 1960). André Mandouze, *La révolution algérienne par les textes* (Paris: Maspero, 1963), brings together a collection of FLN documents. Until Courrière's work is completed, translated, and analyzed however, the best single volume remains that of Quandt, already mentioned.

Among social-science periodicals on Algeria, the *Annales Algériennes de Géographie* (Algiers, irregular) are broader in scope than their title might suggest, and the *Revue Algérienne des Sciences Juridique, Economique et Politique* (Algiers, irregular) narrower, but both are useful.

TUNISIA

There are at least two candidates for the most satisfactory treatment of independent Tunisia. Charles Micaud, Leon Carl Brown, and Clement Henry Moore, *Tunisia: The Politics of Modernization* (New York: Praeger Publishers, 1964) covers (historical) society, contemporary polity, and the economy in a well-coordinated fashion. Clement Henry Moore, *Tunisia Since Independence* (Berkeley: University of California Press, 1965), is the best study of a Third World single-party system and also has a good chapter on decision-making and outputs (the making of the Plan). The fact that it is possible to do research in Tunisia, and that Tunisia is regarded as something of a "model" nation, helps these studies, of course, but they are still valuable half a decade after they were written. They also prepared the ground for later works. One such is Lars Rudebeck, *Party and People: A Study of Political Change in Tunisia* (New York: Praeger Publishers, 1969), which refines the single-party concept and investigates its operation, particularly on the local level. Raimunde Germann, *Verwaltung und Einheitspartei in Tunisien* (Zurich: Europe, 1968), probes further into party-state relations. Charles Debbasch, *La république tunisienne* (Paris: Librairie Générale de Droit et de Jurisprudence, 1962), is a basic work but colorless and somewhat out of date. Two popular general works are rich in color without any loss of precision or insight: Michel Zeraffa, *Tunisia* (New York: Viking Press, 1965), and Jean Duvignaud, *La Tunisie* (Lausanne: Rencontre, 1965). Gabriel Ardant, *La Tunisie d'aujourd'hui et de demain* (Paris: Calmann-Levy, 1961), is in a class by itself; it is a thoughtful interpretative essay on Tunisian society that will be pertinent for a long time.

Much less work has been done in the economic field than in the socio-political area. The most important work is Roger Genoud, *L'évolution de l'économie tunisienne* (Geneva: Courrier, 1965), which not only portrays change and imbalance in the colonial and independent Tunisian economy but also draws useful developmental concepts from the experience. P.L. Reynand, *Economie généralisée et seuils de croissance* (Paris: Genin, 1962), Moncef Guen, *La Tunisie indépendante face à son économie* (Paris: Presses Universitaires de France, 1961), and Ghazi Duwaji, *Economic Development in Tunisia: The Impact and Course of Government Planning* (New York: Praeger Publishers, 1967), are also useful. Labor unions are well covered in Willard A. Beling, *Modernization and*

African Labor: A Tunisian Case Study (New York: Praeger Publishers, 1965). A comprehensive geographical background to the Tunisian economy is given in Jean Despois, *La Tunisie: ses régions* (Paris: Armand Colin, 1961); rural transformation is examined by Jean Poncet, *Paysages et problèmes ruraux en Tunisie* (Paris: Presses Universitaires de France, 1962) and François Charbonnier, *Les reformes afraires: La Tunisie* (Paris: Fondation nationale des sciences politiques, 1964).

Before passing to a unique aspect of Tunisian studies, mention should be made of the numerous shorter treatments of Tunisian polity and society in collected works: Charles Gallagher, "Tunisia," in Gwendolen Carter (ed.), *African One-Party States* (Ithaca, N.Y.: Cornell University Press, 1962); Clement Henry Moore, "Mass Party Regimes in Africa," in Herbert Spiro (ed.), *Africa: The Primacy of Politics* (New York: Random House, 1966), an excellent addendum to Moore's *Tunisia Since Independence;* and Leon Carl Brown, "Tunisia," in James S. Coleman (ed.), *Education and Political Development* (Princeton, N.J.: Princeton University Press, 1965).

One indication of the advanced stage of development of Tunisian studies (and of the thrust of colonial scholarship everywhere in the Maghrib) is that the focus on the total society has been supplemented with numerous good studies on the local level, most of them in sociology and anthropology. A few sociological studies have been done on regions and aspects of Tunis: Paul Sebag, *L'évolution d'un ghetto nord-africain: la Hara de Tunis* (Paris: Presses Universitaires de France, 1959); M. ben Salem *et al., Un faubourg de Tunis: Saida Manoubia* (Paris: Presses Universitaires de France, 1960); and *Enquète sur les salaries de la région de Tunis* (Paris: Presses Universitaires de France, 1956). F. Bonniard, *La Tunisie de Nord* (Paris: Geuthner, 1934) and Jean Despois, *La Tunisie oriental: Sahel et Basse-Steppe* (Paris: Presses Universitaires de France, 1955), and thorough geographical studies of the mountains and the Sahel; Roger Coque, *Nabeul et ses environs* (Paris: Presses Universitaires de France, 1964), is an analysis of a coastal town from the demographic point of view. A number of rural areas and agglomerations have been the subject of excellent in-depth sociological and structural anthropological studies: These include, on a village, Jean Duvignaud, *Change at Shebika* (New York: Pantheon Books, 1970); on a hamlet, Pierre Bardin, *La vie d'un douar* (Paris: Mouton, 1965); on a tribe, A. Bessis, *et al., Le Territoire des Ouled Sidi Ali ben Aoun* (Paris: Presses Universitaires de France, 1956); on a region, Azzedine Makhlouf, *Structure agraire et modernisation de l'agriculture dans la plaine du Kef* (Tunis: CERES, 1968). Tunisia has also inspired a spectrum of sociological studies on personal relationships, ranging from the social psychological interpretation of André Demeersemen, *La famille tunisienne et les temps nouveaux* (Tunis: Maison Tunisienne de l'Edition, 1967), to the sensitive case studies of Henri de Montety, *Femmes de Tunisie* (Paris: Mouton, 1958).

Two quality periodicals specialize in Tunisian social science; *Etudes de Sociologie Tunisienne* (Tunis, quarterly) and *Revue Tunisienne de Sciences Sociales* (Tunis, quarterly); such studies also sometimes appear in *IBLA* (Tunis, quarterly).

LIBYA

If it is difficult to select the single best book on Morocco, Algeria, or Tunisia, the same is true – but for opposite reasons – of Libya. There are few notable works, and – significantly – none is of any help in understanding the military coup that ended the monarchy in 1969. Majid Khadduri, *Modern Libya: A Study in Political Development* (Baltimore Md.: Johns Hopkins Press, 1963), has a misleading subtitle, for it is a detailed political history. It is complemented by *The Economic Development of Libya* (Baltimore Md.: Johns Hopkins Press, 1960), which has the strengths and weaknesses of a World Bank report. An earlier view of the Libyan economy is Agnes Lockwood, "Libya, Building a Desert Economy," *International Conciliation*, No. 512 (March, 1957); Rawle Farley, *Planning for Development in Libya* (New York: Praeger Publishers, 1971) examines in detail the problems of capital – surplus under development. Two studies of the Senusi brotherhood, the predominant institution in Libya, are valuable adjuncts to the understanding of the country: E. E. Evans-Pritchard, *The Sanusi of Cyrenaica* (London and New York: Oxford University Press, 1949), and Nicola Ziadeh, *Sanusiyah: A Study of a Revivalist Movement in Islam* (Leyden: Brill, 1958). Three other narrower studies stand out: Ismail Raghib Khalidi, *Constitutional Development in Libya* (Beirut: Khayat's, 1956), a legalistic analysis; L. Ekblom, *Structures foncières: Ghat, Mourzouk, Ghadames* (Lund: Geografish Institutet, 1968), a treatise in rural human geography; and John Norman, *Labor and Politics in Libya and Arab Africa* (New York: Bookman, 1965), and unusual political study. The best general book on Libya is Pierre Rossi, *La Libye* (Lausanne: Rencontre, 1965).

While it is encouraging that such books as Farley's, Khadduri's and Norman's could be researched and written, the possibilities for further research in Libya in the near future are not good. The one hope lies in such cooperative efforts as currently exist between the University of Durham and the Libyan University, which prepared the way for studies such as Salem Ali Hajjaj, *The New Libya: A Geographic, Social, Economic, and Political Study* (Tripoli, 1967). A fuller bibliography which also includes historical works can be found in the notes to Jacques Roumani,"Libya and the Military Revolution,"pp. 346–62 in this reader.

BIBLIOGRAPHIES

The reviews and listings of books on North Africa published in *Maghreb* and the *Annuaire de l'Afrique du Nord* are fairly complete, up to date, and sound in judgment. *The Middle East Journal* (Washington, D.C., quarterly) also carries extensive listings and some reviews on the Maghrib; the *International Journal of Middle East Studies* reviews more important works.

Four earlier articles provide a broad background to the preceding pages: Benjamin Rivlin, "A Selective Survey of the Literature in the Social Sciences and Related Fields on Modern North Africa," *American Political Science Review*, XLVIII (1954), 826-48; Roger Le Tourneau, *et al.*, "L'Afrique du Nord: Etat des Travaux, *Revue Française de Science Politique*, IX (1959), 411-53; Manfred Halpern, "New Perspectives in the Study of North Africa," *Journal of Modern African Studies*, III (1965), 103-14; and 'Abdelkabir Khatali, *Bilan de la sociologie marocaine* (Rabat: Association pour la recherche en sciences humaines, 1968). Also useful are Helen Conover, *North and Northwest Africa: A Selected Annotated List of Writings, 1951-1957* (Washington, D.C.: Library of Congress, 1957, reprinted by Greenwood press, New York); and Norman R. Bennett, *A*

Study Guide for Morocco and *A Study Guide for Tunisia* (Boston: Boston University African Studies Center, 1968). Greedwood Periodicals (New York) publishes a *Current Bibliography on African Affairs* which includes North African countries, and a *Special Bibliographic Series,* which thus far has included an issue (vol. V, no. 2, 1967) on Algeria.

INDEX